Islam in Iran

SUNY Series in Near Eastern Studies
Said Amir Arjomand, Editor

I. P. PETRUSHEVSKY

Islam in Iran

Translated by Hubert Evans

State University of New York Press
Albany

First published in U.S.A. by
State University of New York Press, Albany

For information, address State University of New York
Press, State University Plaza, Albany, N.Y., 12246

Library of Congress Cataloging in Publication Data

Petrushevskii, I. P.(Il'ia Pavlovich), 1898-1977.
Islam in Iran.

Translation cf: Islam v Irane v VII-XV vekakh.
Bibliography: p.
1. Islam—Iran—History. 2. Islam. I. Title.
BP63.I68P413 1985 297'.0955 84-24087
ISBN 0—88706—070—6

Typesetting by The Word Factory, Rossendale
Printed in Great Britain at the
University Press, Cambridge

Contents

Preface

Ilya Pavlovich Petrushevsky (1898–1977) was born in Kiev and spent most of his early academic career in the Azerbaijan SSR, in country which, throughout most of its recorded history, has formed part of the Islamic world, and where the majority of the population speaks a Turkish language. His first major publication was concerned with the troubled history of one of the peoples of Daghestan in the Caucasus. This was followed by studies of the colonial policy of Imperial Russia in the region and of the history of feudal society there and in Armenia. After 1936 he worked in Leningrad in the historical and oriental institutes and was for twenty years Professor of the History of the Near East at the University. What was probably his most important original research was incorporated in a survey of agriculture and agrarian conditions in Iran in the thirteenth and fourteenth centuries, published in 1960. It has not been translated into any West European language, but its conclusions are summarised in a chapter on socio-economic conditions in Iran under the Mongol dynasty of the Il-Khans which Petrushevsky contributed to volume v of the *Cambridge History of Iran* (1968).

The book now so ably translated by Hubert Evans was published in 1966 as *Islam v Irane. Kurs lektsii* (Islam in Iran: A course of lectures). The title does not do justice to its scope. It is an introduction, at once concise and comprehensive, to those aspects of Islam, legal, social and doctrinal, which are relevant to the history of Iran, many of which are of course equally relevant to the history of other Muslim countries, so that any student of classical Islamic society will find it valuable. In particular it embodies the results of prolonged and profound research into the relation between religious dissidence and social discontent in mediaeval Islam, and into the character and fortunes of some of the resulting rebellions.

The perspective of this book may be somewhat unfamiliar to the English-speaking reader. This is not because the author's interpretation of events is explicitly Marxist; this is equally true of the work of many of the most eminent contemporary French orientalists. It is rather because in Western Europe and America generally Islam is conceived primarily as it has been manifested in the Arab countries and, where the British are concerned, the Indian sub-continent. For Russians contact with Islam has meant above all contact with Iranian and Turkish Muslims, whether as neighbours, subjects or fellow-citizens. It is salutary and stimulating for the balance to be adjusted by such works as this, which epitomises a long lifetime of research by one of the most distinguished orientalists of his generation.

C. F. BECKINGHAM, FBA

Introduction
The rise of Islam

The rise of Islam in Arabia at the beginning of the seventh century is closely coupled with the shaping of a class society among the northern Arabs at that time. In fact Islam was the ideological casing of that social movement, nascent as yet, which culminated in the creation of an Arab state and the expansion of this, militarily and politically, far beyond the limits of the peninsula. This movement, called by Marx 'the Muslim revolution'[1] and by Engels 'the religious revolution of Muhammad',[2] quickly acquired an international character. Iran, the countries of Central Asia and Transcaucasia, the former Byzantine provinces of the eastern and southern Mediterranean — all were soon brought into the body of the Arab state, or Caliphate, and within the embrace of Islam.

The social system of North Arabia before Islam has been little studied, and practically all we know for certain is that the patriarchal structure had collapsed by the beginning of the seventh century and that a class society had replaced it. About this class society two positions have been taken in Soviet scholarship.

According to the first of these, a slave-owning economy had been building up during the sixth and early seventh centuries in the Ḥijāz (round about Mecca and Medīna which lay on the trans-Arabian caravan route) parallel with the already existing slave-owning society of the South. In Central Arabia, mainly a cattle-breeding, nomadic country, the decay of the patriarchal way of life proceeded much more slowly; although even here the conditions favouring the formation of class were present: an aristocracy of rich men had made its appearance — owners of land, of enormous herds and of enslaved prisoners — who would often participate in the caravan trade; and over against them were the poor — who had nothing but their freedom. The slave-owning economy did not develop into the predominant 'mode of production' among the Arabs, inasmuch as later on, after the conquests of the seventh century, they were drawn into the general process of feudalization which had been going on intensively in the areas of South West Asia named above. But because the slave-owning style of society had not yet vanished in those countries by the date of the conquests, it did not vanish among the Arabs either; indeed, for a while it gained ground. On the whole, feudal relations took shape in Arab society after the great conquests of the first half of the seventh century, while the system of slavery was retained.

According to this school of thought, then, the disintegration of the patriarchal community and the formation of a slave-owning system in the Ḥijāz pre-conditioned the rise of Islam; and only after the conquests did Islam gradually develop into the religion of a feudal society. This theory has been advanced on the basis of original sources by Ye. A. Belyayev of Moscow,[3] and is also adopted in the writings of A. Yu. Yakubovskiy, S. P. Tolstov,[4] and some others.

The second point of view is that in North Arabia no less than in the South the decay of patriarchal society had set in to such effect that early feudal relations were already being forged and were dominant here even before the great conquests. Therefore (the argument runs) Islam was from the very start the religion of a feudal regime which was then crystallizing in the Arab community. This view has been stated — if tentatively and without much elaboration — by N. V. Pigulevskaya,[5] and (with more conviction) by N. A. Smirnov.[6] It finds detailed expression in a thoughtful article by a young Moscow scholar L. I. Nadiradze[7] whose study of original sources leads him to conclude that the growth of slave labour in Arabia before Islam had been feeble. Without committing himself on the nature of North Arabian society at the beginning of the seventh century, he is inclined to see in this phenomenon, as also in the prevalence of the *métayage* system, the pre-condition of future feudal relations in the area.

The present writer subscribes to the former of these interpretations. However, one must realize that the intricate problem of pre-Islamic Arabian society is far from being solved, and that both positions are merely working hypotheses pending a final solution in the future. The only certainty is that Islam was the reverberation, so to speak, of the crumbling patriarchal order that made place for class among the northern Arabs. The biting edge of the new preaching was turned primarily against this dying order, against the morality and ideas belonging to the old Arab paganism.

Extensive research[8] has been done on pre-Islamic Arabia and the rise of Islam, chiefly by Western scholars including: T. Nöldeke, R. Dozy, Snouck Hurgronje, J. Wellhausen, C. Becker, I. Goldziher, H. Grimme, L. Caetani, D. Margoliouth, H. Lammens and T. Andrae.[9] Since the present work is not a history of the Arabs or of early Islam in its Arabian setting, we shall dwell very briefly on these themes and refer the reader to the writers just listed for any deeper study.

The tribes of Arabia were divided according to ethnic provenance into the southern or Yemenite group (Qaḥṭān and Kahlān) and the northern group (Muḍar and Rabi'a), and these in their turn were split into clans and families. Many had in a distant past migrated to the north. By the beginning of the seventh century the majority of the northern Arabs were still nomads, raising mainly camels (which were very important for the caravans and as cavalry in warfare) but also goats and sheep. Horses were rare and very costly. Agriculture was of the oasis variety which meant the cultivation of barley, dates, grapes and fruit-trees. Pasture was in common ownership, but cattle, slaves and plots of land were already in individual hands. Within the sub-tribe and the clan a property stratification was already present.

The caravan route by which the Byzantine provinces of Syria, Palestine and Egypt conducted their transit trade with Ethiopia and India used the Yemen as their go-between. It ran parallel to the western littoral from the rich south through the Ḥijāz and so to the Mediterranean. But when the Yemen fell to Sāsānian Iran (572) the kings of that house saw to it that Indian goods for Byzantium passed through Iran instead of the Yemen, and Yemen trade declined in consequence. This factor, added to the social stratification and resultant stresses within the tribes, brought about an economic crisis in Arabia.

On the caravan route from Syria to the Yemen, in the Ḥijāz neighbourhood, lay Mecca. Ptolemy, the Greek geographer, mentions it as early as the second century calling it Makoraba, which is derived from the south Arab word *maqrab* meaning 'sanctuary'. It was the site of one of the most revered pagan shrines in pre-Islamic Arabia, which in Muḥammad's day went by the name of Ka'ba. In the winter months the town attracted crowds of worshippers from various parts of the peninsula, and was the scene of a fair at which the nomadic Bedouin exchanged the produce of their economy, namely hides, wool and livestock, for grain and dates and the artifacts of urban craftsmanship. It also served as a station on the line from Syria to the Yemen for warehousing and reloading.

Mecca itself was a bare, barren and dismal spot permitting no agriculture in its immediate environs.[10] Its inhabitants could only supplement their commerce by handicraft and settled livestock raising. But not far off was the fertile oasis of Ṭā'if with its broad gardens and vineyards peopled by the Thaqīf tribe, and many rich Meccans owned cultivated plots there.

At the beginning of our era the north Arabian tribe of Quraysh (of the Muḍar group) lived in Mecca, the several clans occupying their own quarters of the town. Home and foreign trade with its opportunities to accumulate wealth brought about marked inequalities in status. There were very rich families occupied in business and usury, like the Umayyads; and there were poor families engaged in petty trade, handicraft and livestock raising, like the Banū Hāshim from whom the Founder of the Faith came.

Up to Islam the order of things at Mecca was slave-owning. The merchants put their slaves to work not simply as domestic servants but in production: slaves tended their masters' herds, tilled their fields and cultivated their gardens situated in the nearby oases. They were aliens, mostly Ethiopians and negroes, and the treatment they got from their owners, as is clear from some incidents in Muḥammad's biography, was often cruel.

The Meccans participated in the transit caravans from the Yemen and once or twice a year would fit out and despatch caravans to Syria. A merchant's return was never less than fifty per cent of his investment and sometimes it touched one hundred per cent. Exports from Mecca to Syria were raw materials, treated skins, silver in bullion from the mines of Arabia, the best raisins from the Ṭā'if oasis and dates. Transit goods were, from the Yemen: incense, aloes, sandalwood, cassia, tanned hides; from Africa: gold dust and dusky slaves of both sexes; from India: cinnamon, pepper and other spices or aromatic substances, ivory and costly fabrics. While disposing of all this to Syria, the Meccan merchants imported from there Byzantine silks and woollens, purple cloth of sheep's wool, other cloth, glass vessels, hardware, weapons and luxury goods; also olive-oil, other vegetable oils and grain. The three last items the Bedouin would market at the Mecca Fair. An example tells us something of the scale of this trade: a caravan fitted out by the Meccans for despatch to Syria in the winter of 624 was loaded with merchandise to the value of fifty thousand mithqals, forty thousand in goods belonging to various wealthy members of the Umayyad or other Quraysh. Hundreds of well-armed men would accompany the caravans; besides the merchants there went guides, camel-drivers and hired detachments of Bedouin nomads as guards. As to usury, the Meccan merchants levied from fifty to one hundred per cent on the loan, their motto being 'dīnār for dīnār'.[11]

As yet there were in Mecca no more than the rudiments of a 'polis', or autonomous city-state. Each clan managed itself, and there were no organs of established authority — no court of law, no police, no prison.

Occasionally a council of elders (*malā'*) met in a special building on the square near the Ka'ba named *dāru 'n-nadwa* or 'house of assembly' to decide matters touching the different families, but this Council possessed no means of compelling the unruly to submit to its decisions.

Some two hundred miles south of Mecca lay Yathrib — the Iathrippa of the Greeks — known after Islam as Medīna, 'The City'. At the beginning of the seventh century it was an agricultural oasis possessing arable land, gardens and vineyards. It contained five settlements of particular tribes, of which the Aws and Khazraj professed paganism and the other three Judaism.

The loosening of the patriarchal clan system, the growth of private ownership of land and the inequality of property in general, the increasing contradictions between the aristocracy and the ordinary tribesmen — these factors had combined to stir northern Arabia. A fermentation was set up in which the preconditions of a class society were bred. The way out of the crisis was a pan-Arabian state capable of overcoming tribal separatism. For this a new ideology was demanded, and since mediaeval society, to quote Engels, knew 'only one form of ideology: religion and theology' there had to be a new religious system.

Apropos of Christianity and Islam, Engels said, 'it can be asserted that broad historical movements take on a religious colouring'.[12] This is why the appearance of Islam in Arabia and thereafter on the world stage — for it is one of the three 'world religions' — is not to be thought of as the result only of the preaching of a solitary man, Muḥammad. The new religion had material, social and economic foundations. The old Arab patriarchal society with its clan-organization, its tribal dissension and enmity, was breaking up, and the attendant primitive paganism with its astral, animist and tribal deities had likewise to fall. A novel religious ideology had to replace it, based on monotheism and on the assertion of communion and brotherhood in the faith in counterpoise to tribal discord. An ideology of that nature and no other could fire the new all-Arab state.

The new religion, matching the requirements of the newly formed social system, could not be pieced together without some debt to other religions, especially those developed religions of neighbouring societies already at the stage of class formation. These borrowings were from Judaism, Christianity, Zoroastrianism and (to a smaller degree) Manicheism and Gnosticism.[13] But something else, chiefly in the way of ritual practice, entered Islam from the old Arab religion which from now on the Muslims called *Jāhiliyya* (literally 'ignorance'), Barbarism.[14]

Perhaps the most revered, though far from the only sanctuary of the northern Arabs was, as mentioned, the Ka'ba at Mecca. This brought renown and influence to the town. It was simply a walled rectangular courtyard with idols of different deities set in its enclosure. The more accurate word for these was 'betil' (Semit. *bayt il*, house of God), and they consisted of vertically placed stones. According to tradition there were three hundred and sixty of these idols representing the whole pantheon of the northern Arabs. Here too was The Black Stone which survived paganism. Possession of the Ka'ba naturally conferred considerable religious authority on the aristocratic Quraysh whose several clans had taken upon themselves the duty of performing the ceremonies of worship at the annual Winter pilgrimage. These pagan northern Arabs, it should be explained, not only believed in a multitude of deities and jinns, or demons, but had some conception of a supreme god whom they called Allāh (contraction of *al-ilāh*, 'god'; *il* being the common Semitic root for expressing the concept 'god') and Allāh ta 'ālā, 'All Highest God'. It was a very hazy conception, however, the Arabs never having evolved a mythology resembling that of the ancient Greeks.

It was inevitable that the breakdown of the patriarchal system should bring about the disintegration of the religious ideology associated with it and that the Arabs, northern and southern alike, in seeking a new *Weltanschauung* in lieu of the old polytheism, should have been sensitive to the mature religions of neighbouring countries which were well on the road to feudal development.

The first of the outside monotheistic religions to have asserted itself on Arab ground was Judaism.

Jewish emigrants from the Roman Empire engaged in commerce, handicraft and agriculture had brought this with them, chiefly to such centres as the towns of Yemen, the oases of northern Ḥijāz — particularly Yathrib (Medīna), where, as has been said, three tribal settlements professed it — and Khaybar (to the north of Medīna). There were also Jews in the Ṭā'if oasis, who frequently visited Mecca as merchants.

The second monotheistic religion was Christianity. This had been penetrating Arabia by three routes: 1 From Syria through the agency of Arabs in the Ghassānid kingdom, who, along with their kings, had turned Christian of the Monophysite sect at the close of the fifth century; 2 Through Ḥīra, capital of the Arab Lakhmite kingdom; 3 From Ethiopia where it had established itself in the Axum kingdom as far back as the fourth century. It was widespread in Yemen, where

Najran, a town in the south of over twenty thousand inhabitants, was entirely Christian by the beginning of the sixth century, having its churches and a bishop's residence. It was to be found in other townships of Arabia, as well; for example there was a church in the Yamāma district east of Najd in the centre of the peninsula. The Christians shared the same callings as the Jews, and often hawked their goods through the towns, oases and Bedouin stations; but unlike Judaism, Christianity had made headway among the nomads who might embrace it in whole tribes, as in the case of the Taghlib and Namir and part of the Bakr.

But which branch of Christianity influenced early Islam? The Christianized Arabs were evidently for the most part Monophysites with some Nestorians; possibly, too, there were some Orthodox (Chalcedonites who accepted the findings of the Council of Chalcedon, 451). But none of these could possibly have been the source from which Islam took certain elements of Christian belief, for all three churches recognize the divine nature of Jesus Christ, albeit with variants in the formulation of this.[15] Whereas in Islam's teaching 'Īsā al-Masīḥ (Jesus the Messiah) was human; he was one of the great prophets and the immediate predecessor of Muḥammad, the last of the prophets. Now such a belief came closest to the teaching of the Judaeo-Christians, called also Ebionites (from Hebr. *ebionim* 'the poor'), one of the most archaic of the Christian sects.[16] Unlike the others, this sect had not broken its initial ties with Judaism; it accepted the observance of Mosaic law, i.e. of the Jewish rites, as binding. Jesus they considered a human prophet, a Messiah and saviour sent by God, but they denied his divine nature, and the dogma of the Trinity. They had their gospel, a so-called 'Gospel according to the Hebrews' (Kata Hebraious) in a Semitic language (Aramaic?), not acknowledged by the official church, which has not come down to us. There are grounds for supposing that the Christians whom Muḥammad met and talked with in Mecca were Judaeo-Christians, and it also seems that the major poet and monotheist of old Arabia, al-A'shā Maymūn b. Qays of the tribe Qays, who shortly before his death (*c.* 629) composed a panegyric in praise of Muḥammad hailing him as prophet, was a Christian of this sect.

Although the Christians of Arabia (except in Ḥīra, the Ghassānid territory, Yemen, and 'Omān) lacked robust and organized church communities, anchorite monks living in solitude or in groups in the wilderness, e.g. in the valley *Wādī 'l-Qura* in Ḥijāz, were numerous. Such monks (*rāhib*, pl. *ruhbān*) are commonly pictured in the folk songs of old Arabia, and these ascetics of the desert were known to Muḥammad, who refers to them with respect.[17]

With Zoroastrianism the first Muslims could have become acquainted, not only through Jews and Christians who had assimilated something of that religion but, as Goldziher suggests, from Persians at first hand. For Persian merchants were certainly in Arabia, in Yemen notably; and Zoroastrianism was widespread in Baḥrayn.

Besides the Jews and Christians there was a group of monotheists in pre-Islamic Arabia identified with neither — the Ḥanīfs (*Ḥanīf*, pl. *Hunafā*). The etymology of the word is obscure and various explanations have been given of its original meaning.[18] Our knowledge of the Ḥanīfs is scanty: apparently they had experienced the influence of Judaism and Christianity and taken the quintessence of both: belief in One God, and condemnation of polytheism and idol-worship; and they were noticeably drawn towards asceticism and the hermit's life. At the same time they had reservations; they would not take either Judaism or Christianity whole, preferring a more simple and primitive religion, something more accessible and more acceptable to the ordinary Arab. The Arab poets distinguished Ḥanīfs from both Jews and Christians.[19]

Muḥammad knew Ḥanīfs and regarded them as followers of a 'pure and true' religion, and it is in this sense that they are mentioned in the Koran[20] where they are contrasted with the idolaters. The Prophet saw in them the disciples of the old religion of Abraham;[21] and his biographer, Ibn Hishām, similarly equates Ḥanīfism (*Ḥanīfiyya*) with Abraham's faith and uses the word *ḥanīf* as synonymous with Muslim. Ibn Hishām names four Ḥanīfs who were contemporaries of Muḥammad at Mecca,[22] one being Waraqa b. Nawfal, kinsman of the Prophet's first wife Khadīja. It is of course impossible historically to connect the Ḥanīfs with the legendary preaching of Abraham in Arabia; there are no grounds for holding them to be the latterday adherents of a mythical 'pristine monotheism' which certain Western Islamists would have us suppose was the original religion of the Arabs. On the contrary, Ḥanīfism was a relatively new phenomenon in the history of Arabia (as was the belief in One God, Allah, among the pagans of the north). It expressed the yearning for monotheism prompted by a crisis in the social order of pre-Islamic Arabia and in the religious ideology that had served so far. Islam in this sense can be regarded as a development of Ḥanīfism.[23]

It is worth remarking of Jews, Christians and Ḥanīfs in pagan Arabia that all three used the name Allah for God, and there was thus nothing specifically Muslim in the term.

Let us turn now to the story of the rise of Islam. Muḥammed is its acknowledged founder. But it may be confidently asserted that if the requisite conditions of a new class society had not been present in Arabia, if there had not been a wasting away of the old Jāhiliyya and if a monotheistic movement had not been pitted against it, then there would have been no Muḥammad; or else he would have remained misunderstood, solitary, and been quickly forgotten. Without the above noted social and ideological premise the new world-religion of Islam would not have been able to assume shape and strength.

History does not command the written testimony of contemporaries about Muḥammad, and save for a few passages the Holy Book is not a source for his biography. The Traditions about his life, achievements and utterances, the Ḥadīth[24] as they are called, long propagated by word of mouth and only reduced to writing later on, are very largely unreliable, as Goldziher and other Islamists have established. The earliest biography founded on the Ḥadīth, that by Ibn Isḥāq (d. 767), did not appear until the mid-eighth century, and has only come down to us in a recension by Ibn Hishām (d. 834)[25] and in incomplete, if copious, extracts in the pages of the historian aṭ-Ṭabarī (d. 923). Scholars are nowadays satisfied that much of what Muslim Tradition imparts about the Prophet belongs to the realm of legend.

Muḥammad himself is undoubtedly an historical person. The first Caliphs and those in their entourage based their authority on their kinship with Muḥammad or intimacy with him, and evidently they could not have claimed a mythical figure as their kinsman, teacher and contemporary.[26] But with the passage of time much legend accumulated, especially about the Meccan period of his career. His biography in the form in which Muslim tradition accepted it probably contains more invention than authenticity, and historical criticism is not always successful in separating the two. However, that body of tradition commends itself to all Muslims, and consequently everyone engaged in the study of Islam must attend to it. We shall therefore attend here, as concisely as possible, to the turning-points in Muḥammad's life as handed down.

Muḥammad came of the tribe of the Quraysh, which controlled Mecca — and of the Hāshimite clan. His grandfather 'Abdu 'l-Muṭṭalib and his father 'Abdullāh hardly emerge from the mists, but the latter, is seems, was a modest trader who on his death left his widow Āmina no more than five camels, some sheep and a female slave. Āmina herself died when her son Muḥammad was only six.

He had been born in Mecca in 570/571; but this date may or may not be reliable. Tradition may have wanted him to be born then so as to make it 'The Year of the Elephant', the year of the ill-fated expedition of Abraha, Viceroy of Yemen, against Mecca. From then until his migration to Medīna, his *Hijra* in the summer of 622, not a single date is verifiable.

In Sura XCIII the Koran speaks of God's having found Muḥammad a homeless orphan, impoverished and sunk in pagan delusion; He gave him shelter, enriched him and set him on the straight path enjoining him henceforward not to oppress the orphan nor to chase off the beggar with a shout, but to be merciful. The boy Muḥammad tended the goats and sheep of his uncle Abū Ṭālib, but it was all the latter could do to give his nephew the barest sustenance. Then, as a young man, Muḥammad entered the service of a high-born and wealthy widow named Khadīja. This energetic lady was in the caravan trade with Syria, and her employee's duties were those of salesman in the enterprise. He won such favour in her eyes that at the age of twenty-four he married her, although she was forty. In spite of the difference in years the marriage turned out happily. Khadīja presented him with several children, of whom only one, Fāṭima, his beloved daughter, survived him — and then only just, for she died, like him, in 632. All his days he retained his attachment to Khadīja; in her lifetime he took no other wife, and after her death he would every so often arrange the entertainment of poor people in her memory. He was a compassionate man, and in his affluence was tireless in helping the orphaned and the indigent.

Marriage conferred material security. It is doubtful if he took any really active part in Khadīja's business; it is more probable that, freed from the anxiety about his daily bread which had harassed him hitherto, he indulged his peculiar bent. He loved conversing on religious topics with Jews and Christians, and from his talks got some grasp, albeit general and inaccurate, of the religions of both. To begin with, he had no clear picture of the differences between Judaism and

Christianity; for him, what mattered was the monotheistic idea and the circumstance that God's revelation had been received through prophets.[27] It is said that he had meetings, in particular, with Christian monks, and this is attested by a close resemblance between the eschatological verses of the Koran and the hymns of a well-known sixth-century figure in Syrian Christianity, the mystic Yefrem Sirin. This resemblance — and it is not one of general conception merely, which would be unremarkable, but of expression, form and style — has been established by Professor Tor Andrae of Uppsala.[28] Undoubtedly Muḥammad gained his knowledge of Christianity and Judaism in oral conversation, and not from books (which is not to suggest, of course, that he was illiterate). He had moved, too, in the circles of 'God-seekers' and Ḥanīfs frequented by Khadīja's cousin, Waraqa b. Nawfal. Thus Muḥammad gradually rehearsed his performance as a preacher.

There is nothing to be wondered at in the fact that Muḥammad, like many of his contemporaries, became a convinced monotheist hating idols and polytheists. It is much more difficult to understand how the conviction was born in him that he was a prophet chosen by God in the line of the prophets of old, and that upon him had been laid by God the mission of resurrecting in Arabia the ancient faith of Abraham. We must assume it was natural for Muḥammad, in the age in which he lived, to account for his religious yearnings and meditations as divine enlightenment. And from his word about such heavenly intimations, his followers, and later the Muslim theologians, little by little made up stories of visions, of the appearances of a God-sent spiritual go-between (whether the Holy Spirit or the Archangel Gabriel) who communicated to Muḥammad revelations from the eternal 'celestial book'.[29] Undeniably there is the possibility of hallucinations in Muḥammad's case. His own references to a 'spirit' or 'holy spirit' which appeared to him by day in the name of God were sufficiently obscure.[30] The Koran talks also of nocturnal visions[31] which were evidently dreams induced by sleep; during one of these Muḥammad, in his own words, saw 'him' (judging by the context, a spirit, and not God Himself, as people later explained) 'by the lote-tree of the furthest limit, there where is the garden of refuge (meaning paradise)'.[32] Again, there was one of these visions or slumbers in which Muḥammad was transported from the Forbidden Mosque (*al-masjidu 'l-ḥarām*, i.e. the Ka'ba) to the 'Farthest Mosque' (*al-masjidu 'l-aqṣā*).[33] In the sequel the Muslims embroidered this into the legend of the Ascension, (*mi'rāj*) whereby the Prophet was carried by angels to the

Rock of Solomon's Temple at Jerusalem; and at the turn of the seventh and eighth centuries, under the Caliph 'Abdu 'l-Malik a sacred complex, the Ḥaramu 'sh-Sharīf, was built containing the sanctuary Qubbatu 'ṣ-Ṣakhra (Dome of the Rock) and the al-Aqṣā Mosque.

Muḥammad is said to have begun preaching about 609/610. His own family were the first to believe in him: his wife Khadīja, who was ever his trusting friend; his daughters Ruqiyya, Umm Kulthum and Fāṭima; his cousin the youthful 'Ali (son of his uncle Abū Ṭālib) who later married Fāṭima and became the fourth Caliph.[34] There followed suit: his adopted son, the freedman Zayd b. Ḥāritha; the wealthy merchant Abū Bakr (the future first Caliph); Muḥammad's kinsman Zubayr; another kinsman Sa'd b. Abī Waqqāṣ, victorious commander on the field of Qādisiyya (637); the merchants Ṭalḥa and 'Abdu'r-Raḥmān b. 'Awf, of whom the latter had amassed a fortune; 'Uthmān b. 'Affān of the aristocratic Umayyad branch of the Quraysh tribe, who married the beautiful Ruqiyya, and was to be third Caliph. Other early converts were the herdsman 'Abdullah b. Mas'ūd, a former slave who was to be one of the most prominent of the Prophet's associates, and the trader 'Abdullāh b. Sa'd.

But any wider success was slow in coming. The Meccan aristocracy of money-lenders and slave-owners viewed Muḥammad's preaching with an unconcealed hostility which did not spring from any religious fanaticism. It was simply that Muḥhammad's condemnation of idolatry seemed to them to endanger Mecca's commercial and political position. His teaching could overthrow the idolatrous worship of the Ka'ba, ruin the pilgrimage and the Fair, and consequently reduce both trade and influence. So they conceived a hatred of it. The wealthy Abū Sufyān, head of the Umayyads, his wife Hind, 'Amr b. Hishām (bitterest of all Muḥammad's enemies and dubbed Abū Jahl 'Father of Ignorance' by the converts), Muḥammad's uncle 'Abdu 'l-'Uzzā (lit. Slave of the Goddess 'Uzzā) b. 'Abdu 'l-Muṭṭalib, whom he nicknamed Abū Lahab, 'Father of Hell's Flame' and condemned to torment in the hereafter[35] — these led the attack. They resolved not to kill him — which would have brought on them a blood-feud with the whole Hāshimite clan — but to wear him down with persecution and mockery.

Some five years after the first revelation and the commencement of his ministry the Prophet's following in Mecca totalled one hundred and fifty, of whom many were paupers and slaves. We must not infer from this that Islam (which in Arabic means submission to the One

God) held *per se* anything consonant with the aspirations and interests of these unfortunate people; the more since there was nothing socialistic about it, in spite of Grimme's theory. Admittedly Muḥammad castigated 'Those who give short measure' (*al-muṭaffifīn*) in his revelations, intending of course the Meccan merchants,[36] and censured their attachment to wealth and their penchant for its accumulation, *takāthur*,[37] since this made men forget about God and the life to come. He also said that the nobles (*akābir*) of Mecca and elsewhere were sinful;[38] but his censure was of wealth acquired by dishonourable means and not of wealth as such: it became a sin when its possession caused men to forget God and the retribution awaiting them beyond the grave. There was nothing new or original in this kind of preaching: it occurs in the prophetic books of the Bible and in the Gospels. But wealth, acquired honestly (from the standpoint of religious law) and combined with the performance of religious obligations such as charity,[39] was regarded by Muḥammad, both in the Meccan and Medīna periods, as wholly lawful. He never denounced either private property or slave-ownership; and he pointedly pronounced it legal to turn over prisoners of war to slavery, merely recommending masters of slaves to be lenient in their treatment of those over whom 'the right hand has seized control'.[40] The conversion of some slaves to Islam in its first phase is easily explained: they were aware that their masters loathed and persecuted Muḥammad for his condemnation of their iniquitous money-grubbing; to them he was a friend and supporter, and the Day of Judgment he foretold was, as they saw it, the day of retribution in store for their masters. The latter of course reacted by making these hapless, defenceless people the target of their hatred, and we are told that the first martyrs of Islam were male and female slaves. A number of these converts were redeemed from their owners by rich Muslims; Abū Bakr, for instance, who was an enthusiast in the cause of Islam, spent nearly all his substance (thirty-five thousand dirhems out of forty thousand) on religious needs, particularly the redemption of Muslim slaves. Others of the slave and unprivileged class, one-hundred-and-one in all, made up their minds to emigrate to Christian Ethiopia so as to escape persecution. This left Mecca with fifty-two Muslims(*c.* 615).

Initially Muḥammad did not think of himself as propagating a new faith; he was simply preaching Ḥanīf doctrine. Identifying Ḥanīf belief with his own, he applied the term Muslim to the Ḥanīfs and to his own followers indifferently; indeed it is possible that the words *Muslim* and *Islam* were actually borrowed from the former. In the Meccan period he also regarded Jews and Christians as his co-religionists, having at that stage, as already remarked, no more than a superficial understanding of what their religions meant to them. Of the differences between Judaism and Christianity and between the sects of the latter he had no clear conception, nor did he attach importance to such differences. He fastened on what united Jews, Christians and Ḥanīfs, not divided them: namely, the monotheistic idea; the doctrine of divine revelation sent down to men through prophets, of the end of the world, of the Day of Judgment, of hell and paradise; the repudiation of idol worship, and so forth. Thus there was nothing new in Muḥammad's teaching in that period except that he had added himself to the band of prophets who had gone before.

In that first phase he was particularly attracted by the idea of the coming end of the world, the Day of Judgment that would follow it, and the requital awaiting believers (i.e. monotheists) and polytheists, the righteous and the impious. The eschatological idea, common to Jews and Christians at definite stages in their religions, was reflected repeatedly in Jewish and early Christian writings of the first centuries of our era, notably in the Apocalypse (Gk. 'revelation') attributed to John the Apostle but actually written, modern research supposes, by an unknown Christian of the Hebrews apparently between 67 and 69 AD. Fantastic, vivid pictures of the catastrophic end of the world, and of the Judgment Day, resembling those portrayed in the Apocalypse, featured in the Koran,[41] and it is likely that Muḥammad at the start of his career — though he abandoned this position later — thought the end of things to be near.

He communicated his sermons to his listeners as revelations received from God through the medium of a Spirit acting as his mentor. They were written down by his hearers on palm-leaves, flat bones and stones, or else, and more often, learned by heart and declaimed in the recitative just as rhapsodists would learn and chant the verses of old Arabian poesie. Later, after his death, the fragments of revelations were assembled, edited and made into the Holy Book of the Muslims, the Koran.[42]

After the emigration of the contingent to Ethiopia, numbers only picked up slowly, though the conversion around this time of Muḥammad's uncle Ḥamza b. 'Abdu 'l-Muṭṭalib, (a warrior of renown, subsequently to enjoy the sobriquet 'Lion of Allāh and his Prophet'), and of 'Umar b. al-Khaṭṭāb a young man of twenty-six, of courage, energy and practical bent who would one day be second Caliph, were an asset. 'Umar's adhesion, especially, was of value because of his resolute character and organizing talent. Muḥammad, Abū Bakr and 'Umar supplied one another's deficiencies and made a team capable of leading the community.

But fresh disasters soon befell the Muslims in Mecca. A meeting of clan elders in the Assembly House required the Hāshimites, under pain of excommunication by the other clans, to deny Muḥammad his title to protection. The Hāshimites had no sympathy with Islam, but they were unprepared to depart from the old Arab custom whereby each member defended his clan and each clan defended each of its clansmen even when in the wrong. So then excommunication and boycott were imposed on the whole clan, except Abū Lahab, and the prohibition to take part in the Mecca-based caravans brought the Hāshimites to the brink of ruin. However, in a couple of years the excommunication was lifted, on the advice of the elders, in spite of the opposite pleadings of Abū Jahl.

Muḥammad's plight did not improve. First his wife died, and then his much loved uncle Abū Ṭālib, elder of the Hāshimites. On the latter's death, seniority in the clan passed to Abū Lahab who hated the Prophet and his Muslims. Muḥammad now seldom left his house for fear of indignities, and things became so difficult that he realized it was impossible to remain on in Mecca. His first thought was to move to the Ṭā'if oasis with his following. He actually set out accompanied by his adopted son Zayd b. Ḥāritha, but was met by a hail of stones and forced back. However, he found friends in the Yathrib oasis with the Aws and Khazraj who, it will be remembered, were living there as settled agriculturists. They detested the rich Meccan upper-class partly out of old tribal animosity and partly because many of their agriculturists were in debt to the Meccan usurers. As the enemy of the Meccan aristocracy Muḥammad was their natural ally, and on two occasions (between 620 and 622) meetings took place between them and the Muslims in the little desert centre of 'Aqaba. A pact was concluded and endorsed with a pledge; the Aws and Khazraj binding themselves to receive Muḥammad and his Muslims in Medīna and take up arms, if need be, on their behalf. The Muslims were to be treated as a special community. The Prophet's uncle 'Abbās b. 'Abdu 'l-Muṭṭalib was instrumental in conducting the negotiations, it is said. Unlike the majority of the Hāshimites he was a merchant of consequence, engaged in the Meccan caravans, issued loans in silver on interest, had a garden and vineyard at Ṭā'if, and was authorized to sell water from the well Zam Zam to pilgrims visiting Mecca.[43] He was not yet a Muslim, but he endeavoured to keep on good terms both with the converts and their opponents. And he was the ancestor of the 'Abbāsid house which in later history (750–1258) furnished the dynasty of that name.

The Muslims proceeded without delay to move in small parties to Medīna, 'Umar being in the first batch. They totalled at most one-hundred-and-fifty souls (not counting slaves and the emigrants to Ethiopia), so that there was no difficulty in organizing the exodus. Muḥammad, Abū Bakr and 'Alī brought up the rear.

The migration of the Muslims and their Prophet to Medīna earned the name *Hijra* in tradition. This word has sometimes been wrongly translated 'flight'; actually the root *hajara* signifies 'to cease associating with', 'to leave one's tribe', 'to migrate'; hence *hijra* 'migration', *muhājir* (pl. *muhājirūn*) 'migrant'. This last term began to be applied to those who had migrated with Muḥammad from Mecca,[44] whereas those Medinese who adopted Islam were designated *anṣār* (sing. *nāṣir*, 'helper' from the root *naṣara* 'to help', 'to defend'). As to the date of the Migration (meaning Muḥammad's own move) opinions vary: the most commonly held places it on the eighth of the month Rabī' u 'l-awwal in the Muslim lunar calendar, or 20 September, in the year 622. The Muslim chronology is reckoned from this event, though only legend would affirm that Muḥammad himself took it as the beginning of a new era. Previously the Arabs of Ḥijāz had counted from the Year of the Elephant.[45] The question of introducing a new chronology was raised under Caliph 'Umar from sixteen to eighteen years later (637–639) when it was decided, possibly at 'Alī's instance, to adopt the year of the Hijra as the opening of a Muslim era. But since a lunar calendar was in use, the actual day of the *Hijra* was not adopted as the opening day of the new era, but the first day of the first month (Muḥarram) of the year in question according to the lunar calendar,[46] and corresponding to our 16 July 622.

Thanks to his success in reconciling the rivalries of the Aws and Khazraj, Muḥammad became the *de facto* head of Medīna for all purposes, and the first decade of the era saw him cooperating with 'Umar and Abū Bakr and developing into a talented politician. Tradition hands down the contents of a document, usually acknowledged authentic, amounting to the Statutes of the Medīna Muslim community compiled in the terms of the treaty with the Aws and Khazraj.[47] From this document it is evident that Muḥammad, the religious head of his community, was simultaneously the political head, the legislator and judge of the whole of Medīna. In keeping with their faith, the Muslim leaders denied the validity of tribal and clan traditions; but they arrived at a compromise with them instead of assailing them forthwith. The inhabitants were required to consider themselves a political entity in which all enjoyed equal rights irrespective of tribal affiliation or religion. If any one committed murder, he could expect no protection in his tribe, whichever it was; there was to be an end of tribal enmity and vendetta; disputes between tribes would be settled by Muḥammad. In other respects, each tribe retained its autonomy and could deal and conclude agreements with other tribes outside the Medīna oasis with the exception of the Quraysh, who were classed as enemies. The Muslim community was recognized as an autonomous group on the same footing as the tribes of the oasis.

Full religious tolerance was the rule. Muḥammad proclaimed the principle that 'there is no compulsion in Islam',[48] and in practice the Muslims, Jews, Christians and Pagans were free to go their own way. In the event, many of the Aws and Khazraj chose to adopt Islam.

The community became better organized and the foundations of that ritual which was one day to become highly complicated were laid. The first mosque, *masjid*, was built: a bare house giving on to a courtyard encircled by other structures, and adjacent to the Prophet's dwelling. It was not only a house of prayer, but the venue of community meetings and receptions of envoys, and so forth. Hours were fixed for daily prayers, at which Muḥammad himself, or else Abū Bakr or 'Umar, officiated as *imām*, i.e. leader of the congregation; and a *mu'adhdhin* was designated in the person of an Ethiopian, a former slave named Bilal, whose function it was to utter the *ādhān*, i.e. invitation to prayer. Rules were framed for ablution and fasting.[49]

In this community of Muhājirīn and Anṣār, all ties based on the kinship of blood were denied on the principle that 'in Islam all men are brothers'. The brotherhood in point was not, of course, nor could it be, a genuine social equality, for class relations were asserting themselves even then. Muḥammad's preaching contained no appeal to equalization, no utopian socialism. Nevertheless, the idea of equality for the Muslims irrespective of origin and clan allegiance was an important preliminary step towards the political unification first of the Medinese Arabs and then of the Arabs everywhere. Ibn Khaldūn, the fourteenth-century historian and philosopher, maintained that the Bedouin would not have been capable of fashioning a powerful state, had they not been imbued with religious enthusiasm thanks to a prophet.[50] But in fact the case hinged less on enthusiasm and a prophet's personality than on the idea of religious communion able to obviate tribal discord and tribal separatism.

The foundations of an all-Arab Islamic state were laid in the Medīna period in the sense that the political unification of the Medīna oasis was the germ of such a state. Islam was henceforward not only a religious trend, it was a political factor. Arabia's unification and the creation of the Caliphate were brought about by the build-up of a class society, but it was Islam that hastened that process, hastened unification. A handful of Companions of the Prophet (*aṣḥāb* or *ṣaḥaba*, sing. *ṣāhib*, from *ṣaḥiba* 'to be a friend', 'to accompany') in the sequel, under the first Caliphs, formed and led a new governing class of aristocrats who turned into feudal lords after the conquests.

It was in Medīna that the Muslims became definitely classified as 'People of the Book' (*ahlu 'l-kitāb*) — first along with the Jews and then with the Christians. From the amorphous monotheistic movement, a variety of Ḥanīfism which was all it had been in Mecca, Islam was fashioned into a self-contained religion. This, of course, did not occur overnight.

Though he soon broke with the Jews, Muḥammad continued for some time longer to hope for an intimate union with the Christians. The Koran says in one place that the most stubborn enemies of the Muslims are the Jews and Polytheists, and that the true friends are the Nazarenes (Christians) with their priests and monks.[51] But by the end of his Medīna period Muḥammad broke with the Christians too, apparently at the time when frontier clashes were starting with Byzantine units. The break with Jews and Christians was caused less by religious disagreements than by their unwillingness to acknowledge Muḥammad as a prophet. While relations became openly hostile with the Jewish tribes of Medīna, the situation *vis-à-vis* the Aws and Khazraj was just as bad: there were numbers of secret enemies among the tribesmen who, having outwardly embraced the faith, were covertly working against the Prophet and trying to undo the community from within. These people were given the name Munāfiqs ('hypocrites', 'dissemblers').

Settled in Medīna, Muḥammad and his lieutenants showed no inclination to desist from the struggle with the Meccan aristocracy. Their design, evidently, was to paralyse its commercial operations by severing the caravan route from Mecca to Syria which passed close to Medīna. Early in 623 the Muslims swooped on a caravan and plundered it; and next year an attack on another caravan which was returning from Syria developed into a full-size engagement known as the Battle of Badr (March 624). The Meccans were beaten;[52] some perished, some were taken prisoner. Among the killed was Islam's worst enemy Abū Jahl, and the son of Abū Sufyān Ḥanẓala. Of the prisoners, certain out-and-out foes of Islam were put to death, but the rest either accepted Islam or were released on ransom.[53] Muḥammad's uncle 'Abbās, of whom mention has been made, fought in the ranks of the pagans in this battle, and was captured; but he was allowed to return to Mecca to become, with Muḥammad's approval, a secret agent there.

There had been three hundred and seventeen Muslims against six hundred Meccans. Only two or three of the former were on horseback;[54] the rest were on foot or on camels. Each horseman was allotted a triple share of the spoils of war, and one-fifth of the total was set aside for the Prophet and his family, or for orphans and paupers. In his own words, this distribution of booty was revealed to him.[55]

This battle was of great consequence for it gave Muḥammad a name far afield as well as unlimited power in Medīna. Next year (625) the Muslims once more pillaged a Meccan caravan, and in reprisal Abū Sufyān led three thousand men against Medīna. A thousand Muslims went out to resist them but some three hundred Munāfiqs of their number deserted and came back, leaving their comrades to suffer defeat near Mt Uḥud. The Prophet's uncle Ḥamza, Lion of Allāh, fell in the fight. But the Meccans failed to exploit their victory, made no effort to take Medīna, and simply went off home. Muḥammad was able to explain things away without loss of face: there had been a lack of discipline, and treachery by the Munāfiqs.

In 627 Abū Sufyān led a larger force against Medīna, of perhaps ten thousand men, including four thousand Meccan and allied tribesmen and a body of Ethiopian mercenaries. Great danger hung over Medīna, but in six days the Muslims ringed their city with a ditch (*khandaq*) and communicating trenches. Story has it that this method of defence was suggested by Salmān al-Fārisī, a Persian and erstwhile prisoner-slave who after conversion had become one of Muḥammad's closest Companions. In investing Medīna the enemy were helped by the Jewish tribe Banū Qurayẓa; but quarrels arose among the besiegers and in three weeks the Meccan force under Abū Sufyān withdrew from the camp and departed. The remaining tribesmen had no option but to do likewise. After they had gone, the Muslims sacked the Banū Qurayẓa settlement (it was now the last of the tribes professing Judaism in the Medīna oasis, the other two having been vanquished and evicted earlier on). The men of the Banū Qurayẓa were beheaded, and the women and children given in slavery to the Bedouin of Najd in exchange for camels and weapons. Their lands and property were distributed to the Muslims.

In 628 the Prophet set out for Mecca with fifteen hundred Companions, but was met by an opposing force. After prolonged parleying with the Quraysh he concluded a sworn pact (*bay'a*) at Ḥudaybiya the clauses of which provided for a ten years' truce; permission to Muslim pilgrims to visit the Ka'ba on condition they were unarmed but for the sword; and an obligation on Muḥammad not to attack Meccan caravans. The Muslim leadership rated this treaty a diplomatic success; for though it avoided the designation of prophet in its reference to Muḥammad, it broke new ground in putting him on equal footing with the Quraysh aristocracy. But the Muslim rank and file, who detested that oligarchy and had dreamed of a victorious march on Mecca, were exceedingly displeased. For the first time a rift showed itself in the community: among the top people led by Muḥammad, Abū Bakr and 'Umar the aim was to get a *modus vivendi* with the Meccans; lower down the aim was to overthrow them.

Politically, however, Muḥammad's authority grew after Ḥudaybiya. Various tribes at loggerheads with Mecca recognized his power as paramount, and he was willing to treat with these without necessarily requiring their adherence to Islam. And individual members of the Quraysh, hitherto hostile to the Faith, now began to cross over; notably Khālid b. al-Walīd, victor at Uḥud, and 'Amr b. al-'Aṣ (or b. al-'Āṣī), both of them renowned captains under the Caliphate. Indifferent to religion, they perceived that Islam had become a serious force in politics which it was expedient to join. As regards the Quraysh as a whole, the Muslim leadership in deciding to treat with them was firm in its mind that any compromise must be conditional on an acceptance of Islam — at least an outward acceptance. And meantime the Meccan Quraysh had changed their own attitude. They were not believers all of a sudden in the One God and the prophetic mission of Muḥammad, no; but they were aware now of Islam as a political force that could weld all Arabia. Abū Sufyān himself renounced his enmity with Muḥammad and gave him his daughter in marriage, an act which in those days customarily signified a readiness for a political alliance. The Meccans saw they had an instrument to hand which they could use to their advantage, and it is not unlikely that Abū Sufyān and his set were by then actually weighing the chances of a united Arabia's subjugating the outside territories through which the trade-routes ran, connecting the Mediterranean with Asia. Conquests of this kind would assist

Arabia out of an economic depression and it was evident by now that they could best be organized under the banner of Islam.

In early January 630 Muḥammad with ten thousand warriors, Medinese and allies, approached Mecca. Mecca prepared to resist, but Muḥammad had 'Abbās in his camp, who was now an avowed partisan and Muslim, and he contrived a meeting between the Muslim leadership and Abū Sufyān. The latter negotiated the surrender of Mecca with the Prophet on terms favourable to his own clan and personal friends: the safety of all Meccans — except a few dozen inveterate enemies of Islam from whom the amnesty was withheld — was guaranteed provided they stayed at home or else took refuge either in the enclosure of the Ka'ba sanctuary or at Abū Sufyān's country villa; and the Meccans would undertake to accept Islam. (The talks were kept secret from the bulk of the Muslims.) The entry of the Muslim troops into Mecca passed off almost without bloodshed. The Ka'ba was emptied of its idols and made into the principal Muslim temple, the Forbidden Mosque (*masjidu 'l-ḥaram*). To the mass of the Quraysh, needless to say, submission to the new faith had nothing to do with conviction; it was a matter of political necessity.

Abū Sufyān's calculations proved correct. He and his fellow-members of the Umayyad clan, together with his other supporters, not only saved their privileged position but began to play a prominent part at the summit of the Arab Muslim State. In fourteen years the head of that state would be an Umayyad, 'Uthmān b. 'Affān; and in a further fifteen years Abū Sufyān's son Mu'āwiya would found the dynasty of Umayyad Caliphs. His kinsmen and partisans would enjoy to the full the benefits of the great Arab conquests, annexing lands from the Christian holders in Syria and other provinces, and collecting slaves and all sorts of chattels as the spoils of war.

In 630–631 the Ṭā'if oasis and a very large part of Arabia were constrained to submit to Muḥammad. Mostly the submission was accompanied by the formal adoption of Islam and the destruction of idols. The Prophet's policy was to rest content with such outward adherence in the beginning, judging that genuine faith would come afterwards, whether in the first or some following generation. This calculation was justified: the islamization of Arabia was soon complete.

Even after the surrender of Mecca, Muḥammad stayed on in Medīna. The leader of practically all Arabia did not take the royal title of *malik*,[56] and his life remained simple, resembling that of any well-to-do citizen. But there was one respect in which it had changed from pre–Migration days: after Khadīja's death, he began to take other wives. When he died he left nine wives, and his life's total was fourteen, not counting slave-concubines. V.V. Bartol'd is doubtless right in believing that his career in this regard was not due to any later access of sensuality, but to the ancient Arab idea that a harem was necessary to sustain the dignity of a political chief. Marriage to Abū Bakr's daughter 'Ā'isha, to 'Umar's daughter Ḥafṣa, and later to Abū Sufyān's daughter Umm Ḥabīb, and so on, was contracted in the wish to strengthen personal ties with his associates or indispensable allies. While convinced that God had permitted him as Prophet marriages without limit,[57] he restricted the number of legal wives who could be kept simultaneously to four in the case of all other Muslims, and he did not positively encourage polygamy at all.[58] He sought no riches or luxury but provided for his own household and clan, laying down that one-fifth (*khums*) of any booty must go as subsistence to his descendants and kinsfolk, to the widows and orphans of those fallen in Holy War, and to the destitute and vagrant.[59] His character, too, in the Medīna period underwent some change. This is understandable; in Mecca he was an unrecognized and persecuted preacher, but in Medīna he became a politician, a ruler and legislator; displaying gifts of diplomacy and generalship, even when allowance is made for the contribution in both spheres of the talented 'Umar.

Muḥammad aged prematurely. He performed his last *ḥajj* (pilgrimage) to Mecca in the spring of 632, but by summer took to his bed, and on 13 Rabī'ul-awwal, he died. He left no instructions to meet this event, and obviously neither he nor his Companions expected his death to come so quickly. He was buried in Medīna, and his tomb was subsequently given the status of a holy object second only to the Ka'ba, and became a place of pilgrimage.

I

Iran's obedience to Islam
The warring Sunnī, Shī'ite and Khārijite currents

The unexpected death of Muḥammad was followed by disputes between the Muhājirs and the Helpers which only the tact and authority of 'Umar set at rest. Both sides recognized Abū Bakr as head of the Muslim community — and therefore of the Arab State, since the religious community and the state were indistinguishable ideas. So Abū Bakr, like his descendants after him, was named Caliph: that is, 'deputy', 'vice-gerent' of the Prophet[1] (Ar. *khalīfa* pl. *khulafā'* from *khalafa* 'to follow', 'to replace' someone).

The thirty-year regime of the first Caliphs (Abū Bakr, 632–634; 'Umar I, 634–644; 'Uthmān, 644–656; and 'Alī, 656–661)[2] was a period of wide conquest. This was facilitated by the extreme exhaustion of Sāsānian Iran and Byzantium, in the aftermath of twenty-four years of warfare between them; and in the case of Iran a specific cause of Arab victory was the separatist temper of the local Dihqāns or feudal chieftains, and a consequent weakness of central power in the person of the King of Kings (*Shāhinshāh*). The Arab conquest of the Byzantine provinces amounting to about two-thirds of the whole Empire, is no part of our theme, and we shall not advert to it except to remark that it took place almost simultaneously with that of the dominions of Sāsānian Iran. Palestine, Syria, Upper Mesopotamia and Egypt were conquered between 634 and 642. The subjugation of Transcaucasia started in 640 but did not finish until the early eighth century. Asia Minor was repeatedly invaded, without being conquered properly. The frontier between the Byzantine Empire and the Caliphate was stabilized at the beginning of the eighth century so as to run along the Taurus mountains and the upper reaches of the Euphrates.

The fate of Sāsānian Iran was different. The Arabs, commanded by Muthannā b. Ḥāritha, invaded Sāsānian Mesopotamia early in 633, and in March took Ḥīra, the former capital of the Lakhmites. Carrying the day in 'the chain fight',[3] Muthannā crossed the Euphrates. In May of the same year Khālid b. al-Walīd won a victory over the Persians near Ullays, and early next year his army was thrown into Syria. At this stage the Persians took the offensive. In November their commander Rustam, the Spahbadh, or Captain, of Khurāsān who had a couple of years before helped to put the King of Kings, the young Yazdigird III (grandson of Khusraw II), on the throne, tempted the Arab army across the Euphrates and then surrounded it. The Arabs suffered a severe defeat at Qussu'n-Nāṭif in the 'Battle of the Bridge', alluding to the pontoon at that point of the river on the road from Ḥīra to Ctesiphon; but thanks to Muthannā's presence of mind and energetic action they succeeded in extricating themselves and recrossing the Euphrates. They had their revenge in 635 at the battle of Buwayb, near Ḥīra, when they wiped out a large Persian force commanded by Mihrān.

Yazdigird's government was compelled to realize that it had hitherto underestimated the Arab danger, notwithstanding that information was available to them about the victory the Arabs had scored over the main Byzantine army on the Yarmuk, a tributary of the Jordan.[4] The Spahbadh Rustam had already decided to call up the military class (*arteshtārān*) in a general mobilization, but this required, with equipment, more than a year to carry out. It was not until the autumn of 636 that the huge Persian army found itself encamped near the little borough of Qādisiyya, close to Ḥīra. The Arab camp, to whose command 'Umar had appointed the old Muhājir, Sa'd b. Abī Waqqāṣ, had been pitched only a short distance away. The well-armed and splendid cavalry of Iran, supported by enormous elephants carrying towers for the marksmen on their backs, looked on the Arabs with contempt — sun-scorched, dusty, shaggy camel-men in torn dirty clothes and sandals on their bare feet, with swords sheathed in rags, and shields of ox-hide.

Battle was joined at the beginning of 637 and lasted three (some say four) days. The fight was hard fought. The Persians had been reinforced by some units of Armenian Naharars (propertied princes), but the Arabs got their reinforcements too from Syria. On the last day the wind raised a sandstorm in the faces of the Iranian warriors — in this the Arabs saw the intervention of Allah — and it put the finishing touch to the Persian defeat. Rustam fell on the field, and the great national standard of Iran was captured by the Arabs.

When Yazdigird learned of the disaster at Qādisiyya he hastily left Ctesiphon, the Sāsānian capital on the Tigris, and fled to Ḥulwān in the Zagros Mountains. The abandoned capital was presently taken by the Arabs (June 637). No defence had been put up, but since the inhabitants were unable to treat with the attackers about its capitulation, it was given over to plunder. Part of the inhabitants were slaughtered, part led away into slavery. The total amount of booty, i.e. money with valuables, was put at nine hundred million dirhems.

After once again defeating the Persians at Jalūlā, east of the Tigris, late in 637, the Arabs were in control of the whole of Mesopotamia (Iraq). Camp-towns were established: at Baṣra where the Shaṭṭu 'l-'Arab discharges itself into the Persian Gulf (635); and at Kūfa west of the Euphrates near Ḥīra (638). These became administrative centres, and subsequently great nurseries of Arabic culture. Iraq with its Semitic population of Syrians and Hebrews was arabicized relatively quickly.

Next the Arabs occupied Ḥulwān and moved into the Iranian uplands. A decisive engagement took place at Nahāwand, south of Hamadān, in which the enemy lost both the day, and their commander Fīrūzān (642). In 643 they went on to take Zanjān, Qazwīn, Ray (near the modern Tehran), and Qūmis; and concluded a formal treaty of submission with Qazwīn. Hamadān, Qum, Kāshān and Iṣfahān were captured in 644, and Yazdigird had to flee from the last named to Iṣṭakhr in Fārs. Then the Arabs invaded Fārs by sea from Baḥrayn and by land from Khūzistān. The Dihqāns offered a long and staunch resistance but their militia under Shahrak, the Marzubān of Fārs, was broken in a bloody encounter at Rayshahr, near Tawwaj. Iṣṭakhr submitted in 648 by treaty concluded with Abū Mūsā al-'Ash'arī, but its people rose the following year and murdered the garrison. The Arabs thereupon besieged, took and sacked it, did to death forty thousand of its men, and sent its women and children into slavery (649). In conquering Fārs, the Arab leaders seized a number of rich estates, and it is on record that the family of Ḥanḍala b. Tamīm of Baḥrayn headed the list of new proprietors.[5] But there were numerous Dihqāns of Fārs who kept their lands, castles and feudal rights in return for formal homage to the conquerors.

Yazdigird had meantime hurried to Kirmān, and from there to Sīstān (649). When the Arabs invaded those parts, the Shahinshah repaired to Khurāsān (650). His situation was now tragic, for after the battle of Nahāwand he had neither troops nor power. He passed from one district to the next with a small band and his retinue, hoping for the support of the vassal potentates and princes of whom there were so many in east Iran. But these saw no sense in bolstering up a King of Kings shorn of authority; each one made haste to be rid of him, and passed him on to the next, obtaining a receipt that he had handed him over alive and unharmed and was therefore without further responsibility. The separatist behaviour of these feudal lords, it will be remembered, was one reason why Iran lost its independence. Some offered to treat with the conquerors and save their estates and privileges against payment of tribute; others indeed fought courageously, but their resistance was uncoordinated, and the Arabs crushed them one by one.

In 651 the Arabs mastered Khurāsān.[6] Yazdigird headed for the Merv oasis, and was there betrayed by a local princeling. This person, Mahuiya by name, involved him in a conflict with a horde of nomads in the region of Balkh, and when Yazdigird had lost the last of his men in a fight with them near Merv and arrived on foot at the gates of that city with a few companions (in some versions, one), Mahuiya refused to allow him in. Various accounts exist of his end; the majority are to the effect that he took shelter at a mill on the banks of the river Murghāb, and that the miller, tempted by the Shāhinshāh's jewels, despatched him at night in his sleep. (Some variants say he did this on secret orders from Mahuiya.) He threw the body into the river where it was found by local Christians. The bishop of Merv, or Metropolitan, Iliya, buried the last of the Sāsānian house in consideration of the fact that his grandmother had been Shīrīn the Good, a Syrian and beloved wife of Khusraw II Aparwīz, the protectress of Christians in Iran.[7] According to another account, Yazdigird was robbed and murdered by a certain stone-mason, and the inhabitants of Merv buried his body in a wooden coffin.[8] Mahuiya submitted to the Arabs, on the undertaking to pay a contribution in wheat, barley, valuables and money to the sum of one million dirhems.

In 651 Sāsānian power collapsed. Almost the whole of Iran was overrun by the Arabs, as far as the Amū Daryā in the north-east. Only Balkh, Ghūr, Zābulistān and Kābul remained independent, plus the Caspian-shore districts of Daylam, Gīlān and Ṭabaristān. These resisted stubbornly and Daylam, Ghūr and Kābul never fell to the Arabs; the others submitted later — Balkh, for instance, finally gave way in 707. Some parts of the country suffered grievously under the conquest, the peaceful inhabitants of both sexes being put to slavery. This was especially seen in Iraq, Khūzistān and Fārs; but many towns and ruling Dihqāns chose subordination on terms of tribute. Thus the Marzubān of Nīshāpūr committed himself to pay seven hundred thousand dirhems and four hundred pack-loads of saffron; the Dihqān of Abīward, four hundred thousand dirhems; and so on.[9] Balādhurī, and sometimes other historians, have recorded the contents of such engagements. Normally the treaties guaranteed the inhabitants the freedom to profess their faith, Zoroastrian, Christian, or Jewish; their personal liberty; and their property; in exchange for which, they pledged themselves to acknowledge the paramountcy of the Arab regime, forswearing treason, and to pay outright a contribution and thereafter the tax imposed on foreigners.

The conquest of Iran and its incorporation in the Caliphate were fraught with consequences, the first of which was the movement of entire tribes, settled and nomadic, into the new domain. Many quarters in the conquered towns were peopled by Arabs of a particular tribe and given the name of that tribe. V. V. Bartol'd has pointed out how the immigration proceeded 'first, by pitching military camps in which the Caliph's deputies lived; and second by the seizure of defined territories by Bedouin tribes. The camps quickly became centres of urban life, places where the stamp of Muslim culture could impress itself effectively'.[10] By the tenth-century it was no uncommon thing for a city — Qum is a case in point — to have more Arabs than other citizens and to use Arabic as its principal language. There were many Arab landowners by now in the country, and the greater part of the land reserve was state-controlled. The peasants in occupation were considered hereditary tenants and exploited directly through its financial machine by the government. In Iraq, Khūzistān and possibly elsewhere the state lands represented the largest category of ownership.

The newcomers introduced Arabic as the literary and official language, and as the religious language of all who professed Islam. This is not to say that Iranian culture died. On the contrary, it even affected the Arabs themselves and during the century that followed the conquest many a work of Middle Persian (Pahlavi) literature was translated into Arabic. But Arabic certainly became the language of letters *par excellence*, and was soon enjoying the status of an international tongue in West Asia and North Africa. The Persian Dihqāns not only learned it but were no whit inferior to the Arabs in their use of it, and from the eighth to tenth centuries the poetry of Iran and Central Asia began to be composed in it.[11] Not only Persians in general, but the patriotic iranophiles hostile to Arab pretentions who called themselves *Shu'ūbiyya* wrote in it. Its alphabet became widely adopted and ousted the former Pahlavi script of Aramaic (i.e. also Semitic) origin. It was also Arabic that sponsored Modern Persian, the newly evolved *Fārsi* or *Darī* which had its birth by the ninth century in poetry, and of which a Qaṣīda of 'Abbās of Merv, 809, is the earliest example. This language made its way into historical[12] and geographical[13] writing in the second half of the tenth century, and into mysticism in the eleventh century. But in the exact sciences, philosophy, Muslim theology and law, Arabic had pride of place even after this.

Another effect of the conquest, as great as any, was the propagation of Islam. Islam gradually supplanted Zoroastrianism, the old religion of the Persians, and if it did not wholly dislodge Christianity (which had spread between the third and seventh centuries, especially in the towns) it set a limit to its further expansion. A few Persians, mostly Dihqāns and townsmen, had gone over to Islam in the mid-seventh century, but real success took time. In the early stage the attitude to these conversions was as follows: the neophyte was breaking with his people and becoming an Arab. But since among the Arabs themselves (even those who had moved into Iran) the division into tribes and clans persisted, the new convert, be he Persian or anything else, had to join an Arab tribal community, and (to cap it all) not as a member possessing equal rights but as a client (*mawlā* pl. *mawālī* from the root *waliā* 'to be intimate with', 'to join someone'). Although this violated the principle enunciated by Muḥammad of equality of all Muslims irrespective of origin, the custom continued nevertheless. In Wars for the Faith the *Mawlā* fought in the contingent of the tribe of which he was client. These *Mawālī* were quite numerous, and while their status was considered inferior to that of Arabs, it did not prevent their holding high posts, especially in the finance department where there were no Arab officials of training and experience.

Under the Umayyad Caliphs (661–750) the progress of Islam was slow. Tradition says that the bulk of the most fanatical and irreconcilable Zoroastrians moved to Hormuz, and thence to Gujarāt in India[14] and, according to the Russian Iranist K. A. Inostrantsev, there were several successive expulsions of the 'Guebres', as the Muslims began to call them, to India.[15] But in spite of everything Zoroastrians were still plentiful in the tenth century: the geographer Iṣṭakhrī in that century allows one to understand that in Fārs the Fire Worshippers were in the majority in rural areas and that hardly a village was without its Fire Temple.[16] They were so numerous that they did not wear on their clothing the distinguishing badge which Muslim law prescribed for foreigners.[17] Where the Dihqāns, as often was the case in tenth-century Fārs, were still Zoroastrian, they would afford their coreligionists shelter in their mountain castles such as the one at Jiṣṣ. It was at this castle at Jiṣṣ, as Iṣṭakhrī tells us, that pictures and stories of the kings, heroes and great victories of ancient Iran were preserved on scrolls.[18] Zoroastrianism was still flourishing in the Caspian littoral of Ṭabaristān, Gīlān and Daylam in the second half of the ninth century, but in Khurāsān on the other hand, somewhat before that time, the Dihqāns and most of the populace were Muslim. One must not forget, of course, that even many of the nobles in Khurāsān were secretly Zoroastrian right into the tenth century. There were many of the religion in Kirmān[19] and in Jibāl, in north-west Iran,[20] and the tenth century author Muṭahhar Muqaddasī (or Maqdisī)[21] describes a large Khurramite community[22] in the Māsabadān circuit in the west of the country.[23] So much for the situation in the tenth century.

In the next century the overwhelming majority of the population of Iran was Muslim, and information about the Zoroastrians is almost non-existent in literature from then on. Ibn al-Balkhī, author of an historical geography in Persian entitled 'Fārs nāma' written in the second decade of the twelfth century makes no mention of them in Fārs. By the beginning of the sixteenth century they were only to be found, and in very small numbers at that, in Kirmān and the Yazd oasis, and here and there in scattered spots of which Gabrābād near Iṣfahān was one. (There are none there today.)

Let us now revert to the overall condition of the Caliphate in the period of the conquests. Under the first four Caliphs (632–661) the formation of a class society went on with vigour. The process was hastened by the military successes. Although the basic reserve of available lands in the subjugated dominions was declared the property of the Muslim community — which meant in actual fact, of the Arab state — not a few lands were seized, as has been said, by individuals belonging to the elite. In the next period (seventh to ninth centuries) the early feudal society of the Caliphate, retaining its slave-owning and patriarchal structures, crystallized. A feudalized nobility was created from the Prophet's kinsmen of the Hāshimite clan, from the Companions, whether Muhājir or Anṣār, from members of certain old Meccan clans notably the Umayyad, and from some of the ex–tribal chiefs. This new nobility grew rich in the wars, from which it derived estates and a colossal quantity of booty in money, gold, silver, woven fabrics, herds of horses and cattle, and thousands of slaves fit for exploitation in agriculture,[24] livestock raising and handicraft.[25] The emergence of class was as yet concealed by the theocratic form of the regime: the religious community and the Arab state were indistinguishable. It was considered that the administration must be built upon the divine book and the precepts of the Prophet (Koran and *Sunna*). No line was drawn between the spiritual and secular functions of the Caliph (imāmate and amīrate) — and only later did these show signs of diverging.[26] Officially the principle of the equality of Muslims was acknowledged, even though it had in practice become a fiction.

'Uthmān's Caliphate was a triumph for the Umayyads (from whom he sprang) and their supporters; in other words, for the Meccan aristocratic clique[27] which had only embraced Islam out of political necessity. 'Uthmān himself, old Muhājir and son-in-law of the Prophet, was a weak character, but devout, and he sought no personal riches. He surrounded himself with his own kinsmen and in particular allowed himself to be influenced by al-Ḥakam, cousin of Abū Sufyān and uncle of the Prophet, a man of substance and formerly antagonistic to Islam. Al-Ḥakam's son Marwān became the Caliph's principal adviser, and the civil and military posts were filled by the family or its henchmen. These posts had perquisites in the way of lands and riches, and Syria, the most lucrative appointment of all, went to Abū Sufyān's son Mu'āwiya. Now such proofs of social exclusiveness and aristocratic privilege inevitably excited the strong resentment of the Arab people, and it was at that juncture in 'Uthmān's reign that a coterie was formed of those who supported 'Alī b. Abī Ṭālib, the Prophet's son-in-law and husband of his beloved daughter Fāṭima. It became known as *Shī'at 'Alī* or 'Alī's Party, whence the name Shī'ites. Initially, at the election of the first Caliph only three of the Companions had backed 'Alī: namely, Abū Dharr al-Ghifārī, Miqdād al-Aswad and Salmān the Persian,[28] — and they were not listened to. During 'Uthmān's reign, however, in the general discontent of the lower echelons of the community, 'Alī's name grew very popular, and Abū Dharr (d. 653) chose the moment to found a real party. In Damascus, where Mu'āwiya was governor, he preached against the luxury and greed of the ruling clique and against social inequality, and proclaimed the title of the Prophet's family to the Imāmate — which meant 'Alī and his two sons by Fāṭima, Ḥasan (b. 624/625) and Ḥusayn (b. 625/626). The governor sent him back to 'Uthmān at Medīna, but this did not stop his preaching in the same tone there.

To begin with, the Shī'ites were only a political group favouring 'Alī's Caliphate (or Imāmate) as much for his intimate connection with the Prophet's family as for his personal qualities. Inasmuch as the theocracy admitted no clear distinction between Islamic society and state — or, to put it otherwise, between religion and politics — they based their principle of succession on the former. Long afterwards tradition endorsed this, claiming that the Prophet himself had declared 'Alī his successor at the pool named Ghadīru 'l-Khumm.

Wellhausen called the Shī'ites and Khārijites[29] the religious and political opposition to the Umayyads.[30]

The Shī'ites represented a religious trend, becoming in the sequel a great branch of Islam opposed to the official or, to use the conventional expression, orthodox Islam whose followers insisted on the 'electivity' of the Caliph and were later named Sunnīs[31] or People of the Custom and the Community — *ahlu 's-sunna wa 'l-milla*. The Shī'ite religious theory was due to 'Abdullāh b. Sabā, who like Abū Dharr was 'Uthmān's contemporary. He is said to have been a Jew from Yemen and a recent convert, well read in the Jewish and Christian scriptures and delighting in theological controversy. He pointed out that each of the great prophets of old had his aide or executor (*waṣī*): Moses had Aaron, Jeremiah had Baruch, Jesus had the Apostle Peter; and in the case of the Prophet Muḥammad this *waṣī* could be none other than 'Alī. He also formulated the doctrine of the 'return', *raj'a* (from *raja'a* 'to return') of Muḥammad, relying on one passage in the Koran,[32] and preached that as Jesus must come back, so must Muḥammad. This doctrine of palingenesis, as Wellhausen has shown, was later fused in Extreme Shī'ite[33] teaching with that of the Prophet's rebirth in 'Alī and of the incarnation of the soul of 'Alī in succeeding Imams. 'Abdullāh b. Sabā was the forerunner of the Extreme Shī'ites in the sense that he did not content himself with asserting 'Alī's claims but went the length of almost deifying him.

In the atmosphere of general dissatisfaction, exaggerated hopes were pinned on 'Alī. This son-in-law of Muḥammad was revered and adored not only by the Shī'ites but, as time passed, by the Sunnīs; all uniting to treat him after his death as a hero of romance. By the close of 'Uthmān's reign, 'Alī was well past fifty. He was bald, thick-set, short, swarthy; he had large eyes and a grave regard and he wore a long white beard.[34] Brought up by Muḥammad, he was deeply devoted to him and the cause of Islam, and was one of the half-dozen people closest to him, and among the ten Companions who were promised paradise in their lifetime. Religious to the point of enthusiasm, 'Alī was sincere and honest, and uncommonly scrupulous in the matter of morals. He was a stranger to ambition and avarice. Beyond doubt he was a brave and staunch warrior, present at Badr and the battle of Uḥud (where he received sixteen wounds), and in almost all Muḥammad's wars. In course of time his exploits in the field were so embellished as to sound like fairy tales.[35] But this soldier and poet who possessed the qualities befitting his reputation as a saint — legend ascribed many miracles to him, *karāmāt* — totally lacked the capacity of a statesman. An extreme scrupulosity, the outcome of his religion, made him dread his responsibility before God, dread the shedding of Muslim blood; and consequently he was indecisive and inclined to compromise. A mind wholly obsessed by the religious, neither dynamic nor flexible, took decisions slowly and implemented them even more slowly. The fear of being blamed for personal ambition often restrained him from resolute action against his enemies. But for the Shī'ites who idolized him almost more than Muḥammad, 'Alī was not only Imam but saint and hero, the ideal Knight of Islam.

Some nineteenth-century scholars maintained that Shī'ism was a creation of the Persians, the specifically Iranian understanding of Islam, 'the reaction' as one of them put it 'of the Iranian spirit against Arabism'. Carra de Vaux, R. Dozy and A. Müller were so persuaded. But this theory is inspired by the pseudo-scientific idea — very strongly entrenched in the minds of Western European scholars — that ideologies are tied to race, that there are religions belonging to given races. To add to the trouble, the concept 'race' meaning a definite inherited anthropological type was confused with the concept 'people' meaning a community of cultural type as conveyed by the Russian word *narodnost'*. Hence there was a temptation to detect a religion of the Arab race in Sunnī Islam, but a religion of the Iranian race or 'a reaction of the Iranian spirit against Arabism' in Shī'ite Islam and Ṣūfism. In fact there have never been racially determined religions in history any more than there have been racially determined ideologies. The story of Christianity, Manicheism, Islam and Buddhism demonstrates that these syncretic religions have been propagated on the basis of social and cultural community, and experienced a lengthy phase of consolidation among the most diverse peoples and races. The internal currents and ramifications of these religions were unconnected with the psychological peculiarities of a given people or *narodnost'*, let alone a given race.

Historically, moreover, the hypothesis of an Iranian origin of Shī'ism is false and has nowadays been rejected. Wellhausen has pointed out that the first Shī'ites were not *Mawālī* (Persians) but Arabs, and that the rudiments of the ideas of Shī'ism go back to 'Abdullāh b. Sabā, the Yemenite of Jewish extraction; and has drawn the conclusion that the dogmatics of Shī'ism came from the Jews rather than the Iranians. Actually the doctrine of the prophets' returning (*raj'a*) first made its appearance in biblical Judaism (cf. the belief in the return of Elijah and Enoch) and from it passed to the Christians who thought John the Baptist to be Elijah reborn. In Wellhausen's view the idea of the prophet-monarch as sovereign representative of God's power on earth also entered Islam from the Jews.[36] He may possibly be right, provided he is talking strictly of the sources of Shī'ite dogma. But its later evolution, especially the doctrine of the divine illumination (*nūr-i Muḥammadī*) of the Imam-descendants of the Prophet, dear to the Extreme Shī'ites with their ideas of rebirth (Gk. *palingenesis* Ar. *raj'a*), or transmigration of souls, of the prophets (Gk. *metempsychosis*; Ar. *tanāsukhu 'l-arwāḥ*) surely took place in an Islamic Arab setting already instinct, be it remembered, with certain constructions of Hellenistic philosophy.

In the sequel, of course, the various tendencies of Shī'ism spread both in Iran and in an Arab — and, later, to some extent in a Turkic — environment; while Sunnī Islam, for its part, spread both in the Arab — or else Turkic — environment and in an Iranian ambience. During the tenth to fifteenth centuries in Iran both Sunnīsm and Shī'ism increased; the former principally among the feudal lords and the burghers, the latter among village-folk and the urban lower class.

To revert to the time of Caliph 'Uthmān. Popular discontent grew in the years 653 to 655, and there were even some aristocrats who ranged themselves with the opposition. These were old Muhājirs resentful of the way they had been elbowed aside by the Ummayad party. Two of their number were Ṭalḥa and Zubayr.

In the month of Shawwāl 35 AH, corresponding to April 656, three contingents raised in Kūfa, Baṣra and Egypt arrived at Medīna on the pretext of performing the Lesser Pilgrimage (*'umra*) and encamped at the gates. The Kūfa force was led by Malik b. al-Ashtar, and 'Abdullāh b. Sabā was with the Egyptian contingent; but the bulk of the *soi-disant* pilgrims were of the Arab lower orders, many of whom entertained Shī'ite sympathies and were counting on 'Alī's assistance. 'Alī vacillated. Ṭalḥa and Zubayr while pretending to be neutral secretly egged on the malcontents. The opposition aristocrats as a whole hesitated to allow the latter to enter; all they wanted was to take advantage of this demonstration at the gates to put themselves in power. What followed is far from clear in its details. The earliest sources depicting these events belong to 'Abbāsid times when public opinion was hostile to the Umayyads and their role in the Caliphate, and it is therefore difficult to rely on their impartiality. They make out that 'Uthmān, with 'Alī as intermediary, negotiated with the malcontents and promised to meet their grievance by recalling the provincial governors, but that the Egyptian contingent at that moment intercepted a letter from 'Uthmān bearing his seal addressed to their governor Ibn Abī Sarkh. This document directed the latter to seize the instigators of the mutiny when they should return to Egypt and chop off their hands and feet. Incensed by this act of treachery the contingent rose and entered the city, laid siege to 'Uthmān's house and demanded his abdication. 'Uthmān refused. The insurgents calculated they could force his hand by starving him out. The siege had gone on for ten weeks — it was 18 Dhu 'l-Ḥijja 35 AH = 17 June 656 — when a rumour was circulated that reinforcements despatched by the governors of Baṣra and Damascus were on their way to the Caliph's aid. Unable now to delay, the rebels crossed the flat roofs of the adjacent buildings, burst into 'Uthmān's house, scattered his guard and murdered him. 'Alī, Ṭalḥa and Zubayr were naturally at pains to ward off any suspicion of complicity.

The Egyptians now proposed 'Alī as Caliph. The Kūfa and Baṣra contingents concurred, and finally the Medinese assented. But not so Ṭalḥa and Zubayr who hastened to Mecca where, encouraged by the energetic 'Ā'isha 'Mother of the Orthodox', they chose revolt. The general Sa'd b. Abī Waqqāṣ likewise declined to recognize 'Alī. Much more dangerous however to 'Alī's cause was Mu'āwiya who, it will be remembered, was governor of Syria. His entourage being exclusively pro-Ummayad, he was in a good position to accuse 'Alī of being privy to 'Uthmān's murder, and formally to proclaim himself his avenger.

As usual 'Alī was irresolute. He dismissed the killers from his circle and also got rid of 'Abdullāh b. Sabā whose immoderate praise, almost apotheosis, of his person was compromising him with the orthodox. His slow reactions allowed the partisans of Ṭalḥa and Zubayr to seize Baṣra. Tardily his army moved there in December 656, and he defeated his opponents near the city. 'Ā'isha was taken prisoner but 'Alī released her out of respect; Ṭalḥa was mortally wounded and Zubayr slain while trying to escape. The faction these three had formed of old Muhājirs was shattered, and 'Alī entered Baṣra.

In the month of Ṣafar 37 AH = July 657, 'Alī's army encountered the Syrian Arabs under Mu'āwiya and his recent associate 'Amr b. al-'Āṣ at Ṣiffīn, south of Raqqa on the Euphrates. On the second day of the battle 'Alī's right wing under Malik al-Ashtar and his centre commanded by himself broke the enemy and pressed him hard, partly no doubt thanks to the fanatical bravery of 'Alī's regiment of Readers (*Qurrā'*) who knew the Koran by heart.[37] Only a stratagem of 'Amr b. al-'Āṣ averted total defeat: he ordered Mu'āwiya's troops to fasten scrolls of the Koran to their lances, summoning all as it were to the judgment of the divine book. 'Alī stopped the fight, and under pressure from his advisers (some of whom like al-Ash'ath b. Qays and Abū Mūsā al-Ash'arī were at heart opposed to him) agreed to talks.

This proof of irresolution and an inclination to compromise on the part of 'Alī and the leaders of his faction caused a massive withdrawal of support. Many rallied to the cry *Lā ḥukma illā li'llāh*! ('There is no arbitration except God's'), their case being that God's judgment had already been passed in the shape of 'Alī's victory over Mu'āwiya, and that to negotiate was to flout that judgment. The masses had found a religious formula to express their unwillingness to have any truck with the aristocratic Umayyad party. Thus disappointed in 'Alī as their leader, twelve thousand of them quitted his camp and made their own near Nahrawān in Iraq close to the spurs of the Zagros range. There they elected a new Caliph, 'Abdullāh b. Wahb, one of their own ranks.

In this cleavage of the party it was the spokesmen of the common people — men who countered the domination of the aristocratic Ummayads not with the personal interests of 'Alī and his family the 'Alids, but with the equality of all Muslims — who broke away. A new self-governing offshoot of the Faith had come into being — the Khārijites (*khārijī* pl. *khawārij* from the root *kharaja* 'to go out', 'to secede'), the Seceders. Like the Shī'ites, they were to begin with a purely political party and only in the sequel turned into a religious sect. We shall speak later of their doctrine and historical importance.

The name Shī'ites was thenceforward reserved for those of 'Alī's partisans who stayed faithful to him and his descendants and to the idea of an hereditary Imamate or Caliphate. Their elite, to all appearance, consisted mainly of that self-same new nobility (rapidly becoming feudal) which furnished the leadership of the Umayyad party, and it is this social affinity which to some extent explains the propensity of 'Alī and his entourage to come to terms with it. For Mu'āwiya's supporters, of course, the proposal to negotiate was merely a ruse to gain time.

Civil war was renewed in 658. But first 'Alī had to deal with the Khārijites — his advisers insisted on that. He destroyed their camp at Nahrawān, but not their morale. Reconciliation between Shī'ites and Khārijites was from then on impossible. As 'Alī was coming out of the mosque at Kūfa he was mortally wounded by a sword thrust in the head delivered by a Khārijite named Ibn Muljam. He died two days later on 17 Ramaḍān 40 AH = 24 January 661. By that date Mu'āwiya had already been proclaimed Caliph at Jerusalem.

Upon ‘Alī’s death the civil war, in which the odds for the past two years had been manifestly on the side of Mu‘āwiya, ended. ‘Alī’s elder son Ḥasan whom the Shī‘ites deemed the second Imam-Caliph was a flaccid, passive man who made a pact with Mu‘āwiya resigning his claims in return for a fortune (some say of two million dirhems) in money and estates, and settled in Medīna. Mu‘āwiya declared an amnesty and was presently acknowledged in all the provinces. He chose Damascus as his capital, since his power derived from the Arab tribes that had settled in Syria. Under the Umayyad dynasty now inaugurated (661) the Caliphate was converted into an early feudal- type society having a patriarchal structure among the Arab, Iranian and other slave-owning nomads. It was a secular state, and as such it excited the opposition of the Muhājirs and Helpers who were for a theocracy. The centre of this opposition was Medīna.

The Shī‘ites and Khārijites consistently remained the most dangerous foes of the regime. Umayyad home policy hinged on oppression of the masses, and inequality — both as between Muslims and Dhimmīs (non-Muslims) and as between Arabs and non-Arabs. Revolts were frequent and those engineered by the Khārijites always relied on the common people — peasants, impoverished Bedouin, urban artisans, slaves — whether they happened to be Muslim or not. As regards the Shī‘ites, although their leaders, i.e. the ‘Alids and their entourage, as has been pointed out, were affluent land-owners, they constituted an elite in opposition, excluded by the hated Umayyads from power, and were not unsuccessful in prevailing on the lower orders again and again to fight their cause for them. In early days the Shī‘ites had been Arab to a man, but now under the Umayyads many clients joined them, particularly in Iraq and Iran. These *Mawālī* were naturally anxious to liberate themselves from their humiliating position in the tribes and win equal rights with the original Arab members, and the Shī‘ites promised them just this.

Mu‘āwiya’s death in 680 was the signal for an anti-Umayyad drive. A deputation went from Kūfa to Mecca to approach ‘Alī’s second son Ḥusayn, whom the Shī‘ites had recognized as third Imam on the death of his brother Ḥasan, second Imam, in 669, with an invitation to come to Kūfa and lead a revolt against the new Umayyad Caliph Yazīd I b. Mu‘āwiya. Having sent his cousin Muslim b. ‘Aqīl ahead, Ḥusayn set out with a small force. Unfortunately, the revolt of the Kūfa Shī‘ites was put down by the governor of Kūfa ‘Ubaydullāh b. Ziyād. Muslim perished before reaching his destination, and when Ḥusayn received the sad news on the road he did not want, or was unable, to go back. Some of his men deserted him, and he pitched camp, with the few who remained loyal, at a waterless site near the small habitation of Kerbelā, not far from Kūfa. Towards the end he had with him only seventy fighting men, including eighteen of his cousins and their wives and children. The Umayyad commander ʿUmar b. Saʿd b. Abī Waqqāṣ[38] brought four thousand men to blockade the camp. He called upon Ḥusayn to surrender himself to Yazīd's clemency, but Ḥusayn did not deign to answer. For one whole week he and his people suffered the agony of thirst; then, on the evening of 9 Muḥarram 61 AH = 9 October 680, according to Ṭabarī's account, he made his last will and testament and spent the remainder of the night praying. Next morning, after the common prayer, and watched by the women and children, he made a sortie against the enemy. At first the Caliph's troops held back, nobody in their ranks wishing to incur the odium of slaying the grandson of the Prophet; but presently they set upon him *en masse* so that none should bear individual responsibility. He fell in the unequal contest, victim of thirty-three stabs and thirty-four slashes. His comrades died with him and their heads were sent to Yazīd in Damascus. The latter affected distress at what had happened, declaring that he had not ordered Ḥusayn's killing. He freed the captive wives and children of Ḥusayn and his kinsmen and let them return to Medīna.[39]

The tragedy of Kerbelā left a deep mark on contemporary Islam, and led the Shīʿites to make a regular cult of their third Imam, saint and martyr, whose presumed tomb became a principal holy object and place of pilgrimage.

Meantime the drive against the Umayyads had not ended. Medīna rose in 680; and in Mecca, ʿAbdullāh, son of Zubayr the well-known Companion of whom mention has been made above, was actually proclaimed Caliph. His troops were also engaged in Iraq. Twelve years went by like this before the general rising could be suppressed (692).

Shīʿism, a purely political party to begin with, was transformed into a religious trend in the seventy years that separated the death of Ḥusayn from the establishment of the ʿAbbāsid dynasty in 750, the momentum in this process being provided by the martyrdom of ʿAlī and Ḥusayn. Wellhausen considers the most trustworthy source for early Shīʿism to be Abū Mikhnaf,[40] a pupil of the pupils of the Companions of the Prophet and compiler of the Traditions (d. 774). His writings have not come down to us but they are largely reproduced in Ṭabarī's Annals.

Soon after Ḥusayn's passing, a secret society was founded in Kūfa of one hundred Shī'ites, none below sixty years of age, of whom the old Companion Sulaymān b. Ṣurad was Shaykh. Its slogan was 'Vengeance for the death of Ḥusayn' and it grew so rapidly that in November 684 four thousand of these rebels proceeded to Kerbelā and then, crossing the Euphrates, moved against Ras al 'Ayn only to be defeated and almost annihilated. Also in Kūfa, but quite independently, a certain Mukhtār b. Abī 'Ubayd, an Arab noble of the Thaqīf, propertied in the locality, was busy in the Shī'ite cause; and when he learned that Ḥusayn was on the move towards Kūfa, this man of sixty rounded up his clients, who were peasants, and went forth to greet him. After the disaster at Kerbelā he was arrested, but being later released returned to Kūfa and devoted himself to propaganda as the agent, he said, of the third son of the Imam 'Alī, Muḥammad b. al-Ḥanafiyya.

Muḥammad b. al-Ḥanafiyya (b. 637 d. 700) was 'Alī's son by a slave-prisoner of the tribe Ḥanīfa,[41] not by his wife Fāṭima, and hence the surname, 'Son of the Ḥanīfa Woman'. It is said that this stepbrother of Ḥusayn had outstanding ability as well as complete devotion; and it is a fact that a section of Shī'ites headed by Mukhtār recognized him as Imam in succession to Ḥusayn since the 'Alīds had no other competent leader, Ḥusayn's children being minor. The majority, however, while respecting him, felt they could not hail him as their Imam because he was not the son of the Prophet's daughter. His supporters were later to compose the Kaysānite offshoot of Shī'ism.[42]

In October 685 Kūfa, being then in the hands of the anti-Caliph 'Abdullāh b. az-Zubayr, witnessed a Shī'ite rising in which the city was seized. The *de facto* leader was Mukhtār who had been preaching sermons in the mosque which he claimed were inspired by the Archangel Gabriel. He had entrusted the military side to Ibrāhīm son of Malik al-Ashtar the distinguished general of Caliph 'Alī. The treasury was plundered and its contents distributed among the rebels, each man getting from two hundred to five hundred dirhems. Many of Ḥusayn's killers and Ummayad partisans generally were executed. Ibrāhīm followed up with a brilliant victory over Ummayad troops in Upper Iraq (Muḥarram 67 AH = August 686). But the movement had forked into *Ashrāf* and *Mawālī*; in other words into aristocratic Arabs and client Iranians of lower station. When Mukhtār stood by the latter on the principle of equality in Islam, the Ashrāf were alienated and withdrew their loyalty. The depleted Shī'ite army was defeated by the anti-Caliph's[43] forces who then re-entered Kūfa. Mukhtār locked himself in the citadel with his followers and after being beleaguered for four months, made a sortie and fell fighting (April 687).

Muḥammad b. Ḥanafiyya's attitude to Mukhtār's revolt had been cautious and ambivalent: he neglected to come to Iraq and link up with the insurgents, but neither did he dissociate himself from them; he was either waiting to see how things would turn out or else he was put off by the rebellion's democratic bias. Indeed he hardly lived up to his position as head of the central Shī'ite group. To the end of his days (700) he was too passive — which is why the Umayyads did not persecute him.

Simultaneously with the Shī'ite resistance a still more formidable Khārijite movement had been put in train. In its ranks it counted the indigent Bedouin, peasants, artisans whether Arab or Persian (the latter of course *Mawālī*, clients), and runaway slaves belonging to various tribes. But before discussing this movement it will be well to say something about the ideology of the Khārijites.

The main article in their doctrine was the recognition of the equality of all Muslims. They held that the Believers must dominate the Dhimmīs in the conquered countries, the latter paying capitation and land taxes from which they themselves were exempt. But within the Islamic society complete equality must reign; lands in the conquered provinces must belong to the community (or, what was the same, to the state). Nor was it simply a legal equality on which they insisted as between Arabs and non-Arabs; their ideal was social equality as well. In their doctrine on the Caliphate they were sharply separated both from the orthodox Sunnī[44] and from the Shī'ite positions.[45] They held that the Imam-Caliph, i.e. the spiritual and political head of the religious community-state, must be elected; all Believers, no matter what their origin, participating in the election. The person chosen need not be of the Quraysh, as the Sunnīs postulated — he could be a negro slave, if he were worthy of the post. They did not attach any sacred meaning to the title: the Caliph in their eyes was neither teacher of the Faith nor sovereign, he was merely the executive officer of the community of Believers, military leader and protector of the common weal. The community which chose him had automatically the right to remove him, even to judge him and sentence him to death, if he should govern badly, turn out a tyrant, or betray the interests of the community for the sake of personal gain. They held, moreover, that any society physically cut off from others could elect its own Imam, so that there might easily be several Imams at the same time in different places. Hence all the leaders of Khārijite movements were called Imams, Caliphs, and Amīrs of the Believers. And so central was it in Khārijite doctrine that the Caliphate was not the property of any one family, that not a single Imam of theirs was of the Quraysh. In a word, they conceived of sovereignty as something belonging to the community of Believers and the Caliph as the responsible agent of that community.

They acknowledged the first two Caliphs, Abū Bakr and 'Umar, to be lawful, but not 'Uthmān. 'Alī was only lawful, in their view, until he consented to settle the dispute with Mu'āwiya by negotiation 'instead of being satisfied with the judgment of God'. They did not recognize the Umayyads or the 'Abbāsids after them, and they did not recognize the hereditary Imamate of the 'Alids.

They were implacably opposed to the huge land ownership which the Muslim aristocracy enjoyed, being indeed, in principle opposed to any social inequality inside the community. Some even held that slaves should be emancipated on conversion to Islam, Muslim-slave being a contradiction in terms. In short, the Khārijites of the seventh to ninth centuries were members of a movement that relied on broad popular support, and expressed political views distinctly radical for those days.

This political theory rested primarily on their religion. On strictly religious issues they differed but little from orthodox Sunnī Islam, provided we mean by that the primitive Islam as it was in the first decades of its existence, without the innovations which the Sunnīs added later. The Khārijites did not accept the doctrine of an uncreated Koran, denied the authenticity of Sūra XII, usually rejected *ijmā'* and always *qiyās*,[46] admitted no pilgrimage except that to Mecca, and forbade the cult of saints; though they compensated for this last item by gradually introducing the veneration of martyrs, i.e. Khārijites who had died for their cause. They were distinguished by a rigid observance of fasting, prayer and ritual and by austerity in morals. They came to maintain that a Muslim who has fallen into a state of grievous sin ceases to be a Believer and becomes infidel, even as the man who doubts the truth of his faith. A single false step can excommunicate a person from the Muslim (meaning Khārijite) community, into which he can only be received back after public repentance and proof of earnest works.

This religious doctrine was translated into politics: false Imams, or unlawful Caliphs who had departed from the Book of God (the Koran, principle of theocracy) as had the Umayyads in signal fashion, had fallen into a state of grievous sin: *ergo* they had ceased to be Believers and had become infidels. Not only can there be no submission to them, but Holy War must be waged against them, and every enemy falling into Khārijite hands in such a war slaughtered as recreant. This slaughter of apostates (which word broadly signified all non-Khārijite Muslims) was to start with only a practical measure, but it was afterwards raised to the status of a religious principle named *isti'rāḍ*.

The already mentioned Abū Mikhnaf whose account is preserved in Ṭabarī's Annals states that four sub-sects had emerged by the date of Yazīd's death in 683 named after their leaders. These were: Azraqites (*azāriqa*), Ṣufrites (*ṣufriyya*), Bayhasites (*bayhasiyya*) and Ibāḍites or Abāḍites (*ibāḍiyya, abāḍiyya*). Of these the most extreme was the first. Nāfi' b. al-Azraq who is regarded as its founder was, according to some, the son of a Greek blacksmith who after being a prisoner-slave of the Arabs became a freedman.[47] He pushed the principle of religious slaughter to extreme lengths, holding that it applied not only to the enemies of the Khārijites but to the stay-at-home Khārijites who were too passive to go off to Holy War. He therefore required of his followers (1) rupture with the stay-at-homes; (2) recognition as apostates of all who failed to flock to his insurrectionist camp; (3) gruelling cross-examination (*miḥna*) in the faith of all who did join. He taught that it is allowable to kill women and children as well as men in war with enemies of the faith.

In the seventh century, these Khārijites, and particularly the Azraqite sub-sect, were relentless in fighting the oppressors of the people whom they branded as apostates. Brave, ever ready to die for the cause, they sold their lives dearly on the battlefield, convinced that the blessings of paradise would be the wages of their blood. A characteristic of their warfare was the participation of women: towards the end of the century the Azraqite heroine Umm Ḥakīm was much renowned and, bent on a martyr's death, would cry: 'Tired am I of washing my head and rubbing it with oil. Is there none here that would rid me of this burden?' The Umayyad governor of Iraq 'Ubaydullāh b. Ziyād, a rabid persecutor of the Khārijites, to cool the ardour of these women, gave orders that the corpses of those dying in battle should be stripped and left naked on the field. It is worth remarking that the fanatical hatred these extreme Khārijites displayed towards the Muslims outside their own sect was combined with a generous toleration of Jews and Christians; these, in Azraqite understanding, had not betrayed the teaching of their prophets Moses and Jesus,[48] and therefore *isti'rāḍ* did not extend to them. Certain Khārijite leaders even thought it proper to accord equality of rights with Muslims (meaning, of course, Khārijites) to such Jews and Christians as should agree to acknowledge Muḥammad as Prophet with a stipulation added: Muḥammad was Prophet for the Arabs, but not for us.

The most moderate of the sub-sects was the Ibāḍite, otherwise Abāḍite, who took this name from ‘Abdullāh b. Ibāḍ or Abāḍ (*floruit* second half of seventh century). Its members were revolted by the exaggerated fanaticism of the Azraqites, particularly by the requirement of compulsory slaughter of all non-Khārijites. And their position in regard to the Umayyad Caliphate was less uncompromising, though they did hold it to be illegitimate.

There were some fitful risings of the Khārijites in Baṣra from 661 onwards, and in Kūfa in 677. But the great Khārijite Resistance occupied the thirteen years 684 to 697. The movement was directed simultaneously against three separate opponents, viz. the Umayyad Caliph ‘Abdu ’l-Malik, his sworn enemy the anti-Caliph ‘Abdullāh b. az-Zubayr, and the Shī‘ites. The arrangement of dates in the sources is confused and contradictory, and the chronology here adopted is that established by Wellhausen.[49]

In 684 Baṣra and Lower Iraq were in the hands of ‘Abdullāh b. az-Zubayr, the Kūfa region was held by Shī‘ite rebels under Mukhtār b. Abī‘Ubayd as already mentioned above, and the Umayyad troops were in Upper Iraq and Jazīra. Ibn al-Azraq had three hundred men under him when he made his camp in the Aḥwāz neighbourhood of Khūzistān. There were already pockets of Khārijite insurgents on the marshes east of Baṣra, on the east bank of the Tigris and on the Kārun river. The sect had also just achieved success in Yamāma and Baḥrayn where Najda b. ‘Āmir of the Ḥanīf tribe had been proclaimed local Caliph by the Khārijites. To him, we may note, was due the emancipation of four thousand slaves engaged on Mu‘āwiya’s estates at Yamāma, where the Khārijites held out until 693. Meanwhile Nāfi‘ b. al-Azraq had fallen in a bloody fight at Dulab, on the Kārun, Dujayl as the Arabs called it (684/5). The Azraqites replaced him as Caliph by ‘Ubaydullāh b. Makhūz. They were now getting so many Persians in their ranks — peasants who had risen against Arab taskmasters — that opponents derided them as a ‘mob of riff-raff’. In May of the next year they suffered defeat in battle with Ibn az-Zubayr’s army at Sillabr east of the Kārun, and again their Caliph was among those killed. They evacuated Aḥwāz and made for the Zagros mountains; but when once again worsted at Sābūr in Fārs, they retreated to Kirmān which was entirely in their hands and which became their permanent base.[50] They brought their depleted contingents to strength and moved again through Fārs and Aḥwāz to Baṣra. Muṣ'ab b. az-Zubayr, brother of the anti-Caliph, came out against them and they fell back towards Madā'in (Ctesiphon) and thence re-entered Iran through the Zagros. They raided Ray and besieged Iṣfahān for several months without succeeding in taking it. In May 689 they elected the intrepid Qaṭarī b. al-Fujā'a, a well-known poet, as their Caliph. Under his command they proceeded to Kirmān and after an interval of rest and recruitment crossed the Kārun once more and pitched camp on the east bank of the Shaṭṭu 'l-'Arab opposite Baṣra. In autumn 691 the defeat and death of Muṣ'ab occurred and when this news reached his general, Muhallab, the latter transferred his allegiance to the Umayyads and continued the struggle with the Azraqites in their name. But Caliph 'Abdu 'l-Malik stripped him of his command and entrusted it to two Umayyads: first, to Khālid and then to 'Abdu 'l-'Azīz his brother. Again the Azraqites retired to Kirmān, but inflicted a fearful defeat on 'Abdu 'l-'Azīz at Dārābjird in Fārs. 'Abdu 'l-'Azīz lost most of his troops and had to flee so hastily that his wife, a noted beauty, fell into enemy hands and — in accordance with Azraqite principle — was callously butchered. The victor pursued the fugitives, took Khūzistān and came as far as the Shaṭṭu 'l-'Arab.

Hostilities were dragging on with varying success when Caliph 'Abdu 'l-Malik appointed Ḥajjāj b. Yūsuf governor of the eastern provinces (late 694). This gifted soldier and excessively ruthless administrator was an ardent champion of the feudal-aristocratic policy of the Umayyads, and it is therefore no accident that bourgeois historians like Wellhausen, Becker and Lammens extol him to the skies, giving him credit for 'the pacification of Iraq' and 'the recovery of fertility' in this province. The fact is there were two sides to his character. He carried out vast irrigation schemes in Mesopotamia and the Kārun basin, constructed the town Wāsiṭ on the Euphrates, and rescued the revenue by efficient taxation. This had touched two hundred and fourteen million dirhems in the first half of the sixth century, but had dwindled to one hundred and twenty million under 'Umar I and one hundred million under Mu'āwiya. Ḥajjāj raised it to one hundred and thirty-five million. But recovery and pacification were only the obverse of the coin: turn it and there were popular risings drowned in blood, non-Arab (new Muslim) agriculturists saddled with the *kharāj* which was formerly exacted from people of other religions alone; peasants compelled to wear badges of lead round their necks indicating their place of residence so that they should not be able to make off to the towns and evade payment of *kharāj* or the *corvée* on canal-reconstruction and on building towns, citadels and government offices. The sources tell us that during Ḥajjāj's tenure of appointment one hundred and thirty thousand persons perished at the executioner's hands, and that when he died there were fifty thousand men and thirty thousand women in the gaols.

Ḥajjāj had appointed Muhallab to take command against the Azraqites. When these retired to Fārs, Muhallab followed them with superior and well-equipped forces and took up a fortified position at Kāzarūn. Desultory hostilities ensued around Sābūr and Iṣṭakhr for one year; after which the Azraqites vacated Fārs and retired early in 696 to Kirmān, which was theirs, and where they made Jīruft their headquarters. There the struggle dragged on for a year and a half. Ḥajjāj, indeed, suspected Muhallab of deliberately protracting the war so as to cling to his command, but it is more likely that he was putting his hopes on starvation, epidemic and discord. As to the last he was not without reason; for the Azraqite camp in Kirmān had splintered. The majority of the Arabs remained loyal to Ibn al-Fujā'a, whereas the *Mawālī* numbering eight thousand, and a minority of the Arabs, elected a new leader called 'Abd Rabbihi.[51] In some accounts there are two Azraqite leaders bearing this sobriquet, an Elder and a Younger, of which the present is the Younger. Anyhow, matters culminated in bloodshed. Ibn al-Fujā'a departed with his loyalists to Ṭabaristān (nowadays Māzandarān), and the *Mawālī* stayed where they were with 'Abd Rabbihi, to be almost wiped out by Muhallab's troops in the autumn of 697 after a six-month struggle. It will be seen that the Azraqite principle of equality of all Believers irrespective of ethnic affiliation did not in practice ensure harmony in their own camp.

Those who had left for Ṭabaristān evidently hoped to hold out for a long time in that wooded mountainous country with its difficult approaches. But they failed to win the sympathy of the local peasants, who were still Zoroastrians to a man, and indeed estranged them by imposing a high poll-tax (*jizya*). Presently the forces sent to hunt them down arrived, and engaging them in a certain gorge routed them utterly. Ibn al-Fujā'a fell fighting. His comrade-in-arms 'Abīda b. Hilāl repaired to a mountain fastness in Qūmis where he and his men remained beleaguered until, exhausted by hunger, they sallied out to their death (697).

Before the Azraqite rising had been crushed in this fashion, a Ṣufrite revolt broke out in the upper reaches of the Tigris where for the previous twenty years their local spiritual head, the saint Ṣāliḥ b.

Musarriḥ had been preaching and exhorting the people to bestir themselves in the name of God, be revenged on those in power for their sins, and join battle with the false Imams and their godless following. They rose in the town of Dārā in May 695. Their number was not more than one hundred and twenty to start with, but it grew quickly. However, Ḥajjāj had four thousand soldiers available to throw against them, and in the ensuing fight Ṣāliḥ was killed. A gifted leader replaced him in the person of Shabīb b. Yazīd ash-Shaybānī. The tactical method now adopted with success was sometimes to employ small mobile detachments of one to two hundred men, sometimes to move *en masse*, as the circumstances warranted. The state treasuries were rifled and the collection of taxes was interrupted. This went on in Central Iraq between Kūfa, Madā'in and the Jūkhā district on the Tigris, an old pocket of Khārijite activity. In the summer of 696 they gained Madā'in and consolidated their position. They scattered a force which Ḥajjāj immediately flung against them, and crossing the Euphrates encamped near Kūfa itself. Ḥajjāj could not depend on the Kūfans as the latter had no wish to fight for him, and he only succeeded in repelling the Khārijites thanks to reinforcements from Syria. But Shabīb suffered major losses in two engagements, and in the autumn decided to fall back on Kirmān and join forces with the Azraqites there. At the passage of the Kārun he was the last of everybody to cross, and was hardly on the pontoon bridge when his stallion reared. He was thrown into the water and, weighed down by his armour, was drowned.

The sources relate that Shabīb excelled his companions in stature, physical strength, and fortitude. Humane, he would often save his prisoners from the fate which the Khārijite code prescribed by allowing them a chance to escape — and this earned him the censure of his fellows. It also earned him the respect of the Christians in Iraq who, if they did not enter his army, constantly went out of their way to help him.[52] Further, he was disinterested, and once unloaded from a pack-mule the money apportioned him after rifling a treasury, and threw it into a canal. This unusual man was accompanied on his campaigns by his mother, a Greek woman and one-time prisoner, and his wife, who met her end in the attack by Ḥajjāj's troops on the Khārijite camp near Kūfa.

The Khārijite Resistance had spent itself and after Shabīb's death was soon suppressed (697).

In both of the above-described Khārijite risings one is struck by the breadth of the stage from the upper Tigris to Kirmān and Ṭabaristān, and by the amazing persistence and will-power of the actors. The popular, mainly peasant, character of the movement of 684 to 697 is beyond doubt, and hardly surprising considering that the first Khārijites who seceded from 'Alī in 657 were Bedouin to a man. At the same time it had its weak side in that fanaticism which caused Khārijites to look on other Muslims as apostates and therefore enemies. How could the broad mass of the Bedouin, the peasants, the urban poor give their support to people so persuaded? 'The extreme fanaticism', Ye. A. Belyayev remarks, 'of these implacable, narrow-minded fighters, drove them into a bitter conflict not only with the Caliphate authorities but with the Muslim population which was quite unable to distinguish between their religious convictions and their political views. Again and again they destroyed a working populace without pity for woman or child. Herein lay a reason of the weakness besetting the Khārijite movement, herein an explanation why it had only a relative success. Although the Khārijites came out against oppression and exploitation, the religious fanaticism of these sectarians engendered nothing but discord among the workers, so that any concerted struggle against feudal exploitation in the Caliphate was hampered.'[53] On top of this were the dissensions to which we have referred, and the fragmentation into sub-sects. The twelfth century Shahrastānī recorded that he knew eight of these, and at one time apparently there were as many as twenty.

For all that, the Khārijites held out, and were an even greater political force through the whole of the eighth century. They had their centres in the Berber districts of Africa, in West Arabia, Oman (where there were Ibaḍites), around Mosul and Jūkhā on the Tigris, and in Khūzistān, Khurāsān and Sīstān. They were constantly in revolt, some of their sects flying a white banner, and others a black banner. Only a few of these risings can be noted here. There was that of Ḥārith b. Surayj in Khurāsān in 734.[54] Then, ten years later, under the last of the Umayyads, the iron-willed and inexorable Marwān II (744–750), a major revolt was led in Iraq by Ḍahhāk b. Qays. Kūfa and Wāsiṭ were captured in 745, and the alleged number of insurgents in the following year was one hundred and twenty thousand, including many women who fought in armour alongside their men. Ḍahhāk took Mosul, defeated Marwān's son 'Abdullāh and besieged him at Niṣībīn. But Marwān himself now moved on Jazīra and overwhelmed the Khārijites at Kafartūt in bloody combat (September 746). Ḍahhāk was among the killed. The Khārijites then lost Mosul and Kūfa, but they still had forty thousand troops, and with these they retreated through Ḥulwān into Khūzistān and Fārs. There, finally, they were beaten and dispersed in 747.[55] Wellhausen points out that whereas in the seventh century the Khārijites fought with comparatively small forces reckoned in hundreds or thousands of men, an insurrection now would unite formidable masses of the population numbered in their tens and hundreds of thousands. His explanation of this is that they were now glad, possibly having learned from past mistakes, to receive people of different opinions from theirs, and to act on the principle that 'he that is not against us is for us'.[56] Risings on this scale shook the Caliphate badly.

The principal centre of Khārijism in Iran with effect from the eighth century was Sīstān. There were repeated incitements to peasant revolt in this area. At the turn of the eighth century there was an important rising led by Abū Ḥamza, and revolts continued to occur both in the ninth century and after.[57] The noted geographer and traveller Yāqūt ar-Rūmī al-Ḥamawī writing early in the thirteenth century states that there were many Khārijites in Sīstān, all of them professing their faith quite openly, and that the township of Raqub was peopled exclusively by them.[58] Obviously they had by that time changed into a peaceable sect locally. They seem, too, to have earned a reputation as honest and just people above the average. Yāqūt has an anecdote in which he cites a merchant who had been to Sīstān. This man called at a craftsman's shop to buy something and fell to arguing about the price. The craftsman took gentle exception: 'Brother, know that I am a Khārijite and therefore never deviate from justice and truth. I should be ashamed to cause thee even the slightest loss.' The merchant then questioned the locals and convinced himself of the correctness of what the craftsman was asking. The Sīstān Khārijites practised mutual aid and philanthropy so generously, Yāqūt says, that nowhere were the poor helped with such zeal or the weak protected with such energy as in their midst.[59]

The irreconcilable Azraqite element, however, persisted.[60] It was behind a great insurrection of dark-skinned African slaves, the Zanj as they were called, in Lower Iraq and Khūzistān, for which it furnished a leader in the person of 'Alī b. Muḥammad, better known under his nickname Lord of the Zanj (Ṣāḥibu'z-Zanj) or Caliph of the Zanj.[61] This resistance, presently spreading to the poorest of the Bedouin and the peasants, held out for fourteen years (869–883) and shook the 'Abbāsid Caliphate not a little.

We must come back to the eighth century and discusss one more anti-Umayyad party of religious and political temper. This was the following of a Quraysh family, the 'Abbāsids, so named after their ancestor 'Abbās, the Prophet's uncle.[62] During the Umayyad Caliphate the 'Abbāsids did not count politically but were large landed proprietors enjoying respect as kinsmen of the Prophet. As such they began to noise it abroad that *they* deserved the Caliphate rather than the Umayyads who were alien to the Prophet's family, being descendants of his enemies Abū Sufyān and Ḥakam. This was voiced most effectively by 'Abbās' great grandson, the clever and bold Muḥammad b. 'Alī b. 'Abdullāh b. 'Abbās.

The power of the Umayyads rested on a narrow basis socially. They were abominated not only by the humble Bedouin, and by peasants and townsmen in their myriads, but also by many of the landed-proprietor class — particularly the Persian Dihqāns — by Arab partisans of theocracy in Medīna and elsewhere, and by the Shī'ites who supported the 'Alid claim to the Caliphate. The 'Abbāsids added to this total of disaffection. Moreover, in contrast to the ineffectual 'Alids they were, or had on their side, dynamic people with political vision. A secret organization of adherents centred on Kūfa came into being in the first quarter of the eighth century, under the direction (in the name of the 'Abbāsid Imam Muḥammad b. 'Alī) of an energetic Persian, Buqayr b. Māhān.[63] Propaganda, known as *da'wa*, was conducted here and there, and local branches were formed which grew apace, notwithstanding arrest, flogging, and execution. The missionaries' aim was to win over all the disaffected elements, Arab and non-Arab, Shī'ites, Khārijites and even non-Muslims.[64] They were fortunate in enlisting as one of their canvassers the Imam of the Kaysānite group of the Shī'ites, Abū Hāshim (the son of Muḥammad Ibnu 'l-Ḥanafiyya) who on his deathbed declared that after him the Imamate must cross to the house of 'Abbās. In preaching at the popular level they implied that when the Caliphate passed to the 'Abbāsids, Muslims would be relieved of the kharāj, non-Muslims required to pay this and the jizya only at an equitable assessment, and villagers exempted from forced labour. These were dangerous tactics calculated, as the event showed, to invite embarrassing demands. One of the missionaries, a certain Khidāsh, who was emissary in Khurāsān even started advocating the old Mazdak ideals of social equality and the common ownership of lands.

The pro-'Abbāsid revolt in Khurāsān of 747–750 is well documented in Ṭabarī's Annals and elsewhere, but there are nevertheless details not contained in the abridged version[65] of that work (edited by de Goeje) which alone has come down to us. Luckily, however, the work of an anonymous Arab historian of the early eleventh century who had Ṭabarī's full version in front of him has been discovered by V. I. Belyayev[66] and made available to scholarship in a recent edition.[67]

The leader of the revolt was Abū Muslim. Accounts differ about his origin[68] but there is agreement that he had been a slave in his youth. His master 'Īsā b. Ma'qil had been arrested as pro-'Abbāsid and the slave would visit him in gaol. In this way he became acquainted with Buqayr b. Māhān, also detained, who was much taken by the young man's unusual personality and who, on release, purchased him for four hundred dirhems and made a present of him to the 'Abbāsid Imam Ibrāhīm b. Muḥammad. The latter freed Abū Muslim, named him his client and sent him as his emissary to the Merv oasis to prepare the rising. On the appointed day (25 Ramaḍān 129 AH = 9 July 747) beacons were lighted and four thousand insurgents assembled, wearing black clothing and carrying black flags.[69] Simultaneously the whole of north Khurāsān rose. Iranian peasants constituted the bulk of the rebels, and we read of the inhabitants of sixty villages arriving in a single day;[70] but artisans, Iranian landed proprietors, Dihqāns, South Arabian Yemenite tribes, who had settled in Khurāsān and were dissatisfied with Caliph Marwān II, and many slaves, also responded to the call. For these slaves a separate section of the camp was set aside; and when their owners, also in the camp, protested at these reception arrangements, Abū Muslim ordered the public crier to hail the slaves, saying: 'The Amīr commands you to go back to your masters'. Then it was the slaves' turn to protest; but Abū Muslim rejoined: 'The crier rightly announced that slaves should go back to their lords. But attention! Your lords are the Family of Muḥammad', i.e. the 'Abbāsids.[71] So the slaves remained where they were.

In its religious composition the revolution was no less motley: Sunnīs, Shī'ites of the Kaysānite persuasion, Sīstān Khārijites,[72] Zoroastrians and Khurramites rubbed shoulders. In the mass, of course, the peasantry, artisans and slaves had resorted to arms in the hope of delivery from an oppressive yoke, and not for the sake of the 'Abbāsids at all. Consequently the name of the pretender Imam Ibrāhīm was by no means revealed to everybody: many of the rebels were simply asked to pronounce an impersonal oath of allegiance: 'To him that be welcome to all of the Family of the Prophet Muḥammad.'[73] This wording was especially useful when it came to winning over the Shī'ites and the 'Alid family: when the masses were told that the revolt had been started in defence of the claims of the 'Family of the Prophet' (the Hāshimites) there was an ambiguity, for the expression might be applied equally well to the 'Alids or the 'Abbāsids. As a result many Shīlim's sympathies were with the democratic aspirations of the lower orders; in other words, he was a fellow-traveller in the pro-'Abbāsid party rather than its devoted agent. Revolution slid into real civil war which swept across Iran and Iraq. The Umayyad forces were beaten near Ṭūs, in Gurgān, at Nahāwand and on the Greater Zāb river, and in January 750 they surrendered. Abū'l-'Abbās Ṣaffāḥ was proclaimed Caliph in the mosque at Kūfa.

Thus was founded the 'Abbāsid Dynasty which endured until 1258.[74] Its first two Caliphs, Ṣaffāḥ (750–754) and his brother Abū Ja'far Manṣūr (754–775), once safely on their thrones, gave short shrift to the popular elements who had put them there, and broke their demagogic promises. They adopted blatantly aristocratic policies, and could not wait to be done with their old comrades-in-arms whose popularity they, of course, feared. Abū Muslim's democratic leanings were well known. He was setting out on ḥajj to Mecca and was passing through Iraq when Manṣūr invited him to visit his residence. It was a trap, and he was murdered as soon as he reached the Caliph's headquarters (February 755). His murder moved the peasantry of Iran to indignation. The Khurramites had actually revered him as the incarnation of God, and those who henceforward directed the peasant movements in Iran and Central Asia, not only Khurramites but Shī'ites too,[75] were apt to give out that they were disciples carrying on his work.

The revolution of 747–749 which installed the 'Abbāsid Caliphate was fraught with consequences alike for Iran's people and for Islam. In the first place the 'Abbāsid victory furthered the feudal order and the ownership of land. Under Caliph Manṣūr the masses, so far from gaining anything, were subjected to heavier taxes and obligations than ever, and many a peasant rising, whether beneath the scarlet or white banner of the different Khārijite sub-sects or beneath the green standard of the Shī'ites, bore witness to the general resentment. Indeed peasant revolt was the salient feature of Iran's whole history from the mid-eighth to the mid-ninth century.

The second consequence of 'Abbāsid victory was to fix once and for all the frontier between the opposed politico-religious trends in Islam: between the assortment of Shī'ites and Khārijites on the one side and orthodox Sunnī Islam on the other. The latter now became the ideological form of the Caliphate's feudal state; which, though it remained in essence as secular as its Umayyad predecessor, exerted itself to clothe its authority in the garment of a theocracy. The 'Abbāsids surrounded themselves with *Faqihs* or jurist-theologians

'Abbāsids surrounded themselves with *Faqihs* or jurist-theologians who regarded the Caliph as the head of a college of Mujtahids or senior ecclesiastics. At the same time they smacked down hard on the Kaysānites who had supported them in the revolution and elbowed aside the rest of the Shī'ites. They did not touch the 'Alids so long as they were inoffensive, but set their spies to keep watch on them and in case of suspicion would arrest or poison them. The Shī'ites of every description, being in the opposition, had the backing of the lower orders again and again.[76]

The third consequence of 'Abbāsid victory was the 'iranization' of the Caliphate (*isti'jām*, from *a'jam*, pl. *a'ājim*, meaning originally 'silent', 'dumb', then *par excellence* Iranians, Persians: cf. the Russian words *nemoy* 'dumb', and *nemets* 'a German'). The 'Abbāsids, having been indebted to the Dihqāns for assistance in the revolution, rewarded these landed proprietors with high government posts. Though the state language, culture and religion remained Arab, the Caliphate bore from now on a semi-Iranian character, thanks to a wide assimilation of tradition dating from the Sāsānian epoch. This reconciled the Dihqāns to domination by the Caliphate, and induced many of them who were still Zoroastrian to embrace Islam in the Sunnī form. Thenceforward Sunnism was the ruling class ideology of Iran, and Shī'ism the ideology of the political and not infrequently social opposition; and so things were to remain until the end of the fifteenth century when the Ṣafawid Kingdom took shape.

II
Dogma and ritual

We have said that Islam is a syncretic religion. It absorbed and combined in its system elements of Judaism, Christianity, the old Arabian and especially North Arabian pagan ritual, and Zoroastrianism; and also, to some extent, Gnosticism and Manicheism. But since it had its birth in an early seventh-century North Arab community hardly yet amounting to a class society and still awaiting a social and cultural development, it could only take in elements from the religions of more advanced neighbours such as Byzantium and Iran in a simplified form. In the beginning, like all religions of backward societies it paid little heed to dogmatics, and placed the emphasis rather on the ceremonies and rules of the religious life. For that elaboration of doctrine which is the mark of religion wherever a community is at the feudal and bourgeois stage, it had to wait until the Caliphate evolved into a feudal society between the ninth and twelfth centuries. For the moment it drew no distinction between dogmatics and ritual, any more than it did between religion and law, between religious community and state, between spiritual and secular authority.

The word *Islām* (from *salama* in one of the meanings of the IV Form of this verb — 'to submit to') means 'submissiveness to God'; whence *Muslim*, 'submissive to God'. The term *islām* occurs only eight times in the Koran,[1] but is supplemented by two other terms, *īmān* 'faith' (from *amina* 'to be assured') and *dīn*. As regards this last term, the Arabs in effect had three words of identical sound (*dīn*) but of dissimilar provenance and primary sense: viz. Aramaic–Hebrew *din* 'judgment', 'verdict', 'decision';[2] old Arabic *dīn* 'custom'; Middle Persian *din* (or *dan*) 'faith', 'religion' — this last having crossed into Arabic without change of meaning in the pre-Islamic period. In consequence the word *dīn* was employed in various senses: it could designate all religion in general, but was more often used for the Muslim religion. Frequently, again, it means the aggregate of the religious obligations of the Muslims, as distinct from *īmān* which is Muslim faith. Shahrastānī[3] cites a definition ascribed to Muḥammad according to which *dīn* includes *islām*, i.e. the Five Pillars or basic rules of the Muslim religion; whilst *īmān* is faith in the truth of Islam; and *iḥsān* is moral virtue. *Īmān* supposes inner conviction (*i'tiqād*); its confession by word (*iqrār*); and good works (*a'māl*).

The doctrine of the Five Pillars of the Faith was worked out quite early. The Five Pillars (*arkān s. rukn*) are: (1) Confession of Faith, *shahāda* (the Arabic word is from the root *shahida* 'to witness' which has a V Form *tashahhada* 'to pronounce confession of faith'); (2) Prayer, *ṣalāt* (pl. *salawāt*; Persian synon. *namāz*); (3) Fasting, *ṣawm* (cf. Hebrew *som*); (4) Compulsory Alms, *zakāt*; (5) Pilgrimage to the Temple of the Ka'ba at Mecca, *ḥajj*.

The first pillar, the word of witness, is expressed in the formula 'There is no God but the One God (Allah) and Muḥammad is the Apostle of God.'[4] These two phrases, which every Muslim[5] is under obligation to pronounce, convey the two fundamental dogmas of Islam: (a) the creed of monotheism and (b) the avowal of Muḥammad's prophetic mission. Let us look at them separately.

The dogma of the Oneness of God, *tawḥīd*, monotheism, is explicit and unremittent. Islam teaches that there are no other gods than Allah and that to admit their existence is the most heinous of sins. As has been said,[6] Allah was known to the northern Arabs in pagan times before Islam as the supreme but not the only deity. The word *Allāh* came from the Arabic *ilāh* ('god', 'deity' in general, cf. the all-Semit. root *el*, *il*; Hebrew *eloah*;[7] Syr. *eloho*, *alaha*). The Allah of Islam is to be identified with the Yahwa (Yehova in another reading) of Judaism, and with God the Father in Christianity. The latter's Trinitarian belief postulating Unity in three persons or hypostases, which had its foundation in Hellenistic speculative philosophy, was rejected by Muḥammad because Three in One seemed to him not only contradictory but, to put it plainly, polytheism (*shirk* 'the giving of associates to God'). In Islamic doctrine God has no associates in his being, has not been born, and has not begotten sons or daughters. If this was a reply to the doctrine of the Trinity, it was even more pointedly aimed at the old Arab paganism with its male and female deities. Islam usually calls these pagan false gods, contrasted with the One God (Allah), *aṣnām* or *awthān* (Syrian *sanam*, *wathan*) 'idols'.

Allah, Islam teaches, is the One (*al-wāḥid*)[8] existing in and for himself; is the Living (*al-ḥayy*),[9] the Eternal (*aṣ-ṣamad*).[10] He 'is the first and the last, the manifest and the hidden, he knows all things';[11] is Lord of the Worlds (*rabbu 'l-'ālamīn*),[12] the Holy King (*al-maliku 'l-*

quddūs)[13] King of the Judgment Day (*malik yawmi' d-dīn*),[14] Best of Judges (*khayru 'l-hākimīn*).[15] He is the Light (*an-nūr*),[16] Absolute Truth (*al-ḥaqq*),[17] the Creator (*al-khāliq*),[18] the Giver of Life (*al-muḥyī*), the Giver of Death (*al-mumīt*). He 'created man out of a clot of blood'[19] and 'granted man knowledge through the reed-pen';[20] he 'is closer to man than his own neck vein',[21] is Mighty (*al-qādir*),[22] Strong (*al-qawī*), he Knows (*al-'ālim*), Sees (*al-baṣīr*), Hears (*as-samī'*),[23] and so forth. Many more epithets and attributes (*ṣifāt*) are ascribed to him in the Koran. As in Christianity his picture has two aspects; on the one side God is menacing, stern, violent (*al-jabbār*),[24] he threatens the disobedient with blazing flames[25] and the infidel with the eternal fire of Gehenna,[26] he 'thrusts from the path whom he pleases and guides aright him that has turned to him'.[27] On the other side, God is merciful and clement (*ar-raḥmān ar-raḥīm*),[28] is the pardoner of sins (*al-ghafūr, al-ghaffār*),[29] is the Giver (*al-wahhāb*), the Nourisher (*ar-razzāq*), Loving (*al-wadūd*).[30] It will be noticed that the Koran couples the metaphysical notion of God with his anthropomorphic (Gk. *anthrōpos* 'man', and *morphē* 'shape') picture; speaking of his sitting on the throne,[31] of his hands,[32] eyes,[33] face,[34] etc. This presentation, of course, was appropriate to the level of development of the Arabs of that day who conceived their pre-Islamic pagan deities in this manner, yet the Koran itself avoids clear indication whether such expressions are to be understood literally or as pure metaphor. Consequently, when a system of dogmatics was evolved in the eighth and ninth centuries there were theologians who inclined to anthropomorphism and others who repudiated it.

The Muslim conception of God, then, is strictly and consistently monotheistic and theocentric. The chief idea of the Koran is God and his Oneness; he is absolute, above the world which is his creation. But what relationship there is between God and the world, between God and man is a question to which the Koran has no clear answer — and a question, evidently, which was of small interest to Muḥammad himself. The Arabian prophet was not a thinker with much love of system, and he did not try to bequeath a finished theology — that was to be the preoccupation of divines in the centuries which followed.[35]

Allah, Islam holds, has as his devoted servants the angels, not eternal beings but his creatures, who act as intermediaries between himself and man.[36] And every man has two guardian angels. Four angels are archangels above the rest: Jabrā'īl (Gabriel) who transmits the divine revelation to the prophets, Mikā'īl (Michael) who sees to the feeding of all God's creatures, 'Azrā'īl[37] the Angel of Death who receives the souls of the departed, and Isrāfīl (Seraphil) the Angel of the Resurrection and the Judgment Day who announces its coming with his trump. The whole notion was borrowed, even down to the names of the archangels, from the Jews and Christians, but with this difference that in the Muslim rendering the angels stand below the prophets. Another borrowing from the same source was the tradition that one of the angels was fallen, overthrown by God and cursed by him: namely, *Iblīs* (corruption of the Greek *diabolos* 'devil') otherwise *Shayṭān* (from Ethiopian *satana*). But here again there is an item of originality in the reason why the Devil was cursed: he had refused out of pride to bow before the most perfect of God's creations to wit, man, to whom all the other angels had done reverence at God's bidding. God despatched him to Gehenna (Hebrew-Arabic *Jahannam*) whither sinners must follow him.[38] A third borrowing is the Biblical account of the Fall of the first parents of human creation Adam (*Ādam*) and Eve (*Ḥawwā*), led astray by the tempting of the Devil, and of their banishment from the earthly paradise. Lastly, Muḥammad conserved from pre-Islamic Arabia a belief in the elemental spirits of nature, male and female, called Jinns, which Islam portrayed as creations of Allah out of pure fire from before the time of man,[39] some of whom adopted the true Faith while others remained infidel; and later Muslims took from the Zoroastrians a belief in Dīvs, demons[40] subordinate to the Devil and enemies of men and of God.

We come to the second of the two dogmas, the doctrine of Muḥammad as Prophet. This was closely associated with the teaching about prophets in general and about the Holy Writ sent down through them by God to men. The Islamic doctrine here — Islamic in the sense that it was elaborated by Islam on a Jewish-Christian foundation — held that there were high-ranking prophets styled 'apostles' (*rasūl* pl. *rusul*) each of whom was sent to a specific tribe or people, and ordinary prophets (Ar. Hebr. *nabī*) of whom there were many, charged with the continuation of the preaching begun by the apostles. Amongst the highest apostles Islam recognizes the Biblical figures of Adam (*Ādam*), Noah (*Nūh*), Abraham (*Ibrāhīm*), Moses (*Mūsā*) and Jesus Christ (*'Īsā al-Masīḥ*); and three taken from pre-Islamic legend: Shu'ayb, Hūd and Sāliḥ;[41] and the last of the line is Muḥammad. It is not altogether clear from the Koran that Muḥammad rated himself higher than the apostles he acknowledged as his predecessors, notably Abraham, Moses and Jesus; but in time the Muslims began to regard him as the highest of the apostles, and to thrust the cult of his predecessors into the background. The names of certain other prophets taken from the Bible are: Old Testament — Lot (Lūṭ), Job (Ayyūb), Aaron (Hārūn), David (Dā'ūd), Solomon (Sulaymān), Elijah (Ilyās),[42] Isaac (Isḥāq), Jacob (Ya'qūb), Jonah (Yūnus); New Testament — Zechariah (Zakariyā), John the Baptist (Yaḥyā), the Virgin Mary (Maryam). Then there were some prophets, the invention of purely Muslim legend, who were later on identified with Biblical prophets: Dhu 'l-Kifl with Enoch; Khiḍr with Ilyās. And finally certain additions were made to the ordinary prophets, e.g. Alexander of Macedon (al-Iskandar Dhu 'l-Qarnayn, 'The Two Horned')[43] and the Christian Saint George (Jūrjīs). The total thus composed was given out as three hundred and thirteen apostles and some one hundred and twenty-four thousand ordinary prophets. Muḥammad is recognized as the last and greatest, the Door of Prophecy and the Seal of the Prophets, after whom there can be none. Subsequent legend endowed him with the power to work miracles; but while not denying this to former prophets, and especially Jesus, he did not ascribe it to himself.

Koranic references to the Old Testament prophets are based on the Talmud and Midrash rather than directly on the Bible. They depart somewhat from Jewish tradition. Thus Abraham arrives in Arabia and turns out to be the builder of the Ka'ba temple; his son by Hagar, Ismā'īl[44], becomes his immediate successor and is regarded as the forefather of the Arabs. There is more, however, in the Koran about Jesus Christ ('Īsā al-Masīḥ from Hebr. *Mashiah*, Messiah, 'the Anointed'; Gk. synon. *Christos*) than about any of the preceding prophets. Certain episodes are derived from the Apocryphal Gospels,[45] notably the Gospel of the Childhood of Christ as it is called, though probably not at first hand but from the oral accounts of the heretical Christians with whom Muḥammad mixed. His presentation of Jesus is contradictory: on the one hand, he rejects the Christian doctrine of Jesus as God-man, the Son of God, the second hypostasis of the Triune God; for Muḥammad Jesus is only the Son of Mary,[46] or the Servant (*'abd*) of God,[47] one of the six supreme prophets, the Apostles.[48] On the other hand, the Koran does acknowledge the virginal conception of Jesus by Mary, recounting this almost in the manner of the New Testament.[49] The conception of Jesus, in the Koran, happened at the single word of God: 'Be' (*Kun*);[50] Jesus is the Word (*Kalima*) of God brought down by him into Mary; is the Spirit (*rūḥ*) of God.[51] The Koran follows the New Testament in allusions to Zechariah and John the Baptist, but Mary the mother of Jesus is confused with Mary the sister of Moses and Aaron, being called 'daughter of 'Imrān' who is the Biblical Amram. The New Testament story of the Crucifixion and Resurrection is not reproduced. Instead the story in the Koran is that the Jews wanted to kill Jesus, but did not kill him since God saved him by substituting someone resembling him.[52] It was a version that occasioned a wealth of commentary by the theologians of later date, one invention being that the man crucified in Jesus' place was Simon of Cyrene. The Koran recognizes the Ascension, and also ascribes various miracles to Jesus not mentioned in the canonical Gospels but figuring in the apocryphal Gospel of the Childhood of Christ: such as that he began to speak immediately after he was born, that as a child he would fashion little birds out of clay and give them life, and so on. It makes out that Muḥammad's prophetic mission was foretold by Jesus: 'Sons of Israel! I am God's apostle to you, fulfilling the Law which is in your hands and announcing the glad tidings of an apostle who shall come after me whose name is Aḥmad.'[53] This passage in the Koran is based on the canonical Gospel according to St John where Jesus promised the Believers the advent of the Paraclete.[54] Muslims assume the text of the Gospel to be corrupt in this sentence and that Paraklētos (Gk. *paraclētos* 'comforter') should properly read Perikleitos (Gk. *pericleitos* 'famous') which has the sense which the two synonymous names Aḥmad/Muḥammad bear in Arabic. The introduction of the cult of Jesus and the Koran's assertion, with apparent verisimilitude, that the Paraclete foretold by him was none other than Muḥammad, so impressed the contemporary Christian world that it needed only the conquest of Syria, Egypt, North Africa and Spain in the seventh and eighth centuries (which made it look as though God himself was on the side of the Arabs) to bring many Christians joyfully into the acceptance of Islam.

Bound up with this teaching about the prophets was the doctrine of the divine revelation transmitted to the peoples through them. Thus, according to the Koran, Abraham,[55] Moses,[56] David,[57] and Jesus[58] received scrolls (*ṣuḥuf*) of Holy Writ (*al-kitāb*) from God: Moses was sent the Torah (*tawrāt*), i.e. the Pentateuch, David the Psalms (*zabūr*), Jesus the Gospel (*injīl*). But, continues the Koran, the sacred books thus granted by God to the Jews and the Christians were later falsified by them instead of being kept true to their originals.[59] Muslims also believe that besides the four books named,[60] no less than one hundred other books are comprehended in Holy Writ: these are ten books sent down to Adam, fifty to Seth, thirty to Idris (commonly identified with the Biblical Enoch) and ten to Abraham. In their initial form all the books of revelation are held to have differed from the Koran in arrangement, structure and language, but to have been absolutely identical with it in content. From this the inference was that the divine book exists eternally, its content being communicated from time to time to mankind through the prophets. This is at the root of the subsequent dogma of an uncreated Koran existing from all eternity.[61] Further, if the transcript sent down to Abraham, Moses, David, Jesus and the other prophets did not differ from the Koran in subject-matter, then it followed that Islam was not some new-fangled religion but the self-same, age-old, true religion of monotheism which the emissaries of God had been preaching from time immemorial.

The Muslims made their own, and elaborated, the legend of the Antichrist. The false Messiah (*al-Masīḥ ad-Dajjāl* or simply *ad-Dajjāl*, 'The Deceiver') must appear before the end of the world, and behave as the servant of the Devil and the enemy of God and all who believe in him. Dajjāl is chained to a rock on the sea coast whither demons bring him food.[62] He shall appear after Yājūj and Mājūj (the biblical Gog and Magog, legendary barbarian tribes living somewhere in the depths of Asia) break down the wall raised against them by Alexander of Macedon.[63] In some variants the Antichrist is to appear either in Kūfa or in the Jewish quarter of Iṣfahān, or in Khurāsān. He will reign over the whole earth, inaugurate a terrible persecution of all Believers, and destroy the temples. His rule, however, will not be prolonged beyond forty days, after which he will be overthrown and slain by the Mahdī, the revivalist sent by God. (To begin with, the Mahdī was identified with Christ, but later represented as a person apart.) The Second Coming of Jesus will follow; after which will come the resurrection of the dead[64] and the Day of Judgment upon all mankind, living and departed. Jesus will open the proceedings, there and then testifying that he never called himself God and that the Christians distorted his teaching. After this, the living and the risen, Muslims and infidels, will pass through the tribunal of God; all, except prophets and martyrs will be confronted with registers in which their doings, good and wicked, have been entered. These deeds will be weighed in the scales, and their authors either favoured with the bliss of paradise or cast down into Gehenna.[65]

The debt to Christian and Jewish legend is clear in these beliefs, notwithstanding the additional detail (and incidentally the Jewish–Christian presentation itself was scarcely original but under obligation to Zoroastrianism). As between Jewish and Christian tradition, Islam took its belief in the resurrection of the dead in the flesh from the former, the Christians being less definite on the point;

but from the latter its belief that the abode of the dead in hell or paradise until the Day of Resurrection is provisional pending the final determination of their fate.

Islam's picture of hell is not substantially different from that of Zoroastrian–Jewish–Christian tradition, which in its turn reflected the beliefs of the ancient Greeks and of the Assyrians with their legend of Ishtar. The actual name of hell is taken from the Jews: (*Jahannam* from Hebrew *ge hinnom*), i.e. 'The Valley of Hinnom',[66] the Gehenna of the Gospels. So that Islam's hell, as the Dutch scholar R. Dozy put it, is 'the imitation of an imitation'. Hell is pictured as consisting of seven Gates, i.e. departments or tiers, each earmarked for a particular category of sinner, and arranged one above the other so as to form a capacious funnel.[67] The entire Gehenna is spanned by the bridge Ṣirāṭ (lit. way, road, and possibly from the Latin *stratum* of the same meaning) slender as a hair. All the dead must cross by this bridge. The righteous do so easily, but the sinners lose their foothold and fall into the abyss. The tortures of Gehenna are multifarious, and vary for the different categories of sinner; but fire is the chief ingredient. While the Koran gives no clear indication whether the pains of hell will be everlasting, many theologians later on tended to hold that this would not be so, at any rate for Muslims, and postulated a purgatory. Al-Ash'arī, who was of the school of those denying the eternity of hell fire, relied on a saying in the Ḥadīth attributed to Muḥammad: He (God) shall lead people out of Gehenna after they are burned and charred.' This tenet, with its insistence of course on the limitation to Muslims, became general.

Similarly the notion of paradise is traceable to a Zoroastrian–Jewish–Christian source: the very name *firdaws* is taken from the Persians through the Greeks. But here again the Muslims added their own contribution: for example the presence of youths attending to the true Believers, and of black-eyed houris[68] (*ḥūr* black-eyed) fair of face, allotted as their mistresses. Sale's[69] view that the myth of the Houris is of Zoroastrian origin is refuted by Dozy.[70] Generally speaking Muslim authors portray paradise as a luxuriant, shady garden with rivers, streams and murmuring fountains, pomegranate trees and palms; and though the Medīna, or post-Migration, Sūras of the Koran are studiously silent about the houris who figure in the early Meccan Sūras,[71] the bulk of Muslims had so taken these beautiful damsels to their hearts that succeeding generations could not be expected to dismiss them. The Koran states clearly that paradise is for women as well as men; they will be there together with their husbands.[72] It did not extend to all Believers the promise of communion with God in paradise, or even the sight of him, and later doctrine specified that this privilege would be restricted in upper paradise to prophets and saints or walīs (*walī* pl. *awliyā'*; lit. 'the near ones [to God]').

These conceptions of hell and paradise with its houris were materialistic and sensual, and indeed have remained so to this day for the generality of Muslims. Keener minds, however, and notably the mystics (Ṣūfīs) were at pains to explain the pictures of a sensual paradise allegorically, or else to stipulate that there are two aspects of paradise: sensual for coarse and mean natures, and a purely spiritual one for higher, more refined souls.

Before leaving the subject of dogma we must touch on predestination as this was expounded in the Koran. The doctrine was that God created men together with their good and bad thoughts and acts, and predestined some for salvation and others for destruction:[73] 'There is no soul that can have belief except by God's permission.'[74] But simultaneously he threatens sinners, or at all events non-Muslims, with the punishment of eternal damnation.[75] It was only later that the Muslims became conscious of the inherent contradiction in withholding free will and at the same time imposing responsibility for faith and works, and many were the controversies that ensued.[76] But for the moment, in Muḥammad's day and under the first Caliphs, this dogma was a very useful instrument in the hand of the newly emerged state: it declared the Prophet's mission and his political authority, first in Medīna and then in all Arabia, to be predestined; and it gave the same sanction to the rule of the Caliphs who succeeded him. Moreover, the fatalism implicit in it stimulated fearlessness and daring in the conquering armies of the Arabs whose troops were 'champions of the Faith'. No danger of battle could dismay the soldier who knew the hour of his death to be pre-ordained by God.

Let us pass to ritual and the moral duties required of the Believer. This side of the Faith, as has been pointed out, occupied a more important place in early Islam than dogmatics. The fact that of the Five Pillars of the Faith only the First Pillar dealing with the Oneness of God and Muḥammad's Prophetic Mission is concerned with dogmatics, betrays this. The remaining four, which we shall now be looking at, are ritualistic disciplines: namely prayer, fasting, almsgiving and the pilgrimage.

The Second Pillar of Islam is prayer, or more precisely the regulation prayer (*ṣalāt)* governed by a fixed ritual. It has to be uttered in set phrases and in Arabic,[77] at the hours appointed for it; and if possible in a mosque of the quarter or village.[78] It is accompanied by established postures and gestures such as uplifting the hands, bowing the head or from the hips, kneeling and prostration. The ordered cycle of positions with the uttered words appropriate to them constitutes a *rak'a*,[79] and each prayer consists of from two to four rak'as depending on the time of day. Further, the worshipper must turn his face towards the sacred city of Mecca and its Ka'ba, this direction being known as the *qibla*.[80]

In more detail the procedure is this. The Believer spreads his prayer-mat (*sajjāda*), which as it were detaches him from the world about him. He may do this in a mosque, at home or in the open air indifferently, provided he avoids unclean places such as slaughter houses, execution-sites, lavatories, and so on. He stands on the mat and either to himself or aloud declares his intention (*nīya*) to perform the prayer (morning, noon, or whichever it be) for the sake of God. Having lifted his hands to the level of his ears he pronounces the formula: God is Most Great (*Allāhu akbar*). Then, still standing, he lays his left hand on his right and recites the first chapter (*Sūra*) of the Koran, Al-Fātiḥa ('Opening' as a door to the Scripture). This to the Muslim is what 'Our Father' is to the Christian, and indeed its content is reminiscent of the Lord's Prayer. After this, he kneels and sits back in one movement, his palms touching his knees; then stands up and raises his hands and exclaims: 'Allah hearkens to him that praises him.' Again he comes to his knees and prostrates himself with the palms of his hands and his nose on the ground. This prostration is termed *sujūd* (from the same root *sajada* which yields *sajjāda* and *masjid*, 'mosque'). He now sits back again on the haunches and then comes forward again into a second prostration. This round of movements and utterances composes one rak'a.

At first the custom was to pray three times a day, as can be gathered from the Koran, but in the end the rule of five daily prayers was confirmed. These are: (1) Morning Prayer (*ṣalātu 'ṣ-ṣubḥ*) at daybreak just before the sun is up: two rak'as; (2) Noon Prayer (*ṣalātu 'ẓ-ẓuhr*): four rak'as; (3) Afternoon Prayer (*ṣalātu 'l-'aṣr*) half-way between mid-day and sundown: four rak'as; (4) Sunset Prayer (*ṣalātu 'l-maghrib*) immediately after sundown: three rak'as; (5) Night Prayer before retiring to sleep (*ṣalātu 'l - 'ishā'*) usually offered about two hours after the Sunset Prayer. The Persian names are respectively *namāz-i bāmdād*; *namāz-i pīshīn*; *namāz-i dīgar*; *namāz-i shām*; and *namāz-i khoftan*.

The hours of each prayer are announced by a Muezzin[81] (*mu'adhdhin*, from *adhana* 'to call to') of a mosque. The call to prayer (*ādhān*) is chanted in the following formula: 'Allah is Most Great.' [Twice][82] 'I bear witness that there is no god except Allah.' [Twice] 'I bear witness that Muḥammad is verily the Apostle of God.' [Twice] 'Come ye to the prayer, come ye to salvation.' [Twice; and before the dawn prayer, the words 'Prayer is better than sleep' are added.] 'Allah is Most Great' [Twice], 'there is no god except Allah.' The *ādhān* is the first invitation to prayer, and a second invitation is voiced just before the prayer begins, called *iqāma* (from *qāma* 'to rise'), the formula being the same as in the first invitation. Among the Sunnīs, except the Ḥanafite school, the *iqāma* is chanted once; among the Shī'ites it is said twice. Books of the Sharī'a recommend the Believer to recite the *iqāma* to himself when praying on his own at home or in the open air. The *ādhān* and *iqāma* are likewise used in the invitation to Friday service in the congregational mosque.

Prayer is preceded by ritual ablution, of which there are two kinds: (1) *Wuḍū'*, or minor ablution of the face, arms to the elbows, and feet, requisite before each prayer; and (2) *ghusl*, or complete ablution of the whole body to cleanse it of ritual uncleanliness termed *janāba*.[83] All ablution, like all prayer, to be valid, must include a statement of intention (*nīya*) to the effect that the act is being performed for God, and not for any other object such, for example, as bodily cleanliness. The conception of ritual impurity is very carefully thought out in Islam, and in the technical context is remote from the idea of physical impurity. The water for ablution has to be running,[84] and so courtyards of mosques commonly have basins with flowing water or fountains. If for some reason there be no water near at hand, it is permissible to perform the ablution with sand.

On Fridays a general service is celebrated at noon which in theory all adult male Muslims are expected to attend. The emphasis is on the gathering, and in the Ḥanafite school[85] a quorum of forty is expressly stipulated.[86] The weekly service takes place in a mosque appointed for the purpose called either the Friday (Jum'a) or the Congregational (Jāmi') Masjid[87] and includes a public homily termed *Khuṭba* from the pulpit, in which the Prayer Leader[88] petitions God to bless the ruling sovereign and the entire community of Believers before proceeding to the sermon. At one time women were present in closed galleries or separate enclosures; but nowadays this is only observed in Shī'ite communities, and will thus still be seen in Iran. But in Central Asia the womenfolk now pray at home. Friday is essentially the day for weekly worship; it is not a holiday comparable to the Jewish Sabbath or the Christian Sunday, and people open their stalls and workshops and go about their usual business after divine service.

Apart from the above regulation prayers, Islam recognizes supererogatory prayers, *munājāt*, performed in private at any hour of the day or night — but preferably night. Considered pleasing to God but not compulsory, they are peculiar in this that they may be said in any language and phrased in any words provided these be decorous.

The Third Pillar is the fast (*ṣawm*). Laid down by the Koran, this enjoins total abstinence from food and drink of every kind, as also from the routine pleasures,[89] between dawn and darkness 'when it is no longer possible to distinguish a white thread from a black', during the thirty days of the month of Ramaḍān.[90] It is thus more exacting than the Christian fast. By night all that has been forbidden becomes lawful and the Believer may take normal nourishment.[91] The fast is prescribed by the Koran.[92] If the fast be broken for sufficient cause such as soldiering for the Faith, or on a journey, or in sickness, the Believer must make up the number of lost days; and if it be broken for insufficient reason he must not only do this but in addition must distribute alms to the poor. Pregnant women and nursing-mothers, children and juveniles are exempt, and the elderly of both sexes may substitute alms-giving. In practice the more pious parents make their children observe the fast. For rich people it is of course no hardship, for they can gorge twice nightly, rest in the day, read the Koran at home or in the mosque, and sleep. But it is very hard on the artisans, peasants, poor, slaves, labourers and servants, particularly when Ramaḍān falls in summer: they then have to work throughout the long summer days in 30 or 40 °centigrade in the shade on an empty stomach and without so much as a cup of water.

The breaking of the fast is celebrated in a formal festival (*'īdu 'l-fiṭr*), on 1. Shawwāl and following days, that overflows from the mosque itself into every sphere of life outside.

The voluntary principle is remembered, as with prayers, and fasting is approved at any time of the year.

The Fourth Pillar enjoined in the Koran[93] is obligatory alms-giving (*zakāt*, lit. 'cleaning'). Originally this was regarded as being made over to society for distribution in its totality to the poor, to widows and other lonely women, orphans and the helpless. But since Muslim society from its inception in Medīna was a state as much as a religious community, secular as much as spiritual, the proceeds of zakāt were in practice at the disposal of the authorities. The latter being temporal, even under the Umayyads (661–750), were not slow to allocate most of the amount to the needs of state, reserving but an insignificant fraction for charitable relief. So zakāt, regarded in theory as compulsory alms-giving, became in practice a tax. Payable by adult Muslims alone and in no case by non-Muslims,[94] it is assessed on households and the incomes of trade or handicraft at one-fortieth, i.e. 2½ per cent; but on livestock raising it may be as much as 12 per cent. In parenthesis it should be mentioned that other more burdensome taxes were substituted for zakāt in later mediaeval Iran (thirteenth century) like the Mongol *tamghā* on trade and handicraft and the *mawāshī*, otherwise *chōbān-begī*, on livestock-raising. For a third time the supererogatory principle is respected, and just as voluntary prayers and fasting are acceptable, so Islam recommends free-will offerings (*ṣadaqa*). Charity in this proper sense is thought to facilitate salvation and is widely practised as a redemption for sin and an insurance against the torments of Gehenna. It either takes the form of direct assistance to the indigent, and Dervishes especially, or (in the case of the landed gentry and merchant princes) of endowments in money, estates and immovable property (*waqf*)[95] to support mosques, madrasas and charitable institutions like hospitals, orphanages and vagrants' homes.

The Fifth Pillar is the pilgrimage, (*ḥajj*, Hebr. *hag*) to the sacred city of Mecca with its Ka'ba. All Muslims are required to perform this once in their lifetime, provided they are in a condition to undertake so lengthy a journey. This limits the obligation to those who are wealthy enough and independent enough, and exempts the needy, the helpless, women, slaves and dependants of every type. But many poor people and women do in fact make the pilgrimage. The ḥajj has to coincide with the Sacrificial Festival on 10 Dhu 'l-Ḥijja called *'Īdu 'l-aḍḥā* or *'Īdu 'l-qurbān* (the *Bayrām* of Turkey) — one of the two chief festivals of Islam,[96] and connected with the legendary building of the Sanctuary by the prophet Abraham and his receiving the Black Stone from the hands of the Archangel Gabriel. The attendant ceremonies at 'Arafāt, the well Zam Zam, Muzdalifa, Minā, and other places in the neighbourhood of Mecca, which are part and parcel of the ḥajj, are all of them linked with the story of Abraham and his son Ismā'īl. Actually, (as is now reasonably established) the basis of the ritual was an old Arab paganistic practice whose original meaning had been largely forgotten by Muḥammad's time. But since Islam was retaining the Ka'ba itself with the Black Stone in the ḥajj ritual, it was necessary to give an interpretation of these ceremonies in the spirit of the Muslim religion. So the Ka'ba was made out to be the sanctuary of the One God, constructed by Adam, restored by Abraham and afterwards occupied by the idolaters and, lastly, made clean by Muḥammad; the Black Stone became the gift of paradise; and little by little the legendary tale of Abraham was worked into a form in which it could explain the ceremonial of the ḥajj.

To take part in the Feast of the Sacrifice and even to visit Mecca and Medīna at all belonged exclusively to the Muslim, and it was not until the nineteenth century[97] that a few Europeans, of whom the first was the German Burckhardt in 1814, managed to get there in disguise. Another of their number, the Dutch Arabist Snouck Hurgronje, has given perhaps the best description of Mecca, the Ka'ba and the ḥajj.[98]

The Ka'ba kept its pristine simplicity. Ignoring the abortive attempt of 'Abdullāh b. az-Zubayr to rebuild it in 685, which contemporaries condemned as a sinful innovation, no steps were ever taken to replace the plain cubiform structure set in its rectangular court with something more magnificent and grand. Simple, it was also unique and was not treated as the prototype for other mosques.

The pilgrims from each province usually formed a caravan and set out on a date calculated to bring them to Mecca by 7 Dhu 'l-Ḥijja. *En route* they would visit the Prophet's tomb at Medīna and would sometimes have even been to the Dome of the Rock at Jerusalem, to which, according to legend, Muḥammad had been transported by angels. Having reached Arabia's holy territory, the pilgrim dons the garment called *iḥrām*, consisting of two plain strips of cloth, one of which he winds round his waist and the other of which he throws over his shoulders. Thus dressed and with head uncovered, he progresses the rest of his way. This includes a visit to the Vale of Minā on 8 Dhu 'l-Ḥijja; a visit to Mount 'Arafāt, twelve miles from Mecca where the Meccan Qāḍī delivers a sermon on 9 Dhu 'l-Ḥijja; a running walk from Muzdalifa to Minā with a symbolic stone-throwing at the Devil at three places on the way on the morning of 10 Dhu 'l-Ḥijja;[99] and finally the sacrificing of animals whether camels, oxen, sheep or goats. This last is performed not only in the Vale of Minā on 10 Dhu 'l-Ḥijja but everywhere throughout Muslim countries. The culminating ceremony consists of going seven times round the Ka'ba (*ṭawāf*) and kissing the Black Stone; after which the pilgrim goes to the rock of Abraham's Station (Maqām Ibrāhīm) prays there, drinks from the holy well Zam Zam, and runs between two small eminences called Ṣafā and Marwa. Usually 12 Dhu 'l-

Ḥijja sees the end of the pilgrimage, and the pilgrim returns to his native land to bear henceforward the respected title of Ḥajjī.

There is also a Lesser Pilgrimage called *'umra* which involves visiting Mecca at any period of the year other than the Feast of the Sacrifice, and performing the ḥajj ceremonies but without the sacrifice. Approved of as an act pleasing to God, it is not of comparable value with the Great Pilgrimage.

Islam lays one more obligation on Believers, which, though not numbered among the Five Pillars, has not been inferior to them in its practical effect. This is Holy War, *jihād*, (from *jahada*, III Form *jāhada*, 'to strive', 'to make effort', 'fight') or *ghazā'*, *ghazwa*, plural *ghazawāt* (from *ghazā* 'to campaign', 'to wage war'). The doctrine evolved gradually. Its germ is visible in the Medīna Sūras relating to the military action of the Medinese Muslims against the Meccan pagans and the Medīna Jewish tribes. The idea took on a new meaning in the age of conquest, roughly 632–751, when it became an instrument of Caliphate policy. The wars of expansion, and the wars later waged by the Muslim states that emerged from the ruins of the Caliphate, though they were with non-Muslims, were prompted by economic and political considerations much more than by religion; but invariably the theory of *jihād* as gradually evolved by the jurists was applied to them. On this theory the world is divided into theatres: the Province of Islam, *dāru 'l-islām*, otherwise Province of the Faith, *dāru'd-dīn*, and the Province of War, *dāru 'l-ḥarb*. The first is any country under Muslim government and administered on the basis of Muslim law — even if the majority of the population is not Muslim. To begin with this Province was coterminous with the Caliphate, and later it embraced the totality of Muslim states. The second is every country peopled by infidels or else by Muslims under the dominion of infidel rulers.[100] Some schools of jurists recognize a third theatre, the Province of Peace, *dāru'ṣ-ṣulḥ*, signifying non-Muslim countries governed by non-Muslim sovereigns considering themselves vassals and tributaries of a Muslim empire; such as were, for instance, Georgia and Nubia in the Middle Ages. Theoretically the Muslims are in a state of perpetual war with the people of the second theatre, but it is allowable to conclude a truce of not more than ten years with them.[101]

Of the infidels in debate (*kāfir*, plural *kāfirūn* or *kuffār*, originally 'ungrateful' to God for the gift of revelation,[102] then the conventional term for 'non-Believer', 'non-Muslim')[103] there are various recognized categories in law. People of the Book (*ahlu 'l-kitāb*) were the most leniently treated by the jurists: so named in the Koran were the Jews, the Christians and the Sabians who in their day had been sent a scripture through their prophets. Sabian is an undefined term about whose meaning there was much dispute in later times; it is possible that the Sabians were the Ḥanīfs or the gnostic sect of Mandaeans, otherwise Mughtasilites, in Iraq who are there even now.[104] However that may be, Muslim law permits an attitude of tolerance in the case of People of the Book, though only on condition that they bow to the authority of the Muslim state and commit themselves to the payment of the *jizya* prescribed for people of other faiths. Infidels in this category, that is to say, subjects or Dhimmīs (*ahlu'dh-dhimma* 'people under protection') are personally free but politically without rights; enjoy, that is, a limited citizenship. Where People of the Book decline this form of submission, Holy War has to be waged against them as with other infidels, e.g. Zoroastrians and idolaters. However, in practice the status of Dhimmī was soon extended even to such out-and-out infidels — provided, of course, they accepted it — though in theory Dhimmīs were always People of the Book and in no case pagans.

In the Sharī'a Holy War is an obligation, but again only on those who are in a condition to take part in it. It is not compulsory for the poor who cannot obtain horses and arms or tear themselves from their homes, nor for the infirm, cripples, the old, women and slaves.

Different schools argued whether any war with infidels was Holy War — which was the position of Abū Ḥanīfa, eponymous founder of the Ḥanafite sect — or whether only a defensive war is intended where the infidels attack the Muslims — which is the position of the other schools and, apparently, of Muḥammad himself. But since the majority of Sunnīs at the present time belong to the Ḥanafite school, any war whatever with infidels is usually held to be War for the Faith.

A whole literature grew on the subject of *jihād*. Neglecting controversial points, some main items of interest are these. When about to start hostilities with infidels the Imam (in this context, the head of the Muslim community and simultaneously its secular sovereign) must first suggest their adherence to Islam, but he is not required to renew the proposition. Supposing wars to be repeated with the same non-Muslim state — the wars with Byzantium in the seventh to tenth centuries, for instance — there is no obligation to send envoys to advocate such adherence each time. Then, when war does begin, the infidels are offered three choices. They can embrace Islam and become brethren in the faith; in which case any future wars that might have to be fought with them would not amount to Holy War. (In principle it is held that Muslims must not fight each other unless one side be in the wrong, but in practice, of course, this had no application.) The second choice the infidels can exercise is to decline Islam and stick to their own faith, but on the stipulation that they will accept a subordinate status and pledge themselves to the payment of a poll-tax; will enter, that is, the class of Dhimmīs. The remaining choice they have is to fight it out.

If the fight takes place, a code comes into operation. About all the minor rules the schools are not unanimous, but the divines are at one on the major regulations which are as follows. During *jihād* in a Province of War, it is legal to kill the males[105] with the exception of the old and the children: these together with all women must be spared. Nor is it permissible to kill monks who are anchorites; but if they live in urban monasteries it is quite lawful to despatch them. The male population, unless it has previously acquiesced in the status of Dhimmī, can either be put to the sword by the Muslim soldiery or taken into captivity, since they are classed as spoils of war. Sūra VIII sanctifies the law on these spoils of war and indicates how they are to be divided. It was a favourite Sūra for commanders to read to their troops before battle so as to ensure their enthusiasm. All movable property seized in *jihād* qualified as spoils, but land was pointedly excluded from the definition, the theory being that this was automatically transferred to the ownership of the community as a whole — which was tantamount to saying that it was placed at the disposal of the state. In effect therefore spoils meant cattle, horses, valuables of every description, gold, silver, money, clothing, fabrics and prisoners of both sexes. Distribution was ordered as follows: in early days the horseman received three times as much as the foot soldier or camel-rider, having regard to the scarcity of the horse in the pre-Islamic period; but during the conquests, when the horse became less of a rarity, the cavalry received only twice the infantry's portion. Before actual distribution one-fifth of the total (*khums*) was set aside for the use of the Prophet's descendants and associates, the poor, orphans, etc. In practice it was simply made over to the Imam as head of state either in kind or in the money equivalent of the articles. The rest of the booty would then be divided as explained.

Being classified as spoils of war, the prisoners also came in for distribution. The theory here was that the Imam was entitled to release them on ransom, or exchange them for Muslim prisoners or even let them go unconditionally, as an alternative to consigning them to slavery and permitting their distribution among the soldiers. Release, however, was hardly ever the practice in early days and only of rare occurrence in the later Middle Ages. The general rule was that prisoners were turned over to slavery and distributed with that status among those who had fought for the Faith, a procedure eminently convenient to the feudal society of the Near and Middle East countries in which serfdom was so long implicit.

Of the juridical standing of slaves we shall speak later, when we come to discuss Muslim law.[106]

Islam prescribed only two holidays in the sense of days of rest: these were the two principal festivals in the calendar which have been mentioned already — the Breaking of the Fast on 1 Shawwāl and the Feast of the Sacrifice on 10 Dhu 'l-Ḥijja. These two with their special prayers and universal rejoicing are apt to go on, even in modern Islam, for three or four days. The lesser celebrations that gradually found place in the calendar were marked by special prayers, but did not interrupt ordinary work except at the moment of divine service. Such were: the first ten days in the month of Muḥarram — the New Year and time of mourning to commemorate the martyrdom of the Imam Ḥusayn;[107] 12 Ṣafar, birthday of the Prophet; 27 Rajab, the beginning of his prophetic mission; 28 Rajab, the night of his Ascension;[108] 27 Ramaḍān,[109] the 'Night of Predestination' (*laylatu 'l-qadr*) — meaning the night on which, according to legend, the Koran was sent down to Muḥammad in revelation; the night on which the fate of each human being is decided in heaven; on which his wishes, the subject of his earnest prayer, will be entertained by God and, maybe, brought to pass; a night therefore on which the pious keep vigil in the mosque, praying and reciting the Koran.

There are other festivals peculiar to the Shī'ites.[110]

Let us briefly touch on some further institutions. The Muslims, like the Jews, clung to the ceremony of circumcision (*khitān*) of boys, regarding it as the symbol of membership of the community. The jurists were not entirely in agreement as to whether the circumcision of adult converts to Islam was obligatory, and there is evidence that it was anyhow not demanded of Central Asian neophytes in the early eighth century. Unlike the Jews the Muslims do not perform the operation on the newborn, but delay it until the child is anything from six to thirteen or even until he attains full puberty at fifteen years of age. Any barber at all may perform it.

As everybody knows, Islam allows polygamy. The free Muslim may have up to four legal wives simultaneously[111] and any number of concubines he pleases,[112] but a slave is restricted to two wives. Because of easy divorce a man could of course marry more often, since there was nothing to stop his discarding his partners and contracting new marriages indefinitely. Thus the second Shīʿite Imam Ḥasan, elder son of the fourth Caliph ʿAlī, went on marrying and divorcing from his youth onwards so that his legal wives totalled seventy.[113] However one must remember polygamy existed long before Islam among Arabs, Persians and Jews of old, and that it was something to restrict the number of legal wives, with whom a man might cohabit simultaneously, to four. Moreover Islam abolished certain archaic forms of matrimony prevalent among the pre-Islamic Arabs certainly until the early seventh century, namely the matriarchal marriage and polyandry. The seclusion of women and the institution of the harem (*ḥarīm* 'the forbidden, women's half of the house') and of eunuchs were borrowed from the Persians. It should be added that two passages in Sūra IV 'Women'[114] have sometimes been interpreted as proving the Koran's preference for monogamy. The first passage reads: 'If ye fear that ye may not act with equity to all of them (meaning your wives) then marry one only'; and the second: 'And ye are never in a condition to dispense equal justice to your wives, although ye wished this'. Comparing these two passages some have concluded that the Koran only acquiesced in polygamy and advocated monogamy, and this interpretation is strongly favoured by the modernists of our day who categorically repudiate polygamy. In any case polygamy was in practice confined to the nobility and the rich; the majority of Muslims have been satisfied with one wife, and the institution of concubinage, widely prevalent in the Middle Ages when slave-women were cheap, has likewise practically disappeared throughout Islam.

Islam condemned and abolished the old Arabian custom of putting newborn unwanted girls to death, and instituted a number of prohibitions respecting marriage between close relatives.[115] It did indeed assert the inequality of husband and wife: 'Husbands stand above wives since God gave them superiority and because they spend their substance on their wives';[116] but this attitude was universal in the Middle Ages and not peculiar. Besides, although a husband may bring a disobedient wife to her senses and even beat her,[117] there must be no violence, and a lenient treatment of the wife is recommended. Divorce was fairly easy,[118] especially for the husband.[119] It will be examined in Chapter VII, and the Shīʿite 'temporary' marriage in Chapter X.

If Islam, generally speaking, regards woman as a being inferior to man and holds that the care lavished on her and her children impedes the Believer in the performance of his obligations to God, the Koran selects two women who are perfect, — Āsiya the wife of Pharaoh, and Mary the Mother of Jesus;[120] telling of the latter 'The Angels have said: "O Mary, God has chosen and purified thee, chosen thee before the women of all the worlds".'[121] Subsequently Khadīja the Prophet's first wife, 'Ā'isha[122] 'Mother of the Orthodox', and Fāṭima the daughter of Muḥammad and wife of 'Alī b. Abī Ṭālib were added. And still later there were further additions to the list of saintly women; notably the eighth-century devotee Rābi'a, and another Fāṭima (sister of the eighth Imam of the Shī'ites 'Alī Riḍā) whose tomb at Qum is a considerable place of pilgrimage. So the saints in Islam are not all men.

The burial of the dead (*dafn*) must be effected as quickly as possible, preferably on the day of death and at all events on the morrow. The deceased is washed, usually by those whose profession it is to do this, and wrapped in a shroud (*kafan*). A special prayer is pronounced over the body (*ṣalātu 'l-mawt*) and the Koran is read. Then they put it in a coffin and carry it to the cemetery at a quick pace, repeating prayers in raised voices as they go. If the earth is damp and crumbling they lower it into the grave, dug to a man's height, in its coffin: but otherwise they remove it from the coffin and bury it in its shroud. They are careful to turn the deceased on his right side in such a way that his face is towards the *qibla*; also they put pieces of paper in the grave on which Koranic sayings are written such as 'In the name of God the Gracious, the Merciful!' The object is that the angels Nakīr and Munkar who, in Muslim teaching, present themselves to interrogate the deceased even in the grave, should know that a Believer is buried here, and not an infidel. In the Middle Ages it was common for devout Muslims to ensure in their last will and testament that other proofs of their creed should go with them to the grave. The twelfth century Syrian Arab amir Usāma b. Munqidh tells in his interesting memoirs how his father, having spent all his life copying out the Koran, arranged in his will that the fourteen transcripts thus prepared should be buried alongside him. Another case of this mediaeval practice was that of the Turkish Sultan Bāyazīd II Darwīsh (1481–1512) whose testament required that a chest containing the dust of Holy Wars, brushed by him from his clothing during his campaigns against the infidels, should accompany him to the grave to prove his participation in ghazawāt.

Islam deprecates mourning. However, pre-Islamic custom proved stronger than precept, and professional mourners are to be found in many Muslim countries, especially Iran. But Islam does prescribe visits to the tombs of the rightous, particularly those of saints, and lays down rules for the purpose. Of the cult of the prophets we have said something above; that of the saints, their tombs and their relics was non-existent in early Islam, but it developed later and flourished no less than in Christianity.[123]

The Muslim prohibitions relating to food were lighter than the Jewish, and in effect come down to the use of wine and the flesh of pig. It is true that birds of prey, carrion, anything strangled or not slaughtered in Allah's name but in the name of another and false god, not, that is, according to Muslim ritual, come under the ban; but these prohibitions are of no practical importance, since there would be little temptation to touch such things even without them. Of the two main prohibitions, that against pork has taken firm hold, especially in Iran.[124] But the zealous have never really succeeded in stopping the preparation, sale and consumption of wine, particularly in Iran and Central Asia. All the evidence of history and literature is there to show that the rich and noble in these countries drank the wine of the grape daily and openly,[125] and that it was only the unusually pious, and of course the very poor, who did not.

We have spoken of places of worship without describing them. The principal building, the mosque (*masjid*, lit. 'place of bowing down to God') traces its origin as a place of community-prayer to the hall said to have been constructed by Muḥammad alongside his house in Medīna, without however being modelled on this architecturally. The architectural tradition is not older than the hinge of the seventh and eighth centuries when Byzantine master-builders[126] invited by the Umayyads introduced the Hellenistic style which the Arabs assimilated and developed. There were cases, too, where Christian churches were converted into mosques with the necessary reorientation (if the word is permissible) towards Mecca instead of towards the east. Mosques multiplied as time went on, because people could hardly attend the city mosque five times a day. That mosque became associated specifically with Friday prayers and designated 'Friday' or 'Congregational', while minor mosques sprang up in different quarters or out in the rural area for the five regular daily prayers. In mediaeval Iran the mosque in the sector served also as an assembly hall at the disposal of the inhabitants of the quarter. As towns grew in size the congregational mosque sometimes proved inadequate, and by the later Middle Ages there would often be several congregational mosques and hundreds of the lesser mosques[127] in one and the same city, not to speak of domestic places of worship (*muṣallā*)[128] at the villas of the nobility and rich. It was part of the same process that congregational mosques, once confined to towns, should become a feature of the larger rural centres, as we learn from the tenth-century Arabic-language geographers. There was, however, an elasticity in all this. Friday prayers with an attendance of forty worshippers and upwards could always be said in a lesser mosque, or indeed in the open air in the absence of a suitable building; and the nomads, having as a rule no mosques, habitually prayed out of doors, all the congregation turning towards Mecca.

The rear wall of every mosque is always aligned towards Mecca (*qibla*), and in it is the *Miḥrāb* (in some big mosques several miḥrābs). Originally this only indicated the direction in which the Believer had to turn his face when praying, but later it came to be regarded as something holy in its own right like the Christian altar. It consists of a niche, which may be square, semi-circular or polyhedral, decorated with Koranic texts. By the end of the eighth century people in Iran, influenced by Zoroastrian practice, were placing lamps in front of the miḥrāb; and at a later stage candles and lanterns (*qandīl*) in the Christian manner; and they began spreading carpets. To the right of the miḥrāb may be set a raised pulpit for the prayer leader and preacher (*minbar*, plural *manābir*, from *nabara*, VIII Form *intabara* 'to go into the pulpit'), gained by a staircase. This minbar, which is used for Friday prayers, is found only in congregational mosques.

In the cities of Central Asia and some parts of Persia, special 'festival' mosques (Pers. *namāzgāh*) are found. These have spacious forecourts and are intended to accommodate the entire population of the town on the two great feast days of the Breaking of the Fast (*'īdu 'l-fiṭr*) and the Festival of the Sacrifice (*'īdu 'l-qurbān*).[129]

The passage of time brought variety in architecture. Iran for example had two styles which predominated. The first, introduced by the conquerors, repeated the layout and characteristics of the early mosques of Syria (notably the Umayyad Mosque in Damascus, early eighth century), of Egypt (The Great Mosque of 'Amr in Fusṭāṭ, seventh century) and of Iraq (the Great Mosque at Kūfa, seventh century). It featured a square or rectangular court framed with arcades and galleries, and equipped with a basin or fountain for ablution; and opening on to this court is the prayer-hall, usually flat-roofed, and broader than it is long,[130] with several rows of columns,[131] a miḥrāb and a minbar. The hall is joined to the court by open arches supported on columns or pillars. The oldest examples in this style are: the Mosque of the Caliph Mahdī at Ray near Tehran (late eighth century), of which only the foundation has been preserved; the Mosque of Tarī-Khāna at Dāmghān (ninth century); the congregational Mosque at Nā'in (tenth century); and the Mosque at Damāwand (eleventh century).[132]

The second style perpetuates the architectural tradition of Sāsānian times. The chief portion is the *ḥaram* or sanctuary with principal miḥrāb and minbar, consisting of a comparatively small square or octagonal building without columns, covered with a dome that may be conical, round or (slightly later) ellipsoidal or shaped like a ribbed melon. It has a rectangular portal (*pīshṭāq*) with a high porch (*aywān*) under a curved or lanceted arch. The actual entrance leading to the *ḥaram* is shaped like the porch, but is much smaller. Sometimes prayer places are found along the flanks of the *ḥaram*, separated from it by rows of columns or pillars in narrow naves with vaulted ceilings in the arches. Such prayer places have their own miḥrābs. The square or rectangular forecourt, already mentioned, is often on two levels. It has access to the *ḥaram* through the main *aywān*, and also has three more of these lofty *aywāns*, one in the centre of each of the enclosing walls. The lanceted arch was dominant in mosques of this style by the eleventh to twelfth centuries. Examples are the congregational Mosques in Nayrīz, Gulpāyagān, Qazwīn, Ardistān, the Old Friday Mosque in Iṣfahān (eleventh century),[133] the famous Blue Mosque at Tabrīz (fifteenth century), the Gawhar Shād Mosque at Mashhad (fifteenth century),[134] the Ṣafawid Mosque at Ardabīl (sixteenth century) and the splendid Shāh Mosque at Iṣfahān (early seventeenth century).

Religious painting is forbidden in Islam, the representation of God or man or any living creature being regarded as conducive to idolatry. This, therefore, is absent in mosques,[135] but there is compensation in the lavish ornamentation of walls, aywāns, minbar and miḥrāb: geometric, star-shaped and stylized plant-designs combine with equally stylized Arabic inscriptions — Koranic texts — in Kufic, Naskh, Thulth, and other varieties of penmanship. This ornamentation is supplemented with brick and terra cotta tiles, and carving in stone or alabaster. From the twelfth century, and still more so from the fourteenth century, the fashion developed in Iran and the adjacent countries of facing walls, aywāns and cupolas with glazed faïence or polychrome mosaic embellished with patterned inscriptions. Miḥrābs and minbars were similarly decorated with carvings in stone, wood, alabaster and marble, and given a revetment of faïence or lustrous tiling. Fretted alabaster miḥrābs have been preserved in the mosques of Iṣfahān, Abarqūh, Bisṭām and elsewhere; a miḥrab in one of the side oratories of the Masjid-i Jum'a at Iṣfahān, a gift of the Mongol Khan Uljāytū in 1310, being particularly noteworthy. A highly artistic miḥrāb from Kāshān dating from 1226 has also been preserved.

The mausoleum (*mazār*) over the tombs of Shī'ite Imams and their descendants (imāmzādas all such were dubbed) and other saints common in Iran, comes into the category of places of worship, and is often joined to small domed mosques.

Minarets (*manāra* or *minār*, from *nāra* 'to shine') were associated with mosques from olden times. These towers, from which the mu'adhdhin intones the call to prayer, first made their appearance in Syria under the Umayyads, but experts surmise that they have a link with the Western that is, Hellenistic, memorial column or perhaps an Iranian and even a Buddhist prototype — though this last is extremely doubtful. In Islam they are far from uniform architecturally. One of the most ancient, the ninth-century Minaru 'l-Mālwiya at Sāmarrā near Baghdad, is fifty metres high, in the shape of a truncated cone, and with an outside spiral staircase; whereas the oldest preserved examples in Iran are octagonal towers; witness the splendid early-eleventh-century minaret at Ghazna, and those at Dāmghān, Samnān, Iṣfahān and elsewhere. But the later type is a slender, tall cylindrical tower tapering towards the top, well illustrated by the twelfth-century Ṣīn Mosque minaret, the thirteenth-century Rāhrawān Minār, and the twelfth/thirteenth-century Sarābān Minār, forty-four metres in height, all at Iṣfahān. Then again one frequently meets the combination of an octagonal base and a circular top, as exemplified by the Chihil Dukhtarān Minār built in 1107 and the twelfth/thirteenth-century Ziyār Minār — once more at Iṣfahān. All the later minarets have a winding staircase inside leading to the clerestory or balcony (Pers. *guldasta*). They are usually ornate with brick mosaic or glazed tiles, and twin minarets thus decorated are also set on either side of the entrance-aywān. At the present time the primary function of the minaret has fallen into oblivion in Iran where the ādhān is nowadays proclaimed from the entrance-aywān. A low wooden cage is located over the latter for the purpose, and minarets are simply part of the architectural décor.[136]

The role of the madrasa, or school, was prominent. (Lit. *madrasa* is 'place of teaching', from *darasa* 'to teach'. The same root yields *dars* 'lesson', *tadrīs*, 'teaching', *mudarris* 'teacher', *midras* 'place where the Koran is read',[137] in Persian *dars-khāna*. Cf. Hebrew and Syrian root *drš* 'to teach', whence Hebrew *midraš*, 'teaching in' the sense of interpretation of the religious law: Hebrew *beit ha midraš* 'house of teaching' 'school', 'synagogue:'[138] Syr.*madraše* 'lesson in verse'.) In the early days of Islam, divines held occasional classes in the larger mosques, and even permanent courses of lectures might be given there. Then, by the tenth century, a theological-law school as such took shape, known as *madrasa*, in the eastern part of the empire, i.e. Central Asia and Khurāsān, whence it was afterwards carried to the western provinces. In Bartol'd's view this 'Muslim High-School', as we may call it, owed nothing to the Syrian Christian Schools.[139] It was modelled, he thinks, on the Buddhist Monastery Schools, or rather the Manichean Monastery Schools of Central Asia.[140] But proof is lacking. What we know is that the madrasa was simultaneously a school and a hostel where students lived an ascetic life in their separate cells, attended lectures and read selected books. Women were not allowed on the premises, and married students could only absent themselves once a week to visit their wives. No physical work was permitted, but students had to look after themselves and prepare their own food. The teaching was conducted in Arabic and the basic subjects were theology and law, study and exegesis (*Tafsīr*) of the Koran, and the Ḥadīth; but some madrasas taught secular subjects as well, and in any case there would always be Arabic grammar and philology, and logic in the syllabus. No term was prescribed for the training offered, and students might stay on and sit at the feet of their masters all their lives.[141] Like the mosque, the madrasa was maintained by waqfs — that is, income-bearing properties such as lands farmed by a settled peasant population, gardens, vineyards, mills; or else, in the case of towns, shops and entire bazaars.[142] The resultant revenue went entirely on the maintenance of the teaching and other staff, and on upkeep of buildings. The latter would vary very much from country to country. In Central Asia and Iran the architectural plan resembled that of the congregational mosque, comprising a rectangular or square court framed with arcades and often in two tiers, having four lofty aywāns; the cells (*ḥujra*) were under the arches flanking the court, and the lecture rooms (*dars-khāna*) at its corners. Very often in the countries named the madrasa of early days would be part and parcel of a Dervish community,[143] and only in process of time was the distinction made between the two. The combination of a madrasa with a mosque, often a congregational mosque, also became usual in those parts.

The leader of the daily or Friday prayers, standing in front of the rows of worshippers is named Imam (*imām,* plural *a'imma* 'standing in front', from *amma* 'to stand in front').[144] At the dawn of Islam this function was performed by Muḥammad himself in the Medīna community, or else by Abū Bakr or 'Umar who sometimes deputized for him. Under the first four Caliphs and the Umayyads, Friday prayer in the capital — Medīna to begin with, and later Damascus — was led by the Caliph, but in the provinces by the governors or their subordinates, and in the field by the army commanders. The practice derived from the theocratic idea in which religious society and the state were the same thing. There was no separate clerical order for the simple reason that the representative of the secular authority was automatically the spiritual director. Under the 'Abbāsids a professional class of *Fuqahā*, doctors of law and theology,[145] emerged who came to be regarded as experts and, so to speak, custodians of the Islamic creed. From the religious standpoint these divines are not comparable to Christian bishops or priests; they are not the bearers of any divine grace, they are not consecrated, have no exclusive right to officiate at religious ceremonies and no right at all to excommunicate or forgive sins. But in practice the order of *fuqahā*, or *'ulamā*, as they were alternatively called, began to play a part in society similar to some extent to that of the Christian clergy, and for this reason they are sometimes inaccurately referred to, in literature on the subject, as the Muslim clergy. It is more correct to think of them as a class of doctors of divinity and law which crystallized as feudal society progressed in the countries of the Caliphate, a class structure being characteristic of such a society in its developed stage.

Theoretically any adult Muslim can officiate as Imam provided he knows the rules of the regulation prayers and sufficient Arabic, but from 'Abbāsid times it became the practice to entrust specified persons with the duties concerned. And the designation itself gradually acquired a triple meaning:

1 Among the Sunnī the Imam is the head, in theory the elected head, of the community and state, the supreme depository of spiritual and secular power. In this sense Imam is the same as Caliph, and this Imam-Caliph was termed the Great Imam (*al-imāmu 'l-kabīr*), and his dignity the Great Imamate (*al-imāmatu 'l-kubrā*), as distinct from the Imam who is prayer-leader in the mosque. The name Great Imam, it should be noticed in passing, was also given to the eponymous founders of the Sunnī Madhhabs, or schools, of *fuqahā*.[146]

2 Among the Shī'ites the Imam is the hereditary head of the com-

munity and state, descendant of the family of Muḥammad and his son-in-law ʿAlī, husband of his daughter Fāṭima, the dignity of office being awarded not by human choice but divine command.[147]

3 The prayer-leader at the mosque belongs to the category of junior Imam (*al-imāmu 'ṣ-ṣaghīr*) performing the Junior Imamate (*al-imāmatu 's-sughrā*). In the case of congregational mosques he is drawn from the ranks of the trained *fuqahā*, but in ordinary mosques an elementary training will be enough for nomination if the individual is of moral and pious reputation. In this sense of prayer-leader the Shīʿites prefer the Persian term *pīshnamāz* to the Arabic term *imām*. Mu'adhdhins are rather like the junior Imams in that their appointment depends on general suitability and not specialized training.

Lastly, the Elders (Shaykhs or Pīrs) of Dervish brotherhoods constitute a body of spiritual preceptors. These represented the mystical trend in Islam and more will be said of them in the chapter on Ṣūfism.[148]

It remains to touch briefly on toleration. Modern Western and pre-revolution Russian scholars, including Bartol'd,[149] have given wide currency to the idea that Islam was extremely tolerant of other religions compared with mediaeval Christianity. This is not entirely true. Islam was not an immutable ideology — any more than Christianity was — which could be viewed and grasped, as something static. Tolerance and fanaticism alternated in different periods and in differing degrees of intensity depending on factors outside religion such as the political or economic conjuncture. During the conquests the Arabs were very tolerant of the Christians and Jews in the countries they overran, because at that stage religious exclusiveness was still alien to them. The Koran seemed to warrant this broad tolerance: it alluded to Jews and Christians as People of the Book who had received their revelation from the prophets Moses and Jesus whom the Muslims of that day looked upon as equated with Muḥammad in dignity. Political expedience dictated such leniency because the Christian population preponderated in the conquered territories, and there was everything to be said in favour of reconciling the new subjects with the dominion of the Caliphate and coaxing them to make due payment of tribute. Again, political considerations forced the Caliphate to invite the Zoroastrians to become Dhimmīs,[150] although the Koran expressly named Christians, Jews and Sabians alone as qualified for such lenient treatment. The Umayyads and the first ʿAbbāsids were, generally speaking, very tolerant — quite unlike the contemporary Byzantine

Emperors — and until the end of the eighth century, to go by reliable sources, there was no oppression of people of other faiths in the Caliphate.[151]

However, Islam became less and less tolerant as society became more and more feudal; for intolerance and exclusiveness are commonly attributes of feudal societies and feudal religions. It was Hārūn ar-Rashīd (786–809) who began the policy of persecution by ordering the destruction of churches in 'the provinces marching with Byzantium' (*ath-Thughūr*), and imposing legal restrictions on Christians, Jews and Zoroastrians. It was later pretended that these really went back to Caliph 'Umar I, having been laid down in his treaty with the Patriarch Sophronius on the surrender of Jerusalem in 637. The original text of this treaty has not come down to us, and the many variants offered in the pages of the Arab historians, as the Russian Arabist N. A. Mednikov has shown, are later inventions.[152] The disabilities were endorsed and intensified under Caliph Mutawakkil (847–861) who made Dhimmīs ineligible for the civil service, prohibited their children from attending Muslim schools, increased the capitation tax (*jizya*) to which they were liable, compelled them to wear distinguishing badges on their clothing, to place images of devils over the entrance to their homes, and to ride only mules and asses, and destroyed all churches and synagogues built since the conquest.

There was pronounced fanaticism among the Muslim masses from the early tenth century (and not from the days of the Crusades as certain historians have imagined). In that century pogroms of Christians occurred in Syria and Egypt,[153] and of Zoroastrians in Iran, and a drive of unprecedented cruelty was launched against both Jews and Christians in the former area under Caliph Ḥākim (996–1021).[154] Egypt was to grow accustomed to such massacres in the fourteenth century. In Iran the ban on entry into government employ was several times repeated and notably under the Seljūq Sultan Ṭughril Beg (1038–1063), and a wave of Jewish pogroms swept the country and Iraq as well, particularly Baghdad, in 1289.[155] The restoration of Islam as the state religion under the Mongol Ghāzān Khān in 1295 after nearly seventy years of rule by Khans who were pagan, touched off an explosion of fanaticism in that year and again in 1297 at the expense of the urban Christians and Jews of Iran and Iraq.[156] Buddhism, too, which had gained hold in Iran after the Mongol invasion was prohibited.

It would be easy to multiply such random examples, but these can here suffice. The situation of the Dhimmīs in Muslim states at different periods changed now for the better, now for worse at the unstable dictate of economics or politics. Practice was apt to depart from the legal theory of Fiqh. Theoretically the *Ḥanafite* school treats Dhimmīs more leniently and more condescendingly than does any of the other Sunnī sects, and more leniently than the Shī'ites do. Yet in Ottoman Turkey where Ḥanafite law was state law, the position of Christians was worse than under the Ṣafawids in sixteenth and seventeenth-century Iran where Shī'ism prevailed. Politics explained the divergence of practice from theory. Turkey, constantly at war with one or other of the states of Christian Europe, went through phases of distrust of her own Christian subjects. On the other hand, Ṣafawid Iran, at daggers drawn with Ottoman Turkey, looked to certain European powers as military allies, and utilized the services of Christians, mainly Armenian merchants and Catholic missionaries, both as commercial agents for the silk export and as diplomatic agents in the states concerned. Jews were better off in Ottoman Turkey at the time than in Ṣafawid Iran.

The overall legal position of Dhimmīs in the mediaeval Muslim states reminds one strongly of that of the Jews in most West European states — the Holy Roman Empire, Poland, Venice, and so on. Dhimmīs remained at liberty to practise their religious observances (though they were prohibited from building new places of worship and had to content themselves with repairing the old ones), but they did not enjoy full civic rights.[157]

Even on paper the attitude of the theologians gradually hardened. Under the Umayyads the Peoples of the Book had been sharply distinguished from the pagan polytheists.[158] But in subsequent theological thought Islam came to be portrayed as the sole genuinely monotheistic religion in the world, whereas the Christians and the Jews were a sub-classification under the general head of polytheists. The offence of the Christians was the doctrine of the Trinity with its implicit deification of Jesus, and the offence of the Jews was their idolization of the Prophet Ezra ('Uzayr), though in fact of course the Jews were innocent of this.[159] Hence the clause in the disqualifying act touching the Peoples of the Book, worded: Let them not noise their discourses on 'Uzayr and Messiah,[160] meaning that Jews must not speak of the divinity of Ezra in the presence of Muslims, nor Christians of the divinity of Christ.

Persecution of Muslim sectarians and heretics, notably the Ismā'īlīs and extreme Shī'ites, began in Mutawakkil's time and was accompanied by attacks on freethinkers, dualists — the Zindīqs, that is

Manicheans and Khurramites — and also on materialists and atheists (*ad-dahriyya*).[161] At times it would rage, as under the Seljūqs, and people would be executed and burned at the stake; at times it would die down. In all cases it was sporadic and exhibited neither the method nor the inflexibility of, for instance, the persecution of heretics and men of other faiths in Spain and Portugal under the Inquisition.

III
The Koran

The Koran, in Arabic *al-qur'ān*, is a collection of precepts, homilies and discourses communicated by Muḥammad to his followers at various times as revelations sent down to him by Allah in sleep or in a state of ecstasy through an intermediary spirit whom he took to be the Holy Ghost[1] or else the Angel Gabriel.[2] These revelations, assuming them to be such, were sometimes written down by the Believers on palm leaves, flat bones and occasionally parchment, but more often learned by heart and committed to memory. The fervent Companions got the Koran by heart rather as the rhapsodists memorized the rich oral poetry of the Arabs.

The Koran to Muslims is what the Old Testament is to the Jews, and the Gospel is to the Christians: it is their Holy Book, the foundation of their religion. It has always been read, and is still read, in mosque, school or home as part of the daily routine. Whereas European scholars may see it as the work of the Prophet Muḥammad, it is nothing of the sort in the eyes of believing Muslims: here, to their thinking, are the *ipsissima verba* of God himself. To quote Theodore Nöldeke: 'The Koran in Muslim belief is the word of God, and offers itself as such. For setting aside Sūra I,[3] which is a prayer for people to use, and the very few passages where Muḥammad (VI 104, 114; XXVI 93; XLII 8) or the Angels (XIX 65; XXXVII 164 *et seq.*) are speaking in the first person without the usual introductory "He spoke", "He says", the speaker is always God himself in the first person singular or more readily, as befits majesty, the first person plural. The Koran itself defines the revelation it contains as follows: it is the original text, existing in heaven, the "Mother Book" (XLIII 3),[4] the "Secret Book" (V 77),[5] the "Preserved Tablet" (LXXXV 21);[6] and from this original, fragment after fragment has been sent down to the Prophet through the mediation of an angel designated a "Spirit" (XXVI 193), or the "Holy Ghost" (XVI 104) or, much later on "Gabriel" (II 91). This go-between declaimed the revelation before the Prophet and repeated it so that it might afterwards be published to the people (XXXVII 6).'[7]

Thus Muḥammad brought it home to his followers that the Koran is a revelation from the celestial divine book. He went further and let it be known that the same celestial book had in parts been communicated to earlier prophets before his day:[8] the Torah had been sent down to Moses, the Psalms to David, the Gospel to Jesus Christ; and for that reason Jews and Christians are named People of the Book (*ahlu 'l-kitāb*). The latter's scriptures in their pristine shape, as he maintained, did not differ from the Koran except in language and form. In content they were identical. However, what the Jews had been sent was a portion of Holy Writ[9] which contained certain revelations applicable only to them (for instance, the celebration of the Sabbath) and not to Muslims, and in order to explain why the Jewish scriptures as known in his day did not coincide with the Koran, Muḥammad asserted that the Jews had forgotten some items in the revelation made to them,[10] and concealed others,[11] and had transposed certain words of scripture from their proper context and distorted them.[12] Later on he reproached the Christians with the same behaviour, so the net result was that Islam did not look like a new religion at all. On the contrary, it was the unique eternal religion of the One God which at different times had been laid bare to Abraham, Moses, David and Jesus, to name no other prophets, and had then been in part forgotten, in part perverted. Muḥammad had in consequence been chosen by God to restore the one original faith — the faith of Abraham, Moses, David and Jesus — and the Koran was the genuine Book of God. The general conception of revelation as something transmitted to people through prophets corresponded completely with both Jewish and Christian ideas on the matter.

The actual word 'Koran' (*qur'ān* from the root *qara'a* 'to read') has commonly been rendered as 'reading', and this translation is undoubtedly endorsed by certain passages in the text.[13] But a much more usual meaning of the word *qara'a* at the time was 'to declaim aloud' or 'to recite', and by no means necessarily from a book, but rather by heart. There are places in the Koran where the word is employed precisely in this sense.[14] Contemporary scholarship has therefore come to give the word 'Koran' the exact meaning 'declamation', i.e. the reciting aloud of Muslim scripture. The word *kitāb*, Holy Writ, occurs as a synonym, and Muḥammad used the two words indifferently not only to denote the aggregate of the revelations from which a single book was to be made and edited after his death, but for each separate revelation whether lengthy or (as more often) brief. For each of these separate revelations or fragments of the supposed celestial book, he also used the word *sūra*, and this name was taken over after his time to denote the separate chapters of the edited Koran.[15] Nöldeke derives the word from the late-Hebrew *shura*, a 'row', whence 'line',[16] but Muḥammad apparently associated it with the idea of a celestial book, and there is little doubt that everyone in his day understood by *sūra* an extract from that book.[17] The Koranic Sūras consist of verses termed even in Muḥammad's life *āyāt*, lit. 'sign of the times' and so 'miracle' (cf. Hebr. *ot* of the same meaning).

It must be borne in mind that the Sūras in the recension of the Koran which we have, differ from those Sūras which Muḥammad's listeners noted down or memorized as revelations communicated to him. He never hesitated to add new verses of 'revelation' to old Sūras; and when the Koran came to be edited,[18] verses often went into this or that Sūra though they belonged to another date.

It is hard to say whether the language of the Koran reflects the dialect spoken at the time in the Ḥijāz and Mecca particularly, for no examples of that dialect have come down to us. Karl Vollers held that the Koran is written in the popular conversational idiom of the Northern Arabs of the day,[19] but Nöldeke rejected this as being uncorroborated either by tradition or linguistic data, and noted too that the absence of vowel signs in the oldest text of the Koran precludes judgment on whether there were any peculiarities of pronunciation in Muḥammad's day. What can be affirmed is that the language employed is much different from that of Arab poetry in the sixth/seventh centuries. There are many grammatical divergences from the literary language, and a considerable vocabulary is borrowed from the other Semitic tongues Hebrew, Aramaic, Syriac and Old Ethiopian (Geʿez), the loan words being as often as not distorted and given a sense they did not bear in their original setting.[20] Although Muḥammad declared that the revelation was sent down to him in pure Arabic,[21] European scholars have remarked on the many irregularities: the artificial constructions, frequent grammatical non-correspondence of subject and predicate, non-agreement of principal clause with subordinate clause, and so on. The shortcomings of language were enough to cause one eminent Semitic authority, J. Wellhausen, to pronounce (with violent exaggeration) that 'the Koran is written in thoroughly un-Arabic Arabic.'[22]

The literary form of the Koran is rhymed prose, known to the Arabs as *sajʿ*, in which juxtaposed verses end in assonant words taking the place of rhyme, or in phrases repeated like a refrain. The result is a distinctive poetry, as may be gauged from say, the highly figurative Sūras XVI and LXVIII. It is particularly in the early Meccan chapters that passion and animation are abundant and expressed in vivid imagery. Take the picture of the Earth and the Souls before Doomsday: 'When the sun shall be wrapped around in darkness, when the stars shall grow dim, when the mountains shall move from their places, when the she-camel ten months gone with young shall be idle, when the wild beasts shall crowd, when the seas shall boil, when the souls shall be united, and when the girl buried alive shall be asked for what crime she has been done to death, when the scrolls shall be unwound and when the pall of the sky shall be lifted, when Gehenna shall flare up and Paradise shall draw near — then shall every soul know what it has made ready for itself.'[23] Or another fragment on the same subject: 'Yea, when the Earth shall be minutely ground and become little pieces, when thy Lord [*rabbuka*] shall come and with him Angels standing row upon row, on that day when Gehenna [*al-jahannam*] shall be nigh, on that day man shall meditate, but what shall this meditation bring him?'[24] Or this: 'The day will be when the Unbelievers shall come forth from the graves as hurriedly as men rush to the uplifted standard of war. Disgrace shall haunt them and they shall cast down their eyes. Such shall be this day with which they are threatened in advance.'[25] Or again: 'Ask pardon of your Lord, for he is ready to forgive, and he will command the heavens to pour down plentiful rain for you, and will multiply your estate and sons, give you gardens, and give you rivers.'[26] The precepts and admonitions of these Meccan Sūras are commonly reinforced by passionate oaths: 'I swear by the sunset, by the night and what grows dark in it, by the moon when she is full:'[27] 'I swear by the heaven, I swear by the morning star (*aṭ-ṭāriq*)'; 'Oh, if there were one to make thee understand what it is, this morning star — it is the star (*an-najm*) shining brightly';[28] 'I swear by the heaven that pours down the rain, by the earth that brings forth vegetation',[29] etc. Unfortunately Muḥammad's early poetical style became drier and drier, more and more prosaic and monotonous, so that most European critics consider that the Koran judged as literature does not bear comparison with the contemporary Arabic poetry — which was still oral and only committed to writing in eighth/ninth-century recensions — and that there is on the whole more rhetoric in it than poetry.[30] In every Muslim milieu of course the Koran became recognized as an unmatched literary monument, and if literary standards were still those of pre-Islamic poetry, the development of the language from now on was to be governed largely by the Koran.

The Koran together with the Ḥadith,[31] or Tradition, supplied the basis of theology and jurisprudence — those two 'roots' of the Sharī'a or Muslim Law. Interpretation of the Koran postulated a painstaking study of its vocabulary and grammatical structure; which in turn stimulated philology and lexicography as separate disciplines. And in the sequel of course, it was the Holy Book combined with the Tradition that became one of the three sources of Arab historiography.[32]

When Muḥammad died, the Koran was a chaotic jumble of fragmented revelations which various Companions had either recorded in writing or stored safely in their memories. Muslim tradition has it that apprehension arose in Abū Bakr's Caliphate lest this Koran might be wholly or partially lost, seeing that many of the Companions who knew long fragments of it by heart had perished in the carnage of battle against Musaylima and the other false prophets directing the separatist movements in 11 AH (632/3). Caetani, however, has shown that those who fell in these fights were mostly neophytes who could not possibly have been knowledgeable on the Koran.[33] Apparently it was 'Umar who was responsible for the initiative in piecing together a connected canonical text, imagining perhaps that the inculcation of a definitive Koran might anticipate discord among the Muslims, and particularly quarrels over power. Much obscurity surrounds the compilation, and the only authentic detail is that Caliph Abū Bakr acting on 'Umar's advice entrusted the editing to the twenty-two-year-old Zayd b. Thābit who had been Muḥammad's secretary in the closing years of his life. Zayd was to collect and collate, and embody in a connected text, all the fragments of Koran that had been preserved in the notes or the memories of individuals, and this task he discharged. The collated whole was transcribed on separate sheets (*aṣ-ṣuḥuf*) in bold handwriting without diacritical points and vowel signs; 'Umar apparently supervising Zayd's work as it progressed.

This first redaction bore no official character, and was merely designed for the private use of the leadership of the community — Abū Bakr, 'Umar and Abū 'Ubayd — and was therefore not reproduced in copies. But in the reign of the first three Caliphs other editions made their appearance, at the instance of particular Companions, which differed from Zayd's alike in the layout and arrangement of Sūras and their parts, and in the reading of individual passages. According to tradition the editors of these versions were Ubayy b. Ka'b, 'Abdullāh b. Mas'ūd, Abū Mūsā al-Ash'arī and Miqdād b. 'Amr[34] — all of them Companions. Some idea of the Ubayy and Mas'ūd editions can be gained from Ibn Nadīm's *Fihrist*[35] which tells us that the former included two chapters not in the official recension (i.e. the second Zayd redaction, see below), and that the latter did not contain Sūras CXIII and CXIV. There was also a fifth version, probably identical with the first Zayd redaction, which later on served as the basis of the official Koran compiled under Caliph 'Uthmān.[36]

The existence of various versions of the text, even though they might differ only on points of detail, evidently endangered the potential harmony and concord of the community, and therefore 'Uthmān decided to bring out an official edition or, to put it otherwise, a canonical text of the Koran obligatory for all the Muslims. Once again Zayd b. Thābit, who was living in Medīna, was entrusted with the task (651). Helped by other Companions, he proceeded to acquire whatever notes were in the hands of private persons and to collate these. When the continuous canonical version had been completed, the notes were not returned to their owners but burned at 'Uthmān's orders so as to ensure that the new official edition, sometimes termed the second Zayd redaction, should be universally received as the unique text. No time was lost in preparing four copies in the new edition, the intention being that every Koran thereafter should be a facsimile of one of the four.

There is every justification for holding that 'Uthmān and his entourage, or in other words the Umayyads and their supporters, no less than 'Umar at an earlier stage, were actuated more by political considerations than by religious zeal in their wish for a definitive Koran. Factions had already formed, conventionally termed Partisans of the Umayyads and Partisans of 'Alī (Shī'at 'Alī). There was popular dissatisfaction with the aristocratic leadership whose interests the Umayyad House was backing; and apparently 'Uthmān and his group, foreseeing the inevitable struggle for power, wanted to strengthen their position and were at pains to see that no variants of the Koran should be available which might touch off quarrels with, or be an instrument in the hands of, their opponents. There are grounds for conjecture that certain changes favourable to the pro-Umayyad faction were made in the text of the Divine Book at the time of this recension.

'Uthmān's calculation that his authorized version would be universally accepted, and that competing versions would disappear was only partly right, and even wrong in the short term. It was not feasible to withdraw from circulation and destroy all the old scrolls; and if it had been, there were still plenty of people left who knew the former versions by heart. A protest came from 'Abdullāh b. Mas'ūd who, as has been said, had produced an early edition,[37] and it carried weight because this acknowledged expert had been as close to the Prophet as anybody. Second, there was sharp criticism from the Shī'ites who accused Zayd — and, it would appear, not without cause — of trying to please 'Uthmān and the Umayyads by removing all verses that spoke of 'Alī and the Prophet's bias in his favour, and of his right to the succession. To prove their case they maintained that in a number of passages the text of the authorized version was disconnected and seemed to be intentionally obscure; there were dark hints, in these places, at certain goings-on inside the Medīna community, and also threats directed against the enemies of Islam, albeit without any names being given as a rule. It was to be supposed that the text had been tampered with in these passages and the names in them removed.[38] Mas'ūd and the Shī'ites combined in repudiating Sūras CXIII and CXIV, and the Khārijites rejected Sūra XII.[39]

Thus the 'Uthmān version failed in the beginning to win general acceptance, and certainly until the tenth century the Ubayy and Mas'ūd recensions were current here and there. But since such unauthorized scrolls were systematically pulled in and destroyed at the command of the Caliphs and their provincial governors, it was inevitable that all rival recensions should disappear within a few centuries. Consequently even the Shī'ites and Khārijites who held the authorized version to be corrupt in places had to accept it, for want of anything better. All Muslims were in the same case, and there were even many Sunnīs who did not think the text faultless and would permit themselves departures from it. For even now when the Koran was read divergences would occur because different Readers, or *qurrā'* (pl. of *qāri'*) who had memorized and grown up with a variant reading, naturally retained this as against the 'Uthmān version they had in their hands. The variant reading, and consequently the alternative understanding of a given passage, was promoted too, and perhaps more significantly, by the imperfection of Arabic writing at that time. Neither vowel signs, indicating the short and to some extent the long vowels, nor diacritical points differentiating consonants of similar shape but separate value, were yet in ordinary use. When letters of identical shape had more than one value, resultant words might admit more than one meaning; and when vowelling was absent it was difficult to recognize grammatical forms, and to grasp for instance whether a verb was active or passive. It is unknown at what date diacritical points, probably on the pattern of Syriac lettering, were introduced into Arabic;[40] but if this improvement was invented before Islam, it had not been brought into use by the time the Koran was being edited. This only happened in the interval between the end of the first century AH (equivalent to the first decade of the eighth century of our era) — the time of the Arabo-Egyptian papyri — and the second half of the second century AH (equivalent to the 760s to the 820s of our era).[41] And when it did happen, it of course failed to establish the definitive way of reciting the Koran. The insertion of diacritical points and vowel signs[42] in a text which had not employed them previously led to endless argument as to what consonants or vowels were really intended in the disputed words. Many variant readings were the result, and in certain cities of the Caliphate, notably Medīna, Mecca, Baṣra and Kūfa there arose schools of Readers each of which owed obedience to a chosen master. Abū ʻAmr b. al-ʻAlā (d. *c.* 770) of the Baṣra school and al-Kisāʼī (d. not later than 805) of the Kūfa school and almost the father of Arab philology, were prominent among these authorities on Koranic exegesis. At first the authority of these teachers was handed down orally, but in the ninth century treatises on the variants in the canonical Koran appeared. These were soon superseded, however, by the ʻBook of the Seven' (*kitābu 's-sabʻa*) of Abū Bakr b. Mujāhidi 't-Tamīmi al-Baṣrī (b. 859, d. 936) which became the basis of all subsequent guides to the reading of the Koran (*ʻilmu 'l-qurāʼa*) and was the acknowledged classic in the eleventh century.[43] It has not come down to us, but we know that Ibn Mujāhid's method involved a comparison of the readings of the seven most authoritative Readers of past centuries, Abū ʻAmr and al-Kisāʼī among them.

The incoherent material at Zayd's disposal did not lend itself to treatment according to subject-matter or to chronology, and all he could do was to arrange the Sūras in order of diminishing length. Thus the longest are placed at the beginning of the continuous text (Sūras II, III, IV, etc.), and the shortest nearer the end, the very shortest being CXII. Exceptions to this rule are Sūra I, ʻal-Fātiḥa', which has pride of place as a principal prayer, and Sūras CXIII and CXIV, which, although slightly longer than CXII nevertheless are appropriate to the close because they contain charms that guard against the machinations of the Devil or the evil spirits and evil men who do his bidding.[44] There was nothing novel in such an arrangement; it was common practice in the case of those collections of poetic works which the Arabs termed Dīwāns, and had been adopted with complete consistency in Ibn Masʻūd's recension.

The text of the ʻUthmān edition which we have, consists of one hundred and fourteen chapters or Sūras, and six thousand two hundred and six verses or Āyāt. As Sūras varied in size, the volume of verses in each was not fixed: Sūra II, 'The Cow', consists of two hundred and eighty-five verses, Sūra III, 'The Family of 'Imrān', of two hundred, Sūra IV, 'Women', of one hundred and seventy-five, and so on; whereas Sūras XCVII to CXIV have from three to ten verses apiece. Some verses contain no more than two or three words, but some run to half a page. The Sūras have headings which either indicate the subject matter of the chapter, e.g. Sūra VIII 'The Spoils of War', Sūra IX 'Penitence', Sūra XII 'Joseph', Sūra XIX 'Mary', Sūra XXI 'The Prophets', Sūra LXXV 'The Resurrection', etc; or else — and more frequently — a subject merely mentioned in the beginning or, it may be, in the body of the chapter, e.g. Sūra XIV 'Abraham', Sūra XVII 'The Children of Israel', Sūra XXX 'The Greeks', Sūra XXXV 'The Angels', Sūra XLVIII 'The Victory', Sūra LII 'The Mountain', Sūra LIII 'The Star', Sūra LIV 'The Moon', Sūra LV 'The Merciful', Sūra LXIII 'The Hypocrites', etc. These chapter titles were given sometime after Muḥammad's death, and the Christian theologian John of Damascus (earlier than 750) cites several of them.[45]

In the text of the Koran which has come down to us a few Sūras have mysterious letters of the alphabet in lieu of a heading, and certain others have such letters immediately in front of the title. Twenty-nine Sūras are labelled in this way. For example Sūra XX has ṬA (or ṬH); Sūras XL to XLVI have ḤM;[46] Sūras XXVI to XXVIII have ṬSM;[47] Sūras II, III and XXIX to XXXII have ALM; Sūras X to XV have ALR.[48] Muslim theologians have taken these letters for abbreviations of words of mystical meaning and the secret of which is known to God alone. But European scholars have attempted other explanations. The hypothesis which has most verisimilitude is that of Nöldeke who thought that the letters were inserted by Zayd and were the monograms of the names of the owners of the notes furnished him during the preparation of his connected text.[49] In fact ḤM could well be deciphered as Ḥamza, ALM as al-Mughīra, ALR as az-Zubayr,[50] ṬH as Ṭalḥa, and so on; but other combinations do not yield their secret.

Nöldeke, and after him Hirschfeld and Bauer, made much of the point that a given combination of letters tended to be prefixed to several Sūras in succession. This suggested a preliminary collection of notes already marshalled and examined which Zayd respected;[51] in which case the letters are abbreviated names of the owners of the particular series of notes. It was also possible, as Hirschfeld admitted, that the letters might be the initials of joint owners of a single note: for example ṬH instead of standing for Ṭalḥa could mean 'Ṭalḥa and Abū

Hurayra'. Nöldeke later offered a different explanation of the cryptic letters, but it has not found favour and has not superseded his first hypothesis as developed by Hirschfeld.

Islamic scholarship has given an affirmative answer to the question whether the Koran is genuine and whether Muḥammad is its author, at least so far as the basic text goes.[52] If the style varies as between its different — presumably earlier and later — parts, the book as a whole does bear the imprint of its author's personality. The difference in style can be explained, as scholars have noted, by changes in Muḥammad's psychological make-up over the twenty-two years (roughly between 610 and 632) during which the Koran was being pieced together bit by bit. Sides to his character developed in Medīna which were not displayed earlier. His dominant mood became more sober, dry and prosaic, and this was communicated to the revelations belonging to the Medīna period of his life.

At the same time, it is idle to pretend that the entire Koran has been handed down in its original form in the 'Uthmān canonical text (that is, the Zayd edition). The fact that the Ubayy version contains two chapters missing in the 'Authorized Version' and that certain fragments in the recension of Abū Mūsā al-Ash'arī likewise failed to find their way into the 'Uthmān text, is proof enough that the latter does not include all the original notes of revelations; does not, in other words, include the whole Koran.

As to whether there are interpolations, *a priori* one would think there must be some. But they can hardly have been significant, for otherwise the insertions would have been disputed and contested by the owners of other versions.

The order in which the Sūras and even separate fragments were arranged in the 'Uthmān edition was, as we have said, arbitrary: it bears no relation whatever to the chronological sequence of the parts of the Koran. All Sūras, indeed, are marked 'Meccan' or else 'Medinese' but there is no more precise indication of date than that. Moreover, certain Meccan revelations have been introduced into Medinese Sūras and there are certain Medinese fragments in Meccan Sūras.

European scholars have laboured to establish the chronology of the parts of the book. The task has been the harder in that the Koran itself contains very few allusions to historical events that might permit one to date the passages narrating them. Those few include: Sūra XXX which speaks, obviously, of the defeat of the Byzantine forces in Syria[53] by the Persians and the temporary seizure of the province between 611 and 614. Sūra VIII, 'The Spoils of War', clearly made its appearance after the battle of Badr in 624 when the Muslims for the first time took much plunder from the Meccan idolaters and had to lay down the principle of its division. Sura XXXIII contains clear allusions to the Battle of the Ditch in verses 9 to 25, and to the massacre and captivity of the Jewish tribe Qurayẓa[54] (without naming it) in verses 26 and 27; which together determine the date of this Sūra as the spring of 627. Sūra XLVIII on the face of it is connected with the treaty of Ḥudaybiya with the Meccans in 628. But passages that may thus be linked with known events are scarce, and no coherent picture of the chronology of the Koran can be got from them. The Tradition is no more informative in this regard, and the Biographies of the Prophet by Ibn Ishāq (used by Ṭabarī) and by Ibn Hishām are of almost no help in assigning dates. Consequently the Islamists have had to resort to a different criterion, viz, the comparative study of peculiarities of style, vocabulary, specific expressions and also of psychological mood exhibited in the various sections of the Book. This test cannot, of course, result in an absolutely trustworthy chronology, but it has permitted the greater part of the Sūras, especially the Medīna Sūras, to be cast into proper sequence. Gustav Weil[55] began this research and A. Sprenger[56] continued it, but it was Nöldeke[57] who drew up a chronological table for the whole Koran, postulating four periods for the component sections, three associated with Mecca and one with Medīna. Grimme[58] was responsible for another chart of this sort, but it was very artificial; and a third scheme by Hirschfeld[59] amounted to no more than an elaboration of what Nöldeke had done.

In the latter's classic arrangement the Sūras of the first Meccan period are in effect those which Zayd had put for the most part at the end. They are distinguished by brevity, rhythm, and an accomplished style, and are the most poetic; they are imbued with passionate feeling, sincerity and conviction. The favourite theme of the Sūras in this period is the awaited Resurrection of the Dead, the Judgment Day, and the terrible fate in store for the idolaters and those who do not believe in the One God. In other words the subject-matter here is eschatology. Nöldeke establishes the following sequence of forty-eight Sūras: XCVI, LXXIV, CXI, CVI, CVIII, CIV, CVII, CII, CV, XCII, XC, XCIV, XCIII, XCVII, LXXXVI, XCI, LXXX, LXVIII, LXXXVII, XCV, CIII, LXXXV, LXXIII, CI, XCIX, LXXXII, LXXXI, LIII, LXXXIV, C, LXXIX, LXXVII, LXXVIII, LXXXVIII, LXXXIX, LXXV, LXXXIII, LXIX, LI, LII, LVI, LXX, LV, CXII, CIX, CXIII, CXIV, I.

The Sūras of the second Meccan period are less marked by passion and are quieter in tone. The name of God is commonly replaced by the epithet 'the Merciful' (rahmān), whence the conventional name 'the Rahmān Sūras'. Allah's imperative 'Say' (*qul*) is frequently encountered, and the principal theme is divine unity. The Sūras are longer than in the first period. They number twenty-one, and the sequence submitted is: LIV, XXXVII, LXXI, LXXVI, XLIV, L, XX, XXVI, XV, XIX, XXXVIII, XXXVI, XLIII, LXXII, LXVII, XXIII, XXI, XXV, XVII, XXVII, XVIII.

The Sūras of the third Meccan period abound in repetitions, and the style is drier and rhetorical rather than poetical. Many passages, accounting for one thousand five hundred verses, are occupied with stories about the prophets before Muhammad. There is much homily and the tone is oratorical. The suggested sequence of the twenty-one Sūras is: XXXII, XLI, XLV, XVI, XXX, XI, XIV, XII, XL, XXVIII, XXXIX, XXIX, XXXI, XLII, X, XXXIV, XXXV, VII, XLVI, VI, XIII.

The Sūras of the fourth, or Medīna, period are close to the third Meccan period in style. Since the Medīna period is the phase of Muḥammad's career which is best known, the contents are here at their clearest. Personal religious sentiments, sermons on belief in the One God, are no longer to the fore: instead of preaching about the Wrath to come and the next world Muḥammad had now to attend to the needs of the Muslim community here below. The Medīna Sūras are therefore devoted to uncoordinated decrees of legal character on family, marriage and divorce, penalties for specified offences, the vendetta, Holy War, spoils of battle and their distribution, and so on. There is nothing resembling a connected code founded on religion: that was to be the work of subsequent generations and took at least three centuries. The Sūras contain a number of allusions and even direct pointers to happenings inside and outside the community in the period 622–632, even if there are scarcely any chronological landmarks within the decade. Good examples are the attacks on the Hypocrites who were undermining the community from inside; and Muḥammad's final break with the Jews is also clearly mirrored in these Sūras. Earlier on in Mecca the Prophet had supposed the faith of the Jews and Christians to be at bottom identical with his;[60] but in Medīna he drew a line of demarcation first between Muslims and Jews and then, after a pause, between Muslims and Christians. That he went on hoping for union with the Christians for some time is attested by more than one passage, e.g. 'Of all people the most bitterly hostile to the Believers are the Jews and polytheists; and the most genuinely friendly towards the Believers are they that call themselves Nazarenes (*naṣārā*), and this because there are priests and monks (*qissīsūn wa ruhbān*) among them, and they are not proud.'[61] At this stage, as the quotation shows, the Koran is violently opposed to the Jews, and Sūra II, 'The Cow' — the longest in the Book — abounds in lunges against them.[62] But by the end of the period the Koran is extending its attacks to the Christians as well, the latter now becoming the target of reproach for their doctrine of the Trinity.[63] In both cases the rupture resulted from Muḥammad's teaching that the original religion of monotheism was not connected either with the Jews or with the Christians, but had been preached among the Arabs by God's emissary Abraham and by his son, the prophet Ismā'īl; and that the Ka'ba was the temple in which Abraham prayed. In this Medīna period of the Koran Muḥammad spoke much of Jesus Christ as God's messenger and as Messiah, and sought to show that the teaching of Jesus was identical with Islam but that it had been corrupted by the Christians with the passage of time. Jesus is pictured also as the immediate precursor of Muḥammad and as having foretold the latter's prophetic mission.[64] As V. V. Bartol'd remarked, 'Muḥammad's attitude to Jews and Christians was determined by their attitude to his community rather than by religious differences.'[65]

The idea of Holy War as a religious obligation and the associated idea of the legality of appropriating spoils taken from the enemy were introduced in the Medīna period.[66] Here too Jesus figures, the institution of War for the Faith being ascribed to him and his apostles.[67]

Coming to Nöldeke's table for the fourth (Medīna) period, there are twenty-four Sūras in the following sequence: II, XCVIII, LXIV, LXII, VIII, XLVII, III, LXI, LVII, IV, LXV, LIX, XXXIII, LXIII, XXIV, LVIII, XXII, XLVIII, LXVI, LX, CX, XLIX, IX, V. Many authorities, Nöldeke among them, take verse 5 of this concluding Sūra V to be the last revelation of Muḥammad before his death, containing as it does the Prophet's farewell to his flock.[68]

It is evident that no chronological chart of the Koran, whether that of Nöldeke or another, can hope to be more than hypothetical. At best the positioning of a given Sūra will be governed by its main content and not by all its verses. Examples are easy to find, but one will do: Sūra V, 'The Table', is considered by Nöldeke and most other students of Islam to be the very last on the strength of its dominant part, but the attitude to the Christians expressed in this Sūra is so far from uniform throughout as to prove that the relevant verses belong to a variety of dates.[69] The sequence can only be established approximately.

The contents of the Koran, it will have been seen, are multifarious indeed. The Sūras of the Medīna period which bear largely a homiletic and legal character were directed, as Goldziher has noticed, 'against the barbarity of Arab paganism in matters of worship and social life and in the tribal *Weltanschauung* of the Arabs'.[70] At odds with the old Arab Jāhiliyya, Muḥammad and his Koran were *ipso facto* at war with the tenacious vestigial forms of the decaying patriarchal system and clan routine of pre-Islamic Arabia, reprobating tribal isolation and enmity, the blood-feud,[71] irregular sexual relations, female infanticide, etc. The Koran mirrored the new social attitudes of a dawning class society and pointed to a new way of life and a new religious outlook. It took the important historical step of repudiating the discord of the tribes, of advertising the brotherhood of all the Muslims irrespective of origin, colour,[72] national allegiance and language, and of announcing that the Believers constituted a single religious, ethical, political community. The approach was eminently compatible with the interests of a nascent class society and a new Arab state.

There are many Jewish and Christian elements in the Koran, as in the Muslim religion generally. The former on the whole outweigh the properly Christian, or New Testament, contribution, but much that is 'Old Testament' could obviously have just as well been taken indirectly from Christians as directly from Jews. V. V. Bartol'd thinks that the Meccan Sūras betray Christian rather than Jewish influence, and points out that 'among the Biblical stories that got into the Koran there is not a single one that could not have been borrowed from the Christian circles' in which Muḥammad moved.[73] In the Medīna Sūras, of course, much may well have been taken direct from Jews; though even so, the Biblical stories are much more likely to have been borrowed from the Jewish Haggadah than direct from the books of the Old Testament. The Christology of the Koran is founded on the apocryphal 'Gospel of the Childhood of Christ' and also, in all probability, on the opinions of Judaean-Christians.[74]

Finally, the Koran contains certain parallels with the Psalms of David and the Mishnah from Jewish literature, and with St Luke's Gospel and the Epistle to the Corinthians from Christian literature.[75]

All these borrowings and parallels that found their way into the Koran were apparently received at third hand through oral transmission by Jewish Talmudists and Christian monks. That they did not come direct from the Jewish or Christian books is proved by the frequent inaccuracies, sometimes the glaring mistakes, committed when Jewish and Christian traditions are imported: e.g. Mary the sister of Moses is identified with Mary the mother of Jesus; there is no clear picture of the chronological order of the prophets; the deification of Ezra ('Uzayr) is ascribed to the Jews, and the adoration of Mary to the Christians — without any warrant; and so forth.

Jostling these Jewish and Christian components are certain Gnostic and Zoroastrian elements. Once again the acquisition was at third hand, casual and unsystematic. Goldziher[76] detects the influence of Gnosticism in the famous 'Verse on Light' (*āyatu 'n-nūr*):[77] 'Allah is the light of the heavens and of the earth. His light is as if a niche, in which a lamp is set, in a glass, and the glass is as it were a star of pearl. It is lit from a blessed olive tree neither of the east nor of the west, the oil whereof is ready to ignite although no fire touch it. Light upon Light. Allah will lead to the light whom he pleases, and Allah propounds parables unto men. Allah has knowledge of everything.' However, D. B. Macdonald finds the influence here purely Christian.[78] Zoroastrianism is mostly apparent in the picture of paradise and hell with its horrors, which reached the Koran through the medium of Jews and Christians who themselves had in their time assimilated this imagery from Zoroastrian sources.

Want of originality in its subject-matter did not interfere in the slightest with the impact which the Koran had on the Believers; for not knowing the Jewish and Christian scriptures, the Arabs found the Koranic ideas novel to a degree. And after the conquests this very absence of originality psychologically facilitated the adoption of Islam by numerous Christians, Jews and Zoroastrians who found so much in the Koran that was akin to the religious assumptions they had grown up with. The influence of the Koran was even more profound on the Muslims of succeeding generations than on Muḥammad's contemporaries. The Book was digested from childhood, read repeatedly, commented on by the teachers in school; and when schooldays were over and adult age began, the faithful acquired the habit of reading it, or listening to it being read, day in, day out. It became for them the Book of Books, a volume of prescribed prayer, a code of religious practice and social usage, of daily behaviour and manners. In their esteem it was unsurpassed, peerless, matchless — in other words, a miracle (*i'jāz*) which Men and Jinn put together could not have wrought.[79]

Its style deeply affected subsequent Arabic literature, both poetry and prose: law, theology, mysticism and even Arabo-Persian philosophy arrived at their terminology with the aid of its vocabulary.

Yet it would be wrong to suppose all the dogma, ethic and law of Islam to have been given in the Koran.[80] Islam does not culminate there. Goldziher and many Islamists after him have demonstrated that Islam was no more something fashioned instanteneously and once and for all than any other religion. Like any other religion, it evolved over the centuries and was the mirror of the changing social environment in which it had its being. The Koran is one source, but it is emphatically not the single source for its study.

Little by little the theologians and jurists built upon the Koran their theology in its many branches. First and foremost, this was the 'science' of reading the Book, *'ilmu 'l-qirā'a*, of which something has been said above.[81] The attitude of Muḥammad and the original Islamic society towards a particular point of faith or behaviour, as also towards those beyond the pale, altered according to the circumstances, the time and the place — what was said in Mecca often lost all meaning in Medīna. In consequence there were contradictions in the Koran, and to explain these away the Prophet said that some revelations had been sent down to him only for the occasion and then been rescinded by subsequent revelations.[82] The Believers did not attempt to understand how a celestial, divine and eternal, Book could contain injunctions valid only for the moment and liable to supersession by fresh ones, but they did as time passed demand to know which must be considered as 'abrogating', *nāsikh* (from *nasakha*, in one of its meanings 'to annul') and which as 'abrogated', *mansūkh*. So while Zayd b. Thābit had been content to include all revelations in his canonical text without distinction, theologians gradually came to admit this new branch of study termed *'ilmu 'n-nāsikh wa 'l-mansūkh*. More accurately, this was not so much a branch as the offshoot of a branch; the branch itself being the discipline of exegesis designed to piece together a commentary on the Koran that should conform to the standards of philosophy and theology: *'ilmu 't-tafsīr* (*tafsīr* 'clarification' from *fasara* 'to elucidate'). The founder of this Koranic Exegesis or *Tafsīr*, whose authority all later commentators acknowledged, was 'Abdullāh b. 'Abbās, the Prophet's cousin; but real headway dated from the second century AH (eighth century of our era) onwards. The literature is vast and the following are only the most reputed and authoritative of its Sunnī exponents:

1 Ṭabarī, Muḥammad b. Jarīr, 838–923. A Persian from Ṭabaristān, he was a celebrated historian as well as jurist. His *Tafsīr*, 'fundamental and of enormous range',[83] marshalled everything previously done in the province of exegesis and won wide popularity.[84]

2 Tha'labī, Abū Isḥāq Aḥmad b. Muhammad Nīshāpūrī, d. 1036. A jurist of the Shāfi'ite school, he was author of *Kitābu 'l-kashf wa 'l-bayān 'an tafsīra 'l-qur'ān* (An Exposition of Kuranic Exegesis).[85]
3 Zamakhsharī, Abū 'l-Qāsim Maḥmūd b. 'Umar, 1074–1143. A native of Khwārazm, he wrote the *Kashshāf 'an ḥaqā'iqi 't-tanzīl* (Discoverer of the Truths of Revelation'). Mu'tazilite heretic though he was, his *Tafsīr* won acceptance even among conservative Sunnīs who admitted it subject to corrections in the orthodox spirit. For instance his expression: 'Praise to God who created (*khalaqa*) the Koran' was amended to '. . . who sent down (*anzala*) the Koran'.[86] Zamakhsharī tilted at interpretations that implied anthropomorphism.
4 Bayḍāwī (*Beyzavī* in the Persian pronunciation), 'Abdullāh b. 'Umar, d. between 1282 and 1316. Son of the supreme Qāḍī of Fārs. His *Tafsīr*[87] entitled *Anwāru 't-tanzīl wa asrāru 't-ta'wīl* ('Gleams of Revelation and Secrets of Interpretation') was based on Zamakhsharī's *Kashshāf* and many other sources. Nöldeke says of it: 'It is nowadays regarded by Sunnīs as the best, and as almost sacred. Its chief quality is that it gives a colossal mass of material a concise form. But it is badly wanting in accuracy, and of all the branches of learning it touches — historical exegesis, lexicography, grammar, dialectic, the science of style, and much else — none receives full treatment.'[88]
5 Rāzī (i.e. 'of Ray'), Fakhru 'd-dīn, d. 1209. This Persian encyclopaedist achieved renown with his *Mafātiḥu 'l-ghayb* ('Keys to the Unseen') otherwise entitled *Tafsīru 'l-kabīr* ('Great Commentary'). This *Tafsīr* is anti-Mu'tazilite and also anti-Ẓāhirite; in other words, it is as much against exaggerated literalism as against rationalism.[89]
6, 7 Al-Maḥallī, Jalālu 'd-dīn, d. 1459, and his pupil Suyūṭī, also Jalālu 'd-dīn, d. 1505. These were two Egyptian theologians, the first of whom began and the second completed the *Tafsīru 'l-Jalālayn* ('Commentary by the two Jalāls').[90] Suyūṭī further wrote *Al-itqān fi-'ulūmi 'l-qur'ān* ('Research on Koranic studies') a sort of introduction to the critical study of the Koran.[91]

Shī'ite *Tafsīr* will be dealt with in the relevant chapter.[92]

Koranic Exegesis had room for allegorical interpretation, *ta'wīl* as it was termed, nor was it only the Shī'ite authors who indulged in this. The Muslim mystics as a class were given to it, and the name of Muḥyi 'd-dīn Muḥammad b. 'Alī al-Andalusī, 1165–1240, the noted Ṣūfi pantheist, is memorable in this context.[93] Among the one hundred and fifty extant works of this prolific writer is a Book of *Tafsīr* which Brockelmann describes in a picturesque phrase as 'a Sūfic transliteration of the Koran'.[94] In it the hidden meaning is pushed to extreme lengths. For instance Sūra XII containing the legend of the Biblical Joseph is interpreted as a drama of the warring qualities of the human soul where Jacob stands for intellect, Joseph for the sentient heart, and his ten brothers are five inmost and five superficial senses.

All the above works on *Tafsīr* were written in Arabic, although many of their authors were Persians.

The original manuscript of the 'Uthmān Koran has not come down to us, although numerous codices purporting to be the genuine Koran of the Caliph 'Uthmān have been preserved — dark stains and all. These are 'the traces of 'Uthmān's blood'[95] unless we prefer to call them pious forgeries. One of these alleged 'Uthmān Korans, complete with bloodstains and certainly very ancient, was in the Mosque of Khwāja Aḥrār at Samarqand, and an object of veneration. It has now been transferred to the library of the Institute of Oriental Studies of the Uzbek SSR Academy of Sciences. The odd manuscript going back to the first two centuries AH has been preserved here and there, and codices dating from the succeeding centuries are plentiful.

In the East lithographed and printed editions are very numerous. Muslims hold that the Koran was sent down in Arabic and that translation from this is not pleasing to God. Consequently Korans have habitually been published in the original tongue with, if need be, notes in Persian, Turkish, etc., in lieu of translation. Alternatively in these eastern lithographed editions there is an interlinear translation in small lettering of all the Arabic words not current in the language of the edition — Persian,[96] Turkish, Turkic languages, Urdu or whatever it be.

The Christian countries of Western Europe had no notion of the contents of the Koran (or indeed of Islam itself) until the twelfth century when a very incomplete Latin rendering both of the Book and of Ibn Hishām's Life of the Prophet was prepared in Toledo under the instructions of the Abbot of the famous Cluny Monastery in France, Peter the Venerable (d. 1156). In 1543 this Latin Koran, till then only in manuscript, was printed in Basel by Theodore Bibliander in three volumes with a foreword by Martin Luther and Philipp Melanchthon, the Lutheran theologian. German, Dutch, French, English and other versions were published in the seventeenth to nineteenth centuries.[97]

The first full Russian translation direct from the Arabic to see the light was that of G. S. Sablukov (1804–80), Professor at the Kazan Ecclesiastical Academy.[98] A version of the oldest Meccan Sūras was made by the eminent Russian Arabist A. Ye. Krymskiy[99] at the turn of the century. But the latest and most complete Russian translation is the work of that great Arabist of our day, the Russian Soviet scholar Academician I. Yu. Krachkovskiy, which was finished before his death in 1951 and published posthumously.[100]

A critical edition of the full text was published by Gustav Flügel,[101] and the same scholar also produced the best Concordance of the Koran.[102]

IV
The sources of Muslim law

In the original Islamic community the Koran was the only source of law, as it was the only source of dogma. But this source proved inadequate to the rapidly expanding commitments of Empire (632–*c.* 751) and was gradually supplemented by a second source. This was Tradition (*sunna*).

In the countries of South-West Asia, Central Asia and North Africa which the Arabs overran in those years of conquest, they encountered an early feudal-type society that was much more complex economically, socially and culturally than anything to which they were accustomed. The land system, urban development, property law, the organs of power, social conditions — all were far in advance of what they had left behind in Arabia. They were up against questions for which the Koran had no answer. But since the state had not yet diverged from the Muslim community, or politics from religion, or public law from precepts of piety, all answers to the questions posed by the new environment had to be founded on some religious authority. It was in this situation that the Arabs began to refer to the supposed words and actions of the Prophet Muḥammad — and in doing so did not disdain the pious fraud. Gradually the Muslim Tradition, or Sunna, took shape.

The word *sunna* meant originally 'path', 'correct direction', and then figuratively 'custom handed down from ancestors', 'tradition'. In pre-Islamic Arabia it denoted the unwritten corpus of ethical injunctions, the common law of the patriarchal society of the North. With the advent of a class society and Islam, this pagan Sunna was superseded by a Muslim Sunna; such items as were taken over by the new Sunna always being given out as the Prophet's own precepts. The same applied to the many borrowings from Byzantine and Sāsānian law, or from Christian, Jewish and Zoroastrian tradition: all the rulings that accrued from the great conquests were alleged to have issued from the Prophet.

The main area in which the Koran needed to be supplemented by the Muslim Sunna was juridical. Public law, criminal law, property law, and family law had to be given their norms, but the unaided Koranic text was too flimsy a support. The Sunna was based on a vast number of Ḥadīth. This word *hadīth* (pl. aḥādith, from *ḥadatha*) means 'report', 'anecdote', or in a narrow sense 'quotation'; and in the special context it signifies the tradition regarding the words and actions of the Prophet Muḥammad.

Legal injunctions, precepts about rites, rules of ritual purity, decrees as to food, standards of morality and behaviour in everyday affairs — all these were derived from this or that Ḥadīth. Frequently, too, the practical application of a given Koranic instruction would be settled on the basis of some Ḥadīth more or less connected with the Koranic text in debate. Besides, there were Ḥadīth of historical character containing details of the Biography of Muḥammad or his Companions, i.e. Meccan Muhājirs or Medinese Anṣār. Ḥadīth similarly supplied the material for the books known as 'Wars of Islam' (*kutubu 'l-maghāzī*) in the eighth/ninth centuries, dealing with the campaigns of Muḥammad and the Companions,[1] which were quite a genre of early narrative literature in Arabic; and also for Biographies of the Prophet. In this way the Ḥadīth qualify amongst other things as a source for the early history of Islam, albeit one demanding a highly critical approach.

The Companions — kinsmen, friends, associates and pupils of the Prophet — who had gone on living in Medīna after his death were first and foremost regarded as the custodians and transmitters of the Ḥadīth: notably 'Umar b. al-Khaṭṭāb and his son 'Abdullāh b. 'Umar (d. 693); Caliph 'Alī b. 'Alī Ṭālib; the well-known Companions Ṭalḥa and az-Zubayr; the close friend of the Prophet, and very popular Abū Ḥurayra (d. 677) who had up to eight hundred pupils and was held to have transmitted three thousand five hundred Ḥadīth; one of the conquerors of Iran, 'Abdullāh b. 'Āmir (d. 679); the Koranic scholar 'Abdullāh b. Mas'ūd (d. 653), reputed transmitter of eight hundred and forty-eight Ḥadīth; the Prophet's secretary and editor of the Koran, Zayd b. Thābit; and Muhammad's widow 'Āisha (d. 678), reputed transmitter of twelve hundred and ten Ḥadīth. Many more Companions of the Prophet, or even simply his contemporaries, were presently included in the category of custodians; and after them their pupils (*tābi'*, pl. *tābi'ūn*), and the pupils of their pupils, were similarly thought of as guardians of the sacred lore. Eminent among these in succeeding generations were 'Āmir b. Sharāḥīl ash-Sha'bī (d. 723); 'Urwa b. Zubayr (d. 714);[2] his pupil Muḥammad az-Zuhrī (d. 742); Wahb b. Munabbih (d. 728); and Mūsā b. 'Uqba (d. 758). Such people devoted their lives to tracking down and collecting Ḥadīth: ash-Sha'bī, for example, is said to have interrogated five hundred Companions and amassed a quantity of Ḥadīth. Keeping and compiling proceeded orally to begin with, and depended on memory; but later it became the custom to write down the Ḥadīth on parchment and make them into volumes. The professional collector was called a Muḥaddith, a term usually translated in Western scholarship as Traditionist.

Just as Koranic study, as we saw, led to the science known as Tafsīr,[3] so now the study of the Ḥadīth evolved into a parallel science of Tradition. And from these two departments of religious literature emerged Divinity and Law, the twin branches of the Muslim Way (Sharī'a). However, much time was to pass before any clear distinction was drawn between them.

Research on the Ḥadith and Sunna, in the modern sense of the word, has been mostly the work of the Hungarian Ignaz Goldziher and the Dutch scholar Snouck Hurgronje.[4]

By the beginning of the eighth century there were three Academies of Ḥadīth: the Medīna school to which 'Urwa b. Zubayr and az-Zuhrī belonged; the Iraq school at Kūfa represented by ash-Sha'bī; and the Syrian school at Damascus. The Medīna school was unbending in its strict othodoxy and fidelity to traditions of the time of Muḥammad and the first four 'righteous' Caliphs, and was particularly concerned with the Prophet's Biography and his campaigns. It was in this spirit of strait puritanism that the school expelled the Prophet's first real biographer Muḥammad b. Isḥāq whom it suspected of the Qadarite heresy.[5] It upheld the theocratic principle and was therefore in opposition to the secular policy and administrative method of the Umayyad Caliphs.

According to received opinion each Ḥadīth had to consist of two parts: (1) *isnād* (lit. 'support'), i.e. enumeration of the transmitters, and (2) *matn* ('text'), i.e. specific contents. Thus in the model Ḥadīth the obligatory *isnād* would first be adduced: 'A says: I was told by B, who had it from C, who was informed by D, to whom E had passed it, having got it from F, that he heard how God's Messenger (God bless and salute him!) spoke to such-and-such effect'. Or ' . . . that E related that he saw how the Prophet (Peace on him and his Family!) on such-and-such an occasion acted thus-and-thus'. Then would come the *matn*, embodying the anecdote about the utterance or action of Muḥammad.[6] Some species of criticism was certainly not alien to the Traditionists in an effort to secure authenticity, but it was emphatically not of a sort to satisfy present-day standards of investigation. The criterion established by the eighth century was that the *isnād* must show an unbroken chain of transmitters who in their turn must be well known, of unsullied reputation, and accounted people of the Faith, worthy of esteem, truthful. The technical term for them was *rijāl* (lit. 'men' sing. *rajul*), and their check from the angle of reliability was *al-jarḥ wa 't-ta'dīl* (lit. 'challenge of witnesses and corroboration'). The sifting of reliable from unreliable transmitters became practically a separate department of study called *ma'rifatu 'r-rijāl* (lit. 'knowledge of the men'), and manuals were published entitled *Ṭabaqāt* ('categories') which listed in alphabetical order and by 'categories' whatever biographical matter was available on all the known Companions, their pupils, Muḥammad's contemporaries, and other transmitters of Ḥadīth. The 'Ṭabaqāt' by Ibn Sa'd (d. 845), and the Dictionary of Companions by Ibnu 'l-Athīr,[7] author of the famous History *Al-kāmil fi 't-ta'rīkh*, are signal examples of such works of reference. Other volumes in this genre dealt with the 'weak' (*ḍa'īf* pl. *ḍu'afā'*) transmitters of Ḥadīth who were undeserving of credence.

The more respected the transmitter, especially should he be the last, i.e. the earliest, in the chain of *isnād*, the more conclusive the trustworthiness of the Ḥadīth going back to him was held to be. It was thought impossible, for instance, not to believe a Ḥadīth which was traceable to such persons as Abū Ḥurayra or 'Ā'isha, and the risk that a false Ḥadīth might be pinned without any foundation in fact to an unexceptionable name was totally ignored. Again, provided the *isnād* passed muster, an absurdity in the body of the Ḥadīth, such as a glaring anachronism, bothered nobody. One Ḥadīth, attributed to Muḥammad, spoke of a visit to the baths by the Faithful, although everybody knew that the Arabs had no such thing in the Prophet's day and only learned this luxury from the Byzantine provinces after the conquest. Where a Ḥadīth was rejected on the score of subject-matter — and this was sufficiently rare — it was because the contents were inadmissible in the light of eighth-century ideas of orthodoxy or because they contradicted other Ḥadīth dealing with the same topic. Nevertheless all Ḥadīth were not regarded as being of equal value, but were divided into three classes according to the degree of their presumed credibility (of conditionally accepted credibility, as it was put). If the whole chain of transmitters occasioned no sort of doubt, the particular Ḥadīth was named *ṣaḥīḥ*, 'trustworthy'. But if there were flaws in the chain because, it might be, one of the enumerated persons was little known or else not irreproachable in the eyes of all, or because there was a missing link (e.g. 'A says: B told me, what somebody told him having got it from C'), the resulting Ḥadīth would be *ḥasan*, 'good', meaning that without being valuable it was held admissible. Lastly, if there were persons in the chain unacceptable from the standpoint of orthodoxy or moral reputation, the Ḥadīth was held to be doubtful and labelled *ḍa'īf*, 'weak'. The Ḥadīth with an unbroken chain was called *muttaṣil*, 'continuous', and one with gaps in the chain was *munqaṭi'*, 'interrupted'. Where the pupil or *tābi'* was indicated in the *isnād* but it was not made known from which of the Companions he had heard the report, the Ḥadīth was *mursal* 'having a gap'. Not every Ḥadīth relied on the speech or action of the Prophet: one that ascended to him was termed *marfū'*, 'raised up (to him)', but one that alluded to the words or acts of Companions was *mawqūf*, lit. 'stopped'. One that only depended on a Tābi' or Successor, i.e. on the first generation of pupils of Companions, was *maqṭū'*, 'truncated'. The Ḥadīth qualified as *maqṭū'* or as *mursal* would be accepted by some theologians and rejected by others.

A sequence of reporters going back to one earliest informant, in other words to one Companion — Abū Ḥurayra for instance — was termed a *ṭarīq* (pl. *ṭuruq*, lit. 'path'). If one and the same Ḥadīth was handed down by several ṭarīqs, i.e. was traceable to several Companions, it was *mutawātir*, 'consistent'. A Ḥadīth traceable in this way to three Companions was *mashhūr*, 'famous'; to two Companions *'azīz* 'rare'; and to one Companion *aḥadī*, 'solitary'. The Ḥadīth for which many parallel ṭarīqs could vouch, i.e. where instead of one human chain ascending to one Companion, there were several ascending to several Companions, was naturally accounted the best of all.

The oldest collections of Ḥadīth were compiled according to ṭarīqs; that is, the Companions of the Prophet were listed in alphabetical order and under each name the Ḥadīth issuing from the particular fountain head would be supplied. This principle of compilation was known as *'alā 'r-rijāl*, 'on (the names of) the earliest reporters'. Of the extant collections of this type two are celebrated. One is the *Muwaṭṭa'* or Beaten Track of Mālik b. Anas (d. 795), eponymous founder of the Mālikite system.[8] It contains one thousand, seven hundred Ḥadīth which the author thought genuine by the standards of criticism to which reference has been made above. The second is the *Musnad*, (lit. 'consolidated') a work by Aḥmad b. Ḥanbal (d. 855) who founded the Ḥanbalite school, containing over three thousand entries.[9]

More popular and with a wider circulation were collections of a later type called *Muṣannaf* (lit. 'sorted out') in which the Ḥadīth are arranged according to subject-matter instead of informants. This method was called *'alā 'l-abwāb* 'according to the rubrics' (from *bāb* 'chapter' pl. *abwāb*). The most authoritiative and admired in Sunnī circles [10] were six in number, whence the description *al-kutubu 's-sitta,* 'The Six Books'.[11] These were:

1 *Al-Jāmi'u 'ṣ-Ṣaḥīḥ*, abbreviated to *aṣ-Ṣaḥīḥ*, 'The Genuine', of Abū 'Abdullāh Muḥammad of Bukhārā (810–870). More skilfully composed than earlier ones, this collection was arranged according to subject-matter and contained not only Ḥadīth connected with jurisprudence and ritual observances — which interested contemporaries most — but Ḥadīth bearing on the life of the Prophet and his Companions and even on the historical events and ethnographical aspects of his period. The author brought a good deal of criticism to his task (in the qualified mediaeval Muslim sense), for he tells us that he collected six hundred thousand Ḥadīth, but only passed seven thousand, two hundred and fifty as fit for inclusion; that is, not much more than one per cent. The work has enjoyed immense prestige in the Muslim world and has frequently been republished in the East.

2 The collection made by Muslim Nishāpūrī (817–875), also entitled *Ṣaḥīḥ*, has commanded appreciation on the same scale. In this case some three hundred thousand Ḥadīth were examined of which only twelve thousand, or four per cent, stood up to scrutiny.

3 The *Sunan* or 'Custom', by Ibn Māja (d. 886).

4 The collection bearing the same title *Sunan*, of Abū Dāwūd al-Sijistānī (d. 888).

5 *Al-Jāmi'*, or 'Collection', of Muḥammad at-Tirmidhī, 'of Termez' (d. 892).

6 The *Sunan* of an-Nisā'ī (d. 915) pupil of Abū Dāwūd, a native of Nisā near the modern Ashkhābād.

All the above Six Books have a great vogue among Sunnīs and are highly esteemed as approved depositories of Tradition, but it must be emphasized that the first two are in a class apart. The remaining four are far less finished in arrangement and presentation. Their authors are prone to accept any Ḥadīth that is not demonstrably false or, to express it otherwise, have a much less critical approach than Bukhārī and Muslim. Further, they were preoccupied with Ḥadīth dealing with ritual and law — to put it better, with legal casuistry, — and neglected the Ḥadīth of biographical and historical interest. Consequently they are scarcely on a par with the first two as source books for the historian, being purely practical in their purpose and concerned with what is permitted and what is prohibited in law and in life. They answered men's questions about ceremonial behaviour, food, dress, social conduct, business agreements, the ownership of slaves, and so forth.

As has been said earlier, the standards of criticism employed by the average Muḥaddith were not of a sort to guard against the proliferation of the fictitious Ḥadīth. It must be remembered, too, that the whole activity involved in discovering hitherto unknown items of Tradition, with its peregrinations to places where Successors or their descendants might be tracked down and interrograted, was held to be pleasing to God. So the Muḥaddith who wanted to secure an official cachet for some pet opinion was always under grave temptation to invent an appropriate Ḥadīth and back it by an *isnād* strong enough to ensure its eventual acceptance as genuine. Fabrication was so rife that theologians of standing in the eighth and ninth centuries like Mālik b. Anas, Muslim and Shāfiʿī, voiced their dismay; but this unfortunately did not deter the bulk of their fellows, whether contemporary or later, from recognizing practically any Ḥadīth which did not too obviously sin against *isnād* or orthodoxy.

Modern European scholarship in this field, led by Ignaz Goldziher, rejects the vast majority of Ḥadīth on the following argument. After the great conquests there was a demand for a rigid legal system, and it was soon realized by the Arabs that there was much in Byzantine and Sāsānian law that was vital to the needs of the nascent feudal society of their Caliphate. But whatever juridical rulings were borrowed from these sources had to be offered to the Muslim public as the oral precepts of the Prophet himself, preserved and handed down through the Companions. The same consideration applied to the ceremonial and domestic rules which the conquerors adopted from their Christian, Jewish and Zoroastrian subjects: so these too were accordingly served up as Apostolic injunctions. Goldziher has demonstrated that Jewish and Christian attitudes derived from the New Testament and the apocryphal scriptures, as also random gleanings from the Greek philosophers, were launched upon the Muslim commonalty in the dress of Ḥadīth purporting to convey the utterances of Muḥammad. It was the same with more specifically theological rulings about paradise and hell, the Last Judgment and the Resurrection, about the prophets of old, and so on. Nowhere, Goldziher points out, is the impact of Christianity, Judaism and Zoroastrianism, and of Byzantine–Syrian–Coptic and Iranian culture upon Islam more apparent than in the Ḥadīth.

A community which persisted in the fusion of religion and politics, and whose social upheavals wore the dress of sectarianism, took easily to the fabrication of Ḥadīth. In the struggle for power waged by contenders like the ʿAlid, Umayyad or ʿAbbāsid parties, each side tried to bolster its position with sayings allegedly emanating from the Prophet himself. Then, too, people took advantage of the prevalent belief that Muḥammad had predicted coming events and appraised them. Thus the Ṣūfis, representing the mystical, ascetic pull in Islam which to some degree mirrored the temper of the urban poor, affirmed that the Prophet had foreseen and foretold the appearance of social inequality in Islam, the growth of wealth and luxury, and the tyranny of 'the princes of this world' — meaning the governing classes. And Ḥadīth to support this would be disseminated. Or again, as theological controversy intensified and sects broke away, the Sunnī divines did not scruple to fabricate Ḥadīth transmitting the Prophet's own condemnation of these 'heretics' whose heresies (Khārijite, for instance, or Qadarite) he was alleged to have predicted and censured in advance. A whole class of Ḥadīth contains Apostolic utterances about cities conquered long after Muḥammad's death, in which the Prophet is made to praise the excellent natural and climatic amenities of these places, and the exemplary morals and unadulterated faith of the inhabitants. Beyond doubt such Ḥadīth were concocted in the circle of the ruling set in the cities concerned much after they had fallen to the Arabs, for the greater glory of themselves and an enviable reputation in the Muslim world. Such Ḥadīth are commonly quoted in the pages of histories of Iṣfahān, Herāt, Balkh, etc.

Most of the Ḥadīth — and the exceptions are those that convey biographical matter about the Prophet and the Companions — are thus unauthentic when considered as historical testimony going back to Muḥammad. But it does not follow from this that they have no value as a source of history. Very largely composed between the second half of the seventh and the end of the ninth century, they reflect the social conditions and the march of events in the Caliphate, together with the attitude to law which was crystallizing during that period. As such they are source material for the study of the social and civic development of the countries concerned in their phase of early feudalism. Thanks it was to the body of Tradition thus fabricated that Muslim society in the lands bordering the Mediterranean was able to absorb the socio-legal and ideological heritage of the areas of Roman-Byzantine and Iranian culture which the Arabs had overrun.

V
The elaboration of Sunnī law

The collection and creation of Ḥadīth materially helped both dogma and law — but especially the latter — to develop. It also stimulated the science of law, termed *Fiqh*. The early feudal society of the Caliphate in the seventh to ninth centuries was, in theory anyhow, theocratic: the religious community was the state. It followed that the doctors of divinity formed one profession with the jurists, were even perhaps lawyers rather than divines. An English student of Islam, D. B. Macdonald, makes the point that the word *fiqh* in Arabic originally meant knowledge in general and was a synonym for *'ilm*, then came to mean knowledge of religious law, and finally casuistry or the application of religious and legal rulings to special cases; and that the word *faqīh*, 'theologian', from the same root, meant first a cultured person, later a theologian and then a casuist. It is well said. The word *faqīh* is therefore best, if cumbrously, rendered 'jurisconsult-theologian': in the sequel, these doctors of divinity would be the lords spiritual of the body politic.

Initially the Koran was regarded as the unique 'root', or *aṣl*, of dogma and law, but by Umayyad times the Ḥadīth had qualified as a second root. Enthusiasm for their collection, committal to the written page, codification and study was the corollary. But the resultant Sunna was no more systematic than the activity which brought it into being; it was amorphous and, more than that, without answers to the latest needs of a constantly developing feudal regime. So the second 'root' proved insufficient.

Moreover legal rules hardened in the mould of a religion eternal by definition were bound to grow obsolete with the passage of time. Professor A. E. Shmidt, the Russian Islamist, says apropos of this: 'The close connection of law with religion which long persisted, was fatal to the former. Legal norms belonging to a far-off patriarchal past,[1] because they possessed religious sanction, were not susceptible of revocation or replacement; they were bound to become antiquated because life had succeeded in overtaking them and building a set of conditions totally unforeseen in the period from which they dated. Law which cannot come to terms with the life men lead loses all meaning. And so it was with Muslim law which became an abstract discipline out of touch with reality.'[2]

But this did not happen till much later when feudalism had made strides. For the time being, under the Umayyads and even more so under the 'Abbāsids, generations of divines laboured to produce a code fit to cope with the calls of society. The 'Abbāsid Caliphs who posed not only as secular Amīrs in command of the Muslim world but as spiritual Imams, tirelessly patronized the collection, study and teaching of the Sunna. Centres for the study of the Ḥadīth had been opened in Medīna, Kūfa and Damascus under the Umayyads, but it was under the 'Abbasids that proper courses of instruction were organized. Those in charge of them were not long in discovering not merely that the Koran and Ḥadīth in combination were incapable of supplying answers to many questions of dogma and law, but that they were, as sources, very difficult to use at all. The Koran had many obscure passages and many that cancelled one another; Ḥadīth on one and the same subject were often in flat contradiction. To escape from this quandary the Faqīhs enunciated the theory of *naskh*, 'abrogation' of one Koranic saying by another deemed later or more general. A whole literature presently concerned itself with the 'abrogating' (*nāsikh*) and 'abrogated' (*mansūkh*) texts. The same theory was applied to the Ḥadīth, and in both cases engendered fierce controversy. No sort of written evidence could be called, and it became apparent that what was needed was a new source of law.

Two tendencies of marked dissimilarity began to separate the eighth-century Sunnī divines. On the one hand there were the so-called *Aṣḥābu 'r-Ra'y*, 'defenders of opinion', who favoured logical inference or the rational speculative method. These were pre-eminently of the Syrian theological school in Damascus or else the Iraq school at Kūfa, and later Baṣra and Baghdad as well. They were the product, that is, of places where a feudal system, a rich urban life, and a considerable culture had preceded the Arab conquest. They did not of course dislodge the Koran and Sunna from the high seat of authority, but they held it admissible to base decisions on logical inference whenever these two 'roots' of law were without an answer to the questions posed by the novel circumstances of a society growing on feudal lines. Their motive in resorting to the intellectual method was to serve the Muslim community, and in introducing new legal norms they took pains that these should respect the spirit of Muslim law. In the more strictly religious context of Koran and Ḥadīth they similarly held that a rational, instead of a literal, interpretation was frequently allowable. In thus admitting the validity of personal opinion they were opening the door to rationalism — but not too wide. They had indeed great fear of deviating from orthodoxy, and themselves laid it down that the rational method was only legitimate where an analogy was forthcoming in the particular Koranic passage or the particular Ḥadīth. Such analogy they termed *qiyās* 'comparison'. So here was a new 'root' of law — qiyās.

An example would be this. If an infidel from the Province of War, i.e. any non-Muslim state, arrives in a Muslim country as merchant or envoy armed with a safe-conduct and then commits fornication or larceny, can he be punished? Muslim law is inapplicable to him. But here is where Qiyās comes in: if a Muslim stole something from such a foreigner the former, under Muslim law, would be liable to have his hand cut off, and by analogy one can proceed against a foreigner guilty of the same offence. Or take another example: according to the Koran VIII 42, one-fifth of the spoils of war must be set aside for the Caliph. By analogy, it was argued, the Caliph must be alloted one-fifth of the income from mines, fisheries and the salt-industry. The most active exponent of *ra'y* and *qiyās* was the illustrious Faqīh of the Iraq School, Abū Ḥanīfa, founder of the Ḥanafite system of law.

The *Aṣḥābu 'r-Ra'y*, it need hardly be said, limited this exercise of reason in matters of dogma and law to trained theologians; it was never intended for the mass of Believers. Even so, conservative divines were haunted by the prospect of 'opinion' rending the community, and enunciated the principle that Qiyās must not be applied to the given case unless the consensus of properly authorized theologians was in favour. The technical term for this unanimous decision of the religious authorities was *ijmā'* (from *jama'a* 'to collect, unify'; IV Form *ajma'a* 'to concur, settle conjointly').

So now there were four 'roots' of law: Koran,[3] Tradition, Qiyās and Ijmā'. All orthodox theologians were step by step to accord their assent to the two new roots, if not with an entirely uniform understanding of the scope of their application. But meantime the old-fashioned were up in arms against what they saw as an 'innovation' (*bid'a* from *bada'a,* 'to invent, introduce something new'). Chiefly these were the representatives of the Medīna school who had found themselves in opposition to the Umayyads because the latter had created a secular state at the expense of the theocratic ideal dating from Muḥammad and the first four Caliphs. The change had been an 'innovation' and they were hostile to anything that savoured of this. When the 'Abbāsids secured the throne, these old-world doctors hopefully awaited a full-scale restoration of theocracy. It was a reactionary Utopia, but they clung to it. Their guiding principle was that divine law and not human opinion — unless it were the opinion of the Prophet — had binding force in matters of dogma. First of all, they said, the Divine Book must be consulted in all qustions and if no directions could be found there, then the Sunna of God's Apostle must be followed. This earned them the sobriquet *Aṣḥābu 'l-Ḥadīth*, defenders of tradition, in opposition to their fellows who were defenders of reason. They were doubtless men of ancient piety but their attitude was calculated to encourage fraud, for in order to steer clear of the rational method and Qiyās they had merely to hit on a new Ḥadīth complete with suitable isnād.

Between these extreme tendencies certain theologians opted for a middle course. And in the long term circumstances proved too strong for the defenders of tradition: those who to begin with had repudiated *qiyās* and *ijmā'* grudgingly admitted their restricted validity.

These eddying currents inside orthodox Sunnī Islam led to the formation of several schools called Madhhabs (*madhhab*, pl. *madhhāhib*, lit. 'way of doing', then as technical term 'doctrine'). It is a gross mistake to confuse these, as is too often done, with sects. A sect (from Lat. *sectare* 'to separate') implies a religious group which splinters from the dominant church or community, breaks off relations and thereafter goes its own way. In Islam, the Khārijites and Shī'ites for example, were sects which separated from the Sunnīs, the People of the Custom and the Community, nevermore to be reunited. With Madhhabs the case was otherwise. They might differ on the application of the rational method to questions of law and ceremonial practice, but their disciples remained members of the orthodox Sunnī community. The parallel is rather with the Catholic theological schools of the Middle Ages where the followers of Saint Augustine, Thomas Aquinas and Duns Scotus differed on detail but nevertheless within the framework of the Church.

The four Madhhabs deserving closest attention are those which survive to this day. In chronological order they are:

1 *Ḥanafites*. The eponymous founder[4] of this school, the Imam an-Nu'mān Abū Ḥanīfa (*c.* 696–767), was one of the most illustrious of Muslim theologians. The grandson of a Persian captive, he spent the greater part of his life lecturing on Fiqh at Kūfa. He expounded his system orally, and the various works attributed to him are of doubtful authorship. He was foremost among the defenders of reason and

analogy, but Western scholarship in the past has erred in classing him and his followers as liberal progressives. The Ḥanafites took their stance firmly on orthodoxy, and it would be more correct to say that they were opportunists trying to adapt the unbending Sharī'a to the practical needs of life.[5] In applying *ra'y* and *qiyās*, they employed the principle of *istiḥsān* or 'approval' (from *ḥasana* 'to be good'): which meant that where two possible logical conclusions presented themselves, the criterion of choice must be the welfare of the community or state. For example: the Koran and Ḥadīth inflict punishment for surreptitious thieving, but say nothing about open pillage and robbery. The Ḥanafites held that the principle of public advantage prompts the extension of the penalty envisaged for thieves to robbers.

The Ḥanafites are further distinguished from the rest of the Madhhabs by the use they make of secular law as a supplement to religious law; that is to say, of the body of local custom which had accumulated before Islam and was known as *'āda* and *'urf* together with the statues and regulations issued by secular authority known as *qānūn* (Gk. kanōn). Hence the Ḥanafite system of law is much more flexible and convenient in the secular sphere; and the nomads in particular welcomed it, inasmuch as it enabled them to retain their old patriarchal habits. For the same reason this system appealed to the Turkic peoples when they embraced Islam. Finally the Ḥanafite school was more tolerant than the others of Christians and Jews.

The outstanding doctors of this school were Abū Yūsuf Ya'qūb (d. 795), author of *Kitābu 'l-Kharāj* (Book on Land Tax) written for Caliph Hārūn ar-Rashīd (786–809), and Muḥammad ash-Shaybānī (d. 804), author of *Al Jāmi'u 'ṣ-Ṣaghīr*, both of them well-known pupils of Abū Ḥanīfa; Māturīdī (d.*c* 944), one of the founders of the new theological system called *kalām*;[6] Qudūrī (d. 1036), author of *Al-Mukhtaṣar* (Short Guide to Fiqh); Burhānu 'd-Dīn 'Alī Marghinānī (d. 1197), author of another Guide entitled *Al-Hidāya*.

At the present date the Ḥanafites unquestionably preponderate among the Sunnīs in all the Turkic countries except the Ādharbāyjānīs, from the Uygurs in the East to the Turks in the West, as also among the Muslims of China, India and Syria. In the Ottoman Empire this was the state Madhhab, and all Qāḍīs, whilst at liberty to join any of the Sunnī Madhhabs they pleased, were obliged to judge and issue juridical decrees or Fatwas (*fatwā*, pl. *fatāwā*) in conformity with the Ḥanafite system.

2 *Mālikites*. The founder of their Madhhab was the Imam Mālik b. Anas who has been mentioned already. Staunch defenders of tradition,

the Mālikites were intolerant and rejected rational interpretation of the Koran, even if they admitted a strictly limited application of logic and Qiyās. In so far as they resorted to the latter, it had to be sanctioned by *istiṣlāh*,'improvement', a principle close to the Ḥanafite *istiḥsān*. Strongest in Ḥijāz and Medīna, they were also to be found in Upper Egypt, North Africa and Arab Spain (where they constituted the official Madhhab) by the ninth century. In mediaeval Iran and Central Asia their role was negligible.

In present times this school predominates in Tunisia, Algeria, Morocco, and West Africa, and is not without following in the Sudan and Upper Egypt.

3 *Shāfi'ites*. The eponymous founder of this Madhhab was the Imam Muḥammad b. Idrīs ash-Shāfi'ī (d. 820) who taught in Syria and later in Egypt. In his *Risāla*, or Treatise,[7] he set out to construct a methodology of law that should accurately define the meaning and scope of the four 'roots'. His system is a compromise between the Ḥanafite position and the Mālikite position with a certain bias towards the latter. While recognizing logical conclusion and Qiyās, the Shāfi'ites attempt to control their application. They frown on *istiḥsān* as giving too much latitude to subjective opinion, and prefer their own principle *istiṣḥāb* ('the search for a connection with something known') whenever they address themselves to Qiyās: that is, they accept the rules of Fiqh as applicable to the given situation until it be proved that this has changed. An example: where a person is absent for many years and no one knows if he is still living, can his heirs enter into enjoyment of his estate? The Ḥanafites answer this question in the affirmative, but the Shāfi'ites object that in the absence of proof to the contrary the owner of the property must be deemed to be alive. It should be added that the Ḥanafites themselves flirted with this principle as time passed in conjunction with their own *istiḥsān*.

In the Middle Ages the Shāfi'ites were probably as numerous as the Ḥanafites, and predominated in Iraq, Syria, Ḥijāz and Egypt. The school was even strong in Iran,[8] where the feudal lords and patricians of the towns were Shāfi'ites until the beginning of the sixteenth century.

The principal Shāfi'ite lawyers were Abu 'l-Ḥasan al-Māwardī of Baghdad (974–1058) author of a celebrated work on politics *Al Aḥkāmu 's-Sulṭāniyya* which portrayed his ideal of a Muslim state; Abu 'l-Ḥasan 'Alī al-Ash'arī (873–935), one of the architects of the new *Kalām*: Juwaynī of Khurāsān (d. 1085) known by the title Imāmu 'l-Ḥaramayn ('Imam of the Two Sacred Cities'), and former mystic; Abū

Shujā‘ Iṣfahānī, (d. *c.* 1106); the Imam Abū Ḥāmid Muḥammad b. Muḥammad al-Ghazālī (1058–1111) a Persian from Khurāsān and a figure towering above all other Muslim theologians;[9] Abū Zakariyyā an-Nawawī (d. 1278); and Jalālu ’d-Dīn as-Suyūṭī (d. 1505), author of a well-known *Tafsīr* and juridical work. All these left many writings on the Shāfi‘ite system. Finally there was the great statesman, historian and savant of Iran, Rashīdu ’d-Dīn Faḍlullāh al-Hamadānī, surnamed Aṭ-Ṭabīb, The Physician, (1247–1318) who wrote three works on the tenets of this school.

At the present date this Madhhab predominates in the UAR, East Africa, and Indonesia (mainly Java, Sumatra and Kalimantan) and is also widespread in Syria and South Arabia.

4 *Ḥanbalites.* The Imam Aḥmad b. Ḥanbal (d. 855) who gave his name to this school and is accounted its founder, was primarily an authority on the Ḥadīth rather than the creator of a Madhhab, and it was left to his pupils to coordinate his thought. Living in Baghdad, he had attended ash-Shāfi‘ī’s lectures; but it does not seem that his ideas strayed from the narrow boundaries set by the defenders of tradition. An extreme intolerance of all innovation in matters of faith, a literalism and a repudiation of any rational interpretation of the scriptures characterized the system named after him. Gradually, it is true, the Ḥanbalites came to allow Qiyās and Ijmā‘ but within limits. They insisted on their own definition of the latter as a consensus of the actual Companions of the Prophet, without heed to what succeeding generations of teachers might have held. While to the former, Qiyās, they consented to resort only when the search for a ruling in the Koran or Ḥadīth had proved hopeless. Their refusal to give opinion the least play in religion is matched by a rigid insistence on the observances and rules enjoined by the Sharī‘a, so that the Ḥanbalites in a word are the most fanatical of all the Muslims. Another stand they took was against the worship of saints and the pilgrimages to their tombs. This cult had become common in the ninth/tenth centuries, perhaps under Christian influence, and the Ḥanbalites viewed it as an innovation prejudicial to the Oneness of God.

The Madhhab gained much ground in the reaction which set in throughout the Caliphate after the collapse of the Mu‘tazilites, or heretical rationalists, who had dominated the scene[10] for a while (827–851). Between the tenth and fourteenth centuries its following was large and its social and pedagogical role outstanding in all parts of the Muslim world. Even in Iran where it was of course nowhere in a majority, it made its presence felt, and Muqaddasī writes of Ḥanbalites in Iṣfahan, Ray and other cities in the tenth century. On the turn of the thirteenth and fourteenth centuries a notable theologian of this school, Taqiyyu 'd-Dīn Ibn Taymiyya (d. 1328), made a most fanatical attack on 'Innovation' which in the net result injured the Ḥanbalites by the animosity it excited towards them. Indeed narrow-mindedness, a primitive fanaticism, the estrangement of their system from everyday reality and anything outside the customary round, brought about the school's decline so that nowadays it has hardly any vogue except in Najd and Ḥijāz, plus some insignificant coteries in Cairo and Syria. Yet Ḥanbalite principles had their victory, and Ibn Taymiyya his reward, in the celebrated Wahhābite movement which engulfed the semi-patriarchal society of Najd in the eighteenth century.[11]

These then are the four Madhhabs. There were some others which have disappeared without trace, viz.

5 The school founded by al-Awzā'ī (d. 774) in Syria. It spread westwards as far as Spain, but was dislodged from there by the Mālikites. It was squeezed out of Syria by the Shāfi'ites. Its adherents used the method of *ra'y*.

6 The school founded by the Baṣra theologian Sufyān ath-Thawr (d. 778). This too spread to Spain and was forced out by the Mālikites. It had vanished by the beginning of the eleventh century.

7 The Jarīrites taking their name from the father of the famous historian Muhammad b. Jarīr aṭ-Ṭabarī, a native of Ṭabaristān (Māzandarān). The son was himself a notable representative of this school, and wrote a thirty-volume *Tafsīr*[12] and a work on Fiqh. The Jarīrites were vigorous opponents of the Ḥanbalites.

8 The Ẓāhirites. The founder of this school was Dāwūd b. 'Alī 'Iṣfahānī, surnamed aẓ-Ẓāhirī (d. 883). Founded in the phase of orthodox reaction against the rationalists, this school reasserted as emphatically as the Ḥanbalites themselves the method of the *Aṣḥābu 'l-Ḥadīth*. It was slavishly literal in its understanding of the Koran and Tradition, and as its name *ẓāhir*, 'outward', implied, discountenanced an inner (*bāṭin*), hidden, rationalistic or allegorical interpretation of the texts. However, these 'literalists', like others, were eventually obliged to make some reluctant concessions to Qiyās and Ijmā', as Goldziher brings out in his detailed study of their history and systems.[13] During the tenth to thirteenth centuries the Ẓāhirites were widely in evidence in all Muslim territories from Central Asia and Iran to Arab Spain, and in the last named successfully rivalled the Mālikites for a time. The Spaniard Ibn Ḥazm, author of a work on religions and philosophical schools, was a Ẓāhirite.

The Ḥanafites on the one side, and the Ḥanbalites ranged with the Ẓāhirites on the other, constituted the two poles, so to speak, of orthodox Sunnī theology.

As has been said, the arguments between the schools arose largely over legal and ritualistic rulings; but as these involved Koranic interpretation, dogma was automatically in debate. A typical dispute of the kind was on anthropomorphism, i.e. the presentation of God in human image (from Greek *anthrōpos*, 'man', and *morphē*, 'shape', 'likeness'; Arabic synon. *tashbīh*, from *shabiha* 'to be like'). Such a conception of God was normal among the socially and culturally backward Arabs of the early seventh century when Islam emerged, and if the Koran does not say outright that God is in man's likeness, it speaks many times of his hands and eyes, of his sitting on a throne, of his seeing, of his hearing, etc. These expressions naturally caused no bewilderment in the days of Muḥammad and the first Caliphs, but they had a different reception when Islam had expanded to the erstwhile Byzantine and Iranian Provinces where people were familiar with Greek philosophy and more complex religious constructions. Many Muslims then began to be troubled by Koranic utterances suggestive of primitive anthropomorphism.[14] The theologians approached the given passages in various ways. Some were inclined to regard them as metaphorical and intended to convey divine attributes (*ṣifāt*) which it is beyond the power of human language to explain directly; while others, like the Ḥanbalites and Ẓāhirites, were out-and-out literalists who insisted on taking the words in their primary sense. The Mālikites compromised: that God sits on his throne is indubitable, they said; but how this comes to pass is impossible for the reasoning faculty to grasp; it is obligatory to believe in it, and forbidden to question it. That is, we must believe in these passages without trying to fathom them.

Nowadays all the four surviving schools are recognized to be equally orthodox, and they live in harmony.[15] But this peaceable relationship took time to achieve. Apart from the wordy warfare of the schools in the ninth and succeeding centuries, there were occasions when the theological conflict got caught up with the political bid for power. Thus there were armed clashes not simply between Sunnī and Shī'ite opponents, but between Shāfi'ites and Ḥanafites in certain towns of Iran in the late twelfth and early thirteenth centuries which verged on actual civil war. The learned traveller Yāqūt al-Ḥamawī tells us in his Geographical Dictionary, the Mu'jamu 'l-Buldān, that in the great city of Ray one quarter would be fighting against the next, with barricades between them, that whole sectors were ruined, and that no fewer than one hundred thousand of the inhabitants perished in the course of these violent disturbances. Similar conditions were witnessed in Iṣfahān,[16] Nīshāpūr, and elsewhere. 'It is difficult to imagine', comments Bartol'd, 'that insignificant religious and legal differences between two equally orthodox schools were the real cause of these prolonged disorders. Rather is it apparent that religion was only the banner in the fight for economic advantage between city elements and between town and countryside'.[17] The urban upper set in Iran at that date, consisting of local feudal chieftains allied with powerful merchants, was Sunnī-Shāfi'ite; the middle-class townsmen, modest traders and artisans, were Sunnī-Ḥanafite; and the surrounding peasantry and the urban poor were Shī'ites. It was a class struggle conducted under an ideological cover.

The recognition of the four 'roots' of Muslim law led to the further doctrine of the division of the content of this law into roots (*uṣūl*), i.e. sources, and branches (*furū'*, pl. of *far'*), i.e. concrete issues settled on the basis of those roots. Nowadays only the opinions of the eponymous founder Imams of the existing Madhhabs, and not those of the founders of vanished schools, are given weight.

Gradually the doctrine arose that all Muslims are divided into two main categories: (1) Mujtahids (*mujtahid,* techn. term 'having attained', from *jahada* 'to endeavour'), and (2) Muqallids (*muqallid,* techn. term 'imitating', 'pupil', from *qalada* 'to twist, bind'). Islam had acquiesced in the emergence of an order of divines which functioned in its feudal society somewhat as the priesthood in Christendom — and the Mujtahids were the senior members of this order. They alone are competent to pronounce on religious or legal questions and issue fatwās. All the rest of the Muslims, including the junior members of the clerical order, are named Muqallids whose station implies the unquestioning acceptance of the decisions of the Mujtahids. They are not themselves entitled to discuss, or air their views on, matters of theology and law. Every Muqallid is bound to acknowledge the authority of an appointed Mujtahid and follow his lead, and this link of Muqallid with Mujtahid is termed *taqlīd* ('imitation', from *qalada*).

Each of these two categories again has three grades. The Mujtahids of the highest grade are the authorities competent to pronounce on the 'roots' of theology and law — in other words, the Companions and their successors down to and including the Imams who founded the

Madhhabs. The Mujtahids of the middle grade are those entitled to express an opinion on the 'branches', i.e. on particular questions of theology and law — the pupils perpetuating the teaching of the Imams. It should be said in parenthesis that figures of the stature of al-Māturīdī, al-Ash'arī and al-Ghazālī in practice wielded as much authority as the Mujtahids of the first period. In our own day there are no Sunnī Mujtahids of the two upper grades, but only of the lowest.[18] These are not authorized to utter opinions touching either questions of *uṣūl* or *furū'*, and can only cite and expound to Muqallids what the Mujtahids of the two superior grades have said and decided, and compose fatwās based on their rulings to meet special cases. They are thus specialists, and frequently specialists of the highest authority; but their competence is limited to the writings of the senior Mujtahids. They cannot elaborate theology and law on their own — and in any event these subjects, long congealed in their moulds, were insusceptible of further evolution.

So the Mujtahids having been originally interpreters of dogma and law, then authors of treatises on the Sharī'a, ended up as jurisconsults and casuists whose duty it was to give findings, based on the opinion of the ancient authorities, on concrete cases affecting everyday life. Hence the enthusiasm the Faqīhs displayed for the examination of the most miscellaneous cases, some of them unlikely ever to occur in practice.

As an approach to the law, both Sunnī and Shī'ite,[19] a stereotype was prepared which considered under separate headings all conceivable cases that might arise in the whole legal field including religious ritual, and the circumstances of family and public life. There were two main rubrics: *Ḥalāl* ('allowed, permissible, legal act or case', from *ḥalla,* 'to untie, unravel') and *Ḥarām* ('forbidden, disallowed', and by extension 'prohibited to somebody', 'sacred', from *ḥarama,* 'to be forbidden').[20] Then later refinements were made in the stereotype resulting in five more fractional rubrics, viz:

1 *Wājib* ('obligatory') or *Farḍ* (meaning the same) are all actions and opinions binding under the *Sharī'a*, or religious law. *Wājib* behaviour is in its turn subdivided into *farḍu 'l 'ayn*, i.e. conduct absolutely compulsory for all Muslims such as ablution, the five daily prayers, attendance at the mosque; and *farḍu 'l-kifāya*, i.e. acts which are compulsory only for those who can perform them, such as the discharge of their responsibilities by Imams or mu'adhdhins, or participation in Holy War.

2 *Mandūb* ('recommended') are such actions as are good and laudable from the standpoint of the Faith, but not compulsory. A person performing these is entitled to expect his reward in the next life, but if he

fails to perform them he will not be brought to book. Examples are the supererogatory prayers and fasts, acts of clemency and the like.

3 *Mubāḥ* or *Jā'iz* is anything permitted in the narrow sense of the word, whose performance does not attract God's approbation or reward. Examples here are eating, sleeping, amusing oneself, marrying. All these are allowable without earning credit in heaven. They are neither good nor bad, but indifferent.

4 *Makrūh* (lit. 'unbecoming'; techn. term 'unapproved') are actions which are undesirable from the point of view of the Faith but which are not forbidden outright. For the salvation of the soul it were better not to do these things, but the doing of them does not expose a person to punishment in this world or the next.

5 *Maḥẓūr* ('forbidden', from *ḥaẓara* 'to forbid'), synonymous with *Ḥarām*, are deeds, thoughts, and things prohibited without qualification for the Muslim and attracting penalty as sins both in this world and the hereafter.

In these five categories of Muslim behaviour the blend of religion and law, so characteristic of the entire Sharī'a, is particularly striking. Precepts and prohibitions of an ethical and ritualistic nature, e.g. the ban on drinking wine, wearing silk garments and gold rings, eating off silver plate, etc., are placed on a par with the injunctions in the sphere of criminal and civil law such as the prohibition of murder, usury, sale of standing corn or of weapons to infidels in Holy War, etc. The conception of sin and the conception of crime or law-breaking pass freely into each other.

Casuistry was fertile in stratagems (*ḥīla*) to evade the Sharī'a prescriptions and prohibitions. Thus, while it is unlawful to put on silk clothing, there is no objection to wearing it over a cotton lining, since the silk is then not in contact with the body. It is unlawful to eat off gold or silver plate or to drink from a gold or silver goblet, but one may take the proposed food from a gold dish, lay it on a china plate, and eat off that; or pour the drink from a silver jug into an earthenware or glass cup, and drink from that. It is forbidden to sell a Koran, but not to make a present of it against payment for the binding and paper.

Up to now we have been speaking exclusively of Sunnī law. Shī'ite law was based on the same principles, and exhibits the same blending of ethical, religious and legal notions, the same formalism and casuistry. It departs from Sunnī (chiefly Shāfi'ite) law only in a few regards; namely, in its theory of the state and in certain juridical and ritualistic particulars. We shall pause on this subject later.[21]

The identity of religion and law, with the consequent entrusting of legal processes and justice to a clerical order, affected the whole tenor of life as led in the Muslim countries. Even commercial agreements and deeds relating to land-tenure or house-property or loans were drawn up in Qāḍīs' courts. The impact of religion, as a result, on social and private activities, even on the daily round, was immensely deeper than in Christendom or the Far East where public, criminal and civil law did not depend on religion and church, and where legislation was the province of the secular power. Because laws rested on religious principles that were deemed eternal and immutable, the Faqīhs strove to resist the inroads of change and to keep legislation as close as possible to the ideal of theocracy. But economics, productive relations and culture could not stand still at the bidding of the Faqīhs, and so law lagged more and more behind life, and after the twelfth/thirteenth centuries was left congealed and divorced from actual practice.

VI
Muslim public law

The most we can hope to do here is to give the reader a general idea of Muslim public law as this was interpreted by the two main Sunnī schools, the Ḥanafite and the Shāfi'ite, which were predominant in the greater part of the Muslim countries (including Iran until early in the sixteenth century).

From the standpoint of Fiqh the ideal society is theocracy, in which the political as well as the spiritual power is in the hands of the religious leaders. Even by Umayyad times, however, theocracy had become a fiction, and the state was in reality secular. Meantime the Muḥaddith and the Faqīh clung obstinately to their ideal, with the result that the theory of public law which they evolved ignored the flow of history. It did not envisage a real Muslim state at all, but the state as it ought to be — according to the zealots. Consequently the Muslim theory of the state is the province of theologians, and has something highly artificial about it. These divines contemplated a Caliphate based on the unyielding principles of religion, given once and for all, immutable; they did not deign to take stock of the changes that were driving society along feudal lines. The gap between Fiqh and actual conditions went on widening.

The Koran gives no instructions how to build the state; and it does not mention the Caliph. The office of the latter as Muḥammad's deputy arose from the need which the governing set experienced of a central control strong enough to retain power over the mass — the Bedouin, the land-owners and the townspeople — and also to propel it against the Byzantine and Iranian provinces. The Caliph's authority from the very start was religious in so far as he was Imam, political in so far as he was Amir, but nobody had any clear conception of the range of his responsibilities. This only emerged as the early feudal state of the Arabs itself developed.

Indeed the elaboration of the theocratic theory went on for several centuries. In an endeavour to associate it with the Koran, the divines built the theory on the verse: 'Believers! Obey God, obey his Messenger and the holders of power among you.'[1] The utterance here about power is vague enough; but the commentators, especially Bayḍāwī, take 'holders of power' to mean the Imam-Caliph, the divines competent to expound the Sharī'a, the Qāḍīs, and the Captains in Holy War.

The most authoritative work on Sunnī public law containing the legal theory of the Caliphate was by common consent *Al-Aḥkāmu 's-Sulṭāniyya* ('Laws of Government')[2] by the Shāfi'ite jurist al-Māwardī, Abu 'l-Ḥasan 'Alī b. Muḥammad, 974–1058. It was written in Baghdad when the Caliphate was no longer a single state, but had given place to a number of feudal dominions, and when the orthodox 'Abbāsids retained only a shadow of spiritual authority and no political authority whatever: this having been seized by the 'Amirs of the Amirs' of the Iranian Daylamite dynasty, the Buwayhids (in Persian Āl-i Buviye), 945–1055. What Māwardī pictures is not an existing state but an ideal theocracy; 'he is describing' says Brockelmann 'the ideal of Muslim public law which had possibly never existed, and in any case did not exist in his own day'.[3]

Māwardī considers the Caliphate an institution established by God himself for the protection of the Faith and the guarantee of a just administration in the world. The Caliph combines in his person the spiritual power of the Great Imamate (*al-imāmatu 'l-kubrā*) and the political power of the Amirate (*imāra*, from the root *amara* 'to command'; whence the title *amīru 'l-mu'minīn,* Commander of the Faithful) inherited by him in succession from the Prophet. There can be only one Caliph (or Imam in the sense of Great Imam)[4] at a time, and his authority extends to the entire world; and it follows that the united Muslim state must sooner or later become a universal state, all the infidels having submitted to the Muslims.

The Caliph, says Māwardī, should possess the following qualities: irreproachable moral reputation; the necessary knowledge of jurisprudence and theology; unimpaired hearing, sight and speech, and a sound body; the wisdom needed in handling affairs of state; fearlessness adequate to defend the Province of Islam and carry war to the infidels; and descent from the tribe Quraysh from which the Prophet came. There are two ways of filling the post: popular election — Māwardī considers this the desirable method — and nomination of his successor by a reigning Caliph. For an election, two categories of Muslims must assemble: namely, those who are entitled to elect and those on whom the choice may fall. The latter are the Quraysh by descent and the former are persons satisfying three conditions: that they are Muslims of unblemished repute; have enough knowledge to be able to decide which of the candidates has most qualifications for the appointment, and possess the mental faculties calculated to ensure the best selection.

On the face of it, these criteria for recruiting the electors seem somewhat diffuse, and Māwardī proceeds to narrow the field: the electors are to be people enjoying influence and recognition in the community (that is, in the state), and having authority 'to tie and untie' (or 'settle' and 'liberate', *'aqada wa ḥalla*). In other words, they must be Mujtahids, trusted theologians and high officials. In principle everybody so qualified can participate in the election no matter whether he be at the Caliph's residence or abroad in the provinces, but Māwardī himself only allows an election at which the voters are restricted to qualified persons present in the residence at the moment of the Caliph's death; adding a remark to the effect that this is not law (*shar'*) but custom (*'urf*), justified by precedents. These electors, he says, must assemble in the cathedral mosque at the residence, and discuss the merits of the candidates and choose the one they recognize to be most worthy of the office. In arriving at their decision they will take into account the prevailing circumstances. If the election is held in time of war or disturbance, it is proper to choose a man of the Quraysh who has made his name as an able soldier; but if the prospect is peaceful, an experienced administrator will be preferable. There is no agreeement among the jurists as to the quorum. Some admit the legality of an election by even five voters, relying on the fact that the dying 'Umar I nominated a college of five Companions to appoint his successor, viz, 'Alī b. Abī Ṭālib, 'Uthmān b. 'Affān, az-Zubayr, Sa'd b. Abī Waqqāṣ and 'Abdu 'r-Raḥmān b. 'Awf — the second being in the event chosen. Others, like the Ash'arite school,[5] hold that a single person of authority can perform a valid election.

The second method of filling the office — that is, nomination of his successor by the ruling Caliph — was recognized by the consensus (*ijmā'*) of all Sunnī Mujtahids, the finding being based on the precedent of Abū Bakr's designation of 'Umar to succeed him. Certain jurists even gave the Caliph the right to nominate three successors who should follow him in office one after the other, the precedent here being Hārūn ar-Rashīd's nomination of his three sons in the order: Amīn, Ma'mūn and Mu'taṣim. However, all concurred in adding that a Caliph's nomination of his own successor required, to make it valid, the endorsement of the Mujtahids and Muslim 'community' assembled in the cathedral mosque of the capital, and an oath of allegiance to him (*bay'a*) taken by the orthodox.

The election procedure laid down by Māwardī and accepted by most of the jurists was never put into effect. Under the Umayyads the Caliphate was hereditary in practice; and so it was under the 'Abbāsids, though without specific provision for inheritance in the direct line. Another factor was that from the early ninth century these 'Abbāsid Caliphs could not stay on the throne without armed support; which meant that real power passed to the officers of the Horse Guards. Palace revolutions, in which the Turkish ghulāms of the Guard took the initiative, became the usual means of overthrowing one, and installing another, Caliph — albeit always from within the 'Abbāsid family. A pathetic example of the pawn in the hands of the royal guard was the talented poet and 'One-day-Caliph' Ibnu 'l-Mu'tazz, son of the Caliph of that name by a slave-woman, who was proclaimed successor to Muqtadir in a palace revolution on 20 Rabī'u 'l-Awwal 296 AH (= 17 December 908) but lost his throne in another revolt on the same day, and his life just afterwards.

In any case very few of the Caliphs, Umayyad or 'Abbāsid, possessed the qualities which Māwardī judged necessary, and altogether there were never any proper elections. The only item to which the 'Abbāsids did pay heed — and this in order to support the Faqīh class — was the formal sanctioning of each new Caliph's appointment by a gathering of Mujtahids, theologians and dignitaries of state in the cathedral mosque at the residence.

Before leaving the subject we must just remark that Khārijite and Shī'ite views on the laws of succession to the Caliphate differ sharply from those of the Sunnī jurists.[6]

Māwardī regards the relationship between Caliph and Muslim community as a bilateral agreement (*'aqd*) whereby both sides assume specific responsibilities. The Caliph's obligations are the following: the security of Islam and its fundamental principles; the passing of sentence in court proceedings and the settlement of disputes inside the community; the safeguarding of the correct and uninterrupted exercise of public worship, and the personal discharge of the functions of Imam in the Friday Mosque at the residence; the putting into effect of the criminal statutes; the recovery of taxes under the law; the payment of annual salaries to various military and civil grades from the state treasury; the selection of senior officials and the appointment of other personnel to run the taxation circuits; and the supervision of state affairs with a close watch on the organs of administration.

Other jurists reduced the Caliph's responsibilities to four: the role of Imam at the Friday service in the residence; the law-court; tax-collection; and War for the Faith.

The *khuṭba*[7] and the *sikka* were the symbols of his authority on the periphery of the empire. His name was pronounced in the course of the sermon (*khuṭba*) in all congregational mosques, and chased on the money (*sikka*) issued by all the mints in the Caliphate.

War with the infidels, then, was regarded as one of the Caliph's principal obligations, and was dignified with the name of War in the Path of God (*fī sabīl illāh*). When the great conquests of the non-Muslims — Byzantines, Franks, Christians of Northern Spain, Khazars, nomads of the steppes — ceased, such wars lost their cachet and degenerated into raids and razzias for the sake of spoil. D. B. Macdonald has pointed out that as early as the 'Abbāsids the view had won acceptance that the Caliph must undertake at least one such invasion of the Province of War annually. Either he himself had to take command as Grand Imam, or else the governor (Amir) of the frontier concerned, or a specially designated general, might do so. The Amir or commander would receive a directive from the Caliph simply to conduct the military operation; or he might get plenary powers covering the division of booty, the fate of prisoners of both sexes (whether they were to be distributed as spoils of war among the army, or exchanged with Muslim prisoners, or released on ransom) and the right to conclude a truce.

Besides War for the Faith, whose rules have been discussed in an earlier chapter,[8] Muslim law envisages internal wars, *ḥurūbu 'l-masāliḥ*. These are wars with 'mutineers', and the relevant rules will be noticed in a later place.[9] As regards wars between Muslims, no provision was made, since theocratic theory contemplated nothing less than a unique, united Muslim state; and even after the collapse of the 'Abbāsid Caliphate in the tenth century the fiction of its existence was preserved, independent Muslim sovereigns being considered vice-gerents of the Caliph. Wars between Muslim states had by this time become a common phenomenon, and in the absence of properly formulated rules the two sides would endeavour to refrain, first, from indiscriminate plunder and devastation of the territories affected by the hostilities and, second, from turning over prisoners of war into slavery and capturing peaceful inhabitants (should these be Muslims) in the theatre.

The obligations of the people, according to Māwardī, are obedience to a legally elected Caliph, assistance and cooperation. If a Caliph should turn out unjust and neglectful of the responsibilities spoken of above, the community, on this same theory, might depose him; and such dethronement might likewise be justified if the Caliph lost his mental faculties — or indeed his sight or hearing. But other bodily infirmities did not attract the penalty of deposition. Māwardī said that dismissal of a Caliph had to be voted by an assembly of the people (meaning the inhabitants of the capital) in the congregational mosque; at which a person of influence, Mujtahid or dignitary, must pronounce a charge, accompanying his accusation by the symbolical removal of a ring from his finger, or a shoe from his foot, and the hurling of this to the ground with the words: 'As I have cast away this ring (or shoe), so do I discard so-and-so.' Those present had to voice their concurrence, simultaneously shedding a shoe or a turban or some other article of clothing. Needless to say, theory was here straying very far from the realities, either of Māwardī's eleventh century or of much earlier days. The dethronement of a Caliph, like his induction, was usually the consequence of military or palace revolution, and even more often of popular insurrection, e.g. the end of 'Uthmān in 656, and the overthrow of the Umayyad dynasty in 749/750.

Theoretically the Caliph enjoyed executive, but not legislative authority. He could not alter existing criminal or civil legislation since this, according to the ideal of theocracy, rested on the religious authority of the four Roots of Fiqh and was, as such, immovable. Any edict or tax regulation or court decision he could only give out with the consent of the Mujtahids, and on the basis of a juridical finding (fatwā) of theirs recognizing a particular administrative act or court verdict as — from the point of view of Fiqh — *ḥalāl* (lawful) or *ḥarām* (unlawful). Under the Umayyads this arrangement was consistently disregarded, the state authority being in point of fact purely secular. And so it remained, basically, under the 'Abbāsids, even though they valued the support of the order of Faqīhs and wished to create the impression that the ideal of theocracy was actually in being. The Caliph was now regarded primarily as the head of a college of Mujtahids, and several of the 'Abbāsid Caliphs made a habit of summoning their theologians and listening to their views before issuing an edict. However, there were others who showed no such deference; and in any case pressure from the Caliph, or the clique that controlled him, would always be the determining factor.

The theocratic Caliphate pictured by the Sunnī theorists was above all things lawful. It was not despotic. The Caliph's authority was established by God for the benefit of the community and that community was entitled to elect and depose him. On his side he could only exercise his legislative and judicial powers within the rigid and permanent framework of a hallowed Fiqh, and in concert with the theologians who were guardians of this law. On the other hand there existed no institutions representative of the 'people' which might actually curb the Caliph's power.

In theory the Muslim community was one of equals, but in practice it was divided into exploiters and exploited. The Caliphate was not a mechanism designed to defend the interests of an ideal theocratic society (*al-umma*); it was adapted to defend the interests of feudal exploiters. The historical reality bore small resemblance to Māwardī's ideal. Between the seventh and early tenth centuries the state became more and more saddled with centralization. State ownership of land and the extension of irrigation in agriculture contributed to this result. In the case of government lands the state itself exploited the peasant holders through its finance officials, feudal rent coinciding with taxation;[10] and an enlarged canal system postulated a strong central authority to administer it. Besides which, while the wars of conquest were being waged, the governing class was interested in a strong centre personified by a Caliph as organizer of these campaigns and commander in the field. Hence the exceptionally strong and practically unbounded authority of the Umayyad Caliphs and of the 'Abbāsids until Mutawakkil (847–861). Bartol'd has pointed out that the temporal always outweighed the spiritual in the Caliph's authority, and although ideally there should have been no legislation other than the Sharī'a, in fact secular legislation had made its appearance in the form of edicts, regulations (*qānūn*), 'urf and 'āda. This, as it were, amplified and amended the religious law: the police court (*shurṭa*)[11], which took definite shape under the 'Abbāsids, supplemented and corrected the court of the Qāḍīs. As regards the spiritual component of the Caliph's authority — his Imamate — this, even in theory and without thinking of facts, was hedged by limitations, and purely protective: that is, he was only supposed to guard the position enjoyed by Islam in the state, thwart encroachments on it, punish its enemies and conduct Holy War.

It is a mistake to imagine the Caliph as a sort of Muslim equivalent of the Pope. It is necessary to say this because such a picture is all too frequent even in academic writing. Unlike the Pope, the Caliph was not invested with 'holiness'; he could not introduce new dogmas or rites or any innovation whatsoever. He was not the indisputable authority in questions of religion; on the contrary, he was obliged to consult the

Mujtahids with reference to whom he was *primus inter pares*. Nobody admitted the Caliph's authority to forgive sins on the pattern of the papal indulgences, or to condemn the souls of the dead to the torments of hell, or to excommunicate people (as the Popes did, sometimes even in political controversy). Still less could the Caliph place whole provinces under an interdict, i.e. a prohibition debarring the clergy from celebrating divine service — this would in any event have been impossible in Islam where a specialist priesthood was not needed for the performance of community worship in the mosque. Finally, no Sunnī theologian ever thought of the Caliph as infallible in matters of faith, whereas this was taught of the Pope as early as the Middle Ages and declared dogma in 1870. As Lammens, the French Arabist and Islamist puts it, the Caliph is 'not a high priest but only a temporal defender of the Sharī'a.[12] And to quote Goldziher, he 'is not an authority in the teaching body'.[13]

After the Mongol conquerors had done away with the 'Abbāsid Caliphate[14] by taking Baghdad, putting Musta'ṣim to death and butchering the males of the 'Abbāsid family, the Muslim world was never again to know a single Caliph recognized by all the Sunnīs. Certain members of the 'Abbāsid family or persons posing as such, it is true, made good their escape and turned up in Cairo. Here in 1261 the Mameluke Sultan Baybars (1260–77) proclaimed one of these alleged 'Abbāsids, Aḥmad by name, Caliph; and thenceforward the Mamelukes always had a so-called 'Abbāsid Caliph at their court, exercising exclusively spiritual authority. However, that authority had no meaning beyond the confines of the Mameluke Sultanate of Egypt, Syria and Ḥijāz, and most other Sunnī countries withheld their recognition.

These historical developments were to be reflected in the Sunnī theory of the Caliphate. The jurists began to admit the possibility of a third way of filling the Caliph's post, viz. recognition under duress (*ba'yatu 'l-qahriyya*). They contended that, in times of trouble when there is no legally installed Caliph universally acknowledged, it is permissible to recognize a sovereign who has asserted himself by force, so that the Muslim community should be delivered from its troubles, its anarchy and its internecine strife. Such a sovereign, if he rules in conformity with the Sharī'a, can be considered the lawful head of state — in other words, Caliph. But if he does not rule on the basis of the Sharī'a, he is a tyrant (*ẓālim*). The eminent divine Ibn Jamā'a, Badru'd-Din Muḥammad (1241–1333), Qāḍī in Jerusalem and then

Chief Qāḍī in Cairo, author of *Taḥrīru 'l-aḥkām fī tadbīr ahli 'l-islām* (Laws for the sake of order among the Muslims), subscribed strongly to this opinion. He even asserts that if the ruler who has seized power is ignorant of the Sharī'a, unjust and debauched, he must still be obeyed; and that if another usurper rises up against him and ousts him, then this successor must be obeyed. Muslim law in its later period, as von Kremer remarks, 'was reduced to the theory that might is right'.[15] From then on it recognized the ideological bankruptcy of the artificial constructions of the old Islamic theory of the Caliphate, and notably that of Māwardī. There was to be no more talk of the Caliphate as a bilateral agreement between Caliph and people, and of the latter's right to depose an unjust occupant of the throne.

Ibn Khaldūn (1332–1406), greatest of Muslim historians and unique among them for his conception of the historical process (based on a recognition of the influence of natural environment on the development of communities and civilizations), also had his theory of the Caliphate. He rejected the principle of theocracy and boldly treated the Caliphate as a secular authority which must rest on the sword and the pen. By the first he meant the armed forces, and by the second the *dīwān*, i.e. the civil service administering the departments of state — financial, taxation, postal, and so on. He repudiated the requirement on which Māwardī and the former jurists had insisted that the Caliph must be of the Quraysh from which the Prophet himself came, arguing that the earlier authorities had wrongly interpreted Muḥammad's Ḥadīth on this point. Nor does he consider a knowledge of theology and jurisprudence and the sense of justice to be essential qualifcations for the appointment, for the reason that any estimate of such qualities in the particular person is invariably subjective. To his thinking, the only qualification that can properly be demanded is physical and mental fitness. The Caliph must be a strong and capable ruler, and he is no Caliph who allows one of his military or civil subordinates to order him about. Such a ruler is a mere captive deprived of his freedom of action and incompetent to discharge the duties of the Imam Caliph. Consequently, when the 'Abbāsid Quraysh handed over real power to the Buwayhids, they thereby showed themselves incapable of fulfilling the obligations of Caliphs.[16]

These new theories of the Caliphate, whose first premise was the possession of real power, had their effect on the Muslim states of the fifteenth and succeeding centuries. For instance, the jurists in the Tīmūrid State (Central Asia and Iran) came to the decision that as soon as the Sultan Shāhrukh (1405–47) was in possession of *de facto* power which every one recognized, and ruled his Muslim community in conformity with the Sharī'a, he was automatically a lawful Imam and Caliph.[17] Similarly Sultan Uways of the Jalā'ir dynasty in Western Iran and Ādharbāyjān (1356–74) was recognized Imam-Caliph.[18]

Irrespective of the manner in which a Caliph — or other Muslim sovereign after the disintegration of the Caliphate — has obtained power, Muslim law requires his subjects to obey him. That greatest of theologians, the Persian al-Ghazālī (d. 1111), requires obedience to the reigning monarch, since firm, and even cruel, rule is better than civil war. The 'Abbāsids relied on this Ḥadīth attributed to the Prophet: 'Obedience to me is obedience to God, and obedience to the Imam[19] is obedience to me. Wherefore a rebel against me is a rebel against God, and a rebel against the Imam is a rebel against me.'[20] For those that have risen against the Imam-Caliph, whether feudal lords or popular insurgents, Muslim law ordains as punishment the cutting off of hands and feet, and crucifixion, relying on the Koranic verses: 'For them that fight against God and his Apostle and strive to stir up dishonesty on earth, the recompense shall be that they be slain, or crucified, or have their right hand and left foot cut off, or be banished the land.'[21]

The law hardly reflected the fact of the early feudal society's division into classes, and was content with the ideas appropriate to the pre-feudal transitional period under the first four Caliphs. It therefore treats of only three lawful groups in society: free Muslims, allegedly equal in the sight of the law; Dhimmīs of other faiths (*ahlu 'dh-dhimma*),[22] free but without full citizenship; and slaves.[23] The feudal ownership of land was mirrored just as unfaithfully in the law. The Faqīhs had their eyes on the Koran and the Ḥadīth instead of on actual affairs, and their classification of the categories of land was vague and unreal. Treating of land primarily, but also of water and irrigation works, Fiqh recognizes three principal categories of ownership with three corresponding categories of land: these are, state lands (*arḍu 'l-mamlaka*; in Persian *arāḍī-yi dīwān*); waqfs; and privately owned lands (*milk*, *mulk*, pl. *amlāk*, 'immovable property').[24]

State lands, according to the interpretation given, are those which had come into the common ownership of the Muslim community as a result of the conquest of a particular country, and they constituted the biggest category.[25] The state ownership was here combined with tenure by the community or by small private cultivators; that is, by peasants holding parcels of land. Such lands were directly exploited by the state through the officials of the Finance Department who levied a land-tax (*kharāj*) from the peasants which was tantamount to feudal rent. The revenues from these lands went into the Treasury (*baytu 'l-māl*) to cover the pay and pensions of the Prophet's descendants, and of military and civil officers. In other words, this territorial fund met the upkeep of the 'serving' nobility, military and feudal, of the Caliphate.

Waqf lands were those bequeathed (*mawqūf*, pl. *mawqūfāt*) by the Caliph or moneyed people in support of religious foundations like mosques, madrasas and shrines or else charitable institutions such as hospitals, asylums for the aged and homeless, etc. A portion of the profits from these lands went towards the maintenance of Imams, teachers and members of the clerical class; the latter being indeed largely provided for from this source.[26] The donor could lay down conditions by deed (*waqf nāma*) for the disposal of the income from the given property — whether arable land, gardens, vineyards, canals or karezes,[27] herds; or (in the case of towns) caravanserais, shops and bazars — and might stipulate the nomination of himself and thereafter his descendants as trustee, *mutawallī*, of the waqf. Such trustees received a fixed share, usually ten per cent, of the income. Waqf properties were as a rule tax-free. They could not be sold or otherwise alienated and were not liable to confiscation, and for this reason many a land-owner found this pious act of giving his estates in *waqf* to be advantageous. He could keep the office of mutawallī, and the consequent management of the funds, inside the family and be exempt from taxation and protected from confiscation into the bargain.

Private lands (*milk*, *mulk*) were those belonging to their proprietors (*māliks*) on terms of absolute ownership. They could be sold, or given as gifts, or bestowed in waqf, or inherited by heirs, at discretion and without special permission. As a category of feudal ownership of land and water, they corresponded to the European *allodium*, the Russian *votchina*, and the Armenian *khayrenik*. The divines pronounced mulk to include the lands of killed or fugitive enemies which had accrued to the Muslims by conquest; lands whose owners had embraced Islam in the hour of their defeat; and waste lands (*mawāt*), i.e. lands previously lying idle which had been irrigated, tilled and settled by Muslims. In Fars mulk lands even predominated until the heyday of the Buwayhid dynasty.[28]

As feudal society matured, other categories of land ownership emerged which were either not envisaged or else inadequately dealt with in Muslim law. Thus the system of *iqṭā'*[29] (lit. 'allotment', from *qaṭa'a* 'to cut'; IV Form *aqṭa'a* 'to allot'), or feudal ownership conditional upon service to the state, became widespread. Initially the arrangement carried the right to receive rent without the right to dispose of the property, i.e. it was a 'benefice' in the technical meaning of the term. And this is the sense it bears in Māwardī's text[30] where he discusses the attitude of Fiqh towards it. But later on, between the tenth and fourteenth centuries, in various Muslim countries it grew, in practice at first and then formally, into a hereditary military fief.

Muslim law recognizes the following state taxes:
1 *zakāt*, the tax on crafts, trade and cattle-breeding. 2 *kharāj*, land-tax levied either in kind as a fraction of the yield (*kharāj muqāsama*) or in cash at specified rates on each *jarīb* (approx. 2,600 m^2) of land irrespective of the size of the crop (*kharāj masaḥa*). 3 *'ushr* (P. *dehyak*, 'one-tenth') a lessened land-tax at ten per cent of the crop or profits from privileged lands (see below). 4 *jizya*, poll-tax levied in money exclusively from Dhimmīs. 5 *khums*, 'one-fifth', the portion of the spoils of Holy War to be placed at the Caliph's disposal.

Zakāt was levied only from Muslims, and jizya only from non-Muslims. At first, in the seventh century, jizya and even kharāj were levied exclusively from certain non-Muslims — namely, from such as were owners or holders of cultivated land. Muslims who owned land did not pay kharāj but only 'ushr, and the adoption of Islam by a non-Muslim earned him exemption from jizya and kharāj. These two were frequently not differentiated but regarded as a single tax on non-Muslims, their very names being used as synonyms. But from about 700, after the reforms of Ḥajjāj, 'Abdu 'l-Malik's imperious viceroy in the eastern provinces, it became usual in those parts of the empire to distinguish the jizya or poll-tax (which went on being levied from non-Muslims alone) from the kharāj or land-tax. By now the adoption of Islam no longer released the husbandman from liability to kharāj; land on which kharāj had earlier been assessed remained so taxable for good and all, irrespective of whether the owner or holder was Muslim or non-Muslim.

For tax assessment, lands were classed under three heads: kharāj lands, 'ushr lands, and 'free and cleared' (*ḥurr wa khāliṣ*) lands, exempt from all dues. The first were mainly state lands with peasants in possession; and the second were usually mulk lands, being, according to the criterion laid down by the divines, lands whose owners had adopted Islam immediately after the conquest. In the Iran of the tenth to fourteenth centuries, 'ushr was levied on mulk lands as a universal rule. The third, i.e. tax-free lands, were: (a) waqf lands; (b) specified mulk lands which had obtained a certificate of clearance from the head of state — this privilege being also automatically accorded to any owner who gifted two-thirds of his territories to the state, in respect of the remaining one-third:) (c) iqṭā‘ lands.

The five kinds of tax that have been mentioned were regarded as lawful (*ḥalāl*), their recovery being founded on the Sharī‘a. But with the intensification of feudal exploitation in the Middle Ages, ‘extraordinary taxes’ (‘*awāriḍ*)[31] were introduced, such as collections for the maintenance of troops or different civil installations, and dozens of miscellaneous contributions whether monetary or in kind (grain, dates, raw silk, cotton, etc.). These collections, not prescribed in Sharī‘a law, were viewed as sanctioned by custom (‘*urfī*) and given the generic name *takālīf* (pl. of *taklīf*, ‘burden’, ‘obligation’) in distinction from taxes based on the Sharī‘a.

Muslim law knows no categories of serfs and of peasants in bondage to feudal masters. In actual fact the second of these of course existed; but feudal bondage was not considered as personal bondage; it was land bondage by virtue of the fact of the peasant's holding a plot of state land or waqf land, or iqṭā‘. The doctors classed this feudal bondage as a lease, and most often a hereditary lease, of land to the peasant by the landowner in consideration of rent either in money (*ijāra*) or in kind, amounting to anything from one-tenth to two-thirds of the harvest — depending on whether the peasant received only the land from the proprietor or canal irrigation water and seed and draught oxen as well — in which case it was called *muzāra‘a* (techn. term meaning ‘métayage’, from *zara‘a* ‘to sow, till’; whence *zāri‘*, ‘husbandman’, *muzāri‘* ‘métayer’).[32] In point of fact the ‘consideration’ was nothing less than feudal rent. But no attachment to the land was involved; the peasants (*ra‘āyā*, pl. of *ra‘iyya*, from *ra‘ā* ‘to graze’, lit. ‘herd’, ‘flock’; originally anything ‘subject’, then ‘taxable class’ and so ‘peasantry’) in the Caliphate, and particularly Iran and Central Asia, were not prohibited from movement until the thirteenth century. The factor of attachment to the soil was only introduced by the Mongol conquerors.[33]

The centrally administered state of early feudal type with wazīrs, dīwān, government postal service, royal depots, etc., was not the creation of the Arab conquerors. It was inherited mainly from Sāsānian Iran but also to some extent from Byzantium, and then developed and made more complex by the Arabs outside the context of Fiqh. We shall therefore not dwell upon it here.[34]

VII
The criminal and civil law of Islam

In Muslim jurisprudence there was no really complete system of criminal law. The basis being religion, the concept of crime merges with the concept of sin. In comparison with Roman-Byzantine law, Fiqh in consequence wears a strangely antiquated look. For example, the subject of law is not the person but the family; murder is regarded not as an offence against society, but as an offence against the family of the victim. The Sharī'a retained the vendetta and it retained the 'blood price' which we meet with in the *Russkaya Pravda* or 'Russian Right', that earliest document of our own law, under the name of *vira*, and also in the legal systems of barbarous Western Europe, under the name of *wergeld*, from the fifth to the ninth centuries, — that is, until feudalism had developed. The features of Fiqh here listed are survivals from the clan- and tribal-custom of pre-Islamic pagan Arabia; in other words, remnants of a patriarchal order which Arab society clung to when it entered the feudal phase.

As against this, many other features of the criminal system of Islam were far in advance of the legislation obtaining in Western Europe, not only under the full feudalism of the eleventh to fifteenth centuries but even under the absolutism of the sixteenth to eighteenth centuries. Thus, according to Fiqh, only the adult, the mentally sound and the free can be fully answerable for a transgression; minors, the mentally sick and slaves are not responsible or have a limited responsibility. Muslim law does not allow the use of torture (which several European countries employed as late as the eighteenth century) nor does it countenance 'the divine decision' whether in the shape of the *ordalia*, the ordeal by fire and water, or of the legal duel between plaintiff and respondent, as practised in Western Europe and Russia in the Middle Ages. It does not tolerate, or very exceptionally, a lengthy term of imprisonment. Its criminal procedure was marked by speed and expedition and was innocent of the judicial delay, sometimes amounting to years, and the consequent ruinous costs, which characterized European and Russian courts even in the last century.

In what follows we shall examine certain aspects of the criminal law as interpreted by the two principal Sunnī schools, the Ḥanafite and the Shāfi'īte; and afterwards do the same for civil law. Shī'ite law is very close to the Shāfi'ite position, and such points of difference as there are will be noted in the chapter specifically dealing with the Shī'ites.[1]

The criminal law recognizes three categories of infringement, and associates with each its own type of punishment or *'adhab* (pl. *a'dhiba*, lit. 'torment', from *'adhdhaba* II Form of *'adhaba*, 'to torture'). By this term Fiqh intends both terrestrial penalties determined by the Sharī'a court and the pains of the next world sanctioned by God. The terrestrial punishments are of four kinds: *qiṣāṣ*, *diya*, *ḥadd*, and *ta'zīr*. The three categories of infringement are: (1) Offences punishable by *qiṣāṣ* or *diya*; (2) Offences punishable by *ḥadd*; (3) Lesser offences for which merely correctional punishment, or *ta'zīr*, is prescribed. Let us look at these in more detail.

1 Acts of bloodshed attracting the vendetta (*qiṣāṣ*) or compensation (*diya*). This category contains such crimes as manslaughter, injury, mutilation, etc., which Fiqh regards as offences against the victim and his family alike, and the penalty for which is described as *ḥaqq ādam* —a right of man. As has been said, it is in this more than any other section of the criminal law that the vestiges of the old Arab, and particularly Bedouin, patriarchal law of custom with its blood-feud are apparent. In pre-Islamic Arabia an obligation lay on the entire clan of the slain to take vengeance on the murderer's clan, and the murderer's clan in its turn responded with vengeance for vengeance. One murder therefore set in train a succession of fresh murders by the parties to the feud. Muḥammad modified this law of vendetta so that in Islam vengeance is taken on the murderer alone and not on his kinsmen. Also, if the family of the murdered — it is 'family' now, and not clan or tribe — chooses to be satisfied with compensation (*diya*) in lieu of blood (*qiṣāṣ*), then the obligation to guarantee the payment is confined to the murderer's family.

Having thus allowed a limited vendetta,[2] the Koran nevertheless recommends the relatives of the slain to pardon the slayer, since forgiveness is pleasing to God: 'If thou raisest thy hand against me, to slay me, I will not raise my hand against thee, to slay thee; for I fear God, the Lord of the Worlds.'[3] Thus, on the question of revenge, as on so many questions, the ethic of Islam is midway between the Jewish ethic of 'an eye for an eye and a tooth for a tooth'[4] and the Christian ethic which prohibits men from assuming God's role: 'Vengeance is mine; I will repay, saith the Lord.'[5] Islam is, as it were, saying to the relatives of the slain: You have the right to take revenge, but it will be better for you to forgive. It is this attitude to forgiveness that enables Fiqh to contemplate *diya* as an alternative to blood.

Where the family does not agree to accept *diya*, the law of vendetta is enforced. This may either be carried out by the public executioner or by the delivery of the murderer to the family of the slain so that the relatives themselves may put the murderer to death. The Shāfi'ites hold that the murderer ought to be killed in exactly the manner in which he has done his victim to death; and the Ḥanafites think the murderer should be despatched with a sharp blade and in such a way that death is quick and with the least possible agony, e.g. by beheading.

A distinction is drawn between premeditated (*ta'ammudī*) murder, done with intent (*'amd*), and unintentional manslaughter by error (*khaṭa'*), e.g. by the negligence or inexperience of physicians and surgeons. For premeditated murder *qiṣāṣ*, or execution, is the penalty unless the relatives consent to *diya*, or compensation. In the latter event the Shāfi'ites impose an atonement in addition to *diya*, called *kaffara*, which consists of a two-month fast or the setting at liberty of a Muslim slave. Inadvertent manslaughter is not punishable with death but only with *diya*. Likewise *diya* alone is contemplated for the murder of another's slave by a free man (in which case the compensation is payable to the slave's master) or for the murder of a Dhimmī by a Muslim. The Ḥanafites, it is true, allowed *qiṣāṣ* as well when a Dhimmī was murdered — in theory; in practice it was almost invariably commuted into *diya*. If a slave murders a free man, his master either hands him over to the dead man's relatives for them to despatch him; or else, at their wish, pays them *diya* — even if he has to sell the slave to do this.

In a case of premeditated murder, *diya* has to be paid at once; but the time limit is three years in a case of unintentional manslaughter. Full *diya* is reckoned at 100 camels,[6] equivalent in money to 1000 dinars (12,000 dirhems according to the Shāfi'ites; 10,000 according to the Ḥanafites). This *diya* is technically known as *mukhaffafa*, 'without majoration'; but where the *diya* is imposed in aggravating circumstances, for example in the murder of near relatives, or in murder accompanied by robbery, or in murder committed within the radius of the Holy Cities of Mecca and Medīna, then it is *mughallaẓa*, 'heavy', amounting to 100 she-camels or 1333⅓ dinars.

Only half the full *diya* is payable for the murder of a woman. For the murder of a Dhimmī by a Muslim, Abu Ḥanīfa allows the payment of full *diya*, while the Mālikites fix it at one-half and the Shāfi'ites at one-third. The murder of a Zoroastrian or pagan attracts a penalty of one-fifteenth of the full *diya* (800 dirhems). If a murderer is insolvent, his nearest kinsmen must bear the *diya* for him. Where the murder is perpetrated by a juvenile or person of unsound mind, *qiṣāṣ* does not apply, and the *diya* payable is a charge in the first case on the young person's relatives and in the second case on the local authorities.

Where the murderer kills several persons the *qiṣāṣ* prescribed is the same as for one victim; but if the relatives of the victims consent to *diya*, this has to be paid in respect of each one of the victims. Where several persons murder one person, all are liable to *qiṣāṣ*; or if *diya* be accepted, each one has to pay it. Murder is not punishable when committed under duress or at the command, even if illegal, of one in authority — in both cases the author of the compulsion is responsible — or in defence of one's life or property.

Mutilation can be grievous or less grave: the former might be depriving a one-eyed man of his remaining eye, cutting out the tongue, cutting off the ears with consequent loss of hearing, chopping off both hands or both feet or ten fingers. The guilty party is then liable either to *qiṣaṣ* (meaning here mutilation identical with that inflicted) or else to full *diya* on the same scale as for murder, according to the injured party's preference. In cases of less grave mutilation there is no *qiṣāṣ* and only partial *diya*: for the deprivation of one eye, one hand or one foot, half the full sum; for damage to the brain or harm to the abdomen, one-third; for the loss of a finger, one-tenth; for knocking out a tooth, one-twentieth or five camels; and so forth. For causing miscarriage to a free woman the penalty is one-twentieth of the full *diya*, and for causing it to a female slave it is one-tenth of her value.

The law made a painstaking list of these crimes of physical violence, but could not be expected to legislate for every possible variety of this; where there was a doubt, the judge would consult the authority of the Mujtahids. But it ignored recidivism: the relapse into these crimes was punishable with the same penalty as the first offence.

Since the punishment of these crimes of bloodshed was based on 'the right of the person', i.e. the right of the sufferer or his family or guardian or master as the case might be, so the proceedings could only be instituted on the complaint of the said persons, and they alone were entitled to bring *qiṣāṣ* into effect or to commute it into *diya*.

2 Offences punishable by means of *ḥadd* (pl. *ḥudūd*, 'bounds' or 'limits' of divine patience). These are offences for which punishment is provided for in the Koran. The term is taken from the passage: 'Such bounds are set by God; draw ye not nigh to them for fear of trans-

gressing them."[7] The doctors held such offences to be specifically against God, and their punishment a 'right of God' – *ḥaqq Allāh*. In contrast with crimes in the preceding category where the punishment is a right of man, these are unforgivable; their punishment derives from the will of God as expressed in Holy Writ, and consequently the alternative of compensation is not in point. But even here, irresponsible persons such as juveniles and the feeble-minded and those acting under duress or misapprehension are not liable.

One of the offences in this category is adultery (*zinā'*). In the case of the man this means connection with any woman not his in the sight of the law: that is, with a woman who is neither his wife nor his concubine;[8] in the woman's case it is intercourse with a man other than her husband or, if she be a slave, her master. The Shāfi'ites and Ḥanafites hold that the guilty of either sex, being free, adult, sound of mind and legally married, must be stoned; but that if any one of these conditions be absent — if for example, one of the guilty pair be unmarried — both parties must be punished with a hundred strokes of the lash.[9] A slave, male or female, merits fifty strokes. In practice severe penalties for adultery were seldom enforced because the declaration of the injured husband, even is he had surprised the erring wife in the act, was insufficient to obtain a verdict: there had to be the corroboration of four eye-witnesses, which could only be forthcoming in rare instances.

Pederasty is punishable in the same way as adultery; but, though accounted a major sin, the practice, very widespread in Iran and Central Asia during the Middle Ages, usually went unpunished.[10] Sodomy, necrophilia and onanism are punishable with twenty-five strokes.

Calumny (*qadhf*) in the narrow sense of a false accusation of adultery,[11] is punishable with whipping; a free man receives eighty strokes, and a slave half the number. A husband who has charged his wife with infidelity but failed to prove it is liable to the same penalty; but he may evade this by pronouncing a formula of execration, *li'ān*, which entails divorce.

The use of the wine of the grape, *khamr*, is forbidden by the Koran,[12] and the divines extended the prohibition to all fermented drinks. Different authorities fix the penalty at anything from forty to eighty strokes for a free man and half the amount for a slave, but people viewed this sin very indulgently in the Middle Ages, particularly in Iran — and incidentally it is the same today. Such literary works as the already mentioned *Qābūs nāma*,[13] the *Tārīkh-i Bayhaqī*, the poetry of Nizārī and Ḥāfiẓ and much besides, prove the uninhibited drinking of wine among people of position. It was openly offered at the royal banquets[14] of the Ghaznawids, Seljūqs, Khwārazm-shāhs, and Tīmūrids. Actually it was only drunkenness in the streets that was punished, and then far from always.

Stealing, *sirqa* (from *saraqa* 'to thieve'; whence *sarrāq*, 'thief') is punishable by cutting off the right hand;[15] and a second offence by cutting off the left foot. A thief who twice relapses merits the loss of his left hand, according to the Shāfi'ites, or imprisonment according to the Ḥanafites; all these penalties being applicable provided the stolen article be worth at least ten dirhems (Ḥanafite school) or three dirhems (Shāfi'ite school). The professors distinguish theft from the illegal acquisition (*ghaṣb*) of another's goods and chattels — immovable property, slaves of both sexes, money or articles deposited for safekeeping. If *ghaṣb* be shown, the party committing it (*ghāṣib*) is obliged to return the property to the rightful owner or pay its value, but he is not liable to any punishment. It is noticeable that although Muslim law generally speaking protects private property much more jealously than the right of the person, yet the punishments Fiqh imposes for stealing are less severe than those obtaining in the West where a man might be hanged for a trifling theft in the Middle Ages, or sent to penal servitude for filching a loaf or a morsel of meat in the France or England of the early nineteenth century.

The Koran intends by theft the secret pilfering of another's property; and the doctors relying on the theory of Qiyās[16] extended the same punishment to burglary and pillage. Highway robbers (*qaṭṭā'u 'ṭ-ṭarīq*), if only guilty of plunder, are to have the right hand cut off: but if the act is accompanied by murder, they are to be executed by beheading or hanging. Members of a gang are deemed to be accomplices, and all must suffer for the action of one.

Fiqh reckons apostasy (*ridda*) an extremely grave offence, and though the Koran itself omits to define the appropriate punishment, the doctors found support in the Ḥadīth for their conclusion that it attracts a penalty under the right of God (*ḥaqq Allāh*) heading. Consequently it was assigned to the category of crime to which the *ḥudūd* punishments are applicable. The apostate (*murtadd*) not only ceases to be a member of the Muslim community but loses all civic status: his marriage is dissolved, his men and female slaves are set free, and his estate is confiscated; he himself, if apprehended, is provisionally imprisoned. The Shāfi'ites think he ought to be accorded three days' grace for people to remonstrate with him and give him a chance to repent and thereby escape execution; the Ḥanafites, while admitting the desirability of such remonstration do not deem it obligatory; the Mālikites account it unnecessary, and the Ẓāhirites categorically denounce every such approach and condemn the apostate to instant execution. Certain of the Faqīhs thought a distinction should be made between apostates born and bred in a Muslim family and those who had crossed over to Islam from Judaism or Christianity and in whose case the apostasy was a relapse. These doctors favoured leniency towards the second, to the end that penitence and absolution might follow (and in this attitude the Shī'ite Faqīhs too concurred.) If the apostate refuses to respond to the entreaty to repent (*istiṭāba*), then of course there is nothing for it but execution. The Ḥanafites (and the Shī'ites likewise) consider that only the male apostate is liable to execution; in the woman's case it must be commuted to imprisonment until such time as she repents. Shāfi'ites, Mālikites and Ẓāhirites condemn to death the apostate of either sex. A slave is liable to execution just as a free man.

The apostates *par excellence* were those who embraced an alien faith. These were usually Christians and Zoroastrians, more rarely Jews and Manicheans, who had adopted Islam when their country was overrun by Muslim troops, so as to avoid captivity and slavery, or perhaps in times of persecution, but had continued the clandestine confession of their former faith and brought up their children in it. If this came to light, they or their descendants were labelled apostates. When such officially listed Muslims of secretly Christian persuasion were caught, or voluntarily declared their Christianity in order to redeem by martyrdom their sin, or that of their forefathers, of reluctant conversion to Islam, they were executed. This commonly occurred in Ottoman Turkey where entire villages might be involved, and in Arab Spain. Many Jews were in the same situation in Iṣfahān and other cities of Iran after the drives against them under Shāh 'Abbās II in the 1650s.[17] The famous scholar Ibnu 'l-Muqaffa', a Persian, and an Iranian patriot, was executed in 757 on a charge of secret profession of Zoroastrianism.

The followers of certain heresies which had deviated seriously from the basic dogmas of Islam were placed on the same footing as apostates. The 'Extreme' (*ghulāt*) Shī'ites who idolized 'Alī were of this number.[18] They were punished along with apostates and condemned on charges of witchcraft. Out-and-out atheists were treated the same.

According to Fiqh a rebel (Arab. Pers. *bāghī*, 'making an attempt upon something.' Arab. *mufsid*, 'seditionary') is he who, without repudiating Islam declines to fulfil the requirements of the Sharī'a; for example, to pay taxes, or to obey the lawful Caliph or local ruler. Unless they repent in time such persons are to suffer execution and the confiscation of their estate; are exposed, that is, to the same penalty as apostates save for the detail that they are not denied Muslim burial. However, there is this rider that Abū Ḥanīfa considered a rebel against the Caliph to be on a par with a recreant from the Faith and hence to have forfeited the right to burial in the Muslim way.

If whole provinces are in the grip of heresy and armed revolt, troops have to be despatched there, and if the insurgents are out-and-out apostates (*murtadd*) or heretics, war has to be waged with them as with infidels, i.e. they must be slaughtered, executed, their wives and children led into slavery, their country laid waste and their property treated as spoils of battle. But if the insurgents are not absolute recreants from Islam, they may only be killed on the field or executed by the sentence of a court; they may not be done to death without trial, neither may they or their wives and children be led into slavery, nor may their country be devastated; and the property of the inhabitants of the province that has risen is not within the definition of spoils destined for distribution among the warriors. The slain and executed rebels must be buried according to Muslim ritual. So think the Shāfi'ites and Mālikites. But the Ḥanafites hold that every revolt against a lawful Muslim ruler who observes the Sharī'a, and is not a tyrant, *ẓālim*, riding roughshod over it, can be classified as apostasy;[19] so that war with such must be waged as with non-believers; must involve, that is, mass slaughter, the turning over of women and children into captivity and slavery, and the wholesale pillage of the province.

It will not escape notice that the views of the doctors on this issue, particularly the Ḥanafites among them, reflected the interest of the governing class.

Every rising of peasants, artisans or Bedouin, provoked by feudal exploitation or the oppression of the authorities, could be construed as 'rebellion' or even 'apostasy'; and this was all the easier since popular agitation in the Muslim lands, like anti-feudal agitation in the West during the Middle Ages, was apt to wear the disguise of religious difference.[20] Peasant and artisan revolts in the Iran of the seventh to fifteenth centuries as a rule had a Khurramite,[21] Khārijite, Moderate Shī'ite or Carmathian-Isfmā'īlī complexion.[22]

In the event of the Dhimmīs of an entire province rising against the government — as did the Armenians, for example, and Georgian

Christians against the eighth/ninth century Caliphate, and the Christian Copts of Egypt against Ma'mūn — the troops sent to deal with them were ordered to treat them as non-believers or apostates.

Blasphemy and abuse of the prophets is punishable in the same way as apostasy except that remonstrance is not allowed, the offence being unpardonable. Also, not only Muslims are liable but Dhimmīs and pagans as well. Two Muslim witnesses must testify in court for a verdict to be obtained. Blasphemy and detraction of Muḥammad were in practice punished with death,[23] but disparagement of other prophets was usually awarded a prison sentence.[24]

3 Such infringements of the law as do not attract *qiṣāṣ* or *diya* or *ḥudūd* are awarded *ta'zīr*, 'correctional punishment'. Seizure of somebody else's dwelling, flight from the battlefield, false accusation,[25] perjury, breach of the peace — these are examples of offences in this category. The aim of *ta'zīr*, the doctors taught, is correction; and consequently a judge has a wide discretion in the approach he makes to the culprit, and in the penalty he imposes: this might be a simple warning or reprimand, a box on the ear, a fine, the birch (not more than thirty-nine strokes), exile, imprisonment (for a term not exceeding six months according to the Ḥanafite and Shāfi'ite schools). A judge might also blacken the guilty man's face, cut his beard off, have him paraded through the streets in disgrace, and make him ride a donkey back to front. The *ta'zīr* punishment could be waived at the instance of the injured party.

In its family and marriage regulations the Sharī'a retained certain items of the patriarchal clan system of old Arabia. One of these was the obligation of the bridegroom (or else his relatives or guardian) to pay the bride a marriage settlement called *mahr*. This is done by formal engagement, the amount being either fixed *à l'amiable* (in which event it was *mahr musammā*, 'named settlement') or the same as that received by other girls and women of the bride's family at the time of their marriage (in which case it was *mahru 'l-mithl*, 'settlement after the example'). The actual sum varies greatly, depending on the financial status of the bridegroom's family; but more is, as a rule, expected for a virgin bride than for a woman who has been married once or several times before. The marriage portion becomes the bride's own property — not that of her family; there is here a departure from pre-Islamic custom under which it was payable to her clan so as to compensate it for the loss of a girl.

Legal matrimony (*nikāḥ*) strictly requires both partners to be Muslims, but the Ḥanafite school tolerates the marriage of a Muslim man with a Christian woman or a Jewess (though not with a Zoroastrian or pagan woman) without requiring her to change her faith. The Shāfi'ites and others make no such concession.[26] All the law schools concur in discountenancing the legal union of a Muslim woman and a Dhimmī, much less a pagan.

Marriage is forbidden up to the third degree of blood kinship (*nisba*), and also with the relatives of a foster-mother up to the second degree. Two brothers may not marry two sisters; nor may a man wed two sisters either simultaneously or successively. A man must not marry (or take in concubinage, if a slave is concerned) a woman with whose mother, daughter or sister he is in a state of marriage (or connection). A host of further prohibitions under blood- and foster-relationship are scrupulously provided for by the jurists.

All the schools concur that a free man may not have more than four lawful wives at the same time,[27] but that he may after divorcing one of them replace her by another. A woman may marry again after the death of her husband or after divorce, and the number of remarriages contracted is without limit.

Theoretically Fiqh disallows marriage under compulsion; both the youth and the girl being required to signify their consent. But a girl below the age of puberty can be given in marriage by her father or grandfather — or by a guardian (*walī*) if he be a close relative[28] — without her being consulted. This was even the rule, seeing that girls were customarily married early — at between thirteen and fifteen years of age, and sometimes at the age of nine. When, as so often happened, the marriage was arranged by the parents of the future partners, the young couple set eyes on each other for the first time on the day of betrothal. However, thanks to easy divorce such alliances seldom led to tragedy. An adult woman, whether widow or divorcee, who remarries — there is a consensus of the schools on this point — must express her consent plainly so as to obviate the possibility of pressure by any of her relatives.

As between master and female-slave only cohabitation is allowable, and if the master intends marriage he must first free the woman.

A legal marriage cannot be contracted with a woman previously convicted of adultery.

The jurists recommend that so far as practicable the partners to a marriage contract should have parity in age, social position and means. A written agreement in a prescribed form conveying their consent, or that of their guardians on their behalf, is invariably requisite, and this must be drawn up in the presence of witnesses, and usually with the Qāḍī in attendance and the Imam of the nearest mosque — the latter to read a Sūra of the Koran and offer a prayer. These formalities can be performed either at home or in the mosque. The wedding ceremonies and feast that follow the formalities are based on the custom of the country concerned, and not on Fiqh.

The Sharī'a obliges the wife to obey her husband, but the latter's authority only extends to her person, and not to her property. Unlike Europe's feudal, and afterwards bourgeois, legislation under which the husband has the wife's property and dowry at his disposal,[29] Muslim law asserts the separateness of the property of the partners; the husband has no control over the movable or immovable estate of the wife. All expenditure on the maintenance of the family and home and on the upbringing of the children is his, and his alone. If there are two, three, or four wives in the household the husband must afford each of them separate accommodation and servants (at least one female slave or hired maidservant apiece) and generally create a style of living for her in the way of food, dress, and lodging, etc., not inferior to that she enjoyed in her father's home. He is bound to show all his wives uniform attention. The wife can enter into contracts, leases or other agreements through an attorney, and may, if she pleases, designate her husband as such.

Under these conditions polygamy is only within the reach of the privileged. The majority of Muslims, being peasants and workers, have at all times had to be content with one wife. Moreover, the seclusion of women prescribed by Fiqh postulates the division of the house into the men's half open to guests, and the women's half which only the husband, sons and very near male relations may visit. The rural masses and urban poor could not comply with this. The further obligation that women should be veiled out of doors was only heeded in the towns. It was never observed among agriculturists and nomads.

Divorce in general is easy. A husband can divorce his wife at any time and without any fault on her part; though he must, of course, let her keep her marriage portion or pay up any fraction of it that may still be owing. This form of divorce is called *ṭalāq* (lit. 'repudiation'). To have legal effect the *ṭalāq* formula has to be uttered by the husband three times. It frequently happens in family life that a husband, having thus divorced his partner in the heat of the moment, will afterwards regret it. Fiqh in such circumstances prohibits their reunion unless the wife provisionally marries another and this other husband then divorces her. In practice somebody, frequently a distant relation or friend of the husband, is called in to assume the role (with or without an honorarium) of temporary bridegroom and release the woman on the morrow of the sham marriage. The husband *ad interim* is described as *muḥallil*, 'one who makes lawful'.

A wife can obtain divorce on application to the court if her husband fails to perform his obligations towards her as summarized above, or omits to have intercourse, or has deserted the home. This annulment is known as *faskh* (lit. 'revocation', 'dissolution') and its consequences are the same as those involved in *ṭalāq*. A wife may also get a divorce in agreement with her husband on payment to him of such compensation, *'iwāḍ* (lit. 'equivalent') for loss of wife as the Qāḍī determines. Divorce of this sort is named *khal'* (lit. 'abrogation'), and is final in the sense that marriage between the partners cannot be contracted again.

When a husband is convinced of his wife's infidelity but cannot prove it in court for want of the necessary evidence of four witnesses, it is open to him to swear to the rightness of his cause, having poured imprecations upon her. The wife in her turn may swear that she is innocent and curse him back. The effect of this procedure is that the wife cannot then be accused of adultery, nor the husband of calumny; but the marriage between them is dissolved without possibility of renewal. The formula used in this kind of divorce is called *li'ān* ('cursing'). If the wife is pregnant, and the *li'ān* is pronounced by the husband before the delivery, then he is not deemed to be the father of the child.

A widow or divorced woman cannot remarry until the elapse of a term of waiting known as *'idda*. For a widow this lasts four months and ten days, and for a divorcee three menstrual periods (*qurū'*). The purpose of the *'idda* is to disclose whether the woman is not pregnant by her former husband; if it turns out that she is, then the fatherhood of the future child is established and she cannot go through with the new marriage until the elapse of forty days from the lying-in.

A one-sided view is commonly taken of the status of woman in Muslim countries. Admittedly woman in the Muslim East was denied equal rights with man and was dependent on father or husband, but it must be remembered that she was in practically the same condition in the Christian West where there was no polygamy and no seclusion. Furthermore, her rights in respect of property and family life were guarded in Muslim countries as they were never guarded in the West.

Here, even as late as the nineteenth century it was always considered a father's imprescriptible right to marry off a young son or to give a daughter in marriage while yet a girl, at his own discretion and without reference to their wishes; and divorce in Western countries and in Russia remained difficult and frequently impossible to obtain not simply after a church marriage but a civil one, right into the present century. As against this, Muslim law looks kindly on the dissolution of an unsuccessful union.

Children are legitimate if born in legal wedlock, but so are the children of a female-slave by her master, provided he recognizes them as his;[30] and where that is the case, no distinction is drawn in law between a wife's children and those of a bondwoman. It was no rare thing for the son of a Caliph or Sultan and a slave mother to inherit the throne. Children are illegitimate if born of undeniable adultery (*zinā'*), but also where the husband withholds recognition and resorts to *li'ān*.

The maintenance (*nafaqa*) and upbringing (*ḥiḍāna*) of the children is a charge on the father, although daughters actually remain until marriage, and boys until circumcision, under the mother's care in the women's quarters. In case of divorce, minor children, i.e. boys until they are seven, girls until the age of puberty, stay with the mother: thereafter in Ḥanafite law they return to the father unless he consents to their staying on with their mother; and in Shāfi'ite law they can choose, being of age, which parent to live with. The parent deprived of custody is entitled to visit the child.

In place of a deceased father some very close relation of his, or else a person designated in his will or the nominee of the Qāḍī, acts as guardian (*walī*). Women, the incapacitated such as slaves, juveniles and idiots are ineligible, and so are non-believers and Muslims of dissolute report. Guardianship (*walā'*) continues until the children are of age, full maturity being taken to be the fifteenth birthday at the outside. The Qāḍī supervises these arrangements.

The law of inheritance is marked by complexity and confusion because of the intricacy of family connections under a system of polygamy, concubinage,[31] ready divorce and remarriage, not to speak of the difficulty of reconciling the conflicting instructions of the Koran on the subject.[32] Indeed if the Koranic directions be followed to the letter, the shares apportionable to the various legal heirs come to more than one hundred per cent of the total inheritance. To establish the rights of an heir to a particular fraction, the jurists have recourse to involved calculations of the degrees of kinship. We need only pause briefly on the cases that arise.

The will itself (*waṣiyya*) must be drawn up in the presence of at least two wintesses.[33] The testator (*muwaṣṣī*) has to appoint his executor (*waṣī*). He may dispose of one-third of his estate as he chooses, leaving sums of money, lands or effects to whom he desires, or bequeathing some property in *waqf*, or setting certain of his slaves at liberty. These last two items are accounted pleasing to God and inserted in the will 'for the sake of salvation'. The remaining two-thirds of the estate must be divided among such of his relations as have prescriptive rights as heirs. A person who receives a share of the inheritance by testament is known as *muwaṣṣā lahu*, 'optional legatee', while the prescribed heir is *wārith*. The immediate relatives whose rights are stipulated by the Koran, viz. father or paternal grandfather, son or grandson, daughter, brother, sister, wife, mother, are called *ahlu 'l-farḍ* or *aṣḥābu 'l-farā'id*, members of the family inheriting as of legal right. Each of the *ahlu 'l-farḍ* receives the portion laid down by the Koran: for instance, a wife gets one-quarter of the inheritance if there are no children, and one-eighth if there are children; a mother correspondingly one-third and one-sixth; sons inherit twice as much as daughters. Failing any *ahlu 'l-farḍ*, the inheritance passes to the less immediate blood-relations.

The latter are men and women in the male line and called *'aṣabāt*, 'agnatic kin'. These are subdivided into : *'aṣabāt bi-nafsihi*, literally 'heirs by themselves', i.e. males inheriting in mere virtue of the blood relationship; *'aṣabāt bi-ghayrihi*, literally 'heirs thanks to another', and meaning here kinswomen such as sisters, granddaughters, etc.; and *'aṣabāt ma'a ghayrihi*, literally 'heirs together with another' and meaning kinswomen associated with another of a different category, e.g. half-sisters who inherit along with their mother.

If the categories of kinsfolk described above as *ahlu 'l-farḍ* and *'aṣabāt* are both of them wanting, then the relations in the female line *dhu 'l-arḥām* (from *raḥm*, pl. *arḥām*, 'womb') — are admitted to the inheritance e.g. uterine sisters, children and grandchildren of a daughter, maternal uncle or aunt, etc. The above, of course, pertains to the Sunnī schools; the Shī'ite law of inheritance differs considerably.

Of the law on the ownership of land and the categories of landed property a short account has already been given in Chapter VI.

Let us next outline the attitude of Fiqh to obligations and agreements. The subject is without system and all proper classification is wanting — though the Egyptian scholar Sh. Shafiq has lately gone some way towards a general account of the relevant Ḥanafite ordinances.[34]

To begin with one may pick on obligations arising from the necessity for someone to make good a loss, *maḍarra* (from *ḍarra* 'to harm'); for example, the obligation of a person who has unlawfully appropriated another's property — a *ghāṣib* or 'usurper'[35] — to restore it to its rightful owner. The law here is not concerned to punish the offender, and the question is limited to restitution.

Then there are obligations arising from a vow (*nadhr*); for instance, a promise to perform pilgrimage or make atonement (*kaffara*, 'expiation') for some sin or crime. *Kaffara* might consist of fasting, giving a Muslim slave his freedom, or nourishing or clothing a number, and usually some dozens, of poor people. The fulfilment of any sort of promise, but particularly one of religious character, is obligatory.

Obligations are also created by contracts (*'aqd*, pl. *'uqūd*, lit. 'tying', from *'aqada* 'to bind') concluded between two parties in pursuance of a proposition, *ījāb*, by the one, and its acceptance, *qabūl*, by the other. In law, a contract must have three components called 'pillars' (*arkān*): the negotiating parties, *al-muta'āqidān*; their willing consent, *ikhtiyār*; and the matter under agreement, *ma'qūd 'alayhi*. The contracting persons must be competent and entitled to the free disposal of their property, *iṭlāqu 't-taṣarruf*. A contract is automatically void if its contents contravene the Sharī'a or are otherwise immoral. Fiqh takes the position that agreements envisaging economic advantage must proceed on the principle of permissible (*ḥalāl*) profit based on honest work, and it therefore holds agreements involving usury (*ribā*) to be illegal. Usury is regarded as extortion, condemned by the Koran,[36] and forbidden whether in the shape of straight loans at a percentage or in the shape of agreements in which the possibility of extracting interest is implicit. On the same principle agreements savouring of speculation, insecurity, fraud and risk, *gharar* (from *gharra*, 'to delude, cheat') are prohibited. In practice, however, the prohibition of *ribā* and *gharar* was always circumvented by various shifts (*ḥīla*) and casuistry.

Swallowing the fiction of the equality of all the Muslims, the law looks on the contracting parties as enjoying equal rights. Needless to say, in a feudal and class society men were not equal, and many a contract pretending to be between equals in reality placed one party at the mercy of the other. Such was the *'aqdu' z-zar'*, on sowings, where the peasant was given an area to sow under the métayage system (*muzāra'a*): under this arrangement the peasant on his holding was dependent on his feudal master, and the payment in the form of a portion of the crop was nothing but feudal rent. A marriage was likewise regarded as a contract, *'aqdu -zawāj*, and here again a relationship of dependence, this time of wife upon husband, was secured.

A commercial deal, embodied in a deed, *'aqdu 'l-bay'*, is considered in law as one of the various forms of barter. The special meaning of the word *bay'* is 'sale and purchase', but in the more general sense it is the handing over by one party of some object into the ownership of the other party, the latter letting the first party have some equivalent by way of exchange — *'iwāḍ* ('recompense'). This equivalent can be expressed in money or goods or services. Besides the simple *'aqdu 'l-bay'* in the special meaning of sale and purchase where an article is 'bartered' for its money equivalent, there is the barter of one commodity for another, termed *'aqdu 'l-muqāyaḍa* (from *qāḍa* 'to exchange'): there is the changing of money, *'aqdu 'ṣ-ṣarf* (*ṣarf*, 'changing, spending'; *ṣarrāf*, 'shroff'); and there is the peaceful settlement, *'aqdu 'ṣ-ṣulḥ*; and so on.

The law treats in detail of such further types of agreement as: the pledge, *rahn*, i.e. something given as security for the payment of a debt; the power of attorney, *wakala*, when the principal, *muwakkil*, entrusts to a person chosen by him as his confidential agent, *wakīl*, any commercial operation or financial deal; and the partnership or company, *shirka*.

A partnership is ordinarily an association created for the conduct of trade or other business to which each associate, *shārik*, makes a certain contribution in money, valuables, or wares. There are various classes of partnership depending on the aims and on the conditions binding the members. Such trading companies were very common in the Near East and Central Asia throughout the Middle Ages, and several of them had merchant capital at their disposal on a scale which enabled them to control the caravan trade in the countries concerned. In many cities the companies had their own caravanserais which served simultaneously as hostelries for merchants on tour, warehouses for merchandise and a rendezvous for concluding bargains through a broker (*dallāl*). They would equip enormous caravans with hundreds or thousands of camels, saddle-horses and pack-horses, and personnel including merchants, slaves, servants, guides, and the armed guard against marauders.[37] In large transactions payment was made by cheque — the very word *chek* is Persian — on presentation of which the sum of money due could be received not only in the place where the bargain was struck but in other towns. The influence of some of these companies was so great that, in the words of the eleventh-century historian Abū Shujā 'ar-Rudhrawārī, cheques drawn in the Maghrib were cashed in the eastern provinces of the Caliphate quicker than a receipt of *kharāj* reached the Treasury. And when the Seljūq Sultan Malik Shāh crossed the Amū Daryā with his army in 1089, he ordered that the owners of boats should be paid by cheques on shroffs residing at Antioch on the Orontes in Syria.

Besides the ordinary partnership postulating contributions in money or merchandise, Fiqh allows the formation of (a) societies to which the members bring no contribution; for example, of persons lacking ready money but enjoying enough credit to enable them to operate jointly — the *shirkatu 'l-wujūh* — and (b) corporations of artisans — the *shirkatu 'ṣ-ṣanā'i'*.

Let us look once more at the legal position of the Dhimmīs.[38] We saw that these were non-Muslim subjects of the state who were supposed to be either Christians or Jews, that is People of the Book, *ahlu 'l-kitāb*, but that practical motives impelled the rulers to extend the Dhimmī status to Zoroastrians, Hindus and other polytheists. The jurists argued that the position of the Dhimmīs was based on a treaty of protection, *'aqdu 'dh-dhimma*, irrespective of whether this had in actual fact been concluded with them upon the conquest of their country by the Muslims. In accordance with this notion, the Dhimmīs were communities of outside religious persuasion who had submitted to the Muslims at the time of their conquest, and had bound themselves to obey the state and to pay the *jizya* or poll-tax recoverable from non-Muslims and also the *kharāj* or land-tax.[39] In return the Muslim state offered the Dhimmīs protection, permitted them (within limits) the profession of their faith and the exercise of their cult, and guaranteed them freedom of person and property.[40] The Dhimmīs on this theory were communities on their own, but not exempt from certain disabilities *vis-à-vis* the Muslims. They enjoyed a degree of self-government in virtue of the religious laws binding in their case (in the case of the Christians this meant canon law and Byzantine civil law, and also the Syrian codes; in the case of the Jews, it meant the Torah and Talmud), and were ruled over by their own spiritual heads: the Christians by the local bishop (*usquf*), metropolitan (*maṭrān*) or patriarch (*baṭrīq*); the Jews by the local rabbi (*khabīr*); and the Zoroastrians by their mobed (*mu'bad*). These lords spiritual of the Dhimmīs pleaded the cause of their communities or churches before the authorities,[41] sat in judgment over the members, controlled the schools and the books published in their jurisdictions, and were empowered to punish heretics and recreants from their faith provided these were not persons desirous of adopting Islam. They also had certain personal privileges.

The transfer of the administration of justice to these clerical personages was perfectly in keeping with the theory that the Sharī'a was intended uniquely for the Muslims: the Dhimmīs had to judged by their own codes. The result was that Christian bishops and Jewish rabbis exercised judicial and administrative powers in the Caliphate which they never had in Byzantium and other Christian states; their exalted status being indeed in pointed contrast with the condition of inferiority and submissiveness of their flocks.

If a Muslim and a Christian, or a Muslim and a Jew, went to law with each other, the parties had to be tried under Muslim law before a Qāḍī.

Here we are not concerned with the attitude of Islam to the Jewish and Christian religions — this has been discussed in an earlier chapter[42] — but only with the position of the Dhimmīs in the sight of the law. As has been said, this was founded on a theoretical treaty between them and the state. The treaty was deemed to be violated, in so far as he was personally a party to it, by any Dhimmī who permitted himself insulting references, in public and in the hearing of Muslim witnesses, to the Prophet and the Faith. It was likewise held to have been broken if the Dhimmī (1) failed to pay *jizya* and *kharāj*; (2) struck a Muslim; (3) entered into marriage — illegal from the standpoint of Fiqh — or simply into a union with a Muslim woman. If these things happened, he could, depending on circumstances, be put to death or sold into slavery. A mass refusal to pay *kharāj*, or obey the authorities, was viewed as a collective violation of the treaty in the particular province, and troops accompanied by volunteers, *ghāzīs* or champions of the Faith, would be sent there to wage Holy War on the 'infidels'.

As we saw, the legal disabilities were very mild in the first two centuries, but they were increased thereafter. Tradition ascribes the imposition of a multitude of major and minor restrictions to 'Umar I; but in fact the sources prove that these were hardly in evidence until the end of the eighth century, and were not decreed in a large way until even later. The more time went on, the more numerous they became. They varied in the systems of the different schools: the Ḥanafites were comparatively lenient in their treatment of the Dhimmīs, the Shāfi'ites less so; the Mālikites were harsh, and the Ḥanbalites and Ẓāhirites the most hostile and least tolerant.[43] However, practice depended on country and period: the restrictions might in one place or age be mercilessly implemented, and in another place or age very slackly observed.

The following regulations were common to all the schools. Dhimmīs had to pay *jizya* and *kharāj*. They had to entertain Muslim travellers in their homes for three consecutive days per visit, supplying them lodging, food and fodder for their horses. In effect the civil and military personnel of the postal service was here contemplated (and incidentally the obligation was subsequently extended to Muslim ryots as well). Then Dhimmīs were not entitled to carry weapons. They could not appear as witnesses in a Sharī'a court of law. In theory they might not be land-owners but only land-holders. However, in Iran, as also in Transcaucasia in the later Middle Ages, to judge by the fairly copious documentation of the sources, Dhimmīs of noble rank used to purchase villages as 'mulk' and even bequeath immovable property in 'waqf' to Christian monasteries.[44] Dhimmīs could not participate in artisan corporations, and there were also certain of the trading societies which they were not entitled to join.[45]

At least from the time of Caliph Mutawakkil, they were compelled to wear distinguishing marks on their clothing. To go by the sources, the Christians in eleventh-century Iran wore a peculiar leather belt known as *zunnār*, and the Jews two patches, one on the chest and the other on the back, of a colour contrasting with that of the garment.[46] Dhimmīs were not authorized to ride horses: they might only ride mules and asses, and had to dismount from these and give passage whenever they met a Muslim. Their domestic life had to be quiet and modest, and their houses neither higher nor more showy than those of the Muslims around them. They could not own Muslim slaves, though they could have non-Muslim slaves (whether of their own or another faith).

The Koran enjoins that Dhimmīs shall pay the poll-tax 'with their own hand, as being inferiors'.[47] The Ḥanafite interpretation of this passage is that they had to pay in conformity with their income, and acknowledging their subordination. But the Mālikites took the text to intend this: the Dhimmī, whether Christian or Jewish, must present himself at the Dīwān and hand over the sum due to the Amir,[48] personally and not through an agent;[49] after which, (the Mālikites continue) the Amir strikes him with his fist on the back of the head, repeating 'Pay the tax, O enemy of the One God!'; whereupon the servant of the Dīwān chases him out. But this procedure, apparently, was rarely put into practice even in the Mālikite countries of Maghrib and Arab Spain. In Iran, where the Shāfi'ites and Ḥanafites held the field until the sixteenth century, there was no such custom.

The following juridical cases will illustrate the extent to which the Ḥanafite attitude towards the Dhimmīs was more tolerant than that of the Shāfi'ites. Can a Christian or Jew obtain idle lands (*mawāt*) for cultivation on terms of *iqṭā'*? He can, reply the Ḥanafites. He cannot, object the Shāfi'ites. Can a Muslim rent his house to a Christian or Jew? No, say the Shāfi'ites, since the Dhimmī tenant may construct a church or synagogue in the house; in which event the Muslim becomes an accessory to a sin. Yes, say the Ḥanafites, since the Muslim having leased the house is not answerable for the way the tenant uses it. Can a Muslim accept an inheritance from a Christian or Jew? He cannot, the Shāfi'ites assert, since there may be unclean objects such as swine and wine on the inherited premises. He can, the Ḥanafites rejoin, since the swine can be driven out into the street and the wine poured onto the ground, and the property then taken over. Can a Christian or Jew enter a mosque? He can, the Ḥanafites answer, as long as he conducts himself in the holy building with decorum. He cannot, the Shāfi'ites retort, because he does not perform the ritual ablutions and is consequently impure.

It was against the law to turn Dhimmīs over to slavery; and while the Caliphate endured as a single whole, the rule was scrupulously heeded. But when it collapsed, the resultant states, when at war with one another, did not hesitate to make slaves of the Dhimmīs they captured from the opposite side. It was from this angle more than any other that their situation worsened by comparison with what it had been in the opening centuries of Islam.

As is well known, slavery obtained in Muslim countries until recent times. Islamic law did not, it goes without saying, invent the institution; it retained something that was present in Sāsānian Iran and Byzantium alike when the Arabs overran their territories in the seventh century. In the course of the conquests, great numbers of people of both sexes were taken prisoner and enslaved.[50] As the centuries progressed, male and female slaves were utilized throughout the 'Province of Islam', i.e. Dāru 'l. Islām, and particularly in Iran not merely as menials and odalisques but in production, whether on irrigation works or in agriculture, or in tending the flocks — this among the nomads — or in handicraft or in the mines.[51] In other words a slave-owning structure persisted for a long time in the early feudal societies of the Caliphate, and survivals of that structure were present in the later feudal societies of the Near and Middle East. This was one of the peculiarities of Eastern feudalism as compared with feudal societies in the West, where — if we except Spain and parts of Italy — slavery went out at an early stage.

All the schools of law consider slavery, which is sanctified by the

Koran, to be a legal and necessary institution of the Muslim community. Fiqh recognizes three principal sources of it: (1) the capture of infidel prisoners in the course of Holy War; (2) sale and purchase; (3) descent from slave parents.[52] It will be noticed that (2) and (3) come in the end back to (1), since the people who were on sale were those turned over to slavery in result of war or plundering raids,[53] and those born in a condition of slavery would be descendants of enslaved captives.

The general principle was that only prisoners of faiths other than Islam could be turned into slaves, but the conversion to Islam of those already in the position of slaves did not entail freedom. And since slaves of other faiths living in a Muslim environment commonly embraced Islam in the second or third, if not in the first, generation, the number of Muslim slaves rapidly multiplied. Conversion, it must be added, was rather the effect of atmosphere and way of life than of pressure and compulsion on the part of the owner.

The law does not contemplate slavery for debt in the case of Muslims, but it allows the enslavement of Dhimmīs for non-payment of *jizya* and *kharāj*. It does not recognize the right of Muslim parents to sell their children as slaves.

In common with the ancient slave-owning societies the Muslim community considers the slave (*'abd*, pl. *'abūd*,[54] 'bondman'; *mamlūk*, pl. *mamālīk*, 'mameluke'; *ghulām*,[55] *raqīq*, 'boy'; Pers. *banda*,[56] pl. *bandagān*, or *barda*, pl. *bardagān*) and the bondwoman (*jariyya*, 'female slave' in general; *surriyya*, 'concubine'; Pers. *kanīz*, *kanīzak*, 'girl')[57] as chattels, movable possessions of the owner who is lord and master (*rabb*, *ṣāḥib*; Pers. *khudāwand*). The owner could dispose of them as he pleased; by sale, by gift, by bequest. Slaves were legally incapable; they had no right to property and if they had effects of any description these, like the Roman peculium, were deemed to belong to the master and to be usable only with his consent.

Not a few Western orientalists, scholars and travellers — Edward Lane, Snouck Hurgronje[58] and J. L. Burckhardt among them — have been prone to expatiate on the mildness and humanity of Muslim slavery. The Koran, it is true, taught the master to be mild in his treatment of the slaves,[59] but this was a counsel of moral perfection which was not reinforced by any legal sanction whatsoever: the master could put the slave to any task, hire him out, or pledge him as guarantee for the payment of a debt to sombody. He could inflict corporal as well as other punishment on his slaves, male or female, and even put them to death. The murder of a bondman or bondwoman by the owner was not punishable, and only if it was 'without cause' would atonement (*kaffāra*) be required of him.

Muslim law, like the late Byzantine law (cf. the codes of Theodosius II and Justinian I) recognizes the right of slaves to have a legitimate family, but this humane measure was so hedged about by limitations as to lose much of its value. To begin with, marriages contracted by prisoners of war before their capture and enslavement are deemed dissolved; and second, both in law and in practice the members of a family taken prisoner were straightaway separated and distributed among the victors, or sold off one by one. A slave child may not be removed from his mother while he is still in need of her care, but even the relatively humane Ḥanafites interpret this as seven years of age, and the other jurists permit the removal of the child considerably earlier. To be legal, marriage between slaves had to be contracted when they already had slave status, but such a marriage postulated the owner's agreement. Even then, the latter could at any moment break up the family, by making the husand divorce his wife — a very simple affair in a Muslim milieu — or selling off the whole family, one here one there. The upshot was that a slave family was a dependent unit whose existence was wholly contingent on the master's will.

An owner could take any female slave as his concubine; being merely under obligation in the case of recent purchase to wait one menstrual period (*qur'*) to see whether she was pregnant, and if so to establish paternity. To be sure, the jurists said that the woman in question had to be Muslim, Christian or Jewish (the Shāfi'ites even ruled out the Christian woman and the Jewess), but in real life such limitations were waived. The Sharī'a strictly forbids a master to prostitute a bondwoman, but this humane rule was often defied in practice.

All large cities had their slave markets, and the slave trade was amenable to very exact legislation. The slaver enjoyed all an owner's rights until the moment of sale, and as the eleventh-century author of the *Qābūs-nāma* puts it: 'the slave must fear the slaver, as the ass the horse-breeder.'[60] Admitting the right of inspection by the prospective purchaser, the jurists stipulate that this shall be seemly, and the Ḥanafites insist that the inspection of a female slave must be limited to her face. But in practice these rules were ignored: the author of the *Qābūs-nāma* advises his adolescent son when buying a male or female slave[61] not only to examine eyes, eyebrows, nose, lips, teeth and hair but to make sure of the comeliness of the entire body. 'At the time of purchase' says this author 'make the slave lie down and feel him over on both sides and ascertain carefully whether he has a tender spot or a swelling anywhere . . . and when looking for these signs of latent troubles, neglect not the obvious ailments like the odour from the mouth and nose, fistulas, deafness, impeded speech, stutter, and see whether the gait be upright, the gums regular and healthy — so that there is no cheating.'[62]

Fugitive slaves had to be arrested by anybody who spotted them, and returned to the owner, or, if the latter could not be found, placed temporarily in gaol.[63]

Fiqh draws a distinction between common slaves over whom the master's authority is absolute (the technical designation was then *qīn*) and privileged slaves including the *ma'dhūn, mudabbar, mukātab* and *umm walad.* By the term *ma'dhūn* was meant a slave who had received *idhn*, i.e. 'permission' from his master to conduct the latter's business affairs (for example, to trade in his name, be his travelling salesman, conclude commercial agreements, manage his estate, and so forth), or else to engage in some craft and enjoy the earnings. The *mudabbar* was the slave who had the *tadbīr*, i.e. 'undertaking' or 'promise' of his master in the formula 'When I die, thou shalt become free'. The *mukātab* was the one who had a *kitāba*, or written agreement with his master under which he committed himself to redeem his freedom for a fixed sum by a specified date. There was no getting out of this engagement for the master; and when the redemption figure was paid up, the slave got his freedom. The *mukātab* was entitled to his peculium and own earnings, and might not be sold or given as a gift to any one else; while the female counterpart, the *mukātaba*, could not be forced to cohabit with her master.

The *umm walad* (lit. 'mother of a child') was a slave concubine who had borne her master at least one child, boy or girl, whom he recognized as his. She could not be sold or given to another, and on her master's death received her freedom automatically; provided at least one of her children by him was living at the time. The children were equated in law with those of a lawful wife; that is to say, they were legitimate and free from the moment of birth.

A slave could belong to several masters who, having purchased him jointly, exploited him together. But where a female slave was joint-property, only one of the coproprietors could have the right of cohabitation with her, exercising this with the consent of the others.

The setting free of Muslim slaves is an act pleasing to God; and one which, according to a Tradition attributed to Muḥammad, can save the soul from the eternal torments of hell.[64] The occasions on which this act was performed for religious motives, by way of atonement (*kaffara*) for a sin or for the sake of salvation, were not infrequent: the best known instance was when 'Abdu 'r-Raḥmān b. 'Awf, one of the ten closest Companions of the Prophet, freed, on his death in 652, no less than thirty thousand of his slaves (one can only imagine how many he had altogether!). But it would be wrong to see something specifically Muslim in such acts: the practice of freeing slaves for religious motives was usual enough in Christian countries like Byzantium, and in the slave-owning societies of antiquity — and in big numbers, as we can learn from the inscriptions of the temple at Delphi. This manumission of slaves, or their ransoming, of course hinged wholly on the master's volition, except in cases where the emancipation was based on law. The Shī'ites and a minority of the Sunnī jurists hold that only Muslim slaves may be given their liberty, but the Ḥanafites allow the manumission of all People of the Book. Where the slave is jointly owned, one of the co-owners can free him; the words used in such cases being 'So-and-so has freed the hand (or some other named part of the body) of slave so-and-so'. A declaration of this sort involved release on condition that the manumitting partner committed himself to refund his associates the amounts they had contributed at the time of purchase.

As in Ancient Rome, the freedman was regarded as the client (*mawlā*) of his erstwhile master and remained under his tutelage for the rest of his days. He needed the consent of his patron (*walī*) before giving his daughter in marriage, and if he died a natural or violent death leaving no heirs, his patron took over the inheritance and also the blood price, *diya*. If minor children survived him, the patron became the guardian of these boys and girls until they were of age, and then saw to their marriage. It will thus be seen that manumission did not amount to complete independence in the Muslim world any more than in Rome; the tie between client and patron was, theoretically anyhow, indissoluble.

As has been said already, the enslavement of a free Muslim is impossible in law, and so long as the empire kept its unity this regulation was scrupulously adhered to. But infringements grew common after the collapse of the Caliphate, and particularly after the inroads of the Turks and Mongols. The Oghuz Turks of Balkh (*ghuzziyya*) who were unquestionably of the Faith,[65] when they routed the Seljūq Sultan Sanjar in 1153 and laid waste Khorāsān, carried off a crowd of Muslims from Ṭūs, Nīshāpūr and elsewhere into slavery.[66] Again, it was after their adoption of Islam that the Mongol Il-Khans of Iran conquered Gīlān in 1307 and (as we know from the pages of Ḥāfiẓ-i Abrū) enslaved many of the inhabitants. And in the sixteenth century the Sunnī lawyers in Ottoman Turkey and Central Asia declared it legal to turn over Persian and Ādharbāyjānī Shī'ites to slavery. So in the late Middle Ages adherence to Islam certainly shielded nobody in this regard.

We come now to justice and legal procedure. Theoretically the right to administer the law belonged to the Imam Caliphs, and many of them did on occasion perform that function in their residence. But usually, whether at his residence or on the periphery, the Caliph delegated his judicial duties to a special judge, a Qāḍī (lit. 'he who decides'; pl. *quḍāt*). The first mention of such an appointment relates to 'Umar I's time. Nominees received from the Caliphs — and after the split up of the empire, from the Sultans and other sovereigns — a diploma called *manshūr*, which was read out in the mosques of the circuit in which the given Qāḍī was to have his jurisdiction (*qaḍā'*). The capital of a province had a Chief Justice, known as the Qāḍī of Qāḍīs (*qāḍī 'l-quḍāt*).

Fiqh viewed the Qāḍī's responsibilities as a religious duty towards the Muslim community; it required him to be a Muslim, to have received a specialized training as a cleric, to have studied the Sharī'a and to be versed in case-law. In the first centuries of Islam Qāḍīs were frequently of the Mujtahid class; but later on were recruited from among Muqallids who had learned their jurisprudence, and would pronounce their findings on the basis of the decisions of Mujtahids of the school to which they themselves were affiliated. In Iran until the assertion of Shī'ism early in the sixteenth century, the Qāḍīs were usually Shāfi'ite or Ḥanafite, and in such large towns as Ray or Nīshāpūr the Shāfi'ites and Ḥanafites, and sometimes the adherents of other schools too, would often each have their own Qāḍī.

It was held that a Qāḍī must be both experienced in jurisprudence and a person enjoying the reputation of a religious, just and incorruptible man. In theory he was not to receive any salary or honorarium, much less to accept any inducement or bribe from the litigants; and well-to-do people of independent means were therefore thought to be suitable for selection. But in practice Qāḍīs commonly drew a stipend from the treasury (*baytu 'l-māl*) or a pension from the income of waqf properties. Notwithstanding, there was at no time any dearth of 'bad Qāḍīs' as they were called — grasping, bribable, obsequious towards the secular authorities, and ignorant of the law.

A Qāḍī had to dispense justice on prescribed days and in a courtroom (*maḥkama*) — or, it might be, a mosque; and before each sitting had to perform ablution and prayer in the mosque. According to Shāfi'ite and Ḥanafite observance he sat, during sessions, facing Mecca; but according to Shī'ite observance, with his back to it. He must display complete impartiality *vis-à-vis* the litigant parties: the plaintiff (*mudda'ī*) and respondent (*mudda'ā 'alayhi*); not betraying the slightest bias and not expressing his opinion on the merits of the case until the hearing is over. He must invite the plaintiff and respondent to sit down, unless one of the litigants is a Dhimmī: in that event, he requests the Muslim to be seated and keeps the Dhimmī standing.

In the Sharī'a court there is no prosecutor and no counsel for the defence; the idea is that the Qāḍī so to speak combines the functions of both. The parties plead in person or (which is regular for women) through an attorney; the plaintiff has the right to object to the respondent's attorney and demand personal attendance. No cause can be adjudicated in the absence of the respondent or his attorney. If there were Qāḍīs of the different schools in one and the same district, as was customary in Iran until the sixteenth century, then the choice of Qāḍī lay, under Ḥanafite law, with the plaintiff; and under Shāfi'ite law, with the respondent.

During the trial of more or less complicated cases, the Qāḍī invited experienced Faqīhs to take part in the hearing and consulted them before pronouncing judgment. He had at his disposal a staff consisting of one or more clerks (*kātib*), a commissionaire (*bawwāb*) and a messenger (*rasūl*) whose responsibility it was to fetch the respondent and witnesses to court. Hearings were open to all wishing to attend. In principle a case had to be decided in the course of one day and could be adjourned only in exceptional circumstances. Decisions had to be based on religious law; that is, the Koran, the Traditions, Qiyās and Ijmā'; they could not be based on local custom (*'urf, 'āda*). Personal conviction, or information that had come to the Qāḍī privately, was not relevant.

Fiqh recognizes three sorts of proof: confession (*iqrār*); the deposition of witnesses (*shuhūd*, plural of *shāhid*); and the oath (*yamīn*).

Confession both in civil and criminal cases is a corroboration: it endorses the justice of the claim or charge. It must be voluntary and without pressure or persuasion from any quarter. It cannot be retracted in 'right of man' (*ḥaqq ādam*) proceedings, i.e. those civil and also blood cases which are amenable to the *qiṣāṣ* and *diya*; but it can be withdrawn in 'right of God' (*ḥaqq Allāh*) proceedings which are punishable under the heading *ḥudūd*.[67] If the respondent or accused on the other hand denies the allegation he is described as *munkir* 'denying', and his denial is *inkār*.

The Sharīʿa court sets the greatest store by deposition, and this is usually the determining factor. In the majority of court cases, civil and criminal alike, at least two witnesses are required, who have to be Muslim of the male sex, adult (except in 'blood' proceedings where the testimony of minors is admissible), and capable in the widest sense. This means that they must not be of another religion, or lunatics, or mental defectives, or slaves; and that even Muslims of bad reputation are ruled out, e.g. non-Mosque-goers, libertines, drunkards, gamblers, notorious pederasts, thieves and members of the criminal world. Such importance is attached to the personal qualities of a potential witness that the Qāḍī is empowered to appoint not less than two investigators (*muzakkī*, lit. 'purifying') to sift and report on his moral make-up. A respondent may himself challenge the witnesses called, but not without sufficient justification.

A witness is not required to take the oath, but must preface his statement with the word *ashhadu*, 'I testify'. His evidence amounts to proof if it supports the terms of the allegation as to time, place and essentials. He can go back on his statement at any time before sentence is pronounced. A false witness, detected as such after the sentence has ben passed, must make material amends to the injured party and in addition undergo corrective punishment, *taʿzīr*, which is generally flogging and imprisonment.

If the plaintiff is unable to produce reliable and trustworthy witnesses, or succeeds in producing only one male deponent, he may call on the respondent to swear that he is not guilty or, alternatively, that he righteously repudiates the allegation. To be valid an oath must be spontaneous and accompanied by the invocation *bismillāh*, 'in the name of God';[68] and uttered by a person capable in law: it is accounted more responsible and hence more convincing if the invocation is expanded to include some of the divine epithets: e.g. *bismillāhi 'r-raḥmāni 'r-raḥīmi, rabbu 'l-ʿālamīn* 'in the name of God the Compassionate, the Merciful; Lord of the Worlds', or if the oath is repeated several times (a maximim of fifty times is laid down in certain special cases). If the litigant invited to swear an oath be a Dhimmī, the wording of the invocation will be suitably changed; the Jew saying 'in the name of God who sent down the Torah (i.e. the Pentateuch) to Moses', and the Christian saying 'in the name of God who sent down the Gospel to Jesus.' A false oath, if proved to be such, is punishable with a correctional penalty, *taʿzīr*.

It is worth noticing that the law does not attach great importance to documentary evidence. Indeed in the first centuries the jurists ignored the possibility of the production of written proof altogether, and it was not until later times that they recognized that documents might have the force of proof — provided the respondent conceded that the document, perhaps a promissory note, was really written by him, or provided, where a contract between the parties was at issue, that the deed had been attested at the time by witnesses and bore their seals.

The stages of the hearing in court were usually these. The *mudda'ī* (that is, plaintiff in civil suits or injured party in criminal proceedings) stated his case in the presence of the Qāḍī and the *mudda' ā 'alayhi* (that is, respondent or accused). The Qāḍī to begin with attempted to reconcile the parties; but if he failed in this, he demanded of the respondent/accused whether he acknowledged the justice of the suit/charge. Three courses were open to the latter: he could admit the allegation, or deny it, or keep silent. If he admitted it, he was *muqirr* ('making confession') and the case was over. The Qāḍī then awarded damages or pronounced sentence, as appropriate.

If the allegation was denied, the plaintiff proceeded to call his witnesses. In case of their default the hearing was postponed, but usually not for more than three days. If the witnesses attended, were reliable and made credible statements, the court pronounced judgment in favour of the plaintiff/injured party. If defaulting witnesses did not appear on a second summons, or if there were no witnesses at all, or if there were no quorum, the respondent was invited to swear to the rightness of his position. If he did so in the set form, the court refused the plaintiff satisfaction. The oath was sufficient to clear the arraigned person in civil suits, and in cases of stealing and mutilation. In the rest of criminal cases oaths were usually not invited; as soon as the charge fell to the ground for want of proof, the accused was declared acquitted without being asked to swear.

If the respondent merely held his peace, the judge tried gentle persuasion, for any kind of pressure, let alone torture, was prohibited, as we have remarked. And if he was not to be prevailed upon but persisted in his silence, his attitude was taken as corroboration of his wrongdoing.

There was no appeal from the Qāḍī's judgment.

The duties of the Qāḍī were not limited to court proceedings. There was no such person as a notary among the Muslims, and it was the Qāḍī who attested wills, agreements, marriage contracts, deeds of purchase, instruments dividing family property, and the like. He had the wardship of orphans and abandoned children, or else nominated guardians for these. And it was for him, with the assistance of subordinate officials, to see that the judgments he passed in court were duly implemented.

The larger mediaeval cities, particuarly those of Iran, had, side by side with the Sharī'a court, an institution whose task it was to see that the religious and moral precepts of Islam were respected. This was the *ḥisba* ('Accounts Office', in the initial meaning, from *ḥasaba* 'to count'), which came, while the Caliphate was still in its heyday, to be the service charged with the surveillance of morals and public behaviour as these were defined in the Sharī'a; and since the hub of civic life in the mediaeval cities of the East was always the market-place,[69] the *ḥisba* became an inspectorate of morals and bazaars. It was under the superintendence of an officer called *muḥtasib* appointed from the clerical class, as befitted one whose duties were a religious responsibility. In the feudal city of Iran he held a post of high honour in the civic hierarchy, ranking with the Ra'īs, the Qāḍī, the Imams of cathedral mosques, and the doyen of the Sayyids descended from the Prophet.

The *muḥtasib* saw to it that the citizens attended the mosque faithfully, that the mu'adhdhins intoned the call to prayer punctually, and that no one openly broke the fast in the month of Ramaḍān. He saw to it that women did not appear unveiled in the streets, or converse with men in the bazaars except to make a purchase from a trader or place an order with an artisan; he supervised the baths and all places of resort; he arrested drunkards, gamblers, and drug addicts (i.e. takers of bhang, otherwise hashish, Indian hemp, and — from the thirteenth century onwards — opium.) He prosecuted prostitutes,[70] catamites on hire, street musicians, professional mourners, etc. But above all he made war on drunkenness.

He was assisted in these tasks by a staff of experts, 'arīfs as they were called (*'arīf* 'knowing') and wardens who patrolled the bazaars and artisan quarters. Though he was not authorized to fix market prices, or to compel the observance of these, he checked weights and measures, and was on the look-out for dishonesty. Nothing was more common in the Middle Ages than for traders to sell adulterated or spurious goods; dairymen diluted the milk, chandlers dealt in imitation musk; and so on. The *muḥtasib* had also the prevention of cruelty to slaves and animals within his competence. Punishment imposed by him was classed as correctional, *ta'zīr*: the offender might have a taste of the knout or the lash, or have to wear the cap of disgrace (*ṭurṭūr*), or be paraded through the streets seated back-to-front on a donkey.

House-entry and house-search were not the *muḥtasib*'s prerogative, but he sometimes acted as though it were. We know from the sources of cases where *muḥtasibs* with their agents broke into premises on the suspicion that men were using them for carousals with women; or else searched cellars for wine, and if they found it poured it on to the ground from the pitchers, and punished the transgressors. The most zealous *muḥtasibs* even dared to enter the royal palace with the same aim. Ulugh Beg, son of the Tīmūrid Sultan Shāhrukh and a man of worldly tastes, was giving a wine party in his country palace outside Samarqand when the *muḥtasib* Sayyid 'Āshiq made his appearance and said: 'Thou hast done away with the faith of Muḥammad and introduced the habits of the Kafirs.' To which Ulugh Beg replied: 'Thou hast merited fame by thy descent from the Sayyids, by thy knowledge of the Sharī'a, and hast attained ripe age: manifestly, thou wishest also to be a martyr and therefore speakest roughly. But I shall not satisfy thy desire.'[71] On another occasion, the same *muḥtasib* arrived at a banquet at the house of the Shaykhu 'l-Islam in Samarqand to which singing women had been invited, and reproached his host caustically, saying 'O Shaykhu 'l-Islam Without Islam, in which of the schools is it permissible for men and women to sit together and sing?'[72]

Sharī'a justice could not entirely satisfy the demands of the sovereign in a state which, however much it might be a theocracy in legal theory, had from Umayyad days been really a secular despotism. And if Qāḍīs frequently displayed their independence in the trial of cases and refused to be browbeaten by temporal authority, they had no powers to institute proceedings or arrest a criminal (even an obvious murderer) or suspect, unless there were a complaint by the injured party or his relatives, just as they had no right to force a confession from the accused or subject him to torture.

Meanwhile, thanks to the growth of city life throughout the empire, it was becoming increasingly difficult for the feudal authorities to control the lower strata of the urban population. There was a 'lumpenproletariat' in the large towns, and an army of beggars. In Iran the latter (*sāsiyān* or *sāsāniyān*) had their corporation and their own jargon. Then there were professional wrestlers, *pahlawānān*, and associations, *aṣnāf*, of artisans, who were often arms manufacturers or owners of arms. All these people constituted an unmanageable and frequently unruly element which supplied the human material of anti-feudal revolt. The towns were also a breeding-ground of crime which, for the reasons explained, it was difficult if not impossible for feudal authority to suppress through the agency of the Sharīʿa courts. Lastly, the towns of seventh to twelfth century Iran had many Zoroastrians, Jews and Christians over whom those courts had no jurisdiction.

All these considerations led the Caliphs — and the process began even in the reign of ʿAbdu ʾl-Malik (685–705) — to hand over some of their judicial functions in the cities to a military police. It was under the ʿAbbāsids that a force of that nature (*shurṭa*) took proper shape. Strictly the *shurṭa* was the royal guard (first of the Caliphs and then of the other dynasts — Sāmānid, Buwayhid, Ghaznawid, etc.) whose detachments were quartered in the cities and entrusted with police duties. The commandant of each detachment, called *Ṣāḥibu ʾsh-Shurṭa*, (in thirteenth to fifteenth century Iran, *dārūgha*,[73] and under the Ṣafawids, *dīwān begī*) had powers of arrest and torture on suspicion, without waiting for a complaint to be lodged. He could also institute inquiries on his own initiative, acting on the reports of his secret agents *(munhiyān)* recruited from various sections of the populace, and could interrogate any witnesses he pleased including the Dhimmīs who could not be subpoenaed by the Sharīʿa court, as also drunkards, drug fiends, those frequenting the low haunts and taverns, and the denizens generally of the underworld; the people, in fact, who on occasion might furnish valuable information in the course of a criminal investigation. His concern was not only with crimes of violence like murder, rape, abduction and robbery; it was also with political activity aimed at agitation and revolt. Having completed an investigation and caught the culprit, he was empowered to pass sentence extending to the death penalty. The forms the punishment might take were barbarous in the extreme and quite outside the purview of the Sharīʿa: for example, flaying, impaling, breaking of bones. With civil and family law, of course, he had nothing to do; the jurisdiction of the Qāḍī remained exclusive in that contect.

It will therefore be seen that from the late seventh century until the very close of the feudal age the Muslim world acquiesced in the arrangement of a secular police court able to try cases on the basis of royal ordinances (*qānūn*) or else local or nomadic custom (*ʿurf, ʿāda*), which functioned parallel with the spiritual Sharīʿa court of the Qāḍī, and was much more arbitrary and harsh in its operation. The dualism of the judiciary no more than corresponded with the inherent dualism of the Muslim state in feudal times, which was theocratic in theory and secular in its historical experience.

VIII

Theological disputes The Murjites, Qadarites and Mu'tazilites

In early Islam, as in Christianity, the doctrinal system, or theology in the narrow sense, made its appearance much later than the religion itself. The chief interest lay in questions of law and ritual. We saw in Chapter II how there was little distinction between theology and law, and how the theologians were simultaneously, indeed primarily, jurists.

Nevertheless by the end of the seventh century, coteries and schools had emerged in which the Muslims were already discussing such matters as sin, predestination and free will, and the nature and attributes of God. 'From the first centuries of its existence', says Bartol'd, 'Islam produced the same controversies on God and his relation to man as did Christianity; the explanation of this being partly the direct impact of Christian upon Muslim dogmatics and partly the similarity of the two religions themselves.'[1]

By this time the idea had already taken shape in Islam that sins are of two sorts: great or grievous — and the most heinous of these was unbelief — and small. Argument arose whether a person who had fallen into a state of grievous sin could be considered a Muslim. The Khārijites maintained that such a person ceases to be Muslim and must be regarded as an apostate; while their opponents, the Murjites, retorted that Islam is larger than wickedness and that even a great sinner, provided he keeps his faith intact remains a Muslim and will not be doomed to eternal torment in the hereafter.

This controversy had its direct bearing on the contemporary political scene. The Khārijites did not recognize the Caliphs of the Umayyad dynasty; they held them to be usurpers and tyrants on their record of grievous sin. The sin in point was that they had let slip the dogs of war within the Muslim community — the reference was to the first internecine war of 656–661 — and that almost all the Caliphs of the dynasty had been hypocrites professing Islam more from political necessity than from conviction. So the Kharijite case was that a Caliph being thus in a state of grievous sin is not only not Caliph but not Muslim, against whom Holy War must be waged as against any infidel ruler. In this way doctrine furnished justification for risings against the authority of the Umayyads. On the other hand the Murjites contended that since a Muslim is not excommunicated by reason of his state of grievous sin, even a sinful Caliph must be obeyed; and they consequently opted for loyalty to the Umayyads.

With this controversy was closely connected another, viz. about predestination. Soon after 622 the Medīna community accepted it as dogma — it was corroborated by the 'Medīna' Sūras of the Koran — that each man's life and behaviour are determined by God in advance. The Arabic word *qadar* was originally understood as 'might' in the sense of God's power to accomplish no matter what, and hence the word acquired the meaning 'predetermination': God is the creator of his people including all their thoughts and works. Now at the same time the Koran imposed on Believers the moral responsibility for their misdeeds and threatened their punishment beyond the grave. Muḥammad did not explain how man could be without volition respecting his works and yet answerable for what he did. He was not a theologian expounding a system; he was a preacher-politician and in the Medīna phase of his career a politician primarily. Grimme has shown how the preaching of predestination assumed growing importance in proportion as the political authority of Muḥammad gained ground.

The dogma was a very handy ideological instrument of Holy War. For it could be impressed on the Muslim warrior that, whatsoever danger loomed in battle, he would come through alive if he were not predestined to die that day; but that were he so destined, die he must even though he stopped at home. The doctrine led, then, to fatalism and contributed to valour in the Fighters for the Faith. And it had political weight; since, clearly, predestination underpinned not only the competence of Muḥammad's mission and his standing in the first Arab state but also the subsequent authority of his successors, the Caliphs. That was why the Orthodox Caliphs and the Umayyads adhered so steadfastly to it.

The intrinsic contradiction in the doctrine of predetermination was of course not yet recognized in the comparatively primitive setting of Medīna, and Arabia generally, in which Islam was being moulded: arguments about predestination were there unthinkable. But when Islam started to expand in the countries of ancient culture — both Hellenistic and Iranian — which the Arabs presently conquered, the doctrine brought embarrassment to many. People now put the question: how can man be answerable for his works if these do not depend on his will? How can evil actions be predetermined by a God who cannot be the author of evil?

In Egypt, Syria, Iraq and Iran the controversy about predestination and free will among the Muslims was apparently nourished by the identical dispute proceeding in Christian quarters. Christianity too had its predestinarians (St Augustine, d. 430), and its champions of free will (John of Damascus, eighth century); but neither one nor other of these competing tenets had been so universally accepted as to qualify as a dogma. The two ran on parallel lines. Much later on, at the Reformation, predestination was to be staunchly defended by the Protestants, especially the Calvinists. The Calvinists were a bourgeoisie in the period of primary accumulation of capital, to whom the doctrine was the religious expression of the economic law of competition in a budding capitalist society. But it was only, of course, at the stage of the growth of capitalist relations, and in Europe, that the doctrine took on this complexion. In an Islamic environment, as stated, its significance was different: there it served as the ideological basis for the legality of the Caliphs' authority.

In the eighth and ninth centuries the predestination/free will controversy involved everybody in bitter debate — everybody, that is, except the Murjites whose decision was to take *no* decision. On the one side the absolute predestinarians, who had become known as Jabarites (*jabariyya*, from *jabr* 'compulsion', 'coercion'), contended that God in creating a person also creates that person's character, potentialities and future behaviour, so that there is no room for freedom of will; no man, they said, can control his affairs one whit. The Jabarites were the out-and-out determinists.

Countering them was a school which had apparently made itself felt even before the eighth century opened whose adherents, called Qadarites (*qadariyya*),[2] took as their point of departure the thesis that God is only conceivable as a being possessed of the quality of justice (*'adl*). Now granted that God is just he cannot perform unjust actions. It follows that human wickedness, covering the whole gamut of social injustice, oppression, hypocrisy and crime upon earth, cannot be traced back to God, for this would contradict the concept of divine justice. And the same thesis ruled out the possibility of a God preordaining men to certain acts and then inflicting punishment by way of retribution in the world to come. The Qadarites said that God, possessing the characteristic of free will himself, could not but create men with the same characteristic.

From the premise, then, that the will is free flowed the doctrine of human responsibility. Logically such an attitude was more consistent than the orthodox position on predestination, but the latter was a very present help in time of trouble — in this case the wars of conquest to which the Caliphate was committed. It endorsed a blind obedience to the Umayyad cause: once concede that historical events are prearranged by God, and the sway of the Umayyads was something that none might resist. So the *Jabariyya* were listed as loyal supporters of the regime, whereas the *Qadariyya* together with certain Shīʿite sects were associated with the movement against it. It was probably about this time that the Ḥadīth, or 'Tradition', was faked which ascribed to the Prophet the saying that the Qadarites were Zoroastrians (*majūs*), and a second Ḥadīth to the effect that they were adversaries of God. Neither tradition, evidently, could have been invented earlier than the eighth century.

The opponents of the Qadarites sought to refute them as follows: If the Qadarites allow man his choice to do or not to do, they are committing themselves to the position that man creates his own acts; is, in the Arabic phrase, *khāliqu 'l-afʿāl.* But in that case they are exalting man as a second creator. On this reasoning the Qadarites were accused of being Zoroastrians, i.e. dualists. It is worth remarking in this place that since a rigorous dogma of monotheism is the very foundation of Islam, rival divines always tended to charge one another with polytheism. The Qadarites reacted sharply: God created man with a free will and to that extent man is master of his behaviour, yes; but that does not imply that he is the creator of it.

As time went on, the Qadarite creed was taken over and elaborated by the Muʿtazilite school. Even the label Qadarite was transferred to this new setting, and little by little the two doctrines coalesced.

In Muslim tradition the Muʿtazilite school traces its origin to the circle of Ḥasan of Baṣra (642–728). A pupil of his named Wāṣil b. 'Aṭā, accompanied by another pupil 'Amr b. 'Ubayd, 'separated' (*iʿtazala*) from his teacher and founded his own school. His disciples were called Muʿtazilites (*al-mu ʿtazila*, from *iʿtazala*, 'to go away, withdraw, separate'; the VIII form of the verb *ʿazala*; meaning 'those who parted, went off'; in a word, 'the renegades').

This Wāṣil stoutly defended the doctrine of free will, and some traditions have it that Ḥasan of Baṣra himself was with him in this. But where the split came was on the separate issue, how the Muslim fallen into grievous error is to be classified. Is he a Believer or is he not? In opposition to the Murjite view that the grievous sinner remains a Believer notwithstanding, and in opposition to the Khārijite view that he becomes *kāfir*, infidel, Ḥasan of Baṣra had stated his own view that such a person is a hypocrite, *munāfiq*.[3] Breaking with the master, Wāṣil and his companion held that the Muslim in a condition of grievous sin ceases to be a Believer but does not become an Unbeliever: he occupies an intermediate position expressed by the Arabic formula *manzila bayna 'l-manzilatayn*.

The dispute was on the face of it purely scholastic but in fact it impinged on politics, for the Mu'tazilites made use of this position of theirs to argue that whenever it was not clear who had right on his side in any conflict between Muslims — and the conflict in mind was that of the fourth Caliph 'Alī first with 'Ā'isha, Ṭalḥa and Zubayr and then with the Umayyads — the part of the Believer was to take a neutral stand.

This example illustrates how important it is for the historian of our day to acquaint himself with the religious attitudes of the Middle Ages, however tedious and obsolete they now seem, since they had in those times an actual bearing on the life of the community.

The disagreements of Wāṣil and 'Amr with Ḥasan of Baṣra, as with the body of orthodox opinion, were not too serious to begin with. But they hardened as the Mu'tazilites gradually fashioned their system into one of unabashed rationalism. Certain orthodox divines, like the so-called Aṣḥābu 'r-Ra'y, had already toyed with the argument from reason in questions of law, but the Mu'tazilites were the first theological school in Islam to employ the rationalistic and logical approach in religious questions and even to succumb to the influence of ancient Greek philosophy in their thinking.

The second half of the eighth and the entire ninth century (when Manṣūr and his successors were Caliphs) were marked by an energetic programme of translation. Works on the exact sciences (cosmography, mathematics, medicine, etc.), logic and philosophy[4] were rendered from the Greek — usually not direct but first into Syriac and then into Arabic; Syrian Christians playing a leading part in the operation. It was then, too, that the 'newest', or 'modern' method, as men called it, came into vogue in the educated feudal society of Arabic speech. This was the resort to the postulates of Greek logic and philosophy, as also to a philosophical terminology, and the first people to apply the method to theology were the Mu'tazilites. Among those who thus brought the Mu'tazilite doctrine to a pitch of perfection was the erudite encyclopaedist Jāḥiẓ (d. 869 at the age of ninety).

The Mu'tazilite heresy, then, was a theological school looking for guidance from speculative philosophy (it even interested itself in atomistic theory and pronounced that space and time are concourses of atoms). Rationalistic, it rejected mysticism, repudiating all possibility of knowing the deity through intuition and feeling, all prospect of the direct communion of man with God. It discarded the blind, literal acceptance of the Traditions of the Prophet (the Ḥadīth) on which the Ḥanbalites, Ẓāhirites and others insisted; and although it proclaimed the Koran to be the fountain-head of religious truth, it allowed a free allegorical interpretation of the Book in a search for the inner meaning. On this account the Mu'tazilites together with the other scholastic theologians in Islam were often termed Bāṭinites (*al-bāṭiniyya*, from *bāṭin* 'inner' as opposed to the literalist Ẓāhirites, *aẓ-ẓāhiriyya*, from ẓāhir 'outer').

In spite of all this it would be quite wrong to see in the Mu'tazilites a variety of free-thinkers pretending to some new, coldly scientific *Weltanschauung.* They did not pit reason against faith, science against religion: to the last they stood on religious ground, and it never occurred to them to desert the position of theism, i.e. the postulate of God as first cause and centre of the universe. If they used the methods, arguments, and terminology of Aristotelian logic and philosophy, they did so in order to fortify the real bastions of Islam as they understood these. Their rationalism remained within bounds; their logic and philosophy were the handmaids, no more, of their theology.

The appearance of this fully fashioned system of speculative theology in the ninth century was in itself a sign that Islam had moved into the stage of a feudal religion. For such a system there was no place in the original slave-owning Islamic community. The religions of slave-owning societies either lack dogmatics altogether and are content with myths and rites — witness the religions of Ancient Greece and Rome; or else they have their dogmatics in a primary, embryonic form — witness Zoroastrianism in the first centuries of our era, early Christianity till the third century, and early Islam of the seventh century. The developed system usually occurs as soon as feudalism is reached — one thinks immediately of the scholastic theology which emerged in Christianity in the Middle Ages. In the Christian context and in Islam alike, there was this strikingly similar effort to harmonize religion with philosophy; and the explanation of the resemblance in their theology is not so much the shared roots of the two faiths, nor their interaction, as the common character they now bore as religions of feudal societies.

The cardinal positions of the system, or 'roots' (*aṣl*) in the idiom of the Mu'tazilites themselves, must now be looked at more closely. They were five:

1 *Aṣlu 't-tawḥīd* The Root of the Avowal of Unity, i.e. the doctrine of God. Under this heading were combined two theses: the rejection of anthropomorphism and the assertion of the created Koran.

The Mu'tazilites strenuously opposed the representation of God in human image. Anthropomorphism, known as *tashbīh* in Islamic literature (from the verb *shabiha* 'to be like'), was characteristic of early Islam, as generally of the religions of slave-owning societies. The Koran speaks of God as being seated on a throne,[5] of his having face,[6] eyes,[7] hands,[8] etc. These expressions supplied grounds for representing Allah in the form of a human being, and some orthodox Madhhabs, e.g. the Ḥanbalites and Ẓāhirites, before and after the ninth century, insisted on the literal understanding of such passages; while others, e.g. the Mālikites, taught a blind acceptance of the passages without pausing to explain what the words meant. The Mu'tazilites for their part held that the expressions must be taken as mere metaphor.

To Mu'tazilite thinking the concept of God as a spiritual essence precluded the attribution to him of human characteristics. To ascribe to God such human qualities as strength, the propensity to anger and vengeance, omnipotence, omniscience, etc., was just as naïve, they said, as to picture him sitting on a throne in human shape. Moreover, thus to conceive of the attributes as realities on their own would mean entertaining them as separate hypostases and lead straight to polytheism. So they either denied the possibility of speaking of the attributes of the Deity at all, or else (as in the case for instance of al-'Allāf and al-Jubbā'ī) allowing the possibility of attributes, asserted that these were identical with God's essence and inseparable from it.

In short the Mu'tazilites conceived God as a pure Unity indefinable in human terms, without resemblance to his creatures, men, and unknowable by them either through seeing[9], or through reasoning, or through intuitive feeling. Unity, spirituality, indefinability, unknowability — these were the ingredients in their doctrine of the Deity.

The Mu'tazilites rejected the traditional doctrine of an eternal and uncreated Koran, reasoning that if it were not created by God but existed eternally side by side with him then the same categories of eternity and uncreatedness would belong to it as to him. This would involve the recognition of the Koran as a second divinity; would, in other words, amount to that polytheism which all Muslims dreaded. The One God, they said, is alone eternal and uncreated; and since it is impossible to admit a parallel to him, it follows logically that the Koran is not eternal, but is created by that same unique divinity. And they proceeded to call the orthodox Muslims dualists.

In this thesis of a created Koran something very important to their rationalism was latent: because the Koran is only one among Allah's creations, it could now be argued, there is neither possibility nor need to take every single passage in it literally and without discussion. Of course the Mu'tazilites acknowledged it to be Holy Writ inasmuch as it had been produced by God, but they claimed that the holiness only pertained to the overall contents, the principles and ideas, and by no means applied to each expression, each letter. These expressions could be every bit as contingent and down to the human plane as the hide, ink, and so forth, with the assistance of which the Koran had been reduced to writing. Thus the Mu'tazilites, telling themselves that they were not doing violence to any of its fundamental messages, felt free to interpret individual sentences allegorically in an endeavour to lay bare the hidden sense of Scripture.

2 *Aṣlu 'l-'adl*, 'The Root of Justice'. The Mu'tazilite doctrine of free will was ultimately derived from the universal Muslim account of divine justice, but more immediately it was a better reasoned, better balanced version of Qadarite teaching. Since God is just, argued the Mu'tazilites, he can only perform what is just, reasonable and expedient; he cannot be a source of evil and injustice, cannot be author of the wicked and senseless acts to which men are prone. It is impossible to allow that God, having withheld free will from man and having preordained him to his whole range of behaviour, should thereafter punish him for his sins. The fountain of evil is not God but the free will accorded by God to his creatures, beginning with the Angels and the Devil. In the Judaic, Christian and Muslim tradition alike the Devil was originally one of the Angels who betrayed God and became his enemy, and did so precisely in the exercise of this freedom of will; and similarly men perform their actions, good and bad, in the enjoyment of the free will implanted in them by God. On this reasoning, said the Mu'tazilites, paradise and hell are the just compensation for the life men have led. If men did not possess the choice between good and evil and, consequently, were not answerable for their conduct, then paradise and hell would be extreme injustice. Needless to say, of course, the Mu'tazilites did not understand the bliss of paradise and the torment of hell in the literal and material sense in which the followers of the original Islam conceived them.

Not surprisingly the Mu'tazilites earned the labels of those in whose tracks they walked. Ascribing to man *qadar* or full control over his actions they, too, in the polemic of the orthodox Muslims were no better than Qadarites and polytheists — people who thought of man as creating his destiny and allowed not one creator but many.

3 *Aṣlu 'l-wa'd wa 'l-wa'īd*, 'The Root of Admonition and Commination'. This was the applied ethic which classed sin as minor and major, and taught that God through the medium of the Koran admonishes in the case of the venial sin but promises condign punishment for grievous sin. A particular article of Mu'tazilite faith under this heading was that the likening of God to his creation, *tashbīh Allāh ilā khalqihi*, was among the mortal sins.

4 *Aṣlu 'l-manzila bayna 'l-manzilatayn*, 'The Root of the Intermediate Stage'. The meaning of this thesis has been explained above.[10]

5 *Aṣlu 'l-amr wa 'n-nahy*, 'The Root of Command and Prohibition'. This Koranic expression meant the obligation of the leaders of the community or — what was the same thing — the state, to indicate with precision which acts are compulsory and which are forbidden. In practice it sanctioned the unrestricted spiritual and secular authority of the Imam (in the sense of the head of the community and state) within, of course, the limits of Islamic law. The Mu'tazilite interpretation of the ruling was this: the Imam-Caliph has the right, and is moreover under obligation, to assert the Faith not only by speech and pen but by the sword; in other words, to assert it not merely by preaching and written edict but by the persecution of all heretics. It goes without saying that the state profession of Faith binding on all the Muslims, which the Mu'tazilites here contemplated, was their own creed. For all their rationalism they had no sympathy with religious free-thinking.

We must now dwell on the historical fortunes of the Mu'tazilites. They were one of the factions that supported the 'Abbāsids at the time of their movement against the Umayyads in the second quarter of the eighth century, and in the sequel the early 'Abbāsid Caliphs while they did not embrace their creed did not persecute it. The Mu'tazilites were free to propagate their teaching and deliver lectures, and they founded academies first in Baṣra and then in Kūfa, Baghdad, Shirāz, Nīshāpūr, Damascus, Fusṭāṭ (Egypt) and in the cities of Arab Spain. Among these the Baṣra school (adorned by Abū 'Hudhayl

Muḥammad al-'Allāf, d.*c.* 841, an-Naẓẓām, d.*c.* 845, and his pupil the polymath Jāḥiẓ, d. 869), and the Baghdad school (Ja'far b. Mubāshir, d. 848, and Ja'far al-Ḥarb d. 850) achieved particular renown, and became the rallying points of the most cultivated in the feudal society of the Caliphate.

Moreover, the Caliphate's initiative in translating Greek works through the Syriac and thus spreading a knowledge of ancient philosophy, suited the Mu'tazilite book admirably, for new questions were now being put for which the traditionalist theologians were unprepared. The Mu'tazilites came out with the answers and caused a literary boom in philosophy and the exact sciences, as well as in theology and law.

Under the seventh 'Abbāsid Caliph Ma'mūn (813–833), the Mu'tazilite doctrine became the state religion. The Caliph was driven by political necessity. He had shocked the orthodox and the Arab population generally by conspiring with the Persian nobility to do away with his brother Amīn in order to win the throne for himself. He had even been on the verge of leaning on the moderate Shī'ites for support,[11] but this had been too much for the Sunnīs, and armed resistance resulted in Baghdad and elsewhere. Ma'mūn had been compelled to alter course abruptly, break his pact with the Shī'ites and come back to Baghdad.[12]

In this situation the expediency of a compulsory state religion was brought home to him. Political opponents of the realm were apt to make religion their cover; popular movements — and these had been incessant since the latter half of the preceding century — operated under the Khārijite or Shī'ite or Khurramite banner as the case might be. The way to deal with these,[13] as indeed with indiscipline among the feudal barons, was, the Caliph thought, to introduce a single creed binding upon all the Muslims.

An aim of this kind was something quite new in Islam. In the first two centuries of its existence it had been a motley gathering of persuasions, schools, and juristic sects. Not to speak of the downright heresies, like Shī'ism and Khārijism which had broken away from orthodox Islam, there were the various Madhhabs into which the people of the Sunna had themselves been divided: Ḥanbalites, Mālikites, Ḥanafites, Shāfi'ites — all had their differences. There were no synods as in Christianity competent to take binding decisions, and it was difficult for the faithful to know what was orthodox and what was heretical. There was no coherent system of dogmas prescribed by the state.

Now it was precisely the principle of such a compulsory official denomination that the Mu'tazilites had enunciated. It was, as we saw, a sign of the times. Slave-owning societies are not characterized by exclusiveness in religion but tolerate the co-existence of rival cults. It had been so in Christian lands, and it had been so in the Muslim empire. It is feudalism that brings in the obligatory official creed.

From Ma'mūn's standpoint Mu'tazilite doctrine had still other things to recommend it. It was in harmony with the spirit of philosophical inquiry that had gained much ground in the Caliphate, and it answered the cultural requirements of the educated elite in feudal and urban society which was dissatisfied with the narrow-mindedness of divines engrossed in compiling the Traditions and in bickering about the minutiae of the Sharī'a. More than all, there was the political relevance of its teaching on free will and personal responsibility at a moment when public unrest had come close to disturbing the stability of the empire. It would not be open to agitators to plead that their risings were predestined and independent of their own volition.

Ma'mūn proceeded by stages. He began by according recognition and protection to the doctrine, and then proposed to his people the acceptance of, if not the entire system, at least the *aṣlu 't-tawḥīd* which, as explained already, was crucial. The corresponding decree was issued in 212 AH (= 827). It was left to a second decree promulgated in 218 AH (= 833) to make all Qāḍīs, theologians and jurists liable to inquisition: whoever declined to accept the Mu'tazilite dogmas was to face exile. A special authority was set up called *miḥna*, a sort of inquisitional court,[14] and we know that the eminent jurist Imām Aḥmad b. Ḥanbal, founder of the Ḥanbalite Madhhab, was summoned before this body and sentenced to banishment to the frontier province of Cilicia accompanied by all who shared his views.

Throughout the reigns of Ma'mūn's successors Mu'taṣim (833–842) and Wāthiq (842–847), the Mu'tazilite doctrine continued to enjoy the patronage of the state. A censorship had by now been applied to all the utterances of the theological opposition, and those divines or officials who clung to the dogma of the uncreated Koran were dismissed and punished. In 834 Imām Aḥmad b. Ḥanbal was once more summoned, and this time sentenced to flogging. There was no respite. In 845 when an exchange of prisoners between the Caliphate and Byzantium was arranged, the Caliph's officers cross-questioned the returning Muslims. Those who concurred that the Koran was created and that God is invisible even in the hereafter, were allowed in; but those denying these Mu'tazilite dogmas were herded back into Byzantine territory.[15]

However, this policy of coercion had limited results. The new creed was only adopted at the apex of society; at the popular levels the Muslims remained fiercely resentful of the Mu'tazilite rationalistic interpretation of the familiar tenets, and the old-fashioned divines were as recalcitrant as ever.

The next Caliph Mutawakkil (847–861) was a calculating man who saw these things. Since his own particular enemies were the Shī'ites, it was tempting to him to swing back to the old orthodoxy. He began (850) by prohibiting discussion of Koranic texts, and the following year declared the doctrine of a created Koran as heresy. The Chief Qāḍī, Aḥmad b. Abī Du'ād, was dismissed and traditional Sunnism re-installed.

The principle of persecution which the Mu'tazilites had laid down was retained, only now the Mu'tazilites were among its victims. Even more were the Khārijites and the Zindīqs (this term connoting Khurramites, Manicheans and atheists) the target of attack. The whole rationalistic school suffered. Even the Christians and Jews whom Islamic law had always tolerated were put under heavy constraint, being excluded from the civil service, forbidden to ride on horseback, made to wear distinctive dress and place images of devils on their houses. Official Islam had become intolerant.

But the real vengeance Mutawakkil reserved for the heretics who were also his political foes, namely the Shī'ites, and he even went to the length of destroying the mausoleum of Ḥusayn, their third Imam, at Kerbela.

By comparison with the other 'heretics', the Mu'tazilites consisted of quite small closed groups of upper-class people remote from the masses, and persecution in their case was neither thorough nor sustained. Sporadic drives against them were undertaken, for instance in Iran, during the reign of Sultan Maḥmūd of Ghazna (998–1030) and that of the first Seljūq Ṭughril Beg (1038–63), but afterwards they petered out.

Consequently the Mu'tazilite schools in Baṣra and Baghdad not only continued to flourish in the tenth century but actually spread their teaching eastwards to Iran and Central Asia, so that presently there were schools in Ray, Kirmisin, Iṣfahān, Nīshāpūr, Gurgān, Nasaf and Khwārazm. Prominent among the professors were al-Jubbā'ī (d. 916), principal of the Baṣra school; his son and successor Abū Ḥamīd 'Abdu's-Salām (d.933) who much elaborated the doctrine; the distinguished theologian 'Abdu 'l-Jabbār, also of the Baṣra school, who migrated to Ray in 971 to found the school there; and, last in the line, the great Zamakhsharī of Khwārazm.[16] In the eleventh and twelfth centuries the Iran schools still carried on, but in the next century suffered sadly in the general devastation of the Mongol invasion. Even then the *coup de grâce* seems to have been postponed, for Ḥamdullah Mustawfi Qazwīnī's Geography of Iran can still speak about Mu'tazilites in Hamadān around 1340.[17]

But if the doctrine as such vanished, the ideas behind it lived on. For example, even Sunnī divines were later to repudiate anthropomorphism on occasion, if not always with sincerity.[18] Its basic assumptions, viz. the denial of the human attributes of God; the created Koran; indeterminism — these were very soon assimilated by the Shī'ite theologians (especially of the Zaydi denomination) and through their agency took root in Iran. How widely these ideas were current there among the educated can be proved by some lines from the great Persian poet Firdawsi, author of the celebrated *Shāhnāma*, an indubitable Shī'ite:

> Above Name or Symbol, beyond Thought,
> He is the Creator of the sublime Essence.
> With thine eyes thou shalt not behold Him;
> So why tire them with looking?[19]

IX
A scholastic theology (Kalām)
The veneration of saints

We have seen how the Mu'tazilites were denounced in Mutawakkil's reign, and the traditional Sunnī orthodoxy re-instated as the official creed (851). However, the Mu'tazilites were still a power which the old-fashioned Sunnīs would have to reckon with. Their chief asset had been their rationalism. They had taken their weapon from the arsenal of philosophy, whereas the Sunnīs as yet lacked any proper system of dogmatics. The Sunnī doctors were as engrossed as ever in the Koran and the Tradition, and in the ninth and tenth centuries these were no longer sufficient to satisfy the intellectual curiosity of the educated. Persecution was not the answer. The crying need was for some new 'orthodox' system of dogmatics capable of fighting the Mu'tazilites and their philosopher friends on an ideological front.

It happened that a new orthodoxy of this kind had been preconditioned by the growth of feudalism in the empire. Around the late ninth or early tenth century, the countries of the Caliphate, Iran among them, entered the phase of advanced feudal societies characterized by: the expansion of private (both conditional and unconditional) ownership of land at the expanse of state ownership; the transformation of the immense majority of peasants into feudal dependants; and the shaping of the feudal type of town with its specific structure and culture. Such societies are peculiarly prone to scholasticism in their thinking; that is, to a philosophy based on purely speculative and logical arguments in justification of prevailing religious doctrine.

The term *kalām* (lit. 'word', then techn. term, 'system of dogmatics', from *kalama* in one of its meanings, 'to speak': cf. Gk. *logos* 'word', then 'thought', 'teaching') was applied to this new orthodox scholastic theology. Previously this term had connoted both the science of canon law and the rudimentary theology of the day, there being, as has been said, no clear demarcation between law and theology, between jurist and theologian. But now the term Fiqh began to be reserved for canon law, while Kalām signified scholastic theology; the Faqīh henceforward was the jurist, while the specialist in dogmatics began to be called *mutakallim* (lit. 'speaking'; techn. term 'theologian'). A line was drawn between theology and law — even if it was never to be a very clearly defined line.

Kalām was founded by al-Ash'arī and al-Māturīdī in the tenth century, though these two theologians were doubtless not without their precursors.

Abu 'l-Ḥasan 'Alī b. Ismā'īl al-Ash'arī (b. Baṣra 873 or 874; d. Baghdad 935 or 941)[1] was to begin with a Mu'tazilite, a pupil of al-Jubbā'ī, his stepfather (d. 915), but after intensive study of the Ḥadīth came to the conclusion that the Mu'tazilite system was incompatible with Islam. So having broken with it, he joined the Shāfi'ite school and became its disciple on questions of law. But the theology he constructed was his own, and known as the Ash'arite system.

He defended Sunnī orthodoxy by reasoned argument, and not exclusively with citations from the Koran and the Tradition as the previous doctors had done. From a position of orthodoxy he attacked the Mu'tazilites with their own weapon, borrowing his arguments from logic and philosophy. One must not, of course, exaggerate the place these arguments occupy, for his system is certainly no would-be reconciliation of Mu'tazilite thinking with the old piety. It was an attempt to adapt Mu'tazilite method to the cause; and the cause was the vindication of orthodox positions. *Au fond* his system is profoundly conservative and admits no compromise with Mu'tazilite views. He consciously strove to keep as close as possible to the findings of the old theologians, and it was no accident that he was so ready to cite the most conservative of their number, namely Ibn Ḥanbal, elucidating and corroborating what the latter had said by the arguments of reason and logic. 'The dogmatic constructions of Ash'arī', Bartol'd says, 'are not indicative either of profundity of thought or of deep philosophical knowledge'.[2]

Ash'arī is supposed to have been a most prolific author. The twelfth-century historian Ibn 'Asākir gives a list of ninety-nine works, and others even speak of three hundred. But only a few are extant, and Brockelmann mentions no more than six.[3]

In his apology of the dogma of an eternal, uncreated Koran, Ash'arī calls in logic to argue that the Creator is eternal along with his Word, and his Word is the Koran. He endeavoured to reconcile predestination and the doctrine of man's responsibility for his actions in the hereafter by choosing the middle ground between those who were for unqualified determinism (*jabariyya*) and those who were for free will (*qadariyya*).[4] He distinguishes the concepts *qaḍā'* (lit. 'decision', 'sentence', from *qaḍā* 'to decide') and *qadar*: the former is God's will, his omniscience and his everlasting relationship with things, whereas the latter signifies the origin of things in response to God's will. *Qaḍā'* is God's eternal, universal decision about the world; and *qadar* is the particular application of this decision in the realm of time, an individual act with respect to man. God created man together with his future actions and the capacity to perform them, said Ash'arī, and the creation was an act of will on God's part. But it is the nature of man with his individual consciousness to appropriate to himself the things and actions connected with him; and thanks to this appropriation, *iktisāb* (from *kasaba*, in one of its meanings 'to acquire') man considers his deeds and the will to do them to be his own, although in reality these deeds are to be explained as a particular act of the creative will of God, individual in the case of each separate person. Thus does man appropriate to himself what God has willed, and the appropriation prompts him to imagine that he possesses a free will and a free choice. And hence the notion that man determines his choice of action.

The construction Ash'arī puts on the matter may be logically brilliant enough, but it is quite unconvincing philosophically. It does not eliminate the Jabarite view that man is just an automaton, the passive instrument of Allah's will; nor does it begin to explain how man, possessing a merely imaginary free will and being in point of fact a machine, can be held responsible for his actions and rewarded for them in paradise or hell. On Ash'arī's argument, requital in the next life for action in this has no moral justification, seeing that the absolute authority of God's will is taken for granted in every human action. Logically the difference between good and evil now vanishes altogether. Ash'arī had not really advanced from the position of Ibn Ḥanbal and the other orthodox teachers.

Ash'arī rejected both the anthropomorphism of the conservative thinkers and the Mu'tazilite opinion that it is impossible to ascribe attributes (*ṣifāt*) to God. But in each case his denial savoured of formal logic and was hardly of substance. He maintained that the idea of God's hands, face, etc., only amounts to anthropomorphism if these are consciously likened to human hands, a human face, etc. But if one believes in the face or hands of God and of his sitting on his throne, and so on, without trying to explain these Koranic expressions to oneself, to believe *bilā kayf*, 'without asking "How?"', i.e. 'putting no questions and demanding no explanations', then this belief will be orthodox truth, remote equally from anthropomorphism, or *tashbīh*, and from the Mu'tazilite denial of the existence of God's attributes, or *ta'ṭīl* (from *'aṭala* in one of its meanings 'to be deprived').

The Ash'arities took *tashbīh* (as understood by their master) and *ta'ṭīl* to be equally grave heresies. The former, it was thought, leads to paganism, since the likening to man is of the essence of the pagan representation of the deity; while the latter renders the idea of God so colourless and abstract that, if pushed, it leads logically to atheism. So they were soon calling the anthropomorphists (*mushabbiha*) idolaters, and the deniers of the attributes of God (*mu'aṭṭila*) atheists. It should be noted in parenthesis that the *mushabbiha* and *mu'aṭṭila* were not sects; partisans of *tashbīh* and *ta'ṭīl* could be encountered in the different schools and sects; and the very meaning of the two ideas was long disputed not simply as between schools but within a single Madhhab. Settling, then, their own meaning of *tashbīh*, the Ash'arites fell to exonerating Ibn Ḥanbal from charges of anthropomorphism, and even cast him in the role of authority for the refutation of the teaching of the *mushabbiha* and the *mu'aṭṭila*. By no means all subsequent theologians concurred with them on this point. The eleventh-century Ẓāhirite Ibn Ḥazm, a literalist and conservative like Ibn Ḥanbal, reproached the latter for coming so near to those who thought that God had a body. And the tenth-century author of the well-known encyclopedia *Mafātiḥu 'l-'ulūm* (Keys of the Sciences), Abū 'Abdallāh Muḥammad al-Kātib al-Khwārazmī, bluntly labelled the Ash'arites themselves *mushabbiha*.[5] There were other items, however, where the Ash'arite Kalām found favour with the later divines. This, for instance, was the case with the dogma that Muslims who have fallen into grievous sin nevertheless remain Believers, that condemnation to the pains of hell will be only temporary for Muslims, and that the intercession of the prophets can liberate the souls of sinners from Gehenna.

The disciples in Ash'arī's circle elaborated his system. The best known among them were al-Bāqillānī (d. 1013), Isfarā'inī, 'Abdu 'l-Malik al-Juwaynī (who had the title Imāmu 'l-Ḥaramayn, 'Imam of the Two Holy Cities'), al-Qushayrī, and al-Ghazālī; the last three being men of Khurāsān, mystics, and living in the eleventh century.

The Shāfi'ite school was the first to adopt the Ash'arite system and since this Madhhab was particularly in vogue in Iran, it was able to consolidate its position there before the tenth century was out. Elsewhere the system was apt to be disputed before acceptance, notwithstanding its conservative character, and spread less fast, and less easily. The Ḥanbalites, in spite of the honour in which Ash'arī had held their founder-teacher, became open enemies; and under the first Seljūq Sultan Ṭughril Beg, conqueror of Iran (1038–63), the

Ash'arites were declared heretics, and persecuted. Under his successor Alp Arslan (1063–72), the vizier, the famous Niẓāmu' 'l-Mulk who was himself a Shāfi'ite, convinced the Sultan of the orthodoxy of the Ash'arites, and so managed to put a stop to the persecutions. In course of time, the Ash'arite Kalām won recognition in all the Sunnī countries,[6] and became firmly entrenched in Iran.

Simultaneously with Ash'arī, but independently, the Ḥanafite theologian Abū Manṣūr Muḥammad b. Maḥmūd al-Māturīdī, surnamed Mutakallim as-Samarqandī, was working out his own system. Next to nothing is reported of his life except that he was born in the village of Māturīd near Samarqand,[7] and died in that city in 944. Of his writings, his *Kitāb ta'wīlāt al-Qu'rān* (Book of Interpretations of the Koran) is well known. His Kalām differed but little from that of Ash'arī, so that Brockelmann can record that 'the divergences of view between him and al-Ash'arī are immaterial, and in no sense are they of principle like those which separate Ḥanafite from Shāfi'ite law'.[8] The Sunnī theologians enumerate thirteen items of deviation between the two founders of Kalām: six of content and seven of form.[9] On predestination and free will Māturīdī, unlike Ash'arī, was committed to the teaching of his master Abū Ḥanīfa, and held that bad actions are performed with God's assent (*irāda*) — otherwise they could not be performed at all — but not at his wish (*riḍwān*). God created man with freedom of will or, what is the same, freedom of choice (*ikhtiyār*) so that man can do things at his discretion and be rewarded or punished for them after death. In good actions God helps him, but in bad actions abandons him, and only acquiesces in the commission of sin. There is thus justification for asserting the moral responsibility of man. But the contradiction is of course not cleared up between human freedom and the absolute creative omnipotence which is God's. On anthropomorphism and the attributes of God, the Māturīdites, while rejecting *tashbīh* and *ta'ṭīl* alike, preferred to express themselves *per negativum*: it is impossible to set boundaries to the idea of God, impossible to measure and count him (i.e. give a quantitative definition of his attributes); impossible to divide him (i.e. consider his attributes separately); impossible to piece him together from his parts (i.e. to conceive of him as the sum of his characteristics).

Māturīdī's system won as much favour with the Ḥanafites as did Ash'arī's system with the Shāfi'ites, and it therefore prospered; notably in East Iran (Khurāsān) and Central Asia where the Ḥanafite Madhhab was strong. But with the passage of time these two systems, which were so close to one another, were accepted indifferently wherever there were Sunnīs.

In their polemic with the Mu'tazilites the adherents of both used the weapon of their opponents, their method, their terminology and their arguments taken from logic and philosophy — without, however, alluding to the philosophers directly. As an historical phenomenon, Kalām in the Islamic countries was analogous to the scholastic theology in Catholic Europe; in both cases certain of the positions of Aristotle, suitably treated, were utilized in the defence of religion; in both cases philosophy was regarded as a handy instrument to shore up the orthodox theology. The schoolmen of the West coined the phrase 'Philosophia est ancilla theologiae' (Philosophy is the handmaiden of theology), and this exactly describes the relationship of philosophy to Kalām in the Muslim East. The exponents of Kalām were employing philosophy and logic to strengthen and vindicate the dogmas; there was never any question of revising these from philosophical positions, and Kalām was in this respect quite unlike the Mu'tazilite doctrine which had set out to criticize. The view of certain Western Islamists that Kalām was a reformation is therefore untenable. One could no more think of al-Ash'arī and al-Māturīdī as reformers of Islam than one could call Thomas Aquinas or Albert the Great reformers of Western Christianity.

The successor of al-Ash'arī, and the greatest figure in dogmatic theology, was al-Ghazālī (1058–1111). Abū Ḥamīd Muḥyi 'd-Dīn Muḥammad b. Muḥammad aṭ-Ṭūsī al-Ghazālī[10] (or al-Ghazzālī in an alternative spelling) was a Persian, born in Ṭūs, who studied in Nīshāpūr where he attended the lectures of Juwaynī, the Imāmu 'l-Ḥaramayn, who was both Ash'arite and Ṣūfī. In youth he frequented a Ṣufī circle; but this had little impact on him at the time, his main preoccupations being theology and law. His study of these made him critical and sceptical, though he was officially affiliated to the Shāfi'ite school to which his master belonged. On the latter's death in 1075 he set out for Baghdad, and entered the coterie of Niẓāmu 'l-Mulk (1018–92) the celebrated Persian vizier of the Seljūq Sultan Malik-Shāh, and author of the *Siyāsatnāma* (Book of Government). It was a society in which the leading divines and jurists moved, and in it Ghazālī quickly earned a reputation as a skilful controversialist who had shone in many a debate. The caravans leaving Baghdad for the other Muslim countries spread the report of this new luminary in Kalām.

In 1091 Ghazālī became a mudarris, or professor, at the Niẓāmiyya Madrasa, the famed university Niẓāmu 'l-Mulk had founded in Baghdad. Three hundred students listened to his lectures. Outwardly his career was brilliant, but he knew himself to be unhappy: he had turned into a confirmed sceptic, as he himself acknowledged later; and having lost his faith in Islam and in God, had found nothing to build upon in their place. He was at odds with himself. And the more he studied the systems of the philosophers, the more he doubted the very possibility of the knowledge of objective truth on the basis of philosophy. But he kept these opinions to himself, and continued to lecture on Shāfi'ite law, and to publish polemical treatises against the Ta'līmites (Qarāmiṭa),[11] Ismā'īlīs, Imāmī Shī'ites and other heretics. In other words he was a dissembler, masquerading as the defender of the Faith.

This inward conflict and moral disgust with his career did not cease to torture him. He has depicted his ideological gropings and the evolution of his *Weltanschauung* with notable psychological skill in his work *Munqidh mina 'ḍ-Ḍalāl*, or Deliverer from Error. Four years (1091–95) of search in the pages of the philosophers had brought him to agnosticism and scepticism. These had not satisfied him, but he had seen no way to overcome them, and had concluded that reason was in its nature powerless to acquaint the mind with truth. This pessimistic outcome drove him to prosecute the search along a different path — that of intuition. So he reverted to Ṣūfism from which he had turned aside in youth, but which now seemed to him a sheet anchor. Between the months of Rajab and Dhu 'l-Qa'da 488 AH (from July to November 1095 of our era) he lived, as he tells us, through a grave inner crisis: his earlier mystical mood, seemingly long ago abandoned but actually dormant in him, and especially the fear of the tortures of hell awaiting the Unbelievers which had been instilled in him in childhood, took possession of him with fresh strength. Ṣūfism gave him back his religious faith. He experienced a 'shattering of the personality' (Pers. *shikast-i nafs*) and felt he must 'break his life in pieces'.

He handed over his chair in the Niẓāmiyya Madrasa to his brother Majdu 'd-Dīn Aḥmad al-Ghazālī, gave up his honourable and lucrative status, and without the knowledge of his friends and relations slipped out of Baghdad dressed as a Dervish. He spent eleven years in his wanderings, seeking peace of mind and the solace of a new outlook on life through voluntary poverty, asceticism and contemplation. He visited Mecca, Damascus, Alexandria; for two years he lived as a hermit in the hills about Jerusalem; and in the solitude of this phase wrote his chief works. In 499 AH = 1106 AD Ghazālī returned to the world of affairs, took up teaching at Damascus and Baghdad, and accepted the invitation of the vizier Fakhru 'l-Mulk, the son of Niẓāmu 'l-Mulk, to lecture at the Niẓāmiyya college[12] in Nīshāpūr. But this resumption of academic life was brief. With a few of his pupils he retired to a Khānaqāh, or Dervish retreat, he had founded in his native city of Ṭus, and there he was to die in the month of Jumādī 'ul-ūlā 505 AH, or 1111 of our era.

He was thus a Muslim Abelard who became a Muslim Francis of Assisi.[13] His conversion from scepticism and agnosticism to religion and mysticism made a great impression on his contemporaries, but there were some, even in his lifetime, who voiced their doubts about its sincerity. They observed that if a man in his early years can conduct a polemic with the Ismā'īlīs and other heretics without believing in what he writes, the sincerity of his later writings will not be above suspicion. There were suggestions that his renunciation of the world and flight from Baghdad had been prompted by political motives. In 1095, before this flight, the Seljūq Sultan Barkiyāruq had overpowered and slain his uncle Tutush who was a rival for the throne; and before that, the 'Abbāsid Caliph Mustaẓhir (theoretically suzerain of all the Muslim rulers, but politically powerless and only a shadowy spiritual authority) had been supporting Tutush. So might not Ghazālī, who was prominent in the Caliph's entourage and high in his counsels, have apprehended the Sultan's vengeance? The fact that he returned to Baghdad immediately after Barkiyāruq's death in 498 AH = 1104/5 AD, pointed to that conclusion.

Ghazālī left a large literary legacy, most of it in Arabic. Brockelmann lists sixty-nine extant works of his on theology, ethics, Ṣufism, Fiqh, philosophy, and even poetry.[14] And much else was attributed to him. Towards the last years of his life he was recognized in Sunnī circles as a major theologian, and was honoured with the titles Muḥyi 'd-Dīn, 'Renewer[15] of the Faith', and Ḥujjatu 'l-Islām, 'Proof of Islam'. After he died his authority was further strengthened, and his fame as a Sunnī divine eclipsed that of all his predecessors. 'Could there have been a prophet after Muḥammad', said Jalālu 'd-Dīn Suyūṭī, the noted commentator on the Koran in the late fifteenth century, 'it would unquestionably have been al-Ghazālī'.

His principal work on theology and Ṣūfism, the *Iḥyā'u 'Ulūmi 'd-Dīn*, 'Revivification of the Religious Sciences', is an exposition of his whole system.[16] It is divided into two parts, each of them consisting of two 'quarters' (*rub'*), and each quarter contains ten books. Selections from this monumental survey have been translated into the European languages. In style, layout, literary method and logical argument it stands apart from the stereotyped compositions of previous divines and Mutakallims, is off 'the beaten track of the smug theologians' as Goldziher put it; but even so, it took time for it to win almost universal recognition as the supreme example of theological writing. To render it more generally accessible, the author made an abridgement in Persian — not often did he write in that language — under the title *Kīmiyā-yi Sa'ādat*, or 'The Philosopher's Stone of Happiness'.[17] Of his other works only a few can here be recalled: a work on systematic theology *Jawāhiru 'l-Qur'ān* (Jewels of the Koran); *Mishkātu 'l-Anwār* (Niche of the Lamps)[18] dealing with the different Madhhabs and the extent to which private opinions may be compatible with orthodoxy; *Al-maḍnūn bihi 'alā ghayr ahlihi* (On what it is not proper to disclose to the inexperienced); *Mīzānu 'l-'amal* (The Balance of Deeds), on good works;[19] *Mi'yāru 'l-'ilm* (Touchstone of Science) on logic and logical method; *Tahāfutu 'l-Falāsifa* (Mutual Refutation of the Philosophers,[20] being a polemic against the philosphical trends of the author's age; a sort of introduction to this work in the form of a treatise entitled *Maqāṣidu 'l Falāsifa* (Aims of the Philosophers) setting forth their doctrines on various questions;[21] and *Al-munqidh mina 'ḍ-Ḍalāl*,[22] the already mentioned autobiographical Apologia.

Ghazālī did not try to portray himself in his works as an innovator, but only as restoring an Islam wrongly understood or distorted by the theologians; and, like the Christian Fathers of the Church, he borrowed not a little from the very people whose systems he called in question. 'His teaching on God, the world and the human soul' observes T. de Boer,[23] 'exhibits many elements, alien to early Islam, that go back to pagan wisdom[24], partly through Christian and Jewish mediation and partly through the mediation of latter-day Muslims'. He understood how inopportune any attempt would be to build a religious *Weltanschauung*, suiting the educational level of his day, on the petty dogmatic subtleties of the theologians or the legal casuistry of the jurists. Yet though he had long concluded that he must not build on a foundation of philosophy, and had indeed made it one of his chief aims to resist the philosophical currents of his time, he saw no need to rid himself entirely of its influence. Particular philosophical ideas could be enlisted in defence of the positions he had chosen; philosophy could be the handmaiden of his theology. But holding that the arguments employed by earlier theologians had too often contributed to perplexity and doubt, he decided that his own faith and his own system could rest only on mysticism. Like the Ṣūfis he preferred a private, emotional faith, for it had become clear to him that a knowledge of God was possible through intuition, inner illumination, ecstasy. To him such inner experience alone was real.

Until the eleventh century, Ṣūfism was a trend on its own in Islam, outside the Madhhabs, and either frowned upon or ignored by the Faqīhs and Mutakallims. It was Ghazālī's achievement to reconcile a moderate Ṣūfism with orthodoxy, and to make it an integral part of Islamic thought — here completing what his teachers al-Qushayrī and the Imāmu 'l-Ḥaramayn, both of them Ṣūfis, had begun. But to Ghazālī as Ṣūfī we shall return in a later chapter;[25] here we are discussing him as philosopher and theologian.

We saw that one of his chief endeavours was to combat the philosophical tendencies of his day and age. He was the first of the Mutakallims to have made a thorough study of the subject. He divided the philosophers into Materialists (*dahriyya*),[26] Naturalists (*ṭabī'iyyūn* from *ṭabī'ī* 'natural'. Gk. synonym *phusikoi*) and Metaphysicians (*ilāhiyyūn*). By these last he intended Socrates, Plato, Aristotle, the Aristotelians and the Neo-Platonists. The Materialists are frequently mentioned, and always with detestation, by the ninth- to twelfth-century Muslim authors, but not much exact information is vouchsafed, possibly intentionally, about their doctrine. Only this much is known, that they rejected the idea of a divine Creator, denied that the soul subsisted independently of the body and was immortal, and held matter and the world to be eternal. They were numerous, but their outstanding names are not reported, and nothing is on record about their writings, which were no doubt consigned to the flames at different times. We may guess that all free thinkers of whatever complexion were termed *dahriyya* by their contemporaries.

The Naturalists were eclectics going back to Pythagorean doctrines fused with the elements of other systems,[27] who recognized God as the First Cause but held that his work terminated when he made the world. Everything since then is governed by natural laws, they said; man is a moving mechanism *sui generis*, whose thinking is part of his activity and ends with his death. They rejected the immortality of the soul and the life of the world to come. The famous tenth-century Ikhwānu 'ṣ-Ṣafā (lit. 'Brothers of Purity', or 'Brothers of Sincerity', sometimes translated 'True Friends' or 'True Brethren'), who had affinities with the Carmathians, were affiliated with them.[28]

The Metaphysicians were the Aristotelians of the day who were strongly tinged with a revised, rationalistic Neo-Platonism.[29] Their great names were: al-Kindī (ninth century), al-Fārābī (*c.* 870–950), Ibn Sīnā (980–1037)[30] and Ibn al-Haytham (965–1039).[31] Some of their attitudes were materialistic. Altogether theirs was the philosophy which Ghazālī regarded as the most dangerous rival to orthodox Islam, and at them he directed the full blast of his polemic; doing this, characteristically, without dismissing all that they wrote or withholding all his esteem.

Ghazālī took philosophy to include the exact sciences, of which he counted six: mathematics (with which went astronomy and cosmography), physics (together with medicine, chemistry, zoology and botany), logic, economics, metaphysics and ethics. Whilst rating them all highly he put mathematics, logic and physics above the rest since these were both necessary and indifferent towards theology; whereas metaphysics, in the sense of speculative philosophy, too often took up positions that were hostile to Islam and amounted to heresy.

Attacking the doctrine of the Aristotelians on the eternity of the world, he charged them with a contradiction: they saw the world as limited in space but eternal in time; whereas, logically, if time is without end, space is without limit. Space and time, Ghazālī maintained, are the correlations of our ideas which God creates in us; the infinity flows from God in whom causality and activity are united. The intellectualist philosophers (like the Neo-Platonists and the Aristotelians) explained causality as the acts whether of God, the soul, nature or chance, and they restricted God's activity to the single initial act of giving the world its beginning; whereas Ghazālī rested his entire construction of the relationship between God and the world upon the divine will. According to him, the operative power of God the Creator cannot be limited in space and time, but God himself can so limit his creature. Only God is infinite and eternal; the world is finite and not everlasting.

Ghazālī repudiates the Neo-Platonist doctrine of the emanation of the world (Lat. *emanatio*; Ar. synon. *ṣudūr*) from God which the Aristotelians of his age, including Ibn Sīnā, had adopted, and which the extreme Ṣūfīs also had assimilated in its rather different mystical aspect. According to this doctrine the world proceeded from God, but not as a result of his creative will; the emanation or outflowing of the world from the deity was an act of natural necessity because the primary source had come to its plenitude. The subsequent stages of emanation are: Universal Reason, the world of ideas (or of the ideal prototypes of all things), Universal Soul, the isolated souls of people, original matter, and the material world. Thus on the theory of emanation, God, the world, and man are only links in the general process of the universe's construction, connected by a natural historical law. It was a doctrine that, logically pursued, led to pantheism, i.e. to the position that God and the universe are identical (Gk. *pan* 'all', and *theos* 'God'). And pantheism could be apprehended and explained in either of its two aspects: there was the mystical aspect which appealed to the Neo-Platonists and extreme Ṣūfis, epitomized in the sentence: 'The whole world is the manifestation of a single divine force, the world is divine in its nature and lives in God'; and there was the rationalistic, essentially (if not always consciously) atheistic aspect. This appealed to the Aristotelians, who had 'rationalized' the Neo-Platonist doctrine of emanation, and is summarized in the sentence: 'God is the universe with all its spheres; consequently, God is nothing else than nature with her regularity of law; there is no God outside the world and nature'. Ghazālī rejects both aspects of pantheism and affirms that the world is the result not of emanation but of the conscious creative will of God, and that the action of his will is prolonged without interruption after the creation.

The doctrine of emanation implied the denial of God's foreknowledge and conscious premeditated action. But to Ghazālī will and knowledge are eternal attributes of the deity and are exhibited not only in a universal context, as Ibn Sīnā thought, but in particular phenomena. God's will and consciousness comprehend the general and the particular as well.

Allah is the God of Adam, Noah, Abraham, Moses, Jesus and Muḥammad; is a living personality, a pure spirit possessing consciousness and freedom of will and action. Ghazālī discards both the anthropomorphic representation of God (*tashbīh*), dear to naïve faith, and the Mu'tazilite conception of God as a nondescript unity lacking attributes (*ta'ṭīl*). He agrees that God possesses many attributes, but their multitude does not, he contends, damage the oneness of his being. The anthropomorphic attributes named in the Koran, like hands, eyes and so on, must be understood in another, a loftier and purely spiritual sense. Among God's attributes Ghazālī finds will, consciousness, omniscience, omnipotence, ubiquity transcending space, eternity, the good, and love. Thanks to his omnipresence God is nearer to his creatures than they can imagine, nearer than their own neck vein.[32] It was but a step from this last Koranic utterance to the Ṣūfi doctrine of the possibility of direct personal communion between man and God by means of inner illumination.

Closely connected with his teaching about God is his doctrine on the soul. Ghazālī maintains that the human soul differs in its essence from all the other creations, and from the sensual world. Taking as his point of departure the Koran[33] and a tradition that is common to Jews, Christians and Muslims, to the effect that God created man in his own image and likeness, Ghazālī argues it would be absurd to suppose that God has an outward appearance corresponding to that of a man, and therefore 'likeness' must here be understood in the sense of spiritual likeness. The human soul is a spiritual substance (*jawhar rūḥānī*) harbouring a reflection of the divine substance; it does not submit to measurement or localization, is neither in the body nor outside it; in other words, is non-spatial. It belongs to the spiritual world, not to the material world of sense. However, in contrast to the pure Neo-Platonists and extreme Ṣūfī pantheists Ghazālī holds that the nature of the human soul is not identical with the nature of the divine spirit; the nature of the soul is not divine but only godlike — it is like the divine spirit in essence and qualities and in its acts. For this reason the soul is capable of knowing itself and knowing God: 'He that knoweth his own soul shall know his Lord' says the Ḥadīth.

Just as the first manifestation of the deity in the world was, in Ghazālī's argument, not thought but will (the imperative 'Be' is the act of creation), the volitional act is also the primary act in the human soul, inasmuch as the latter is godlike. His conception of self-recognition could be expressed in the formula: 'I wish, therefore I am' — *volo, ergo sum.*[34] Consequently, if freedom of will is inherent in God, it is likewise inherent in the human soul — and man's free will becomes reconcilable with God's omnipotence. The human soul is a microcosm as against the macrocosm of the higher spiritual world; and just as God directs the world, so the human soul directs its body. This body belongs to the sensual world, and is a microcosm in comparison with the macrocosm of the sensual world and corresponds to the latter in all its parts. The souls of people are alone immortal, and not their bodies.

Ghazālī accepts in general terms the gnostic and idealistic notion of the Neo-Platonists and various other philosophers, and of the mystics, that there is a hierarchy of worlds; that over the material world of the senses there is set a spiritual world of ideas, that over this is the world of angels, and finally, towering over all, God. But in accepting a hierarchy, he has his own conception of the way the worlds composing it are correlated. He postulates three worlds: the lowest world of sensual things (*'ālamu 'l-mulk,* 'world of possession');[35] the middle world of the ideal prototypes of things (*'ālamu 'l-jabarūt,* 'world of power')[36] corresponding to the Neo-Platonists' world of ideas; and the highest world (*'ālamu 'l-malakūt,* 'World of the dominion of the Lord'). These worlds of Ghazālī do not correspond with the Islamic doctrine of the seven heavenly spheres. They are extra-spatial and the main difference between them is that the *'ālamu 'l-mulk* is in continual change and evolution, while the *'ālamu 'l-malakūt* exists in virtue of a timeless immutable decision (*qaḍā'*; *al-qudratu 'l-azaliyya*) and is therefore eternally conserved in one and the same state; and the *'ālamu 'l-jabarūt* occupies a middle position between these. The pure souls of men belong to the *'ālamu 'l-malakūt*; they have issued from it and will return to it after death: but in earthly life they may come into contact with this upper world in sleep, rapture, ecstasy — and such are the souls of the prophets, the saints and the mystics.

Now although the nature of the soul is in its essence godlike, the reflection of the deity is not equal in all souls, and there are three sorts of soul just as there is a hierarchy of three worlds. There are people in whom the influence of the sensual world prevails over their spiritual beginning. These people are incapable of consistent spiritual activity and must content themselves with the Koran and the Tradition and obedience to the authority of the Mujtahids: the doctrine that is binding on all will be the bread of their life, since they are not capable of grasping the inner sense of Holy Writ; for them philosophy is poison. Ghazālī asserts that the higher secrets of religion, the esoteric doctrine, should be withheld from the lower souls, and he develops this thesis in his tractate *Al-maḍnūn bihi 'alā ghayr ahlihi* of which we have spoken. Similarly, the study of Kalām is not a universal obligation (*farḍu 'l-'ayn*) of all Believers, but is only for those who have the requisite aptitude (it is, in other words, *farḍu 'l-kifāya*).[37] People of this kind are the inquiring souls striving to comprehend what is in-accessible to the crowd; they want to raise their faith to the grade of knowledge. The danger that lies in wait for them in their yearning is that they may easily slide into doubt, heresy or disbelief, particularly if they fall under the influence of philosophers. For this kind of person therefore, dogmatics and a polemic with philosophy from theological positions are most useful medicines. The higher souls are those who are competent to grasp the highest truth, divine reality, through inner enlightenment and ecstasy: to wit, the souls of the prophets, saints and mystics (*'ārifūn,* pl. of *'ārif* 'having knowledge' of God).

Ghazālī's grading of souls is based on their capacity for spiritual activity. But it is obvious that his opposition between the profane crowd which can only believe blindly and obey authority, and the people of superior spiritual performance no more than mirrors in a religious form the hierarchic structure of an advanced feudal society with its sharp contrast between obedient inferiors and ruling superiors.

Ghazālī tried consistently to adjust his system to the dogmatics of orthodox Islam. He accepted the uncreated, eternal Koran, and held that Koran, Torah (Pentateuch), Injīl (Gospel) and Zabūr (Psalms of David) were one and the same divine book, communicated by revelation to God's apostles, and existing eternally in his Essence.[38] He thought that the buried bodies of the dead would not rise but that, on the Day of Judgment, souls would be clothed in new bodies completely in keeping with people's inner make-up. Hell's torments would be spiritual as well as physical. In his own age, as he himself emphasized, fear of hell was almost universal. Eloquent Muslim preachers intimidated their audiences with their pictures of its horrors, and would provoke tears, swoons, nervous crises, sometimes insanity and even death. This terror, he found, had ceased to be salutary, for it led souls to despair, and it ought, he thought, to be combined with hope in divine mercy. Fear and hope are the two 'wings' of the spiritual life, or (in another metaphor) they are the bridle and the spur: the bridle restrains the steed and prevents it from turning aside from the direct path, and the spur impels the steed to make for the goal more quickly.

Ghazālī joined issue with the Bāṭinites (Ismā'īlīs) and Mu'tazilites, but his attitude was otherwise forbearing. He accorded equal recognition to all the Sunnī Madhhabs, and he tolerated the Moderate Shī'ites, and also the Christians[39] and Jews. He was in character here with most of the Ṣūfīs, and while conducting his polemic with the philosophers he did not omit, as we have seen, to speak of the Neo-Platonists and Aristotelians with respect, and to underline that they were only heretics and not non-believers, inasmuch as they recognized the existence of God.

Incontestably Ghazālī is a figure of capital importance in Muslim scholasticism. His distinguished service to theology was to furnish Kalām with logical method and put it in possession of philosophy's weapon and philosophy's terminology. Even greater was the service he rendered moderate Ṣūfism in reconciling it with theology, and proclaiming intuition and inner experience to be the sole means of getting to know absolute truth. It was Ghazālī who gave the Ṣūfīs their secure position in the Muslim community.

His book *Tahāfutu 'l-Falāsifa*, directed principally against al-Fārābī and Ibn Sīnā, produced a deep impression on his contemporaries and was greeted with delight by the Mutakallims and Ṣūfīs. It was designed to undermine the very foundations of the speculative philosophy of the

Aristotelians and Neo-Platonists, and demonstrated the impossibility of achieving a knowledge of objective truth by their methods. D. B. Macdonald remarks how in this book Ghazālī reaches the extremity of intellectual scepticism and, seven hundred years before Hume, destroys causality with the biting edge of his dialectic and proclaims that we cannot know the reality of cause and effect but only that one phenomenon follows on another.[40] The work called forth a rejoinder from the philosophers. The celebrated Western Arab, Ibn Rushd (1126–1199), known to mediaeval Europe under the name Averroes, shared the philosophic trend of Kindī, Fārābī and Ibn Sīnā, and wrote in answer to the *Tahāfut* his treatise *Tahāfutu 'l-Tahāfut* or 'Refutation of the Refutation'.

As has been said, the Ghazālī system of Kalām or, more accurately, the Ash'arite–Ghazālī system, gained general acceptance in the Sunnī countries reasonably quickly — and not simply in Iraq and Iran but in the Maghrib and Arab Spain. No more than a handful, and those not very influential, of the Ḥanbalite Madhhab, like Ibn Taymiyya (1263–1328), persisted in the naïve positions of early Islamic literalism and more or less frank anthropomorphism, lumping Ash'arī, Ghazālī and the Ṣūfis with the whole company of philosophers and accusing them of heresy.

The influence exerted by Ash'arī, Māturīdī and Ghazālī was enough to excite a fairly general condemnation of anthropomorphism (*tashbīh*), but there were still pockets of resistance. Apart from the Ḥanbalites there were the Karrāmites in Iran (*Karrāmiyya*, after the name of Abū 'Abdullāh Muḥammad b. Karrām). These could be classed as anthropomorphists to the extent that they ascribed a body (*jism*) to God, though the sectaries themselves rebutted the charge on the argument that 'body' in their usage meant 'substance' and that there was no question of its having members and shape. The sect flourished in Khurāsān in the tenth century but underwent persecution in the following century. However, on the evidence of Fakhru 'd-Dīn Rāzī it was still alive in the early thirteenth century. It did not vanish until after the Mongol conquest.[41]

Some of Ghazālī's works, notably his *Tahāfutu 'l-Falāsifa*, were translated into Hebrew, and from Hebrew into Latin.[42] Thus gaining admission to Christian Europe, they had their effect on the Catholic scholastics and mystics, like Raymond Lully and Meister Eckhart. This is accounted for partly by a certain community of approach — the paths along which religious ideology developed under feudalism being identical in West and East — but even more by the common ideological roots of Muslim and Christian scholasticism, viz. the teaching of Plato, the amalgam of Neo-Platonism and Aristotelianism, and a general tendency to make philosophy the 'handmaiden' of theology and mysticism. The *Tahāfut* pleased the Christian, as it had pleased the Muslim, theologians; whereas Ibn Rushd's rejoinder was condemned by the bishops of Paris and Canterbury and by Oxford University. And there is no doubt that Ghazālī's thought influenced such outstanding exponents of scholasticism in Western Europe as Thomas Aquinas.

One other aspect of Ghazālī's achievement deserves to be noticed — he destroyed the bond between theology and Fiqh. Macdonald observes that although he was among the greatest of jurisconsults he deprived Fiqh of the high standing it had enjoyed, castigated its casuistry and compelled people to think of it as something unconnected with religion.[43] Henceforward it was possible to adhere to a given Madhhab on questions of law, and yet express theological views quite alien to it. Thus 'Abdullāh Anṣārī and 'Abdu 'l-Qādir of Gīlān were accounted Ḥanbalites in matters of law, but were at the same time Ṣūfis; and Ḥanbalite objection to Ṣūfism was beside the point. Again, Ibnu 'l-'Arabī was held to be a Ẓāhirite or Literalist on legal questions and simultaneously an extreme Ṣūfī pantheist and advocate of the allegorical interpretation (*ta'wīl*) of the Koran.[44]

Ghazālī's writings have yet to receive the critical study they deserve.[45]

With effect from Ghazālī the shaping of Kalām can be regarded as basically complete. Of its other exponents who in one way or another kept up his work, his brother Aḥmad al Ghazālī (d. 1126) and the Māturīdites Abū Ḥafṣ 'Umar an-Nasafī (1068–1142) and Taftāzānī (d. 1391) may be named. The battle with the philosophers was carried on indefatigably by Ghazālī's well-known follower Fakhru 'd-Dīn Muḥammad Rāzī (1149–1209), a Persian from Ray, author of the Koranic commentary *Mafātiḥu 'l-Ghayb* (Keys of the Unseen), a compendium on speculative philosophy *Muḥaṣṣal afkāri 'l-Mutaqaddimīn wa 'l-Muta'akhkhirīn* (Synopsis of Views of Previous and Recent Writers') and an encyclopaedia *Jāmi'u 'l-'Ulūm* (Collection of Knowledge). Fakhru 'd-Dīn Rāzī, like Ghazālī, combined Kalām with Ṣūfism and challenged the philosophers from the positions Ghazālī had indicated. 'Abdu 'r-Raḥmān al-Ījī (d. 1355), author of *Al-mawāqif fī 'ilmi 'l-Kalām* (Basic Attitudes of the Science of Kalām), likewise accused philosophy of heresy. The theologians were by this time making the point that there is a true philosophy and a false: the former is Kalām in the system of Ghazālī and his successors, but the philosophy of the Aristotelians and Neo-Platonists is false philosophy. In the period of al-Ījī and al-Taftāzānī, says Macdonald, philosophy was finally dethroned and reduced to the status of a handmaid and protectress of theology.[46] Attacked and persecuted by the theologians, philosophy as an independent discipline wilted progressively between the twelfth and fourteenth centuries, and very nearly disappeared. Nor were the theologians and the feudal system at their back content with the exposure of the philosophers in books and addresses; even under the Seljūqs in eleventh-century Iran and Iraq, acts of persecution had started which were to continue and extend on occasion to the professors of the exact sciences. For all that Ghazālī himself had prized those sciences highly, the Faqīhs and Mutakallims of the twelfth and thirteenth centuries could be observed venting their fanatical fury on them. In 1214 the library of a Baghdad philosopher who had just died was set on fire by a mob, and a Muslim preacher with his own hand cast into the flames a book on astronomy by Ibn al-Haytham because he had discovered 'the ill-starred mark of accursed atheism' in its portrayal of the terrestrial globe.[47] Of course this battle of the Mutakallims and Faqīhs with the philosophers was very far from being the only cause of the ideological reaction and cultural lag noticeable in the Near and Middle East from the eleventh century onwards. A variety of factors contributed. There were the devastating invasions and dominion of the Nomads — Turks in the eleventh/twelfth, Mongols in the thirteenth/fourteenth centuries; there were the Crusades which shifted the trade hegemony in the Mediterranean countries to the Europeans; there was the general economic decline of Iran and adjacent areas which was accentuated by Mongol domination; and finally there was the persecution undertaken by the state authority itself of heresies which were apt to be the ideological cover for popular and anti-feudal movements.

Among the signs that Islam, Sunnī and Shī'ite, had flowered into the religion of an advanced feudal society was the spread of saint-worship and the veneration of tombs. Early Islam had condemned a cult that was rooted in the pre-Islamic past of both Arabs and Persians. It had been perfectly prepared to admit the holiness of its remarkable men, but it forbade the worship of these saintly characters and their sepulchres. The Koran censures any appeal to angels, saints or pagan idols; to turn to anyone with a prayer for intercession before God is defined as *shirk*, 'the assignment of colleagues'. 'They worship besides God', says one passage, 'those that can neither harm them nor bring them benefit: they say, These are intercessors for us with God.'[48] Another passage reads: 'They to whom ye pray besides God created nothing but are themselves created; are dead, not living, and they know not when they shall be raised. Your God is the One God'.[49]

In the early stages of the Faith a person outstandingly pious and devout had enjoyed a certain deference, and was called *walī* (pl. *awliyā*, the near to God, from *waliya*, 'to be near'; whence also *ahlu 'l-wilāya*, 'holy people'). Then, step by step, as Islam evolved into the religion of a developed feudal society with its hierarchic structure, the superstitious belief in mediators between God and men, which had never been absent at the popular level, was legitimized. A doctrine on the hierarchy of saints resulted. The *walī* who had simply been a man of piety is turned into a saint who can mediate between men and God, is endowed with divine grace, is a thaumaturge.

Saint-worship will occupy us but briefly here, and the reader desirous of fuller information is referred to the works of that high authority Ignaz Goldziher.[50]

Initially, then, the cult flourished in Islam as a popular belief without the official sanction of the Mujtahids and Faqīhs. The holy who received veneration were of various grades. The first regular cult to develop was that of Muḥammad to whom miracles galore, omniscience and supernatural powers were attributed; then came the veneration of other prophets; then of certain relations of Muḥammad, especially 'Alī, Fāṭima, Ḥusayn, etc.; then of the Companions and their disciples the Tābi'ūn; then of the Imams who had given their names to the Madhhabs like Abū Ḥanīfa; then of respected theologians and martyrs generally. Nor did this exhaust the selection. There were even certain Christian saints in the assemblage whose worship had engrafted itself upon Islam, as for example St George (Jurjīs), the Seven Sleepers of Ephesus, and the Virgin Mary.[51] There were also various pre-Islamic local holy men, heroes who were often legendary, and even pagan deities attached to particular localities, who were promoted to the company of Muslim saints. The re-appraisal of ancient cults in the light of new beliefs came easily to Islam.[52]

The heroic story of the Arab Conquests invited the cult of martyrs who had fallen in Holy War, and the Shī'ites and Khārijites were peculiarly given to the veneration of such warrior saints. Then there were the patron saints of the crafts and callings; sometimes these would be one or other of the prophets, sometimes a local man of piety, sometimes a hero or other personage usually legendary. The historian Hammer-Purgstall, drawing his information from the Turkish traveller Evliyā Chelebī who was in West Iran in the seventeenth century, has compiled a list of patrons of crafts and guilds showing the regions where the worship of each was prevalent.

The Ṣūfī mystics and the Dervish brotherhoods associated with them[53] did much to further the veneration of the holy, and it is these Dervishes and spiritual mentors who actually compiled the largest contingent of Muslim saints. The gift of working miracles was ascribed to the saints at an early stage. The hagiographers enumerated twenty types of miracle including: *tatawwur* 'change', i.e. the faculty of assuming various forms and shapes, and of being transported in a trice to the most remote places; *iḥyā'ul-mawt* 'raising the dead'; rescuing wayfarers from danger; curing diseases, etc. Pious women were venerated too; but, as in Christianity, they were far fewer than the men.

The Faqīhs, for their part, to begin with withheld their official recognition of saint-worship and of that belief in invocations and miracles to which the mass of the Muslims had always been prone. Certain of them, like the rationalist Mu'tazilites even viewed miracles as sorcery (*siḥr*). But between the tenth and thirteenth centuries the Ash'arite and Māturīdite systems of Kalām increasingly accepted the legitimacy of saint-worship. The Imāmu 'l-Ḥaramayn, al-Ghazālī in his *Iḥyā'u 'Ulūmi' d-Dīn*, and Fakhru 'd-Dīn Rāzī in his Commentary on the Koran, strove to give the belief in saints and their marvels the sanction of orthodox dogmatics. The views propounded by the very architects of Kalām could not but win over the Mutakallims and Faqīhs, and presently only a handful of not very influential Ḥanbalites (those dyed in the wool conservatives who fought every innovation) led by Ibn Taymiyya, continued to fulminate against the worship of saints and pilgrimage to their tombs. They did so in vain, and in Iran particularly, were scarcely an influence to be reckoned with.

The legalization of saint-worship by the official theology was perfectly in keeping, as has been said, with Islam's character as the religion of a feudal world. The doctors naturally took pains to present this veneration in a way that did not outrage the Koran or the established creed. They began to produce Ḥadīth like the following: 'He that comes forth in enmity towards a *walī*, hath declared open war on Allah'.[54] They now taught that although the saints cannot work miracles on their own, Allah acts through them, for he may choose any instrument whatsoever to perform his wonders; and this need not be a human agent — it can be an inanimate object such as a tomb, a relic, or a spring. Prophets are above saints: prophets are conscious of their high degree and of the mission conferred on them by God, whereas saints are sometimes unaware of their status. Miracles wrought by God through the prophets are higher than ones performed through saints. The miracles of prophets are therefore termed *āya*, 'a sign' (pl. *āyāt*),[55] whilst the miracles of saints are *karamāt*, 'generosities' (sing. *karāma*, from *karuma* 'to be generous'; whence *ṣāḥibu' 'l-karamāt*, 'thaumaturge'). No longer did the doctors rate such wonders as sorcery achieved with the Devil's assistance; no longer was the worship of tombs and relics confounded with idolatry. Islam of course had no synods and no centralized authority like the Pope's, so that no canonization of saints could take place as in Christianity. Nevertheless there emerged a large number of recognized saints, whose worship might be universal or might be local.

The doctors, then, legalized saint-worship. But the Ṣūfīs had done most to inculcate it. It was they who invented the doctrine that apart from the dead saints who intercede with God for men, there is in constant existence a whole hierarchy of living saints, unfamiliar to the mass of Muslims, *rijālu 'l-ghayb*, 'undetected men', living in poverty and obscurity but yet possessing such spiritual power that the whole world is guarded from evil by their prayers.[56]

As in Christianity, saint-worship found expression in the veneration of tombs and relics, and journeys to these. The visiting of tombs was sanctified by the consensus (*ijmāʿ*) of the religious authorities, and regulations were prescribed governing the pilgrimages. The pilgrimage is termed *ziyāra* ('visit') and it was soon accepted that ziyāra to the sepulchres of certain particularly revered Imams, Shaykhs and other holy men — for example, to the tomb of the Imam 'Alī at Najaf, or of the Imam Husayn at Kerbelā — could rank with the Lesser Pilgrimage (*'umra*) to Mecca.[57] In Iran the favourite places of pilgrimage apart from the tombs of the Shī'ite Imams[58] are those of the Ṣūfī Shaykhs such as: Bāyazīd Bisṭāmi in the town of Bisṭām; of Aḥmad Jām at Turbat-i Shaykh Jām, and of Ḥaydar at Turbat-i Ḥaydarī (both these two being in Khurāsān); of Ṣafiyyu 'd-Dīn Ardabīlī, ancestor of the Ṣafawid dynasty, in Ardabīl; of Akhī Farrukh Zanjānī in Zanjān; and of Shah Niʿmatullāh Kirmānī in the little township of Māhān near Kirmān. Mausoleums, mosques and Dervish convents were commonly to be found hard by the tombs, and these gathered a healthy income from the pilgrims who arrived to pray for the intercession of the saints.

Ibn Baṭṭūṭa in the fourteenth century cites a typical case. In the town of Kāzarūn in Fārs was the monastery (*zāwiya*) of Shaykh Abū Isḥāq Ibrāhīm al-Kāzarūnī (*floruit* eleventh century).[59] Merchants conducting maritime trade with India and China usually prayed to this saint to save them from the terrifying storms of the Indian Ocean and the no less terrifying pirates. When setting out on a voyage they would make a vow to donate a sum of money to the monastery for which promissory notes would be drawn up. On the safe return of the vessel to harbour the votaries of the Zāwiya would go on board, produce the notes and receive the promised sum from each merchant. No ship arriving from India or China, says Ibn Baṭṭūṭa, failed to pay in an amount reckoned in thousands of dinars. Certain of the Dervishes and Murīds (novices) of the shaykh would solicit alms (*ṣadaqa*) for themselves. The suppliant was handed an assignment (*barāt*) worded: 'Let him that has taken upon himself a vow to Shaykh Abū Isḥāq, give on account of the sum of the vow so-much to so-and-so'. A silver seal bearing the Shaykh's monogram was smeared with red dye and the impression stamped on the document. Assignments would be for one thousand or one hundred dinars in silver, or for lesser sums. The possessor of the assignment duly appeared in front of the merchant who had made the vow, and obtained payment of the sum named in the document and wrote a receipt on the back.[60] On one occasion Muḥammad, Sultan of Hindustan (evidently Muḥammad Shāh b. Tughluq, 1325–51), paid ten thousand dinars in fulfilment of a vow. It is easy to imagine how prosperous the community of this Shaykh grew on votive offerings of the sort.

Coming now to relics (*āthār*, pl. of *athar*), it is clear that the collection of bits of hair, pieces of clothing, prayer mats (*sajjāda*), sandals, turbans, etc., allegedly left behind by Imams and Ṣūfī Shaykhs, or even by the Prophet himself — and the commerce in these things — go a very long way back in Islam. In the Shī'ite city of Qum in the ninth century thirty-thousand dirhems were offered for a portion of a garment of an 'Alid who was still living.[61] Many similar examples are quoted in Goldziher's pages.[62] Often the relics were patently false, and even many a tomb was demonstrably not authentic. Caliph 'Alī had two tombs. In the twelfth century a sepulchre 'came to light' for the first time in the neighbourhood of Balkh which had an inscription attesting that it was the tomb of the Lion of God, 'Alī, fourth Caliph and first Imam of the Shī'ites. It was then demolished by the Mongols and forgotten. But in 885 AH = 1480/81, the Tomb of 'Alī was rediscovered. The Tīmūrid Sultan Bayqarā with his Amirs and entourage arrived to do it reverence. As its authenticity was unquestioned, a mosque and mausoleum were raised on it, and in the course of four centuries this locality grew so rich from the pilgrim traffic that the large city of Mazār-i Sharīf sprang up there. And it did not embarrass the Believers in the slightest that Caliph 'Alī had never been near Balkh to anybody's knowledge, or that there had long been a sepulchre of 'Alī in Najaf also serving as a noted resort of pilgrimage — whose genuineness, incidentally, was also doubtful. A vast hagiographical literature accumulated in both Sunnī and Shī'ite Islam consisting of lives of the prophets, Imams and saints, embellished with the inevitable stories of miracles; and, as a genre of its own, guidebooks to the holy sites and burial places in the different towns.

Sometimes an ancient religious tradition would persist that had no connection with Muḥammadanism at all. There were so-called graves of nameless saints in Iran and Central Asia which on the face of it were sites where Zoroastrian deities or pre-Islamic heroes had once been worshipped. The veneration of trees and sources, which the zealots of Islam so often combated in the first centuries of the Hijra, is similarly a survival of an immemorial nature worship. A sacred tree grew in the courtyard of one of the mosques at Qazwīn which was felled in Mutawakkil's reign. However, the veneration of the spot did not cease, and in a typical explanation it was given out that a saint had been buried there. But after the tenth/eleventh centuries the worship of sacred trees and springs became as intimately woven into the texture of Islam as saint-worship. Trees hung with rags, and worshipped as holy, and sacred springs abound in Iran. People come to them to pray, and it enters nobody's head to doubt the genuinely Muslim character of these essentially pre-Muslim shrines.

Along with this gradual assimilation of pagan beliefs went another tendency, highly characteristic of Islam between the ninth and twelfth centuries, viz. the preaching to the masses of humility, patience in adversity or poverty, and contentment with one's lot. It was an indication that the Faith had advanced into the religion of a feudal society. The growing influence of the theologians and jurists as a class, the spread of mysticism and the Dervish orders, the increase in Waqf lands and in the wealth of pious and charitable foundations, testified to the same development.

X
The moderate Shī'ites

The story of the Shī'ite branch of Islam has received much less attention than the story of Sunnī Islam. In 1924 E. G. Browne wrote: 'We still possess no comprehensive and authoritative statement of Shī'a doctrine in any European language'[1] and it is doubtful whether his judgment calls for amendment even today.

In the opening decades of Islam, as has been said,[2] Shī'ism was a political current. Shī'ism was *Shī'at 'Alī*, "Alī's Party', just as there was *Shī'at 'Abbāsiyya*, 'the 'Abbāsid Party'. It is true that 'Abdullāh b. Sabā endeavoured to give it a religious justification while 'Uthmān was still Caliph, but this idea did not gain ground until it was elaborated by his followers a good deal later. It needed time and the fire of civil war and revolt for Shī'ism to harden into a doctrine, and qualify as a branch of Islam.

Ash-Shahrastānī (1071–1153) in his *Kitābu 'l-Milal wa 'n-Niḥal* (Book of Religious and Philosophical Schools) defines it thus: The Shī'ites are those who take the side of the Prophet's son-in-law 'Alī, recognizing his exclusive right to the status of Imam and Caliph. The Shī'ites hold that the title to the Imamate can belong to no one except the descendants of 'Alī and Fāṭima (Muḥammad having no male posterity): it depends, that is to say, on the principle of inheritance and not on a particular individual's suitability — and this is the essence of Shī'ite belief. The Imam cannot be freely chosen by the Muslim community as the Sunnīs think; he is Imam by virtue of his inherited dignity which cannot be transmitted to any other person or group. Shī'ites believe that the Imams are innocent of sin, infallible in their principles, deeds and faith. They permit 'the prudent concealment' (*taqiyya*) of their beliefs if there is danger of persecution, though certain of them[3] do not concur on this point. The actual transmission of the Imamate to a particular descendant of the 'Alids is the occasion for differences of opinion and schism. Their principal divisions are the Kaysānīs, the Zaydīs, the Imāmīs, the Extremists (*ghāliyya*), and the Ismā'īlīs.[4]

The main general positions of Shī'ism will be stated here, without reference to all the details that were gradually worked out by the several groups into which this branch of Islam divided. We should use the word 'branch' in speaking of Shī'ism, and not 'sect' of Islam. To consider it a sect, Ye. A. Belyayev remarks, 'is only possible if we adopt the standpoint of orthodox Sunnīs. But if we attend to the ideology and organization of the Shī'ites as these developed historically, and above all to their specific influence in the countries of Islam, we must regard Shī'ism as one of the two fundamental directions taken by the Muslim religion'.[5] Of these two basic directions or branches, Sunnism was always preponderant in most countries, and even in Iran until the close of the fifteeenth century. But if the Shī'ites were in most places a minority, this was often energetic to a degree, influencing popular movements and social thought, and challenging the Sunnism of the feudal state. If proof were wanted of the vitality of Shī'ism throughout the whole age of feudalism, it could be seen in the way it never ceased to throw out new shoots. The five principal divisions noticed by Shahrastānī forked in their turn into many minor ones.

The first three of those five — Kaysānīs, Zaydīs and Imāmīs — can be referred to as Moderate Shī'ites, since their deviation from orthodox Islam did not go beyond their conception of the Imamate as something inherited by succession from the 'Alids.[6] On the other hand the Ismā'īlīs and Extremists arrived at doctrines so remote from the basic positions of Islam as to merit the description of independent religions masquerading as Shī'ism. The difference between the Moderate and the Extreme Shī'ites was fundamental and clearly recognized even in the first centuries.[7] The present chapter will be concerned with the former, and the Ismā'īlīs and Extreme Shī'ites will be allotted their space separately.[8]

At the start, the Shī'ites did not advance any religious or doctrinal theory of the Imamate and Caliphate. They simply supported 'Alī's right to these on the score of his being the son-in-law of the Prophet and the person nearest to him. This view was later 'corroborated' by a Tradition they invented to the effect that Muḥammad at the time of his last pilgrimage (another version put it after the Treaty of Hudaybiyya in 628) uttered these words at the Pool Ghadīru 'l-Khumm: 'Whoso acknowledges me as his Lord (*mawlā*), must also acknowledge 'Alī as such.'

Shī'ism crystallized into a religious trend in the interval between the tragic death of the third Shī'ite Imam Ḥusayn in 680 and the establishment of the 'Abbāsid dynasty in 749/50. In this interim, dissensions began to occur inside the Shī'ite camp, occasioned originally by disputes as to which of the 'Alids should be deemed the next Imam. To this item were added differences of opinion about the qualities befitting the Imam, and it was now that the characteristically Shī'ite cult of martyrdom as the direct road to paradise was born. After the death of the first three Imams — namely, 'Alī, his son, the passive Ḥasan, (whom the Shī'ites, however, insisted on considering a martyr, accusing Caliph Mu'āwiya I of having poisoned him) and the latter's brother, the bold and enterprising Ḥusayn — there occurred the first serious breach, and the Kaysānīs detached themselves. The name *Kaysāniyya* designated the group which, while it adored 'Alī, attached no great importance to the personality of Fāṭima, and therefore recognized Ḥusayn's step-brother Muḥammad Ibnu 'l-Ḥanafiyya[9] as having the succession. This Ibnu 'l-Ḥanafiyya, tradition relates, was moreover a man of outstanding ability and was indeed credited subsequently with occult powers, a knowledge of the secret meaning of the heavenly spheres, and so on. His partisans rose in revolt at Kūfa (685–687) under the leadership of Mukhtār b. Abī 'Ubayd.[10] The actual name Kaysānī is apparently derived from Kaysān Abū 'Amr, leader of the clients (*mawālī*) in Mukhtār's army, a fervent Shī'ite who played a distinguished part in the revolt, or else from another Kaysān, a client of 'Alī, who perished at the battle of Ṣiffīn (657). In justification of Ibnu 'l-Ḥanafiyya's claim the Kaysānīs argued that 'Alī had become Imam by spiritual succession and not in virtue of his being the Prophet's son-in-law, and that he had necessarily to transmit this spiritual succession of his to his three sons in the sequence Ḥasan, Ḥusayn and Muḥammad Ibnu 'l-Ḥanafiyya.

The latter's death in about 700 occasioned rifts among the Kaysānīs themselves. Some of them believed that the number of Imams must be limited to four — 'Alī and his three sons — in view of the imminent end of the world; others recognized 'Alī son of Ibnu 'l-Ḥanafiyya as fifth Imam; and a third faction gave this recognition to a second son of his named Abū Hāshim, on the ground that he was supposed to have inherited his father's occult knowledge and was consequently Imam by spiritual succession. On Abū Hāshim's death new sub-sects came into being. One of these combined with the supporters of the 'Abbāsid pretenders to the throne, and the version was circulated that Abū Hāshim on his deathbed had bequeathed his rights to the Imamate to the head of the 'Abbāsid house, 'Imam' Muḥammad b. 'Alī and his descendants. This ramification of the Kaysānīs, the Rāwandīs, took an active part in Abū Muslim's popular insurrection (747–750) which brought the scheming 'Abbāsids to the throne of the Caliphate. Once in power the 'Abbāsids made short work of the democratic elements which had supported them — 'Abū Muslim and Rāwandīs alike. Another Kaysānī sub-sect disbelieved in the death of Ibnu 'l-Ḥanafiyya, maintaining that he had concealed himself in a cave whence he would appear again as Mahdī and establish the reign of justice on earth. Thus the doctrine of the hidden Imam, of his unseen existence (*ghayba*) and return (*raj'a*), had its birth among the Kaysānīs; a doctrine which would afterwards be adopted by other Shī'ite sects — by the Imāmīs notably among the Moderates, and by the Ismā'īlīs and Extremists. Ibn Ḥazm, the eleventh century writer on heresy, speaks of the Kaysānīs as a sect which had vanished by his time.

The immense majority of Shī'ites declined to recognize Muḥammad Ibnu 'l-Ḥanafiyya as fourth Imam since this son of 'Alī was not the son of Fāṭima, and consequently not descended from the Prophet; and on the same grounds they were not prepared to acknowledge Ibnu 'l-Ḥanafiyya's posterity as Sayyids. Two lines of the 'Alids were extant: the descendants of Ḥasan (known as Sayyids or sometimes Sherifs of Ḥasan, or Ḥasanids) and the descendants of Ḥusayn (Ḥusaynī Sayyids or Ḥusaynids). Both lines led private lives under the Umayyads, notwithstanding their wealth and occasional influence. They were viewed with suspicion by the Caliphs with the single exception of 'Umar II, and excluded from the offices of state; and certain of them were put to death as dangerous to the realm. Al-Mas'ūdī supplies a list of those liquidated.[11] The 'Abbāsids, indeed, in the first phase of their power tried to win the 'Alids to their side, but even they were not averse to poisoning or otherwise getting rid of a member of this house whenever their suspicion was aroused. One must however bear in mind that cultivating martyrdom as they did, the Shī'ites wanted to see as many martyrs as possible among the 'Alids and were apt to accuse the Umayyads and 'Abbāsids of poisoning Imams or others belonging to this family without the least evidence. The Government had cause for suspicion. Both under the Umayyads and under the 'Abbāsids, members of one or other of the two 'Alid branches would rebel and seize power temporarily. And sometimes they even succeeded in setting up an 'Alid dynasty in a particular province, as was the case of the Idrīsids (Ḥasanids) in Maghrib, 788–985, and of the Zaydīs (Ḥusaynids) in the Yemen.

The majority of Shī'ites recognized the son of Ḥusayn as fourth Imam, 'Alī by name, called al-Aṣghar, 'The Younger',[12] and also known by his title Zaynu 'l-'Ābidīn 'Ornament of the Servants, i.e. the Pious'.[13] He was captured by the Umayyad troops after the disaster as Kerbelā, but Caliph Yazīd I spared him on account of his youth, and let him go to Medīna where he lived peacefully until his death in 713 or 714. Shī'ite tradition credits this Imam with exceptional piety and virtue,[14] and also makes out that he was poisoned at the instigation of the Umayyad Caliph and so became a martyr. He was buried in Medīna.

Most Shī'ites acknowledged his son Muḥammad, surnamed al-Bāqir, as their fifth Imam. The sobriquet, according to the historian al-Ya'qūbī,[15] was derived from the Arabic root *baqara* 'to cut open, lay bare', and was appropriate because he probed knowledge to its depths. Tradition attributes profound learning to him in the field of religious law and dogmatics, and also tells of his miracles. He lived in peace at Medīna where he was visited by Shī'ite delegations from different provinces, and notably distant Khurāsān. He died around 732 — or 742 according to Mas'ūdī.

It was in the time of this fifth Imam that a new schism occurred. A body of Shī'ites, probably discontented with Muḥammad al-Bāqir's conciliatory temperament, rallied round his energetic brother Zayd b. 'Alī. Zayd was in favour of resolute action against the Umayyads and left Medīna for Kūfa at the invitation of the local Shī'ites to head a rebellion against Caliph Hishām. This dragged on for ten months until it was suppressed in 739/740. Zayd himself was killed by an arrow in battle, and his body suspended from a cross in Kūfa. His severed head was displayed on a pole at Damascus and then at Medīna. But the 'Zaydīs' had become a sect. They were henceforward to be contrasted with those Shī'ites who recognized the Imamate of Muḥammad al-Bāqir, Ja'far aṣ-Ṣādiq and their posterity, and who were styled 'Imāmīs'. We shall touch here on the doctrine and history of the Zaydīs in Iran so as not to revert to this sect afterwards.

Their influence was felt chiefly in the early Middle Ages. These were essentially the Shī'ites whom the Sunnī authors favour with the epithet 'respectable' though that label in justice could have been extended to the Kaysānīs and Imāmīs. As a sect the Zaydīs hold Zayd b. 'Alī to be the fifth Imam, but probably recognition was only accorded after his heroic exploits and martyrdom. There is no evidence that Zayd himself used the title: he seems indeed to have been on good terms with his brother the Imam Muḥammad al-Bāqir and, anyhow until the rebellion in Kūfa, to have accepted his authority.

Mas'ūdī relates how Zayd consulted the Imam before setting out to join the rebels in that city but for all his brother's pleading could not be dissuaded from his purpose.

In common with all Shī'ites the Zaydīs recognize that 'Alī b. Abī Ṭālib had a stronger claim to the Imamate than any of the other Companions, not so much because of his family connection with the Prophet as because of the holiness and spiritual qualities attributed to him. Zaydīs did not, however, ascribe any sacred properties to Imams such as divine manifestation (*ẓuhūr*) or occult, esoteric experience. Their understanding of the Imamate was reasonably close to the Sunnī understanding of it — the Imam is the Defender of the Faith and the Community, but is not a Pontiff and Infallible Lord Spiritual — except, of course, that they held, like all Shī'ites, that the incumbent must be a member of the Prophet's family (*ahlu 'l-bayt*). They do not insist on succession from father to son, which the Imāmīs require, but hold that the community can choose any 'Alid, whether Ḥusaynid or Ḥasanid, depending on his personal qualities. (There was here a departure from Imāmīs, not to speak of Ismā'īlīs and Extremists, to whom personal qualities did not matter for the Imamate.) They thought the choice should fall on the 'Alid who showed himself an active, determined leader capable of winning acceptance or, in other words, gaining the Caliphate. They allowed the co-existence of several Imams in a number of countries, should the relations between these be uneasy or should the Zaydīs have succeeded in creating states in them over which 'Alid Imams could rule. In keeping with their demand that the Imam should be an energetic public figure, they rejected the doctrine of the Hidden Imam which was so prominent in the systems of other Shī'ite sects.

Of all Shī'ites the Zaydīs show the most tolerance in regard to the Sunnīs; their forbearance goes so far that they do not curse the first two Caliphs Abū Bakr and 'Umar.[16] Agreeing with the rest of the Shī'ites that these two were wrongly and illegally elected Caliphs, they think that they were otherwise decent and honourable men. Another item of doctrine brings them close to the Sunnism of the early period: namely, the repudiation of saint-worship and mysticism. (The Sunnīs later abandoned their stand in these two matters, and so did the Imāmī Shī'ites, but the Zaydīs stuck to their position.) They dissociate themselves from the tenet subsequently adopted by most of the Sunnī doctors that the torments of hell will be only temporary even in the case of persons dying without repentance in a condition of grievous sin, provided they be believing Muslims. That is, Zaydīs do not accept the doctrine of purgatory. And they are the only sect of Shī'ism which rejects the principle of *taqiyya*, or prudent concealment of their belief;[17] no doubt because this principle would be inconsistent with the demand the sect made of its members to be active in fighting for the triumph of their community. Lastly, they deny the legality of temporary marriage for a fixed term permitted by the Imāmīs. In theology and dogmatics the Zaydīs assimilated almost the whole Mu'tazilite system with its rejection of anthropormorphism, its denial of predestination and its doctrine of human freedom.

The absence of serious difference with the Sunnīs and a certain tolerance in their regard did not hamper the Zaydīs in the political battle for their ideal of a theocratic state headed by an Imam-Caliph chosen from the 'Alids. It is a paradox that the mildest of the Shī'ites dogmatically were the most active champions of the Shī'ite idea in the eighth and ninth centuries; whereas the Imāmīs who had gone furthest from Sunnism and hated it most, damning the first three Caliphs as usurpers, were politically the most passisve in those centuries. The Sunnī Caliphs found no reason to restrict the liberty of Zaynu 'l-'Ābidīn 'Alī, Muḥammad al-Bāqir or Ja'far aṣ-Ṣādiq because these Imams were aloof from the movements of their day. The political activity of the Imāmīs was of much later date.

In the present state of our knowledge it is not easy to explain this paradox, and one can only suppose that its cause lay in the social composition of the two sects at the time. The fact that the Zaydīs led so many popular movements suggests that theirs was then a popular 'heresy' distinguished by conservatism in religion[18] and activity in politics. We have already noticed the same combination of aims among the Khārijites, who were conservative in so far as they sought to retain intact the original pattern of Islamic faith and precept and dreaded innovation, but radical in their social attitudes.[19] Possibly it is the common social composition of the two groups that explains their common belief that those who commit flagrant (*kabā'ir*) sins cease to be Muslims and are condemned to everlasting torment in hell. From this thesis the two of them inferred the religious obligation to wage Holy War with rulers who had abandoned the early Islamic ideal of theocracy; with the Ummayads, that is, and then with the 'Abbāsid Caliphs whom the Zaydīs thought unlawful and against whom they rose in repeated rebellions.

Such were the ill-starred revolts led by the 'Alids of the Ḥasanid branch, Muḥammad an-Nafsu' z-Zakiyya (762/3) and by Ḥusayn b. 'Alī Ibnu 'l-Ḥasan in the Ḥijāz. In the latter rising the rebels were destroyed almost to a man by 'Abbāsid troops in a crushing defeat at the valley of Fakhkh near Mecca on 8 Dhu 'l-Ḥijja 169 AH = 11 June 786. The Shī'ites afterwards observed this date as a day of mourning comparable to the day of Kerbelā. In Yemen there were successes, 'Alid dynasties being installed several times; and it is of course a country in which the Zaydī persuasion has maintained itself until our own time. In 199 AH = 814/15, the Zaydīs rose in Iraq against Caliph Ma'mūn, and their leader Abū Sarāyā proposed the Ḥasanid 'Alid Muḥammad b. Ṭabāṭabā as Imam and Pretender. But the revolt was suppressed, the Imam died, and Abū Sarāyā was executed.

Historically the most significant Zaydī risings were those of peasant character in the Caspian region in the second half of the ninth and first quarter of the tenth centuries. The two hundred years 750–950 were marked by intense peasant commotion in various parts of Iran, and one of the upheavals, that of the *Muḥammira*, the 'Wearers of Red', led by Bābak (more properly Pāpak), in Ādharbāyjān and the west of the country (816–837) shook the Caliphate to its foundations. Until roughly the thirties inclusive of that century these peasant risings were, so to speak, 'covered' ideologically by the non-Muslim sect of Khurramīs, an offshoot of Zoroastrianism which, like its ideological forerunner the Mazdakī sect in the fifth/sixth centuries, aimed at social equality, the abolition of the private ownership of land and the transfer of estates to free rural communities. But from the middle of the ninth century the ideological leadership of the popular disturbances in Iran shifted to the Shī'ites in the chronological order: Zaydīs, Carmathians and Isma'īlīs, Imāmīs and Extremists. For Shī'ism in mediaeval Iran, as Bartol'd remarked, was widespread in the countryside long before the Ṣafawids, and served as the ideology of the mass movements.[20] The circumstance that Sunnism was the dominant branch of Islam in the Caliphate and in the states that rose on its ruins, while Shī'ism was viewed as a heresy and at times persecuted, was doubtless responsible for this situation.

The Caspian region, consisting of the coastal Gīlān and, south of this, the upland Daylam, Ṭabaristān (now Māzandarān) and Gurgān (Jurjān in its arabicized form), is separated from the rest of Iran by the high Elburz Mountains and impenetrable forests, and it was economically apart. Besides which, the population of Gīlān and Daylam had never been subjugated by the Arabs and remained heathen at least until the mid-ninth century. An early feudal order was here concealed beneath formal patriarchal customs, and self-governing rural communities were still well entrenched. The hillmen of Daylam whose lives were poor and austere in their native land left their homes in large numbers and entered the mercenary armies of the 'Abbāsid Caliphs and local Iranian dynasts. It was the practice in royal courts for the Horse Guard to be composed of bought Turkish slaves and the Foot Guard of young mercenaries from Daylam and Gīlān. Prominent generals like Mardāwīj b. Ziyār, and even certain founders of feudal dynasties, began their careers in the ranks of these mercenaries.[21]

The hills and forests of Daylam and Gīlān afforded the 'Alids a convenient refuge from 'Abbāsid persecution, and their presence helped the spread of Islam in its Shī'ite form to these parts.

When Ṭabaristān was held by the Ṭāhirid Amīr Muḥammad, his local governor Muḥammad b. Aws trebled the taxes and also declared the forests, pastures and uncultivated lands, previously belonging to the rural communities, to be the property of the state.[22] The sorely oppressed peasantry on the Ṭabaristān and Daylam border rebelled and turned to the Zaydī Imam Ḥasan b. Zayd of the Ḥasanī 'Alids who was a refugee in their midst. He assumed command of the rebels in 864 and succeeded in setting up a Shī'ite regime whose sway stretched to Gīlān, Daylam and Ṭabaristān. This Ḥasan b. Zayd who ruled from 864 to 884 was a cultured man, versed in Fiqh and poetics, and of unusual energy. He and his brother and successor, Muḥammad b. Zayd, had constantly to guard against Ṭāhirid or Ṣaffārid or Sāmānid incursions, and every so often these 'Alid Imams would have to dodge the enemy, leaving Ṭabaristān for the maquis of the Daylam uplands while the attack lasted. The Ṣaffārid Ya'qūb wasted forty thousand men, if Ṭabarī be believed, in fruitless attempts to bring down the 'Alid state in the Caspian zone. It only fell to the feudal Sāmānid dominion in 900, when Ismā'īl of that house routed the 'Alid army in a battle in which Muḥammad b. Zayd perished.

Thirteen years later, just after the Sāmānid power in the Caspian belt had been shaken by an invasion of the Russ from the sea, a massive rising of the peasantry occurred again. It was led this time by the Zaydī Imam, the 'Alid Ḥasan b. 'Alī, nicknamed al-Uṭrush, 'The Deaf', who had earlier taken shelter in Daylam. With the assistance of the unprivileged in Ṭabaristān, Gīlān and Daylam, this elderly but energetic and popular man managed to expel both the Sāmānid troops and the feudal barons, or Dihqāns. Al-Bīrūnī regretted that Ḥasan al-Uṭrush had thrown out the local Dihqāns whom Farīdūn, the mythical ancient Iranian king, was supposed to have placed over the people, only to install so many mutineers as land-owners in place of the nobles. However, the sources supply no details of the land revolution: Ṭabarī simply tells us that Ḥasan al-Uṭrush treated the people with benevolence and fairness, and that men had never seen any one else caring so much about justice, good administration and equity. Ḥasan died soon afterwards and in 928 the 'Alid state collapsed under the battering it received from the army of the Ziyārid dynasty, and the old feudal order was restored.

We now pass to the Imāmīs. On the death of Muḥammad al-Bāqir, the Imāmīs recognized his son Ja'far, known as aṣ-Ṣādiq, 'the Veridical', as the sixth Imam (b. *c.* 700; d. 765). Like his father and grandfather before him Ja'far b. Muḥammad abstained from opposition politics — he lived and died peacefully at Medīna — but to make up for it was, according to Shī'ite tradition, a most subtle jurist and theologian who enjoyed the respect even of the Sunnī doctors,[23] and founded his own system of Fiqh which is named after him, the Ja'farite school. In later days, writings were in circulation in the Shī'ite world attributed to him, but his authorship is very doubtful. He was credited with a wide knowledge of astrology, alchemy and other occult sciences, and with exceptional piety and the gift of marvels. Ibn Wāḍiḥ al-Ya'qūbī cites a number of his sayings, or utterances supposedly his, in his History.[24] It was Ja'far who elaborated the doctrine of the Essence of the Imamate and the doctrine of the Light of Muḥammad (*Nūr Muḥammadī*), the light as old as Adam that illuminated all the prophets, Muḥammad himself, and his family.[25] He is noticeably influenced by the Mu'tazilite school in his theology, especially in his rejection of anthropomorphism (*tashbīh*) and his refusal to invest God with attributes taken from the range of human experience. He was not, however, so consistently tied to Mu'tazilite dogmatics as the Zaydīs were, and notably on free will took a *via media* between *jabr* or unqualified determinism, and *tafwīḍ*, God's mandate to humans to choose their behaviour.

While Ja'far lived, the Imāmīs were not, ideologically speaking, an 'entire' sect, for the ultra-Shī'ite elements among them had not yet deserted them. One of his closest confidants, the fanatical and indefatigable Abu 'l-Khaṭṭāb, went so far in his adoration of the Imam as to spread it abroad that he was God incarnate. Ja'far could not allow such a distortion of Islam and removed Abu 'l-Khaṭṭāb from his confidence; acting just as Caliph 'Alī himself had done when he dismissed 'Abdullāh b. Sabā from his entourage for the same offence, appreciating that it would compromise his cause. Abu 'l-Khaṭṭāb founded a separate sect of Extreme Shi'ites — the *Khaṭṭābiyya*.[26] But Ja'far lived to see another split in his community which was of far greater consequence to the history of Shī'ism. Having seven sons he had designated the fourth of these, Mūsā al-Kāẓim, as his successor; but there were those in the community who favoured one or another of the three senior sons — Ismā'īl, 'Abdullāh or Muḥammad — all of whom had asserted their claims. Three splinter groups resulted of which only one, however, was dynamic, viz. the group supporting the eldest son Ismā'īl. Its members presently became known as the Ismā'īlīs (*Ismā'īliyya*). Now Ismā'īl predeceased his father *c.* 762, and consequently could not actually become Imam; but this did not deter the Ismā'īlīs from declaring his son Muḥammad seventh Imam, the moment Ja'far died. These partisans of Muḥammad continued to be known as Ismā'īlīs. With the passage of time it came to light that the differences between them and the Imāmīs went much further and deeper than this dispute about the pretenders. They were the bitterest rivals of the Imāmīs, and occupied a prominent place in the political and cultural affairs of the Muslim countries, and particularly Iran, from the late ninth to the mid-thirteen centuries.[27]

Ja'far died at Medīna while the dispute was at its height, and was buried there in the cemetery called al-Baqī' alongside his father and grandfather. True to form, Shī'ite tradition relates that he had been sent a gift of poisoned fruit by the 'Abbāsid Caliph Manṣūr (754–775) who was fearful of his popularity.

The Imāmīs who remained loyal to Ja'far recognized Mūsā al-Kāẓim as the seventh Imam.[28] Of the latter's life very little that is reliable has come down to us, most of what is on record being no better than legends about the numerous miracles he performed. Mild, generous and tolerant, he is said to have lived in constant dread of arrest or assassination at the behest of the 'Abbāsid Caliphs. Nevertheless he survived the death of his father by some thirty years (765–794), residing comparatively undisturbed at Medīna, and not in penury to judge by his enormous family of eighteen sons and twenty-three daughters, all of them born of slave-mothers — he had no lawful wife — and by Ibn Khallikān's story that Imam Mūsā sent a purse of a thousand dinars to every one who slandered him. Some accounts suggest that he was arrested in the reign of al-Mahdī (775–785) or his successor al-Hādī (785–786) on suspicion of complicity in one of the Khārijite risings in which certain of the 'Alids were involved; but if he was in fact arrested, he was in no real danger and was soon set free. However, he was later suspected of treason again, arrested in Medīna at the orders of Hārūn ar-Rashīd and brought to Baghdad[29] where he was put in prison. The sources are conflicting on the circumstances of his incarceration and death, but agree that he died in a Baghdad gaol in 799. The authorities gave out that he died a natural death, yet the Imāmīs deem him a martyr.

His son 'Alī, better known under his later title 'Alī ar-Riḍā,[30] was acclaimed his successor by the Imāmīs, and so eighth in the line. To begin with he resided in Medīna, but in 816 Caliph Ma'mūn ordered him to be brought to Khurāsān. The summons there is explained as follows. The Caliph had overcome his brother Amīn, his rival for the throne, in 813, but felt too insecure to show his face in Baghdad where they hated him, and stayed in Merv, ingratiating himself with the Iranian barons, or Dihqāns. On the advice of his vizier Faḍl b. Sahl, a Persian, and the latter's brother Ḥasan b. Sahl, Ma'mūn resolved to approach the Moderate Shī'ites and give them a taste of power, hoping that with their help the discontent of the masses might be lessened. When 'Alī arrived in Merv, Ma'mūn conferred on him the title ar-Riḍā and proclaimed him heir apparent (*walī 'ahd*) on 2 Ramaḍān 201 AH = 24 March 817. A ceremonial gathering, said to have numbered thirty-three thousand persons, descendants of 'Abbās the Prophet's uncle, descendants of 'Alī b. Abī Ṭālib, officials and nobles, marked the occasion. To please the Shī'ites, Ma'mūn ordered the official black of the 'Abbāsids (i.e. the colour of the standards and the robes of the dignitaries of state) to be changed to green which was their adopted colour; and had the coinage stamped with 'Alī's name immediately after his own, the inscription reading: 'ar-Riḍā, Imam of the Muslims'. He also gave his daughter, Ḥabība in marriage to the Imam. Much later Shī'ite sources tell of religious conferences and debates held at the Caliph's residence at Merv in which Ma'mūn himself, the Imam 'Alī ar-Riḍā, and not only the Sunnī and Shī'ite, but the Christian, Jewish and even Zoroastrian divines, took part. It is quite possible that the famous Theodore Abū Qurra, Nestorian bishop of Ḥarrān, who recalled his participation in a religious discussion at the court of Caliph Ma'mūn, was alluding to one of the colloquies attended by Imam 'Alī Riḍā.

But the 'Abbāsid Caliph's alliance with the Moderate Shī'ites proved short-lived. It failed to yield the results envisaged. The masses in Iran gained nothing from the volte-face, and a revolt broke out in Baghdad;[31] while the Dihqāns for their part, who were mostly adherents of Sunnism at that time, were annoyed at the Caliph's pro-Shī'ite policy. Everything went to show that the Imāmīs were not then so influential in Iran that the Caliph's wooing of them could help him *vis-à-vis* the general public. So Ma'mūn decided to break with the

Shī'ites. His vizier of Shī'ite proclivities, Faḍl b. Sahl, was murdered at the baths in Sarakhs, at the Caliph's orders it was thought (though Ma'mūn denied it), and Imam 'Alī ar-Riḍā died unexpectedly at Nūqān, one of the villages of Ṭūs in Khurāsān. His end came in late Ṣafar 203 AH = early September 818 after three days of pain from an allegedly poisoned pomegranate[32] (another version makes it a bunch of grapes) he had eaten. Rumour — this time not without foundation, it would appear — attributed the poisioning to Ma'mūn. The latter protested vigorously, mourned the Imam ostentatiously and arranged his obsequies on a grand scale, himself officiating.[33] However, the circumstance that he returned to Baghdad immediately afterwards, broke off relations with the Shī'ites and reintroduced black as the state colour in place of green, was in the general view an ample endorsement of the rumour. Inasmuch as the death of Imam 'Alī Riḍā was thought to have been directly occasioned by Ma'mūn's breach with the Shī'ites, these looked on him as a martyr. He was interred at Sanābād near Ṭūs in the garden which contained the tomb of Hārūn ar-Rashīd (d. 809).

The sepulchre of the eighth Imam became a place of pilgrimage and an object of unrivalled sanctity in the eyes of the Imāmī sect.[34] A settlement sprang up around it which became a complete city known as Mashhad-i 'Alī Riḍā, or simply Mashhad.[35] Enriched by the stream of pilgrims, this gradually supplanted the old town of Ṭūs: the latter had no future, was destroyed by the Mongols and afterwards never properly rebuilt. A mausoleum over the tomb and a magnificent mosque erected alongside by Amīr Fā'iq in the tenth century were demolished by Sabuktagīn, founder of the Ghaznawid dynasty and an enemy of the Shī'ites (977–998), but the mausoleum was restored by his son Maḥmūd (1009) who respected the Imam's memory. In the mid-eleventh century the mausoleum was again pulled down by the Turkish conquerors. It was renovated by private initiative in the first half of the next century and then, for the third time, destroyed in 1220 by the Mongols. But it was also a Mongol who rebuilt it, namely the Il-Khān Uljāytū, called Muḥammad Khudā-Banda, who had embraced the Shī'ite faith (1304–1316). A great mosque adjacent to this mausoleum was constructed at the command, and expense, of Gawhar Shād, queen of the Ṭīmūrid Sultan Shāh-rukh. It was designed by the noted Persian architect Qawāmu 'd-Dīn Shīrāzī and completed in 821 AH = 1418. Decorated with mosaics of multicoloured glazed tiles, it is one of the most remarkable monuments of Persian architecture. The main cupola was covered with gilded slabs

The ninth Imam was Muḥammad surnamed al-Jawād, 'The Generous', and at-Taqī, 'The Devout'. He was the son of 'Alī Riḍā by a bondwoman of unknown origin,[37] and not by his lawful wife Ḥabība, the Caliph's daughter. He remained in Medīna until his father's death when he was between seven and nine. Ma'mūn, wishing to keep him under observation, then assumed formal charge of him, and gave him one of his daughters, Zaynab, in what proved an unhappy marriage. The Imam lived first in Medīna, and then in Baghdad studying theology and jurisprudence. It was a quiet existence so long as Ma'mūn was on the throne — except that his wife repeatedly complained about him to the Caliph; but things changed for the worse under Ma'mūn's brother and successor Mu'taṣim. Shī'ite tradition maintains that Imam Muḥammad Taqī was poisoned with the aid of a kerchief by his wife Zaynab at the instigation of Caliph Mu'taṣim, or according to another version, with sherbet sent him by Mu'taṣim's own hand. These stories are to be questioned, but in any event the ninth Imam died at Baghdad in 835.

The tenth Imam was his son 'Alī surnamed an-Naqī, 'The Pure', by a bondwoman.[38] He was a boy between six and eight years of age when his father died, and he lived in Medīna with his mother, receiving his education. He was subjected to no constraint at all under the Caliphs Mu'taṣim and Wāthiq, but Caliph Mutawakkil was a fanatical Sunnī who persecuted the Mu'tazilites and Shī'ites, prohibited the pilgrimage to the tomb of 'Alī b. Abī Ṭālib and Ḥusayn b. 'Alī, and wrecked the mausoleum of Ḥusayn in Kerbelā. It was not likely that 'Alī an-Naqī would be spared the Caliph's attentions, in spite of his political indifference. In Mas'ūdī's account,[39] spies reported that the Imam had concealed arms and heretical books in his house and was aiming at power. The Caliph thereupon ordered the Captain of the Turkish Guard to proceed to Medīna. This officer broke into the house at night and conducted a search. Nothing incriminating was discovered, but the Imam was brought away first to Baghdad and then to the Caliph's residence at Sāmarrā. His lot from then on was imprisonment; and Shī'ite tradition dwells on the miracles he is supposed to have performed during his detention. Even after Mutawakkil's murder by the Turkish Guard in 861, the Imam was not released. He died in prison in 868 at the age of forty, having spent half his days in confinement.

The eleventh Imam was Ḥasan b. 'Alī surnamed al-'Askarī. Sāmarrā where he spent the greater part of his life was usually called

'Askar, 'Army' or 'Armed Camp' because the royal guard was stationed there, and hence the Imam's sobriquet. He was born of a female slave in 846 or 847, a few years before his father's arrest, and when the latter was imprisoned in Sāmarrā his family was given permission to reside in a private house in the same town. After his father's death and during the reign of Mu'tazz (consequently, between 868 and 869) he was himself imprisoned, but in Baghdad. He remained in detention, too, under the next two Caliphs, Mu'tamid (870–892) being in Shī'ite tradition his chief oppressor. However, Mu'tamid eventually set him at liberty and allowed him to go and live in his father's house at Sāmarrā; but he deprived him of the pension which Sayyids of the 'Alids customarily received as descendants of the Prophet from the *Khums* monies, i.e. the one-fifth of the spoils of war. This Imam had no lawful wife but one of his bondwomen, to whom tradition gave the name Narjis,[40] bore him a son Muḥammad, and a daughter;[41] and it is this only son who was fated to be the last of the Shī'ite Imams. Ḥasan 'Askarī is credited in Shī'ite tradition with numerous miracles and a saintly life, but to all appearance this saintliness was as conventional an attribute in his case as in that of most of the preceding Imams, his ancestors. He died in Sāmarrā in 873 when scarcely twenty-seven years of age. In Shī'ite story he is one more Martyr for the Faith, poisoned by the 'Abbāsid Caliph Mu'tamid.

Information about the twelfth and last Imam of the 'Imāmī' Shī'ites is nebulous in the extreme. Traditions cannot agree whether this son of Ḥasan 'Askarī was born four to five years or two years before his father's death, or even eight months after; but in any case he was a small child when he became Imam. At the age of six, or else at the age of seven or nine, the boy vanished. The various existing accounts of the manner of his disappearance are mostly of fairly late origin. One variant is that he hid himself in the sardab[42] of his own home; another that he disappeared in Sāmarrā; a third that he disappeared in Ḥilla. If the disappearance really took place at all, it could not have been later than 878 and could most probably be accounted for by assassination or abduction of the boy by the enemies of his family, and possibly the agents of Caliph Mu'tamid who needed to get rid of a potential pretender to the throne. However, the very existence of this boy-Imam defies proof. Rumours and different opinions divided the Imāmīs themselves touching both the death of Ḥasan 'Askari and the birth of his son Muḥammad. Some maintained that Ḥasan 'Askarī did have a son Muḥammad, the last Imam, who afterwards vanished; others that there was a son, but that he remained unknown; others that Ḥasan

'Askarī died childless and that the earth was then without Imam in punishment for men's sins. There were even other attitudes, one of these being that Ḥasan 'Askarī never died but concealed himself, and in time will return. So there were Imāmīs who themselves denied the existence of the twelfth Imam Muḥammad, holding Ḥasan 'Askarī, eleventh Imam, to be the last.

However it may be, there were no more visible Imams, and there were those Imāmīs who concluded from this that God had deprived men of the Imamate for their sins. But there were also those who argued that the world cannot exist without an Imam and that if no visible Imam be to hand there must be a hidden Imam, in God's keeping, directing the destinies of the Shī'ite community. When he returns, they said, he will be the Mahdī. The tenacity of the belief in a hidden Imam and his return, *raj'a*, as Mahdī, is evidently to be explained by the fact that the masses did not separate the prospect of his advent from their hope of a social revolution in religious form.

As to the identity of this hidden Imam who continues to live unseen among men pending his return, there was no unanimity. Some thought that while there is a hidden Imam, none can know who he is — whether he is a descendant of Ḥasan 'Askarī or whether he is some other 'Alid; a second group, as stated above, held Ḥasan 'Askarī to be the promised Mahdī; and a third group took the vanished twelfth Imam Muḥammad b. Ḥasan for their Messiah, giving him the titles al-Ḥujja 'The Proof', al-Muntaẓar 'The Awaited', al-Mahdī 'The God-Guided', and Ṣāḥibu 'z-Zamān 'Lord of the Age'. And some believed that the future Mahdī would be the eighth Imam 'Alī Riḍā who had not died but only gone into concealment.

In this welter of opinion the Imami sectarians could not but be divided among themselves. D. B. Macdonald counts as many as eleven of their sub-sects, and it was not, he thinks, until the fifth century AH = the eleventh century AD that the view of those who recognized twelve Imams, and Muḥammad son of Ḥasan 'Askarī as the hidden Mahdī, prevailed. Only then did the Tradition of the Twelve Imams properly emerge at the expense of the competing traditions. The Imāmīs henceforward were called the *Ithnā 'ashariyya*, 'The Twelvers'.

We can here recapitulate the series of Imams in the Tradition of the Twelve: (1) 'Alī b. Abī Ṭālib, al-Murtaḍā 'the Chosen', killed in 661; (2) Ḥasan b. 'Alī, d. 669; (3) Ḥusayn b. 'Alī ash-Shāhid 'the Martyr', killed in 680; (4) 'Alī Zaynu 'l-'Ābidīn, d. 713 or 714; (5) Muḥammad al-Bāqir, d. 732; (6) Ja'far aṣ-Ṣādiq, d. 765; (7) Mūsā al-Kāẓim, died in prison 799; (8) 'Alī ar-Riḍā, d. or poisoned, 818; (9) Muḥammad at-Taqī (Jawād) d. 835; (10) 'Alī an-Naqī, d. or killed, in prison, 868; (11) Ḥasan al-'Askarī, d. 873; (12) Muḥammad al-Mahdī disappeared between 874 and 878.

Of these, 'Alī b. Abī Ṭālib, fourth Caliph and first Imam, and his son Ḥusayn perished by violence, and the twelfth Imam Muḥammad al-Mahdī probably met a violent end (assuming he lived at all). Shī'ite tradition asserts that all the remainder were poisoned by Umayyad or 'Abbāsid Caliphs, but this can only be stated with some verisimilitude in the case of Mūsā al-Kāẓim, 'Alī ar-Riḍā and 'Alī an-Naqī. The poisoning of the rest of the Imams was plainly added by legend, in order that they might qualify for martyrdom. Martyr-worship had such vogue among the Shī'ites that death for the Faith was thought of as the highest merit before God; this was the royal road to paradise, and the saint, to be complete, must needs suffer it.

The sanctity of all Imams was of course a conventional conceit deriving from the claimed character of the Imamate[43] and having nothing to do with the real lives of those who held the office. Apart from 'Alī, Ḥusayn, Muḥammad al-Bāqir and Ja'far aṣ-Ṣādiq, the Imams led idle lives cushioned by material comforts; they had estates, houses, assignment of income from the faithful, and often a pension from the Caliph's *Khums* fund. And they were surrounded by odalisques brought from different countries by the slave traders. Not one of the Imams was an ascetic (*zāhid*); so in order to make them into saints, a much later legend embellished their lives with multifarious miracles and capped their careers with a martyr's death. Actually all the Imams in the series with the exception of the first 'Alī and Ḥusayn ash-Shāhid, it is worth remarking, were indifferent to politics. They preferred the quiet life to the bid for power, and kept out of the Shī'ite risings in the seventh, eighth and ninth centuries.[44] They thus present a contrast to the Zaydī Imams who tended to be politically engaged, and often played the lead in popular movements.

The tombs of the Imams became places of pilgrimage without loss of time; and not only for Shī'ites but for Sunnīs, the latter revering 'Alī, Ḥusayn and others as 'Alids and saints. The presumed[45] tombs are the following: of 'Alī b. Abī Ṭālib at Najaf in Arab Iraq on the Euphrates; of Ḥasan b. 'Alī, 'Alī Zaynu 'l-'Ābidīn, Muḥammad al-Bāqir and Ja'far aṣ-Ṣādiq at Medīna in the al-Baqī' burial-ground;[46] of Ḥusayn b. 'Alī at Kerbelā in Arab Iraq near Ḥilla; of Mūsā al-Kāẓim and Muḥammad Taqī at Kaẓimayn near Baghdad; of 'Alī ar-Riḍā at Mashhad; and of 'Alī an-Naqī and Ḥasan al-'Askarī at Sāmarrā. These shrines were supplemented as objects of unremitting Shī'ite pilgrimage by the tombs of other descendants of the Imams, the so-named *Imām-zādas*;[47] in which category the graves of Fāṭima, sister of the eighth Imam 'Alī Riḍā, in Qum and of the saintly 'Abdu 'l-'Aẓīm, descended from the second Imam Ḥasan, a close associate of the Imams Muḥammad Taqī and 'Alī Naqī, and a Faqīh and ascetic, in the borough of Shah 'Abdu 'l-'Aẓīm near Tehran, are especially venerated. Mausoleums with mosques adjacent were erected at all these 'Alid shrines.

Until 940, more than sixty years after the occultation of the twelfth Imam, the Imāmī community was administered by *wakīls* or 'regents'. The fourth of these deputies of the hidden Imam, one 'Alī b. Muḥammad of Sāmarrā, expiring in the forties of the century, designated nobody as his successor on his death bed. He was persuaded, as was all his community, that as many years had now elapsed since the last Imam's disappearance the times of trouble were at hand. The Carmathian popular risings had posed the question of social revolution and the establishment of a reign of justice on earth. Baghdad had been taken by the Buwayhids, and the Ismā'īlī Caliphate of the Fāṭimids had been installed in Africa. All these happenings were interpreted as signs of the imminent advent of the Mahdī, and therefore there was no sense in nominating another deputy *ad interim*. Thenceforward the Imāmī community had no visible acknowledged leader. Tradition gives the name Lesser Concealment to the period of direction through deputies, and Great Concealment of the Twelfth Imam to the period opening after 940.[48]

The Iranian (Daylamite) dynasty of the Buwayhids (935–1055) in West Iran and Iraq which seized Baghdad in 945 practically stripped the 'Abbāsid Caliphs of their political power[49] and left them with nothing but a shadowy spiritual authority. Its founders were Moderate Shī'ites of the Zaydī persuasion, whereas succeeding Buwayhids declared themselves to be Sunnīs while inwardly sympathizing with the Shī'ites, or at all events treating the Moderates among them with consideration. A long period had now set in when the Imāmīs and Zaydīs of West Iran could profess their faith with reasonable freedom and attend undisturbed to the elaboration of their dogmatics and law.

A mistaken view persists that one of the main differences between Sunnīs and Shī'ites is that the latter do not accept the Sunna. 'This is a radical error', remarks Goldziher, 'probably due in most cases to an antithesis between the terms *Sunna* and *Shī'a*, which completely misinterprets the essence of Shī'ism. No Shī'ite would tolerate being called an opponent of the principle of the Sunna'.[50] Only the Shī'ite Sunna does not coincide with the Sunnī Sunna. The Shī'ites have their own Ḥadīth, usually termed *Akhbār* (pl. of *khabar*, 'news') which rely on other *isnāds*, or warrants: in their traditions, the references are to what the Imams of the 'Alids have communicated. They reject for the most part Ḥadīth founded on *isnāds* going back to the Companions who deliberately opposed 'Alī, e.g. 'Ā'isha, Ṭalḥa, and az-Zubayr. So in effect the Shī'ite collections contain the traditions reporting the utterances and acts of the Prophet Muḥammad, of 'Alī and of the latter's descendants, the Imams.

There are however many Ḥadīth which are accepted by Sunnīs and Shī'ites alike, and, as Goldziher puts it, 'we often have to realize that a great quantity of the Traditions are common to both.[51] These differ only in the names of the authorities on whom reliance is placed. Where the Ḥadīth of the Sunnīs are favourable to, or anyhow do not contradict, the view of the Shī'ites, the theologians of the latter rely on the canonical collections of their adversaries without the slightest hesitation.'[52]

The Shī'ite Ḥadīth and their Collections are of much later origin than those of the Sunnīs, and betray even more glaring forgeries and figments, as Goldziher has shown.[53] The works of the Zaydī authors, beginning with Qāsim b. Ibrāhīm al-Ḥasanī (d. 860) and his successors, on Fiqh and dogmatics have been listed by C. Brockelmann.[54] The Imāmīs deem Ja'far aṣ-Ṣādiq, the sixth Imam, to be the founder of their system, but the Imāmī Collections of the Tradition and works on Fiqh which have come down to us are not earlier than the second half of the ninth century. Detailed information on them is contained in the *Fihrist*, or Index, of Muḥammad an-Nadīm (995), among other sources.[55] One of the well-known Imāmī compilers of the Tradition was Muḥammad b. al-Ḥasan al-Qummī (d. 903), and a still more authoritative Imāmī Faqīh was Muḥammad b. Ya'qūb al-Kulaynī,[56] who died in Baghdad in 939. He was responsible for a comprehensive work entitled *Al Kāfī fī 'ilmi 'd-dīn*, or Compendium on Theology. This is divided into two parts, one devoted to *uṣūl* and the other to *furū'*; and it comprises over sixteen thousand Ḥadīth: of which five thousand and seventy-two are trustworthy (*ṣaḥīḥ*); nine thousand, four hundred and eighty-five weak (*ḍa'īf*), meaning that the recorders themselves recognize them to be unreliable; and the remainder accepted by those recorders with reservations. The most noted Imāmī theologian of the tenth century was Abū Ja'far Muḥammad b. 'Alī al-Qummī, more familiar under the names Ibn Bābuyya (or Ibn Bābawayh in the arabicized spelling) and aṣ-Ṣadūq, 'The Sincere'. He came from Khurāsān to Baghdad in 955 and expired there in 991. As many as three hundred writings were attributed to him, of which about ten have come down, including a Legal Guide containing some four thousand, five hundred Ḥadith, entitled *Man lā yaḥḍuruhu 'l-faqīh*, a sort of 'Everyman's Lawyer'.[57] Qāḍī Nu'mān Muḥammad b. Ḥayyān (d. 974), who lived in Egypt and was a Mālikite before becoming an Imāmī Shī'ite, composed a digest on Imāmī Law which the Ismā'īlīs too adopted as a manual on exoteric doctrine suitable for their uninitiated public.[58] Another acknowledged Imāmī authority was Abū 'Abdullāh Muḥammad b. an-Nu'mān al-Baghdādī al-Mufīd (d. 1022), author of numerous works, allegedly two hundred, of which only four have survived. But it is his pupil Muḥammad b. Ḥasan aṭ-Ṭūsī (d. 1067/8 at the age of seventy-three) who won even more fame among the Imāmīs. Having left his native Ṭūs in Khurāsān as a youth, he settled in Baghdad. After the fall of the Buwayhid dynasty in 1055 and the shift of power to the Seljūqids, the Shi'ites began to be persecuted, and aṭ-Ṭūsī found himself accused of cursing certain Companions who were opponents of 'Alī. He managed to clear himself, but was compelled to quit Baghdad (where his house was burned down by Sunnīs) and repair to Najaf where he presently died. His *Fihrist*, or 'Index', a biographical work, is a mine of information on Shī'ite literature. Two other works of his, namely the *Tahdhību 'l-Aḥkām*, ('Amendment of Legal Findings') and the *Istibṣār* ('Investigation') combined with the works by al-Kulaynī and Ibn Bābawayh cited above, constitute in Imāmī parlance the Four Books (*al-kutubu 'l-arba'a*), and their authors are the Three Muḥammads, accounted the highest authorities produced by the tenth and eleventh centuries. All the works enumerated in this paragraph were of course written in Arabic.

A phase of stern Sunnī reaction set in under the Ghaznawids in East Iran, and more so under the Seljūqids. Even the Moderate Shī'ites, not to speak of the Ismā'īlīs and Extremists, suffered periodic persecution and were driven, Faqīhs included, to conceal their belief and pretend to be Sunnīs. These were consequently inauspicious years for Shī'ite literature, and between the mid-eleventh century and the Mongol invasion in the earlier thirteenth the sole theologian the Imāmīs had of note was Shaykh aṭ-Ṭabarsī of Mashhad and Sabzawār who brought out a Koranic commentary which was well received, the *Jāmi'u 'l-Jawāmi' fi-Tafsīri 'l-Qur'ān* ('Collection of Collections on Koranic Exegesis').[59]

Under the Mongols the Imāmīs went unmolested. The conquerors themselves were to embrace Islam in 1295, and meantime they showed themselves tolerant of all creeds and sects, or else indifferent in matters of religion. Certain of the Il-Khāns, like Hūlāgū and Abāqā, found it politically expedient to pose as patrons of the Christians and Buddhists — and Arghūn added the Jews to these — but the point was that nobody was persecuted. And when the Il Khāns became Muslims, one of them, Uljāytū Khān (Sultan Muḥammad Khudā-Banda, 1304–16) chose the Imāmī sect of Shī'ism. This, it is true, was a personal affair and he did not succeed in making the state as such follow suit: the Sunnī Faqīhs, Shāfi'ite and Ḥanafite, were too strong, and the bulk of the Persian barons were of course Sunnīs at that time.

The outstanding Shī'ite authorities in this period were Najmu 'd-Dīn Ja'far b. Muḥammad al-Ḥillī (d. 1275) and his nephew on his mother's side, Jamālu 'd-Dīn Ḥasan Ibnu 'l-Muṭahhar al-Ḥillī, dubbed in Persian 'Allāme-yi Ḥillī, the Sage of Ḥilla[60] (d. 1326), who is credited with having converted Uljāytū Khān to Shī'ism. The elder of the two wrote a classic on Imāmī law entitled *Sharā'i'u 'l-Islām* ('Laws of Islam')[61] and the younger had many books, perhaps seventy-five, to his name of which a few are extant. To be mentioned here are: a study of the Imamate, *Minhāju 'l-Karāma fī Ma'rifati 'l-Imāma* ('The Way of Grace in the Knowledge of the Imamate') in ten chapters with a supplement on the principles of Shī'ite theology; a work on the foundations of Shī'ite belief, *Minhāju 'l-Yaqīn fī Uṣūli 'd-Dīn* ('The Way of Certainty in the Elements of Faith'); and a handbook of Imāmī law, *Tadhkiratu 'l-Fuqahā* ('The Faqīhs' Guide') in three volumes. These two authors eclipsed all previous Imāmī scholars in fame, and when Shī'ism asserted its hold on Iran later on in Ṣafawid days, the writings of the Ḥilla divines became the standard textbooks of the Imāmīs on dogmatics and law.

Imāmī theologians bring their dogmatics under these five heads of belief (*uṣūlu 'd-dīn*): *tawḥīd*, the Oneness of God, the dogma of monotheism; *'adl*, justice, the belief in divine equity; *nabuwwa*, prophecy, the recognition of the prophetic mission of Muḥammad and of his precursors, the earlier prophets; *imāma*, the acknowledgement of the community's need of hereditary Imams of the family of 'Alī; and *qiyāma*, resurrection (otherwise called *ma'ād*, 'the place of return', techn. term 'future life'), the belief in the Day of Judgment and the world beyond the grave. Four out of these five basic dogmas, viz. *tawḥīd*, *'adl*, *nabuwwa* and *qiyāma*, are shared with the Sunnīs; albeit *'adl* is here understood rather in the Mu'tazilite sense with its denial of unconditional predestination. On the other hand the doctrine of the Imamate as expounded by the Imāmī Shī'ites, the *Ithnā-'ashariyya*, is radically at variance with the Sunnī conception of the Caliphate. This doctrine is the cornerstone of their dogmatics. Whereas the Imam-Caliph of the Sunnīs possesses no sacred characteristics and is not looked up to as a teacher,[62] 'the Imam of the Shī'ites, having personal qualities which God has imparted to him, is a leader and a teacher of Islam, is the heir to the rank of the Prophet. He rules and teaches in the name of God. . . . He is lifted from the ruck of mankind by his superhuman virtues'.[63] The Sunnī theologians attribute an inherent immunity from sin, *'iṣma*, to Muḥammad; in Shī'ite thinking *'iṣma* is an innate quality not only of Muḥammad but of the Imams as well.

As if this were not enough, the Shī'ites (except the Zaydīs) consider the Imam to be the born medium of divine manifestation — *ẓuhūr*. The rudiments of this idea were already in the Koran, where Jesus is the 'divine word'.[64] But Muḥammad claimed no such thing for himself: it was the Shī'ites who developed the doctrine of an everlasting divine light — *Nūr-i Muḥammadī*. From the time of Adam's creation this divine light went on passing from one descendant of his to another, at God's selection; then after visiting a series of prophets, it illumined Muḥammad's grandfather 'Abdu 'l-Muṭṭalib: after him it became divided; part fell on Muḥammad's father 'Abdullāh and next on the Prophet himself, while the other part lent its radiance to 'Abdullāh's brother Abū Ṭālib, and then to his son 'Alī. From 'Alī the divine effulgence shone in a line of Imams descended from him, from generation to generation. It was the manifestation of this divine light that made the particular 'Alid the Imam of his time, and gave him the spiritual powers of a superman: whence the Imam's innocence, his immunity from sin and error, his infallibility in judgment and word and act.

Such was the Imāmī Shī'ite conception of the Imamate. 'This', observes Goldziher 'is roughly what the Moderate Shī'ite thinks about his Imams. We do not, it is true, find any nicely formulated statement of the theory, but we need not hesitate to regard it as the universally accepted view.'[65] The doctrine still fell short of deification, being only the notion of a divine light in certain men. But for the mass of simple Believers unversed in theological subtleties the avenue leading to the idolization (*ḥulūl*) of the Imams had been thrown open. The Extreme Shī'ites pursued it to its end.[66]

It will thus be seen that Imāmī doctrine requires of its followers not only a belief in the One God, in the prophetic mission of Muḥammad and his forerunners, and in the revelation sent down in the Koran, but also a belief in the Imam of the time who is chosen by God to be the vehicle of a portion of the divine light and an immaculate (*ma'ṣūm*) teacher leading the Believers to everlasting bliss. Without knowing the Imam of the age it is not possible to save the soul, according to the Imāmīs; knowledge of the genuine Imam and walking in his steps are the necessary conditions of salvation. In virtue of the Imam's inborn infallibility, each direction of his, each opinion, must be considered evident and indubitable truth. If the Imam's opinion should contradict our direct sense-perception, then it were proper to show preference to his opinion by reason of the infallibility of its source, since the organs of sense of ordinary people may mislead badly. For the Sunnīs the highest authority is the *ijmā'* — the consensus of the religious teachers,[67] — but the highest authority for the Imāmīs is the Imam of the time. Admittedly the Shī'ite jurists recognized the principle of *ijmā'*; but with this vital reservation that a consensus can only be achieved through the good offices of the Imam. Goldziher has written: 'If we want to put in a nutshell the difference between the Islam of the Sunnīs and the Islam of the Shī'ites, we can say the first is the Church founded on *ijmā'* and the second is the Church founded on authority.'[68]

The Shī'ites also believe that the Imams must possess a secret knowledge embracing the whole content of religion, the occult sciences and all world-history. This knowledge had been disclosed to 'Alī and transmitted through him to the other Imams in sequence. It includes the inner (*bāṭin*) hidden sense of the Koran which is withheld from the uninitiated, a comprehension of the secrets of nature, and an understanding of the inside meaning of all the events of the history of mankind from Adam until the day of the resurrection of the dead. It followed that the Imam was privy to the future, knew the historical figures to come and everything which would be accomplished after his own death. Muḥammad had said that unlike Jesus he had not been granted the gift of working miracles, but the Imāmī Traditionists ascribe thousands of miracles to each of the Imams.

Without the Imam's guidance there is no salvation; more than that, the world cannot exist without him. So after the disappearance of Muḥammad b. Ḥasan, allegedly twelfth in the line, a way out was found in the doctrine of the veiled Imam. The idea was not new. One of the branches of the Kaysānīs had already maintained that their Imam Muḥammad Ibnu 'l-Ḥanafiyya had not died, but lived on unseen; and subsequently the Ismā'īlīs claimed hidden Imams after the death of their seventh pontiff Muḥammad b. Ismā'īl.[69] The Imāmīs simply followed suit, developing the theory of *ghayba* in more detail than the other sects. According to their doctrine *ghayba* signifies the state of things when the divinely chosen person is withdrawn at the will of God from the gaze of the world's inhabitants; in that state he lives on unseen, his life being miraculously prolonged, it may be for hundreds and even thousands of years. Ibn Bābawayh explained that the hidden Imam who is generally invisible to all may on occasion become visible to an elite, for instance religious preceptors, enter into communion with them and give them directions and advice. In this manner the veiled Imam watches vigilantly over the destinies of his community, and guides it from behind his screen.

Closely bound up with the cult of the Imams, particularly that of the first Imam 'Alī and the third Imam Ḥusayn, was the martyr motive. The Sunnīs did not press this motive since Sunnism became the state religion, official and triumphant. On the other hand it was understandable that the idea of the majesty of martyrdom, of purification by suffering, of the tragic fate of the noble family of 'Alī, should beckon to the persecuted and frequently clandestine community of the Imāmī Shī'ites. With them the cult of the martyrs attained virtually the sort of importance it had in Christianity. The legend which turned all Imams into martyrs, the mourning in memory of the catastrophe at Kerbelā on 10 Muḥarram, the traditional date of that event,[70] the observance of Ghadīru 'l-Khumm day,[71] the reading of the lives of the saints, the pilgrimage to their shrines (more in vogue among Shī'ites than among Sunnīs) — all this was evidence of the martyr-worship from which Imam-worship was scarcely separable.

Shī'ites, and particularly the Imāmīs, mentally equated the return of the hidden Imam with the advent of the Mahdī, a sort of Messiah appointed to appear at the end of the world. The idea was not alien to the Sunnīs even. Originally the Mahdī was thought of as none other than Jesus Christ who in the common creed of the Muslims must herald the approach of the Day of Judgment; and only afterwards was he thought of as a separate person. But as Goldziher has observed 'in Sunnī Islam the pious expectation of the Mahdī, for all that it was endorsed by the Ḥadīth and had its theological justification, never attained the status of a dogma; it is never more than a mythological embellishment of the ideal of the future, a supplement to the orthodox understanding of the world'.[72] To the Sunnīs the Mahdī is only the announcer of the imminent end of the world, an ill-defined and colourless figure whose place is not large in religious belief: he does not seem to be a specific person in their eyes. And they hold on the basis of their Ḥadīth that the name of the Mahdī has to be the same as that of the Prophet — Muḥammad b. ʿAbdullāh — and on this account do not acknowledge as such the twelfth Imam of the Imāmīs who was called Muḥammad b. Ḥasan.

As against this, the Shīʿite belief in the advent of a Mahdī — in the case of the Imāmīs it was not differentiated from a belief in the return of their twelfth Imam whom they called consequently Muḥammad Mahdī — amounted to a principal dogma. The belief was that on his return the Imam Mahdī would continue the work of the Prophet, reassert the flouted rights of his divinely chosen family, and restore the original Islam including the theocracy on which the Sunnī Caliphs had trampled. Therewithal, he would 'fill the world with truth and justice', and would 'remove tyrants and tyranny which is the violence done by some to others' — so read two favourite Ḥadīth of the Shīʿites. In the language of the same Ḥadīth, he is Lord of the Sword — *Ṣāḥibu 's-Sayf* — meaning that in setting up the reign of truth and justice upon earth he would head an armed revolt of Shīʿites against the tyrants, who were the Sunnī rulers, and with God's help vanquish them.

It is here that the messianic idea joined forces with the hopes which the artisans, peasants and poverty-stricken nomads had of a social revolution. This explains why Shīʿism in Iran, Syria, Asia Minor and Yemen, as Bartol'd noted and more modern research has confirmed, flourished mainly in a rural setting.[73] Shīʿism was the ideological expression of mass aspirations; belief in the return of the Imam Mahdī was the idea of social revolution expressed in religious terms. In the popular imagination he was pictured as the reformer of the existing order, the deliverer from want, sorrow and oppression. And the whole messianic theme, including the martyr-cult, was what seemed specially attractive about this persecuted faith of Shīʿism to a people whose life under feudal conditions was often one long martyrdom.

Some passages in literature show how strong was the expectation of the Mahdī among the Shīʿites of Iran. Yāqūt relates that in early thirteenth-century Kāshān, which was one of the main nurseries of Shīʿism, the city elders would go out beyond the gates every morning leading a saddled and richly caparisoned white horse by the bridle, in case of the sudden appearance of him who was daily awaited. He never does appear, adds Yāqūt with some scepticism, but this does not reduce their faith one whit.[74] Something similar was done in another Shīʿite hotbed, the town of Sabzawār, during the regime of the Sarbadārs[75] there in the fourteenth century. Each day, morning and evening, they tethered a saddled steed on the main square in the hope that the Lord of the Age might come.[76] And of course there was never any dearth of self-styled Mahdīs.

Periodic persecution on the one hand and the need for clandestine propaganda on the other led the Shī'ites not only to approve the 'prudent concealment of faith' but positively raise it to the level of a principle. It is termed *taqiyya* (lit. 'circumspection') and *kitmān* (concealment), and based on a rather arbitrary interpretation of a sentence in the Koran: 'Whether ye hide that which is in your breasts, or whether ye declare it, God knows it.'[77] The Ḥanafites permit the Believer in exceptional circumstances, but emphatically not as a rule, to deny his faith aloud in order to avoid the risk of death to himself or his family, provided that he makes a mental reservation (cf. the *reservatio mentalis* of the Jesuits who accepted the same principle) repudiating in his heart the words he has uttered aloud. The Shī'ites go much further. They not only allow, they oblige their adherents living in a country where there is persecution, to conceal their convictions, play the hypocrite and talk as though they are not Shī'ites. Moreover, in addition to making his mental reservation that he does not believe what he is perforce saying aloud, the Shī'ite must curse the enemies of his faith and their ideas. The inward cursing of the enemies of his faith is his moral obligation.

In one of the Imāmī traditions it is related that a certain Shī'ite addressed the sixth Imam Ja'far aṣ-Ṣādiq, saying: 'O descendant of the Prophet, I am not capable of actively supporting your cause; the only thing I can do is inwardly to repudiate your enemies and curse them. What then am I worth?' The Imam answered him: 'My father gave me this instruction imparted to him by his father, who had it from his father, the third Imam Ḥusayn, who heard it from the mouth of the Prophet: Whoso is too weak to help us the members of the House (*ahlu 'l-bayt*) to gain the victory, but in his own cell heaps curses on our enemies, him do the Guardian Angels glorify as blessed; they pray to God for him, saying: "O God thou hast had pity on this thy servant who does all that he is in a condition to do; if he could do more, he would assuredly do it." And the voice comes forth from the Lord: "I have heard your petition, and am merciful to his soul; it shall be received by me among the souls of the elect and good."' All branches of the Shī'ites follow the *taqiyya* principle except the Zaydīs. The Ismā'īlīs and Extremists (Druzes, Anṣārīs, Ḥurūfīs, 'Alī-Ilāhīs and others like them) adhere to it even more consistently.

The religious doctrines of the Imāmīs can thus be seen to revolve on the cult of 'Alī and the Imams in his line. Avowal of the Imam, either declared or else harboured in the silent recesses of the heart, is the very condition of salvation. They like to say: 'The love of 'Alī devours all sins as the fire consumes the dry wood'. And to the general confession of all the Muslims 'There is no God but God, and Muḥammad is the Apostle of God', they add the words 'And 'Alī is the saintly intimate of God' (*wa 'Alī waliyyu 'llāh*).

We have spoken of the Shī'ite debt to Mu'tazilite views. The Imāmīs were more restrained than the Zaydīs in assimilating these; but they accepted the Mu'tazilite theses relating to the Unity of God (*tawḥīd*) and Divine Justice (*'adl*), the first of which repudiated anthropomorphism and the second of which refuted unqualified predestination. Identity with the Mu'tazilite assumptions was here so complete that the Shī'ites did not hesitate to call themselves what the Mu'tazilite called themselves — Supporters of Unitarianism and Divine Justice (*ahlu 't-awḥīd wa 'l 'adl*).[78] Goldziher well observes that when the Shī'ites produce works on dogmatics, the Mu'tazilite text-book always shows through in the approach to the two fundamental issues, one of these occupying a chapter on God's Unity and the other a chapter on God's Justice.[79] In their dogmatics, God created man with freedom of will and responsibility; so that predestination has to be understood as meaning that the actions of the whole of mankind past, present and future, are known to God from all eternity and are consequently inscribed in the book of each man's destiny. The dogma of the existence of an Imam in every age, and of the infallibility of the Imamate, was also indebted to the Mu'tazilite assumptions; for the Justice of God required that he should give mankind a spiritual leader, in every age, immune from error and capable of leading the human race along the path to salvation.

Exegesis,[80] particularly in the case of the Imāmīs, was based on an allegorical understanding of the Koran — *ta'wīl*. It pained the Shī'ites that Holy Writ made no mention of 'Alī b. Abī Ṭālib, but a satisfactory explanation of this omission was ready to hand. The Book, they said, was edited by Zayd b. Thābit at the instance of Caliph 'Uthmān and his Ummayad kinsmen, all of them bitter enemies of the 'Alid house, and to please them certain changes were made in the text, including the removal of the references to 'Alī. It was not demonstrable, but it certainly had the ring of probability. Shī'ites therefore do not consider Zayd's official recension of the Koran, as received by the Sunnīs, to be faultless: they hold that it does not represent the original in its entirety and also that Suras CXIII and CXIV are spurious insertions. They use the official version since no other is in existence, but their theologians feel justified in bringing a critical mind to bear on it. There are places where they prefer a variant reading or else an interpretation of individual words which alters the meaning of the whole sentence, but they keep these emendations to their commentaries without incorporating them in the text. The Koran is recited in mosques as it stands.

If they can manage to find an allusion to ʿAlī even in the Zayd redaction, the Shīʿites will do so, obscurity notwithstanding. Thus in one passage[81] where the adjective *ʿaliyy* ('sublime') occurs as an epithet of the Koran, they see the proper name ʿAlī; and in another,[82] instead of reading *salām ʿalā Ilyāsin* 'Peace on Ilyās (the prophet Elias)' they read 'Peace of ʿAlī, yā sīn'.[83] Again, in certain places[84] where the Koran has the word *umma* ('people', 'religious community'), they suggest *a'imma* ('Imams', pl. of *imām*) which closely resembles it in the Arabic script, so that utterances which relate to the whole Muslim community in the official text of the Koran in Shī'ite exegesis become utterances addressed to the Imams and affirmations of their authority. The title of Sura XVI, 'The Bees', and the passage in that Sūra referring to them,[85] are given an allegorical meaning: the Bees are the Imams of the ʿAlids, and the nectar gathered by them from the flowers and fruits is the salutary teaching which is in the Koran and interpreted to people by the Imams of ʿAlī's line. To the Shīʿites ʿAlī, in consequence, is the Prince of Bees (*amīru 'n-naḥl*). In Sūra II it is said that Moses, commanded by God, told his people to sacrifice a cow, *baqara*.[86] This word in the context, according to the Shīʿites, means ʿĀ'isha, the implacable opponent of ʿAlī; it was she who was to be sacrificed for the good of the Muslim community. The aim of such allegorical interpretations of the text was of course to secure Koranic authority for the doctrine of the exclusive recognition of ʿAlī and the Imams of the ʿAlid line.

Differences of ritual and law as between the Moderate Shīʿites, especially the Imāmīs, and the Sunnī schools were slight on the whole, and very little need be added to what has been said above under the heading of civil and criminal procedure.[87] 'The ritualistic and juridical practice of the Shīʿites', Goldziher concludes, 'does not differ from that of other persuasions in Islam more than usages differ as between one Sunnī Madhhab and the next. The minor and formal differences of detail are on a par with the divergences existing between say, Ḥanafites and Mālikites'.[88]

Just as the Sunnī jurists in their day split up into *Aṣḥābu 'l-Hadīth* or literalists who sought to rely as far as possible on the Koran and Ḥadīth alone, and *Aṣḥābu 'r-Ra'y* who admitted some degree of logical inference and personal opinion, so the Imāmīs for their part had their *Akhbārī*, a minority body of 'traditionist' divines, and their *Uṣūlī*, a majority group of doctors who went to 'the root' of the matter by the process of *qiyās* and an *ijmā'* unifying the rulings of the Mujtahids. The Imāmī theologians of this majority constitute what is known as the Ja'far aṣ-Ṣādiq Madhhab. They reject the Sunnī view that 'the gates of *ijtihād* are now closed', i.e. that there are no more Mujtahids competent to arrive at findings on the roots (*uṣūl*) and branches (*furū'*) of law,[89] and indeed postulate that they do exist and can continue to do so until the advent of the Mahdī. Thus Mujtahids were honoured with the title *Ḥujjatu 'l-Islām*, Proof of Islam, by the Imāmīs and enjoyed every esteem. The highest among them lived in the 'Holy Land' of the Shī'ites, namely Arab Iraq, at Kerbelā, Najaf, Kāẓimayn and Sāmarrā, close to the sacred sepulchres of the Imams. And when Shī'ism had consolidated itself in Iran under the Ṣafawid Shahs, all royal edicts and administrative reforms had to receive the assent of the Mujtahids, and Holy War could not be declared without their sanction.

The essential divergence from the Sunnīs in the civil law is the recognition of the validity of temporary marriage. This was in vogue among the heathen Arabs but was abolished and prohibited, it was traditionally taught, either by the Prophet Muḥammad or by Caliph 'Umar. The Imāmīs considered that the Prophet's intervention was unproved and that of 'Umar illegal, since he was a mere usurper from their standpoint. This temporary union, known as *mut'a* (lit. 'something of use' from the vb. *mutta'a* 'to give, to enjoy') or *ṣīgha* (lit. 'formula'), can be contracted at the desire of the parties (in practice, the man) for a term of anything from one day to ninety-nine lunar years. So in a given case it might either be just a legal form of that prostitution which the Sharī'a prohibits, or it might amount to a permanent alliance with this difference that the woman had none of the rights the Sharī'a confers on the lawful wife — bride-price, inheritance, separate accommodation, servants, etc. Moreover she is so inferior socially to the lawfully wedded wife that Sayyid families do not allow their womenfolk to contract the *mut'a* marriage; and the Imāmī Sharī'a itself, while not prohibiting *mut'a*, characterizes it as disapproved (*makrūh*) in the case of girls. The *mut'a* marriage is in fact legalized cohabitation, comfortable enough for the man since it involves him in none of the obligations he would incur towards a fully wedded wife. It appeals therefore either to the poor who lack the means to support a lawful wife properly or to the very wealthy and aristocratic whom it enables to get round the prohibition against more than four wives. For there is nothing to prevent a man having dozens of *mut'a* wives simultaneously. Where the contract is for a lengthy term the woman may be shackled for life, but the man is not tied at all: at any moment he can release the woman having 'made her a present' of the uncompleted term.

The children of such unions, like children by a slave-woman, are legitimate. On the lapse of the contracted term, or in case of foreclosure by the woman's 'release' or the man's death, the woman is obliged to wait a period of three months and ten days called *'idda* to show whether she is pregnant. In the event of pregnancy she can claim maintenance unless the father prefers to look after the child himself. On the expiry of her *'idda* she is free to enter into another temporary marriage. There is no question of the man paying his partner a *mahr* in a temporary marriage,[90] but a monthly sum is stipulated by way of subsistence. The woman cannot cancel the contract.

Where the temporary marriage is for a brief spell, a written contract is frequently dispensed with; but where it is for a more lengthy term a document is usually executed in roughly this form, or *ṣīgha*:

'Entering into the enjoyment is . . . (here follows the full name with description of the man).

Contributing to the enjoyment, sound of reason, of legal age, capable of acting unaided and mindfully is . . . (here follows the full name of the woman).

Duration: ninety lunar years from today's date, every day and every night.

It shall be binding on the first party: to pay eighteen qrans per mensem.

This agreement of temporary marriage hereby comes into force and effect.'[91]

The contract, like other legal instruments, is authenticated by the Qāḍī's seal and the seals (in place of signatures) of witnesses. It is read aloud and pronounced to be 'the commitment and consent', *ījāb wa qabūl*, of the parties.

For the rest, as has been said, Imāmī law differs from Sunnī law merely on small points, the Imāmīs coming especially close to the Shāfi'ite position. Consequently it was always easy for them to practise 'prudent concealment' in Sunnī states, and pass themselves off as Shāfi'ites.

Some further minor features of the Imāmī system can be noticed. Like the Shāfi'ites the Imāmīs forbid legal marriage (though of course allowing *mut'a*) with a woman of the People of the Book — that is, a Christian or Jewess. They allow the formula of provisional divorce (Pers. *ṭalāq-i raj'at*) which entitles the husband to resume the marriage. The wife in such cases must submit to the husband's wish, and where a divorce is confirmed it is always the father who keeps the children. The Imāmīs did not countenance the setting at liberty of non-Muslim slaves, except that these might be ransomed for money. They condemned to death any one guilty of blasphemy and reviling the Prophet, and even any one reviling the Imams of the 'Alids. They admitted repentance in case of apostasy but only where the person concerned had originally professed another religion, and afterwards embraced Islam and then renounced it. Such a recreant would be accorded thirty days' grace in which to repent.[92] Other apostates were sentenced to death unconditionally, and no plea of penitence was entertainable.

There is a departure from Sunnī law in the matter of 'permissible' (in the sense of not being wine or the flesh of the pig) nourishment. The Sunnīs allow this to be consumed when prepared by Christian or Jewish hands; whereas the Imāmīs forbid its consumption in such a case, and the partaking of anything in company with People of the Book.

A declaration of Holy War (*jihād*) requires the assent of the Imam of the Time or, during the Occultation, that of the Mujtahids. The Imāmī definition of Jihād is not only war with the infidels, it is also war with those who do not acknowledge the authority of the Shī'ite Imams; in other words, with the Sunnīs.

The *iqāma* is announced twice among the Shī'ites. The public cursing of the first three Caliphs Abū Bakr, 'Umar and 'Uthmān was instituted under the Ṣafawids. There are a number of small differences in the performance of the regulation prayers, the ablution and the Pilgrimage. According to the Manual of Imāmī Law adopted in the reign of Shah 'Abbās I called *Jāmi'i 'Abbāsī*, the work of Shaykh Muḥammad Bahā'u 'd-Dīn 'Āmilī, there are seventeen obligatory and fifteen recommended rules for the full ablution, *ghusl*; twenty-one obligatory and twenty recommended rules for the partial ablution, *wuḍū'*; twelve obligatory and seven recommended rules for the ablution with sand, or *tayammum*; and twelve obligatory and fifteen recommended rules for the washing of a corpse.

The Imāmīs celebrate the general Muslim holidays and their own

Saints' Days in addition. Of these the most important is the day of mourning[93] commemorating the catastrophe at Kerbelā in which the third Imam Ḥusayn perished with his adherents. This 'Day' is the ten-day commemoration ('*āshūrā*') beginning on 1 Muḥarram (and thus coinciding with the New Year's Day of the Muslim calendar) and reaching its climax on 10 Muḥarram. The days of grief are marked by passion plays, *ta'zīya*, the recitation of the tragic events, *rawḍa*, and processions in which the participants in times gone past used to exhibit their self-inflicted wounds. Various other dates are set aside for prayer meetings, ziyāras to holy shrines, etc.: the fortieth day after the martyrdom of Imam Ḥusayn and his following, falling on 20 Ṣafar; the day of the death of Fāṭima, daughter of the Prophet and wife of 'Alī, on 13 Jumādī 'ul-ūlā; the birthday of 'Alī on 13 Rajab; the day when he received his mortal wound, on 19 Ramaḍān; and the day of Ghadīru 'l-Khumm on 18 Dhu 'l-Ḥijja. The birthdays and days of 'martyrdom' of the Imams are also observed.

The Shī'ites are less strict than the Sunnīs in their attitude to the representation of the human form, and it is not rare for the prophets, even the Prophet Muḥammad, 'Alī and the other Imams to be depicted in the miniatures illustrating manuscripts,[94] though their faces are generally veiled or shown only in outline. Saints, Ṣufī Shaykhs, and so on, will also figure in such miniatures, and notwithstanding the fact that the religious authorities officially disapproved of sacred pictures, a kind of icon-painting did come into vogue. Frescoes depicting the prophets, Muḥammad himself, and the Imams, are now and then to be met with in mazārs, (mausoleums) at saqqa-khānas[95] (drinking fountains) and even in mosques.[96]

Shī'ism of the Imāmī sect was the gainer when its rivals, the Ismā'īlīs, lost position in Iran in the thirteenth century.[97] From then until the fifteenth century the Imāmīs became widely represented in the country, and repeatedly took the lead in the major movements of the people.

XI
Ismā'īlīs, Carmathians and Extreme Shī'ites

We have been discussing the Moderate Shī'ites — Kaysānīs, Zaydīs and Imāmīs — who did not differ very materially from the Sunnīs except in their doctrine of the hereditary Imamate of the 'Alids. But side by side with these Moderates, a number of sects took shape in 'Abbāsid times whose common denominator was the deification of 'Alī and his descendants, and whom men called the Extreme Shī'ites — the *Ghulāt* (pl. of *ghālī*, from *ghalā*, 'to exceed bounds, exaggerate'). These sects developed in one form or another the ideas of incarnation (*ḥulūl*) and metempsychosis (*tanāsukh*, Lat. *transmigratio*) which were alien to the original Islam. Contemporaries traced these doctrines to 'Abdullāh b. Sabā,[1] the ideological founder of Shī'ism, who had preached the divine character of 'Alī and also the theory of the palingenesis (*raj'a*) of Muḥammad which was later identified with the Extremist doctrine of the reincarnation of the souls of the prophets.

Orthodox theologians, attacking these heresies, distinguished three forms of idolization: there was *ẓuhūr* ('appearance', Lat. *manifestatio*) or the reflection of deity and divine power in a man; there was *ittiḥād* ('unity') or the co-existence in a single soul of the human and the divine principles; and there was *ḥulūl* or the incarnation of God in a man, whose human nature is thereby made divine. Regarding *ẓuhūr* opinions were apt to vary, but *ittiḥād* and *ḥulūl* were condemned by all Sunnī and all Moderate Shī'ite theologians, as well as by all moderate Ṣūfīs,[2] as heretical and foreign to Islam.

Close to the Extremists in some regards was a Shī'ite sect, or more accurately a great offshoot of Shī'ite doctrine dating from the mid-eighth century, which was destined to play an important role in the Middle East and Iran — that of the Ismā'īlīs (*ismā'īliyya*). As Professor Ye. A. Belyayev rightly insists, 'the main reason for the emergence of Ismā'īlism was the way in which class contradictions had asserted themselves in the Baghdad Caliphate by the eighth and ninth centuries'.[3] A progressing feudalism, the strengthened grip of the local barons in Iran, and the increasing burden of taxation combined to excite popular risings of the peasantry. Almost always these wore the cloak of sectarianism. In the eighth and ninth centuries the cloak was often the non-Muslim Khurramī doctrine which harked back to the ideas of the Mazdakites of three hundred years earlier. But as time went on, and particularly in the ninth and tenth centuries, the risings would occur under Moderate or Extreme Shīʿite and Ismāʿīlī leadership.

These religious movements of different persuasions were united in a common disavowal of the Caliphate, whether Umayyad or ʿAbbāsid, and in the ambition to establish universal justice and social equality. Sometimes that idea would be but vaguely conceived and only expressed in slogans, but sometimes (as in the doctrines of the Khurramīs and the Carmathians) it would be more concrete and amount to a system of utopian socialism. The Shīʿite movements shared, besides, the common aim of installing the true Imamate of the ʿAlids and reverting to the theocracy of the unadulterated Islam which was idealized and contrasted with the secular feudal state of the Caliphate. One had here that 'open heresy' which, as Engels points out, is characteristic of popular and opposition movements in the phase of feudalism.[4] Nor would it be possible to disengage the messianic spirit of these different, chiefly Shīʿite, movements from the hopes which the masses placed in a kingdom of justice on earth. The Shīʿite Khabars, or traditions, touching the Mahdī[5] are variations on a single theme: 'He shall fill the earth with truth and justice as now it has been filled with injustice and brute force.'[6]

The rise and spread of Ismāʿīlism must thus be laid at the door of the class contradictions and the movements of popular opposition which became rife in the Caliphate with effect from the seventh and eighth centuries. This social basis or class aspect of early Ismāʿīlism and Carmathianism has been well brought out by two Soviet scholars Ye. A. Belyayev[7] and A. Ye. Bertel's.[8]

But the early history of the Ismāʿīlīs, their organization and doctrine have been inadequately studied up to the present. This is because virtually all the information on the subject (especially for the eighth and ninth centuries), available to European research in the last century and the beginning of this,[9] came from orthodox, and to that extent prejudiced, sources. Those who were out to condemn heresy were readier to distort the Ismāʿīlī doctrine than to study it; and many beliefs were attributed to the Ismāʿīlīs which they had never held, in order to excite the repugnance of all good Muslims. The Ismāʿīlīs were charged with *ḥulūl* and *tanāsukh*, with rejecting the Sharīʿa, with amorality, with atheism; they were said to have gone to the non-Muslim religions for their doctrines. A number of authors, including that of the famous Persian political treatise, the *Siyāsat-nāma* or 'Book of Government' supposedly from the pen of the eleventh-century statesman Niẓāmu 'l-Mulk, lumped the Ismā'īlīs with the Mazdakites, and so comparatively objective a writer on religion and heresy as Shahrastānī harnessed them to sundry Khurramī sects. Very few early Ismā'īlī works having been preserved, it is difficult to tell in what way the initial tenets differed from those which we are familiar with in the tractates of later date. Nevertheless it is now feasible to revise many of the standard opinions held by Islamists about the Ismā'īlīs in the light of recent editions of authentic Isma'īlī texts and of recent research by Bernard Lewis, Louis Massignon, H. Hamdani,[10] and W. Ivanow.[11] As regards the last-named, however, this is the place to say that while he has brought to the surface much that is new in Ismā'īlī history and ideology, his work is marred by his patently apologetic approach.[12] He seeks to clear Ismā'īlism in the eyes of contemporary Muslims of those charges which mediaeval writers and modern scholars have been apt to level at it, and to demonstrate that early Ismā'īlism was very little different from orthodox Islam. Ivanow also contends that there was never the least trace of class struggle or the slightest hint of communistic ideals in its system[13] — a tendentious judgment if ever there was one. One need not appeal to Soviet scholars;[14] one can appeal to Western scholars like Massignon and Hitti who are certainly not Marxist but have explained the socialistic content of the doctrine of the Carmathians by their tie-up with the artisan corporations (*aṣnāf*).[15] The connection of the Ismā'īlīs (and their sideshoot, the Carmathians) with the class struggle in the Caliphate can be taken as proved. Khurramis and Ismā'īlīs/Carmathians had precisely this in common, that they identified themselves with the social movements of their time. And this of course is why the Sunnī authors lumped them together.

The Ismā'īlī sect resulted from a schism among the Shī'ites in the mid-eighth century. The sixth Imam Ja'far aṣ-Ṣādiq had debarred his eldest son Ismā'īl from the succession, and nominated his fourth son Mūsā al-Kāẓim as the next Imam — an act which ancient tradition explained by Ismā'īl's addiction to wine. However that might be, one set of Shī'ites recognized Mūsā al-Kāẓim as seventh Imam, those who took this line becoming known in the sequel as the Twelvers or Imāmīs;[16] and another set stuck to Ismā'īl, arguing that drink is permissible to Imams inasmuch as they are without sin. The real cause of the schism was probably a demand for action voiced by the more radical elements, who were alive to the popular movements that swept through the eastern provinces of the empire not long after the 'Abbāsids secured the throne. So a new ramification of Shī'ism appeared whose following took the name of Ismā'īlīs. The name was reserved for them notwithstanding the fact that Ismā'īl died in 762 three years before his father the sixth Imam, and that it was his eldest son Muḥammad, consequently, whom the sect recognized as seventh Imam. This Muḥammad b. Ismā'īl went into hiding in the Damāwand neighbourhood near Ray to escape the persecution of the 'Abbāsid government; and his descendants, similarly in fear of their lives, were scattered over various lands, Syria and Khurāsān among them. The identity and abode of the one who was acknowledged as the next Imam would only be communicated to a few devoted confidants, and the rest of the Ismā'īlīs did not know so much as the name of their 'hidden' Imam. The succeeding phase of Ismā'īlī history until the early tenth century is termed the Concealment — *satr* (from *satara* 'to hide'). Of the hidden Imams little is known; their very names are variously transmitted in the different sources.[17] Nevertheless the Ismā'īlīs were able to arrange a secret network of much complexity, and energetic propagandists, *du'āt* (sing. *dā'ī*, 'missionary'), set about spreading the gospel of the sect. The halo of secrecy surrounding the 'call', or *da'wa*, proved a powerful attraction, and by the end of the third century AH = the early tenth century of our era, Ismā'īlīs were very numerous in southern Iraq, Baḥrayn, West Iran, Khurāsān, Syria, Egypt and Maghrib.

Apparently quite early on, that is at the turn of the second century AH = eighth/ninth centuries AD, the Ismā'īlīs split into two sub-sects.[18] One of these continued, after Muḥammad b. Ismā'īl's death, to recognize his descendants as hidden Imams, and the adherents of this sub-sect became known thereafter (from, say, the beginning of the tenth century) as Fāṭimid Ismā'īlīs. The other sub-sect clung to the view that there could only be seven Imams, as there were seven principal prophets,[19] all told, and that Muḥammad b. Ismā'īl must therefore be held to be the last Imam. The line of the Imams having ended, it was now for men to await the coming of the seventh prophet, al-Qā'im al-Mahdī, who would arrive not long before the Resurrection or Judgment Day. The members of this sub-sect as acknowledging only seven Imams were styled the *Sab'iyya*, 'The Seveners'. And subsequently, that is in the second half of the ninth century, they adopted another name — Carmathians.

For a long time there was no reason to suppose the division of the Ismā'īlīs would be final. The hidden Imams were shrouded in deep secrecy; they did not enter into contact with the mass of their adherents, and these had never even heard their names. There was therefore no occasion for the two sub-sects to quarrel about whom they did, or did not, recognize; and in fact people often mixed up the two and named both of them Ismā'īlīs, Seveners, and Carmathians indifferently. This was the state of affairs until the beginning of the tenth century.

The origin of this name Carmathian, in Arabic *qarmaṭ*, plural *qarāmiṭa* or *qarmaṭiyya*, has not so far been ascertained, though there have been various hypotheses.[20] Ṭabarī mentions Carmathians for the first time under the year 255 AH (= 869) where he relates that a contingent of fighting-men thus called joined the Zanj rebellion in Lower Iraq and Khūzistān (868-883) alongside the negro slaves and their peasant and Bedouin allies.[21] But it is probable that this secret organization had had its birth in the ranks of small industry earlier than that rebellion. A revolt which was evidently Carmathian occurred in Khurāsān in 873; and some twenty years afterwards there was a major rising in Lower Iraq under the leader Ḥamdān Qarmaṭ who had established a peculiar sort of headquarters near Kūfa in 890. Styled *Dāru 'l Hijra,* Emigration Centre, this had its common purse to which Carmathians were obliged to contribute a fifth of their income. The fraternity held ritual repasts at which the participants ate 'the bread of paradise' — an echo, it may be, of the Christian mystery of the Communion. The ideal they set themselves was to bring in an administrative distribution of 'blessings' or as we should say, consumer goods. The rising was eventually suppressed by imperial forces in 906, after which Lower Iraq was laid waste. Considerably earlier, in 894, the Carmathian revolt had spread to Baḥrayn, where the town of Laḥsā (properly al-Aḥsā') was taken in 899. (Baḥrayn does not refer to the islands in the Gulf, which now constitute the independent state of this name, but to the mainland of eastern Arabia.) Laḥsā became the capital of a sovereign Carmathian community whose sectarians endeavoured to realize their social ideal.[22] Then in 900 revolt broke out in Syria under the leadership of the Carmathian *dā'ī,* Zikruy, or Zikrawayh in the Arabic form. This was put down, but risings went on occurring spasmodically in some districts of Syria and Palestine until the end of the tenth century. On Bīrūnī's showing,[23] the Carmathians were active in India in the thirties of the same century, for this eminent Khwārazmian scholar relates that they seized Multān with its region and set up a state of their own there which was only demolished by Maḥmūd Ghaznawī in 1010/1011. In Khurāsān and Central Asia, Carmathian insurrections were quelled by the Sāmānid Nūḥ b. Naṣr (943–954). However, many Ismā'īlīs of both branches remained in Iran. A massive drive was conducted against them by Maḥmūd Ghaznawī, and it is recorded that when he took Ray from the Buwayhids in 1029 he arrested a large number of local Carmathians and Fāṭimids, and executed them. The artisan component of the sub-sect had been supplemented by Bedouin nomads, but far the biggest intake had been from the peasantry. All these were united by a hatred of the 'Abbāsid Caliphate and the hope of a new order built on social equality.

Parallel with the Carmathians whose agitation in the eastern provinces of the empire has just been outlined, there were the Ismā'īlīs in the west, recognizers of the 'hidden' Imams, who were just as active. The outstanding figure in this sub-sect in the ninth century was 'Abdullāh b. Maymūn (d. *c.* 874). His father Maymūn was a Persian, some say a Zoroastrian, living in Ahwāz, an oculist by profession nicknamed *al-Qaddāḥ* for having carried out an operation for cataract. 'Abdullāh himself, it is said, after studying theology and philosophy became an Ismā'īlī *dā'ī* and preached the gospel of the hidden Imam in Khūzistān. Forced into concealment, he found shelter first in Baṣra and then in Salamiyya in Syria, where he founded a propaganda centre from which missionaries went forth to teach that the coming of the Lord of the Time, *Ṣāḥibu 'z-Zamān*, the Mahdī, was at hand. He also sought a rapprochement with the Carmathians with a view to making the most of the widespread discontent and the internal embarrassments of a Caliphate enfeebled by popular risings. Both Ḥamdān and his relation 'Abdān, a noted writer whose works have been lost, were spoken of as his followers.

Sunnī writers on heresy, and the nineteenth and early twentieth-century scholars who have been influenced by what they wrote, have imputed to 'Abdullāh b. Maymūn the fashioning of an esoteric doctrine (Gk. *esōterikos* 'inner'.[24] Ar. synon. *bāṭin,* 'secret') accessible to the chosen few, as against an exoteric doctine (Gk. *exōterikos* 'outer', Ar. *ẓāhir*) intelligible to the uninitiated. This view, so long entrenched in Islamic scholarship, has now been vigorously disclaimed by W. Ivanow who declares it mere legend. He thinks that the esoteric doctrine of the Ismā'īlīs took shape gradually out of early Shī'ite esotericism as this underwent its own development. In any case, it remains uncertain when and how the secret doctrine of the Ismā'īlīs hardened into shape; but this we know that it was immensely important to the growth and spread of both the sub-sects. The uninitiated were all aware of the existence of this doctrine, and therefore the Ismā'īlīs as such were named Bāṭinīs (*Bāṭiniyya* 'Esoterics' in distinction from *Ẓāhiriyya* 'Externalists' whose doctrine was accessible to all). We shall revert to the esoteric doctrine of the Ismā'īlīs in a moment.

As the tenth century dawned, the missionaries based on the centre in Salamiyya spread the report that the Mahdī had arrived and that he was the Ismā'īlī Imam 'Ubaydullāh whose name had been kept a secret until the last hour. In our present state of knowledge, it cannot be said whether this 'Ubaydullāh was in actual fact the descendant of the seventh Imam Muḥammad b. Ismā'īl of the 'Alids or if he was a daring impostor. Whichever it was, he used the Carmathian agitation in Iraq and Syria in the hope of seizing power. After leading an ill-starred rising in Syria in 900, he abandoned his comrades to the mercy of fate and repaired to Egypt, followed by their curses, and thence to Maghrib. This had long been the scene of momentous events. As early as 895 an energetic and eloquent preacher, Abū 'Abdi'llāh ash-Shī'ī, a native of Yemen and one-time Muḥtaṣib in Baṣra before joining the Ismā'īlīs, had been sent there from the Salamiyya centre. In Tunis where the Aghlabites had ruled since 800, the Berbers were dissatisfied with internal policy and it was easy for Abū 'Abdi'llāh to push them into rebellion. They rose and brought down the local dynasty in 909. This was 'Ubaydullāh's opportunity, and in January 910 he was proclaimed Imam Caliph at Raqqāda, Commander of the Faithful (Amīru 'l-Mu'minīn), and Mahdī. The new dynasty assumed the name Fāṭimid as befitted its claimed descent from 'Alī and his wife Fāṭima, daughter of the Prophet. Its supporters were thenceforward called Fāṭimid Ismā'īlīs.

The Fāṭimid Caliphate, 910–1171, grew into a formidable power. In 969 it forced the rich Egypt into submission, and the Caliph al-Mu'izz founded the new city of Cairo (al-Qāhira) alongside the old Fusṭāṭ and moved his capital there. By the end of the century Maghrib, or a large part of it, Libya, Egypt, Palestine, Syria and Ḥijāz had fallen under Fāṭimid sway. The possession of Egypt in particular, the most highly developed country economically in the Near East, guaranteed immense resources and a war potential. Nor did the rulers of this Ismā'īlī empire omit to spread their gospel beyond their own borders. A missionary centre, *Dāru 'd-Du'āt*, was opened at the Caliph's residence, from which preachers were sent all over the Muslim world. By the dawn of the eleventh century, there was no corner of Iran unaffected by the clandestine message of the Fāṭimids.

The foundation of the Fāṭimid Caliphate in 910 had this result that it drew a definite line of demarcation between its own Ismā'īlīs and the Carmathians. The leaders of the latter were occasionally in touch with the Fāṭimid Caliphs, it is true; but only for immediate political ends, and they neither accepted their paramount authority nor treated them as Imams.

When Ḥamdān Qarmaṭ and 'Abdān inspired and led the agitations at the turn of the ninth and tenth centuries, they claimed to be doing so in the name of the veiled, perhaps mythical, leader of their sect whom they called *Ṣāḥibu 'ẓ-Ẓuhūr* ('possessor of divine manifestation'), whose whereabouts were not made known. And when the Carmathian state was founded in Baḥrayn in 899 with a centre at Laḥsā, its virtually independent leader, the Dā'ī Abū Sa'īd Haṣan al-Jannābī, professed to have been sent there on behalf of the secret head of the sect. No wonder the activities of the Carmathians alarmed the 'Abbāsid government. In the case of Baḥrayn the threat was the greater in that the sect had a following of warlike Bedouin. Abū Sa'īd died in 914, and was succeeded by his son Abū Ṭāhir who ruled for the next thirty years. During his time the Baḥrayn Carmathians repeatedly invaded Lower Iraq and Khūzistān, and cut the caravan routes. But their peak moment was 8 Dhu 'l-Ḥijja 317 = 12 January 930, a day of pilgrimage, when they turned up at Mecca without warning, seized, sacked and partly destroyed the town and led off some thousands of pilgrims and citizens into slavery. That was not the end of the story. The Carmathians were the most radical of the Ismā'īlīs, repudiating most of the rites of orthodox Islam and holding the worship of the Ka'ba to be idolatry. They pillaged the Sanctuary, wrenched the Black Stone from the wall, broke it in two and carried it off with them to Laḥsā.[25] Twenty years were to pass before they consented, under pressure from the Fāṭimid Caliph, to restore it to its place.

Our knowledge of the social order instituted by the Carmathians of Baḥrayn is due to the description of it by an illustrious Ismā'īlī, the Tājīk-Persian poet Nāṣir-i Khusraw who paid a visit to Laḥsā in 1051. We read that the bulk of the population consisted of free peasants and artisans and that the town was encircled by arable lands and groves of date-palms. None of the inhabitants were liable to taxes. The state[26] owned thirty-thousand bought slaves, negroes and Abyssinians, whom it made available to the cultivators gratis for labour in the fields and gardens, as also for repairing buildings and mills. There was a government mill to which the people took their grain and had it ground into flour free of charge. Any cultivator requiring it could obtain a government grant; and a newly arrived artisan settling in Laḥsā received a loan without interest to purchase the tools of his trade and set himself up, which he could refund when it suited him. Usury in any shape or form was forbidden. After Abū Ṭāhir's day, the functions of state were exercised by a college of six Elders (*sādat* pl. of *sayyid* 'lord') assisted by six viziers, and every decision taken by the college had to be unanimous. There was a militia numbering twenty-thousand men.[27]

Such a system can be described as an attempt to establish an old-style free community of farmers and artisans based on slavery. As Ye. A. Belyayev rightly remarks, the ingredient of slavery in the Carmathian community is accounted for by its peasant composition, for 'the Near East peasantry of the Middle Ages in agitating against the feudal state, was striving to revive a social order belonging to the pre- feudal period. And the agricultural communities of the East in that period had normally had their publicly owned slaves'.[28] A point to notice is that the Carmathians, like the Khurramīs indeed, did not extend to slaves the social equality they preached for every one else. They did not reject slavery as an institution, but only wanted to replace the private ownership of slaves by collective ownership. And they could get the slaves either by purchase or by capturing them in the course of their raids on the territories of the Baghdad Caliphate. The Baḥrayn Carmathians having got rid of the regime of the big landlord and the feudal exploitation that went with it, retained slavery — but as a public asset and the basis of their common prosperity.

One thing, however, is indisputable: they did get rid of feudal exploitation and they did attempt to realize their ideal of a free society — even if this was marred by slave-labour. It was a radical programme for those days. Whereas the Fāṭimid Ismā'īlīs had no concrete social programme at all; only vague expectations of the reign of justice that would follow the enthronement of the Mahdī. The first Fāṭimid Caliph, 'Ubaydullāh, having declared himself the Mahdī, actually took it into his head to add to the words of the Tradition, 'he shall fill the earth with justice', the sentence 'And his justice has filled that earth which has fallen under his authority, and he that will come after him shall fill all the rest of the earth with justice'.[29] But needless to say, having become Caliph he introduced no serious reform of any sort; the great estates only passed from their previous proprietors to new ones in his own entourage.

Let us say something about the ideological system of Fāṭimid Ismā'īlism. This was divided into two quite distinct branches. There was the exoteric doctrine, *ẓāhir*, fit to be known by the uninitiated ranks in the sect, and there was the esoteric doctrine, *bāṭin*, disclosed to no more than a few initiates of high degree. This latter, inner body of teaching was regarded as the allegorical interpretation, *ta'wīl*, of the former; there being, as the Ismā'īlī dictum has it, 'nothing outer without inner and, inversely, nothing inner without outer'. In other words, each article of external doctrine has its corresponding article of inward doctrine to elucidate it.

The exoteric branch of the system differed little from Imāmī Shī'ism except on the point that the seventh Imam was not Mūsā al-Kāẓim but Muḥammad b. Ismā'īl, and that after him came the hidden Imams, and after these the Fāṭimid Caliphs. It retained as binding on the mass of Believers (except, that is, the initiates of high degree) almost all the ritualistic and legal decrees of the Sharī'a, notably the regulation prayers, the ablutions, attendance at the mosques, and fasting. It had its own Fiqh, the work of the Imāmī jurist Qāḍī Nu'mān[30] in Egypt in the tenth century. It was, so to speak, the official creed installed by the Fāṭimid Caliphs but with nothing compulsory about it: Imāmīs, Sunnīs of the Mālikite or Ḥanafite schools, Christian Dhimmīs — all these were welcome to pray in their own fashion.[31]

The esoteric branch of the system consisted of two parts: (1) *ta'wīl*, or the allegorical interpretation of the Koran and the Sharī'a. Hell is the condition of ignorance in which the greater portion of mankind abides' and paradise the perfect knowledge which is within the reach of those who ascend the stairs of initiation. (2) *ḥaqā'iq* (pl. of *ḥaqīqa*, 'truth', 'reality'), or a combination of knowledge with theology.

This second was largely unoriginal and eclectic. Most of it had been taken bodily from Neo-Platonism; however not directly, it has now been established, from the Enneads of Plotinus, but from later versions of his idealistic philosophy as rendered by Christian and Jewish authors with some measure of adulteration. Like the Christian and Jewish mystics and the Muslim Ṣūfīs, the Ismā'īlīs found in Neo-Platonism a synthesis of the monotheistic idea and the pluralism of the visible world which strongly appealed to them. They also took over something from Plato; but here again not direct from his writings, for scores of hands came between. And their Natural Philosophy with its doctrine of the organic and the inorganic world was founded on the rationalistic philosophy of Aristotle. The mediaeval authors attribute to them the doctrine of the transmigration of souls, *tanāsukh*, and this may well have been borrowed, though once again not directly, from the neo-Pythagoreans[32] (Ivanow's statement that the idea of metempsychosis was foreign to the Ismāʿīlīs is puzzling, and on the face of it erroneous). Traces of Christianity are perceptible in Ismāʿīlism — its writers quote the New Testament accurately, unlike their orthodox counterparts; and of Christian Gnosticism. Whether the influence of Manicheism is present is doubtful, for Ismāʿīlīs deny the reality of evil and the Devil which is there fundamental. On the whole, the philosophy of Ismāʿīlism is more rationalistic than anything else, but stray elements of mysticism and of magic have found their way into it.

According to the esoteric teaching of Ismāʿīlism, the single source of the plurality of phenomena in the universe is God Most High: He is *al-Ghayb Taʿālā*, the Invisible; *Aḥad*, the One; *Ḥaqq*, Absolute Truth. He has no attributes, is indeterminable, unknowable by men who can have no communion with him. Therefore even to pray to him is impossible. There was here a sharp divergence from both Ṣūfism and Neo-Platonism which asserted the possibility of the direct personal intercourse of man with God. Ismāʿīlism took over from the Neo-Platonists their theory of the origin of the universe but removed the mysticism from it. In its cosmogony, God the Absolute dwells in a state of eternal rest. He is not the immediate creator of the universe, as is taught by Judaism, Christianity and orthodox Islam. By a mere act of will, *amr* ('command') outside time, he has detached from himself the creative essence Universal Reason, *'Aqlu 'l-Kull*. This is the first emanation of the divine nature. It possesses all the attributes of the latter; and the chief one among these is Knowledge. If there are to be prayers, let them be addressed to this. It has many epithets: First, Veil, Spirit, Precedent, etc. In its turn it has given off a second, lower, emanation, Universal Soul, *Nafsu 'l-Kull*; this is imperfect, and its chief attribute is life. Being imperfect, it strives after perfection by exuding fresh emanations: thus it has brought forth Primal Matter, *Hayyūlā* (from Gk. *hulē* 'matter'). The latter has produced the earth, the planets, the constellations and living creatures, and is thus the Initiator, *Mubdiʿ*, of the universe. However, Primal Matter is inert in the sense that it lacks the creative potential, and therefore it can only construct such forms as are pale imitations of the prototypes existing in the Universal Reason. The notions Universal Reason and Universal Soul are borrowed from the Neo-Platonists; the doctrine that transient objects of sensation are only imitations of eternal prototypes or 'ideas' is Plato's, albeit altered. With the Ismāʿīlīs, the Perfect Man, *al-Insānu 'l-Kāmil*, has to have his being on earth as the crown of mankind; in

Plato he is the prototype, or 'idea', in the ideal world of man in the world of sense. Man's appearance is accounted for by the striving of the Universal Soul after perfection.

The seven stages of emanation, viz. God-Most-High-and-Absolute, the Universal Reason, the Universal Soul, Primal Matter, Space, Time and the Perfect Man make up the Sublime World, *'Ālam 'Ulwiy*, which is the seat of creation (*Dāru 'l-Ibdā'*). The world is the macrocosm, *al-'Ālamu 'l-Kabīr*, and man is the microcosm, *al-'Ālamu 'ṣ-Ṣaghīr*; and Ismā'īlī esoteric doctrine emphasizes the parallelism there is between microcosm and macrocosm, between the world of sense and the sublime world. The correspondence, or reflection, of Universal Reason in our world of sense is the Perfect Man: that is, the Prophet — in Ismā'īlī terminology 'the Speaker', *Nāṭiq*; and the correspondence, or reflection, of Universal Soul in the world of sense is his adjutant, called 'the Silent', *Ṣāmit*,[33] otherwise *Asas* ('Basis'), whose task it is to explain to people the inner meaning of the Prophet's utterances and writings by interpretation (*ta'wīl*). Each of the prophets has had such an adjutant: Moses the Nāṭiq had Aaron as Ṣāmit; Jesus Christ had the Apostle Peter; Muḥammad had 'Alī.[34] Nāṭiqs and Ṣāmits have been appearing on earth for mankind's salvation, which is nothing else than the attainment of perfect knowledge — paradise being the allegory of this perfect state.

Answering these seven stages of emanation in the Sublime World, there are seven prophetic cycles marking the life of mankind which are so many sections of the route towards perfection. Each of these cycles is distinguished by the appearance of a Nāṭiq with his Ṣāmit, and six have already occurred, viz. those associated with the coming of Adam, Noah, Abraham, Moses, Jesus and Muḥammad. The seventh will be marked by the advent of the last of the great prophets, al-Qā'im, who shall appear before the end of the world. In each prophetic cycle Imams have followed in the footsteps of the Nāṭiq. The end of the world is due to come when mankind shall have attained perfect understanding through the mediation of Nāṭiqs, Ṣāmits and Imams. Then shall evil, which is nothing but ignorance, vanish, and the world return to its source, the Universal Reason.

It is understandable that Muslim heresy-hunters should have charged the Ismā'īlīs with saying in effect that not a single soul is doomed to the everlasting torments of hell — in their parlance, permanent submersion in ignorance — seeing that knowledge can be arrived at in the course of a series of existences by the process of metempsychosis. It is difficult to say whether this idea prevailed among the early Ismā'īlīs or evolved later. But in any event the Ismā'īlīs did hold that perfect knowledge can only be achieved by an acceptance of the Imam of the Age; which was another way of saying, by becoming an Ismā'īlī.

The strongly knit, ramified organization of the Fāṭimid Ismā'īlīs recognized a hierarchy of degrees of initiation. In ascending order these religious grades were: *Mustajāb* ('accepted'), the neophyte knowing nothing as yet of the esoteric doctrine; *Ma'dhūn* ('permitted'), the learner to whom esoteric doctrine has been partially communicated; *Dā'ī*, the missioner who taught the doctrine and headed local organizations; *Ḥujja* ('Proof'), the chief Dā'ī in charge of a network in an entire area, such as Khurāsān; the Imam; the Ṣāmit; and the Nāṭiq. There were thus seven stages in all. The mass of Believers usually would not rise above the first grade, and rarely rose above the second. Those who achieved the third and fourth constituted the elite of the sect, but even they of course had three unattainable grades above them, viz. those of Imam, Ṣāmit and Nāṭiq.

The Ismā'īlī Sharī'a, worked out by Qāḍī Nu'mān, underwent no further development, and for a very good reason: it only catered for the two lowest grades in the sect. The superior members, initiated into the esoteric doctrine, attached no importance to the Sharī'a. Prayers, interdictions, fasting, and the other prescriptions of the external code were not binding on them.

So much for the doctrine of the Fāṭimid Ismā'īlīs. The Carmathian system approximated to it in essentials, but also had noticeable points of difference. The Divine Essence termed Sublime Light, *Nūr 'Ulwiy*, produced the first emanation which was Glittering Light, *Nūr Sha'sha'ānī*; and this latter gave off the Universal Reason and the Universal Soul, and then primal matter which is Obscure Light, *Nūr Ẓulāmī*. This is blind, passive, inert, unreal, doomed to extinction; it is virtually non-being. All people are not earmarked for perfection or, in other words, salvation, but only the chosen few, viz. prophets, Imams and the initiates. These are sparks thrown off from the Glittering Light into the world of matter or Obscure Light, and it is only the souls of the elect that transmigrate from generation to generation. Other people not belonging to the elite are phantoms of non-being.

The Carmathians had their own degrees of initiation, fixed traditionally by 'Abdān. These degrees were seven in number at first, then ten, and the names, variously reported by different writers, do not coincide with those used by the Fāṭimid Ismā'īlīs. The Carmathian who reached the fourth degree swore an oath to divorce any wife who disclosed the secrets of the sect. Instruction in the esoteric doctrine was imparted by members of the five superior grades, and followed a prescribed method which was to awaken doubt in the pupil's mind and then teach him to conquer it. Because of the emphasis placed on this programme of training (*taʿlīm*), the Carmathians were commonly referred to as the *Taʿlīmiyya*.[35]

In the domain of philosophy proper, Carmathianism had connections with the noted fraternity 'the Brethren of Purity', *Ikhwānu 'ṣ-Ṣafā*, and influenced such thinkers as al-Fārābī (*c.* 870–950) and Ibn Sīnā (980–1037). Something has been said already about the democratic composition of the Carmathian communities and their policy of a social equality adulterated by the collective ownership of slaves, and it will be enough here to add that in Louis Massignon's view it was the Carmathian experiment that inspired the guilds of craftsmen (*aṣnāf*) of Iran and Central Asia.

In their attitude to external practices, ritualistic prohibitions and Fiqh, the Carmathians were even more free-thinking than the Fāṭimid Ismāʿīlīs; for whereas the latter thought ritual and Fiqh to be binding on the lower grades, even these among the Carmathians were allowed to neglect all the observances. Nāṣir-i Khusraw relates that there was no congregational mosque, or any mosque for that matter, in Laḥsā except a small one constructed by a Sunnī resident for his own use. The inhabitants never recited the standard prayers, never heeded the interdictions, retailed and ate the flesh of every animal including cats and dogs. But they did not prevent Sunnīs and mercantile people of other religions settled in their midst from professing their faith and praying in their own fashion. Nāṣir-i Khusraw's report of an absence of fanaticism on their part is perhaps valid for the mid-eleventh century; but at the turn of the ninth and tenth centuries the Carmathians had been fanatical and intolerant in the extreme, especially where Sunnīs were involved.

Unsuccessful risings, fierce persecution under the early Ghaznawids, and internal dissension combined to weaken their communities. As Belyayev has remarked, 'the intense struggle the Carmathians conducted against the Caliphate and Sunnī Islam assumed from the very start the form and quality of a religious sectarian movement. Because they were bigoted fanatics, they turned their weapons not only against the Sunnī Caliphate and its rulers but against every one who refused to accept their doctrine and enter their organization . . . Their armed detachments fell upon peaceful townsmen or countryfolk in a whirlwind of slaughter, pillage and brutality . . . Survivors were taken captive, made over into slavery and sold in their busy markets like any other kind of loot'.[36] Such methods gradually isolated the Carmathians from the peasantry at large, and were perhaps mainly responsible for the extinction of the movement. In Iraq and Iran its influence decayed almost altogether.

On the other hand the Fāṭimid Ismā'īlīs were able to intensify their influence well beyond the confines of their Caliphate. They were not even weakened by the serious schism which detached the Druzes. These followers of ad-Darazī or Duruzī, one of the entourage of the Fāṭimid Caliph al-Ḥākim, deified the latter in the grossest form (*ḥulūl*) and became a sect on their own. But the nursery of this sect was the Lebanon, and it did not affect Iran. When al-Mustanṣir (1036–94) was on the throne, the Fāṭimid empire was evidently at the peak of its political power, and consequently his spiritual authority as Imam stood high. Countless missionaries, receiving their wherewithal from the propaganda centre in Egypt, spread the Ismā'īlī message throughout Iran and recruited adherents. From the date of the Seljūq invasion in 1040 onwards, the Ismā'īlīs in Iran made a point of winning over all elements dissatisifed with the rule of the invaders; doing so the more readily in that the Seljūqids began to invade Syria in the seventies of the century, and thus to collide with the Fāṭimids in real earnest. The strength of their position in Iran and Arab Iraq can be gauged from the fact that there was twice an attempt in the second of these areas to proclaim al-Mustanṣir the rightful Imam Caliph, and to read the khuṭba in his name in place of the 'Abbāsid al-Qā'im.[37] Nāṣir-i Khusraw who visited Cairo in 1047 gives an enthusiastic description of the court which proves how deeply contemporaries were impressed by the power and glory of the Ismā'īlī Fāṭimid dynasty.[38]

The early Seljūq Sultans who conquered Iran were fanatical Sunnīs and persecuted the Shī'ites, and particularly the Ismā'īlīs of both branches, with unremitting energy. It was sometime in the seventies of the eleventh century that Ḥasan b. Ṣabbāḥ al-Ḥimyarī came to the fore. One version says that this Ismā'īlī came of the house of the Ḥimyarī kings of pre-Muslim Yemen; in another version his family began as villagers in Khurāsān. His father moved from Kūfa to Qum, and there Ḥasan was born in an unrecorded year. He was, to begin with, an Imāmī Shī'ite like his father, but in student days at college met the Ismā'īlī Dā'ī surnamed Amīr Ḍarrāb ('Coiner of Money') with whom he had long discussions. He did not allow himself to be convinced, but he was shaken. He then sought the company of other Ismā'īlī Dā'īs, viz. Abū Najm called Sarrāj, 'the Saddler', a certain Mu'min, and 'Abdu 'l-Malik b. 'Aṭṭāsh; the last being the *Ḥujja* in charge of all the clandestine communities of Ādharbāyjān and Persian Iraq. Mu'min admitted Ḥasan b. Ṣabbāḥ formally into the sect, receiving from him, as custom required, the oath of allegiance to the Fāṭimid Caliph al-Mustanṣir. About 1075 Ḥasan went to Iṣfahān where he acted for two years as Ibn 'Aṭṭāsh's deputy. He was then summoned to Cairo and stayed there eighteen months, from the summer of 1078 to January 1080.

At this juncture there were two warring parties at al-Mustanṣir's court; one of which desired to see his eldest son an-Nizār as heir, and the other his second son al-Musta'lī. Those who favoured this second son prevailed. Ḥasan who had meantime given his support to Nizār was compelled by the victorious clique to leave Egypt.[39] He returned to Iṣfahān in the summer of 1081, and subsequently carried on propaganda in favour of Nizār's claims to the Imamate in Yazd, Kirmān, Ṭabaristān and Dāmghān. He gave out that he had secured the secret authorization of Mustanṣir to do so.

The proclamation of Musta'lī as heir to the Imamate split the Fāṭimid Ismā'īlīs into two sub-sects, Nizārīs and Musta'līs. The former were indisputably predominant in Iran and the eastern countries of Islam, whereas the Musta'līs had their following in Egypt and the western territories. And as so often happens in such cases, the dispute did not restrict itself to the claims of the pretenders. The Musta'līs emerged as the more conservative wing of the Ismā'īlīs, while the Nizārīs proceeded to introduce new doctrinal and organizational features which earned their faction the name of the New Propaganda, *Da'watu 'l-Jadīda.*

In 1090 Ḥasan b. Ṣabbāḥ worked his way into the confidence of the owner of the impregnable fortress of Alamūt[40] in the Elburz Mountains, and repaired there with his comrades-in-arms. The host, who was a moderate Shī'ite of the Zaydī persuasion, was mistaken in his guests. They set upon him and put him in irons, and by this stratagem acquired the stronghold. The episode paved the way to the power which the Nizārīs, or Neo-Ismā'īlīs as they are conventionally termed, exercised in Iran from 1090 to 1256. So sustained was their activity that in a very short time a number of the strongholds, castles and fortified towns of the uplands had become theirs through force or guile. Added to Alamūt, they presently had Maymūn-Dizh, Lanbasar,

Dare, Ustūnāwand, and Washm Kūh in the Elburz; Gird-i Kūh near Dāmghān; Ṭabas, Tūn, Turshiz, Zawzan and Khūr in Kūhistān; Shāh-Dizh and Khālanjān near Iṣfahān; Qal'atu 'ṭ-Ṭanbūr in the mountains of Fārs; and Qal'atu 'n-Nāẓir in Khūzistān. And as one stronghold after another fell to them, they would foment risings in the towns of the neighbourhood.

It will be seen that Nizārī dominance was mainly in the Elburz mountains and Kūhistān, and did not depend on territorial continuity. The *de facto* leader was Ḥasan b. Ṣabbāḥ, aided by his energetic disciples, the ra'īs Muẓaffar and the Dā'ī Kiyā, called Buzurg Ummīd or 'Great Hope', who between them had largely engineered the seizure of the fortresses and castles. But the formal head of the Nizārīs of Iran was the Chief Dā'ī Ibn 'Aṭṭāsh[41] who was regarded as the vicar of the hidden Imam, one of the sons of Nizār; Nizār himself having been murdered by the Musta'līs in an Egyptian dungeon. Ibn 'Aṭṭāsh had his residence at Shāh Dizh, and it was from this vantage point that the threat was levelled at the very centre of the Seljūqid state. In the nineties the Nizārīs extended their activities to Syria, now by means of propaganda and now by open insurrection, and found themselves fighting two enemies — the Sunnī feudal lords of the region and the Crusaders who were just then gaining a foothold in Palestine after the First Crusade (1096–1099). In the thirties of the next century they got possession of ten castles in Syria; and by the mid-thirteenth century their strongholds in Iran, according to the historian Rashīdu 'd-Dīn, exceeded one hundred.

The social factors conditioning the New Propaganda movement which the Nizārīs launched in Iran at the turn of the eleventh century are almost undocumented in the sources. In certain of his works[42] Bartol'd expressed the view that the movement was 'a fight between castles and towns', which is a vague enough conclusion founded apparently on the conception of European history in the eleventh to thirteenth centuries as a conflict between would-be self-governing towns and barons in their castles. He subsequently amended this judgment, and suggested that the movement was 'the last struggle of Iranian chivalry with the victorious new age', was 'a union of the land-owning aristocracy and the rural masses against the towns'.[43] Bartol'd, not being a Marxist, had a very defective grasp of the social structure of feudal society. It is nonsense to talk of a unity of interests between land-owners and peasantry (on what possible ground could it be?) and of their combined struggle with the towns as such, without specifying what strata of townspeople are in debate.[44] Bartol'd's amended opinion was revised by A. Yu. Yakubovskiy in roughly the following sense: The Neo-Ismā'īlīs are the representatives of the Dihqāns, i.e. the old Iranian land-owning class, who had been deprived of part of their estates after the Seljūq invasion and elbowed aside by new feudal lords drawn from the Turkman military-nomadic nobility.[45] Latterly, though, he had dropped this view, holding that any finding on the matter must be premature in the present state of our knowledge. However, there has been a recent attempt by Ye. A. Belyayev to revive the Bartol'd–Yakubovskiy theory. The Ismā'īlīs, as he sees it, were not leading the peasants in an anti-feudal struggle, but were simply profiting by that struggle for their own ends.[46]

Bertel's has criticized the Bartol'd thesis together with the amendments, or rather rewordings of it, proposed by subsequent scholars.[47] His argument is convincing. Actually the sole basis for Bartol'd's case is the factual information in the sources that the Nizārīs were in possession of the castles, and that in the course of the fighting they did destroy the towns. Bertel's, relying on Ibnu 'l-Athīr's chronicle and other sources, has rightly pointed out that 'the castles were not the age-old property of the Ismā'īlī Dā'īs. These had seized them, as the sources show, by stratagem and force'.[48] In other words the Ismā'īlīs in possession of the castles were very far from being the old Iranian Dihqāns — the knights as Bartol'd named them; on the contrary, they were the people who had expelled the Dihqāns from the castles and partially annihilated them. Bertel's has further pointed out, no less correctly, that the Neo-Ismā'īlī heresy spread not only among the peasantry (which could still, perhaps, be an instrument in the hands of the Dihqāns) but also 'among the urban population in its lower orders'.[49] To these remarks one might add that the Neo-Ismā'īlīs were in conflict not with the towns as such, but with the Seljūqid state; and that in the course of the struggle certain towns where Seljūq garrisons were stationed happened to suffer badly. It was never a specific aim of the Ismā'īlīs to destroy the towns.

Granted that any verdict on the question would be premature, let us only say that the following working hypothesis will do for the time being: The Neo-Ismā'īlī movement from about the middle of the eleventh to the middle of the twelfth century was fundamentally a movement of peasants and unprivileged townspeople. It was essentially a mass rising against the feudal state (at the time Seljūqid) and a feudal nobility comprising both old Dihqāns and new Seljūqs. But after the Neo-Ismā'īlīs had taken possession of numerous strongholds, castles, fortified towns (in Kūhistān) and lands, the Dā'īs at the summit of their society could not but become new seigneurs. From the mid-twelfth century a conflict of two groups within the Neo-Ismā'īlī persuasion is plainly traceable, one of which, evidently, was democratic and the other of which represented the interests of the new feudal lords. L. V. Stroyeva of Leningrad University is at the moment working on the problem from this angle.[50] It can just be added that many of the Dā'īs at the turn of the eleventh century were of artisan origin, and that Usāma b. Munqidh, a feudal seigneur of Syria who left his memoirs, calls the Nizārīs muzhiks and carders of wool.

In the reign of the Seljūq Sultan Barkiyāruq (1094–1104) mass executions of Ismā'īlīs took place at Nīshāpūr in 1096, and massacres in several cities in 1101. The next Sultan, Muḥammad (1105–18), regarded the Ismā'īlīs as the most dangerous foes his empire had, and did his utmost to crush their rebellion. In 1107 he captured the fortress Shāh Dizh near Iṣfahān, so that Aḥmad b. 'Aṭṭāsh fell into his hands. The Chief Dā'ī was subjected to every humiliation and mockery; then crucified; then transfixed with arrows on the cross from which his body was not removed for seven days. For the succeeding eight years the Seljūq troops ravaged the Alamūt neighbourhood and took several strongholds from the Ismā'īlīs before laying siege to Alamūt itself. Starvation had almost brought the beleaguered to the point of surrender when word came of the death of Sultan Muḥammad. His troops, anticipating dynastic confusion, raised the siege forthwith. Nevertheless the persecution of the Ismā'īlīs went on unabated in the parts of the Seljūq state which lay outside their domains. There was a massacre at Aleppo in 1113 and another at Āmid in 1124 in which seven thousand Ismā'īlīs perished. The Ismā'īlī-controlled areas themselves, however, were scarcely again in serious jeopardy until the Mongol invasion. For their part the Nizārīs answered persecution with a far-reaching terror, and the murder of the political figures opposed to them.[51]

After the death of Ibn 'Aṭṭāsh, Ḥasan b. Ṣabbāḥ who had for so long been at the helm of affairs, assumed formal office as Chief Dā'ī; and when he in his turn died in 1124, the energetic Kiyā Buzurg Ummīd took his place. On Buzurg Ummīd's death the post devolved on his descendants.

Let us look at the doctrine and organization of these Nizārīs, or Neo-Ismā'īlīs.

They reduced the number of rules binding on the lower grades in respect of ritual and law, and they no longer resisted the appeal of Ṣūfī mysticism which had been something wholly alien to early Ismā'īlī thought. This influence is very apparent in the works of the great Ismā'īlī poet and philosopher Nāṣir-i Khusraw (1104–88/9?). The acknowledged head of the sect, of course, was the Imam in the descent of Nizār, but since the Imams after Nizār were 'hidden' and their whereabouts and very names unknown to the mass of Believers, the headship was purely nominal and those on whom it devolved belonged to myth. So the *de facto* head of the sect was the Chief Dā'ī who was deemed the vicar of the hidden Imam and resided at Alamūt. The third holder of the office after Ḥasan b. Ṣabbāḥ, namely Ḥasan II b. Muḥammad b. Kiyā Buzurg Ummīd (1162–1166) gave out that his grandfather had been the descendant of Nizār (a claim which Kiyā had never made for himself), and on this basis took for himself the title Imam which conferred on him the right to require members of the sect to obey him as they would obey the Universal Reason.

The hierarchy as exhibited in the Nizārī organization from the end of the eleventh to the middle of the thirteenth century was, in descending order: *Imam*; *Dā'ī 'd-Du'āt* or 'Chief Dā'i; *Dā'ī 'l-Kabīr* or 'Superior Dā'ī'; *Dā'ī* or 'Ordinary Dā'ī'; *Rafīq* or 'Comrade'; *Lāṣiq* or 'Adherent'; and *Fidā'ī* or 'Self-Sacrificer'. Members of the last two grades were only conversant with the exoteric doctrine; both grades gave their blind obedience to the upper grades, and the *Lāṣiqs* in addition had to swear a specific oath of allegiance to the Imam. The majority in the sect did not ascend beyond these two grades. The *Rafīqs* were partly initiated but nevertheless ranked as among the inferiors. The ordinary Dā'īs in the fourth grade were fully initiated into the esoteric mysteries and along with the senior Dā'īs in the two grades above them constituted the controlling elite. They were exempt from prayer and ritual, and could ignore both the legal prescriptions and the elementary rules of morality. The highest grade was of course open to none but the descendants of 'Alī and Nizār — with this rider that the descendants of Kiyā Buzurg Ummīd were officially recognized from 1164 onwards as being descended from Nizār.

Although the lowest grades largely composed of peasants and artisans had no entry into the mysteries of the sect, they had heard of them and aspired some day to have knowledge of the Secret of Secrets which was the key to the understanding of the universe. The fascination of the mysterious, the harsh discipline, a belief in the limitless power of the head of the sect in the spiritual sphere as well as the material, finally the expectation of the Resurrection Day (Pers. *rūz-i qiyāmat*) associated with the coming of al-Qā'im the Mahdī, and the hope of paradise — it was all irresistibly attractive to the youth who had entered the ranks of the Fidā'īs. These were virile, resolute lads, nurtured on fanaticism and a hatred of the enemies of the sect and brought up in total obedience to those having priority of grade. And from their number terrorists were recruited ready to spy on those who opposed the Nizārīs, report back the intelligence, and then murder them if ordered. This chosen band of young men was tested out by tutors, then taught the rules of conspiracy and the art of disguise, and trained to endure deprivation and to use arms, and in some cases to speak foreign languages. At the command of their leaders the Fidā'īs would strike down public figures — the motive of assassination was invariably political — known for their active opposition to the sect. The victims might be of any religious confession: Sunnīs, Imāmī Shī'ites, Christian Crusaders in Syria, Musta'lī Ismā'īlīs — or fellow Nizārīs suspected of treachery. The young men deputed to accomplish these terrorist missions usually did not survive their victims, but they cared nothing for that. They were convinced that derring-do in the name of the Faith would open the gates of paradise to them with its gardens, palaces, its houris and every sensual enjoyment. Not initiated, they were unaware that paradise as conceived by the esoteric doctrine of their sect was merely an allegory of Perfect Knowledge and purely spiritual delight. And of course the enthusiasm of these young terrorists was also stirred by the class hatred of the sons of peasants and craftsmen for princes and people of wealth.

The Muslims, and the Christians too, have always been of the opinion that the Neo-Ismā'īlī leaders used to drug the young Fidā'ī with hashish[52] in order to steel his resolution for the acts he had to perform. But this is apparently a legend. However, if a legend, it is one so obstinate as to have securely fastened the epithet *Ḥashīshiyyūn* or 'hashish addicts' upon the Nizārīs of Iran and Syria during the twelfth and thirteenth centuries, both in popular speech and in literature. The Persian historians, Rashīdu 'd-Dīn and Ḥamdullāh Qazwīnī for example, subscribed to it. And thanks to the Crusaders this term, disguised as *assassin*, entered Italian and French with the meaning 'Killer'. Others there have been, admittedly, who, suggesting a different derivation, fancied *assassin* to be merely *Ḥasaniyyūn*, 'followers of Ḥasan' — of Ḥasan b. Ṣabbāḥ, that is. Anyhow, the appellation, whatever its true orthography and meaning, did not displace other names by which the Nizārīs were known in Iran, such as the *Bāṭiniyya* and — most common designation of all — Mulḥids (*mulḥid*, pl. *malāḥida*). Mulḥid means 'heretic', but is exclusively applied to Ismā'īlīs of any denomination; whereas the word Rāfidī (*rāfiḍī*, pl. *rawāfiḍ*) also meaning 'heretic', is almost exclusively reserved for Moderate, i.e. Zaydī or Imāmī, Shī'ites.

The Nizārī Assassin had no monopoly of political murder. Ismā'īlī terrorism was not invented by Ḥasan b. Ṣabāḥ, but had been employed by the Ismā'īlīs of Iran before him. It was, as is evident, gradually adopted by the Nizārīs in answer to the savage persecution and violence which the Seljūqid and other rulers practised against them. But admittedly it was from Ḥasan's time that the Nizārī terror assumed really wide proportions. One of its earliest victims, after Alamūt had been seized by Ibn Ṣabbāḥ, was the celebrated Seljūq vizier Niẓāmu 'l-Mulk, the presumed author of the *Siyāsatnāma*. While accompanying Sultan Malikshāh (1072–92) on a journey, he halted near Nahāwand on 10 Ramaḍān 485 (= 14 October 1092), and in the evening was about to enter his wife's tent when he was stopped by a youth of Daylam looking like any petitioner, who suddenly whipped out a knife and dealt him a mortal wound. It was a mode of operating later to become usual, and in fact employed again in the case of the vizier's own son Fakhru 'l-Mulk, also a vizier, in revenge for the execution of numerous Ismā'īlīs in 1111. The Fidā'īs would often shout the name of the Head of the Nizārīs as they settled their account.

In the section devoted to the history of the Ismā'īlīs of Alamūt in Part II of his *Jāmi'u 't-Tawārīkh*, Rashīdu 'd-Dīn furnishes three lists of names of persons assassinated by the Nizārīs in the period covered by Ḥasan b. Ṣabbāḥ, Kiyā Buzurg Ummīd and his son Muḥammad I, i.e. between 1092 and 1162, accompanied by the names of the Assassins.[53] Writing in the beginning of the fourteenth century, the historian was drawing on a Nizārī original source *Sarguzasht-i Sayyidnā*, 'The Story of Our Master' (meaning Ḥasan b. Ṣabbāḥ), which has not come down to us. Among the seventy-five victims listed, there are eight rulers (including the Fāṭimid Caliph and Imam of the Musta'līs, al-Amīr; the 'Abbāsid Caliph Mustarshid and his son and successor Rashīd; and the Seljūq Sultan of Iraq, Dā'ūd, grandson of Malikshāh); six viziers; seventeen generals and provincial governors; six city magistrates; thirteen Qāḍīs and Muftīs of different circuits including Qazwīn, Hamadān, Iṣfahān, Ray, Kirmān, Gurgān, Kūhistān, Tabrīz, and Tiflīs; heads of religious sects such as the *Muqaddam* of the Kirāmīs in Nīshāpūr; the Imam of the Ṭabaristān Zaydīs; courtiers, dignitaries, scholars and sayyids; and some Nizāri traitors, one of them a former Dā'ī. Practically all the individuals named belonged to the military, civil or clerical elite; and being valid only for the period quoted, the lists omit the Christian victims such as Conrad, Marquis of Montferrat (1192). On the evidence here adduced, one terrorist sometimes accounted for two or three victims — which proves that on occasion, anyhow, the killer did manage to escape. If peculiar difficulties were foreseen, three or four or even more Fidā'īs and Rafīqs might be sent from Alamūt for the accomplishment of the errand. Thus the murder of the Fāṭimid Caliph Amīr, son of Musta'lī, at Cairo in 1130 was carried out by seven Rafīqs, and that of the 'Abbāsid Caliph Mustarshid in 1135, near Marāgha, by fourteen. But our sense of proportion must not be lost: terrorism was not the chief method of conducting the struggle. Assassinations like these were usual enough in reprisal for the burning or execution of Nizārīs or at least for savage repression, but propaganda and armed risings of the masses were always more central to Nizārī planning.

When the Nizārī leaders accumulated large reserves of land, they themselves turned into seigneurs. From about 1150 onwards an aristocratic caste can be noticed lording it over the rest. Ḥasan's third successor, Ḥasan II b. Muḥammad b. Kiyā Buzurg Ummīd (1162–66), looked to this large, popular, and socially lower, element for his support. In 1164 he announced himself to be the descendant of 'Alī and Fāṭima, Muḥammad b. Ismā'īl, al-Mustanṣir and Nizār, appropriated on these grounds the grade of Infallible Imam, and proclaimed that the New Era, bringing the end of the world, the Day of Resurrection and Judgment, had dawned. Now in the theory of the Ismā'īlīs they alone were 'resurrected' to a new life in a spiritual paradise, and henceforward the whole exoteric doctrine with its prayers, outward observances and Sharī'a ceased to be binding even on the mass of their Believers. Translated into practice this meant equating the lower rank and file with the upper grade of the sect. Not eighteen months had gone by before Ḥasan II was murdered in the fortress Lanbasar by his brother-in-law, a propertied seigneur of Buwayhid descent and a Moderate Shī'ite — who was acting in all probability at the instigation of those at the summit of the sect. Ḥasan II's son, Muḥammad II avenged his death by butchering the murderer's family, and continued on the lines laid down by his father. The result was that new members of lowly position were attracted to the sect in very large numbers.

Meanwhile, the enriched upper set that had slipped into feudal lordship was getting apprehensive of the enthusiasm and activity of the rank and file. It wanted to secure its estates, castles and privileges, and the teaching about the imminent end of the world did not suit it at all. So it aligned itself with the Sunnī seigneurs in an attempt to bring the masses of the sect to heel. Muḥammad II's son and successor Ḥasan III fell in with this attitude. On the plea of a return to the original Islam of the Prophet's day, he decreed the exoteric doctrine to be once more obligatory, restored the mosques and the lapsed Friday prayers, and made up to the Sunnīs to the extent of ordering the Khuṭba to be read in the name of the ʿAbbāsid Caliph an-Nāṣir and sending his mother on pilgrimage to Mecca. The Sunnīs nicknamed him the New Muslim.[54]

The struggle within the sect was now bitter indeed. Ḥasan III was poisoned in 1220, and Ismāʿīlī doctrine re-instated. His son and successor Muḥammad III reigned but did not rule, being locked up in his palace while each of the two rival groups in the sect, aristocracy and rank and file, claimed to be acting in his name. The aristocratic summit was ready to bow to the Mongol conquerors, so keen was it on holding on to its castles and lands; whereas the rank and file were for Holy War. Muḥammad III was murdered in a drunken stupor, and his son Khurshāh submitted to the demands of Hūlāgū Khān, grandson of Chingīz Khān and founder of the Mongol-type state in Iran. He consented to dismantle his strongholds and deliver the keys of his castles and his treasure, but he failed to redeem his promise of all this in face of the opposition of the rank and file. In the end Hūlāgū besieged and took Alamūt. Khurshāh, having been given a safe-conduct, presented himself at the conqueror's camp in 1256. Hūlāgū sent him from there to his brother the Great Khan Mungke Khān in Mongolia, who promptly ordered him to be put to death. The rank and file fought on. The fortress Gird-i Kūh held out for three years, and it was twenty years before all the fastnesses and castles in Kūhistān had been reduced. But followers of the sect were in the region at least until the middle of the fifteenth century.

At the present day the remnant of the Nizārī branch of Ismaʿilism is scattered. There are Nizārīs in the Maṣyath vicinity of Syria, in Oman to the number of some thousands, here and there in Iran in the mountainous Maḥallāt near Qum, and in north-east Afghanistan where they account for practically the whole population of Badakhshān. Until the 1930s certain of the eastern districts of the Tadjikistan SSR and the entire Pamirs (nowadays the Gorno-Badakhshan Autonomous Oblast') were exclusively peopled by them. But the real home of the Nizārīs is India. Migration to that country had started in the thirteenth century, and went on steadily between the sixteenth and nineteenth centuries. In 1838 the hereditary head of the Nizārīs, now usually styled the first Agha Khan, himself moved from the Maḥallāt region of Iran to settle in India near Bombay. The dynasty claims descent from Kiyā Buzurg Ummīd, and consequently from 'Alī and Fāṭima through the Fāṭimids, and its titular heads who are millionaire land-owners impose a tithe on all their followers. The late Agha Khan, Muḥammad Shāh (1877–1957), received an English education, and rendered distinguished services to the British in India for which he was knighted. He was succeeded by his grandson, Karim, who is at present acknowledged as the forty-eighth Imam of his line. The sect, numbering now more than two hundred-and-fifty thousand followers in India, is entirely non-militant and shows no sympathy with democratic and anticolonial movements, but its Dā'īs go forth from headquarters to preach in the mission field in Africa where Nizārī communities extend as far as Lake Tanganyika.

The Musta'līs (or Proto-Ismā'īlīs as they are sometimes termed in contrast to the Nizārīs who are the Neo-Ismā'īlīs) have also found a home in India. Their gradual migration from Egypt began in the eleventh century via the Yemen and came to rest in Gujarat where they now exceed one hundred and fifty thousand. They are known there as *Bohras*, 'merchants', from the Gujarati word *vohorvu*, 'to trade', a designation which indicates the social structure of the sect at the present time. Like the Ismā'īlīs of the other branch, they have long since abandoned their militancy nor have they anything to do with political causes.

There are many sects of Extreme Shī'ites, all of them characterized by the doctrine of *ḥulūl* and *tanāsukh*,[55] and all of them exhibiting a cleavage between the initiated and the profane following (with some differences of nomenclature) and a disregard of the outward observances and precepts of Islam including mosque-going. In exchange for what was dropped they were apt to evolve their own ritual, which varied from sect to sect. They all practised *taqiyya*, the prudential concealment of their religious opinions to avoid persecution, usually passing themselves off as Sunnīs or, under the Ṣafawids, Moderate Shī'ites; but not infrequently, too, as Dervishes, the outward demeanour of the brotherhoods being always a convenient disguise. We shall here glance at a few sects of the so-called *Ghulāt* or extremist type, with particular reference to those which had Iran for their setting.

One of the earliest was that of the *Khaṭṭābiyya*, thus named after Abu 'l-Khaṭṭāb Muḥammad al-Asadī. This confidant of Ja'far aṣ-Ṣādiq had ascribed divinity to the sixth Imam and been removed from the entourage in consequence; whereupon he had formed his own sect and begun to name himself the incarnation of God. Muḥammad, he said, had transmitted his prophetic dignity to 'Alī, and Ja'far aṣ-Ṣādiq had done so to him. That is, he denied the succession through the 'Alids and taught that the Imamate was a matter of purely spiritual merit — and that Prophets and Imams are incarnations of God. He and his following marched against the troops of the ruler of Kūfa armed with stones and knives and, of course, were scattered. Abu 'l-Khaṭṭāb was taken and impaled; his body was then burned and his severed head despatched to Baghdad (756 or 760). But the sect survived and immediately after the founder's death had over a hundred thousand adherents in Iraq, Iran and Yemen. Its members allowed orthodoxy to none but themselves and, like the Khārijites, were without mercy on others, men, women or children, at the time of their militancy. The sect was still existent in the twelfth/thirteenth centuries.

The Druzes who broke away from Ismā'īlism in the first quarter of the eleventh century identified the Fāṭimid Caliph al-Ḥākim with God on High, and held the Universal Reason and the Universal Soul to be emanations from his sacred person. Having thus deserted the Ismā'īlī position, they became a separate sect of the *Ghulāt* type, following indeed an eclectic religion of their own. We shall not dwell on their fortunes here since they were located in the Lebanon and never made themselves felt in Iran.

The same can be said of the *Nuṣayriyya*, named after the supposed founder of their faith, Ibn Nuṣayr who detached himself from the Imāmīs in the second half of the ninth century. The sect later became localized in north-west Syria. Its doctrine was an eclectic mixture of Shī'ism, Christianity and popular pre-Islamic beliefs. God is an indivisible unity having three hypostases named *Ma'nā*, 'the Meaning', *Ism*, 'the Name', and *Bāb*, 'the Gate'. The Trinity thus composed has periodically been made flesh in the prophets, and the last incarnation coincided with the founding of Islam. The Trinity on that occasion became embodied in 'Alī, Muḥammad and Salmān al-Fārisī; for which reason it is denoted by the group of initials *'Ams*, being the letters *'ayn*, *mīm* and *sīn* with which the names of the three said persons begin. The Nuṣayrīs divided their following into the *khāṣṣa*, or initiated elite, and the *'āmma*, or commoners, somewhat as the Druzes divided theirs into 'spiritual' and merely 'physical' members. The initiated had their holy books which they interpreted allegorically, and did not reveal to the commoners. Worship took place at night in a chapel called *qubba* built on a hillock, usually over the grave of some saint, and priests officiated. There were many borrowings from Christianity, or perhaps more accurately survivals of it, among the Nuṣayrīs: the veneration of Jesus as the divine incarnation, the reverence shown to the apostles and the Christian saints and martyrs, the festivals of Christmas and Easter, the liturgy, and the Eucharistic rite of the cup. But with this there went a belief in metempsychosis.

A considerably later heretical sect is that of the Ḥurūfīs, or 'Literalists'. The *Ḥurūfiyya* (from *ḥurūf*, pl. of *ḥarf* 'letter') had for the inventor of their faith Faḍlullāh of Astarābād (b. *c.* 1340) who preached a 'new revelation' in the years 1386/7. Some sources affirm that he had been sent by Tīmūr to Shīrwān where Tīmūr's son Mīrānshāh murdered him with his own hand in 1393/4; which would explain the peculiar hatred of the Ḥurūfīs for the Tīmūrid dynasty and for Mīrānshāh in particular, whom they renamed Mārān Shāh, 'The King of Snakes' and seem to have regarded as the Antichrist, ad-Dajjāl. Faḍlullāh, called al-Ḥurūfī, was an independent thinker of original views and a prolific writer, his best known work being the treatise *Jāwidān-i Kabīr* (The Great Eternal) written partly in the Astarābād dialect of Persian and partly in Arabic.[56] The sect spread rapidly over the whole of Iran, Ādharbāyjān, Syria and Ottoman Turkey where its propaganda was initiated by 'Alī al-'Ala' (d. 419), one of Faḍlullāh's disciples. The followers were mostly artisans or of the urban intelligentsia, and it was indeed the presence in it of so many progressive-minded people that gave the sect its special stamp. The Ādharbāyjānī poet Nasīmī, who was martyred in Aleppo in 1417, belonged to it; so did the Turkish poets Tamannā'ī (also executed) and Rafī'ī; and so, apparently, did the eminent Persian poet Sayyid Qāsim (1356–1433/4), surnamed Qāsimu 'l-Anwār, 'Distributor of Lights'. Qāsim, who wrote in the Gīlān and Ādharbāyjān dialects as well as in Persian, had originally been a Ṣūfī and Imāmī Shī'ite and a disciple of Shaykh Sadru 'd-Dīn Ardabīlī, the ancestor of the Ṣafawids. He introduced the common ownership of property and communal meals in the Dervish cloister he founded at Herāt.

The Ḥurūfī writers left a large legacy of books, half a dozen of which qualify as principal works. We have already cited the *Jāwidān-i Kabīr*, and can here single out three more: the *Maḥram-nāma* (The Forbidden Book) *c.* 1425, written in the Astarābād dialect; the *'Ishq-nāma* (The Book of Mystical Love) *c.* 1430; and the *Hidāyat-nāma*

(The Book of Guidance). These last two are in Turkish and by Firishta-zāda (Turk. Firishta-oglu; Ar. Ibn Firishta, d. 1469), a disciple of Faḍlullāh. Several of the Ḥurūfī treatises have been edited by the French orientalist Clément Huart with text, translation and notes[57] followed by an essay (also in French) by the eminent Turkish scholar Dr Riza Tëwfiq, better known under the pseudonym Feylesuf Riza.[58]

The doctrine is set out in the *Maḥram-nāma* and other treatises: The Universe exists eternally. The divine origin is reflected in man, in his face and form even, since he has been created in God's likeness. As the movement of the Universe is a recurrent cycle, so also is the history of mankind; each cycle is marked by the appearance of Adam at its beginning and by the Judgment Day at its close. The divine principle shows itself in men in three progressive forms: prophecy, saintliness[59] and incarnation. Muḥammad was the last of the prophets, and 'Alī was the first of the saints; and the last of the saints was the eleventh Shī'ite Imam al-Ḥasan al-'Askari.[60] Faḍlullāh of Astarābād is the first God-incarnate. The Ḥurūfīs borrowed the idea of the mystical significance of the letters (*ḥurūf*) of the Arabic alphabet from the Ismā'īlīs — and of course they get their name *Ḥurūfiyya* from 'the letters'. These served as mystical symbols of the recurrent cycles, and were also mystical signs corresponding to the contours and constituent parts of man's visage. The sect was profoundly influenced by Ṣūfism as well.

It was not long before the Ḥurūfi religion, biased from the start against the Tīmūrids, was attacking the feudalism which the Tīmūrid state, of all states at the time, typified so completely. The Antichrist, *Dajjāl*, as the Ḥurūfīs taught, had already appeared and died in the person of the Tīmūrid Mīrānshāh.[61] Now the advent of Qā'im the Mahdī was to be expected at any moment, who would install the rule of justice and universal equality on earth, and under whom man would no more do violence to man. The relevant passage in the *Maḥram-nāma* reads:

> From long past until this day they [sc. the Ḥurūfīs] have been awaiting the Qā'im of the Imams whose other name in the Tradition is Mahdī. And they have been telling us that he is the Lord of the Sword (*Ṣāḥibu 's-Sayf*), and how there is this Ḥadīth about him: 'He shall fill the earth with truth and righteousness after it has been overflowing with tyranny and brute force.' They have faith that he will remove tyranny, which is the violence of some people over others, through the sword.[62]

It is evident from this that the overthrow of the tyrannical order exemplified in feudalism was envisaged by the Ḥurūfīs as an armed and victorious rebellion under the Mahdī's leadership.

The fifteenth-century Persian source, the *Mujmal* of Faṣīḥī, mentions an attempt on the life of the Tīmūrid Sultan Shāh-rukh (1405–42) in the cathedral mosque at Herāt when he received a stab-wound in the stomach which was to cause him pain ever afterwards. The unknown assailant was killed in the heat of the moment by one of the royal servants, and this hampered the investigation into his identity. However, a key found in his clothing made it possible to trace the house where he had been lodging and so to establish that he was a Ḥurūfī named Aḥmad Lūr, a disciple (*murīd*) of Faḍlullāh of Astarābād. It also came out that there was a Ḥurūfī secret society in existence to which prominent members of the urban intelligentsia belonged. The calligrapher Mawlānā Ma'rūf, who was among those implicated, was sentenced to imprisonment in the tower of the citadel of Ikhtiyāru 'd-Dīn at Herat, and others of the society, including Faḍlullāh's grandson, were executed and burned.[63] Qāsimu 'l-Anwār the poet, to whom allusion has been made above, also came under suspicion of belonging to the Ḥurūfīs, but nothing against him could be proved. He was merely expelled from Khurāsān, and made his way to Samarqand where he died.[64]

Thanks to repression and execution, the Ḥurūfīs did not last long in Iran. But they put down firm roots in Turkey (notwithstanding occasional persecution even there, especially under Sultan Muḥammad II, 1451–81). They practised *taqiyya* freely, passing themselves off as Imāmi Shī'ites, or Sunnīs, or Ṣūfīs. It was in Turkey that they succeeded in making an impression on the leaders of the Bektāshī order of Dervishes. Founded, according to tradition, in the beginning of the fourteenth century by the half-legendary Ḥājjī Bektāsh, this order was very influential in Turkey, Constantinople included, because of its connection with the privileged corps of Janissaries. The order went on officially being a Sunnī brotherhood of Ṣūfīs, but in actual fact a secret doctrine was entertained by its members and passed down from generation to generation which was simply that of the Ḥurūfīs slightly modified.[65]

Another Extreme Shī'ite sect in Iran and the neighbouring countries was that whose members styled themselves the *Ahl-i Ḥaqq*, or 'People of Truth'. This emerged, as Professor Vladimir Minorsky thinks, in the fifteenth century, and gained a wide following among Ādharbāy-jānī and other Turks, as well as among Persians and Kurds. The name the Persian Shīʿites gave it was different from that which the sectaries affected, viz. *ʿAlī-ilāhī*, 'those who deify ʿAlī'. The sect ramified into sub-sects which bore local designations: in Turkey, *Qizil Bash*, echoing their participation in the fifteenth/sixteenth century movement of that name;[66] in Ādharbāyjān, Kāra-Koyūnlū (after the union of Turkmen tribes among whom the sect apparently had its birth) and *Görenler* 'those who see'; in the Rizaiyeh vicinity, *Abdāl-beyī*; in Qazwīn, *Kakāwand*: and in Māzandarān, *Khojāwand*; and so on. The credit goes to Russian and Soviet scholars for having brought to light its beliefs and practices.[67]

The sect is even today to be found in all parts of Iran, although the sectaries conceal their creed and are officially accounted Imāmī Shīʿites. The overwhelming majority are peasants and nomads, or else craftsmen and petty traders in the case of the towns. By origin this sect sprang from a heresy at the popular level, the common folk in the fifteenth/sixteenth centuries actively supporting the Qizil Bash Shīʿites against the Sunnī regimes of the Āk-Koyūnlū and the Ottoman Empire. Against the latter the Asia Minor Turks who were Extreme Shīʿites raised revolts throughout the sixteenth and into the seventeenth century. The sect has long since settled down to peaceful ways. Its chief centre is Kermānshāh, but there is a large following in Tehran and other cities too, and in the rural areas of Iran, Ādharbāyjān and Kurdistān.

Certain European scholars have identified the *Ahl-i Ḥaqq* with the *Nuṣayriyya*, but Russian research has now disproved this theory. They have of course the deification of ʿAlī in common — but all the *Ghulāt* sects share this. And in point of cosmogony, doctrine and worship the two sects are far from being identical.

It would seem that the *Ahl-i Ḥaqq* kept bits and pieces of Ismāʿīlī doctrine. The world and man are the result of five successive emanations of the deity. God fills the whole universe with his being. He is indissolubly One with ʿAlī who existed before time. ʿAlī has become incarnate continuously not only in Adam, Noah, Abraham, Moses, Christ, and Muḥammad — which is what the followers of most of the *Ghulāt*-type sects believed — but in all the prophets that have been, and thereafter in the Imams and saints. (In parenthesis it should be added that the *Ahl-i Ḥaqq* consider, and considered even in his lifetime, that Shah Ismāʿīl I, founder of the Ṣafawid dynasty, was an incarnation of the God-ʿAlī.) The last incarnation of the God-ʿAlī was, as they believe, a certain Shah Muḥammad, or Meḥmed who is said to have lived at the turn of the seventeenth century. And again the God-

'Alī will become incarnate in the hidden Twelfth Imam, the Mahdī who shall return.

V. A. Gordlevskiy describes *Ahl-i Ḥaqq* teaching thus: 'The main item in the doctrine of the sectaries is 'Alī's continuous deification and his no less continuous coming down upon earth. . . . 'Alī is not only a personal God, he is the divine principle as such which dwells everywhere and pervades all. It is only among the people that the abstract philosophical ideas are lost in the deification of 'Alī.'[68]

The *Ahl-i Ḥaqq* doctrine asserts that there are two warring principles in man, *'aql,* 'reason', and *nafs* in the sense of 'passion'. There is no life beyond the grave, paradise and hell being allegories of religious knowledge and ignorance. After death man awaits the passing of his soul into another body. Ethical standards are the victory of the reasoning principle over passion; they are mercy and sympathy. All the *Ahl-i Ḥaqq* repudiate polytheism, practise monogamy and disallow divorce. The women take part in their dancing, which is to all appearance ritualistic, with faces unveiled.

The sub-sects are directed by *Pīrs*, or Elders, who have under them Khādims, subordinate priests, to help them officiate at ceremonies. Sacred groves and the tombs of saints are among their objects of worship, but their most remarkable observance is the oblation made at secret gatherings usually held at night. A ritual meal takes place at which sugar, dūgh (Pers. *dūgh*, separated sour milk with salt) and, it may be, cheese, rice and the sacrificial flesh of ox, ram or cock are eaten. This ritual repast may well go back to the early Christian *agape*, or love feast, from which the Liturgy subsequently developed — not, indeed, directly but through the ritual fraternity meals of the Carmathians. However that may be, the sectaries believe that those participating in the supper are vouchsafed a particle of the divine principle. Before the meal, vent is sometimes given to an enthusiasm reminiscent of the voiced Dhikr of the Dervishes and the Radeniye of the Khlysts[69] in Russia. It is here an ecstatic dance to the sound of stringed instruments, punctuated with the exclamations "Alī!' and 'Ḥaqq!', and accompanied by convulsive movements and contortions, and even with self-torture such as putting hot coals in the mouth.[70]

The sectaries have holy books which they keep secret, the principal one being the *Saranjām* or 'Outcome', written seemingly in the Kermānshāh vicinity. They also have a kind of acathistus in honour of the God-'Alī and in honour of his different incarnations. And they make out that their sect has a much more ancient history than is adumbrated in the sources, asserting for instance that the famous folk-poet Bābā Ṭāhir 'Uryān, who bridged the tenth and eleventh centuries, was of their number.

XII
Mysticism in Islam

Mysticism (from the Gk. adjective *mustikos*, 'mysterious'), as usually understood, is a specific religious attitude admitting the possibility of the direct, personal and intimate communion, or even union, of man with the Godhead through what is termed 'illumination', 'inner experience', 'ecstasy'. Historically, mystical tendencies or, it may be, systems of idealistic philosophy permeated with mysticism, have been wont to appear in the guise of a particular religion, and mostly in the setting of feudalism. Thus: *Neo-Platonism* took shape from the third century within the syncretic religion of the Hellenistic civilization; from the fourth to the seventh centuries Ephraim the Syrian, Isaac the Syrian, Johannes Climacus and, most notably, the pseudo-Dionysius the Areopagite were giving this speculative mysticism its lodgment in Eastern Christianity; in the fourteenth century there came the Hesychasts; in Russia in the fifteenth/sixteenth centuries there were Nil Sorsky and his followers, the so-called 'abstainers from property'; in the ninth century John Scotus Erigena introduced mysticism into Western Christianity, and between the thirteenth and fifteenth centuries Francis of Assisi, Raymond Lully, Meister Eckhart, Ruysbroeck the Admirable, Tauler, Suso, Thomas à Kempis and others were preaching it in the same context; *Kabbalah* (which even had some Christian adherents) wore the dress of mediaeval Judaism; and the systematized Vedānta of Shankarāchārya, otherwise Advaita or Non-dualism, was developed under the aegis of Hinduism in the ninth century and after.

The mystical trend running through these different religions calls attention to the similarity there is between them. This resemblance, let it be said, is not so much a matter of borrowings as of the common path taken by religious ideologies in the course of their development under feudal conditions. As a rule, the mystics showed no great regard for the outward form of the given religion, Muslim, Christian or whatever it might be, and this is why they at times incurred the suspicion and even hostility of the official church. The main impulse almost always arose from asceticism and the idea of the renunciation of the world.

Mysticism achieved an even greater importance and spread in Islam than in Christianity. The term 'Ṣūfism', in Arabic *taṣawwuf*, by which it is universally known in the Muslim world, is derived according to the accepted opinion of Islamists from *ṣūf* 'wool' or 'coarse woollen garment' (Ar. V Form, denominative from *ṣūf*, *taṣawwafa*, 'to clothe oneself in wool'; techn. term 'to become a Ṣūfī'). The term *ṭarīqa*, literally 'path' and technically 'the method of the mystic' (from the root *ṭaraqa*, in one of its meanings 'to go, take the path') is used as a synonym for *taṣawwuf*. It also signifies the preparation for the Ṣūfī way of life, and *ṭarīqas* in the plural are the various orders or brotherhoods of which the general body of the Ṣūfī community is composed.

The study of Ṣūfism has yielded a vast literature in European languages, supplemented by a certain output in Oriental languages during the last decades. In pre-Revolution Russia the three workers in the field were V. A. Zhukovskiy, A. Ye. Krymskiy, and A. E. Schmidt. Soviet writing on the ideology and social roots, and on the history of the individual currents, of Ṣūfism is practically non-existent, except for the pages of the late Ye. E. Bertel's[1] and a few essays on the connection between Ṣūfī trends and popular movements in the East. Western scholars (and we include here the pre-Revolution Russians just named) have always displayed great interest[2] in Ṣūfism, but study has been limited to its ideology and terminology, its ramifications and the problem of its origin. It has been conducted without reference to social antagonisms and social movements in the countries concerned.[3]

Although research on the first four centuries following the Hijra has been carried out with comparative success, it cannot be pretended that any general history of Ṣūfism satisfying the requirements of scholarship has up to now been produced. The task, of course, is one of unusual complexity. As yet the abundant sources not only in Arabic, Persian and Turkish but in Greek, Syriac, Coptic, Hebrew, Sanskrit and Urdu have not been fully tapped — whereas the study of Ṣūfism is unthinkable unless it comprehends the ideological and cultural links of Islam with other religions and philosophies. As yet the numerous branches of Ṣūfism have neither been investigated nor classified; instead, individual Islamists, wedded to their pet systems of idealistic philosophy, have imported a subjective element into their research and tended to see in Ṣūfism what they wanted to find rather than what was really there.

The British orientalist Arthur Arberry, commenting that no adequate history of Ṣūfism has so far been written and that 'der wahre Meister' of Ṣūfī studies has not yet been born, suggests that such a work cannot be undertaken at the present stage of our knowledge and must be the business of scholars to come.[4]

Needless to say, no detailed account of Ṣūfism and its branches must be expected in this short chapter. Our concern here is only to furnish the essential information about Ṣūfism and the part it played in the history of Iran.

The nineteenth-century Western scholars and their Russian confrères were inclined to regard Ṣūfism as of alien birth: it was, as they expressed it, the result of 'borrowings' from non-Muslim religions and philosophical systems, and in this sense it 'overlaid' Islam. It is true that one of the earliest of their number, F. A. Tholuck, was an exception; for having set out from the position that Ṣūfism was a legacy of the Magi, he abandoned this unsubstantiated hypothesis in favour of the view that it was rooted in Islam from its rise and even went back to Muḥammad himself. Other theories of the origin of Ṣūfism have been advanced by more recent scholars. A. Merx, Edward Browne, D. B. Macdonald, M. Asin Palacios, A. Wensinck, F. S. Marsh and Margaret Smith have derived it from the asceticism and mysticism of Eastern Christianity and a Neo-Platonism refashioned in a Christian spirit by Syrian monks. Asin Palacios is often carried away, taking simple parallels in Ṣūfī and Christian theosophy for proof of the debt of the former to the latter.[5] R. Dozy thought he had discovered the springs of Ṣūfism in Iranian, i.e. Zoroastrian/Manichean, influence, and in an Aryan reaction against Arab culture and against Islam as the religion of a Semitic people. The echo is audible here of those racist theories that bedevil the history of religion. And Carra de Vaux's finding was on the same lines, for admitting that the Ṣūfī philosophy of illumination was founded on Neo-Platonism, it was a Neo-Platonism, he insisted, which had received the attention of the Persian sages and undergone a Zoroastrian or rather Manichean treatment.

Yet others like R. Hartmann and Max Horten[6] contended that Ṣūfism came from an Indian source, whether the Vedānta or Buddhism. Hartmann supposed that as Central Asia was the meeting-ground of Zoroastrians, Buddhists and Muslims, it was from there that Indian mysticism and ascetic practices made their entry into Islam through Persian intermediaries. He had a Russian supporter in Gordlevskiy, but the theory was sheer conjecture unwarranted by facts. Once more the racial approach is responsible; Ṣūfism being imagined as an Aryan (Indo-Iranian) revulsion of feeling against Arabism. Max Horten detected the presence of both Buddhism and early Vedānta in Ṣūfism.

So three main theories of the origin of Ṣūfism emerged which can be labelled respectively Christian (or Christian–Neo-Platonist), Iranian and Indian.

Von Kremer advanced a more involved theory which postulates two sources. 'It seems', he says, 'that Ṣūfism actually absorbed two distinct elements, viz. an early, Christian-ascetic element which had been influencing Islam powerfully from its very inception, and a later Buddhist-contemplative element which gained the ascendancy when the authority of the Persians in Islam had increased.' Goldziher adopted this theory with minor changes, and defined the two elements in Ṣūfism as: asceticism — *zuhd* ('abstention' from *zahada,* 'to be without desires', techn. term 'to be a hermit'; whence *zāhid*, pl. *zuhhād*, 'ascetic') and mysticism proper — *taṣawwuf.* Pure asceticism, he held, which was the nearer of the two to orthodox Islam, had its ultimate source in the monasticism of Eastern Christianity, whereas Ṣūfī mysticism was based on speculative philosophy — on Neo-Platonism in the earlier phase and on Buddhism in the later phase.

In the first half of the twentieth century, Reynold Nicholson and Louis Massignon propounded a new theory. They had between them a wider and more thorough acquaintance with the originals of Ṣūfī literature than any of their predecessors in the field, and this led them to hold that Ṣūfism was not a superimposed stratification in Islam: on the contrary, it was something indigenous. It is convenient to label this the Muslim theory. Nicholson took Ṣūfī mysticism to be a natural development of the ascetic tendencies which had asserted themselves in Islam in the course of the first century AH. That Christian asceticism exercised some influence he did not deny; but he maintained that Ṣūfī asceticism and the mysticism that grew from it was at bottom an Islamic phenomenon.

Admittedly, the speculative philosophy of Ṣūfism was due to the influence of a Christianized Neo-Platonism, and there was also little doubt that its more extreme pantheistic ideas evolved under the Indian influences which the Persians introduced.

Massignon was even more consistent in his criticism of the theory that Ṣūfism was of alien birth. You could not, he argued, prove an Indian influence on Ṣūfism by just pointing to the fact that both Muslims and followers of Indian philosophy could be met with in say, Central Asia or Iran. For such a theory to be tenable it was necessary to show that as a matter of fact the exchange of ideas between Islam and Hinduism did take place. As Massignon said, the only right way to demonstrate the presence of a non-Islamic influence in Ṣūfism would have been through study of the authentic works of the exponents of early Ṣūfism — in other words by using the historico-philological method.[7] He emphasized that vital clues were to be found in the terminology employed in the Ṣūfī writings; and in his basic work on the origins of the technical terms of the Ṣūfīs, he put precept into practice.[8] He was able to establish the following sources of their terminology: (1) the vocabulary of the Koran; the Ṣūfīs would pick on obscure, ambiguous passages and give them a novel interpretation; (2) the vocabulary of Arabic-language science of the first centuries of Islam; (3) the vocabulary of the theological schools; (4) the peculiar lingua franca of the polite society of the day which took its loan-words mainly from Aramaic and Syriac but also to some extent from Greek and Pahlavi, and which had been fashioned to meet the demands of the syncretic philosophy of the Levant in the course of the first six hundred years of our era.[9]

Massignon drew attention to the presence of sentences in the Koran itself which could be construed in a spirit of asceticism and mysticism, and deduced from this that Ṣūfism was inherent in Islam and emerged in an Arab setting. If there were certain ideas in it of non-Arab, i.e. Jewish and Christian, provenance, then these ideas had been absorbed into the body of Islam at the very start, being indeed already reflected in the Koran. 'It is from the Koran', he concludes, 'which they [sc. Muslims] were continually reading and pondering over and which they applied to their daily lives, that Islamic mysticism rose and grew. It was founded on a continual re-reading and a continual citation of a whole text revered as sacred, and it owed its characteristic flavour to this circumstance.'[10] He did not rule out the influence of Christian mysticism, and later of Neo-Platonism, on Ṣūfism once this had grown from its Islamic soil, but he classed it as fairly moderate.

All in all it can be taken as established that Ṣūfism arose on Muslim ground, and resulted from the natural development of the Islamic religion under the conditions of a feudal society. Non-Islamic mystical ideologies were not responsible for its appearance, though at a later stage, from the ninth century onwards, these ideologies, and particularly Neo-Platonism, had some bearing on its growth. It is very doubtful whether the writings of Plotinus, Porphyry and the other Neo-Platonists could have affected any of the Ṣūfīs directly, and more probable that Neo-Platonism only reached the Ṣūfīs after it had been doctored by the much later Christian syncretic school of Alexandria and perhaps also of Gundishāpūr,[11] or in the version of the mystics of Eastern Christianity such as the pseudo-Dionysius the Areopagite.

The particular debt to Neo-Platonism is seen in the extreme or pantheistic Ṣūfī doctrine of the world as an emanation of God.[12]

It was evidently not until long afterwards, when Islam had already made its inroad into India, that the pantheism of Vedānta had its impact on certain of the more extreme offshoots of Ṣūfism. As to the hypothesis that Buddhism affected Ṣūfism at some stage, much caution is called for. The central idea in Ṣūfism, alike in its monotheistic and its pantheistic presentation, is the Oneness of God; whereas Buddhism knows nothing of the One God, much less of the One Creator. The idea of Creation, the idea of the emanation of the universe from the Godhead — these are foreign to Buddhism, whether to the pluralistic philosophy of original Buddhism or to the vulgarized popular Buddhism with its multiplicity of Buddhas and Bodhisattvas. Buddhism developed either in the direction of agnosticism and atheism (as in the Hīnayāna school) or else in the direction of polytheism, assimilating the worship of the Tantrist deities of India and the folk-cults of the Far East (as in the case of the Mahāyāna school). It never showed signs of moving towards monotheism or pantheism. The theory of Buddhist influence on Ṣūfism has had its partisans in plenty, but it has never been possible to reconcile it with the facts.

Finally, as M. Asin Palacios well observes, if it is right to speak of the influence Christian asceticism and mysticism had on the development of Ṣūfism, it is no less legitimate to speak of the reverse influence of the Ṣūfīs on the Christian mystics, especially after al-Ghazālī and Ibnu 'l-'Arabī.

The Ṣūfīs themselves dressed the origins of their movement in legend. Their authors portray not only Muḥammad and 'Alī but even the pre-Islamic prophets as Ṣūfīs: Abraham is a Ṣūfī, Moses is a Ṣūfī, Jesus is a Ṣūfī; and al-Ghazālī sees in the last named the ideal Shaykh, the model to be copied. Khiḍr, whom they confounded with Elijah, was another Ṣūfī in their eyes, and came in for widespread veneration. These were the wild exaggerations of legend, but even as a matter of history Ṣūfism is practically as old as Islam. Individual Companions of the Prophet like Abū Hurayra were obviously not strangers to ascetic attitudes, nor was the Koran itself untouched by asceticism. At all events one may speak of Ṣūfism as being a specific trend inside Islam by the time the eighth century was under way.

One of the earliest Ṣūfīs was Ḥasan of Baṣra (642–728). The son of a Christian captive who had embraced Islam in Medīna where he had been brought by his Arab captors, Ḥasan was known as a compiler of Ḥadīth and for his fearless denunciation of the Umayyad Caliphs Yazīd I and 'Abdu 'l-Malik and of the dreaded Ḥajjāj. But it is as an austere ascetic with a following in Baṣra that he has a claim to fame. Tradition relates that he was fond of quoting the Ḥadīth handed down from Abū Hurayra: 'If you knew what I [sc. Muḥammad] know, you would forget how to laugh and would weep indeed.' This pessimistic frame of mind was exceedingly common among the Muslims of the eighth century and, as Goldziher has shown,[13] asceticism (*zuhd*) and a turning of one's back on the world (*al-firār min ad-dunyā*), coupled with a condemnation of the wealth, luxury and idleness of the governing elite in the Caliphate, were the principal ingredients of Ṣūfism at that early stage. And this condemnation of the material pleasures of the ruling class echoed the protest, admittedly the passive protest, of the socially unprivileged.

From it arose the cult of poverty as the ideal prelude to salvation. The early Ṣūfī ascetics, preaching voluntary poverty and scorning the greed for riches, put forth the doctrine of *tawakkul* or 'trust' (from *wakala,* 'to rely on some one'): which meant placing absolute reliance on God without caring about sustenance (*rizq*). The rule of the mendicant ascetics, afterwards to be called Faqīrs or Dervishes, was to beg only enough alms for the day, since to provide oneself with means or nourishment for the future would be an infraction of *tawakkul.* 'It is very significant', says Goldziher, 'that the words which occur more than once in the ascetic maxims of the Gospel[14] about the fowls of the air that neither sow nor reap nor gather into barns and yet are fed by the heavenly Father, occupy a central place in *tawakkul* very nearly in their literal rendering'.[15] The Ṣūfī had to choose as between toil and begging.

The coarse woollen garment called *ṣūf,* which had originally been the garb of the poor and the penitent, became the habit of the ascetic in Caliph 'Abdu 'l-Malik's time,[16] and was to give rise to the terms *taṣawwuf* for the ascetic strain in Islam and *ṣūfī* for the ascetic himself. These words, however, did not acquire their exact terminological sense till later, the original appellation of the ascetic among the Arabs being *zāhid.* And *pace* those who cling to the theory that Ṣūfism was an Aryan reaction to Islam, the whole movement was cradled in Syria, Iraq and Egypt — that is, an Arab home, albeit outside Arabia.

Mysticism — the yearning for personal communion with God and the love for him — is a development of asceticism. It is perhaps no accident that this exalted state manifested itself with remarkable strength among women. Rābi'a (d. 752/3) who headed a circle of female ascetics in Baṣra was renowned as the authoress of love-poetry addressed to the Divinity and is credited with the verse: 'The flame of the love for God burns up the heart'. The emotion here in evidence was not of course peculiar to women, but the point we are making is that asceticism and the mysticism to which it led, had an appeal quite as much for women as for men. Other names than Rābi'a's were only less revered, and one might single out 'Ā'isha, daughter of the sixth Shī'ite Imam Ja'far aṣ-Ṣādiq in the eighth century; Nafīsa of the 'Alids at the turn of that century, famed for her knowledge of theology; Fāṭima of Nīshāpūr (d. 838); and several more.

As time advanced asceticism and mysticism became the basic constituents of the Ṣūfī outlook, and both excited the violent opposition and detestation of the divines. The fact was, an anti-ascetic attitude prevailed in the first centuries of Islam, especially during the reign of the Umayyads. Goldziher,[17] Caetani and Lammens allude to the colossal wealth that accumulated in the Holy Wars. Conquest on the grand scale and the seizure of huge quantities of booty caused the Arabs to cast about for some moral justification of their material success, and they were soon telling themselves that theirs was the reward of fighting for the Faith. This idea of a religious justification of riches was of course upheld in the first instance by the governing class of Arab nobles learning to be feudal seigneurs; but even among the rank and file the hope of legitimate enrichment from the spoils of war, hallowed by Sūra VIII of the Koran, tipped the scales against asceticism. It was left to good Muslims of ascetic leanings to answer that those who took part in Jihād for the sake of the future life were pleasing to God, not those who did so out of earthly avarice.

The enemies of Ṣūfī asceticism were given to quoting the Ḥadīth, actually spurious but ascribed to Muḥammad: 'There is no monkery in Islam'.[18] To this the Ṣūfīs retorted that the Ḥadīth in question relates to Christian monks, and that in any case Ṣūfīs are not monks. While practising their ascetic abstention from the goods of this world, they took no vow of perpetual celibacy. They did not hold marriage to be incompatible with their ideal of life provided it were for the procreation of children and not for the satisfaction of physical passion; but the convention was gradually accepted that so long as a man lived in a Dervish retreat, or led a roaming existence, he must refrain from the marriage-tie.[19] The custom later spread among certain Ṣūfī groups of terminating marital relations after the birth of a first child. The behaviour of Shaykh Bahā'u 'd-Dīn Muḥammad Naqshband, the renowned founder of the Naqshbandī order of Dervishes, who had been married at the age of seventeen, was traditionally held to be exemplary in this regard; for when his wife had borne him a child he did not put her aside, but treated her as a sister thenceforward. Al-Ghazālī's summing-up is that marriage is obligatory for all Muslims with the exception of those who have dedicated their lives to the service of God — meaning Ṣūfīs.

As the eighth century gave place to the ninth, the anti-ascetic mood of the Muslims was passing. The conquests were over and the steady flow of booty had stopped, a feudal society was in the making and class contradictions had become sharper. It was an atmosphere in which the Ṣūfī ethic could expect a better hearing than before, for its condemnation of wealth and luxury, passive though it was, voiced the feelings of large numbers of the downtrodden. Ṣūfism now made headway in the towns, chiefly at the artisan level, among Arabs and Persians alike. Two outstanding Ṣūfīs of Iranian descent, about whom many stories, most of them unreliable, have come down to us, belong to these years, viz. Ibrāhīm b. Adham, a native of the Balkh neighbourhood (d. after 776), and Bishr nicknamed al-Ḥāfī, 'the barefooted', from near Merv (767–827). Both these led their active lives away from home, the first in Syria and the second at Baghdad; but the next hundred years or so were to witness the spread of Ṣūfism within Iran itself, Khurāsān becoming one of its principal centres.

A new stage of development began in the ninth century. The ascetic and mystical tendency of the first stage was little by little subordinated to speculative thought, and numerous systems, or *ṭarīqas* as they were named, in time resulted which robbed Ṣūfism of its earlier unity. All the varied trends of mysticism and esotericism, some of them orthodox and some heretical, some homogeneous and others dissimilar in kind, were lumped under the single term *taṣawwuf*. How multifarious the varieties of Ṣufism eventually became may be gauged from the fact that Nicholson collected no less than seventy-eight separate definitions of its content from written sources up to the eleventh century.

Much study remains to be done on these *ṭarīqas*, and even their classification is far from complete. In the roughest way one can state that with some Ṣūfīs like Bishr al-Ḥāfī and al-Muḥāsibī (d. 857), asceticism dominated everything else, and such mysticism as they permitted themselves did not wander from the path of Muslim orthodoxy. To others, mysticism was in the foreground of thought and feeling, but a controlled mysticism that resisted the extravagances of pantheism and to that extent also clung to the orthodox position. Ma'rūf of Karkh (d. 815/6); his pupil Sarī as-Saqaṭī the Persian (d. *c.* 870); the latter's nephew Junayd, also a Persian, a native of Nahāwand (d. Baghdad 910); Junayd's pupil Rubaym (d. 916); another pupil of his, ash-Shiblī (d. 946); and Muḥammad aṣ-Ṣadafī (d. 879) were in this second category. They and their kind insisted on the observance of the Sharī'a with its ritual and its prohibitions, and their sole endeavour was to spiritualize Islam, changing it from a religion of submission and obedience into a religion of love, from a dry and stale ceremony, engaging (as they put it) the limbs, into an affair of the heart.

The somewhat enigmatic figure of Dhu 'n-Nūn al-Miṣrī, the Copt or Nubian born in Egypt where he died in about 860, stands alone. At home in the late Hellenistic culture of Alexandria, Dhu 'n-Nūn combined this with a knowledge of the occult and alchemy, and yet tradition has it that when hauled before the tribunal of Caliph Mutawakkil he was pronounced to be blamelessly orthodox. He is considered in Ṣūfī annals to have been the first to give a definition of mystical ecstasy (*ḥāl*), and although his doctrine is only known to us from the works of much later authors such as the fifteenth-century Jāmī,[20] he is credited by the Ṣūfīs themselves with having done more than any one else to convert their movement into a system of speculative philosophy. Some scholars, notably Browne and Nicholson, see him as responsible for bringing the influence of pantheistic Neo-Platonism to bear on Ṣūfism, but whether this conclusion is warranted is doubtful.

There was yet another group which, while it did not reject the Sharī'a outright, attached no great importance to it, or even deemed it superfluous in the case of those who had won through to knowledge (*'ārifūn*) and to whom the door to communion with God was open. Ṣūfīs in this category thought that the outward form of a religion, be it Islam, Christianity, Judaism or anything else, was of consequence only to those still inexperienced in mystical adventure. At their head was Shaykh Bāyazīd (more exactly Abū Yazīd Ṭayfūr b. 'Īsā, Sulṭānu 'l-'Ārifīn), a Persian from Bisṭām where he died about 875. His ideas were expounded in the pages of the very much later Ṣūfī authors, Qushayrī and Jullābī Hujwīrī in the eleventh century, Ghazālī in the early twelfth century, Farīdu 'd-Dīn 'Aṭṭār in the twelfth and early thirteenth centuries, and Jāmī in the fifteenth century. His followers constituted a separate community in Iranian Ṣūfism and were known as the *Ṭayfūriyya*.

Another celebrated Ṣūfī was Abu 'l-Mughīth Ḥussayn b. Manṣūr, nicknamed al-Ḥallāj, 'the carder of cotton', after his original calling.[21] A native of Fārs, he was the grandson of a Zoroastrian and was a pupil of Junayd. He was accused of heresy by the Mu'tazilites, damned by the Ẓāhirites and Imāmīs, twice arrested by the 'Abbāsids, and finally, in 922, officially declared a heretic and executed at Baghdad in circumstances of extreme barbarity.[22] His execution was followed some thirteen years later by that of a prominent representative of the same Ṣūfī group, ash-Shalmaghānī, convicted on the same charge. It was a group noted for its advanced asceticism and its use of Dhikr (*dhikr*, lit. 'mention', from *dhakara*, 'to recollect'; techn. term for the special prayer in glorification of Allāh couched in set expressions, either uttered aloud in chorus or murmured quietly to oneself);[23] and for its undoubted adoption of the elements of Neo-Platonism assimilated in a revised, that is, Christianized version. Its members were all more or less inclined to pantheism, albeit a vague pantheism not yet formulated into any kind of system.

It is accepted in Ṣūfī literature that the central idea of *fanā* ('disappearance', 'perishing', from *faniya*, 'to vanish'; whence *dāru 'l-fanā*, 'the transient world') was formulated for the first time by Shaykh Bāyazīd of Bistām. *Fanā*, to the Ṣūfī, is the attainment of the state of perfection when, having stifled his personal will, mundane desires and human characteristics, and thus freed himself from the very apprehension of the world of the senses, he achieves mystical fulfilment and becomes capable of communion with the One God. The understanding of the conception was hardly uniform as between different Ṣūfīs in later days, but at least two aspects of *fanā* are constant — the monotheistic and the pantheistic. On these aspects, and on the origin of the idea, we shall have more to say presently.

By the tenth and eleventh centuries Khurāsān had become a main centre of Ṣūfism. It was here that the disciples of Shaykh Bāyazīd of Bisṭām invited their audiences to ecstasy, and preached rapture and intoxication (*sukr*) with the love for God; it was also here that the pupils of Shaykh Junayd of Baghdad perceived the risk inherent in ecstasy and spiritual drunkenness, namely that the artificially excited Ṣūfī might mistake his fantasies for genuine union with the deity, and held that the only right path for him to follow was that towards sobriety of spirit, *ṣaḥw*, the state of quiet prayer.

Another tendency which gained momentum in Khurāsān was that exemplified by the so-called *Malāmiyya* (from *malāma*, 'censure', from *lāma*, 'to upbraid').[24] These self-reproachers felt that the Ṣūfī, in trying to save his soul, ran the gravest risk of smugness and pride in his ascetic and mystical performance; and that so as not to occasion the praise of others, a Ṣūfī ought to conceal his attainments and endeavour to seem worse than he is, and even excite the irritation and censure of other people by his behaviour. Unfortunately, in practice that behaviour often degenerated into a neglect of the ordinary rules of society and to acting the fool, and to cynicism. The itinerant Dervishes were noticeably prone to this contempt of current morality, recalling the Cynics of antiquity and the half-crazy devotees of Christianity.

It was Khurāsān, too, that nurtured the writers of the systematic accounts of the Ṣūfī theosophy: Abu 'l-Qāsim al-Qushayrī, author of *Risālatu 'l-Qushayriyya* or 'Qushayrite Message', in Arabic (d. 1072); 'Abdu 'l-Malik al-Juwaynī, the Imāmu 'l-Ḥaramayn (d. 1085); and Abu 'l-Ḥasan 'Alī b. 'Uthmān, Jullābī Hujwīrī,[25] author of the widely celebrated compendium entitled *Kashfu 'l-Maḥjūb*, or 'Revelation of the Occult' in Persian which, as it were, unveiled the main positions of moderate Ṣūfism as Junayd had taught it, and also conveyed information on various other tendencies in Ṣūfism and on the more eminent Shaykhs of Syria, Ādharbāyjān, Iran and Central Asia. And it was Khurāsān that produced Abū Ḥamīd Muḥammad al-Ghazālī who was not only a Sunnī theologian of towering stature, but the originator of a system of moderate Ṣūfism of which something will be said below.

It was the usual thing for the lonely Ṣūfī to devote himself to ascetic and mystical exercises without abandoning his permanent occupation in handicraft, retail trade, etc. But between the eighth and tenth centuries a parallel class of Ṣūfīs emerged and soon proliferated, who were professional mendicants. These were designated — as they are to-day — Faqīrs (lit. 'poor men', from *faqura* 'to be poor') or else, and more commonly, Dervishes (Pers. *darwīsh*). In the strict sense the Dervish is the kind of Ṣūfī who either wanders about begging or lives in a hostel, but in a looser sense the word *darwīsh* is used to mean the Ṣūfī of any type. The hostels or retreats[26] in which many Dervishes reside permanently or temporarily are variously styled *khānaqāh, zāwiya* (lit. 'corner'), *takiya* (lit. 'support'), *langar* (lit. 'anchor' and techn. term 'refuge')[27] and *ribāt*. Rules and regulations governed the management of these homes and the spiritual direction of their inmates; the younger of whom would be under the tutelage of the Elder-in-Charge who was the Shaykh or, in Persian, the Pīr. In relation to the novice (*murīd*,[28] 'adept', from *radā* 'to learn') the Shaykh was *murshid* ('director', from *rashada*, 'to go along'; whence *irshād*, 'direction') or *ustād* ('master').[29] Under the guidance of his Shaykh, the Murīd had to undergo a lengthy course of ascetical and contemplative training in preparation for the perfect state to which the *ṭarīqa* beckoned. After his more or less prolonged novitiate[30] the Murīd would be received into the brotherhood, the Shaykh laying upon his shoulders the garment called *khirqa* ('a garment full of holes' from *kharaqa*, in one of its meanings 'to rend') which the Ṣūfī thereafter wore for life. Having been given his *khirqa* he would be allotted his cell in the hostel, and whether he remained there or one day left it, his tie with the Shaykh would never be severed. He abdicated his will, placing himself at the disposal of his Shaykh who in his eyes was the vicar of God himself. Before this spiritual director he would make regular confession of his errors, mental errors included, and would do penitence, *tawba* (from *tāba,* 'to repent'). Al-Ghazālī regarded repentance as the doorway leading to the mystical path and held that it ought to be unceasing, since man is at no moment wholly without fault. He advised the Murīd to enter his sins from day to day in a note-book (*al-jarīda*) and to confess them daily before his Shaykh, supplementing confession by spiritual exercises in the shape of a conscientious self-examination (*al-murāqaba wa 'l-muḥāsaba*) and inward contemplation, otherwise 'mental prayer', *tafakkur* ('reflection', cf. Lat. *meditatio*) to be performed in the privacy of his cell (*khalwa* 'seclusion').

A famous Ṣūfī Shaykh of Khurāsān, Abū Sa'īd Faḍlullāh b. Abī 'l-Khayr of Mahna (968–1049), allows us a glimpse of these exercises. As a young Murīd he lived in the hostel of his Murshid, Abu 'l Faḍl Ḥasan. 'Seven years', he narrates, 'we sat in front of the miḥrāb and said, Allāh, Allāh, Allāh! And always when through human frailty drowsiness or carelessness beset us, a certain warrior (*sipāhī*)) would appear before the miḥrāb, a fiery weapon in his hand, stern and menacing, and would shout at us with all his might: "Say Allāh! O Abū Sa'īd, say Allāh!" In terror and awe of that apparition we would abide ardent and trembling even in sleep, and not permit ourselves to be remiss.'[31] The discipline of 'mental prayer' consisted in the Murīd's shutting himself in his cell, covering his head, and repeating without interruption 'Allāh!' or 'Huwa' (the Arabic for 'He') or one of the epithets of God, or else the phrase *Lā ilāha illā 'llāh*, and concentrating hard on this until his tongue and lips ceased to be aware of producing any sound and the word became engraved on his heart. God's name, it was believed, would thereafter remain imprinted in the Ṣūfī's consciousness for evermore.

The Ṣūfīs based their Dhikr, or invocation of the name of God, on the words of the Koran: 'Say, Allāh!'[32] and 'O Believers, remember

God with frequent remembrance and celebrate his praise early in the morning and at eventide.'[33] The exercise could be performed in solitary silence (then termed *khāfī*, 'hidden') or aloud in company (*jālī*). This voiced Dhikr might be heightened by singing to music, in which case the term for it was *samā*ʿ (lit. 'hearing', techn. term 'the zealous Dervish invocation'). Al-Ghazālī has given this description of such a concert.[34] The Ṣūfī initiates of the community gather in seance without any outsiders or even the novices, to distract their minds from the discipline, and one of their number, the cantor (*qawwāl*, from *qāla*, 'to speak') taking his place in their midst, gives the tune of the hymn in the particular metre and chants to the accompaniment of the musical instruments allowed by custom, such as the tambour, the tambourine, the clarinet, etc. The audience sits motionless, their heads bent, everybody trying not to breathe audibly or fidget and break the spell for his neighbour just when the state of trance is awaited. Suddenly one of the Brethren, fallen into ecstasy, bursts into exclamation and clapping, and dances. The whole assembly imitates his gestures and movements until his rapture passes. Lyrical verses of mystical content, sung to the accompaniment of musical instruments which may be stringed, work on the Ṣūfī's soul and bring it to the state of ecstasy, or *ḥāl* (lit. 'state', from *ḥawila* in one of its meanings 'to be changed into sg.').

Lively disputes went on among the Ṣūfīs of the different groups as to whether this vocal Dhikr with its adjuncts of song, music and ecstatic dancing (*raqs*), or only the quiet Dhikr in sober silence, was admissible.

The hostels multiplied apace so that more than two hundred of them could be counted in Khurāsān alone by the turn of the tenth century. Jullābī, looking at three hundred of the most 'valiant' out of 'the Khurāsān host of God's people', was convinced that 'the sun of love' shone more brightly there than in other places and that 'progress on the mystical path' was 'in the star of Khurāsān'.[35] It was there that the far-famed convents of Shaykhs Abū Saʿīd Faḍlullāh of Mahna, already mentioned,[36] and Abu 'l-Ḥasan Kharaqānī[37] were situated; these, and other retreats like them, housing both permanent or long-term residents and Dervishes only there for the winter. Shaykh Sarī as-Saqaṭī addressing his Ṣūfīs, said: 'Spring is at hand, and the trees are clothed in leaves; it is time for you to go forth on your wanderings about the world.' The soliciting of alms by itinerant Dervishes was accounted entirly legitimate and even helpful for their spiritual advancement (since it could not but put an end to pride and self-ishness), provided the amount collected was only sufficient unto the day. But for Dervishes living in the convent, the steward had the right to collect charitable donations against the future and lay in supplies of rations and fuel.

Abhorrence of the body and self-torture were as highly valued in these Dervish khānaqāhs as in Christian and Buddhist monasteries. Tradition relates that Shaykh Bāyazīd of Bisṭām once addressed his body, saying: 'Nay, nay, O receptacle of every evil! . . . O impure body (*tan-i palīd*) in thirty years thou hast not been cleansed, and, lo!, tomorrow it shall be for thee to present thyself pure before the Pure One.'[38] And Shaykh Abu 'l-Ḥasan Kharaqānī would instruct his Murīds thus: 'Strive to fast as much as possible; and if you set the term of trial at one day, fast three days; and if you set it at three days, fast for four; and go on increasing it up to forty days.'[39] The same Shaykh taught: 'The night shall fall and folk are dropping off to sleep, but do thou apply to thy body the chains, the hair-shirt and the leathern lash (*ghull o palās o tāziyāne-yi charmīn*), so that the All Highest may take compassion on this body, and speak, saying: "My slave, what wishest thou from this body?" Answer: "O God, I wish Thee!" He shall say: "My slave, abandon this miserable body, I am thine."'[40]

Ṣūfism was the ideology common to all Dervishes but there were many ramifications of it. Asked one day what Dervishism was, Shaykh Abu 'l-Ḥasan Kharaqānī replied: 'It is a stream from three sources; one of these is abstention, the second is mercy, and the third is independence of the creatures of God — may He be honoured and glorified!'[41] The independence was in this sense that the Ṣūfī must have no attachment to any of his fellow men, his heart being full to overflowing with the single love for his Creator, the One Friend (Pers. *yār, dūst*) who is God. Towards his fellow creatures he must be merciful, but no more. Abstention implied not merely asceticism and poverty but renunciation of one's own will and 'ego'. 'Lord, grant it to me not to exist', prayed Shaykh Bāyazīd of Bisṭām. 'How long shall this "I" stand between Thee and me?' So asceticism was viewed not as a goal in itself but as a means of loosening the ties of the sensual world, of desire, of self-love; and thereby, as it was thought, of preparing the soul to experience the precious moments of personal communion with the Creator in the state of ecstasy. Though, of course, while the Ṣūfī must thus exert himself to the limit in the performance of his spiritual 'exploits' if he is to attain to that ecstasy, it is God who wills it in the end. Finally, the Ṣūfī must not reckon on reward in the next world — his love for the Friend must be utterly disinterested. 'O God,' said Shaykh Abu 'l-Ḥasan Kharaqānī 'people thank thee for thy generosity, but I am thankful for thine existence; thy chiefest mercy is thine existence. . . . The Lord (*khudāwand*) called out to my heart: "My servant, ask what is necessary to thee!" And I said: "O God, is not thy mere being enough for me that I should ask for anything else?"'[42]

The different branches of Ṣūfism evolved a doctrine of the stations of spiritual perfection, terming these *maqāmāt* (pl. of *maqām*, lit. 'place'; techn. term 'stage on mystical path', from *qāma*, 'to rise, set out'). The number and nomenclature of such stages varied from system to system: Farīdu 'd-Dīn 'Aṭṭār enumerates seven, al-Ghazālī nine (see below). But most commonly four were specified:

1 *Sharī'a* — the Law, i.e. the pious life according to the precepts of the Muslim religion appropriate to all Believers. In the case of Ṣūfīs this stage was envisaged only as a preparation for the mystical way;

2 *Ṭarīqa* — the Path, entailing poverty, contempt of possessions, renunciation of the world and one's will. The Ṣūfī had to become the Murīd of a chosen Shaykh, or Murshid, to whose will and control he would surrender himself absolutely, and under whose guidance he would practise asceticism and the spiritual life;

3 *Ma'rifa* — Gnosis. In this stage the Ṣūfī, having rid himself of sensual desires, was deemed capable of attaining to isolated moments of ecstasy (*ḥāl*) and temporary communion (*wiṣāl*, lit. 'connection', from *waṣala* in one of its meanings, 'to unite') with the One God; and with his Shaykh's permission he could himself be a Murshid of novices from now on;

4 *Ḥaqīqa* — the Truth, a stage reached according to the consensus of Ṣūfī authors by only a few, when the Ṣūfī enjoyed constant intimacy with the absolute truth which is God. For this it was imperative to be completely freed from the impact of the senses and to have entered into the state named *fanā* (see above).

The idea of *fanā* dated from the latter half of the ninth century. Certain Islamists, notably Goldziher and even Nicholson, have seen it as a modification of the Buddhist Nirvāna.[43] But, apart from the fact that the Ṣūfī authors of this period had a most hazy conception of Indian philosophy in general and of Buddhism in particular, the resemblance between Nirvāna and *fanā* is at best superficial. *Au fond* they have nothing to do with each other. *Fanā*, whether in the monotheistic or the pantheistic presentation of it, is bound up with the notion of the communion of the human soul with God: but Buddhism does not know a One God and does not accept the real existence of the soul and personality. The doctrine of God the Creator, or of the emanation of the universe and of man from God, and of the reverse journey (*ma'ād*) of the soul to God, is alien to Buddhism. And Ṣūfism in its turn knows nothing of the Buddhist doctrine of rebirth and of Nirvāna as the deliverance from its chains. It is quite impossible to derive the idea of *fanā*, either in its monotheistic or its pantheistic aspect, from Buddhism.

The doctrine of *fanā* was not uniform throughout the vast extent of Ṣūfism, but there are two basic understandings of it — the monotheistic suiting the attitude of the moderate Ṣūfīs, and the pantheistic to which the extreme Ṣūfīs leaned — which should be noticed. As understood by the moderates, *fanā* was the state in which the soul, having lost the faculty of perceiving the sensual world, thereby becomes capable of knowing God and entering into communion with him. According to Jullābī[44] the soul in this case only loses its attributes, i.e. its empirical existence, but keeps its essence and does not shed its personality: communion with the divinity does not signify merging with him, since human nature cannot be changed into divine nature. The pantheists, on the other hand, thought of the universe and human souls as divine, not in their empirical being but in their very essence. In their thinking, therefore, the gradual liberation of the soul from the impress of sensual existence — disengagement, as they put it — and the discarding by the Ṣūfī of his empirical 'ego', must needs bring him to a state of *fanā* which is a complete dissolution of soul and personality in God, a complete merging with the universal 'ego'. It should be added, however, that for all their pantheistic identification of God with the universe, the extreme Ṣūfīs went on recognizing his personal aspect.

The idea of communion with God in a state of ecstasy led on to the doctrine of 'illumination', or *ishrāq* (lit. 'radiance', from *sharaqa* in one of its meanings, 'to shine'). This was elaborated by numerous Ṣūfī authorities and notably by Shaykh Yaḥyā as-Suhrawardī, who was executed as a heretic in 1191 and hence called al-Maqtūl, 'the Slain'. And closely bound up with 'ecstasy' and 'illumination' is the psychological phenomenon of *shaṭḥ* (lit. 'going out'; techn. term 'going out from one's ego', from *shaṭaḥa* 'to depart') to which Louis Massignon has given careful study.[45] This is the state in which the Ṣūfī, having lost all consciousness of his 'ego', as it were exchanges roles with the divine Friend and begins to speak in his name. It is said that Shaykh Bāyazīd of Bisṭām, for example, replied to some people who had inquired if he were at home: 'Under this roof there is nobody except God.' But the extreme case is that of the aforementioned Manṣūr al-Ḥallāj. He was accused of having exclaimed 'I am the Truth' (*Anā 'l-Ḥaqq*) in one of his ecstasies, and was executed for this assertion. Such theopathic utterances seemed blasphemy to the orthodox Muslims, but the extreme Ṣūfīs read only *shaṭḥ* into the words of al-Ḥallāj and revered him as their saint and martyr.

On this whole subject is should be borne in mind that up to the end of the twelfth century one can only speak of an inclination to pantheism, a pantheistic trend, and not of any pantheistic philosophy. The Ṣūfī movement had to wait for that until the time of Ibnu 'l-'Arabī (see below.)

If the Ṣūfī ideology was the result of socio-historical conditions, the natural development of religious ideas in a feudal society, what, it may be asked, do the Ṣūfī phenomena of ecstasy, *shaṭḥ* and *fanā* represent? We are dealing here with psychic phenomena. Persons of a neuropathic cast of mind, nurtured in mystical ideology, are prone to imaginary sense-perceptions which arise independently of real objects; these sense-perceptions, of course, being subjectively experienced every bit as vividly as the ordinary sense-perceptions. And nothing perhaps was better calculated to induce the para-normal state in which hallucination occurs than the Ṣūfī Dhikr with its singing and music. The ecstasy when it happened would often be accompanied by auditory hallucinations which al-Ghazālī named *khāṭif* (lit. 'catching', from *khaṭafa* 'to grab') and took to be the language of dead beings whose speech strikes the ear of the mystic without his knowing where the sounds proceed from. D. B. Macdonald equates *khāṭif* with the demon (*daimōn*) of Socrates which would warn him in his hours of creative ecstasy. But probaby the so-called pseudo-hallucinations which were studied for the first time by the Russian psychiatrist V. Kh. Kandinskiy are here in point: the subject hears inner voices, sees imaginary forms with the inward sight, etc. Al-Ghazālī describes vision experienced in the state of trance as being extraordinarily vivid and clear, comparable with a flash of lightning, or with the calm radiance of the full moon, or with the dazzling reflection of a polished blade. It should not, needless to say, be supposed that all Ṣūfīs were exceptionally neuropathic types. Singing and music, rhythm, the company of highly strung, excited companions — precisely the attendant circumstances of Dhikr — produce a powerful effect even on entirely normal subjects, greatly intensifying mental activity and the play of the imagination. For the rest — the ecstatic vision and the enthusiasm experienced in trance — the way was suitably paved by training and the ascetic way of life.

The cult of poverty featured prominently in the various *ṭarīqas*.

Many Ṣūfis, like the Spiritual Franciscans whom the Pope persecuted in the thirteenth century, held it to be the ideal condition for the soul's salvation. They condemned riches as the origin of all sin and selfishness, and as a condition positively precluding salvation. The tale of the conversion of Farīdu 'd-Dīn 'Aṭṭār (d. *c.* 1230), though it belongs to legend, is illustrative of the mood of passive protest against wealth which the Ṣūfis in touch with the urban poor were tireless in voicing. The well-known Persian poet and pantheist had in his young days been the owner of a store dealing in drugs and perfumes (*'aṭṭārī*) on the outskirts of Nīshāpūr. One day he was sitting there, as any self-satisfied proprietor would, amid the nimble assistants (*ghulāmān-i chālāk*) at his beck and call, when an idiot Dervish came up and shot him a glance in obvious disapproval of the trade being done. 'Aṭṭār took exception to this and told him to be off. The Dervish answered: 'See here, mister, I travel light and have nothing but this tattered cloak (*khirqa*). I can get out of this bazaar [this world] in a moment, but do you think about your property and your burdens and what destiny holds.' 'What d'you mean, you can "get out"?' asked 'Aṭṭār. 'Watch me!' said the Dervish, and he took off his cloak, laid it beneath his head and made a present of his soul to God. So struck was 'Aṭṭār by this that 'he gave up his shop for anybody to loot (*ghārat*), and renounced the bazaar of this world. He had been of them that own, he was now of them that groan;[46] he had been in the chains of worldly vanity and now put wordly vanity in chains'.[47] He became the Murīd of a certain Ṣūfī Shaykh, and afterwards roamed the earth garbed in the tatters of a mendicant friar.

Again, in the biography of al-Ghazālī the story is told of his becoming a Ṣūfī and turning his face from riches. While Shaykh Badru 'd-Dīn Simāwī (who led a peasant rising in Turkey in 1416) on his conversion to Ṣūfism in Cairo distributed his effects to the poor — except for his books on theology which had preoccupied him before, and these he threw into the Nile.

Modern scholarship believes the third phase of Ṣūfism to have opened in the twelfth century. It was a phase characterized by the following new features:

1 The official Sunnī theology — and the official Shī'ite theology followed suit — made its peace with moderate Ṣūfism and, thanks very largely to al-Ghazālī, the theological authorities pronounced it to be orthodox. Nor was this all; moderate Ṣūfism now became incorporated in the Islamic *Weltanschauung*. Islam from now on was imbued with Ṣūfī ideas.[48]

2 Ṣūfism made even further headway, notably in the towns. To be — or at any rate to be called — a Ṣūfī was henceforward to show that one was abreast of the fashion. Feudal seigneurs and powerful merchants were hardly behind the urban lower classes and the peasants in enrolling themselves as Murīds of the Shaykh of the moment. A good example of this process was the case of Ardabīl, where the bulk of the inhabitants were Murīds of the celebrated Shaykh Ṣafiyyū 'd-Dīn (d. 1334)[49] who gave his name to the Ṣafawid dynasty. Though we must not of course conclude that social differentiation had now lost its place in the Ṣūfī movement as a whole.

3 The various Ṣūfī groups crystallized into immense 'orders' (see below).

4 The distinction between moderate (that is, monotheistic) Ṣūfism and extreme (that is, pantheistic) Ṣūfism became sharper. The pattern of the former was the system worked out by al-Ghazālī;[50] the pattern of the latter was Ibnu 'l-'Arabī's system. We must take a brief look at each of these.

Al-Ghazālī's system is discussed in several of his numerous works, but the classic explanation of it is in the fourth part of his *Iḥyā'u 'ulūmi 'd-Dīn*. His position, all in all, is that of orthodoxy. Asceticism he views as a means of purification and as a preparation for the spiritual life. The mystical path has according to him nine principal stations (*maqāmāt*), each of which is determined by the acquisition of one of the 'saving virtues', or *munjiyyāt*, whose technical names he uses as labels for the stages themselves: (1) Repentance — *at-Tawba*; (2) Patience in Adversity — *aṣ-Ṣabr*; (3) Gratitude to God for sending down blessings — *ash-Shukr*; (4) Fear of God — *al-Khawf*; (5) Hope of Salvation — *ar-Rijā'*; (6) Voluntary Poverty — *al-Faqr*; (7) Renunciation of the World — *az-Zuhd*; (8) Abdication of one's Will — *at-Tawakkul*; (9) Mystical Love for God — *al-Muḥabba*.[51]

It will immediately be noticed that the first five of these constitute the common way of 'piety' suited to all Believers, while the last four are the stations on the specifically mystical path — the *ṭarīqa*.

Each of the stages, al-Ghazālī adds, is itself divided into three stopping-places. Taking the third stage, *ash-Shukr*, for example, the Ṣūfī will, to begin with, train himself to feel gratitude to God for blessings which he might easily have withheld: to wit, that God had created him a living being and not for instance a stone; a conscious person and not an irrational animal; a man and not a woman; physically sound and not lame, blind or one-armed; Muslim and not infidel; good and not evil; and so forth. After this, the Ṣūfī must learn to look on God's mercy as neither more nor less than the means whereby *fanā* may, in due time, be arrived at. Finally, the Ṣūfī must school himself to regard even misfortune as a boon and to thank God for it; since suffering, physical and moral, purifies the soul and in the result brings the Ṣūfī nearer to his goal of *fanā*. He will therefore now not simply tolerate misfortune but rejoice in it; even as he will rejoice in poverty, remembering that material prosperity is the basis of every sort of sin.

The last four stages in al-Ghazālī's *ṭarīqa* are of supreme importance. In the sixth stage, that of Poverty, the Dervish in the first lap contents himself with the small belongings which may be his, without trying to increase them; in the second lap, he must cultivate a positive loathing of riches; and in the third, having by this time accustomed himself to deprivation, he will be sublimely indifferent to both poverty and wealth. The Dervish must never grovel before the rich man, since to do so would be equivalent to setting store by his riches and coveting them. By the end of this sixth stage, he must cut down his possessions to the bare minimum needed for subsistence: the meanest of lodgings, a single garment of coarse fabric, barley-bread with some simple seasoning. So long as he has these indispensable things, al-Ghazālī explains, begging is not permissible; he can engage in honest labour, and preferably in handicraft.[52] If, however, even these few necessaries are not to hand, the Ṣūfī is allowed to beg alms, but only sufficient for the day — unless he be living in a khānaqāh, in which case the ban on the accumulation of charitable donations is lifted. But whether he is on his own or in a convent, he is strictly prohibited from accepting alms if there be the slightest doubt as to whether the donor's estate has been acquired in a manner approved (*ḥalāl*) by the Sharī'a; since by accepting prohibited (*ḥarām*) alms the Ṣūfī becomes an accessary in the rich man's crime. It follows that alms must not be accepted from usurers, tax-collectors, tyrants and the like: from such people not only must nothing be taken, but nothing must be even bought.

The thought underlying the next stage, Renunciation of the World, is that the Ṣūfī must nurse an aversion to all that is 'worldly' in the sense of belonging to the empirical world of appearance, and together with this strive passionately after what is 'heavenly'. This emotion differs essentially from penitence, for there is no question here of repudiating what is sinful and disallowed (*maḥẓūr*) by the Sharī'a: it is a question of repudiating even what is lawful (*mubāḥ*).[53] The ambition to renounce the world arises, according to al-Ghazālī, from the quickened belief that this world affords nothing of value comparable to the future life and to God. In this seventh stage the Ṣūfī's poverty has to be unqualified. He must now have no dwelling of any kind; he must live in a khānaqāh or else roam abroad, spending the night in mosques.[54] But he may, on his wanderings, erect a hut of rushes or clay. Food he must only take once a day — and it must be limited to a bran loaf (*nukhāla*) of six ounces without any flavouring. In the way of property he is allowed one earthenware bowl, old and chipped, for drinking and for washing — 'of the kind Jesus Christ had'.

In the eighth stage the Ṣūfī, having committed himself to God's will, trains himself to want nothing. The principle now is 'inner experience', 'mental sight', 'the divine unity' or *at-tawḥīd.* Convinced that God's will is guiding his life, the Ṣūfī accustoms himself to fear nobody, to rely on nobody, to trust nobody. It would seem that the outcome of this is sheer quietism and complete passiveness, but al-Ghazālī does not agree here with the extreme mystics, and unexpectedly makes a number of stipulations: an obvious danger ought not to be disregarded, nor the physician's treatment scorned; and so on. It goes without saying that Abdication of the Will, which characterizes this stage, signifies also the abandonment of one's empirical 'ego'.

The ninth and last stage, Mystical Love for God, is the summit of the spiritual climb.[55] As many theologians in the opposite camp to Ṣūfism denied the possibility of such love, al-Ghazālī deemed it appropriate to bring in at this point his psychological theory of love as such. This contained actually little that was original, being almost a repetition of what the Neo-Platonists had said on the matter. Love is the direct inclination of the will of the subject towards an object whose perception affords him joy. Al-Ghazālī finds that this inclination is occasioned by any of five principal motives; but most notably when the subject is in the presence of the beautiful (whether the beauty be physical or moral) and likewise when he is in the presence of anything that bears a resemblance to himself. Also, there are two possible forms of love — the love that arises out of gratitude and the love aroused by the disinterested joy which beauty awakens. There is an echo here of Plato's aesthetic ideas.

The mystic, according to al-Ghazālī, knows that God is the prime source of existence — of his private existence, therefore, and that of the whole universe around him — and is the prototype of beauty and perfection. He is conscious, though sometimes but dimly, that there is a certain analogy between his soul and God (the soul in al-Ghazālī's system is not divine but is god-like). These factors combine to provoke love for God in the mystic's heart in both its aspects — the love arising from gratitude and the more exalted disinterested love. But since God is the prime source of love, so he on his part has infinite love for those who yearn for him. In the psychological corroboration of his theory al-Ghazālī introduces the symbolism of earthly love by way of allegory.[56] As the lover separated from his beloved experiences a passionate desire to be united with her and will not be comforted, so the soul, loving God, suffers and aspires to union with him in ecstasy.

Like all the Ṣūfīs, al-Ghazālī considers *fanā* the highest state. He remarks how it is heralded by an emotional trance of such depth as to bring about the anaesthesia of the subject's bodily organs and his entire loss of free will, so that he is in a condition outwardly resembling drunkenness or torpor in which action is unwilled and purely mechanical. Repudiating pantheism and the emanation-theory which presupposes the essential oneness of god and the human soul, al-Ghazālī rejects the interpretation of *fanā* as a complete merging of the soul with God and its dissolution in him. Such an understanding of *fanā*, he insists, is absurd since human nature cannot be converted into divine nature. Communion with the Deity consists in this, that the soul, having lost the faculty of sensing the phenomenal world, becomes capable of picking up the beams of the prime source of existence, otherwise God, like a smoothly polished mirror catching the rays of light (a simile borrowed from Plato). To suppose that the soul and personality are absorbed by God and become part of him is as ridiculous as to attribute to a mirror the colour of an object reflected in it. It will thus be seen that al-Ghazālī, while maintaining that the mystical and supernatural intimacy of the loving soul with the beloved God in the state of *fanā* is real, manages to escape the pitfall of pantheism. His position, he claims is supported by the Ḥadīth which read: 'God is neither in the heavens nor on the earth; God is in the hearts of his faithful servants,' and 'Heaven and earth can in no wise contain me, but the heart of my faithful slave which is loving and meek can contain me.'

Al-Ghazālī's ideas, as has been said, influenced the Muslims profoundly: they also impressed the mediaeval Jewish thinkers such as Maimonides, Yehudah Halevi and Bahya Ibn Pakuda. Rabbis of Spain and Provence rendered various of his works into Latin, and it was in their translations that his thought later on entered the stream of Western mysticism. Raymond Lully, the Dominicans Raymond Martin and Meister Eckhart, the Franciscan John of the Cross, and perhaps even Ignatius Loyola (in his mystical moments) were much indebted to him.[57] Yet somehow the Ṣūfīs of Islam, and particularly those of Iran and Central Asia, never took to his system as they took to the extravagances of pantheistic mysticism. The great exponent of this in its mature form, Ibnu 'l-'Arabī, was of Andalusia, but it was in Iraq, Iran and Central Asia, not Spain or Africa, that the doctrine he developed had its widest appeal.

Abū Bakr Maḥyi 'd-Dīn Muḥammad b. 'Alī al-Ḥātimī 't-Ṭayyi'[58] of Andalusia, better known as Ibnu 'l-'Arabī (1165–1240) was born at Murcia, and studied in Seville and Ceuta. At the age of thirty he left Spain and resided in turn at Tunis, Mecca, Baghdad, Aleppo, Mosul and in Asia Minor (where the Sultan made him a present of a house which he forthwith gave to a beggar), and finally settled at Damascus, where he died. In his views on the religious law he was a Ẓāhirite, rejecting *ra'y*, *qiyās* and *taqlīd* while accepting *ijmā'*;[59] but this careful adherence to the Ẓāhirite prescription in the legal field was curiously combined in his case with an extremely allegorical and esoteric interpretation of the Koran. In his theology he was a pantheist, and as Brockelmann puts it, nobody brought such uninhibited fantasy to mysticism as he.[60] His books, Macdonald says, are a strange amalgam of theosophy and metaphysical paradox resembling the theosophy of our own days.[61] Ibnu 'l-'Arabī was a prolific author, of whose works in Arabic no less than one hundred and fifty of accepted authenticity have come down to us.[62] His principal work *Futūḥātu 'l-Makkiyya*, or 'Meccan Revelations' is an exposition of his mystical system in five hundred and sixty chapters, the five hundred and fifty-ninth being a résumé of the whole. His second best known work is his *Fuṣūṣu 'l-Ḥikam*, or 'Gems of Wisdom',[63] and among the rest his allegorical commentary on the Koran[64] and his dictionary of the Ṣūfī terms, *Al-Iṣṭilāḥātu 'ṣ-Ṣūfiyya*, may be selected for mention. There is also a collection of verses composed during his stay in Mecca in 1214 and dedicated to a noble and learned lady of that place whose intellectual friendship he enjoyed. This has been edited by Nicholson. These voluminous compilations in their high-flown and florid style have secured Ibnu 'l-'Arabī's fame as the greatest of the writers on mysticism in the annals of Islam.

Professor Arberry rightly comments that no adequate study has yet been made of Ibu 'l-'Arabī's works, and that our knowledge of his literary legacy is still in its infancy.[65] The present account of his system will therefore be of the briefest.

His main ideas, in so far as they have been studied, can be summarized thus: God is True Being and nothing exists except God. All things exhibit an essential oneness, and therefore any part of the universe is the same as the whole universe. This oneness of the universal divine essence is the true reality, whereas the external, empirical world which is presented to people's consciousness as real during their life upon earth, is mere illusion. Humanity is one in its essence, albeit plural in its individual manifestations. All things in the universe, including human souls, are emanations of the divine primary source. That is, the divine energy is poured out into the whole universe. However, God is not altogether deprived of the aspect of personality in this process. He possesses a personal consciousness and he can be encountered in communion with the souls of men.

Although Ibnu 'l-'Arabī seems sometimes to imply a distinction between the divine source and its emanations, any dissimilarity between God and the souls of men is in effect obliterated, since the substance of these souls is by hypothesis divine. Souls which have issued from the divine origin in order to realize their vocation return to God after death; and therefore death is nothing but a new birth for life in God. Chosen souls can return to God even during life, having won a preliminary freedom from the yoke of the phenomenal world and from their empirical 'ego', and arrived at knowledge of the essential unity of Creator and creation. *Fanā* is the communion of the soul with God and its complete dissolution in him during the person's life, and is attended by loss of earthly, illusory individuality.

In sum, these ideas on the unity of God and the universe could be epitomized in the formula, 'The existence of the creatures is the very essence of the being of the Creator'.[66] Massignon calls Ibnu 'l-'Arabī's philosophy 'existential monism', this being a translation of the Arabic expression *waḥdatu 'l-wujūd* or 'Unity of Being'. By 'Being' (*wujūd*), it need scarcely be said, Ibnu 'l-'Arabī intended not outward and empirical, but inner and essential Being.

According to Ibnu 'l-'Arabī, free will belongs to illusion: God directs the souls of men. Inasmuch as the soul is divine by its nature and does not possess its own power of choice, all distinction between good and evil vanishes: what man takes for evil has to do with his illusory ephemeral existence, and therefore is unreal. Automatically, the problem of good and bad and man's responsibility for his acts loses all meaning in Ibnu 'l-'Arabī's system. He here, of course, departs radically from Ghazālī who had recognized the reality of evil and its personalized vehicle the Devil, the reality of sin and its destructive effect on the soul, the freedom of the human will and man's consequent responsibility. And he is the very antithesis of Ghazālī and the moderate Ṣūfīs in his doctrine of the essential identity of God and the universe, in his theory of emanation, and in his understanding of *fanā*.

Au fond Ibnu 'l-'Arabī was indifferent to the form of this or that religion, holding the activity of God and the worship of God to be present in all religions.[67] One can always refute belief that is founded on dogma and speculation, he declared, but one cannot refute the personal, intuitive faith that is the religion of the heart. The form of the religion, therefore, does not matter: prayer can be said equally well in Muslim mosque and Christian monastery and Jewish synagogue — and even in a heathen temple before an idol, provided the worshipper believes he is addressing God and not a fetish. Nevertheless, for his own part Ibnu 'l-'Arabī found Islam to be the most convenient form of religion, and Ṣūfism the true philosophy of Islam. In consequence he called himself an orthodox Muslim and recommended Ṣūfīs to keep to the rules of the Sharī'a.

Many orthodox theologians were scandalized by these ideas. They called their author a *Zindīq* (wrongly, for there is no room for dualism in his system) and charged him with the heresies of *ittiḥād* and *ḥulūl*.[68] But he had his ardent defenders, too, and not only in the ranks of the pantheists; while in the Ṣūfī world, especially in Iran, his ideas were welcomed with enthusiasm by large numbers.[69]

Among the Ṣūfī writers kindred spirits were not wanting. One was his fellow-countryman Ibn Sab'īn (d. 1269), a pantheist who believed that 'God is the true reality of all that exists' and whose renown spread from the Muslim East to Western Europe thanks to his replies to certain philosophical questions which the Holy Roman Emperor and King of Sicily, Frederick II of Hohenstaufen (1212–50) had addressed to the sages of Ceuta.[70]

Another was the Persian Kamālu 'd-Dīn 'Abdu 'r-Razzāq al-Kāshānī (also called as-Samarqandī,[71] but mistakenly for he was certainly born in Kāshān). Little is known of this Ṣūfī's career except that he died in 1329/30, but his reputation as a writer was great in Iran, and beyond. Several of his works in Arabic are extant, the most important being a lexicon explaining the technical terms of Ṣūfism, *Al-Iṣṭilāḥātu 'ṣ-Ṣūfiyya*. Others are the commentary he wrote on Ibnu 'l-'Arabī's *Fuṣūṣu 'l-Ḥikam* and an allegorical interpretation of the Koran entitled *Ta'wīlatu 'l-Qur'ān*. He wrote very much in the spirit of Ibnu 'l-'Arabī and defended his 'orthodoxy' against the attacks of the opposition. But in adopting his general conception of the emanation of the universe from God, he declined to go the whole way with him. His pantheistic system is a blend of the metaphysics and theology of the Neo-Platonists with Aristotelianism and Koranic mythology.[72]

Unlike Ibnu 'l-'Arabī, whose idea of the essential unity of the universe had led to a belittling of the individual's status and a denial of his free will, 'Abdu 'r-Razzāq emphasized that this unity co-exists with a plurality of individual emanations. Inasmuch as free will is one of the attributes of the deity, the emanations from him — that is, the individual souls — must likewise possess free will. The question was, how to combine this free will with predetermination. 'Abdu 'r-Razzāq's answer is that the behaviour of the individual has both a primary or remote cause, viz. divine predestination, and a whole group of confused secondary causes which are closer; so that the willed act can be explained as the interaction of various forces. His solution of the problem of evil and human responsibility is simple: evil and sin arise from ignorance and distance from God, and the punishment of imperfect souls in the world to come for their offences in this will serve as a purification, and it will not be everlasting.[73]

In the forefront of the pantheistic mystics stands the great Persian poet Jalālu 'd-Dīn Rūmī (1207–1273). The founder of the Dervish order of the *Mawlawiyya* was born in Balkh but spent nearly all his days at Konya in Asia Minor. He was not a philospher and left no systematic account of his outlook on life, but he gave expression to his ideas in the imagery and symbolism of a poetry which is the glory of his voluminous *Mathnawī-yi-Ma'nawī* and his *Dīwān* or 'Collection of Lyrics', both of them in Persian. Brilliant in form, in beauty of image and lyrical power, his verses, it must be said, contain little originality of thought, being rather the clear echo of the Neo-Platonism preached by preceding pantheistic Ṣūfīs such as Bāyazīd of Bisṭām and Farīdu 'd-Dīn 'Aṭṭār, and, it may be, certain of the mystics of Eastern Christianity. Jalālu 'd-Dīn himself considered that he was heavily indebted to the intellectual and emotional influence of his companion and confidant, the half-demented itinerant Dervish-poet Shams-i Tabrīz.

A favourite theme of Jalālu 'd-Dīn's poetry is the Ṣūfī's need to renounce the 'ego' and the consciousness of individuality — this being the prelude to intimacy with God: the Ṣūfī had to be done with his carnal soul in order to experience the sweet love of the divine Friend. United with the deity in the state of *fanā*, the mystic becomes himself God (that is, part of God); and such a 'man of God' (Pers. *mard-i khudā*), though dwelling among his fellows in obscurity, poverty and contempt, is happy in his nearness to God and rich in the completeness God gives him; he is like a boundless sea, a downpour of pearl without clouds, he is a king in the rags of an ascetic.

Jalālu 'd-Dīn's own career provides a valuable clue to his thought.[74] For him a personal and emotional faith, however primitive and unsophisticated, was always preferable to the dogmatic lecturing of theologians. The tale of Moses and the Shepherd in the *Mathnawī* hinges on this. Man's heart is God's tabernacle, a Ka'ba, a source of insight into divine mystery, and therefore pilgrimages and ritualistic ceremonies are superfluous for those who are treading the path of mysticism. The idea is tirelessly hammered home that the difference between religions is of no moment, for all are rays of a single sun; Muslims, Christians and Jews bicker and fight over form, without realizing that the substance of their creeds is one and the same.

Another theme of his poetry is the rapture of mystical ecstasy, the pantheistic supra-personal consciousness. The poet is aware that he is the servant of the King and is himself King, a speck on the sun and also the sun's orb, a grain of deity and part of mankind, the dawn of morning and the evening sunset, moon and sun, the rose and the rose-garden, Believer and Guebre, sinner and God. We find, too, in his verses the idea of the pre-existence of souls and the idea of the transmigration of souls in a singular and perhaps original treatment: the emanations of God are confronted, as it were, with a climbing stairway of transitions; namely, from inanimate mineral to vegetable, from vegetable to animal, from animal to human endowed with consciousness and capable of faith, from human to angel, and from angel to God.

The extreme pantheism thus pervading Jalālu 'd-Dīn's thought, strangely enough, did not deter Sunnīs from accepting him as orthodox and revering him as a saint.

Ṣūfī mysticism had an immense effect on Persian poetry between the eleventh and fifteenth centuries. The theosophic verses attributed to Shaykh Abū Sa'īd of Mahna[75] are the earliest of the sort that have come down to us, and a long succession of poets from him onwards are imbued with the mystical outlook: Bābā Kūhī of Shīrāz (d. *c.* 1050), 'Abdullāh Anṣārī (1006–1088), Abu 'l-Majd Majdūd Sanā'ī (1048–1141), Shaykh Aḥmad-i Jām (1049–1142), Farīdu 'd-Dīn 'Aṭṭār (d. *c.* 1230), Fakhru 'd-Dīn 'Irāqī (d. 1289),[76] Maḥmūd Shabistarī (d. 1320), Awḥadu 'd-Dīn Kirmānī (d. 1298), Muḥammad Shīrīn Maghribī of Tabrīz (d. 1406/7),[77] Shaykh Sayyid Shāh Ni'matullāh Kirmānī (1330–1431)[78] and Nūru 'd-Dīn 'Abdu 'r-Raḥmān Jāmī (1414–92) are examples. And such poets as Niẓāmu 'd-Dīn Niẓāmī of Ganja (1141–*c.* 1205), Muṣliḥu 'd-Dīn Sa'di of Shīrāz (1284–1391) and Shamsu 'd-Dīn Muḥammad Ḥāfiẓ (d. 1389), although not out-and-out Ṣūfis, were to a greater or lesser extent sensitive to the environment of Ṣūfism and reflected it in their creative work. This Ṣūfī impact on poetry in the centuries named (and even afterwards) is too well known to require much space here, and we shall content ourselves with one aspect of it and no more. In developing a systematic philosophy, Ṣūfism evolved a very rich terminology based, as Louis Massignon has shown, mainly on the Koran. Now Persian poetry, being steeped in this Ṣūfism, appropriated the terminology, supplementing it with its own conventional terms drawn in great part from its native vocabulary. Thus God is conventionally named *dūst*, *yār* (Pers. 'friend', 'beloved'), *kā'su 'l-maḥabba* (Ar. Pers. 'cup of love'), *tarsā bachcha* (Pers. 'Christian child'), *pīr-i mughān* (Pers. 'elder of the Magi'), *khammār* (Ar. 'wine merchant', 'intoxicating'), *may furūsh* or *bāda furūsh* (Pers. with the same meaning). The mystical ecstasy is *may* or *bāda* (Pers. 'wine'), or *mastī* (Pers. 'intoxication'): the gathering-place of Ṣūfis is *kharābāt* (Ar. 'den of thieves', 'tavern'); and the Ṣūfī himself is *'āshiq* (Ar. 'lover') or *rind* (Pers. with Arabicized pl. *runūd*, 'wine-bibber', 'idler') or *kharābātī* (Ar. Pers. 'haunting the tavern'), and so on.[79]

The mystical poets depict their love for God in the terms of sensual love. In Persian mystical poetry, as Bertel's reminds us, 'the words "God", "soul", "prayer", etc., are seldom employed; they are replaced by a phraseology proper to erotic expression'.[80] A person not too familiar with Ṣūfī poetry may in reading it not even suspect that it has to do with religion; and the interpretations of the commentators in that sense are apt to seem false and forced, so real and so clear are the erotic pictures the poet has drawn'. It follows (the same scholar continues) that 'in the presence of Persian love-poetry one is often hard put to it to decide whether one is listening to a Ṣūfī or just to a common debauchee employing his idiom. Even in the most flagrant cases Persian hypocrisy likes to detect in the gay reveller a saintly ascetic celebrating the joys of Paradise'.[81] Under the protective cover of Ṣūfism a poet might sing the praises of wine and sensuality without fearing the revenge of the Faqīhs.

Nor was this the only context in which the specialized terminology allowed those who used it to insert in the form of Ṣūfī teaching a content that was anything but mystical. It would sometimes happen that the Ṣūfī imagery served to camouflage political, religious and philosophical free-thinking, or atomism, or materialism — and even atheism could be introduced in the language of pantheism.[82] Here was a very present help in trouble, to which all who lived in dread of persecution — poets, members of heretical sects and the preachers of humanistic and social gospels unpalatable to the regime — would on occasion resort. It was Jāmi writing in the fifteenth century who said there were two sorts of Ṣūfī authors: there were the genuine mystics and there were those others who borrowed the literary form, allegories and terminology of Ṣūfism in the service of ideas that had nothing in common with it.[83]

We have spoken of the generally reactionary character of Ṣūfism with its ideal of renunciation of the world and withdrawal from the arena, with its quietism implicit in the doctrine of *fanā*. There was often, however, a counter-current in Ṣūfism stirred by the popular discontent with the rapacity, wealth, sloth, luxury and sinful living of the feudal nobles and merchant princes. In so far as this was a Ṣūfī attitude it remained passive, but there were also times when the protest of the masses against feudal oppression was voiced in Ṣūfī language. Of course, when this happened, the guiding ideas of Ṣūfī mysticism were relegated to the background and lost behind social precepts in Ṣūfī form. Engels showed how in the history of Western Europe mysticism was at times the ideological disguise of anti-feudal movements.[84] The same thing took place in Iran.

A further factor served to strengthen the hold of Ṣūfism on Iran during the period we have been discussing. The devastation and impoverishment caused by the invasion of the Seljūqs in the eleventh century, the Balkh Oghuz in the twelfth, the Mongols in the thirteenth, and the hordes of Tīmūr at the turn of the fourteenth century, could not but incline large sections of the people to the pessimism associated with the Ṣūfī outlook on this perishable world, and heighten the appeal of self-abnegation and retirement from the social scene, voluntary poverty, and the like. So the period saw the uncoordinated Dervish convents beginning to amalgamate into large, powerful brotherhoods or 'orders', each with its own system of Ṣūfism, its own saints or eponymous founders, and their successors, the Chief Shaykhs. Each such order, termed *silsila* ('chain' of spiritual succession, from *salsala*, 'to connect, link') or *ṭarīqa* (here in the sense of the specific system of mystical discipline) sent out its shoots over immense areas, until certain of them were playing a role not unlike that of the Catholic monastic orders of Benedictines, Dominicans, Franciscans and Jesuits, or of the half-chivalrous, half-religious Templars and Teutonic Knights.

The view generally entertained by those who are not specialists in the Islamic field is that the Ṣūfī groups (including the extreme pantheists among them) and the Ṣūfī orders grew into self-contained 'sects'. This is quite untrue. They were happy to consider themselves, and be considered, within the pale of Sunnī Islam or Shī'ite Islam but as their mystical trends. To call the Dervish orders 'sects', as is still too often done in Soviet writing, is as incorrect as it would be to describe the Dominican, Franciscan, Jesuit, etc., orders of the Catholic Church as sects. It is quite another thing that the adherents of Extreme Shī'ite sects sometimes gave themselves out as Dervishes of this or that order.

We shall only speak of these orders briefly. They were numerous. Some were founded by Persians in Iran and then spread far beyond its frontiers; while others, founded abroad, took root in Iran. Some were Sunnī, others Shī'ite; and yet others were at home in both branches of Islam. Shī'ites, particularly the Imāmīs and Zaydīs, had for a long time looked askance at Ṣūfism, but in the period now in debate they made their peace with at least some groups of Ṣūfism, and several Dervish orders presently assumed a Shī'ite complexion.

All the orders claim a spiritual succession either from one of the famous Ṣūfī Shaykhs, e.g. Ma'rūf of Karkh and his pupil Sarī as- Saqaṭī, or Junayd, or Bāyazīd of Bisṭām — or indeed from persons who were never Ṣūfīs but whom legend subsequently declared such. For instance, Shī'ite orders trace the chain of affiliation back to one of the Twelve Imams, and often to the first Imam 'Alī; or else to quite mythical figures like the prophet Khiḍr. The orders attracted not only Dervishes in the strict definition of Faqīrs housed in khānaqāhs or solitaries and vagrants, but Ṣūfīs belonging to all classes of society living a family life in their own homes. At the head of an order stands a 'saint' (*walī*) who 'has known God' (*ṣamdānī*); he is the Chief Shaykh commonly called the *Quṭb* or 'Pole', and he will be locally represented by *naqībs*, local Shaykhs, who in turn will have their deputies (*khalīfas*). Each order will boast its own system of *ṭarīqa* which is thought of as having been handed down through the chain of succession from a particular luminary of Ṣūfism, its own repertoire of spiritual exercises and silent or vocal Dhikr, its own statutes, and its own tradition, usually legendary, as to the founding of the order and the transmission of the succession. In certain orders a secret, esoteric and often very far from 'orthodox' doctrine was transmitted, which was disclosed only to a few initiates. However, neither secret doctrine nor open pantheism stood in the way of an order's passing as thoroughly 'orthodox'; and it was even no rare thing for a brotherhood to combine its pantheism with Sunnī fanaticism or Shī'ite fanaticism, as the case might be.

The principal Dervish orders dispersed over Iran between the twelfth and fifteenth centuries were:[85]

1 The *Qādiriyya* This, the most ancient of the brotherhoods, was founded by Shaykh 'Abdu 'l-Qādir Gīlānī (al-Jīlānī in the Arabicized form, b. Gīlān, d. Baghdad 1166) styled al-Quṭbu 'l-A'ẓam. The *quṭb* of the moment would be guardian of the saint's mausoleum which had the principal *zāwiya* of the order just alongside it. Adherents of this Sunnī order are to be found today in all the Muslim countries. They were especially numerous in Iran up to the sixteenth century but were forced to leave after the victory of Shī'ism under the Ṣafawids, 'Abdu 'l-Qādir having been a Sunnī Ḥanbalite fiercely antagonistic to the Shī'ites. The *ṭarīqa* is pantheistic, and its founder is commonly deified in secret. The order has been connected with the guild of fishermen from olden times, and members of this qualify as Dervishes. Green is the symbol of the order.

2 The *Rifā'iyya* Founded by Sayyid Aḥmad Rifā'ī (b. Baṣra, d. 1182), this is an order of itinerant Dervishes tracing its line of succession back to Ma'rūf of Karkh. Its area is the whole of South-West Asia, but with a concentration in Iran.

3 The *Ṭayfūriyya* This order traced its beginning to Bāyazīd Ṭayfūr of Bisṭām, but the chain of succession went back to the fourth Imam Zaynu 'l-'Ābidīn 'Alī. It had both Sunnī and Shī'ite branches. It does not exist nowadays.

4 The *Suhrawardiyya* This order was founded by the Sunnī Shaykh 'Umar as-Suhrawardī.[86]

5 The *Mawlawiyya* or, in the Turkish pronunciation, *Mevleviyye.* Founded in the thirteenth century by the Persian poet Shaykh Jalālu 'd-Dīn Rūmī,[87] its chief convent was at Konya where the Shaykh spent his days and has his mausoleum. It is widespread in Turkey even at the present time. It used to be represented in Iran, but its Dervishes were expelled by the Ṣafawid Shah Ṭahmāsp I for their extravagant pantheistic attitudes. The initiates practise the vocal Dhikr with music and dancing, and hence Europeans usually call them the Whirling or Dancing Dervishes. They were always distinguished by a broad-minded tolerance of Christians and Jews. In the lifetime of Jalālu 'd-Dīn Rūmī, at all events, the order consisted for the most part of the lower classes and artisans.[88] An outward distinguishing mark is the tall cap (*kulāh*) these Dervishes wear.

6 The *Shādhiliyya* Founded by Shādhilī of Morocco (d. 1258), the order was not without some following in Iran.

7 The *Kubrāwiyya* Founded by the Khwārazmian Shaykh Najmu

'd-Dīn Kubrā who perished during the Mongol conquest of Khwārazm, this order was widespread in Central Asia but rather thinly dispersed in Iran. It practises the silent Dhikr.

8 The *Chishtiyya* The chain of succession is in the first instance from Mu'īnu 'd-Dīn Chishtī (d. Ajmer 1236), but it is claimed that it ascends through him to the semi-legendary Ibrāhīm Adham, and then through the latter to the prophet Khiḍr. The centre of the order to begin with was near Herāt but was afterwards transferred to India. The poet Khusraw of Delhi (d. 1325) belonged to it.

9 The *Naqshbandiyya* The accepted founder is Shaykh Bahā'u 'd-Dīn Muḥammad Naqshband, a native of the Bukhārā oasis (1318–89).[89] The word *naqshband* means 'engraver' in Persian, and indicates the calling of the saint and that of his father before him. But though the order gets its name from this Shaykh, it would seem in fact to go back beyond him; and it may well be an offshoot of the *Ṭayfūriyya*. The sources portray Naqshband as an ascetic preaching poverty, utter simplicity[90] and a pantheistic love of all living things; but eventually these early attitudes of his followers degenerated into the exact opposite, viz. an apology of wealth and the existing regime, a religious fanaticism totally incompatible with their pretended pantheism, and a vindication of Holy War on the infidels.[91] The order stretched from the Chinese province of Kansu as far as Kazan and Istanbul, and was particularly well entrenched in Central Asia, Iran and Ādharbāyjān.[92] It possessed a preponderating Sunnī branch and a Shī'ite branch of modest size. It abided by the principle of community-life in khānaqāhs, and frowned on the solitary recluse. It favoured the silent Dhikr. Its Dervishes were recognizable by their sand-coloured *khirqa*.

10 The *Bektāshiyya* This order which was almost exclusively confined to Turkey was founded, tradition said, in Asia Minor in the fourteenth century by the Persian Ḥājjī Bektāshi Walī, a half-legendary person,[93] and was chiefly known for its close connection with the corps of Janissaries. Officially it was always classed as an orthodox Sunnī fraternity, but it was an open secret that it countenanced an esoteric doctrine very near to that of the extreme Shī'ite sect, the Ḥurūfīs.[94] The Bektāshī held all religions to be of equal value, paid no heed to ritualistic performance, and did not even repeat the Dhikr. When the corps of Janissaries was disbanded in 1826, the headquarters of the order moved from Istanbul to Albania. Bektāshīs wore white clothing and a cap of the same colour.

11 The *Ṣefeviyya*, properly *Ṣafawiyya* We shall have something to say about this Shī'ite order in another place.[95]

12 The *Ḥaydariyya* This Shīʿite order, associated with the name of the thirteenth-century Shaykh Ḥaydar of Khurāsān, was spread over the whole of Iran. In the following century, as Ibn Baṭṭūṭa tells us, it was noted for its extreme asceticism and insisted on the celibacy of its Dervishes.[96]

13 The *Niʿmatullāhiyya* This Shīʿite order was founded by the noted Ṣūfī and poet Sayyid Shāh Niʿmatullāh Kirmānī (1330–1431) who claimed descent from the fifth Shīʿite Imam Muḥammad al-Bāqir. Niʿmatullāh lived in Samarqand, Herāt, and Yazd but spent the last twenty-five years of his long life at the convent he founded in the picturesque village of Māhān near Kirmān, where his grave became a place of pilgrimage. He is a saint who attracted great attention, and was given the title 'Shah' in the sense of King of Mystics — a title prefixed ever since to the names of the Chief Shaykhs of the order. He enjoyed the special patronage of the Tīmūrid Sultan Shāhrukh (1405–47), and the Ruler of the Deccan, Aḥmad I Bahmanī (1422–35), would often invite him to his court.[97] Many Ṣūfī tracts are attributed to him, but his principal work is his widely esteemed Diwan of verse.[98] This was redolent of extreme pantheism. In the spirit of Ibnu 'l-ʿArabī's *waḥdatu 'l-wujūd* ('Unity of Being') — the doctrine in fact of the *ṭarīqa* Niʿmatullāh had founded — it abounded in apocalyptic pictures of the disasters to be expected at the end of the world, and spoke much of the advent of the Mahdī and Jesus, and of Doomsday. The order was widely spread in Iran and India, and in some places broke into sub-orders of the parent body.

In the sixteenth and following centuries, that is after the victory of Shīʿism in Iran, the influence of the *Ḥaydariyya* and the *Niʿmatullāhiyya* strengthened, especially over the townspeople. These two orders competed jealously for the favour of the traders' associations and the corporations of artisans (*ṣinf*, pl. *aṣnāf*), and European travellers in the sixteenth, seventeenth and eighteenth centuries have recorded how the citizens of many a town in Iran would be ranged in two groups owing their allegiance to the Ḥaydarīs and the Niʿmatullāhīs respectively.

14 The *Jalāliyya* This Shīʿite order of itinerant Dervishes went back to Shaykh Jalālu 'd-Dīn Bukhārī (1307–83), better known as Shaykh Jalāl and Makhdūm-i Jahānīyān, 'Lord of the Inhabitants of the World'. Its members paid no heed to the Sharīʿa, had a cord around the neck, clipped the moustache and beard very short, and did not wear their hair long and dishevelled like most of the other

Dervishes in Iran. They handed in to their Murshid whatever alms they collected. They were dispersed over Iran, Central Asia and India.

In addition there was a less tidy category of wandering mendicants very numerous in Iran and Central Asia who went by the generic name of Qalandarīs (*Qalandariyya*). This term was used to designate sometimes an independent order, sometimes the branch of one of the other orders such as the *Naqshbandiyya*, and sometimes just Dervishes answerable to no organized fraternity at all.

We have already alluded to the affiliation of particular Ṣūfī orders to the corporations or guilds of different crafts. As this is a question that awaits study it is impossible to say more on it here.

Ṣūfism in the twelfth to fifteenth centuries had no ideological unity, and it would therefore be wrong to speak as though it rested on a single social basis at that time. The milieu from which the different trends of Ṣūfism recruited their adherents was far from homogeneous; added to which, one and the same Dervish order might very well play a shifting role over the years. If some orders, or their branches, to a greater or lesser degree voiced a protest (which would be passive and rarely active) against social oppression, others on the contrary by their advocacy of the contemplative life and a withdrawal from affairs played into the hands of the feudal seigneurs. Nor was this all. There were those who frankly strove to gear Ṣūfism to the defence of the interests of the ruling class. In teaching men to spurn wealth, the Ṣūfīs began to put the accent on contentment with one's lot, patience, submissiveness, non-resistance to force; and it was but a step from this to imply that there was no harm in the Ṣūfī's being rich, if only he did not sell his soul to his riches and allow them to implement violence and sin. The rich Ṣūfī could look on himself not as the owner of his wealth but only as the manager of something God had entrusted to him; he was supposed to spend next to nothing on his personal needs and disburse the rest on religious and charitable causes. Such moral precepts were, of course, harmless since there was nobody to enforce them. Inevitably the Ṣūfī of means not only found his patrons among the seigneurs, he became a spiritual seigneur himself.

A pointed example is the case of 'Ubaydullāh, styled Khwāja Aḥrār (or more accurately, Khwāja-yi Aḥrār, 'Lord of the Nobles', 1403–90) who as Chief Shaykh of the Naqshbandī order was for nearly forty years the leading — and, be it added, most reactionary — personality in the politics of the Central Asian Sultanate of the Tīmūrids. This

Ṣūfī Shaykh and writer was lauded as a saint by his admirers, and he is portrayed as such in the biography which ʻAlī b. Ḥusayn-i Wāʻiẓ Kāshifī wrote of him in the late fifteenth century.[99] But that author also allows us to inspect the reverse side of his ʻsaintʼ. His ʻsaintʼ owned thirteen hundred ʻmulkʼ properties. In a single one of these there were three thousand ʻyoke of oxenʼ plots, (*juft-i ʻawāmil*)[100] and at the rate of one man per plot a labour contingent of three thousand was annually drafted to repair the irrigation channels. Naïvely carried away by what he sees as a mark of God's favour, the author of the biography spells it out that ʻthe substance and estate of the saintly Īshān, his lands, fields and patrimony, and therewith his flocks and herds of livestock and other belongings, movable and immovable, were exceeding great and beyond computationʼ.[101] Besides which, the holy man had laid his hands on practically the whole transit caravan trade on the Merv–Bukhārā–Samarqand route. Changed indeed was the social milieu, and gone the morality, of the leaders of this order — and all in less than one hundred years from the days of Bahāʼu ʼd-Dīn Naqshband. The Ṣūfī poet ʻAbdu ʼr-Raḥmān Jāmī is another example. He got through one hundred thousand kebekī dinars annually on his ordinary expenditure and into the bargain obtained a decree from the Tīmūrid ruler of Khurāsān Sultan Ḥusayn, exempting his estates from all dues to the treasury.[102]

After such men as Ibnu ʼl-ʻArabī and Jamālu ʼd-Dīn Rūmī in the thirteenth and ʻAbdu ʼr-Razzāq Kāshānī in the fourteenth century, Ṣūfism had apparently no more to offer in the realm of thought. Although it spread ever more widely, it had spent its force and was living henceforward on the rehash of old ideas. The mysticism of the Dervish orders became more and more associated in the popular mind with the working of marvels and with the cult of a multitude of holy men and supposedly inspired Shaykhs, living or dead, and with the veneration of their graves and relics. The khānaqāh became more and more the forcing-house of this saint-worship, of superstitions galore, of ignorant fanaticism.

The bulk of the followers had never had much time for the Ṣūfī cosmology, and they now interested themselves in it less than ever, only looking to their Shaykhs for miracles and help in the difficulties of daily life. The more the Shaykhs exerted their hold, the more affluent the Dervish convents became. Feudal barons and civic notables vied in giving them money, goods, valuables, grain, or herds and in assigning them waqf estates; Sultans and Khans would endow them with lands and grant them papers of immunity. The wandering Dervishes, who socially were indistinguishable from the *déclassé* proletariat, came more and more to be an army of professional beggars innocent of Ṣūfism, or indeed of any other faith. There was also another direction in which Ṣūfism could sink into corruption. Certain of the brotherhoods, or their offshoots, deviated into military organizations in which the code of *jihād* replaced the Ṣūfī ideal of spiritual perfection. Such orders would engage in Holy War, otherwise pillaging expeditions, against the infidels of the bordering lands of Georgia, North Caucasus, Russia, the Kalmyk country, India, etc., and bring back booty and captive-slaves as the reward of their piety. This is precisely what happened in the case of the *Ṣefeviyya* whose evolution will be our concern in the next chapter.

XIII
The triumph of Shīʿism in Iran

The defeat of the Nizārī Ismāʿīlīs and the decline of their sway in Iran led to a corresponding strengthening of the hold which the other current of Shīʿism, the Imāmīs or Ithnā-ʿasharīs,[1] exerted over the masses. We have had occasion to quote Bartol'd's observation that Shīʿism in one or another of its forms was the ideological outer cover of Iran's peasant movements.[2] In the fourteenth and fifteenth centuries those movements matured under the outer cover of Shīʿism in conjunction with Ṣūfism. It was a phenomenon exactly analogous to the religious colouring of the popular movements of mediaeval Western Europe to which Engels drew attention when he said: 'The revolutionary opposition to feudalism goes on throughout the Middle Ages; it takes the stage sometimes in the dress of mysticism, sometimes in the dress of open heresy, sometimes in that of armed rebellion, depending on the conditions of the day.'[3] All three of the elements noticed by Engels were present in the popular upheavals of Iran in the period we are considering; that is, sectarianism (Shīʿism), mysticism (Ṣūfism), and armed revolt. The religious colour of class movements in feudal societies, to cite Engels again, 'is explained not by the characteristics of the human heart or by man's religious need . . . but by the whole preceding history of the Middle Ages which knew only one form of ideology: namely, religion and theology'.[4]

The popular movements during the period were responses to the heavy yoke of the Mongol conquerors and to feudal exploitation. Ideologically they were directed against the then predominant Sunnism and also against the 'Great Yāsa' of Chingīz Khan, which sanctioned the institution of serfdom and an oppressive system of taxation imposed on Iran by the Il-Khans. Hence the popular slogans 'Down with Innovations' — meaning the taxes which the Sharīʿa never envisaged — and 'Back to Islam' — an ideal Islam as pictured by the masses. In the countries of the Muslim East the state was much more closely bound up with religion than in the Christian West, and although religion in fact played a subservient role in popular movements, every social idea had to be clothed in it.

Until the beginning of the sixteenth century at least half of Iran, and perhaps more, was Sunnī. Ḥamdullāh Mustawfī of Qazwīn writes in his Geography (*c.* 1340) that Imāmī Shīʿites predominated in the Kūfa, Baṣra and Ḥilla districts of Arab Iraq,[5] and in the Ray, Āba, Qum, Ardistān, Farāhān and Nahāwand districts of Western Iran.[6] In Sāwa town, Shāfiʿite Sunnīs were dominant, but in the surrounding rural area Imāmī Shīʿites preponderated:[7] in Kāshān town Imāmī Shīʿites, but Sunnīs in the rural area.[8] In Gurgān the majority of the inhabitants were Shīʿites.[9] Ḥamdullāh is silent about Māzandarān and Gīlān, but we know from other sources[10] that the bulk of the population there, except for a section of the nobles and townspeople, were strongly Shīʿite of the Imāmī school. He names only one district in Khurāsān where Imāmī-Shīʿites predominated, viz. Bayhaq with its capital Sabzawār.[11] He grants that Bāṭinīs,[12] i.e. Ismāʿīlīs, preponderated in a number of districts in the Elburz Mountains — Daylam, Tawālish (The Two Tālish), Rūdbār and elsewhere, and from other sources we learn that Kūhistān also long remained an Ismāʿīlī hotbed. Ḥamdullāh gives no information about the confessional bias observable in Khūzistān,[13] Kirmān and Sīstān, but in the rest of the provinces Sunnīs undoubtedly predominated.[14]

Admittedly, one must make some allowance for the fact that in a number of localities, rural ones mostly, the residents may have been really Shīʿites but passed themselves off as Sunnīs on the *taqiyya* principle of prudent concealment of one's creed.[15] But even so we should be right in repeating that the majority of the population of Iran counted as Sunnī until the beginning of the sixteenth century. The barons were Sunnīs, and so were the overwhelming majority in the actual towns — Sunnīs of the Shāfiʿite school as far as West Iran was concerned. Ḥamdullāh specifies that Shāfiʿite Sunnīs predominated in the following cities: Iṣfahān, Qazwīn, Abhar, Zanjān, Mizdaqān, Shīrāz, Jarbādhaqān, Yazd, Tabrīz, Ardabīl, Bishkin, Ahar and Nakhjawān.[16] As to Khurāsān there is some uncertainty; for whereas Ḥamdullāh mentions that only a few towns, notably Herāt, Khwāf and Juwayn, were of the Sunnī persuasion,[17] other sources report that the majority of people there were Sunnīs — and of the Ḥanafite school. At all events Sunnism was the official confession of all the state formations of Iran, with the exception of Māzandarān and Gīlān which were Shīʿite principalities.[18]

However, when it came to popular movements aimed simultaneously against the Mongol conquerors and the exploiting barons, the ideological colouring was Shīʿite. The Shīʿites were a minority in relation to the whole of Iran but a highly significant minority, because both active and commanding the sympathy of the peasants and the poor townsmen. We have commented in an earlier chapter on the strength, at this juncture, of the hopes men placed in a Messiah, or Mahdī,[19] whose advent they foresaw as a social revolution in religious form which would put an end to the violence of some over others, would remove the tyrants (meaning the Sunnī rulers) and establish the kingdom of justice on earth.[20]

An impressive, but premature, rising occurred in Fārs in 1265/6 led by one Sayyid Sharafu 'd-Dīn, a self-declared Mahdī, which was put down without mercy.[21] There was then a pause until the 1330s when the break-up of the state of the Il-Khans of the House of Hūlāgū (1335) left Iran in internal confusion. Economic decay, high taxes whose burden was enhanced by the illegal extortions of finance officials, mutually destructive fighting among feudal cliques who contended for power in the name of the puppet Il-Khans they controlled, feudal anarchy, pillage and violence by those who had snatched local authority and by barons turned brigands — all these had combined to ruin the countryside and reduce its husbandry to the lowest level.[22] Especially parlous was the plight of Khurāsān, which had already suffered enough devastation at the time of the mutiny of the Mongol prince Yasāwur (1317–19). The warfare between the feudal cliques here spelled the plundering and molesting of humble folk in the villages and towns. 'There was not a corner', wrote Ḥāfiẓ-i Abrū, 'where some aggressor (*mutaghallib*) or other did not strive to thwart the people and do them wrong.'[23] And in the words of Ẓāhiru 'd-Dīn Mar'ashī, 'the ryots of Khurāsān fell into grievous straits, and tyranny (*ẓulm*) exceeded all bounds; and particularly did the Tājīk people[24] reach the extreme of suffering, their men being tried beyond endurance'.[25] The last of the Mongol Il-Khans, Tūghāy Tīmūr (1336–53), continued to hold out in Gurgān, but his authority was purely nominal.

A rebellion in Khurāsān in 1337 set the tone of the risings which from now on would agitate Iran until the sixteenth century — and not only Iran but the bordering countries where feudal exploitation was equally advanced. Time after time the peasants, the urban poor, and runaway slaves rallied to the standard of revolt. The Sarbadār movements (Pers. *sarbadār*, 'gallows-bird', 'desperado') in Khurāsān, 1337–81, in the Samarqand region in 1365/1366, and in Kirmān in 1373 were part and parcel of this wave of resistance. Other analogous movements were: risings in Māzandarān in 1350–60 and following years, in Gīlān in 1370 and following years, in Sabzawār in 1405, and in Māzandarān in 1406; the Ḥurūfī agitation which swept across the immense tract from Khurāsān to Ottoman Turkey in the first decades of the fifteenth century; the rebellion of the Mevlevi Shaykh Badru 'd-Dīn Simawī and Börklüce Muṣṭafā in Turkey in 1416; and the rising led by the 'precursor' Mahdī Musha'sha' in Khūzistān in 1441 and following years. The ideology common to almost all these popular movements, as has been said, was Shī'ite of the various sects in combination with Ṣūfism; the Dervishes invariably playing a prominent role in them.

The Sarbadār movement in Khurāsān was of the most significance historically. The ideological impulse was supplied by the founder of a particular Dervish order, one Shaykh Khalīfa of Māzandarān. In his youth Khalīfa had been the pupil of Dervish preceptors, but not finding the answers to the questions that tormented him he left their company and himself became a Shaykh — perhaps self-styled, for the sources do not suggest that he received the diploma in the usual way from his Dervish masters. He made his way to Sabzawār in the Bayhaq district, where both the townspeople and the peasants of the neighbourhood were ardent Imāmī Shī'ites, and there set up in a *ḥujra*, or cell, alongside the cathedral mosque and began to propound his own doctrine. What this was, the sources, being unsympathetic to Khalīfa, do not tell us, indicating merely that the Sunnī doctors of Sabzawār accused him of preaching worldly themes (*ḥadīth-i dunyā*, *sukhan-i dunyā*) conflicting with the Sharī'a. His teaching had an immense vogue and the majority of the citizens of Sabzawār enrolled themselves as his Murīds. The Faqīhs then issued a Fatwā condemning the heretic to death, and he soon fell victim to the killers they deputed to execute the sentence. On arriving at the cathedral mosque to attend a lecture on the morning of 22 Rabī'u 'l-Awwal 736 = 9 November 1335, Khalīfa's pupils found their Shaykh hanged on one of the pillars in the forecourt.[26]

Of these pupils one had stood out from the rest. This was Ḥasan Jūrī, a man of peasant origin, evidently, from the village of Jūr. Having successfully terminated a course of training in the madrasa and received the grade of mudarris or reader, he had felt the attraction of Shaykh Khalīfa's gospel and renounced both his teaching career and the official Sunnī allegiance. On the tragic death of his teacher he became a Shaykh, and head of a new order, and departed for Nīshāpūr where he preached with enormous success. Most of his Murīds were artisans (*ṣāḥib-i ḥirfa*) and he himself earned his livelihood by handicraft (*kasb*).[27] Each Murīd on entering the order had to take an oath pledging himself to keep a weapon always at hand 'and he would note down the names of any who did not respond to this call. And he used to tell them: now is the time for concealment; and anon exhort them, saying that as soon as the signal of their Shaykh was given and the time was ripe for overt action it would behove each one of them to prepare his weapon and make ready for the fray'.[28]

It is obvious from this that Ḥasan Jūrī (as also, without doubt, his master Shaykh Khalīfa before him) was using Ṣūfism and Shī'ism as a mere cover for the advocacy of a political revolt, and conceived the spadework towards this as the proper purpose of his spiritual order. It may be supposed that neither of these Shaykhs was a genuine Ṣūfī and only took advantage of the Dervish organization to instil unrest and so prepare the terrain. The order adopted the designation *Ḥasaniyya* after Ḥasan Jūrī's name,[29] and presently gave out that the chain of succession ascended to Shaykh Bāyazīd of Bisṭām and through him to the sixth Shī'ite Imam Ja'far aṣ-Ṣādiq. For three years Ḥasan Jūrī preached in Nīshāpūr and in the Khurāsān cities of Mashhad, Abīward, Khabūshān, Balkh, Herāt, and Khwāf; then visited Tirmidh, Kūhistān and Persian Iraq; then returned to Khurāsān. He had to take shelter at times in caves, until on the orders of Arghūn Shāh, head of the Mongol nomadic nobility in Khurāsān, he was apprehended on the road from Mashhad to Kūhistān along with sixty to seventy of his disciples and incarcerated in the fortress of Ṭāq in the Yāzir district.[30]

Long before this a peasant revolt had broken out in the village of Bashtin in the Bayhaq district. According to one version, an envoy (*īlchī*) of the Mongol fisc happening to be billeted there in the peasant homestead of two brothers, first demanded wine of his hosts and then their wives — whereupon the indignant brothers slew him. The Il-Khan vizier of Khurāsān, 'Alā'u 'd-Dīn Muḥammad Hindū, after in vain requiring the Bashtin villagers to hand over the murderers, sent a military detachment against them. At that the villagers rose openly, and repelled the soldiers.[31] The local land-owner, a descendant of Ḥusaynī Sayyids, had a son named 'Abdu 'r-Razzāq, and just then the latter happened to return to Bashtin. He informed himself of events and took the part of the peasants. A band of daring young spirits, who thought themselves no whit inferior to the hero Rustam, now armed themselves and elected 'Abdu 'r-Razzāq as their leader. A gathering was held at which the peasants declared: 'These men who have taken to themselves the power are doing us much violence. If God on High vouchsafes us aid, we shall remove the tyranny and be done with the tyrants (*ẓālīmān*); if not, then let our heads be on the gibbet (*sar ba dār*), for endure this aggression we cannot.'[32]

The rebellion in Bashtin began, according to the sources, on 12 Sha'ban 737 = 16 March 1337. The majority of the peasants were Murīds of Shaykh Ḥasan Jūrī, and therefore long since prepared for hostilities. Their pre-war strength rapidly increased, and by August they were able to capture the fortified town of Sabzawār and, not long afterwards, the neighbouring towns of Juwayn and Isfarā'in. 'Abdu 'r-Razzāq took the title Amir, minted his money, and ordered his name to be read in the khuṭba. The Sarbadār Kingdom had been founded, and was to endure until 1381.

We have discussed the history of the Sarbadārs of Khurāsān in a separate work,[33] and a brief mention is all that will be appropriate here. The general picture is that the petty land-owners of native stock joined hands with the insurgents in the selfish design of driving the Mongol nobility from their midst. A lasting cleavage in the Sarbadār state resulted, namely, between a moderate element which was involved with these small local land-owners and an extreme element represented by the Dervishes of Shaykh Ḥasan Jūrī's order who relied on the artisans and poorest peasants. The Shaykh himself was rescued from imprisonment in about 1339 and came to Sabzawār to be among this latter element. The partisans of the moderate tendency were designated Sarbadārs proper, and those of the extreme tendency, aspiring to social equality and a distribution of property, took the name of Shaykhites (Pers. *Shaykhiyān*).[34]

The discord between these two elements in the Sarbadār state led to frequent *coups* and changes of ruler — twelve, in fact, in forty-four years. Inevitably these rulers were mostly from among the small land-owners, but pressure from the artisans and peasants did force them into worthwhile concessions. Thus the peasants surrendered all told three-tenths of the yield (in kind), and 'not a dinar' could be demanded above that. Then the ruler with his entourage, officials and military captains, all dressed alike in a plain woollen or camel-hair coat. A common table was laid every day in the ruler's house at which poor man and rich man[35] could sit together. The militia was composed of peasants[36] and petty land-owners, the latter being described in the sources as the Sarbadār nobility (*buzurgān-i sarbadār*). Twelve thousand men were at first entered in the enrolment lists, then eighteen thousand, and finally twenty-two thousand, all of them drawing pay from the treasury. These Sarbadār soldiers were famed for exceptional bravery and their endeavour, as one of the poets put it, was to see that 'from dread of the lances of the Sarbadārs not a single Turk[37] should dare to pitch his tent in Iran'.

In about 1339 the Sarbadār forces routed three contingents of Mongol seigneurs and freed the major city of Nīshāpūr from their grasp. The Sarbadār power now occupied territory from Dāmghān in the west to Jām in the east (500 km), and from Khabūshān in the north to Turshīz in the south (200 km), and it was at this juncture that the second ruler of the kingdom Wajīhu 'd-Dīn Mas'ūd (1338–44) took the title Sultan of Islam and Shāhinshāh of all the Climes.

The last Mongol Il-Khan, Tughāy Tīmūr, who had been leading a nomadic existence in Gurgān with his horde,[38] suffered several defeats at the hands of the Sarbadārs. In the end he invited them to his camp, ostensibly to conclude a treaty of peace but privately thinking to make them drunk and overpower them by the end of the banquet. The Sarbadār ruler, Yaḥyā Kerabī, visited the horde with his general Ḥāfiẓ Shaghānī and three hundred (in another version, one thousand) Sarbadārs. They had tumbled to the Il-Khan's strategem, and decided to forestall him. When the wine cups began to be handed round at the feast in the Il-Khan's marquee, Yaḥyā laid his hand on his head. At this prearranged signal Ḥāfiẓ whipped out a knife from his top-boot and stabbed the Il-Khan in the head, and Yaḥyā quickly dispatched him with a blow from his pole-axe. The Sarbadārs hurled themselves on the Mongols, thus taken unawares, and slaughtered a good proportion of them. The rest took to their heels in panic. 'In the twinkling of an eye', says Ḥāfiẓ-i Abrū, 'the Padshah's horde was annihilated, so that not a trace of it remained'.[39] The Sarbadārs next added Ṭūs and Mashhad to their territory in the east and, albeit only for a short while, the Gurgān and Qūmis areas in the west. They carried out large irrigation works, or rather restored the underground canals, or karezes, in the Ṭūs and Mashhad region.[40] Ḥafiẓ-i Abrū tells of the prosperity of the Bayhaq district under the Sarbadārs, and remarks that Sabzawār at this time was transformed into one of the grandest cities of Iran.[41]

The Imāmī Shī'ite doctrine was installed in the Sarbadār state, and the khuṭba was read with the mention of the Twelve Imams. The regime did not turn out to be a peasant democracy: it was one of small land-owners; which, however, in order to subsist had to make significant concessions to the peasantry. Heads of state drawn from the moderate element were increasingly inclined to copy the traditional Islamic monarchy based on the (Shī'ite) Sharī'a, and the last of their number actually wiped out the extremists altogether, executing their leader Dervish 'Azīz together with seventy of his supporters and banning the order of the *Ḥasaniyya*. If it had lasted longer, the Sarbadār dynasty would probably have lapsed into an ordinary feudal principality.

Very similar was the movement that started in Māzandarān about 1350.[42] A zealous Shī'ite of the Imāmī sect named Qawāmu 'd-Dīn Mar'ashī who had become Shaykh of the *Ḥasaniyya*[43] after Ḥasan Jūrī's death, appeared at the head of a popular *émeute* engineered by the Dervishes. 'The inhabitants of Sārī and Māzandarān', says Dawlatshāh, 'had become his [the Sayyid's] Murīds',[44] and even the ruler of Māzandarān, Kiyā Afrāsiyāb Chulāwī, had been obliged to give himself out as a Murīd of this Shaykh, dressing in 'the garment of poverty', attending the communal baths, and so on — though no doubt 'he was deceiving the people'[45] in thus pretending to be a Dervish.

Anecdotes in the pages of Ẓāhiru 'd-Dīn Mar'ashī make it plain that the Māzandarān Dervishes, who were men of peasant and artisan origin, aimed at an even distribution of the means of consumption and at social equality. He relates how the people of Māzandarān having become Dervishes and true followers of the Shaykh 'also considered Afrāsiyāb as their Murīd and demanded various things of him in the way of weapons and clothing, so that several times when he went to the baths (*ḥammām*), the Dervishes would turn up and take away the clothes he had been wearing, saying: "We too are Murīds, but have no *qabā*;[46] thou art the ruler in these parts and canst command a second one to be tailored, since Dervish so-and-so has taken the other and has put it on." And from Afrāsiyāb's sons they took shields and sabres, saying: "Dervish so-and-so had no weapon and therefore has taken yours. You have plenty, so go and get another."[47] Another time Dervishes came to the private estate of Kiyā Afrāsiyāb at the season of harvesting the rice (*dirow-yi birinj*) and made demands, saying: "The Dervishes, not having sown any rice, beg thee to deign to give them a few kurr[48] of thine." Kiyā had perforce to respond: "Give the Dervishes some kurr of rice." But of their own initiative they went to the paddy field and began to bind up the rice by packloads, counting each such bundle as one kurr, so that if in each bundle there were a hundred kurr they tied up by hundreds; and thus they got a thousand kurr instead of the legitimate number'.[49]

These stories also prove that the Dervishes constituted nothing less than an armed community. The sorely vexed Afrāsiyāb at length broke with them, and cast Shaykh Sayyid Qawāmu 'd-Dīn into prison on a charge of spreading sedition. In answer, an armed party burst into the gaol and freed him. A pitched battle ensued near the town of Āmul, in which the soldiers of Afrāsiyāb were defeated by the insurgent Dervishes and he himself was killed. A so-called Sayyid state of Māzandarān then took shape (1360), resembling in type the Sarbadār regime in Khurāsān. The spiritual and political authority vested in Sayyid Qāwamu 'd-Dīn and after him in his descendants, the successor Shī'ite Sayyids Mar'ashī.

Ten years later, as a result of a similar popular movement inspired by Shī'ite Dervishes and notably Shaykh Sayyid Amīr Kiyā, a second Sayyid state was formed in the eastern part of Gīlān, having its centre at Lāhijān.

In 1365–66 a Sarbadār rebellion occurred in Samarqand, to be suppressed, however, forthwith by Tīmūr.[50] Another broke out in Kirmān in 1373. In this disturbance many of the surrounding *iqṭā'* ('allotment') proprietors and the Faqīhs were executed or imprisoned, and their lands or other property confiscated. The rising was only quelled after a nine-months' siege of Kirmān by the forces of the Muẓaffarid Shāh Shujā'. At last, in 1381 Tīmūr took Sabzawār, and so put an end to the Sarbadār state. An attempted comeback by the Sarbadārs in 1383 failed. After Tīmūr's death, things flared up again in Sabzawār, but his successor Sultan Shāhrukh managed to control the situation.

Meantime the Sayyid state of Māzandarān likewise had known the meaning of disaster, for Tīmūr's troops overthrew it in 1392. However, in 1406 a new rising in Māzandarān brought back the Sayyid state there. Both the Māzandarān regime and the parallel Sayyid regime in Gīlān, now that the fifteenth century had opened, evolved into ordinary petty feudal states.

The Extreme Shī'ites (*ghāliyya*, *ghulāt*) exhibited a galvanic energy under the Tīmūrid dominion in the fifteenth century, and some new sects made their appearance. The Ḥurūfīs, especially, were active in their anti-Tīmūrid propaganda, and the attempt on the life of Sultan Shāhrukh at Herāt in 1427 was an indication of the trend in popular feeling.[51] In 1441/2 the people rose in Khūzistān. Their leader was Sayyid Muḥammad, called Musha'sha' ('the radiant' from *sha'sha'a*, 'to shine'), an Ultra-Shī'ite naming himself precursor (*pīshraw*) of the hidden Imam Mahdī whose imminent return and reign of universal equality and justice he heralded. Ten thousand 'ignoramuses, loafers and thieves' (*juhhāl*, *'ayyārān wa duzdān*), says the historian Ja'farī, employing the terms that feudal writers were wont to apply to the insurgent proletariat and villagers, flocked to his side and raised the standard of revolt in the countryside between Ḥuwayza and Shūshtar. They overthrew and annihilated the dynasty of the local feudal ruler Ṣakhr b. 'Ulyān, and exterminated the nobles and the spiritual lords, i.e. the Sunnī Shaykhs and Sayyids. Ja'farī labels the followers of Musha'sha' Extreme Shī'ites (*ghāliyya*), Fidā'īs (*fidāyyān*, pl. of *fidā'ī*, 'volunteer, ready to lay down his life for the cause'), also Philosophers and Ismā'īlīs (*falāsifa wa ismā'īliyya*), and adds that the rising was accompanied by pillage — meaning, probably, the distribution of the houses, lands and effects of the slain nobles among the insurgents.[52]

This mass rising in Khūzistān alarmed the barons of the neighbouring territories, and the Shīrāz Shaykhu 'l-Islām Nāṣiru 'd-Dīn Jazā 'irī took the field against the insurgents at the head of the feudal militia of Fārs. 'When both armies met', says Ja'farī, 'a mighty battle ensued, and since that community [sc. the following of Musha'sha'] was made up of Fidā'īs who had dedicated themselves to death, it stood firm; and the Shīrāz army turned in flight before it.' Musha'sha' now besieged Ḥuwayza, and the local nobility appealed for help to the prince Isfand of the Turkman dynasty of the Kāra Koyūnlū which controlled Ādharbāyjān, Armenia and Arab Iraq. This prince hastened to the rescue with his troops, and routed the insurgents in a bloody engagement; then ravaged Ḥuwayza and its region, and brought starvation to the land. Musha'sha' escaped, but a few years afterwards returned. Insurrection flared up afresh, and the rebels succeeded in setting up a small Shī'ite dominion of Sarbadār type in the Ḥuwayza region which later on slipped in usual fashion into the standard feudal mould.

It must be supposed that Shī'ism was greatly strengthened as a result of these fourteenth and fifteenth-century movements. After all, its own ideology had been the badge they wore in common. The Sunnī historians were naturally at pains to say as little as possible about the motive forces at work, since equality of opportunity and a fair distribution of property were hardly on the agenda of their feudal masters. We find a much more detailed account of the levelling programme in the pages of the Greek historian Ducas who was a Christian and a stranger to Muslim orthodoxy. His context is the rising under Shaykh Badru 'd-Dīn Simāwī and the Dervish Börklüce Muṣṭafā in Turkey, i.e. Asia Minor and Thrace, in 1416, in which Greek as well as Turkish peasants participated. This Dervish, as Ducas tells us, 'proclaimed the common enjoyment of food, clothing, teams and fields —

everything except wives; saying: I shall go into thy house as into mine, and thou wilt come into my house as into thine, save only the women's part thereof'.[53] The insurgent peasants all wore uniform clothes of the utmost simplicity and went without felt cap or any footwear, took their meals at a common board, and endeavoured to effect an even distribution of material goods.

If we go by such details as are supplied by the writers on the popular upheavals in Iran during the two centuries in question, the social programme of the extreme wing in those movements amounted to: standard dress for all, community-meals, and at least an attempt at an equal distribution of clothing and food. This programme, reflecting the aspirations of the urban and rural poor, was apparently indebted to four sources of inspiration: (1) the social ideas of the fifth and sixth-century Mazdakites, and of the eighth and ninth-century Khurramīs who walked in their steps and whose followers were still to be found in Iran in the fourteenth century; (2) the social Utopia of the Carmathians; (3) the Shī'ite expectation of the Imam Mahdī whose coming would mean the establishment of the rule of justice and equality on earth; and (4) the Ṣūfī ascetic condemnation of wealth and luxury, and the cult of poverty, of which we have spoken in an earlier chapter.[54]

We come now to the most important of the Shī'ite movements in Iran, and the one fraught with lasting consequences politically — the Ṣafawid Qizil Bāsh movement.[55] The Dervish order headed by the hereditary Shaykhs of the Ṣafawid family, in Persian *Ṣafawiyyān*, which came into being under the Mongol dominion, had adopted the name *Ṣafawiyya* after that of Shaykh Ṣafiyyu 'd-Dīn Isḥāq Ardabīlī (1252–1334), the ancestor of the Ṣafawid dynasty, though its real founder apparently was the teacher and father-in-law of that Shaykh, namely Taju 'd-Dīn Zāhid of Gīlān (d. *c.* 1300).

The principal sources for the history of the Ṣafawid-Qizil Bāsh movement are: the Biography of Shaykh Ṣafiyyu 'd-Dīn entitled *Ṣafwatu 'ṣ-Ṣafā*, or 'Purity of Purity', in Persian, compiled sometime after 1358 by the Dervish Tawakkul commonly called Ibn Bazzāz, 'Son of the Draper';[56] the anonymous History of Shah Ismā'īl I;[57] and the well-known historical works of Khwāndamīr,[58] Ḥasan Rūmlū[59] and Mīr Yaḥyā Qazwīnī.[60] These last three authors are distinctly pro-Ṣafawid in their sympathies, but an anti-Ṣafawid and anti-Shī'ite stand is taken by Faḍlullāh b. Rūzbihān Khunjī in his *Ta'rīkh-i 'Ālamārā-yi Amīnī*.[61] A later source, belonging to the second half of the seventeenth century and in many respects untrustworthy, is *Silsilatu 'n-Nasabī Ṣafawiyya* or 'Genealogy of the Ṣafawids' by Shaykh Ḥusayn b. Shaykh Abdāl Zāhidī.

When the Ṣafawid dynasty won the throne of the Shahinshahs of Iran in 1502, it proceeded to assign to itself a Sayyid, and consequently Arab, origin. It was claimed that a genealogical tree had been handed down in the family showing Shaykh Ṣafiyyu 'd-Dīn as twenty-first in the line of descent from the seventh Imam of the Shīʿites, Mūsā Kāẓim. Modern research holds this to be a latter-day legend that did not make its appearance earlier than the mid-fifteenth century;[62] and recently the Iranian scholar Ahmad Kasravī put forward the suggestion that the Ṣafawids were in fact of Kurdish stock. The Turkish historian Zaki Validi Togan has lent his support to this view. But whether it be so or nor, the Ṣafawids living as they did in Ardabīl, became Turkicized and at least until the second half of the fifteenth century their mother-tongue was Ādharī. Shāh Ismāʿīl wrote poetry in this Ādharbāyjān language under the pen-name Khaṭā'ī.

It is possible that the original Dervish circles in which the order of the Ṣafawiyya was cradled[63] were implicated in popular agitation. It is known, for instance, that Shirwānshāh (Akhsitān II, in the reign of the Mongol Il-Khan Arghūn Khān 1284–1291) accused Shaykh Zāhid of Gīlān of distracting his ryots from their agricultural labours, and threatened to demolish the Shaykh's convent in Mughān and drown his Murīds. Further, when Shaykh Ṣafiyyu 'd-Dīn became the successor of Shaykh Zāhid as chief of the order, he too, as his biography, the *Ṣafwatu 'ṣ-Ṣafā*, informs us, had a multitude of Murīds spread among the peasants and village elders in the Ardabīl, Khalkhāl, Bishkin, Mughān, Tālish and Marāgha districts. The same source goes out of its way to name in addition the artisan and trader component of his following, viz. a shawl-maker (*shāldūz*), jewellers, bootmakers (*mūzadūzān*), shoemakers (*kafshdūzān*), bakers (*khabbāzān*), a tanner (*dabbāgh*), a tailor (*khayyāṭ*), carpenters (*najjārān*), weavers (*jāmabāfān*), blacksmiths (*āhangarān*), saddlers (*sarrājān*), diggers of underground-watercourses (*kahrīzkanān*), drapers (*bazzāzān*), a soap-seller (*ṣābūnfurūsh*), and the son of the foreman of the oil-merchants (*pisar-i kulū-yi naftfurūsh*). And finally there is Ḥamdullāh Qazwīnī's statement that most of the inhabitants of Ardabīl were Shaykh Ṣafiyyu 'd-Dīn's Murīds.[64] But already the princes of this world figured importantly among the disciples: for example, the vizier historian Rashīdu 'd-Dīn and his two sons vizier Ghiyāthu 'd-Dīn Muḥammad Rashīdī and Amir Aḥmad Rashīdī, the Ulus Amir

Chūbān, chief of the Mongol nomadic tribe Sulduz, and the Mongol Il-Khan himself, Abū Sa'īd Bahādur Khān (1316–35). Also, as Faḍlullāh b. Rūzbihān tells us, he had the support of the Amirs of the Tālish Wilāyet and the grandees (*kubarā'*) of Rūm, or Asia Minor.[65] Like his teacher Shaykh Zāhid before him, this great Ṣūfī with his Murīds scattered over Gīlān, Rūm, Iṣfahān, Shīrāz and elsewhere, was considered a saint; and many were the wonders attributed to him, especially in saving merchants from the perils of the deep.[66]

On the authority of the *Ṣafwatu 'ṣ-Ṣafā*, Shaykh Ṣafiyyu 'd-Dīn at first had only one *juft* (or 'one-pair plot') of land for sowing and lived on its yield, but by the end of his life he had over twenty villages in 'mulk' property, gifted by various seigneurs, which he bequeathed in 'waqf' to his convent. Shaykhs like Ṣafiyyu' d-Dīn were not obliged to foreswear acquisitions, and so they received numberless donations. The vizier-historian Rashīdu 'd-Dīn once informed the Shaykh by letter that he had allocated him on the occasion of the breaking of the Fast (*'īdu 'l-fiṭr*): 150 jarībs[67] of wheat, 300 jarībs of rice, 400 maunds of butter, 800 maunds of honey, 200 maunds of sour milk, 100 maunds of grape juice, 400 maunds of ordinary sugar, 100 maunds of refined sugar, 30 head of oxen, 130 rams, 190 geese, 600 chickens, 30 bottles of rose-water, and ten thousand dinars in cash. The delivery of these different items was debited to Rashīdu 'd-Dīn in eight district of Ādharbāyjān, according to the apportionment cited in the letter.[68]

It is clear from what has been said that Shaykh Ṣafiyyu 'd-Dīn was hardly the mouthpiece of the aspirations and interests of the masses; on the contrary, he was hand in glove with the barons. But somehow he succeeded in preserving his influence over the peasants and artisans.

His descendants succeeded him as saints and Shaykhs of the order. The first two were Shaykh Ṣadru 'd-Dīn Mūsā (1334–92/3) and Shaykh Khwāja 'Alī, also called Sulṭān 'Alī (1392/3–1429), both of whom resided in Ardabīl. They possessed immense prestige there, albeit without secular authority. The Amirs of the Turkish nomadic tribe Jāgīrlū were still the lords of Ardabīl when the fifteenth century opened, and the sources do not make it clear when and how the Ṣafawids replaced them. But it would seem that the great-grandson of Shaykh Ṣafiyyu 'd-Dīn, Shaykh Ibrāhīm Shaykh-Shāh (1429–47), was already *de facto* ruler of Ardabīl.

There is nowadays sufficient proof that the first Ṣafawid Shaykhs were not Shī'ites. According to Ḥamdullāh Qazwīnī Shaykh Ṣafiyyu 'd-Dīn was a Sunnī of the Shāfi'ite school,[69] and the allegiance of Shaykh Ṣadru 'd-Dīn was not different, at least officially.[70] Nobody knows exactly when the Ṣafawid Shaykhs adopted the Shī'ite doctrine, but Shaykh Khwāja 'Alī in all likelihood was a Shī'ite, and at all events Shaykh Ibrāhīm's son, Shaykh Junayd, was a declared Shī'ite of the Imāmī sect. Although later tradition makes Junayd the fourth successor of Shaykh Ṣafiyyu 'd-Dīn as head of the order (from 1447–60), actually it was the uncle of Junayd, Shaykh Ja'far, who seized office in Ardabīl whether as guardian of his young nephew or as rival pretender to the spiritual headship of the order. Anyhow, he banished Junayd from Ardabīl, and for the next several years the younger man lived the life of an adventurer in various parts of Asia Minor (Rūm). Jean Aubin suggests that disagreement arose between Junayd and Ja'far precisely because the former was an avowed Shī'ite whereas the second clung to the moderate Sunnī tradition of his predecessors.[71] The sources themselves are silent on the subject of Ja'far's religious beliefs.

Junayd found disciples among the warlike Turkish nomads of Asia Minor, and many of them were only too ready to be considered his Ghāzīs. Faḍlullāh b. Rūzbihān comments that 'the Rūm blockheads' had, like the Christians, devised their own Trinity (*thālith-i thalātha*) calling Shaykh Junayd God (*ilāh*) and his son Ḥaydar the Son of God (*ibn-i-Allah*) and extolling him, saying: 'He is the Living One, there is no God except him.'[72] From this it is evident that the mass of Junayd's following consisted of Extreme Shī'ites who believed in the incarnation of God in man. The exile sojourned three years in Diyār Bakr, the capital of Ūzūn Ḥasan Āk-Koyūnlū (1453–78), where the latter gave him his sister Khadīja Begum in marriage. Junayd carried out an attack on Trebizond[73] and though he could not capture it, he laid waste the surroundings and came away with a vast amount of booty including many slaves (1459).[74] Incidentally, the sources (Khawāndamīr, etc.) put Junayd's death in 860 AH = 1456, but it is nowadays accepted that he was still living in 1459.

In that year in fact, backed by Ūzūn Ḥasan, he turned up in Ardabīl — to be ejected forthwith by Shaykh Ja'far who had the support of Jahānshāh Kāra-Koyūnlū. With his martial Turkish Murīd volunteers Junayd now made Holy War on the 'country of the Circassians', i.e. Dāghistān,[75] notwithstanding the protest of Shīrwānshāh Khalīlullāh I, through whose dominions his Ghāzīs had to pass. His force seized spoils and captured prisoners, and then returned to Qārabāgh to winter. The following spring Junayd once more set out to raid Dāghistān. This time Shīrwānshāh, egged on no doubt by Jahānshāh Kāra-Koyūnlū and also influenced by Shaykh Ja'far who had painted Junayd to him as an impostor pretending to be Murshid of the

Ṣafawiyya, decided to offer resistance. In March 1460 battle was joined between Shīrwānshāh's troops and Junayd's Ghāzīs on the banks of the river Samūr, south of Darband. The Ghāzīs were routed, and Junayd himelf fell on the field, tranfixed by an arrow.

His son Ḥaydar took shelter with Ūzūn Ḥasan Āk-Koyūnlū and found so much favour that he married his host's daughter. She was 'Ālamshāh Begum whose mother was the Christian Despina Khātūn, niece of David of the Comneni, last Emperor of Trebizond. Ḥaydar was acclaimed Shaykh and Murshid of the Ṣafawiyya by the majority of his Murīds, but Shaykh Ja'far was at the seat of power in Ardabīl and had the backing of Jahānshāh Kāra-Koyūnlū. However, in 1467 the army of the Kāra-Koyūnlū was defeated by Ūzūn Ḥasan. Jahānshāh himself perished in the fighting, and his vast domains embracing Ādharbāyjān, Armenia, Arab Iraq and Western Iran now passed to the Āk-Koyūnlū dynasty (1468). Thanks to Ūzūn Ḥasan's victory the coast was clear. Shaykh Ḥaydar established his hold on Ardabīl in 1469.

In the fifteenth century the composition of the Ṣafawiyya and the very character and ideology of the order underwent change. Shaykhs Ṣafiyyu 'd-Dīn, Ṣadru 'd-Dīn and Khwāja 'Alī, together with the bulk of their disciples from town and countryside were peaceable mystics: but as the order gained an ever large following among warlike Turkish nomads, these last began to give it a very different stamp. V. Minorsky calls them Turkmans, while O. A. Efendiyev and other scholars of Ādharbāyjān itself prefer to name them Ādharbāyjānīs. It would be more exact to say that these nomadic tribesmen of the Turk Oghuz had not yet hardened into what we would term in Russian a *narodnost'* (like the nomadic tribes of Iran in our day, such as the Qājārs, Qashqā'īs and Afshārs), but their language was certainly Ādharbāyjānī or a group of Turkish dialects akin to it. Between the eleventh and fifteenth centuries the tribes of the Turk Oghuz had come to rest over a wide area embracing Asia Minor, North Syria, the Armenian upland, Ādharbāyjān and Iran, and a portion of them had become an organic part of the tribal units of the Kāra-Koyūnlū and the Āk-Koyūnlū.

It is worth noticing that the Shī'ite propaganda of the Ṣafawid Shaykhs had its main success in remote Asia Minor. In the fifteenth and sixteenth centuries Shī'ism there, as in Iran, was the religious form in which the social opposition to the feudal state (in this case the Ottoman Empire) consisting of poor peasants and nomads, expressed itself. But simultaneously Shī'ism in Asia Minor was also the form in which the political opposition expressed itself. The Ottoman Sultans from Bāyazīd I (1389–1402) onwards had relied chiefly on the Turkish settled seigneurs of Rumelia (the European part of Ottoman Turkey), whereas the nomadic feudal seigneurs of Asia Minor had been thrust into the background. The latter were, moreover, dissatisfied with the centralization policy pursued by the Sultans. Shī'ism had made its entry into Asia Minor as early as the thirteenth century, at the time of Bābā Isḥāq's movement in 1239, and so progressed in the sequel that the Venetian envoys could report in 1514 that four-fifths of its inhabitants were Shī'ites.[76] It is not surprising, therefore, that many Asia Minor Shī'ites, of the nomadic Oghuz especially, accepted the spiritual leadership(*irshād*) of the Ṣafawid Shaykhs, and actually became the principal prop of the order. A very late tradition had it that there were seven of these nomadic Turkish tribes of Asia Minor which had initially announced themselves Murīds of the Safawid Shaykh: namely, the Shāmlū, Rūmlū, Ustājlū, Tekelū, Afshār, Qājār and Dhu 'l-Qadar; but sources as early as the fifteenth century mention other Turkish tribes as well which had joined the Ṣafawids, viz. the Bayat, Qaramānlū, Bayburtlū, and the Ṣūfīs of Qāraj Dāgh. They also add the Iranian Tālish to the list. The Shāmlū and the Rūmlū, it should be explained, accepted the Ṣafawid spiritual hegemony in their totality, while in the case of each of the other tribes only a fraction of the total strength intimated its allegiance.

The influx of these warlike elements changed the character of the Ṣafawiyya, though of course features were still present which recalled the democratic movements of a hundred years or so before. Jean Aubin cites a text where it is said that 'there was neither "thine" nor "mine" in the brotherhood, but they ate all that they had in common';[77] in other words, that community meals were the rule. But doubtless this was only when campaigning. By and large, the Ṣūfī mysticism was shelved; or more accurately, respected as a tradition. Militant Shī'ism and Holy War on the infidels had become the vital ariticles of faith. The tribesmen who were called Murīds, Dervishes or Ṣūfīs, developed a pattern of behaviour which these names did not suggest. Detachments of volunteer Ghāzīs were formed of these one-time nomads who would set out on *ghazwa* against the non-Muslim territories of Georgia, Trebizond and Dāghistān. Shaykh Ḥaydar gave thought to their efficiency, and improved their organization. He also obliged them to wear, instead of their former Turkman cap, a *kulāh* having twelve purple stripes in honour of the Twelve Imams. This headgear was to give currency to the term Qizil Bāsh (Ādharī,

'Red Head') which from now on was applied properly speaking to the nomadic tribe component, but also more loosely to all Murīds whatever, owning allegiance to the Ṣafawid Shaykh. The Qizil Bāshes shaved their beards but let their moustaches grow long, shaved their heads but left a forelock. Before battle they uttered a war-cry in the Ādharbāyjānī language: 'O my Pīr, O my Murshid, may I be a sacrifice for him!'

Thus the Ṣafawiyya evolved in the fifteenth century into a military brotherhood of Turkish nomads, a peculiar sort of semi-spiritual, semi-chivalrous order. Needless to say, in practice the political aims of a Junayd or a Ḥaydar would decisively outweight religious ones, and, as we have seen, when it suited them these Shī'ite Shaykhs were happy to lean on the Sunnī lord of the Āk-Koyūnlū. In their hearts what Junayd and Ḥaydar visualized was a great Shī'ite state with their own dynasty at its head. The slogan 'War for the Faith' was no more than a blind for profitable incursions into Georgia and Dāghistān, and the captives of both sexes brought back from such raids, as Caterino Zeno, the Venetian envoy, reported, would be sold in the slave-market at Ardabīl.[78]

On every such occasion the Qizil Bāshes had to pass through Shīrwān. In 1488 when Shaykh Ḥaydar again set out with his troops for Dāghistān, the Shīrwānshāh turned to his brother-in-law Sultan Ya'qūb Āk-Koyūnlū for help. Ḥaydar was defeated[79] by the joint forces of his opponents at Ṭabasarān (Dāghistān) and fell in the battle, 'having tasted the honey of martyrdom for the Faith'. According to Faḍlullāh b. Rūzbihān 'a numberless mob (*ḥashar*) of the Tālish dressed in blue (*kabūd rakhtān*), of the ill-starred people of Siyāh Kūh [= Qāraj Dāgh], and of the benighted Shāmlū' had taken part in this disastrous campaign.[80] The same author informs us that Ḥaydar had been preaching *ibāḥat*, or 'permissiveness' to his followers, i.e. the legality of actions prohibited by the Sharī'a, and 'the code of the Khurramīs of Bābak'.[81] This amounts to evidence that the Qizil Bāshes entertained the ancient Khurramī notions of social equality; and it perhaps is no accident that the inhabitants of Qāraj Dāgh and Tālish supported the Ṣafawids, seeing that both these districts had been principle centres of Bābak's peasant revolt. Sultan Ya'qūb's assistance to the Shīrwānshāh had not been disinterested: he compelled him to subscribe to an agreement acknowledging himself a vassal of the Āk-Koyūnlū sovereign and binding himself to come to the aid of the latter at the first demand.[82]

The senior Qizil Bāsh officers, who were 'feudalized' nomadic nobles, were, like Junayd and Ḥaydar, Shī'ites of the Imāmī school, but in the rank and file there were many Extreme Shī'ites. Faḍlullāh b. Rūzbihān has this to say: 'Many people from Rūm, Tālish and Siyāh Kūh [Qāraj Dāgh in Ādharbayjānī] flocked to him [Junayd]. It is told that they revered him as their divinity (*ma'būd*) and that, neglecting the obligation of prayer and public worship (*'ibādat*), they looked on their Shaykh as on their Qibla and as on a being deserving of adoration (*masjūd*).'[83] We detect the characteristic features of the doctrine of the Extreme Shī'ites (*ghāliyya*) in this tale. And the fact that the 'Alī-ilāhī,[84] that Extreme Shī'ite sect, were called Qizil Bāshes in Asia Minor right into the present century seems to clinch the matter. Obviously Shaykh Ḥaydar did not share the beliefs of these extremists; but he dared not break with them, since it was mainly they who supplied the volunteers for his army.

After Ḥaydar's death, Sultan Ya'qūb Āk-Koyūnlū took possession of Ardabīl and carried off the Shaykh's minor sons Sulṭān 'Alī, Ibrāhīm and Ismā'īl — the last being not yet two years of age. Ya'qūb's successor Rustam Pādishāh (1492–96) returned the young Sulṭān 'Alī to Ardabīl hoping to make use of him in his struggle with his enemies, but afterwards began to fear him and resolved to be rid of him. A battle was fought near Ardabīl in which four thousand warriors of the Āk-Koyūnlū encountered seven hundred Qizil Bāshes. Sulṭān 'Alī fell on the field, but the boy Ismā'īl was enabled by devoted Red Heads to take shelter in Gīlān (1495).

Meantime the internal situation of the Āk-Koyūnlū state, comprising Ādharbāyjān, Armenia, Arab Iraq and all Western Iran as far as the Dasht-i Kavīr, had deteriorated through feudal fragmentation, civil war among the seigneurs, and the increase of *soyūrghāls*, or fiefs, and 'waqf' lands at the expense of state lands. This last item entailed a steep reduction in revenue, since fiefs enjoyed tax immunity. On top of all this, unchecked feudal exploitation exasperated the masses. The vizier Qāḍī Ṣafiyyu 'd-Dīn 'Īsā Sāwajī in the reign of Sultan Ya'qūb (1490), and the Sultan Aḥmad Pādishāh Āk-Koyūnlū later on (1497), attempted to introduce agrarian reform. They thought to abrogate the tax immunity on 'soyūrghāl' and 'waqf' lands so as to increase the revenue and permit the abolition of duties not based on the Sharī'a, and thus ease the condition of the masses. But both attempts failed through the furious opposition of the military and clerical nobility.[85]

The failure of these attempts at reform, the increase in taxes, and the heavy oppression of the feudal system brought class contradictions to a head. The Āk-Koyūnlū state, that is to say, the whole of West Iran — an area, as has been said, already torn by the warfare of the seigneurs and their separatist ambitions — was seething with discontent. The situation in East Iran — that is, the Khurāsān Sultanate of the Tīmūrids which included Khurāsān, the Merv Oasis, Gurgān, Māzandarān, Sīstān and the western part of present-day Afghanistan with its captial Herāt — was no more stable. Here too the sources dwell on the growing burden of taxation, and on wholesale abuses and embezzlement on the part of the finance officials. By the end of the reign of the decrepit Sultan Ḥusayn Bayqarā (1470–1506), who had now lost all interest in public affairs, the mutinies of the feudal lords had reduced the regime to literal anarchy.

In this state of things the Qizil Bāshes, notwithstanding their reverses hitherto and the deaths of their Shaykhs Junayd, Ḥaydar and Sulṭān 'Alī, were far from thinking the game lost. They were simply waiting for an opportune moment to strike again at the Sunnī heretics of the Āk-Koyūnlū, before marching against the Ottoman Sultans themselves. Such a moment presented itself during the internecine war of the Princes Murād, Alwand and Muḥammadī for the Āk-Koyūnlū throne (1458–1500). A renewed Qizil Bāsh putsch, on a wider front than before, began in the summer of 1499. The twelve-year old Ismā'īl, accompanied by his tutor (*lāla*) Ḥusayn Beg of the Shāmlū tribe, quitted Gīlān for the summer camp of the Ustājlū where he was greeted with enthusiasm. With three hundred Qizil Bāshes he made for Ardabīl, but could not take it. The Amirs of the tribe now counselled him to head westwards, first to Qāra Bāgh and then to Shuragel and so to Kaghizmān and Arzanjān, counting on getting reinforcements there from the Qizil Bāshes of Rūm. By the end of 1499 seven thousand Ghāzīs of the Qizil Bāsh tribes (mostly from Asia Minor and Qāraj Dāgh) had rallied to the banner of the young Ismā'īl. In their winter quarters at Arzanjān the tribal Amirs met once more in conference and elected to march first of all against the Shirwānshāh. But presumably they had to wait for new detachments of Qizil Bāsh Ghāzīs to arrive, for it was only in the autum of 1500 that they actually moved against him. They completely routed his army at Jabānī and took possession of the town of Shamākhā. In the spring of 1501 they seized Baku.[86]

It was also in this spring of 1501 that the Qizil Bāshes defeated Alwand's army and entered Tabrīz. They were temporarily forced to evacuate it when the Āk-Koyūnlū counter-attacked, but they recaptured it in 907 AH = 1502. The youthful Ismā'īl Ṣafawid was forthwith proclaimed Shahinshah of Iran, and took his seat on the throne. His dynasty, it is generally agreed by modern historians, dates from that year.[87]

His first act in Tabrīz was to introduce the Shīʿite khuṭba commemorating the Twelve Imams, and also the public cursing of the initial three Caliphs Abū Bakr, ʿUmar I and ʿUthmān. ʿAnd there went forth a noble and royal edict', Ḥasan Rūmlū narrates, ʿthat men should loosen their tongues in street and square for the profanation and cursing of Abū Bakr, ʿUmar and ʿUthmān, and that they should chop off the heads of any that stood in the way of this.'[88]

Next year the army of Shah Ismāʿīl I, as he must now be styled, defeated that of Sultan Murād Āk-Koyūnlū near Hamadān. Murād himself escaped to Arab Iraq where he held out for another five years; but the fate of his state had been sealed. In that same year 1503 the Shah's armies took Qazwīn, Qum, Kāshān, Iṣfahān, Shīrāz and Kāzarūn; and in the following year Yazd and Kirmān. From 1506 to 1510 the operations were sustained: the Shah campaigned against Armenia, Kurdistān and Arab Iraq; won Vān, Bitlīs and Diyār Bakr; took Baghdad (1508). In East Iran the two Tīmūrid Sultanates of Central Asia and Khurāsān had been overrun between 1499 and 1507 by the roving Uzbeks of the Ulus Shaybān under Muḥammad Shaybānī Khān. In 1510 Shah Ismāʿīl turned his attention there, and gained a decisive victory over the Uzbeks near Merv, which enabled him to annex Gurgān, most of Khurāsān,[89] and Sīstān. Gīlān and Māzandarān had submitted earlier. The Ṣafawid state, destined to endure until 1736, had taken shape.

The Shīʿite Qizil Bāsh movement of 1499 and following years presents a composite picture socially. The leading role in it was undoubtedly played by the fighting Amirs of the Qizil Bāsh Turkish-speaking nomadic tribes, and in the first two years (904–906 AH = 1499–1501) these Amirs with the Ghāzīs of their tribes alone fought under Ismāʿīl's standard. Noble Persian families did enter the Shah's service — Jean Aubin has analysed some examples of their behaviour[90] — but that was later. It was when the success of the Qizil Bāshes was no longer in the balance that the Iranian settled nobility, including the clergy, i.e. the ʿUlamā', Faqīhs and Dervish Shaykhs, and the civil officials, gradually, and eventually in their overwhelming majority, came over to Ismāʿīl's side. But the Qizil Bāshes even so would not perhaps have won through if they had not attracted the support of the ordinary peasants and nomads. The masses had learned to regard Shīʿite movements as such as the vehicle of their own social aspirations, and were not to know that the Qizil Bāshes were different from previous Shī'ite insurrectionists and did not express their interests at all. The Qizil Bāsh leadership only used the support of the masses, whom they looked on as temporary fellow-travellers, for their own advancement on the road to power and conquest.

What then was this Ṣafawid state which nomadic Turkish tribesmen known as Qizil Bāshes had brought into being? One can nowadays write off the opinion of the older bourgeois historians that the Ṣafawid power was an Iranian national state.[91] V. Minorsky sees in it the third phase of 'Turkman'[92] sovereignty in Iran and bordering areas,[93] while O. A. Efendiyev and other scholars of the Adharbayjan SSR view it as an 'Ādharbāyjānī state'. To us it seems nearer the mark to suppose it the same kind of conglomerate empire of countries, *narodnost's* and tribes as the previous mediaeval states on Iranian territory from the 'Abbāsid Caliphate onwards. However the political role in the Ṣafawid state, at any rate until the reforms of 'Abbas I, was monopolized by Ādharbāyjānīs, i.e. by the Qizil Bāsh tribes. They formed the nucleus of the feudal militia, their Amirs divided among themselves the greater part of the land reserve; the principal court dignitaries, the viceroys of provinces, and the military commanders were nominated from their number; and if Persian was used in official correspondence and legal acts, it was their Ādharbāyjānī language that was preferred at court and in the army. The Persian nobility was relegated to second place and had to be content with ecclesiastical and civil offices, the latter mostly in the finance department. The title Shahinshah of Iran did not point to any dominance of the Iranian element. From Sāsānian times it had been connected rather with the notion of universal, world-wide monarchy, just as the title Roman Emperor in mediaeval Europe and the title Chinese Emperor in the Far East had carried the same idea. And Ādharbāyjān was long the hub of the state.

The memoirs of Italian travellers and diplomats bear ample testimony to the fact that Shah Ismā'īl was greatly loved and even deified by the Qizil Bāshes, and was popular with the masses.[94] The peasants and nomads of Iran, Ādharbāyjān and Asia Minor associated him with their long-standing hopes of a reign of justice and universal equality; and he, for his part, owing his throne to their support, could hardly neglect the peasantry altogether. The sources speak of his 'concern for the ryots', but only in general terms without mentioning any concrete measures.[95] There is, it is true, an indication in one place, not entirely reliable, that Shah Ismā'īl restored a tax-regulation of Ūzūn Ḥasan Āk-Koyūnlū under which the land tax (*kharāj*) had been lowered to one-sixth of the yield. However, if this regulation was indeed restored, it was only a palliative. On the whole, the entire system of taxation and feudal obligations was retained intact.

The conclusion, then, is that the social system and state organization of the Ṣafawids more or less perpetuated the arrangements that obtained in the fifteenth century. The composition of the clique of feudal seigneurs in power of course changed,[96] but that was all. Shah Ismāʿīl I himself, as Jean Aubin has remarked, did not display any zeal for social reform, to judge by his 'Diwan' of poetry which contains no hint of such an interest. Neither the warlike Amirs of the devoted Qizil Bāsh tribes nor the 'Ulamā' and civil servants who presently came over to the Ṣafawids, were interested in any serious change of the existing system. They courted the masses for their own ends; and once Shah Ismāʿīl's victory was consolidated, were at pains to see that everything went on, so far as possible, as before.

A very important consequence of the victory of the Qizil Bāshes was the measure installing Shīʿism of the Imāmī school (*madhhab-i Jaʿfarī*, the Madhhab of Imam Jaʿfar Ṣādiq or the Madhhab of the Twelve Imams) for the first time as the state religion in the whole of Iran. The Shīʿite khuṭba was everywhere introduced, as also the public cursing of the first three Caliphs. The Shah himself took care to see that the imprecation should ring out loud and clear, and, it is said, would often exclaim: 'May it be more, not less!'[97] Sunnī sympathies were still fairly strongly entrenched among the 'Ulamā', the nobles and the burghers, and there were some who slipped away to Turkish Sultan or Uzbek Khan and then incited one or other of these to attack the Ṣafawid power. Here and there Sunnīs resisted on the spot, usually passively, and such resistance was ruthlessly repressed. Mass executions and savage tortures took place in Iṣfahān, Shīrāz, Kāzarūn, Yazd and elsewhere. But the greater part of the townspeople and many of the divines chose safety in Shīʿism;[98] and before long the clerical appointments were being filled as much by Faqīhs turned Shīʿite as by Shīʿite Faqīhs. Ḥasan Rūmlū points out how few people there were in this transitional phase with even an elementary knowledge of Shīʿite theology and law, and how few books on these subjects were in circulation.[99] The fact was that Shīʿism had had its appeal as the emblem of a politico-social movement directed against Sunnī rulers, rather than as a religious doctrine. But there was, anyhow, one man in Tabrīz, the capital, of the stature needed to propagate the newly introduced faith, and this was the Qāḍī Naṣrullāh Zaytūnī. He delivered lectures day by day on Imāmī theology (*kalām*) and law (*fiqh*), and popularized a book entitled *Sharāyi'u 'l-Islām* by the thirteenth-century Shaykh Najmu 'd-Dīn Ḥillī as the best available manual of instruction.

Shah Ismā'īl did not succeed in possessing himself of Asia Minor, in spite of the fact that the main body of the Qizil Bāshes came from there. In 917 AH = 1511/12 a rebellion of local Shī'ites, all of them either nomads or peasants, broke out in Asia Minor against the Ottoman Sultan Bāyazīd II. Its leader was a nomad of the Tekelū (from the province Teke-īlī in the south) who called himself Shāh Qulī, 'Slave of the Shah', a name which the enemies of the Qizil Bāshes altered to Shayṭān Qulī, 'Slave of Satan'. The Sultan was compelled to call up a large army to suppress it. A battle was fought near the Kiyuk Chāy river, between Sīwās and Qayṣariyya, in which the Grand Vizier Khādim Pāsha was among the dead. There is also some reason to think that Shāh Qulī himself perished on this field. The survivors of the rebellion escaped to Ṣafawid territory. The Shah had not offered the insurgents any military assistance, and he now received the émigrés with coldness when they arrived at Tabrīz. The explanation to some degree no doubt is that he did not want to bring things to an open breach with Bāyazīd II (who for his part had no wish to go to war with Ismā'īl). But there was another argument for lukewarmness: the Asia Minor Shī'ite community contained many of the Extreme persuasion and it was they who tended to carry the lower classes with them. The Shah and his Qizil Bāsh leadership regarded these extremist travelling companions as potentially dangerous both in the social and the religious context, and they were never willing to back them unreservedly. When the need for these temporary allies passed, the Shah had no compunction in dropping them, and even subjecting them to persecution, albeit not so mercilessly as in the case of the Sunnīs.

But relations with Asia Minor were to change suddenly. Bāyazīd II's successor, Sultan Salīm I The Grim (1512–20), perpetrated a massacre of the local Shī'ites, declared war on Shah Ismā'īl, and defeated his army at the battle of the Chāldirān plain on 1 Rajab 920 = 22 August 1514. Asia Minor was henceforward lost to the Ṣafawids, even though popular risings under the Shī'ite standard continued to occur there throughout the whole of the sixteenth and into the first half of the seventeenth century.

Once it had become the official religion of Iran, Imāmī Shi'ism lost its peculiar status as the ideology of the masses, and evolved into a pillar of feudalism. In the formal sense the Ṣafawid state was a theocracy, a Shī'ite power that was in theory world-wide. In it the Shahinshah could claim not only a political but a spiritual authority as the head of the Imāmī Shi'ites. Legend, promoted to history by the fifteenth century, traced the origin of the Ṣafawids to the seventh Imam Mūsā Kāẓim, and through the latter to 'Alī and Muḥammad, and in virtue of this descent the Shah was the deputy *ad interim* of the hidden twelfth Imam, Muḥammad Mahdī, to whom he would hand over his charge when the day came.[100] This element of theocracy also revealed itself in the way the Shahs of the dynasty continued, like their ancestors, to bear the hereditary title of Grand Shaykh of the *Ṣafawiyya*. European diplomats, merchants and travellers were echoing what they heard around them when they referred to the Shah as 'The Great Ṣūfī'. And just as the royal Ṣafawids were the Shaykhs and Murshids of the order, so the warlike seigneurs and warrior nomads of the Qizil Bāsh tribes went on calling themselves Dervishes and Murīds. It was beside the point that neither the royal incumbents nor their Qizil Bāshes resembled the early Ṣūfīs and Dervishes in their mode of living. The practices and everyday rules of the order were not observed; no thought was given to the ideal of poverty; and the whole attitude of mysticism was forgotten.[101]

In fact, in the ideological sense a complete degeneration of the *Ṣafawiyya* had set in by the sixteenth century. Of its Ṣūfism nothing remained; there was only Shī'ite fanaticism now, dictating the wars with the Sunnīs of Ottoman Turkey and the Uzbek Khanates of Central Asia. But if the order of the *Ṣafawiyya* had become a fiction, it was a fiction by which the royal authority set much store. For the allegiance of the Qizil Bāshes to the Shah was visualized as the obedience of Murīds to their Shaykh — which under the rules of the Dervish orders had to be unlimited, blind, unreasoning. Many of the Qizil Bāsh nobles bore the title *khalīfa*, (signifying here 'deputy' of the Shaykh); and the Senior Deputy of the Shah was styled *Khalīfatu 'l-Khulafā'*, or 'Deputy of the Deputies' of the Shaykh, and supposed to administer the order. The post was one of the most honourable in the kingdom, and existed until the fall of the dynasty.[102] When the dynasty fell, the fictitious order of the *Ṣafawiyya* automatically ceased to be. By the sixteenth century it had already lost all its urban hold; henceforward it had nothing in common with the townspeople. From now until the eighteenth century the artisans and traders of Iran — as, incidentally, many a European traveller had occasion to record — were mostly affiliated to the *Ḥaydariyya* and the *Ni'matullāhiyya*. It will be seen, therefore, that stripped of its fictions the Ṣafawid state was just like any of the previous states, military, feudal and secular, with which Iran had been familiar from the tenth century onwards.

The installation of Imāmī Shīʿism as the national religion and — what was the ultimate outrage in Sunnī eyes — the cursing of the first three Caliphs, coupled with the ruthless execution or victimization of Sunnīs, poisoned relations with the then mighty Ottoman Turkey, the Crimea Khanate and the Uzbek Khanates of Transoxiana and Khwārazm. It may be contended that religious enmity played a purely subordinate part in Iran's wars with these Sunnī states during the sixteenth, seventeenth and eighteenth centuries. This is of course true; but that enmity gave to those wars a blacker hue. The two branches of Islam were vying with each other in frightfulness as never before: for the first time in history Sunnī doctors declared it permissible to enslave Shīʿite prisoners-of-war — it did not matter if they were even Sayyids — and sell them in the market. It was not so much the triumph of Shīʿism in Iran as its fanatical intolerance of Sunnism there from the sixteenth century onwards that caused the Shīʿites to be execrated abroad. Mutual hatred led to the rupture of cultural contacts with Central Asia and the other countries of Sunnī allegiance to the grave detriment of Iran's intellectual life.

Abbreviations
Chapter notes
Bibliography
Index

Abbreviations

AN SSSR	Akademiya Nauk SSSR (USSR Academy of Sciences)
AN AZ.SSR	Akademiya Nauk Azerbaydzhanskoy SSR (Azerbaydzhan SSR Academy of Sciences)
AN UZ.SSR	Akademiya Nauk Uzbekskoy SSR (Uzbek SSR Academy of Sciences)
BGA	*Bibliotheca Geographorum Anabicorum*, Ed. M. J. de Goeje
BI	*Bibliotheca Indica*, Calcutta
BIFAO	*Bulletin de l'Institut Français d'Archéologie de Damas*
BSOS	*Bulletin of the School of Oriental Studies*, University of London
EI	*Encyclopédie de l'Islam*, Leyden-Paris
ERE	*Encyclopaedia of Religion and Ethics*, ed. I. Hastings
GMS	E. J. W. Gibb Memorial Series
GMS NS	E. J. W. Gibb Memorial Series, new series
HS	Works issued by the Hakluyt Society, London
IVAN	Institut Vostokovedeniya Akademii Nauk SSSR (Institute of Oriental Studies of the USSR Academy of Sciences)
JA	*Journal Asiatique*, Paris
JAOS	*Journal of the American Oriental Society*, New Haven
JBBRAS	*Journal of the Bombay branch of the Royal Asiatic Society*

JRAS	*Journal of the Royal Asiatic Society*, London
LB	Lugdunum Batavorum (Leyden)
LGPB	Leningradskaya Gosudarstvennaya Publichnaya Biblioteka (Leningrad State Public Library)
LGU	Leningradskiy Gosudarstvennyy Universitet (Leningrad State University)
MGU	Moskovskiy Gosudarstvennyy Universitet (Moscow State University)
ZDMG	*Zeitschrift der Deutschen Morgenländischen Gesellschaft*
ZVORAO	Zapiski Vostochnogo Otdeleniya (Imp.) Russkogo Arkheologicheskogo Obshchestva. SPG (Notes of the Oriental branch of the Imperial Russian Archaeological Society, St Petersburg)

Chapter notes

Introduction The rise of Islam

1 See K. Marx and F. Engels, *Works*, 28, p. 221.
2 Marx and Engels, *Works*, 28, p. 210.
3 Ye. A. Belyayev, *The Arabs, Islam and the Arab Caliphate in the early Middle Ages*. Also Ye. A. Belyayev, 'Formation of the Arab State and rise of Islam in the seventh century', Papers of the Soviet delegation to XXIII International Congress of Orientalists, Moscow, 1954; Ye. A. Belyayev and A. Yu. Yakubovskiy, 'Arabia to the beginning of the seventh century', in '*World History*', vol. III ch. VII, Moscow, 1957.
4 A. Yu. Yakubovskiy, 'Iraq at the turn of the eighth and ninth centuries', Transactions of the First Session of Arabists, Moscow-Leningrad, 1937. S. P. Tolstov, *Outlines of early Islam*, Moscow, 1932; 'Genesis of feudalism in cattle-breeding nomadic societies.' Proceedings GAIMK (State Academy History of Material Culture) Issue 103, 1934; and *On the tracks of the ancient civilization of Khwarazm*, Moscow-Leningrad, 1948, pp. 318 ff.
5 N. V. Pigulevskaya, *Byzantium on the routes to India*, Moscow-Leningrad, 1951, p. 403.
6 N. A. Smirnov, *Outline of the history of Islamic Studies in USSR*, Moscow, 1954, pp. 181 ff.
7 L. I. Nadiradze, 'The question of slavery in Arabia in the seventh century', in *Questions of history and literature in the countries of the East beyond our borders*, Moscow, 1960.
8 In Russian; besides those indicated, see especially the works of V. V. Bartol'd and A. Ye. Krymskiy (see Bibliography).
9 See Bibliography.
10 Koran XIV 40 speaks of the barrenness of the valley of Mecca.
11 Many facts regarding the economic life of Mecca at the beginning of the seventh century are given in H. Lammens, *La Mecque à la veille de l'hégire*. See also A. von Kremer, *Kulturgeschichte des Orients*, vol. I, ch. II.
12 F. Engels, 'Ludwig Feuerbach and the end of classical German philosophy', Marx and Engels, *Works*, 21, p. 294.
13 Gnosticism (from Gk. *gnōsis* 'knowledge') is the common designation of many doctrines and sects of the first centuries of our era which united the outlook of Christianity (minus the Old Testament element) with the mythology of Eastern Hellenistic paganism and with certain ideas taken from the philosophical systems of the Platonists, Pythagoraeans and Neo-Platonists.
14 On the old Arab religion see J. Wellhausen, *Reste arabischen Heidentums*; I. Goldziher, *Muhammedanische Studien*, vol. I, pp. 219 ff.

15 In the teaching of the Nestorians (who were mostly in Mesopotamia and Iran) the Person of Christ has two natures, human and divine, which exist in separation and without mingling, in two hypostases between which there is only a relative unity. According to the Chalcedonites (orthodox) there are two natures in Christ, divine and human, but these exist inseparably and in one person. The Monophysites (from Gk. *monos*, 'one', and *phusis*, 'nature') held that there is only one nature in Christ, and this divine; that during his life on earth he had a complex of human attributes but not a human substance. The Monophysites were mostly scattered over Armenia, Upper Mesopotamia, Syria, Egypt, and Ethiopia. The Christianity which penetrated Arabia from Syria and Ethiopia was most likely monophysite.
16 On the Ebionites see W. Beveridge, *Ebionism*, pp. 139–45.
17 Koran v 85.
18 Kitābu 'l-Aghānī, xvi, 45; cited in Fr. Buhl, *Hanif.*
19 Fr. Buhl, *Hanif.*
20 Koran x 105; xxii 32; xxx 29; xcviii 4.
21 Koran ii 129; iii 60.
22 Ibn Hishām. p. 120.
23 Among Russian Islamists Ye. A. Belyayev has put forward this theory.
24 On the Ḥadīth see ch. iv.
25 It is known that Ibn Hishām omitted in his work certain episodes in the life of Muḥammad transmitted by Ibn Isḥāq, considering that these compromised the Prophet.
26 Academician I. Yu. Krachkovskiy points out the 'impossibility of a gigantic deception' in the Appendix to his translation of the Koran p. 655 (see Bibliography under 'Koran').
27 Koran xvi 45–6; xxi 7 and other passages.
28 Tor Andrae, *Mohammad, the man and his faith*, pp. 119–24.
D. S. Margoliouth ('Mohammed') says that Muḥammad adopted the eulogistic, solemn style of the Christian monks.
29 See Chapter iii.
30 Koran liii 3 ff; lxxxi 23 ff. In these Suras Muḥammad refers to the spirit simply as 'He'.
31 Koran liii 13 ff; xliv 3; lxxii 1 ff; lxxxi 19 ff; xcvii 1. Sura xcvi (1–5) speaks, apparently, of the first vision.
32 Koran liii 14–15.
33 Koran xvii 1 ff. In admitting the possibility of hallucinations, there is no need to ascribe any particular malady to Muḥammad. Hallucinations, both of sight and hearing, were extremely common in those days among people subject to heightened religious emotion.
34 'Alī at the time was between 8 and 13 years of age. He was known also by the nickname Abū Turāb ('Father of Dust' or 'Earth') presumably given him by Muḥammad. 'Alī's followers, the Shī'ites, thought it an honourable surname. According to T. Nöldeke, on the other hand, it was a derisive nickname invented by 'Alī's enemies.
35 Koran cxi 1–5.
36 'Those who give short measure' — the heading of Sura lxxxiii of the Koran.
37 Koran cii 1–8.

38 Koran VI 123. The pagan nobility, of course, was in question.
39 Koran XCII 5–7; XCVIII 4.
40 Koran IV 40.
41 For details see Chapter II.
42 On this see Chapter III.
43 He retained this privilege even after the consolidation of Islam in Mecca.
44 The designation *muhājir* was thenceforward regarded among Muslims as one of high honour; and subsequently Muslims who had emigrated from a Muslim country conquered by non-Muslims (e.g. by European colonial powers) to a Muslim state, were termed muhājirs.
45 570 of our era is the conventional date, historically incorrect, of the unsuccessful expedition of Abraha, Ethiopian Viceroy of Yemen, against Mecca. According to tradition Abraha had elephants in his army — which the Arabs had never seen before.
46 For details of the Muslim calendar see Chapter II.
47 Ibn Hishām, pp. 341–4; J. Wellhausen, *Das Arabische Reich und sein Sturz*, pp. 1 ff.
48 Koran II 257: *lā ikrāha fī 'd-dīn*.
49 On mosques and ritual in Islam see Chapter II for details.
50 Ibn Khaldūn, French transl. vol. I, p. 313.
51 Koran V 85.
52 Ibn Hishām. pp. 427 ff: Ṭabarī. ser. I, p. 1297.
53 L. I. Nadiradze, in the article already referred to, sees this as a proof of the weak hold of slavery in Arabia. But the instance is not convincing: they did not turn the captives over to slavery because they were of the Quraysh — of the same tribe, that is, as Muḥammad and the Muhājirs — and only those of an outside tribe could be turned over to slavery.
54 Compare with what has been said earlier on the scarcity of horses in pre-Islamic Arabia.
55 Koran VIII 42 ff. The battle of Badr is clearly in point in the passage indicated. On the prescriptions of Islam regarding war with Unbelievers, and on the spoils of war see Chapter II.
56 Which he could have assumed, had he wanted to imitate the Kings of Yemen, and also the Kings of the Arab dynasties — the Ghassanites in Jordan, the Lakhmites to the west of the river Euphrates and the Kindites in Najd.
57 Koran XXXIII 49.
58 On this see Chapter II.
59 Koran VIII 42. For Muḥammad's other legislation see Chapter II.

Chapter I Iran's obedience to Islam

1 Of course none of the Caliphs could dare to arrogate to himself the dignity of Prophet, inasmuch as Muḥammad had earlier on declared that he was the last of the prophets. For the scope of the Caliph's authority see Chapter VI.

2 The much later tradition of Sunni Muslims named these four Caliphs 'Orthodox' (*rāshidūn* 'righteous'), and portrayed the period of their rule as a happy phase of Islamic orthodoxy and pure theocracy. In actual fact the internal policy of these Caliphs was far from uniform.

3 So named because the tradition was that the Persian warriors in the forward ranks chained themselves together.

4 20 August 636.

5 Iṣṭakhrī. p. 158.

6 The boundaries of Khurāsān were very much wider in the Middle Ages than they are now. Khurāsān included the Nīshāpūr, Merv, Balkh and Herāt provinces, i.e. north-east Iran, the south of the present-day Turkmen SSR, and the north and west of present-day Afghanistan.

7 Ṭabarī, ser. I, pp. 2873–83.

8 Ṭabarī, p. 2872.

9 Balādhurī. pp. 403 ff.

10 V. V. Bartol'd, *Muslim World* p. 30.

11 Y. E. Bertel's, *History of Tajik-Persian Literature*, p. 102. Volumes II and III of the anthology of Arabic literature *Yatīmatu 'd-Dahr*, 'Pearl of the Age', in four volumes by Tha'ālibī Nīshāpūrī (early eleventh century) are devoted to the Arabic-language poets of West Iran, and vol. IV to the Arabic-language poets of Khurāsān up to the author's day of whom 119 are numbered.

12 The first historical work in the new Persian was a recension of Ṭabarī's 'History of Prophets and Kings' done by Muḥammad Bal'amī (963). Original historical writings in the new Persian (works of Gardīzī and Abū 'l-Faḍl Bayhaqī) appeared in the eleventh century.

13 The earliest production was the anonymous Geography *Ḥudūdu 'l-'Ālam* 'Boundaries of the World', 372 AH = 982/3. A work on pharmacology had been written in modern Persian by Abū Manṣūr Muwaffaq of Herāt even earlier (between 967 and 976).

14 The descendants of these emigrants, known as Parsees, constitute a large and well-organized community in India.

15 K. A. Inostrantsev, *Sasanian Studies*, p. 6.

16 Iṣṭakhrī. pp. 116 ff.

17 Muqaddasī. p. 421.

18 Iṣṭakhrī. pp. 118, 150.

19 Iṣṭakhrī. p. 164.

20 Muqaddasī. p. 194.

21 Not to be confused with the noted geographer Abū 'Abdullāh Muḥammad b. Aḥmad al-Muqaddasī (or al-Maqdisī) al-Bannā', whom we refer to simply as Muqaddasī.

22 The Khurramites (eighth to tenth centuries), successors of the Mazdakites (sectaries thrown off by Zoroastrianism, fifth to seventh centuries) were advocates of social equality and the common ownership of land.

23 Muṭahhar al-Muqaddasī's work was edited by Huart erroneously under the name of Abū Zayd Aḥmad al-Balkhī (Arabic text and French translation): Cl. Huart, *Le livre de création et de l'histoire*, Paris, 1899–1919, ch. 12.

24 Figures testifying to the glut of slaves in Arab society at that time will be found in H. Lammens, *Etudes sur le siècle des Omayyades*, pp. 33–4; and the same author's *Etudes sur le règne du calife Mo'awiya I*, p. 248. For example, Mu'āwiya b. Abī Sufyān exploited four thousand slaves on his fields and gardens in the Ḥijāz alone, from whose labour he obtained 150 thousand camel-loads of dates and 100 thousand sacks of grain annually. The Ṣāḥib 'Abdu 'r-Raḥmān b. 'Awf had over thirty thousand slaves.

25 A particularly ruthless exploiter of prisoner-slaves was the old muhājir Mughīra b. Shu'ba. Amongst his slaves settled in Medina was a Persian Christian named Fīrūz, a carpenter and stone-mason. This man complained to 'Umar against his master who had demanded an excessive quit-rent of two dirhems a day. The Caliph answered with a joke. Driven to desperation Fīrūz next day mortally wounded 'Umar in the mosque, stabbing him six times with a two-edged dagger.

26 For further details see Chapter VI. 'Umar was also named Commander of the Faithful (*Amīru 'l-Mu'minīn*).

27 We here use the conventional term 'parties' (ḥizb) for the groups that took shape in the time of the first four Caliphs of a more or less distinct social nature and with a political programme.

28 For whom see the Introduction.

29 For the Khārijites see later in the present chapter.

30 J. Wellhausen, *Die religiös-politischen Oppositionsparteien im alten Islam*.

31 From the word *sunna*, 'tradition' (see Chapter IV).

32 Koran XXVIII 85: *Inna 'l-ladhī faraḍa 'alayka 'l-qur'āna larādduka ilā ma'ādin*. 'He that hath made the Koran thy duty will certainly bring thee back to the place of final homecoming'.

33 On the Extreme Shī'ites (*Ghulāt*) see Chapter XI.

34 Mas'ūdī,Tanbīh, pp. 297 ff.

35 Thus Mas'ūdī (Murūj, vol. IV, p. 376) asserts that in the battle of Ṣiffīn (657; for this battle see below) 'Alī struck down 523 enemies in one day.

36 Wellhausen, *Die religiös-politischen Oppositionsparteien* . . .,. pp. 90–92.

37 According to tradition 70 participants in the battle of Badr fought on 'Alī's side.

38 Son of the celebrated Ṣāḥib and general, victorious over the Persians at the battle of Qādisiyya.

39 Wellhausen, *Die religiös-politischen Oppositionsparteien* . . ., pp. 61–7; and the same author's *das arabische Reich und sein Sturz*, pp. 89–92; and H. Lammens, *Etudes sur le règne du calife Mo'awiya I*, pp. 132 ff.

40 Wellhausen, *Die religiös-politischen Oppositionsparteien* . . ., pp. 67–8.

41 She had fallen to 'Alī as his share in the spoils seized by the Muslim troops after the victory over the revolt of the 'False Prophet', Musaylima, whom the Ḥanīfa tribe supported (633).

42 For this sect and its doctrine see Chapter X.

43 Whose deputy in Iran was his brother Muṣ'ab b. az-Zubayr.

44 See Chapter VI.

45 See Chapter X.

46 For *ijmā'* and *qiyās* see Chapter V.

47 Balādhurī, p. 56. According to other sources Ibn al-Azraq was an Arab either of the Tamīm or the Bakr.

48 Whom the Khārijites of that time still looked on as the equals of Muḥammad.
49 Wellhausen, *Die religiös-politischen Oppositionsparteien . . .*, pp. 28–48.
50 Wellhausen, p. 53. footnote 3.
51 Which means 'slave of his lord'.
52 Wellhausen, *Die religiös-politischen Oppositionsparteien . . .*, p. 47.
53 Ye. A. Belyayev, *Muslim Sectarianism*, p. 35.
54 For details see V. V. Bartol'd, *Turkestan . . .*, pp. 248 ff.
55 Ṭabarī, ser. II, pp. 1897 ff. Ibnu 'l-Athīr. vol. V, pp. 254 ff.
56 Wellhausen. *Die religiös-politischen Oppositionsparteien . . .*, p. 51.
57 See T. Kadyrova, *History of peasant movements in Māwarānnahr and Khurāsān in the eighth and ninth centuries.*
58 Yāqūt. *Mu'jamu 'l-Buldān*, vol. III, p. 42.
59 Ibid.
60 For the Khārijites and their risings in the seventh and eighth centuries, see: Wellhausen. op. cit., and also his *Das arabische Reich und sein Sturz*; Brünnow, *Die Charidschiten*; and Ye. A. Belyayev, *Muslim Sectarianism*, pp. 30–38.
61 For the Zanj rebellion see Th. Nöldeke, *Ein Sklavenkrieg im Orient*, pp. 153–84.
62 For this family see the Introduction.
63 For his career see Ṭabarī, ser. II, pp. 1467 ff. and Ibnu 'l-Athīr, vol. V, pp. 93, 101 ff.
64 See V. V. Bartol'd, *Turkestan . . .*, p. 251; A. Yu. Yakubovskiy, *History of the Uzbek SSR*, vol. I, pp. 178–84; and B. Spuler, *Iran in frühislamischer Zeit.*
65 Ṭabarī, ser. II, pp. 1249 ff.
66 V. I. Belyayev, *An anonymous historical manuscript of V. A. Ivanov's collection in the Asiatic Museum.*
67 *An anonymous Arab of the eleventh century*, Arabic text, sheets 249b ff; translation, pp. 85 ff.
68 *An anonymous Arab.* Arabic text, sheets 259a–62a, translation, pp. 96–100.
69 Black was recognized as the official colour of the 'Abbāsids.
70 Ṭabarī, ser. II, p. 1952.
71 *An anonymous Arab*, Arabic text, sheets 264b–65a; translation, p. 104.
72 See Bartol'd, *Turkestan . . .*, p. 252.
73 *An anonymous Arab*, Arabic text, sheet 285b: *li'lriḍā min āl muḥammad*; translation, p. 130.
74 With an interruption from 945 to 1132 when the 'Abbāsid Caliphs were in practice deprived of political authority; this having passed first to the Buwayhid dynasty and afterwards (from 1055) to the Seljūqs.
75 Bartol'd, *Turkestan . . .*, p. 255 (with a reference to the Niẓāmu 'l-Mulk pp. 199, 204).
76 For this see Chapters X and XI.

Chapter II Dogma and ritual

1 See Koran III 17: *Inna 'd-dīna 'inda 'llāhi 'l-islāmu*, 'The true faith before God is Islam'.
2 The word *dīn* has this meaning in Sura I (al-Fāṭiha) of the Koran.
3 Shahrastānī. p. 27.
4 In Arabic: *Lā ilāha 'illa 'llāh wa Muḥammadun rasūlu 'llāh.*
5 A person of another faith who has pronounced this formula before witnesses becomes a Muslim (unless the formula has been quoted simply as a grammatical example). The non-Muslim wishing to embrace Islam attends the Qāḍī's chamber (*maḥkama*), and there pronounces the *shahāda* formula in the presence of Muslim witnesses.
6 In the Introduction.
7 The grammatical plural *elohim*, however, acquired the meaning 'God' in the sing. in Jewish Holy Writ (or, what is the same thing, in the Old Testament of the Bible); the expression *elohim* being a survival of the ancient polytheism.
8 In many passages of the Koran.
9 Koran II 256; III 1.
10 Koran CXII 2.
11 Koran LXII 3: *Huwa 'l-awwalu wa'l-ākhiru wa ẓ-ẓāhiru wa 'l-bāṭinu wa huwa bikulli shay'in 'alīmun.*
12 Koran I 1.
13 Koran LIX 23; LXII 1.
14 Koran I 1.
15 Koran VII 85 and in other places.
16 Koran XXIV 35.
17 Koran XXII 6: *Allāha huwa 'l-ḥaqqu*, also in a series of other passages of the Koran. *Ḥaqq*, besides, is 'absolute reality'.
18 Koran LIX 24.
19 Koran XCVI 2.
20 Koran XCVI 4.
21 Koran L 15: *wa naḥnu aqrabu ilayhi min ḥabli 'l-warīdi.*
22 Koran II 19.
23 These epithets occur in many passages.
24 Koran LIX 23.
25 Koran XCII 14.
26 Koran XCVIII 5.
27 Koran XIII 27.
28 In all Suras of the Koran.
29 Koran VII 154 and many other passages.
30 Koran XI 92; LXXXV 14.
31 Koran XX 4 and other places.
32 Koran V 69 and other places.
33 Koran LIV 14.
34 Koran II 109. The face (*wajh*) of Allah is also mentioned in other passages of the Koran.
35 See Chapters IX, X and XIII.
36 Koran III 33, 40. Among the ordinary angels cited by name are Nakīr

and Munkir who interrogate the dead in the tomb immediately after burial, and Riḍwān, the Guardian of Paradise.

37 'Azrā'īl's name is not actually in the Koran but he occupies an important position in the beliefs of Muslims.

38 Koran XV 26–44 and elsewhere.

39 Koran XV 27.

40 They are also named Shayṭāns, whereas the name Iblīs is reserved for his majesty the Devil, head of the demons and the kingdom of darkness.

41 According to the Koran Hūd was sent to the tribe of 'Ād (the biblical Gad; Koran VII 63 ff.), and Ṣaliḥ to the tribe of Thamūd (Koran VII 71 ff.).

42 In the Koran, Ilyāsin.

43 Koran XVIII 82–9.

44 Koran II 118–21, 127. Ismā'īl is also accounted a prophet. The principal prophets in Islam were given their epithets: Abraham is 'the Friend of God, (*Khalīlu 'llāh*), Moses is 'the Interlocutor of God' (*Kalīmu 'llāh*), and Jesus is 'the Word and Spirit of God' (*Kalima wa rūhu 'llāh*).

45 The apocryphal gospels are those not accepted by the official (orthodox) Christian Church. The Church has recognized only four gospels as 'canonical', out of some dozens that were rejected as apocryphal. (See W. Sanday, 'Bible', ERE, vol. II).

46 Koran III 40 and other passages.

47 Koran XLIII 59.

48 Koran IV 156, 169 and other passages.

49 Koran III 37–43.

50 Koran III 42.

51 Koran IV 169.

52 Koran IV 156: *shubbih lahu*. Some commentators have understood this passage differently: it was the likeness of Jesus, i.e. a phantom created by God to deceive the enemies of Jesus, that was crucified. It is possible that this interpretation echoed that of the heretical Docetists among the Christians who held that the crucifixion was illusory.

53 Koran LXI 6. The name Aḥmad has the same signification as Muḥammad, being formed from the same root *ḥamida* 'to praise', 'to glorify'; whence Aḥmad 'glorious', Muḥammad 'glorified'.

54 Gospel according to St John 16:7.

55 Koran LXXXVII, 19; LIII 38 ff.

56 Koran XXXII 23; XXXIII 7, etc.

57 Koran XVII 57.

58 Koran V 50; LVII 27, etc.

59 Koran II 73; III 72; IV 48; V 16.

60 I.e. the revelations of Abraham, the Torah, the Psalms and the Gospel.

61 See Chapters III and VIII.

62 It is possible that this portion of the legend is influenced by the ancient Greek myth of Prometheus chained to the rock by Zeus.

63 Apparently there is a vague recollection in this legend of the Great Chinese Wall which was supposedly erected by Alexander of Macedon as a barrier against the nomads.

64 The trumpet of the archangel Isrāfīl in Muslim belief must announce the coming of the Day of Judgment.

65 The judgment upon many millions of people, it is assumed, will require much time, and therefore the Day of Resurrection and Judgment will last fifty thousand years.

66 This valley was near Jerusalem. The idol of Moloch stood in it, before which human sacrifices were performed, and it therefore became hateful to the Jewish monotheists.

67 The Spanish Islamist M. Asín Palacios has shown that the influence was two-way; the Muslim version of hell had its effect on Christians in the late Middle Ages and is apparent, incidentally, in Dante's 'Inferno'.

68 In Russian literature the word is no more than approximately rendered 'guriya'.

69 G. Sale, *The Koran*, p. 134.

70 R. Dozy, *Essai sur l'histoire de l'islamisme*, p. 154.

71 Koran LV 70–72; LVI 22.

72 Koran II 23; III 13; IV 60.

73 Koran XIV 4; and textually almost the same in XVI 39 and LXXIV 34.

74 Koran X 100: *wa mā kāna linafsin an tu'mina illā bi-idhni 'llāhi.*

75 Koran XXIII 105–13 and many other passages.

76 See Chapters VIII and IX.

77 Even if the worshipper does not understand the meaning of the formulae, which is often the case with non-Arab Muslims.

78 However *namāz* may be said at home or in the open air. (For mosques in the quarter and congregational Friday mosques see below).

79 For a description of the various prayer-positions see A. Müller, *History of Islam*, vol. I, pp. 216–17: and the Notes to I. Mouradjea d'Ohsson's *Tableau de l'Empire ottoman*, Paris, 1788.

80 Nowadays the direction is often fixed with the aid of a compass.

81 Often distorted in Russian literature into 'muedzin'.

82 This formula is named *takbīr.*

83 For example, after intercourse in marriage, contact with a corpse, swine or dog; and in a variety of other cases.

84 Even polluted running water from stream, canal or river is accounted ritually pure.

85 For the Ḥanafite school (*madhhab*) of Sunnī Muslims see Chapter V.

86 On entering a mosque the Muslim (and also a person of different faith, visiting or looking round a mosque) is required to remove his shoes; but his head must remain covered by turban or hat throughout the visit, as also during prayer.

87 For congregational and local mosques see below.

88 For the term *imām* and its meanings see below.

89 In particular, from perfumes, tobacco and narcotics, games, spectacles and conjugal dalliance.

90 Ramaḍān is the ninth month of the lunar calendar. It is appropriate to note here that the Muslim year is divided into the following 12 lunar months. 1 *Muḥarram*, 2 *Ṣafar*, 3 *Rabī'u 'l-awwal*, 4 *Rabī'u 'th-thānī*, 5 *Jumādā 'l-ūlā*, 6 *Jumādu 'l-ukhrā*, 7 *Rajab*, 8 *Sha'bān*, 9 *Ramaḍān*, 10 *Shawwāl*, 11 *Dhu 'l-qa'da*, 12 *Dhu 'l-ḥijja*. The lunar year has 354 days, and is thus 11 days shorter than the solar year. Therefore, to take an example, the Muslim New Year 1318 AH fell on 1 May in 1900, but the

New Year 1319 AH fell on 20 April 1901. In this way, all months, dates and festivals in the lunar calendar are always so to speak in transition, and may occur at any moment of the year. F. Wüstenfeld constructed a table in German for the coversion of dates in the Muslim calendar into the European calendar, and a similar conversion table has since been published in Russian, L. Izd. Gos. Ermitage, 1940. In Iran and in Islam generally the solar calendar has been used along with the lunar calendar, the Arabic names for the signs of the Zodiac serving as the names of the months.

91 Except, of course, the flesh of the pig and wine which are absolutely prohibited.

92 Koran II 181, 183.

93 Koran II 211; XXX 38 and in other places.

94 On those of other faiths a special poll-tax was imposed — the *jizya* (from the Aramaic *gezit*). For this see Chapter VI.

95 For waqf see Chapter VI.

96 The other great festival is the already mentioned breaking of the fast, the ʻīdu 'l-fiṭr.

97 Not strictly accurate. The occasional European did manage to get there in disguise before the nineteenth century: notably, Ludovico di Varthema, in about 1503, who published an eye-witness account in 1510; Piero da Covilha even earlier; and an Englishman, Joseph Pitts, who was there in 1685 and published his account in 1704. It was not, however, until the nineteenth century with Burckhardt that exploration properly speaking took place.

98 C. Snouck Hurgronje, *Mekka.* A detailed description of the ceremonies of the ḥajj with the legend about Abraham is available in Russian in the translation of R. Dozy's *Essai sur l'histoire de l'Islamisme* (Part II, pp. 11–18 in the Russian edition). See also A. J. Wensinck, *Ka'ba*, pp. 622–30.

99 At each of these three points on the route to the Vale of Minā a large heap of stones (*jamra*) had collected: the Jamratu 'l-ūlā, the Jamratu 'l-wusṭā, and the Jamratu 'l-ʻaqaba. The ritual of pelting the Devil with pebbles gave occasion, as early as Umayyad times, for frivolous poetry, since female pilgrims when casting the pebbles would raise their veils momentarily.

100 However, in the opinion of many Muslim jurists, especially in modern times, Muslim countries conquered by Unbelievers — for instance territories which have become colonies of European states — cannot be viewed as 'Province of War', seeing that 'the non-Muslim pattern of rule there is an anomaly; it must be tolerated only so long as there is no possibility of combating it'.

101 This term may be prolonged by renewal of the armistice treaty.

102 This understanding of the word *kāfir* is to be found in the Koran XVI 57, 85; XXVI 18; and XXX 33.

103 The Persian term *Gabr* means Zoroastrian, and then any infidel (whence Turkish *Gâvur*). Though of different origin from kāfir, the word has come to have the same meaning.

104 See the article: 'Mandaeans', by W. Brandt in ERE, vol. VIII and the bibliography attached to it. In the ninth century it was usual to class with

the Sabaeans the pagans of Ḥarrān (the ancient Carrhae), the only city in Upper Mesopotamia (or al-Jazīra) where the old Hellenism survived until the eleventh century.

105 All the rules that follow extend to peaceful inhabitants, as well as soldiers, in the 'Province of War'.

106 See Chapter VII.

107 This mourning is observed not only by Shī'ites but here and there by Sunnīs too.

108 The legendary night journey of Muḥammad from Mecca to Jerusalem is here intended, when he was transported by angels.

109 Among the Shī'ites 23 Ramaḍān.

110 For the Shī'ite festivals see Chapter X.

111 Koran IV (Sūra, 'Women'), 3 ff.

112 Muslim law draws a sharp distinction between the lawful wife, whose rights are carefully protected, and the kept slave-woman (for which, and for family law in general, see Chapter VII).

113 For which he earned the sobriquet Miṭlāq, 'often divorcing'.

114 Koran IV 3, 128.

115 Koran IV 22–3.

116 Koran IV 38.

117 Ibid.

118 For divorce in more detail see Chapter VII.

119 Koran LXIV 14–15.

120 Koran LXVI 11–12.

121 Koran III 37.

122 Shī'ites, however, do not hold 'Ā'isha in esteem since she was hostile to 'Alī.

123 For this cult see Chapter IX.

124 Even in our day it is frequently observable that atheists brought up and nurtured in a Muslim environment feel an aversion for the flesh of the pig in all forms. Nevertheless it cannot be maintained that this prohibition against eating the flesh of the pig was never violated in Iran. The historian Ẓahīru 'd-Dīn Mar'ashī in his *History of Ṭabaristān* (B. Dorn's edition of the Persian text, St Petersburg, 1850, pp. 344, 346) tells us that Afrāsiyāb Chulawī ruler of Māzandarān in the 1350s openly ate roast pork (*kabāb az gūshti khūk*).

125 For further details on this see I. P. Petrushevskiy. 'Viticulture and wine-making in Iran in the thirteenth and fourteenth centuries', where references are made to the sources.

126 These craftsmen had originally been invited by Caliph Walīd I in 709 to build the Great Mosque of the Umayyads in Damascus on the site of the Cathedral of St John which had been pulled down, except for the south gate with its Greek inscription.

127 In such centres of Islam as Stamboul (more correctly Istanbul, Constantinople) and Cairo, congregational mosques number many dozens.

128 The term *muṣallā* can also mean a place set aside for prayer in the open air. The Persian synonym is *namāzgāh*.

129 Originally the public worship at these festivals was performed in the open.

130 The early Christian church, on the other hand — the basilica — although likewise a columned hall, was usually longitudinal and orientated to the east.
131 Thus the mosque at Nā'in has 11 rows of columns.
132 A similar, but simplified, layout is usual in the small local mosques of the quarter.
133 It was built in the second half of the eleventh century on the site of a burnt-out mosque of the ninth century. It was several times reconstructed and enlarged between the fourteenth and sixteenth centuries. It has 470 vaulted ceilings.
134 Constructed by the noted master-builder Qawāmu 'd-Dīn Shīrāzī in 1417 at the order of Queen Gawhar Shād, wife of the Tīmūrid Sultan Shāhrukh.
135 However, in some Shī'ite mausoleums and even mosques of Iran and Adharbayjan pictures of prophets, imams and saints are now and then met with. See Chapter x.
136 At the present time in Iṣfahān only one minaret is still used for announcing the ādhān (for this see M. Bement Smith, *The Manars of Isfahan*, 'Athar-i Iran', ii, Haarlem, p. 331, note 6).
137 An early Islamic term.
138 Ṭabarī, relying on early traditions, states that a Jewish *beit ha midraš* existed at Medina at the date of the Prophet's migration there.
139 The most noted Syrian Christian (Nestorian) high schools in the fifth to ninth centuries were at Nisibin in Upper Mesopotamia and Gundishāpūr in Khūzistān.
140 There were many Buddhists and Manicheans in Central Asia and the Balkh region at the time of their conquest by the Arabs (seventh to eighth centuries); and there were Manicheans in Samarqand even in the eleventh century.
141 The routine of the Central Asian madrasas of the nineteenth century has been vividly illustrated in the memoirs of the noted Tajik philologist and poet Ṣadru 'd-Dīn Aynī who attended the well-known Bukhārā madrasa, Mīri 'Arab. He thinks that the syllabus of the madrasa had remained unaltered since the fourteenth century. Instruction lasted on the average 16 years, of which 8 were spent on the study of Arabic and grammar.
142 Traders and craftsmen would take waqf shops on lease, and pay the rent to the mosque or madrasa.
143 For Dervishes and their hostels see Chapter xii.
144 In pre-Islamic Arabia the *imām* was originally the caravan conductor who went ahead of the camels; then, by extension, the person conducting any affair. Having this background in pagan Arabia, the word entered the Koran with the sense 'spiritual leader' (Koran ii 118) or 'instructive example' (Koran xv 79).
145 For these see Chapter v.
146 For details on the Sunnī theory of the Imamate-Caliphate see Chapter vi. For the Sunnī Madhhabs and their founders see Chapter v.
147 For details of the Shī'ite theory of the Imamate see Chapter x.
148 See Chapter xii.

149 Bartol'd, *Islam*, p. 81.

150 For the Dhimmīs see page 000 of text.

151 There only occurred isolated cases of persecution of Muslim heretics on political grounds. The information given in certain much later sources about the restrictions imposed on Dhimmīs in the reign of 'Umar II (717–720) is extremely unreliable.

152 See N. A. Mednikov, *Palestine from the Arab conquest to the Crusades*, in the Arab sources. I, pp. 529–613.

153 Mednikov, pp. 809 ff.

154 For details, Mednikov, pp. 847–57.

155 *Tārīkhi Waṣṣāf*, lithographed edition of Persian text. Bombay, 1269 AH = 1852/3, pp. 247 ff.

156 *Histoire de Mar Yabalaha III*, traduite du syriaque, par J. B. Chabot, Paris, 1895, pp. 106–14, 119–21; M. Brosset, *Histoire de la Siounie*, vol. I, St Petersburg, 1870, pp. 260–63.

157 For the legal position of Dhimmīs see Chapter VII.

158 *Mushrik* (pl. *mushrikūn*) 'one who assigns partners' to God, a 'polytheist'; from *sharika* 'to participate', IV Form *ashraka*, 'to make someone a partner', 'to assign partners to God'; whence *shirk* in one of its meanings, 'polytheism'.

159 This charge is based on Koran IX 30: *wa qālati 'l-yahūdu 'uzayrun ibnu 'l-lāhi wa qālati n-naṣārā 'l-masīḥu 'bnu 'llāhi dhālika qawluhum bi-afwāhihim yuḍāhi'ūna qawla 'lladhīna kafarū min qablu qātalahumu 'llāhu anna yu'fakūna*. 'And the Jews said, Ezra is the son of God; and the Christians said, Messiah (= Christ) is the son of God. These words in their mouths are like the words of those who did not believe in former times. May God defeat them! How they are infatuated.'

160 See for instance Māwardī (eleventh century); Russian translation in Mednikov. *Palestine from the Arab conquest*, 4, p. 1337.

161 The term *ad-dahriyya* is taken from Koran XLV 23: 'They said, there is nothing except our immediate life, we die and we live and nothing destroys us except the passage of time (*illā 'd-dahru*)'. For *dahriyya* see M. Horten, *Die philosophische Systeme der spekulativen Theologen im Islam*, Bonn, 1912.

Chapter III The Koran

1 Koran XVI 104: *qul nazzalahu rūḥu 'l-qudusi min rabbika bi 'l-ḥaqqi liyuthabbita 'lladhīna āmanū wa haddā wa bushrā li 'l-muslimīna*. 'Say: in truth the holy spirit sent it (the revelation) down from thy Lord in order to confirm those that believed on the straight path and bring glad tidings to the Muslims'.

2 Gabriel (Jabrā'īl) is named in one of the late Medina Sūras (II 91) as the transmitter of the revelations.

3 Sūra I, '*al-Fātiḥa*', the 'opening', contains the text of the principal prayer of the Muslims. On the term *sūra*, see below.

4 Koran XLIII 3: *ummi 'l-kitābi*, i.e. 'the original text of the book', 'the autograph'.

5 A misprint here: the expression cited by Nöldeke is actually in Koran LVI 77: *fī kitābin maknūnin* 'in a secret book' (or 'writing').

6 Koran LXXXV 21–2: *bal huwa qur'ānun majīdun fī lawḥin maḥfūẓin.* 'Verily this is a glorious Koran on a guarded tablet.'

7 Th. Nöldeke, *Der Qoran*, pp. 23–4.

8 Koran IV 161.

9 Koran III 22: *naṣīban min al-kitābi*; also IV 47.

10 Koran V 16.

11 Koran II 169.

12 Koran IV 48; V 16, 45.

13 Koran XCVI 1–5; *iqra 'bismi rabbika 'lladhī khalaqa, khalaqa 'l-insāna min 'alaqin. iqra 'wa rabukka 'l-akramu 'lladhī 'allama bi 'l-qalami 'allama 'l-insāna mā lam ya'lam.* 'Read, in the name of thy Lord who has created; has created man from a clot of blood. Read, by thy most beneficent Lord, who vouchsafed knowledge by means of the reed-pen, vouchsafed to man knowledge of that which he knew not'. Nöldeke surmised that the word *iqra'* must here be understood as meaning 'preach'. (Th. Nöldeke, *Geschichte des Qorans*, p. 65; and *Der Qoran*, p. 25).

14 Koran LXXV 17, 18; LXXXVII 6 ff., where a warning is introduced not to forget any of the text at the time of reading. It is plain from this that declamation by heart is in point, and not reading from the book (cf. LXIX 19; LXXIII 20 ff.)

15 Nöldeke, *Der Qoran*, p. 25.

16 Ibid.

17 F. Buhl, *Kur'an*.

18 For recensions of the Koran see below.

19 Karl Vollers, *Volkssprache und Umgangsprache im altem Arabien*, Strasburg, 1906.

20 For examples see Nöldeke, *Der Qoran*, pp. 40–41.

21 Koran XXVI 195: *bilisānin 'arabiyyin mubīnin*; also Koran XVI 105.

22 J. Wellhausen, *Skizzen und Vorarbeiten*, I, p. 105: 'Der Koran ist in einem ganz unarabischen Arabisch geschrieben.' On the language of the Koran see also Nöldeke, *Der Qoran*, pp. 37–8; R. Dozy, *Outline of the history of Islam* (Russian edition), pp. 127–8.

23 Koran LXXXI 1–14.

24 Koran LXXXIX 22–4.

25 Koran LXX 43–4.

26 Koran LXXI 9–11.

27 Koran LXXXIV 16–18.

28 Koran LXXXVI 1–3.

29 Koran LXXXVI 11.

30 For details see Nöldeke, *Der Qoran*, pp. 38–40.

31 For the Ḥadīth see Chapter IV.

32 For this see: C. Brockelmann, *Geschichte der arabischen Literatur*, vol. I p. 133.

33 L. Caetani, *Annali dell'Islam*, vol. II, pp. 713 ff.; see also F. Buhl, *Kur'an*.

34 Ibnu 'l-Athīr, vol. III, p. 86.

35 Ibn Nadīm, *Fihrist*, pp. 26 ff.

36 See F. Buhl, *Kur'an*.

37 'Abdullāh b. Mas'ūd was of lowly origin and for that reason not kindly disposed towards 'Uthmān. In his youth he had been a slave of the Hudhayl tribe (Ṭabarī, ser. I, p. 2812) and grazed the herd of his master of the family Banū Zuhra in Mecca, and afterwards became his client. He took part in the battle of Badr where he decapitated Abū Jahl the well-known Qurayshite and principal foe of Muḥammad. He was accounted an excellent scholar both of the Koran and the Ḥadīth. He died at Medina in 653 or 654 (see A. J. Wensinck. 'Ibn Mas'ud', EI, vol. II)

38 It should be remembered that until the taking of Mecca by Muḥammad in 630, the Umayyad family headed by Abū Sufyān were amongst the Prophet's chief enemies. It is possible that certain dark hints and threats contained in the original text of the Koran related to Abū Sufyān and were expunged to please 'Uthmān and the Umayyads.

39 Shahrastānī, p. 95.

40 See Nöldeke, *Geschichte des Qorans*, pp. 305–11.

41 See B. Moritz, 'Arabie. Ecriture arabe', EI, vol. I p. 389.

42 As late as the lifetime of Mālik b. Anas (715–795) vowelling had not been adopted in the scrolls of the Koran.

43 Nöldeke, *Geschichte des Qorans*, pp. 284–98; Brockelmann, *Geschichte der arabischen Literatur*, vol. I, pp. 188–9.

44 These two Sūras, as has been said, were not in the edition of 'Abdullāh b. Mas'ūd.

45 He names the Sūra headings: 'The Cow' (II), 'Woman' (IV), 'The Table' (V), and also 'The Camel', which does not now occur in the Koran. Possibly this last was the heading of VII (now 'The Barriers') or XXVI (now 'The Poets').

46 Ḥ m at the beginning of all the Sūras here numbered, but in Sūra XLII it is Ḥ m 's q.

47 Ṭ s m in XXVI and XXVIII, but ṭ s in XXVII.

48 Ȧ l r at the beginning of all the Sūras here numbered, but a l m r in Sūra XIII.

49 Nöldeke, *Geschichte des Qorans*, pp. 215 ff.

50 Since in the absence of diacritical points a l r could be read also as a z z.

51 See F. Buhl, *Kur'an*.

52 See I. Yu. Krachkovskiy, 'Notes' to his translation of the Koran, pp. 656 ff.

53 Koran XXX 1–5.

54 See Introduction p. 00.

55 G. Weil, *Historisch-Kritische Einleitung in den Koran*.

56 A. Sprenger, *Das Leben und die Lehre des Mohammed*, vols. I–III, Berlin, 1861–5; 2nd edn. 1869 (the chronology of the Koran is traced parallel with the biography of Muḥammad).

57 Th. Nöldeke, *Geschichte des Qorans*, Göttingen, 1860; 2nd edn. 1879; new revised edition under the editorship of F. Schwally, vols I–II, Leipzig, 1909–19. See also Nöldeke, *Der Qoran*.

58 H. Grimme, *Mohammed*, vol. II, *Einleitung in den Koran*.

59 H. Hirschfeld, *New researches in the composition and the exegesis of the Qoran*.

60 This is evident, for instance, from Koran XXIX, 45–6 where the 'People of the Book' are portrayed as like-minded with the Muslims and contrasted with the infidels (kāfirs), and where, incidentally (end of verse 45) it is said: 'Our God and your God is one, and to him are we resigned.' In Sūra XXX, 1–5, Muḥammad speaks of Byzantine Christians as his coreligionists and allies.

61 Koran V 85.

62 Koran II 38–97.

63 Koran V 116; cf. CXII 1–4. But the fact is that Muḥammad had only a vague idea of the Christian doctrine of the Trinity. The Christians hold God the Father, God the Son and the Holy Ghost to be the 'persons' or 'hypostases' of the triune God, whereas Muḥammad supposed the Trinity to consist of God the Father,Christ and Mary (V 116).

64 V. V. Bartol'd, *Islam*, pp. 28–9.

65 Koran LXI 6; for this, see Chapter II, p. 57.

66 Koran II 212, 245; also the greater portion of Sūra VIII; cf. IX 5; LIX 6 ff.

67 Koran LXI 14.

68 Koran V 5: *al-yawma akmaltu lakum dīnakum.* 'Today have I completed your religion for you'. According to I. Yu. Krachkovskiy, 90 Sūras are Meccan Sūras and 24 are Medīna Sūras. See 'Notes' to his translation of the Koran p. 656; cf. 'Notes' p. 499.

69 In V 85, as noted above, it is stated that the Jews are enemies but the Christians are friends, of the Muslims; in verse 17 (which is much later) of the same Sūra it is said that the Christians have forgotten part of the scripture sent down to them; in verse 56 of the same Sūra we read: 'Believers, take neither the Jews nor the Nazarenes (= Christians) for your friends; they are friends one to another . . .'; and in verses 116–18 the Christians are accused of the deification of Jesus and Mary, and a sentence is put in the former's mouth censuring them for having distorted his teaching.

70 I. Goldziher, *Lectures on Islam*, p. 13.

71 For the Koran and the blood-feud, see Chapter VII.

72 No sort of hostility to persons of other race such as Ethiopians, Mongols, etc., was noticeable either among the early Muslims or their successors. Dark-skinned Africans, provided they were not slaves and were Muslim, were not subjected to any discrimination. The treatment of negro slaves was the same as that of any other slaves, no significance being attached to marks of racial difference.

73 Bartol'd, *Islam*, p. 22.

74 See Introduction.

75 For this see Note 1 in A. Ye. Krymskiy's Russian edition of R. Dozy, *Outline of the history of Islam*, p. 111. And in greater detail: A. Geiger, *Was hat Mohammad aus den Judentum aufgenommen*? Bonn, 1883, new edn Leipzig, 1902; H. Hirschfeld, *Jüdische Elemente im Koran*, Berlin, 1873; H. Lammens, 'Les chrétiens de la Mecque à la veille de l'hégire', BIFAO, XIV, and the same author's 'Les juifs de la Mecque à la veille de l'hégire'. BIFAO, VIII; S. M. Zwemer, *The Moslem Christ*, London, 1912; R. Bell, *The origin of Islam in its Christian environment*, London, 1926.

76 Goldziher, *Lectures on Islam*, pp. 14–15.
77 Koran XXIV 35. This verse suggested the name of the whole Sūra — 'Light', (*Sūratu 'n-nūri*).
78 D. B. Macdonald, *Allah*, p. 305, supposes that there are parallels here to the Gospel expression 'God is the Light of the World' and the Nicaean symbol of faith Light of Light (Lat. *lumen ex lumine*), and thinks that the image of the glittering glass lamp in the niche is evoked by the brightly illuminated altar of the Christian church. I. Yu. Krachkovskiy thinks it could be the unextinguishable lamp on Sinai (see Commentary to his translation of the Koran, p. 570, note 14 to Sūra XXIV).
79 Koran II 21; XVII 90.
80 For this, see Appendix to I. Yu. Krachkovskiy's translation of the Koran, p. 654.
81 See earlier in the present Chapter, p. 89.
82 See Koran II 100: 'Whenever we (= God) abrogate a verse, or command thee to forget it, we adduce a better one, or one resembling it.'
83 Brockelmann, *Geschichte der arabischen Literatur*, vol I, p. 143.
84 Complete edition in 30 vols: Cairo 1320 AH = 1902, and following years.
85 See Nöldeke, *Geschichte des Qorans*, p. 76.
86 Ed. W. Nassau-Lees, Calcutta, 1856–9, 2 vols; also Cairo edition 1307 and 1308 AH (1889, 1890) with glosses. For the Mu'tazilites see Chapter VIII.
87 There is a European edition of the text: Beidhawii Commentarius in Coranum, ed. H. O. Fleischer. Lipsiae, 1846–8, 2 vols. For list of oriental editions and commentaries see C. Brockelmann. 'Al-Baidawi'. *EI*.
88 Nöldeke, *Geschichte des Qorans*, p. 29.
89 Edition Cairo 1307 AH = 1889/90; also other oriental editions. For the Ẓāhirites see Chapter V.
90 There are not less than 8 oriental editions, among them the Cairo editions 1305, 1308, 1313 AH = 1887, 1890, 1895.
91 Calcutta edition of text, 1852–4, under English title: *Soyuti's Itqan* . . ., ed. Mawlawies Basheer od-deen and Noor ol-haqq, with an analysis by Dr A. Sprenger (in series Bibliotheca Indica). There is also a Cairo edition 1278 and 1306 AH = 1861 and 1888.
92 See Chapter X.
93 For details see Chapter XII.
94 Brockelmann. *Geschichte der arabischen Literatur*, vol. I, p. 442, 'sufische Umschreibung des Qor'ans'.
95 Killed while reading the Koran.
96 Such as the Tehran lithographed edition 1259 AH = 1843.
97 See list of these translations with bibliography in A. Ye. Krymskiy's article 'On interpretation of the Koran and textbooks for its understanding' in the Appendix to R. Dozy, *Outline of the history of Islam* (Russian edition) pp. 137–43. Also pp. 143–4 for Russian translations of the Koran in the eighteenth and nineteenth centuries.
98 Kazan', 1879; 2nd edn, Kazan', 1896. Both these have only the Russian translation A third edition, Kazan', 1907, has Arabic text with Russian

translation on parallel pages. There is also G. S. Sablukovs 'Appendices to the translation of the Koran' — a sort of comprehensive index to the Koran with a Russian translation — Kazan', 1879, 1898, which has won the high appraisal of I. Yu. Krachkovskiy (*Outline of Arabic Studies in Russia*, p. 183).

99 A. Ye. Krymskiy, *Lectures on the Koran*, Moscow, 1902 (lithogr.)

100 Koran. Translation and Commentary by I. Yu. Krachkovskiy, edited V. I. Belyayev, Moscow, 1963.

101 The first edition came out in Leipzig in 1834. The best modern edition is the Egyptian official one, based on the oldest MSS, Cairo 1337 = 1919.

102 The first edition was published in Leipzig in 1842 with the Latin title: Concordantiae Corani arabicae, ad literarum ordinem et verborum radicem. Subsequently reprinted.

Chapter IV The sources of Muslim law

1 The *Kitābu 'l-maghāzī* of al-Wāqidī (Abū 'Abdullāh Muḥammad b. 'Umar, 747–823) is the most important of these :(see Bibliography).

2 Son of the well-known Companion az-Zubayr and brother of the enemy of the Umayyads, the anti-Caliph, 'Abdullāh b. az-Zubayr (d. 692), on his mother's side a grandson of Caliph Abū Bakr and nephew of 'Ā'isha.

3 See Chapter III.

4 See I. Goldziher, *Muhammedanische Studien*, vol. II; C. Snouck Hurgronje, *Le droit musulman*. Also Th. W. Juynboll. 'Ḥadith', *EI*, vol II.

5 For the Qadarites see Chapter VIII.

6 For examples: I. Goldziher, *Muhammedanische Studien,* vol. II, pp. 6 ff.

7 *Usdu 'l-Ghāba fi Ma'rifati 'ṣ-Ṣahāba*. Cairo, 1280 AH.

8 For the schools (Madhhabs) of the jurist-theologians see Chapter V.

9 For editions see Bibliography to this chapter.

10 For the Shī'ite Tradition see Chapter X.

11 For editions see Bibliography.

Chapter V The elaboration of Sunnī law

1 I.e. in the time of Muḥammad and the first four Caliphs.

2 A. E. Shmidt, *Outline of the history of Islam as a religion*, 'Mir Islama', vol. I, p. 43.

3 Tafsīrs (Commentaries on the Koran) are in effect a supplementary source for Fiqh.

4 Who gave his name to the Madhhab — *Ḥanafiyya*.

5 Of course from the point of view of the governing class.

6 See Chapter IX.

7 Edition: Cairo 1310 and 1312 AH = 1892 and 1895.

8 See Chapter XIII.

9 Further details of al-Ash'arī and al-Ghazālī will be found in Chapters IX and XII.

10 See Chapter VIII.
11 For the Wahhābīs see D. S. Margoliouth, 'Wahhabiya', *EI*, vol. IV. His article cites the relevant literature.
12 See Chapter III.
13 I. Goldziher, *Die Zahiriten*. See also other works of the same author.
14 On these passages in the Koran and on anthropomorphism see Chapter VIII.
15 All four systems are taught at the Muslim University al-Azhar in Cairo. There are four raised daises (maqām) at the Ka'ba, so that the Imam of each of the Madhhabs has one.
16 Qazwīnī. *Nuzhatu 'l-Qulūb*, p. 49.
17 V. V. Bartol'd, *The history of peasant movements in Persia*, pp. 61–2. The author cites Yāqūt and other sources.
18 The Shī'ites think otherwise of Mujtahids — see Chapter X.
19 On theirs especially see Chapter X.
20 In this last meaning, 'a place not accessible to all': Medīna with the Prophet's grave and Mecca with the Ka'ba, the approach to which was barred to non-Muslims.
21 See Chapter X.

Chapter VI Muslim public law

1 Koran IV 62; cf. V 37.
2 The term *sulṭān* (pl. *salāṭīn* fr. *sallaṭa* II Form of *saluṭa* 'to grant power') originally conveyed the abstract idea of 'dominion', 'sovereignty', and also 'authority', 'government'. It was not until the middle of the tenth century that it began to be used for the personal holder of power, the sovereign.
3 C. Brockelmann, *Geschichte der arabischen Literatur*, vol. I, p. 386.
4 For the meaning of the terms 'Great Imam' and 'Lesser Imam' see Chapter II, p. 77.
5 For this see Chapter IX.
6 For the Khārijite theory of the Imamate-Caliphate see Chapter I; and for the Shī'ite theory of the Imamate see Chapter X.
7 See Chapter II.
8 See pp. 66 ff.
9 See p. 142.
10 See K. Marx, *Capital*, vol. III. Marx and Engels, *Works*, 25, pt. II p. 354.
11 On this see p. 165 below.
12 H. Lammens, *L'Islam, croyances et institutions*, p. 120.
13 I. Goldziher, *Lectures on Islam*, pp. 191–2.
14 In 945 Arab Iraq together with Baghdad was seized by the troops of the Iranian dynasty of the Buwayhids (945–1055). Thenceforward the 'Abbāsid Caliphs were in practice deprived of political power and retained only a shadowy spiritual authority. Baghdad came under the sway first of these Buwayhids (945–1055), and thereafter (from 1055) of the Turkman conquerors, the Seljūqs. In theory, however, men continued to recognize the existence of the Caliphate as state, the Buwayhids and

Seljūqs being, by an official fiction, accounted viceroys of the Caliph, from whom they received their investiture, charter and banner. The *khuṭba* and *sikka* (see above) were kept for the Caliph, although in actual fact he was powerless and merely the tool of the ruling dynasty. In 1132 the 'Abbāsids got back their political authority but only within the limits of Arab Iraq and — later — Khūzistān.

15 See A. von Kremer, *Kulturgeschichte des Orients* . . ., vol. I, p. 403.

16 Ibn Khaldūn, French translation, vol. I, pp. 388 ff.

17 See V. V. Bartol'd, *Caliph and Sultan*, pp. 361 ff.

18 In the collection of official documents *Dastūru 'l-Kātib* compiled by Muḥammad b. Hindūshāh Nakhchawānī, passim.

19 In the sense 'Great Imam', i.e. Caliph.

20 Abū Yūsuf Ya'qūb, *Kitābu 'l-Kharāj*, Būlāq, 1302 AH p. 5.

21 Koran V 37.

22 For the Dhimmīs see Chapter II; and for their legal position in the Muslim state see Chapter VII.

23 For the legal position of slaves see Chapter VII.

24 The word *mulk* has another meaning, 'kingdom'.

25 They were first and foremost in Arab Iraq, Khūzistān, Egypt and other provinces with large-scale systems of irrigation and an agriculture dependent on this. They were entirely absent in Ḥijāz and the Arabian peninsula.

26 However, many Faqihs owned 'mulk' property.

27 *Kārīz* or *Kahrīz*, subterranean canal bringing sub-soil water into use for irrigation. Karezes are very much used in Iran.

28 See Ibnu 'l-Balkhī, pp. 171–2.

29 On the evolution of *iqṭā* 'see F. Løkkegaard, *Islamic taxation* . . ., p. 14–91; I. P. Petrushevskiy, *Agriculture and Agrarian Relations in Iran*, pp. 256–69, and the bibliography appended to that work.

30 Māwardī. *Al-Aḥkāmu 's-Sulṭāniyya*, pp. 300–43 (ch. XVII).

31 Supposed to be levied in war or in case of other emergency expenditure, but in practice already being collected annually under Sultan Maḥmūd Ghaznawī (998–1030).

32 For the *métayage* system in the Caliphate see A. Yu. Yakubovskiy. On *métayage* rents in Iraq in the eighth century; as also the literature he has listed.

33 For details see I. P. Petrushevskiy, *Agriculture and Agrarian Relations in Iran* . . ., pp. 319–39.

34 Details of the state machinery will be found in A. von Kremer, *Kulturgeschichte des Orients* . . ., vol. I, pp. 256–469 (chs. VII and VIII); R. Levy, *The social structure of Islam*, pp. 251–457 (chs. VII–IX).

Chapter VII The criminal and civil law of Islam

1 See Chapter X. In the present chapter all terms are Arabic, except where otherwise specified as Persian, etc.

2 Koran XVII 35. The kinsmen are here enjoined not to exceed the bounds of vengeance.

3 Koran v 31. The words here cited are those of Abel addressed to Cain.

4 See Exodus 21:24; Leviticus 24:20; Deuteronomy 19:21.

5 Epistle to the Romans 12:19; cf. The Gospel according to St Luke 6:27–9.

6 Because according to Tradition this was the *diya* paid for the Prophet's father 'Abdullāh by the Prophet's grandfather 'Abdu 'l-Muṭṭalib. Moreover *Fiqh* minutely regulates how the number is to be composed (i.e. how many male camels, how many female, of what age, and so forth) in different cases of payment. The Ḥanafites allow 200 oxen or 2000 sheep as an alternative to the hundred camels.

7 Koran II 183; cf. LXX 31: 'Those that go beyond these bounds are transgressors.'

8 Koran XXIII 6–7; LXX 30. The cohabitation of an owner with his slave women, however many they be, is not accounted fornication.

9 Koran XXIV 2.

10 The author of the eleventh-century Persian *Qābūs-nāma* on how to manage a household, namely the small feudal seigneur 'Unṣuru 'l-Ma'ālī Kā'ūs, frankly advised his son Gīlānshāh to take a female slave in winter (at whose side it is warm) but a boy slave in summer (Qābūs-nāma, ch. 15, p. 49).

11 The precedent for classing calumny of this sort among crimes against God was the well-known episode involving 'Ā'isha, young wife of the already elderly Prophet, whom 'Abdullāh b. Ubayy and others accused of a liaison with the youthful and handsome Ṣafwān b. al-Mu'aṭṭal. The Prophet acknowledged the charge to be false on the basis of a revelation he claimed to have received from God on the subject (Koran XXIV 11 ff.). 'Alī, however, endorsed the accusation, and thereby incurred 'Ā'isha's irreconcilable enmity.

12 Koran II 216; IV 46; V 92.

13 Qābūs-nāma chs 11, 18, pp. 37–9, 53. The author recognizes that all young men drink wine every day, and merely counsels his son to drink prudently 'so that room is left for two or three cupfuls more'.

14 See Bayhaqī, pp. 165, 658–9; and I. Sreznevskiy's edition of R. G. Clavijo's *Journey to the Court of Tīmūr*, St Petersburg, 1880, pp. 279–80.

15 Koran v 42.

16 For *qiyās* see Chapter V.

17 This persecution of the Jews with its tale of confiscation, deportation and torture to compel them to adopt Islam, is narrated with sympathy for the victims by the contemporary Armenian historian Arakel of Tabrīz (see M. Brosset, *Collection d'historiens arméniens*, vol. I, St Petersburg, 1873, Ch. 34, pp. 489–96).

18 For whom see Chapter XI.

19 On the strength of Koran v 37.

20 See F. Engels, 'Peasant war in Germany', Marx and Engels, *Works*, 7, p. 361.

21 A Zoroastrian sect in Iran and Central Asia in the eighth to tenth centuries, the Khurramīs were the successors of the Mazdakites of the fifth and sixth centuries. They aimed at social equality and the transfer of land to free rural communes.

22 For the Carmathians see Chapter XI.

23 However the culprit could declare to the judge that his mind was 'darkened' when he uttered the disparagement, and in that case he was not punished. It is clear from the biographies of Christian martyrs who insulted Muḥammad in order to earn the glory of a martyr's death, that Muslim judges commonly prompted the accused to take this way out; but they refused to avail themselves of it, preferring to achieve their purpose.

24 Jews were sometimes subjected to this punishment for insulting references to the prophet Jesus and his mother Mary. In this context, too, the evidence of two Muslims was required.

25 Except a false or unproved accusation of fornication which was punishable by the *ḥudūd* penalty (see above).

26 Shī'ite law does not allow the legal marriage of a Muslim with a Christian woman or a Jewess, but it does permit temporary marriage with her. For the Shī'ite temporary marriage see Chapter X.

27 But he can, however, have as many slave-concubines as he pleases.

28 If not, the clearly expressed consent of the girl is demanded.

29 For instance under the Napoleonic code the wife has no right to spend her dowry without the permission of the husband; but the latter, on the other hand, can spend his wife's dowry as he pleases.

30 The Ḥanafites consider that the clearly expressed recognition by the father is required for this. But the Shāfi'ites think that a statement by the father is only required in the case of his non-recognition of the child as his, and in the absence of such a refusal of recognition, the child of the slave-woman is automatically acknowledged to be the legitimate son of her master.

31 Inasmuch as children of a slave-concubine inherit along with children of a lawful wife.

32 Koran IV 8–9, 12–16, 175.

33 Koran II 176–7; V 105.

34 Sh. Shafiq. *Essai d'une théorie générale de l'obligation en droit musulman*, Cairo, 1936.

35 See what has been said above on *ghaṣb*.

36 Koran II 276; III 125; XXX 38.

37 In a caravan which set out from Khwārazm for the country of the Volga Bulgar in March 922, and with which travelled the envoy of Caliph Muqtadir, Ibn Faḍlān, there were 3000 pack-horses and camels, and 5000 people.

38 See Chapter II.

39 For *jizya* and *kharāj* see Chapter VI.

40 The contents of a number of such agreements appear in the pages of the ninth-century historian Balādhurī and of other Arab authors.

41 The Nestorian Patriarch Catholicos represented the interests both of his own Church and of other Christians at the court of the 'Abbāsids.

42 See Chapter II.

43 For the standing of Dhimmīs under Shī'ite law see Chapter X.

44 See I. P. Petrushevskiy, *Agriculture and Agrarian Relations in Iran*, pp. 250–51, 253; also the references to sources.

45 Dhimmīs were not admitted to associations of the *shirkatu 'l-mufāwaḍa* category, whose members had to be equal in regard to religion, legal capacity, and the sum contributed.

46 In Iran patches on the clothing of Jews were replaced (but not until the very end of the nineteenth century) by a special buckle worn on the sleeve.

47 Koran IX 29: *'an yadin wa hum ṣāghirūna.*

48 The Amīr in the context is the head of the dīwān.

49 As the Ḥanafites permit.

50 H. Lammens, *Etudes sur le siècle des Omayyades*, Beyrouth, 1930, pp. 33 ff., where the enormous number of prisoners taken by the Arabs is indicated.

51 See I. P. Petrushevskiy, *Application of slave labour in Iran*; as also the author's references to the sources and the relevant literature.

52 In Iran these three categories of slaves were correspondingly termed *asīr* 'prisoner', P. *zarkharīd*, 'bought for gold', P. *khānazād*, 'born in the house'.

53 Apart from slaves captured in wars for the Faith, there were great numbers of slaves brought into the Muslim countries by slave traders from Eastern Europe — *saqlāb*, pl. *saqāliba*, 'Slavs' — from the countries of the Turks, and from India and Africa. The scale of the slave trade can be judged from an example cited by the tenth-century geographer Iṣṭakhrī: one Persian merchant from the Persian Gulf littoral in the course of a summer voyage in 324 AH = 936 brought back 400 barges carrying camphor and 12,000 dusky African slaves.

54 The same word *'abd* forming a second plural *'ibād* was used in the meaning 'slave of God', i.e. simply 'person', or more especially an 'ascetic' or 'shaykh'.

55 The terms *ghulām* and *mamlūk* (our 'Mameluke') had a dual meaning; being either 'a purchased slave' generally or 'a slave-guard', that special category of young foreigner, Turkish, Slav or African, whom the Muslim dynasties were wont to buy from the slave trader for service in the royal horse guards. Semantically there is a parallel between *ghulām*, pl. *ghilmān* (lit. 'young man', then 'slave') and the Russian words *otrok* ('lad') and *molodets* ('youth') which in old Russia were terms indicative of age and then evolved into terms of social status like 'slave', 'servant', 'menial'.

56 The word *banda* has a dual meaning, viz. 'slave', whether in the literal sense or in the figurative sense of 'humble servant' (cf. our use of the expression 'your humble servant' in correspondence), 'loyal servant'; and 'religious devotee'. On the other hand, *barda* is always 'slave' in the primary sense.

57 Here again a term suggesting youthful years has acquired a social signification.

58 C. Snouck Hurgronje, *Mekka*, vol. II, Leiden, 1888, pp. 11–20, 136.

59 Koran IV 40 and other passages.

60 *Qābūs-nāma*, ch. 23, p. 68.

61 In view of the absence of gender in Persian grammar the terms *banda* and *barda* can mean either slave or slave-girl.

62 *Qābūs-nāma*, ch. 23. *andar banda kharīdan*, 'On the purchase of slaves'.
63 Abū Yūsuf Ya'qūb (*Kitābu 'l-Kharāj*, p. 113) says that in the reign of Hārūn ar-Rashīd the prisons of the great and lesser cities held many runaway slaves of both sexes who had been arrested but whose owners had not been found.
64 The belief was that the more slaves the owner released the quicker would his soul be liberated from hell after death.
65 *Ibnu 'l-Athīr*, vol. XI, pp. 116–20.
66 Ibid.
67 See p. 138 above.
68 Without the invocation of the name of Allah the oath is held null and void.
69 The term 'bazaar' covered the entire trading network of the town, including caravanserais, the counters of the brokers and the money-changers, the sectors earmarked for the different branches of industry, the artisans' workshops, etc.
70 Prostitution is strictly prohibited by the Sharī'a, but it existed everywhere throughout the Middle Ages and has continued into modern times.
71 See V. V. Bartol'd, *Ulugh Beg and his time*, p. 104; Note 2, references to the sources.
72 Bartol'd, p. 95 (with allusion to Khwāndamīr. *Ḥabību 's-Siyar*, vol. III, Tehran, p. 219).
73 The term *dārūgha* subsequently acquired other technical meanings in Iran and the adjacent countries, but these need not detain us here.

Chapter VIII Theological disputes

1 V. V. Bartol'd, *Islam*, p. 67–8.
2 Apparently the word *qadar* in this context was understood in the sense of 'power' and more precisely 'a person's power over his actions', otherwise 'freedom of will'.
3 For munāfiqs see Introduction p. 18.
4 However there was no noticeable move to translate the Greek poets and historians into Arabic. Consequently the heritage of ancient classical culture acquired by the Arabs and Muslim Persians was extremely one-sided.
5 Koran XX 4: *ar-raḥmānu 'alā 'l-'arshi 'stawā*. 'The Merciful has set himself firmly on the throne'. Also in other passages of the Koran.
6 Koran II 109; VI 52; XVIII 27.
7 Koran LIV 14.
8 Koran V 69; XXXVIII 75; XLVIII 10.
9 In other words, it is impossible to see him not only here on earth but in the after-life.
10 See p. 170.
11 For this see Chapter X.
12 Ma'mūn lived in Khurāsān for the first years of his reign, not daring even to show his face in Baghdad.

13 It was in Ma'mūn's reign that a large-scale peasant rebellion of the red Khurramīs led by Bābak broke out in Ādharbāyjān and West Iran (816–837).
14 Lit. 'ordeal', from the verb *maḥana* 'to put to the test'. The word comes close in meaning to 'inquisition' (Lat. *inquisitio*, lit. 'inquiry').
15 For details see Ṭabarī, ser. III, pp. 1351–7.
16 For him see Chapter III.
17 Qazwīnī. *Nuzhatu 'l-Qulūb*, p. 71.
18 For this see Chapter IX.
19 Firdawsī, *Shāh-nāma*, vol. I, pp. 4–5.

Chapter IX A scholastic theology (Kalām)

1 For al-Ash'arī and Ash'arites see D. B. Macdonald, *Development of Muslim Theology . . .*, pp. 186–92, 213 ff.; W. Spitta, *Zur Geschichte Abu-l-Hasan's al-Asch'ari*; M. A. Mehren, *Exposé de la réforme de l'islamisme commencée par el-Ash'ari*.
2 V. V. Bartol'd, *Islam*, p. 75.
3 C. Brockelmann, *Geschichte der arabischen Literatur*, vol. I, pp. 194–5. The author omits to include *Al-ibāna 'an uṣūli 'd-diyāna* ('The elucidation of the roots of religion', edited in Hyderabad, India, in 1321 AH = 1903), attributed to al-Ash'arī and undoubtedly his.
4 For this term see Chapter VIII.
5 See R. Strothmann. 'Tashbih'. *EI*, including references to the sources.
6 Al-Ash'arī's doctrine was, in particular, the official ideology of the Almoravid movement in Maghrib and Spain in the eleventh century.
7 Year of birth unknown.
8 See Brockelmann, *Geschichte der arabischen Literatur*, vol. I, p. 195.
9 D. B. Macdonald, *Development of Muslim Theology*, pp. 193 ff.
10 According to the *Kitābu 'l-Ansāb*, or 'Book of Genealogies', of as-Sam'ānī (twelfth century), he was so named after the village Ghazāla near Ṭūs whence his family originated.
11 For whom see Chapter XI.
12 This madrasa too was founded by the Niẓāmu 'l-Mulk.
13 The famous ascetic and mystic with a leaning towards pantheism, the preacher of voluntary poverty, and founder of the Catholic monastic order of Franciscans, or Friars Minor, in Italy (1182–1226).
14 See Brockelmann, *Geschichte der arabischen Literatur*, vol. I, pp. 421–6.
15 Lit. 'vivifier'.
16 Complete edition, Cairo, 1289 AH = 1872. 4 vols.
17 Or 'Alchemy of Happiness'.
18 Or 'Niche of mystical illumination'. The title echoes Koran XXIV 35, where the image of God as Light is portrayed in a metaphor — a wall-niche (*al-mishkāt*) with a glittering lamp.
19 This treatise was translated into Hebrew by Abraam bar Hasdai, and in that rendering made its way to Western Europe.
20 T. J. de Boer's German translation is 'Widerspruch der Philosophen'. Others render 'Destruction of the Philosophers' (Lat. *Destructio*

philosophorum), 'Vanity of the Philosophers' (cf. M. Asín Palacios, *Sens du mot 'tehafot' dans les oeuvres d'al-Ghazali et d'Averroes*).

21 A medieval Latin translation by Gondisalvi was printed in Venice in 1506.

22 There is a French translation by Barbier de Meynard (JA, 7 ser., vol. IX).

23 See T. J. de Boer, *Geschichte der Philosophie im Islam*, p. 146.

24 I.e. to ancient philosophy.

25 See Chapter XII.

26 The term is taken from the Koran XLV 23. For the quotation see Chapter II, Note 161.

27 In particular, with the rationalistically explained elements of Neo-Platonism.

28 See de Boer, *Geschichte der Philosophie im Islam*, pp. 76–89. Fifty-two treatises of this fraternity were published in Cairo in 1347 AH = 1928, in 4 vols.

For Carmathians see Chapter XI.

29 In particular, al-Fārābī and the other representatives of this school accepted as a genuine work of Aristotle his so-called 'Theology' (in Arabic, Uṣulujiyya Arisṭūṭālīs) which is actually apocryphal and came from the Neo-Platonist circle. It is based on the Enneads of Plotinus (third century), the initiator of Neo-Platonism.

30 The mediaeval Europeans called him Avicenna (from the Hebrew Aven Sina).

31 For details of this philosophical trend see de Boer, *Geschichte der Philosophie im Islam*, pp. 90–137.

32 Koran L 15: see p. 54 above for the quotation.

33 Koran XV 29. *fa-idhā sawwaytuhu wa nafakhtu fīhi min rūḥī*. 'When I (= Allah) completely form him (= Adam) and breathe of my spirit into him'. And Koran XXXVIII 72, textually the same.

34 See Macdonald, *Development of Muslim Theology*, p. 232.

35 I.e. that which a person can enjoy with the help of his senses.

36 The expression *'ālamu 'l-jabarūt* was used also by the philosophers in the Neo-Platonist tradition, and by certain Ṣūfīs as well, but in a somewhat different sense, and meant sometimes 'higher world' as compared with *'ālamu 'l-malakūt*. The term *jabarūt* corresponds with the Hebrew *geburah*.

37 For the meaning of *farḍu 'l-'ayn* and *farḍu 'l-kifāya* see p. 119.

38 See Macdonald, *Development of Muslim Theology*, Appendix I, pp. 302–3. (an English translation of the first book of the second part of *Iḥyā'u 'ulūmi 'd-dīn*). For Muslim doctrine on the identity of the contents of the Torah and the New Testament (in the original form) with the Koran see Chapter III.

39 Ghazālī found heresy among the Christians only on two points — the doctrine of the Trinity and the non-recognition of Muḥammad's prophetic mission.

40 Macdonald, *Development of Muslim Theology*, p. 229.

41 For details see D. Margoliouth, *Karramiya*.

42 Al-Ghazālī's name was familiar to mediaeval Western Europe in the form Algazel.

43 D. B. Macdonald, *Ghazali*, p. 155.
44 On the personages named see Chapter XII. For Ḥanbalites and Ẓāhirites see Chapter V.
45 For Ghazālī and his system consult Macdonald, *Ghazali*; the same author's *Life of al-Ghazali*; and his *Development of Muslim Theology*, pp. 215–42; T. J. de Boer, *Geschichte der Philosophie im Islam*, pp. 138–50; R. Nicholson, *A literary history of the Arabs*, pp. 338 ff.; H. Bauer, *Die Dogmatik al-Ghazali's*; M. Asín Palacios, *Algazel — dogmática, moral, ascética*; C. Brockelmann, *Geschichte der arabischen Literatur*, vol. I, pp. 419–26.
46 Macdonald, *Development of Muslim Theology*, p. 269.
47 See de Boer, *Geschichte der Philosophie im Islam*, p. 137.
48 Koran X 19.
49 Koran XVI 20–23; cf. also XIII 17–18; XVIII 102; XXXIX 44.
50 See I. Goldziher, *The Worship of Saints in Islam*, being a Russian translation of five articles from his 'Muhammedanische Studien'. The first of the articles, 'The Veneration of Saints in Islam', is especially relevant (pp. 21–102).
51 Typical examples, with allusion to the sources, are in Goldziher, *The Worship of Saints*, pp. 64, 66. For the veneration of the Virgin Mary in Islam see Chapter II above.
52 Goldziher, pp. 60–61.
53 See Chapter XII.
54 Goldziher, *The Worship of Saints*, p. 98.
55 The same term is also used for a verse of the Koran.
56 For details of this hierarchy of hidden saints see I. Goldziher, 'Abdal', *EI*.
57 On ziyārats see Goldziher, *The Worship of Saints*, pp. 51 ff.
58 See Chapter X.
59 His tomb, incidentally, was visited by the Persian poet Maḥmūd Khwājū of Kirmān (fourteenth century) who dedicated his *Rawḍatu 'l-Anwār* ('Garden of Illumination') to it.
60 Ibn Baṭṭūṭa, vol. II, pp. 88–91; see also I. P. Petrushevskiy, *Urban nobility in the Hūlāgūid state*, 'Soviet Orientalism', Moscow-Leningrad. vol. V, 1948 pp. 104–5.
61 See Goldziher, *The Worship of Saints*, p. 86.
62 Goldziher, pp. 86–96.

Chapter X The moderate Shī'ites

1 E. G. Browne, *A literary history of Persia*, vol. IV, p. 418.
2 See Chapter I.
3 The Zaydī branch; see below in present chapter.
4 Shahrastānī, pp. 108–9; see also Browne, *A literary history*, vol. IV, pp. 16–17.
5 Ye. A. Belyayev, *Muslim Sectarianism*, p. 23.
6 For the Sunnī conception of the Imamate-Caliphate see Chapter VI.
7 See Browne, *A literary history*, vol. II, p. 195.

8 See Chapter XI.
9 For whom see Chapter I.
10 See Chapter I.
11 Mas'udī, *Murūj*, vol. VII, p. 404.
12 He was so called to distinguish him from the elder son, earlier deceased, of Imam Ḥusayn who likewise bore the name 'Alī (and is referred to as 'Alī al-Akbar, 'the Elder').
13 The biographers of Zaynu 'l-'Ābidīn relate that his mother was a Persian princess. According to Ibn Khallikān (thirteenth century), the three captive daughters of the last Sāsānid King of Iran Yazdigird III were brought to Medīna in the reign of Caliph 'Umar I, and the intention was to distribute them among the soldiery along with other captive women as spoils of war. But 'Alī b. Abī Ṭālib objected to this, and with the Caliph's consent gave away all three princesses in marriage — two to sons of 'Umar and Abū Bakr, and the third to his own son Ḥusayn. To the last named this third princess bore a son 'Alī, the future Imam. This story is probably a legend invented in order to make the Imams, and Shī'ism itself, popular in Iran. At the date of 'Umar's death, Yazdigird III was still a youth and could not have had grown-up daughters. Imam 'Alī al-Aṣghar was not born earlier than 654/5. Apparently his Persian mother was a captive slave-woman.
14 Incidentally, he was the first of the Imams to be content with only one wife. She was his first cousin, daughter of the second Imam Ḥasan.
15 Ya'qūbī, *Ta'rīkh*, pt. 2, p. 384.
16 However, they condemn 'Uthmān.
17 For *taqiyya* see later in the present chapter.
18 The Mu'tazilite explanation of certain dogmas was current among the leadership, but was of small interest to the rank-and-file of the sect.
19 For Khārijites see Chapter I.
20 See V. V. Bartol'd, *The history of peasant movements in Persia*, pp. 55 ff., and the same author's *Iran. An historical survey*, p. 33.
21 Musāfirids (Sālārids) in Daylam and Ādharbāyjān, Ziyārids in Gurgan, Buwayhids in West Iran and Arab Iraq (all three in the tenth century).
22 Ṭabarī. ser. III, pp. 1524–5.
23 The Sunnī theologians esteemed Ja'far aṣ-Ṣādiq the more in that his mother had come of the family of Caliph Abū Bakr, also styled 'aṣ-Ṣādiq'.
24 Ya'qūbī, *Ta'rīkh*, pt. 2, pp. 458 ff.
25 This doctrine is expounded in Mas'ūdī, *Murūj*, vol. I, p. 55.
26 For this sect see Chapter XI.
27 For the Ismā'īlīs see Chapter XI.
28 Tradition said that his mother was a Berber (in another variant, an Andalusian, i.e. Spanish) slave, Ḥamida.
29 According to certain later data, in 794.
30 His full title is *Riḍā' min āl Muḥammad* lit. 'the one of the family of Muḥammad to whom preference or favour has been vouchsafed'. It was conferred on him by Caliph Ma'mūn. His mother was a Persian slave who had been chosen to be the friend of his father by the latter's mother Ḥamida. 'Alī was born in 765 or 770.

31 The slogan of this rising was the restoration of Sunnism. The grand-uncle of Ma'mūn, Ibrāhīm b. al-Mahdī was proclaimed Caliph (817). The rising was put down.
32 Ya'qubī, *Ta'rīkh*, pt. 2, p. 550.
33 I.e. as prayer leader.
34 On the word of the traveller Ibn Baṭṭūṭa who was here in the 1330s, the Shī'ite pilgrims, having done obeisance before the sepulchre of Imam 'Alī Riḍā, cast stones at that of Hārūn ar-Rashīd. The tomb of 'Alī Riḍā was the tomb of one of the 'Alīds and of a saint, and Sunnīs venerated it as such.
35 The word *mashhad* (fr. the root *shahida* 'to testify') means 'place of confession' of the faith or, what is the same thing, 'place of martyrdom' for it: whence the expression 'tomb of the martyr'. cf. *shahīd*, pl. *shuhadā* 'confessor' of the faith, 'martyr' for it.
36 For details of the history of the Meshhed holy quarter consult D. M. Donaldson, *The Shī'ite Religion*, pp. 170–87, and references to the sources in that volume.
37 Much later traditions call her variously Nubian, Greek or Copt, but concur that she was Christian.
38 According to Shī'ite tradition she was known as Pearl of Maghrib (the West), and she seems to have been a slave woman from the lands of the West (Western Europe?). She was also called Sūsan (Lily) which was possibly an approximation to the Christian name Susanna.
39 Mas'ūdī, *Murūj*, vol. VII, pp. 379 ff.
40 I.e. 'narcissus'. In another variant her name was Khamṭ ('aromatic milk'). Such names as these and Susan, Banafsha (P. 'violet'), Gulinār (Pers. 'pomegranate blossom') and so on, were commonly given to odalisques of the harem.
41 In Shī'ite tradition, Narjis was a captured Byzantine princess, daughter of Yoshua, son of the Emperor. This was doubtless a legend, since Byzantine sources mention neither a princess of the name nor the fact of any princess falling a prisoner to the Arabs. The story was evidently invented to exalt the origin of the twelfth Imam who was particularly revered by the Shī'ites: on his father's side, a descendant of the Prophet; and on his mother's, a descendant of the Roman Caesar!
42 *Sardāb* (Pers. lit. 'cold water'): a ventilated underground apartment containing a pool to which people could repair in the heat. Sardabs were commonly installed in the well-to-do homes of Iraq and Iran.
43 See later in the present chapter.
44 In this regard 'Alī ar-Riḍā was no exception. He lived in tranquillity at Medīna until 816 when he became the passive tool of Caliph Ma'mūn in the implementation of his political schemes.
45 The genuineness of certain of these tombs, particularly the supposed sepulchre of 'Alī in Najaf, is doubtful.
46 This burial-place was ultimately ravaged, and the mausoleums on it demolished, by the fanatical Wahhābīs who took Medīna and Mecca in 1803/4. (The Wahhābīs repudiated the worship of saints).
47 Properly *imām-zāda* means 'descendant of the Imam', but the word acquired the additional technical meaning in Iran of 'mausoleum of the descendant of the Imam'.

48 For the biographies of the Imams and wakīls in detail see Donaldson, *The Shī'ite Religion*, pp. 1–257.

49 In theory, the 'Abbāsid Caliphate continued to exist, the Buwayhids being the viceroys (with the title 'Amir of Amirs') of the Caliphs and installed by them. This of course was pure fiction: in practice the Caliphs were wholly dependent on the Buwayhids, and mere puppets in their hands.

50 I. Goldziher, *Lectures on Islam*, pp. 212–13.

51 I.e. to Sunnīs and Shī'ites.

52 I. Goldziher, *Lectures*, p. 213.

53 See Goldziher, *Muhammedanische Studien*, vol. II, pp. 111–18.

54 C. Brockelmann, *Geschichte der arabischen Literatur*, vol. I, pp. 185–6.

55 See also Brockelmann, *Geschichte*, vol. I, pp. 186–8; Donaldson, *The Shī'ite Religion*, pp. 281–304.

56 Kulīnī, in a variant, but incorrect, reading.

57 Lit: 'he that has no lawyer at hand'. Lithogr. ed. Tehran 1326 AH = 1908.

58 See Chapter XI.

59 Brockelmann, *Geschichte*, vol. I, p. 405.

60 In the thirteenth to fourteenth centuries Ḥilla in Arab Iraq was a centre of Shī'ite scholastic learning.

61 Ed. 'Abdu 'l-Ibrāhīm 1300 AH = 1882; Russian transl. Kazembek, and French translation A. Querry.

62 For the Sunnī doctrine of Imamate-Caliphate see Chapter VI.

63 Goldziher, *Lectures on Islam*, p. 192; also the same author's *Beiträge zur Literaturgeschichte der Shi'a*, p. 445.

64 Koran III 40.

65 Goldziher, *Lectures on Islam*, p. 192.

66 For the Extreme Shī'ites see Chapter XI.

67 For *ijmā'* see pp. 111 ff.

68 Goldziher, *Lectures on Islam*, p. 200.

69 See Chapter XI.

70 For a detailed description of the celebration and ceremonies of the days of mourning commemorating the death of Ḥusayn, his comrades and companions at Kerbela, as also of the religious mysteries connected with these days (the *'āshūrā'*, in common parlance *shahsay-wahsay*) see K. N. Smirnov, *The Persians: An essay on the religions of Persia*, pp. 83 ff.

71 See p. 242. Smirnov, *The Persians*.

72 Goldziher, *Lectures on Islam*, p. 205.

73 See above p. 209.

74 Yāqūt. *Mu'jamu 'l-Buldān* vol. VI, p. 15.

75 For these see Chapter XIII.

76 Mīrkhwānd, *Rawḍatu 'ṣ-Ṣafā*, Lucknow. p.1088.

77 Koran III 27.

78 See Chapter VIII.

79 Goldziher, *Lectures on Islam*, p. 209.

80 Exegesis (Gk. exēgēsis) is the interpretation, philosophical or dogmatic, of a particular text which is generally ancient and in this case is the text of Holy Writ, the Koran. That branch of theology is called exegetical

which is concerned with establishing and interpreting the texts of the Scriptures (in the case of the Christians the Bible, and in that of the Muslims the Koran).

81 Koran XLIII 3.
82 Koran XXXVII 130.
83 Yā Sīn. The mysterious heading of one of the chapters of the Koran (XXXVI).
84 Koran II 137; III 106 ff.
85 Koran XVI 70: *wa-awḥā rabbuka ilā'n-naḥli* 'And thy Lord gave inspiration unto the bees'.
86 Koran II 63.
87 See Chapter VII.
88 Goldziher, *Lectures on Islam*, p. 209.
89 For this see Chapter V.
90 See Chapter VII.
91 See Smirnov, *The Persians*, p. 123.
92 On the supposition that such a person has not yet managed to assimilate the Muslim faith properly and that his apostasy is in the nature of a relapse into his previous religious views.
93 More accurately days of mourning in the plural. These lasted from the 1st to the 10th of the month of Muḥarram.
94 The writer of these lines has seen a Persian carpet representing the Virgin Mary (in trousers and Persian costume) and the child Jesus.
95 Saqqā-khāna ('house of the water-carrier') is a sort of arbour during the '*āshūrā*' mysteries which is connected with one of the episodes in the tale of the tragedy at Kerbela.
96 A Russian merchant, F. Kotov, who was in Iṣfahān in 1623 wrote: 'And over against that mosque on the left hand was another mosque likewise of stone and traced out in colours, and in it stood 4 Russian ikons in the wall: the Birth of Christ, his Entry into Jerusalem, and, on the other side, the Transfiguration and the Epiphany; and a Russian inscription . . . and they tell that these were brought from the Georgian lands'. (Fedot Kotov, *An excursion to the Persian Kingdom*, p. 13).
97 See Chapter XI.

Chapter XI Ismā'īlīs, Carmathians and Extreme Shī'ites

1 For whom see Chapter I.
2 For Ṣūfism see Chapter XII.
3 Ye. A. Belyayev, *Muslim Sectarianism*, pp. 47 ff.
4 See F. Engels, 'Peasant War in Germany', Marx and Engels, *Works*, 7, p. 361.
5 For Mahdī see pp. 225 ff.
6 W. Ivanow, *The Rise of the Fatimids*, pp. 9 ff.
7 Belyayev, *Muslim Sectarianism*, pp. 47–80.
8 A. Ye. Bertel's, *Nāṣir-i Khusraw and Ismā'īlism*, pp. 51–147.
9 See Bibliography to present chapter.
10 See Bibliography.

11 W. Ivanow, *The Rise of the Fatimids*, also his *Studies in early Ismā'īlism*: and his *Brief survey of the evolution of Ismā'īlism*.

12 Having emigrated from Russia in 1918, he was for long years among the intimates of the Agha Khan, head of the Ismā'īlis of India.

13 W. Ivanow, *The Rise of the Fatimids*, p. 112.

14 Besides the works above indicated of Ye. A. Belyayev and A. Ye. Bertel's, see B. N. Zakhoder, *Muḥammed Nakhshabī*.

15 Ph. K. Hitti, *History of the Arabs*, pp. 444–5. (Hitti calls the Carmathians 'the Bolsheviks of Islam'); L. Massignon, 'Sinf', *EI*, vol. IV.

16 For whom see Chapter X.

17 According to the Fāṭimid version: Muḥammad b. Ismā'īl, 'Abdullāh, Aḥmad, Ḥusayn, 'Ubaydullāh; in the Druze version: Muḥammad b. Ismā'īl, Ismā'īl II, Muḥammad II, Aḥmad, 'Abdullāh, Muḥammad III, Ḥusayn, Aḥmad II, 'Ubaydullāh (nine Imams instead of five); and in the Nizārī version: Muḥammad b. Ismā'īl, Aḥmad, Muḥammad II, 'Abdullāh, 'Ubaydullāh.

18 'Sect', 'sub-sect', 'branch' are convenient terms and no more. Under certain historical conditions a sub-sect can in time evolve into a self-contained sect, and afterwards into a separate religion. This happened to the Druzes who were to begin with a sub-sect of Ismā'īlism.

19 Adam, Noah, Abraham, Moses, Jesus and Muḥammad, according to the common doctrine of all Muslims. And according to the Extreme Shī'ites, the Seventh is al-Qā'im, the Mahdī (a mythical personality) who is due to appear before 'the end of the world'.

20 These are listed in L. Massignon's article 'Karmates'. Note also W. Ivanow's theory (*The Rise of the Fatimids*, p. 99) that the term *qarmaṭ* is derived from the word *karmitha*, 'cultivator', 'peasant', in the Lower Mesopotamian dialect of Syriac, i.e. Aramaic.

21 Ṭabarī. ser. III, p. 1757.

22 For the Carmathian state in Baḥrayn see below in present Chapter.

23 See: Bīrūnī, Arabic text p. 56; English translation vol. I, pp. 116 ff.

24 Whence 'esotericism', the common term denoting concealed religious doctrines disclosed only to a chosen few.

25 According to tradition Abū Ṭāhir used two pieces of the Black Stone as foot rests in the closet.

26 In the original the word *sulṭān* is obviously used in its old sense of 'government' 'authority'.

27 See Nāṣir-i Khusraw, Persian text, pp. 82–4; French translation, pp. 225–9; Russian translation, Ye. E. Bertel's, *Nāṣir-i Khusraw. Ṣafar-nāma*, pp. 179–83. There are some inaccuracies in the translation by Bertel's: instead of 'thirty bought slaves' it should be 'thirty thousand slaves purchased for money' (*sīhazār banda diram kharīda*); and the sentence *āsyāhā bāshad . . . kih mulk-i sulṭān bāshad* should be rendered: 'there are mills . . . belonging to the government' and not 'there are mills belonging to the Sultan'. It is obvious from the context that there was no Sultan in the sense of absolute ruler.

28 Belyayev, *Muslim Sectarianism*, p. 59.

29 W. Ivanow, *The Rise of the Fatimids*, text p. 9; Bertel's, *Nāṣir Khusraw and Ismā'īlism*, p. 82.

30 For whom see p. 221.
31 Except for a brief period of persecution in the time of Caliph al-Ḥākim (996–1021) who cruelly victimized first the Christians and Jews, and at the end of his reign turned his wrath against the Sunnis. The persecution ceased with his death. The official Fāṭimid confession is explained in W. Ivanow, *A Creed of the Fatimids.*
32 Not, of course, from Buddhism as some Islamists have supposed. Buddhist doctrine on regeneration has nothing in common with the idea of metempsychosis. Buddhism rejects the very concepts 'soul', 'personality' and 'unity of consciousness' as illusion; and replaces these by the concept of the stream of consciousness. This stream is liable to interruption (death), and the separated elements of the stream afterwards assemble in fresh combinations. Regeneration thus defined is not the continuation of a previous life in a new body; it is a new life containing only elements of a former one.
33 I.e. not saying anything of his own but only elucidating the words of the Prophet.
34 The *Nāṭiq* and *Ṣāmit*, however, are manifestations of Universal Reason and Universal Soul, but not incarnations (*ḥulūl*) of these, which was what people imputed to Ismā'īli doctrine.
35 For details of the theology and philosophy of the Carmathians see L. Massignon. 'Karmates', *EI.*
36 Belyayev, *Muslim Sectarianism*, p. 60.
37 In 1056 in Wāsiṭ, and in 1058 in Baghdad.
38 *Nāṣir-i Khusraw*, pp. 54, 55 ff.
39 Rashīdu d-Dīn Faḍlullāh (*Jāmi'u 't-Tawārīkh*, section on Ismā'īlī History) pp. 101–2.
40 Properly Āluh-āmūt (Pers.). Some sources translated this name as Eagle's Nest, but it is not clear in what dialect of Iran *āmūt* could mean 'nest'. Another more likely explanation is that Alamūt is a corruption of the words *āluh āmūkht* 'eagle's teaching', i.e. the place where eagles teach their fledgelings to fly. The Ismā'īlīs attached great significance to the fact that the sum of the numerical values (*abjad*) of the letters in the name *Āluh-āmūt* (1 + 30 + 5 + 1 + 40 + 6 + 400) comes to 483, which is the date of the castle's capture by Ḥasan b. Ṣabbāḥ (483 AH = 1090/91).
41 Son of 'Abdu 'l-Malik b. 'Aṭṭāsh, teacher of Ibn Ṣabbāḥ.
42 Two may be noticed: V. V. Bartol'd, *Chivalry and urban life in Persia under the Sāsānids and under Islam*; and his *History of peasant movements in Persia.*
43 Bartol'd, *History of peasant movements*, p. 61.
44 Pointed out in I. P. Petrushevskiy. 'Urban nobility in the Hūlāgūid state', '*Soviet Orientalism*', vol. v, 1948, p. 108.
45 A. Yu Yakubovskiy, *Feudal Society in Central Asia and its trade with Eastern Europe in the tenth to fifteenth centuries*, in the Collection, *Material for the history of the Tajik and Turkmen SSRs*, Pt. I. Leningrad, 1933, pp. 34–5.
46 Belyayev, *Muslim Sectarianism*, pp. 70–72.
47 Bertel's, *Nāṣir-i Khusraw and Ismā'īlism*, pp. 142–7.

48 Bertel's, p. 144.
49 Ibid.
50 See Bibliography.
51 For details see later in this chapter.
52 *Ḥashīsh* (or *bang*), a narcotic produced from hemp. On the method of preparation see Cl. Huart. 'Beng', *EI*, vol. I. In the eleventh and twelfth centuries hashish was as yet little known in Iran. People regarded this narcotic as a secret remedy with which few were acquainted.
53 Rashīdu 'd-Dīn Faḍlullāh (*Jāmi'u 't-Tawārīkh*, section on Ismā'īlī History) pp. 134–7, 144–5, 160–61. These lists indicate the social status of all the victims, but the social condition of the killers is only mentioned in a few cases: Ḥasan *sarrāj* (saddler, twice mentioned, pp. 136, 137); Ḥusayn *sarrāj* (p. 160); Muḥammad *ṣayyād* (fowler or trapper, twice mentioned, pp. 136, 137); and, lastly, a Russian slave (*ghulāmi rūsī*) who murdered Abu 'l-Fatḥ Dihistānī, vizier of the Seljuq Sultan Barkiyāruq in 490 AH = 1097 (p. 135). The Russian slave could well have been one of the many thousands of captives whom the Turk-Kypchaks (the 'Polovtsy' of the Russian sources) drove before them in the course of their raids on Kiev-Russia, and then sold to the countries of South-West Asia through the ports of the Crimea and the slave-dealers. The slave here mentioned had probably escaped to the Nizārīs of Alamūt and embraced their doctrine voluntarily. At all events, he could only have become a Fidā'i terrorist of his own volition. The Qābūs-nāma speaks of Russian slaves in Iran in the eleventh century. (ch. 23, p. 65).
54 I.e. 'newly converted Muslim'; the Sunnis had long refused to recognise Ismā'īlīs as Muslims.
55 See p. 234.
56 Preserved in the libraries of Stambul (Aya Sofya), Leyden and Cambridge.
57 *Textes houroufis*, édités et traduits par Clément Huart, Leyden–London, 1909 (*G M S*, IX).
58 Dr Riza Tëwfiq (Feylesuf Riza), *Etude sur la religion des houroufis*.
59 In the teaching of Orthodox Islam prophets stand above saints. With the Ḥurūfīs, on the contrary, saintliness is much higher than prophecy, being a stage of the divine manifestation.
60 The Ḥurūfīs did not acknowledge the twelfth Imam Muḥammad.
61 Mīrānshāh perished in 1408 in the battle of Sardrūd with the troops of Sultan Aḥmad Jalā'irid and his ally, Amīr Qāra Yūsuf Qāra Qoyūnlū.
62 See *Textes houroufis*, text p. 39; French translation p. 63.
63 From the standpoint of orthodox Islam the burning of a person, or of a corpse (and the consequent deprivation of burial according to Islamic rites) was deemed to be the greatest desecration. The bonfire was the symbol of the flames of hell awaiting the heretic's soul.
64 A translation of the whole extract from the *Mujmal* of Faṣīḥī was published by E. G. Browne in a special number of the journal *Muséon*, Cambridge University Press, 1915. See also Khwāndamīr, vol. III, pt. 3, Bombay edition, 1273 AH = 1856, pp. 127–8.
65 For detailed digressions on the Ḥurūfīs see E. G. Browne, *A Literary History of Persia*, vol. III, pp. 365–75, 449–52; E. J. W. Gibb, *A History of*

Ottoman Poetry, vol. I, London, 1901, pp. 336–88; and also the already mentioned study by Riza Tëwfiq.

66 See Chapter XIII.

67 V. A. Zhukovskiy, *The Sect of the People of Truth, the Ahl-i Ḥaqq in Persia*; V. F. Minorsky, *Material for the study of the Persian sect 'the People of Truth' or 'alī — ilāhī*; (and elsewhere in the same author's works); V. A. Gordlevskiy, *Qāra Qoyūnlū*.

68 Gordlevskiy, p. 15.

69 The Khlysts or 'Flagellants' (from the word *Khlyst* meaning 'whip') were a secret religious sect dating from the seventeenth century whose meetings were associated with singing and ardent invocations termed *radeniye* (which is 'zeal').

70 For a description of the ecstatic invocation see, apart from the literature cited on *Ahl-i Ḥaqq*, Yu. N. Marr, *Ecstasy of the People of Truth Sect*, pp. 248–54.

Chapter XII Mysticism in Islam

1 See Ye. E. Bertel's, *Sufism and Sufi Literature*, Moscow, 1965.

2 In part this interest has been sustained by the religious reaction and the taste for idealism and mysticism among the upper strata in Western capitalist societies these last 60 to 75 years.

3 One of the few exceptions is F. Babinger, *Schejch Bedr ad-din*.

4 A. J. Arberry, *An introduction to the history of Sufism*, pp. 58–61.

5 The extent to which this author exaggerates the influence of Christianity can be gauged from the very title of his work 'El Islam cristianizado' (Islam Christianized), 1931, where he even attempts to trace the pure pantheism of Ibnu 'l-'Arabī (thirteenth century) to a Christian source.

6 See Bibliography.

7 For the works of R. Nicholson and L. Massignon see Bibliography.

8 L. Massignon, *Essai sur les origines du lexique technique de la mystique musulmane*.

9 Massignon, pp. 29–32.

10 Massignon, p. 84.

11 Gundishāpūr (in Ar. Jundaysābūr; Syr. Bet Lapat), a city in Khūzistān founded by Shāpur I (241–272) and peopled by him with Syrian and Greek captives. It became a centre of Syrian Christian (Nestorian) culture in Iran, and a great School of Medicine was established there in the sixth century.

12 See Chapter IX, pp. 189–90.

13 I. Goldziher, *Lectures on Islam*, pp. 136 ff.

14 St Matthew 6:25–34; St Luke 12:22–30.

15 Goldziher, *Lectures*, pp. 140–41; cf. D. B. Macdonald, *Development of Muslim Theology*, pp. 179–80.

16 Goldziher, *Lectures*, p. 142.

17 For anti-ascetic attitudes in the age of the Umayyads, see Goldziher, *Lectures on Islam*, pp. 127–36.

18 *Lā rahbāniyyata fī 'l-Islām*.

19 However Shaykhs would frequently live at convents with their families.
20 For writings attributed to Dhu 'n-Nūn see C. Brockelmann, *Geschichte der arabischen Literatur*, vol. I, pp. 198–99.
21 A work specifically on al-Ḥallāj is L. Massignon, *La passion d'al-Halladj, martyr mystique de l'Islam.*
22 He was publicly flogged, his hands were cut off, he was suspended upside down on a gibbet, he was pelted with stones; and finally he was beheaded and his body burned. For his opinions see below.
23 For Dhikr and Ṣūfī practices generally see below in present chapter.
24 This had its genesis among Junayd's disciples in Iraq, but it gained particular hold in Khurāsān and passed from there to Central Asia.
25 Year of birth and year of death unknown.
26 Certain European authors call these hostels monasteries. This is not quite appropriate since Dervishes, although they practise asceticism, make no vow of celibacy and may, when they leave the hostel, marry or return to a family which they have forsaken for a time.
27 From Fr. *l'ancre.* The term, evidently known from the time of the Crusades, is met with in Jāmī (fifteenth century) in the sense of Dervish cloister.
28 In Turkish and Ādharbāyjānī pronunciation *mürid*, a form in which it has entered Russian. cf. Russian 'myuridizm'.
29 In Central Asia also *īshān* (Pers.), 'they', a term of respect for a teacher.
30 In the Dervish brotherhood founded by the notable Persian poet and Shaykh, Jalālu 'd-Dīn Rūmī (see below in this chapter), the novitiate lasted 1001 days: for 40 days the novice did duty as ostler in the cloister, for another 40 days he cleaned the latrines, for 40 days he carried water, for 40 days he swept the courtyard, for 40 days he fetched firewood, for 40 days he worked as cook, and so on. The discharge of burdensome and humiliating tasks was calculated to break his pride and test his humility and his readiness to carry out whatever the Shaykh ordered, and serve the convent.
31 Ibnu 'l-Munawwar, p. 26; cf. *Ḥālat o Sukhanān*, p. 12.
32 Koran VI 91.
33 Koran XXXIII 41.
34 The corresponding extract from Part IV of the *Iḥyā'u 'ulūmi 'd-dīn* has been published in an English translation, D. B. Macdonald, *Emotional religion in Islam as affected by music and singing.*
35 *Jullābī Hujwīrī*. p. 216.
36 Two biographies of him in Persian both written in the latter half of the twelfth century have been edited by V. A. Zhukovskiy, St Petersburg, 1899: *Ḥālat o Sukhanān-i Shaykh Abī Sa'īd* ('Life and sayings of Shaykh Abū Sa'īd') by an unknown author; and *Asrāru 't-tawḥīd fī maqāmāti 'sh-Shaykh Abī Sa'īd.* ('Secrets of the Knowledge of Divine Unity in the stations of the mystical path of Shaykh Abū Sa'īd') by Muḥammad b. al-Munawwar. N.B. V. A. Zhukovskiy's translation 'Secrets of Unity with God in the exploits of Sh. Abū Sa'īd' is inadequate.
37 His biography (author and date of composition unknown, but not later than twelfth century) has been edited from a unique MS in the British Museum by Ye. E. Bertel's. See Bibliography to Chapter XII.

38 Kharaqānī, Pers. text p. 188; translation p. 216.
39 Kharaqānī, text, p. 181; translation p. 209.
40 Kharaqānī, text, p. 182; translation p. 209.
41 Kharaqānī, text, p. 175. *yakī parhīz dovvom sakhāvat seyyom bī niāz būdan az khalq-i khudā-yi 'azza wa jalla*. The same definition occurs in Faridu 'd-Din 'Aṭṭār, only the order of the sources is changed.
42 Kharaqānī, text, p. 179; translation p. 207.
43 B. Carra de Vaux and M. Asín Palacios detect the source of the idea of *fanā'* in the mysticism of Eastern Christianity.
44 *Jullābī Hujwīrī*, p. 316.
45 Massignon, *Essai sur les origines du lexique*, pp. 95 ff.
46 A play on words: *bāzārī* and *bā zārī*.
47 *Dawlatshāh*, pp. 187–8 (in biography of 'Aṭṭār).
48 See D. B. Macdonald, *The religious attitude and life in Islam*, p. 159.
49 Qazwīnī, *Nuzhatu 'l-Qulūb*, p. 81. Feudal seigneurs, such as the well-known Vizier and historian Rashīdu 'd-Dīn, his sons Vizier Ghiyāthu 'd-Dīn Muḥammad and Amīr Aḥmad Rashīdī, and the Mongol Amir Chūbān, were accounted murīds of this Shaykh.
50 For the Ghazālī system of Kalām see Chapter IX.
51 All these terms are Arabic and have their technical Sufi meaning.
52 In Ṣūfī circles the Arabic proverb had apparently been coined that the craftsman is God's friend — *al-kāsibu habību 'llāh*.
53 Al-Ghazālī wrote a special treatise on 'Contempt of the World', *Dhammu 'd-Dunya*.
54 A common custom of strangers and mendicants in Muslim countries.
55 *Iḥyā'u 'Ulūmi 'd-Dīn*, vol. IV. Cairo, 1289 AH = 1872. pp. 308 ff.
56 This analogy was customary with Ṣūfī authors, and especially the poets.
57 See M. Asín Palacios, *La mystique d'al-Ghazzali*, pp. 101–02.
58 He was held to be a descendant of the half-legendary Ḥātim of Ṭayy.
59 For the meaning of these terms see Chapter V.
60 C. Brockelmann, *Geschichte der arabischen Literatur*, vol. I, p. 441.
61 D. B. Macdonald, *Development of Muslim Theology*, p. 262.
62 For list see C. Brockelmann, *Geschichte der arabische Literatur*, vol. I. pp. 442–8.
63 For the works of Ibnu 'l-'Arabī see Bibliography.
64 See p. 99.
65 Arberry, *An introduction*, p. 58.
66 *Wujūdu 'l-makhlūqāti 'ayn wujūdu 'l-khāliq*.
67 See I. Goldziher, *Die Zahiriten*, Leipzig 1884, p. 132; and the same author's *Lectures on Islam*, p. 157.
68 For the meaning of these terms see p. 234
69 For Ibnu 'l-'Arabī see Bibliography.
70 On the African shore of the Straits of Gibraltar.
71 Sometimes confused with the great (Persian-writing) historian Kamālu 'd-Dīn 'Abdu 'r-Razzāq of Samarqand (1413–1482).
72 See D. B. Macdonald, "Abdu 'r-Razzāq Kāshānī'.
73 For studies on 'Abdu 'r-Razzāq Kāshānī see Bibliography to this chapter.
74 This is included in the biography of the Shaykhs of the Mevlevi order

(for which see below in this chapter) written in the mid-fourteenth century by Afḍalu 'd-Dīn Aflākī, entitled *Manāqibu 'l-'Ārifīn* or 'Stations on the mystical path of those that have had knowledge'. Persian text not published; French translation by Cl. Huart.

75 Abū Sa'īd's biographer Muḥammad b. al-Munawwar maintained that this Shaykh never wrote verses.

76 Pupil of the well-known Ṣūfī Shaykh Ṣadru 'd-Dīn of Konia who had attended in that place his course of lectures on the *Fuṣūṣu 'l-Ḥikam* of Ibnu 'l-'Arabī. Influenced by these lectures, 'Irāqī wrote a philosophical work in prose, the *Lama'āt*, or 'Effulgences'.

77 An ardent follower of Ibnu 'l-'Arabī. His poetical pseudonym Maghribī was accounted for by his having received the Dervish Khirqa in Maghrib from a certain Shaykh who took his spiritual continuity from Ibnu 'l-'Arabī.

78 The eponymous founder of the order of the *Ni'matullāhiyya* (see below).

79 This conventional vocabulary was developed under the influence of Sūfīs of the school of the *Malāmatiyya* (see above) which taught that the Ṣūfī ought to hide his piety behind a mask of flippancy or even cynicism.

80 Allegory and symbolism of this sort were facilitated by the absence of gender in Persian grammar. The words *dūst* and *yār* mean 'friend' and 'beloved', masculine or feminine indifferently. It was left to the reader to guess whom the poet had in mind: whether God the Friend or an inamorata; whether the love that is expressed is mystical or of this earth and sensual.

81 Ye. E. Bertel's, *Outline history of Persian Literature*, pp. 52, 53.

82 See Chapter IX.

83 *Jāmī*. pp. 13 ff.

84 F. Engels, 'Peasant War in Germany', Marx and Engels, *Works*, 7, p. 361.

85 For more details on Dervish orders see L. Massignon. 'Tarika', *EI*, where there is a classification, albeit incomplete, of orders and a bibliography of sources and text-books.

86 Not to be confused with Yaḥyā as-Suhrawardī, surnamed al-Maqtūl, executed in 1191, who founded the order of the *Ishrāqiyya*, 'the Enlightened'.

87 Jalālu 'd-Dīn Rūmī usually called *Mawlānā* ('Our lord'), whence the designation of the order of the *Mawlawiyya*.

88 *Aflākī*, p. 117.

89 For bibliography of sources on Naqshband, A. A. Semenov, *The Bukhārā Shaykh Bahā'u 'd-Dīn*, pp. 202–04, note.

90 According to the biographies his entire property consisted of an old mat and a broken pitcher. He earned his bread by handicraft, and thought it wrong for a Ṣūfī to have servants or slaves. He lived with his wife as with a sister. Invited to the table of the Herāt ruler, he ate nothing at the repast saying that he was a friend of the common people and a Dervish. His tomb, which became a place of pilgrimage, is near Bukhārā.

91 For this evolution of the order see below.

92 By the eighteenth and nineteenth centuries the order had become widespread in Dāghistān. The Naqshbandī ṭarīqa was the ideology of

the movement called 'murīdism', as of its leaders Qāḍī Mullā, Ḥamzat Bek, and Shāmil.

93 But see G. Jacob. 'Die Bektashije', Abh. Königl. Bayerisch. Akad. Wiss. I Kl., XXIV, III Part. Münich, 1909, p. 24. Jacob thinks the real founder of the order was Balim-bābā at the turn of the fifteenth century.

94 See Chapter XI.

95 See Chapter XIII.

96 *Ibn Baṭṭūṭa*, vol. III, pp. 79–80.

97 The biography of this Shaykh and poet, together with the texts relating to him taken from the historical sources, have been published by Jean Aubin (see Bibliography to ch. XII under 'Kermani').

98 Lithogr. edn. of his Dīwān: Tehran 1276 AH = 1860.

99 In Persian, under the title *Rashaḥāti 'Aynu 'l-Ḥayāt* ('Little drops from the spring of life').

100 This term (synonym *juft-i gāw* lit. 'pair of oxen') signifies (a) team of bullocks for ploughing; (b) parcel of land for ploughing, i.e. the plot which can be tilled by one team for a season, here 8–9 hectares. (See P. P. Ivanov, *Husbandry of the Jūybārī Shaykhs*, p. 10, note 4).

101 Kāshifī, pp. 327–8.

102 A copy of the ukase is inserted in the life of Jāmī written by 'Abdu 'l-Wāsi'. For Persian text with Russian translation see A. A. Molchanov, *Description of the tax-system in Herāt in the time of 'Alī Shīr Nawā'ī* in the Collection, *Father of Ubzek Literature*, Tashkent, 1940, pp. 156–61.

Chapter XIII The triumph of Shī'ism in Iran

1 See Chapter X.

2 See Chapter X, p. 209.

3 F. Engels, 'Peasant War in Germany', Marx and Engels, *Works*, 7, p. 361.

4 F. Engels, 'Ludwig Feuerbach and the end of classical German philosophy', Marx and Engels, *Works*, 21, p. 294.

5 Qazwīnī, *Nuzhatu 'l-Qulūb*, pp. 31, 38, 40.

6 Qazwīnī, pp. 45, 60, 67, 68, 69, 74 respectively.

7 Qazwīnī, pp. 62–3.

8 Qazwīnī, pp. 67–8.

9 Qazwīnī, p. 159.

10 In particular on Māzandarān see Dawlatshāh, p. 282; Ẓahīru 'd-Dīn Mar'ashī, pp. 340 ff., 346 (on the enormous influence of the Shī'ite Dervish Shaykh Qawāmu 'd-Dīn — for whom, see below in this chapter).

11 Qazwīnī, p. 150.

12 Qazwīnī, pp. 60–61, 65.

13 It is merely stated that Ḥanafites predominated in Tustar (Qazwīnī, p. 110). Khūzistān is known to have been one of the hotbeds of the Mu'tazilites in the tenth century (see V. V. Bartol'd, *Historico-Geographical Survey of Iran*, p. 129). According to the historian Ja'farī there were many Shī'ites in Khūzistān in the fifteenth century.

14 Only in Hamadān, to go by Ḥamdullāh Qazwīnī (*Nuzhatu 'l-Qulūb*, p. 71), were the inhabitants Mu'tazilites and anthropomorphists (*mushabbiha*). But this information is possibly taken from much earlier sources and it appears to be an anachronism for the fourteenth century.
15 For *taqiyya* see Chapter x.
16 Qazwīnī, *Nuzhatu 'l-Qulūb*, pp. 49, 58, 59, 62, 66, 68, 74, 77, 81, 84, 89, 115. At Marāgha alone Sunnī Ḥanafites predominated (Qazwīnī, p. 87).
17 Qazwīnī, pp. 150, 152, 154.
18 See also N. D. Miklukho-Maklay, *Shī'ism and its social face in Iran at the turn of the fifteenth century*.
19 See Chapter x, pp. 225–6.
20 For details, I. P. Petrushevskiy, *Agriculture and Agrarian Relations in Iran*, pp. 414–6.
21 Waṣṣāf, pp. 191–2.
22 Waṣṣāf tells of the plight of the ryots of Fārs as early as 718 AH = 1318 in consequence of high taxes, and the malpractices and extortion of officials (pp. 630 ff.).
23 Ḥāfiẓ-i Abrū, geograph. works MS. IVAN Uz.SSR, 5361 (without heading), sheet 394 b.
24 All Iranian *narodnost's* were at that time called Tājīk.
25 Ẓahīru 'd-Dīn Mar'ashī, pp. 103–4.
26 The story of Shaykh Khalīfa is told in the pages of *Ḥāfiẓ-i Abrū* (Historic. works MS. IVAN UzSSR 4078, sheets 472a–74a), and *Mīrkhwānd* (Lucknow, 1300 AH = 1883, pp. 1081–84). Both these fifteenth-century authors used in the main the anonymous 'History of the Sarbadārs' which has not come down to us. Dawlatshāh cites an independent version (ed. E. Browne, pp. 277 ff.). For more details see Petrushevskiy, *Agriculture and Agrarian Relations in Iran*, pp. 428–33, and references to sources in the same work.
27 *Ḥāfiẓ-i Abrū*, Historic. Works, MS cited above, sheet 474a.
28 *Ḥāfiẓ-i Abrū*, and also in *Mīrkhwānd*, p. 1083.
29 *Dawlatshāh*, p. 282.
30 *Mīrkhwānd*, pp. 1084–5; *Ḥāfiẓ-i Abrū*, sheets 475b–77b.
31 *Ḥāfiẓ-i Abrū*, sheet 474a; *Mīrkhwānd*, p. 1081; *Mujmali Faṣīḥī* MS INA V-709, sheets 358b–59a. The primary source of this version is the 'History of the Sarbadārs'.
32 *Ḥāfiẓ-i Abrū*, sheet 474a; *Mīrkhwānd*, p. 1081. The name 'Sarbadārs' is thus explained in the 'History of the Sarbadārs'. There were, however, other explanations of it.
33 For details, I. P. Petrushevskiy, *Agriculture and Agrarian Relations*, ch. IX, pp. 409–66, and references to sources.
34 *Ḥāfiẓ-i Abrū*, sheet 479b; *Mīrkhwānd*, p. 1084. These 'Shaykhites' must not be confounded with the very much later sect of the same name.
35 *Mīrkhwānd*, p. 1086; *Dawlatshāh*, p. 287.
36 Cf. Tughāy Tīmūr Khān's remark about the Sarbadār army: 'You are a handful of peasants' (Pers. *shumā musht-i rūstāī*) (*Mīrkhwānd*, p. 1085).
37 Both Mongol and Turkish nomads were referred to as Turks at that time.
38 *Ibn Baṭṭūṭa* (vol. III, pp. 70–71) portrays the warriors of this horde as plunderers and robbers.

39 *Ḥāfiẓ-i Abrū*, Historic. Works MS cited, sheet 480b; *Dawlatshāh*, p. 237; *Mīrkhwānd*, p. 1087.
40 *Dawlatshāh*, p. 283.
41 *Ḥāfiẓ-i Abrū*, Geograph. Works, MS cited, sheet 242b.
42 For details, V. V. Bartol'd, *The place of the Caspian provinces*, pp. 82–4; Petrushevskiy, *Agriculture*, pp. 467–70.
43 *Pīshvā-yi darvīshān-i ḥasaniyya* (*Dawlatshāh*, p. 282). Shaykh Ḥasan Jūrī fell in the battle of Zāwa in 1342 with the army of the Malik of Herāt.
44 Ibid.
45 Ẓahīru 'd-Dīn Mar'ashī, p. 345.
46 A man's outdoor clothing, a sort of kaftan.
47 Ẓahīru 'd-Dīn Mar'ashī, p. 342.
48 *Kurr* (Ar.) is a dry measure, varying in different localities.
49 Ẓahīru 'd-Dīn Mar'ashī, pp. 342, 343.
50 See V. V. Bartol'd, *A popular movement in Samarqand, 1365*; L. V. Stroyeva, *Sarbadārs of Samarqand.*
51 For Ḥurūfīs see Chapter XI.
52 On the revolt of Musha'sha' see V. V. Bartol'd, *A new source on the history of the Tīmūrids* (pp. 23–5), text of unedited Persian work of Ja'farī (fifteenth century). See also V. Minorsky, *Musha'sha'*.
53 Quoted in article, A. S. Stepanov, *The work of Ducas as source for the history of the rising of Börklüe Mustafa*, pp. 99 ff. For this rising see also F. Babinger, *Schejch Bedr ed-din . . .*; A. S. Tveritinova, *Towards the study of the first anti-feudal upheaval in Turkey*; A. D. Novichev, *A peasant rising in Turkey at the beginning of the fifteenth century*.
54 See Chapter XII.
55 See: I. P. Petrushevskiy, *The Ādharbāyjān State in the fifteenth century*; O. A. Efendiyev, *The formation of an Ādharbāyjān Ṣafawid State in the early sixteenth century*; V. Minorsky, *The supporters of the Lords of Ardabīl*; and the same author's *Shaykh Bali-efendi on the Safavids*; H. R. Roemer, *Die Safawiden*; Aḥmad Kasravī, *Shaykh Ṣafī va tabārash* (in Persian); J. Aubin, *Etudes Safavides*, I.

When the present book was still in the press, an article by P. I. Petrov appeared, entitled 'Data in the sources on the composition of the military contingents of Isma'il I'. Petrov's controversy with the present author will be touched on in a special article.
56 The best MS is in LGPB, Catalogue of B. Dorn No. 300 (from the library of the mosque of the Ṣafawids in Ardabīl); also Bombay lithogr. edn. 1323 AH = 1911.
57 Cambridge MS. Add. 202; Br. Mus. Or., 3248; a portion of this work was published (Persian text) by D. Denison Ross (JRAS, April 1896, pp. 249–340).
58 See Bibliography.
59 Of the volumes which have been preserved vol. XI has not been published. In LGPB there is a MS (Catalogue B. Dorn No. 287); vol. XII has been edited by C. N. Seddon.
60 *Lubbu 't-Tawārīkh*. Tehran, 1315 AH sol. = 1936.
61 An abridged English translation has been published by V. F. Minorsky (see Bibliography). The Persian text has not been published.

62 In not a single one of the writings or documents of the fourteenth century is Shaykh Ṣafiyyu 'd-Dīn named as a Sayyid or descendant of the Imams. Nor does Rashīdi 'd-Dīn so style him in his extremely deferential letter to him (Rashīdu 'd-Dīn Faḍlullāh, *Mukātabat-i Rashīdī* pp. 265 ff.).

63 Louis Massignon considers the Ṣafawiyya to be 'an Ādharbāyjānī branch of the Suhrawardiyya'. (L. Massignon. 'Tarika'. *EI*, vol. IV).

64 Qazwīnī, *Nuzhatu 'l-Qulūb*, p. 81.

65 Faḍlullāh b. Rūzbihān Khunjī, p. 62.

66 See I. P. Petrushevskiy, *Urban nobility in the Hūlāgūid State*, p. 104.

67 The jarīb as a measure of weight is the same as the kharwār. The Tabrīz kharwār = 100 maunds = 295 kg; 1 Tabrīz maund = 2950 g.

68 Rashīdu 'd-Dīn Faḍlullāh (*Mukātabat-i Rashīdī*) pp. 265–72.

69 Qazwīnī, *Nuzhatu 'l-Qulūb*, p. 81.

70 Was he not secretly a Shī'ite? It is known that Shī'ites at that time often availed themselves of the rule of *taqiyya* and gave out that they were Sunnīs of the Shāfi'ite school. In favour of this hypothesis is the fact that Shaykh Ṣadru 'd-Dīn's disciple and friend, the mystical poet Qāsimu 'l-Anwār (1357–1434), was a Shī'ite who began as an Imāmī and later joined the Ḥurūfīs.

71 J. Aubin, *Etudes Safavides*, I, p. 46.

72 Faḍlullāh b. Rūzbihān Khunjī, pp. 65–6.

73 Capital of the Greek Trebizond 'empire' (1204–61).

74 See F. I. Uspenskiy, *Outline history of the Trebizond empire*, Leningrad 1929, p. 133, containing references to the fifteenth-century Greek historian Chalcocondyles. The latter calls Junayd 'Shaykh Ertebil', as though this (Ardabīl) were a personal name, not a place-name.

75 Dāghistān was still only to a small extent Islamized in the fifteenth century.

76 See F. Babinger, *Marino Sanuto's Tagebücher als Quelle zur Geschichte der Safawijja*, pp. 34–5.

77 Aubin, *Etudes Safavides*, I, p. 50.

78 Caterino Zeno, pp. 43–4. According to Faḍlullāh b. Rūzbihān's story (p. 70), Ḥaydar took and enslaved 6000 captives in the campaign against 'the country of the Circassians' in 892 AH = 1487.

79 Ḥasan Rūmlū, MS. LGPB sheets 156–8 (in much detail); Khwāndamīr, Bombay edn. vol. III, pt. 4, pp. 16–18; *Sharaf-nāma*, vol. II, St Petersburg, 1862, pp. 127, 133; Iskandar Munshī, Tehran lithogr. edn. 1314 AH = 1896/97, p. 16.

80 See Faḍlullāh b. Rūzbihān Khunjī, p. 71. According to Minorsky's conjecture 'the people dressed in blue' is the peasantry which wore clothing of homespun blue cotton yarn. The Tālish, as is known, were settled peasants, and not nomads. They were the only Iranians who had entered the brotherhood of the Qizil Bāshes.

81 See Faḍlullāh b. Rūzbihān Khunjī, p. 68.

82 The written instrument of the Shīrwānshāh's oath of allegiance is quoted by Ḥasan Rūmlū, loc. cit. For translation and analysis of the text of this instrument see article: I. P. Petrushevskiy, *History of Shīrwān at the end of the fifteenth century*, pp. 87–91.

83 See Faḍlullāh b. Rūzbihān Khunjī, pp. 67–8.
84 See Chapter XII.
85 For details of these attempts at reform see: I. P. Petrushevskiy, *The home policy of Aḥmad Āq-Qoyūnlū*, pp. 144–53; V. Minorsky, *The Aq Qoyunlu and land reforms*.
86 For details see I. P. Petrushevskiy, *The Ādharbāyjān State in the fifteenth century*, pp. 227–35.
87 One ought rather to take the year when Ismā'īl entered Tabrīz for the first time: 906 AH 1500/1.
88 Ḥasan Rūmlū, Persian text, p. 61.
89 Its then limits embraced the Nīshāpūr, Herāt and Merv areas. The Balkh area remained in Uzbek hands.
90 See Aubin, *Etudes Safavides*, I, pp. 53 ff.
91 See I. P. Petrushevskiy, *Ādharbāyjān in the sixteenth and seventeenth centuries*. Collection of articles on the history of Ādharbāyjān, Baku, 1949, pp. 244–6; Aubin, *Etudes Safarides*, I, pp. 37 ff.
92 Understanding by the term 'Turkmens' all the descendants of the Oghuz; of whom a portion had gone into the composition of the Turkmen people, another portion into that of the Ādharbāyjān people, and a third portion into that of the Turkish people.
93 Taking the state of the Seljūqids to be the first phase, and the states of the Kāra-koyūnlū and Āk-koyūnlū to be the second phase.
94 See the memoirs of Angiolello (p. 115) and of an anonymous Venetian merchant (pp. 189 ff.).
95 Khwāndamīr, vol. III, pt. 4, p. 35.
96 See I. P. Petrushevskiy. *Outline history of feudal relations in Ādharbāyjān and Armenia* . . ., ch. II.
97 *Bīsh bād kam ma-bād.*
98 For details see N. D. Miklukho-Maklay, *Shi'ism and its social face.*
99 Ḥasan Rūmlū. Persian text, p. 61.
100 A white horse was always kept ready-saddled at the court of the Ṣafawids in the sixteenth century, against the day of the Imam Mahdī's return; and one of the daughters of the royal family would not be given in marriage, but earmarked as his bride.
101 Anthony Jenkinson (1561), agent of the English 'Muscovy Company', describes the mode of life of one of the representatives of the Qizil Bāsh nobility 'Abdullāh-Khān Ustājlū, Beglerbeg (vice-regent) of Shīrwān. He reports him as a man of middle height, of ferocious aspect, richly clad in lengthy garments of silk and brocade embroidered with pearls and precious stones, the floor of whose marquee was spread with fine rugs, and at whose board 140 dishes and 150 platters of fruit and sweets, making 290 in all, would be served. He was a man who did not sleep at night but made merry with the women of his harem, of whom he had 140, and slept the greater part of the day. At his command Jenkinson would take part, along with the crowd of nobles of the court, in falconry and various diversions and amusements. Of the Qizil Bāshes (whom he mistakenly took to be Persians) Jenkinson narrates that they were proud and brave, considering themselves the best of all peoples, both for their beliefs and piety and for their other qualities. They were martial in

spirit, great lovers of splendid well-caparisoned steeds, and were hot-tempered, cunning and cruel. (See in the Collection: *English travellers in the Moscow State in the sixteenth century*, translation from Engl. by Yu. V. Got'ye, Leningrad, 1937, pp. 203–04, 213.).

102 Tadhkiratu 'l-Mulūk. Persian text, sheets 29b–30a; English translation, p. 55, and commentary by V. F. Minorsky p. 125.

Bibliography

Classics of Marxism-Leninism, in Russian editions

Most of the references below are to K. Marx and F. Engels, *Works*, published in Moscow. Volume numbers and dates are given.

Marx, K., *Capital*, vols. 1–3, in Works, vols. 23–25, parts I and II (1960–61).

——, *Declaration of War: The history of the rise of the Eastern Question*, *Works*, vol. 10 (1958).

——, Letter to Engels of 2 June 1853, *Works*, vol. 28 (1962).

——, *Forms preceding capitalist production*, Gospolitizdat, 1940.

Engels, F., *History of primary Christianity*, *Works*, vol. 22 (1961).

——, *Peasant war in Germany*, *Works*, vol. 7 (1956).

——, *Ludwig Feuerbach and the end of classical German philosophy*, *Works*, vol. 21 (1961).

——, Letter to Marx of 6 June 1853, *Works*, vol. 28 (1962).

——, *Origin of the family, of private property and of the state*, *Works*, vol. 21 (1961).

General literature

Sources

Abu 'l-Ma'ālī, *Bayānu 'l-Adyān*, in Ch. Schefer, *Chrestomathie Persane*, vol. I (Paris, 1883) (extract from Persian text).

Bīrūnī, *Alberuni's Chronologie orientalischer Völker*, hrsg Dr E. Sachau (Leipzig, 1878) (Arabic text).

——, *Chronology of Ancient Nations* . . ., trs Dr E. Sachau (London, 1879).

Wāqidī, *Al-Waqidi, History of Muhammed's campaigns* (Kitab al-maghazi) ed A. von Kremer (Calcutta, 1856) *BI* (Arabic text).

——, *Muhammed in Medina* (Waqidi's Kitab al-maghazi), trs J. Wellhausen (Berlin, 1882) (German translation).

Dawlatshāh, *The Tadhkirat ash-shu 'ara . . . of Dawlatshah*, ed E. G. Browne, (London-Leyden, 1901) (Persian text).

Ibnu 'l-Athīr, *Ibn al-Athiri Chronicon* . . ., ed C. I. Tornberg, vols. I–XIV (LB, 1851–76) (Arabic text and indexes).

Ibnu 'l-Balkhī, *The Fars-nama* . . ., ed G. Le Strange and R. A. Nicholson (London, 1921) GMS NS, 1 (Persian text).

Ibn Baṭṭūṭa, *Voyages d'Ibn Batoutah* . . ., by C. Defrémery and B. Sanguinetti, vols. I–IV (Paris, 1854–9) (Arabic text and parallel French translation).

Ibn Miskawayhi, *see* Miskawayh.

Ibn Nadīm, *Fihrist*, Ibn an-Nadim al-Warraq, *Fihrist*..., ed G. Flügel, vols. I–II (Leipzig, 1871–2) (Arabic text).
Ibn Ḥazm, *Kitābu 'l-fasl fī 'l-milal*, vols. I–V (Cairo, 1317–21 (1899–03)).
Ibn Khaldūn, *Prolégomènes d'Ebn Khaldoun*, published by E. Quatremère, 'Notices et Extraits' vols. XVI–XVIII (Paris, 1858–61) (Arabic text).
——, *Prolégomènes*... trs M. C. [MacGuckin] de Slane, 'Notices et Extraits' vols. XIX–XXI (Paris, 1862–8) (French translation).
Ibn Khallikān, *Ibn Challikani Vitae illustrium virorum*, ed F. Wüstenfeld, fasc I–XIII (Göttingae, 1835–43) (Arabic text).
——, *Ibn Challikan's biographical dictionary*, trs Baron MacGuckin de Slane, vols. I–IV (Paris, 1842–71) (English translation).
Iṣṭakhrī, *Viae regnorum*..., ed M. J. de Goeje (LB, 1870) BGA vol. I, ed 2 (LB, 1927) BGA, vol. I (Arabic text).
Ya'qūbī, Ta'rīkh, *Ibn Wadhih... Historiae*, ed M. T. Houtsma, parts 1–2. (LB, 1883) (Arabic text).
Yāqūt, Irshād, *The Irshad al-arib*... or Dictionary of learned men, ed D. S. Margoliouth, vols. I–VII (London-Leyden, 1907–27) GMS VI/1–7 (Arabic text).
——, Mu'jamu 'l-Buldān, *Yaqut's Geographisches Wörterbuch*, trs F. Wüstenfeld, Bd I–VI (Leipzig, 1866–73) (Arabic text and indexes).
Qazwīnī, Ḥamdullah Mustawfī, *Nuzhatu 'l-Qulūb. The geographical part of Nuzhat al-qulub*..., ed G. Le Strange (Leyden-London, 1915) GMS XXIII/1–2 (Persian text and English translation).

Concordances to the Koran, *Concordantiae Corani Arabicae*, ed G. Flügel (Lipsiae 1898).
Koran: *Corani textus Arabicus*, ed G. Flügel (Lipsiae, 1869) (Arabic text).
——, Al-Qur'ān (Cairo, 1338 (1919–20)) (Arabic text).
——, Al-Qur'ān, ed Ḥājjī Muḥammad Ḥusayn Qajurānī (Tehran, 1341 (1923)) lithogr. (Arabic text with Persian interlinear translation and concordances).
——, Al-Qur'ān, ed Baṣīru 'l-Mulk. (Tehran, 1314 (1896)) lithogr. (Arabic text with parallel Persian translation and kashfu 'l-ayāt — concordance).
——, ed G. S. Sablukov, 3rd edn (Kazan', 1907) (Arabic text with parallel Russian translation).
——, Russian translation commentaries and appendices. Acad. I. Yu. Krachkovskiy, ed V. I. Belyayev (Moscow, 1963).
Maqdisī, *see* Muqaddasī.
Mas'ūdī, Murūj, *Maçoudi, Les prairies d'or*..., C. Barbier de Meynard and Pavet de Courteille, vols. I–IX (Paris, 1861–77) (Arabic text with parallel French translation).
——, Tanbīh, *Kitāb at-tanbīh wa 'l-ishraf*, ed M. J. de Goeje (LB, 1894) BGA vol. VIII (Arabic text).
Mīrkhwānd, Rawḍatu 'ṣ-Ṣafā, vols. I–VII lithogr. edn Persian text in one vol. (Lucknow, 1300 (1883)); Bombay 1266 (1849)); new edn (Tehran, 1338–9 (1959–60) (Persian text and indexes).
Miskawayh (Ibn Miskawayhi), ed Caetani. *The Tajarib al-umam*..., reproduced in facsimile..., by L. Caetani vols. I,V,VI (London, 1909–17) GMS VII (Arabic text).

——, ed Amedroz-Margoliouth, *Experiences of the nations* . . ., vols. V–VI (*The eclipse of the Abbasid Caliphate*, vols. I–II) (Oxford, 1920–1) (Arabic text and English translation).

Muqaddasī (Maqdisī), *Descriptio imperii Moslemici auctore* . . . *al-Moqaddasi*, ed M. Y. de Goeje (LB, 1872) BGA vol. III; 2nd edn (LB, 1906) BGA vol. III (Arabic text).

Niẓāmu 'l-Mulk, *Siasset-Nameh* . . ., ed Ch. Schefer (Paris, 1891) (Persian text).

——, *Siyāsat-nāma* . . ., Russian translation with Introduction and Notes, B. N. Zakhoder (Moscow-Leningrad, 1949).

Sam'ānī, *The Kitab al-ansab* . . ., ed D. S. Margoliouth (Leyden-London, 1912) GMS XX (facsimile of Arabic text).

Ṭabarī, *Annales quos scripsit* . . . *at-Tabari*, ed M. J. de Goeje cum aliis, ser. I–III, vols. I–XIII (LB, 1879–01) (Arabic text with Introduction, Glossary and Indexes).

Ḥājjī Khalīfa, *Kashfu 'ẓ-Ẓunūn 'an asāmī al-Kutub wa 'l-funūn. Lexicon bibliographicum et encyclopaedicum* . . . *primum*, ed G. Flügel, vols. I–VII (Leipzig-London, 1835–58) (Arabic text, Latin translation, Commentaries and Index).

Khwāndamīr, *Ḥabību 's-Siyar*, vols. I–III (Bombay, 1273 (1856–7)) (Lithograph of Persian text); new edn Jalālu 'd-Dīn Humay, vols. I–IV (Tehran, 1333 H.S. (1954)) (Persian text with Editor's Foreword).

Khwārazmī, Abu 'Abdillāh Muḥammad, *Liber Māfatih al-'olum* . . ., ed van Vloten (LB, 1895) (Arabic text).

Shahrastānī, *Kitābu 'l-Milal wa 'l-Niḥal* ed W. Cureton, parts I–II. (London, 1842–6) (Arabic text).

Shahrastānī, *Asch-Schashrastani's Religionsparteien und Philosophenschulen* . . . übersetzt . . . von Th. Haarbrücker. Bd 1–11. (Halle, 1850–1) (German translation).

Further aids to study

Essays and Works of Reference

Ali-Zade A. A., Sotsial'no-ekonomicheskaya i politicheskaya istoriya Azerbaydzhana (Social-economic and political history of Azarbaydzhan) 13th and 14th centuries (Baku, 1956).

Bartol'd, V. V., Iran Istoricheskiy obzor (Iran. Historical Survey) (Tashkent, 1926).

——, Islam (Islam) (Petrograd, 1918).

——, Istoriko-geograficheskiy obzor Irana. (Historico-Geographical Survey of Iran) (St Petersburg, 1903).

——, Istoriya izucheniya Vostoka v Yevrope i v Rossii. (History of oriental studies in Europe and in Russia) 2nd edn (Leningrad, 1925).

——, K istorii Krest'yanskikh dvizhenii v Persii. V sb: Iz dalekogo i blizkogo proshlogo (V chest' N.I. Kareyeva) (History of peasant movements in Persia) In collection 'The remote and recent past' (in honour of N. I. Kareyeva) (Petrograd, 1923).

——, Kul'tura musul'manstva. Culture of Muhammadanism. (Petrograd, 1918).

——, Mesto pricaspiyskikh oblastey v istorii musul'manskogo mira. (The place of the Caspian region in the history of the Muslim world) (Baku, 1925) new edn in V. V. Bartol'd. *Works*, vol. II, pt 1 (Moscow, 1963).

——, Musul'manskiy mir (Vvedeniye v nauku: istoriya) (Muslim World. Introduction to study. History) (Petrograd, 1922).

——, Turkestan v epokhu mongol'skogo nashestviya. (Turkestan down to the Mongol Invasion.) In V. V. Bartol'd, *Works*, vol. I (Moscow, 1963) (new edn supplement).

Belyayev, V. I., Arabskiye istochniki po istorii turkmen i Turkmenii. V kn: Materialy po istorii turkmen i Turkmenii. (Arab sources on the history of the Turkmens and Turkmenia.) In material for the history of the Turkmens and Turkmenia, vol. I. (Moscow-Leningrad, 1939).

——, Musul'manskoye sectanstvo. (Muslim Sectarianism) (Moscow, 1957).

——, Araby, islam i arabskiy khalifat v ranneye srednevekov'ye. (The Arabs, Islam and the Arab Caliphate in the early Middle Ages) (Moscow, 1965).

Bertel's Ye. E., Istoriya persidsko-tadzhikskoy literatury. V kn: Izbn. trudy (History of Persian-Tadzhik Literature) In Y. E. Bertel's *Selected Works* [vol I] (Moscow, 1960).

——, Ocherk istorii persidskoy literatury. (Outline history of Persian Literature.) (Leningrad, 1928).

Ghafurov B. G., Istoriya tadzhikskogo naroda. (History of the Tadzhik people) vol. I, 2nd edn (Moscow, 1952).

Gibb, H. A. R., Arabic Literature (Moscow, 1960).

Goldziher, I., Lectures on Islam (Moscow, 1912) (Russian translation).

Dozy, R., Outline of the history of Islam. Russian translation V. I. Kamenskiy, ed with Foreword and Notes by A. Ye. Krymskiy (St Petersburg, 1904).

Istoriya Irana s drevneyshikh vremën do koñtsa XVIII v. N. V. Pigulevskaya, A. Yu. Yakubovskiy, I. P. Petrushevskiy, L. V. Stroyeva, A. M. Belenitskiy (History of Iran from the most ancient times until the end of the 18th century) (Moscow-Leningrad, 1958).

Ivanov, M. S., Ocherk istorii Irana. (Outline of the history of Iran) (Moscow, 1952).

Klimovich, L. I., Islam Ocherki (Islam. Essays) (Moscow, 1962; new edn, 1965).

Krachkovskiy, I. Yu., Ocherki po istorii russkoy arabistiki (Essays on the history of Arabic studies in Russia, (Moscow-Leningrad, 1950).

Krymskiy, A. Ye., Istoriya Persii, yeyë literatury i dervisheskoy teosofii (History of Persia, of her literature and of her Dervish theosophy.) vols. I–III (Moscow, 1909–17 (lithogr.)).

Massé, A., Islam, Russian translation ed with foreword by Ye. A. Belyayev. (Moscow, 1961).

Mednikov, N. A., Palestina ot zavoyevaniya yeyë arabami do krestovykh pokhodov po arabskim istochnikam. Issledovaniye. Prilozheniya (izbr. otryvki iz soch. arab. istorikov i geografov). V serii: Pravoslavnyy Palestinskiy sbornik (Palestine from the Arab Conquest to the Crusades in Arab sources) vol. 1, Essays; vols. 2–4, Appendices (Selected extracts from the writings of Arab historians and geographers). In series:

Orthodox Palestinian Collection vol. XVII Instalment II. (St Petersburg, 1897–1903).
Müller, A., History of Islam from its foundation to modern times. Russian translation from German, ed N. A. Mednikov, vols. I–III (St Petersburg, 1895–6).
Novichev, A. D., Istoriya Turtsii. (I) Epokha feodalizma (History of Turkey. I. The epoch of feudalism.) (LGU, 1963).
Petrushevskiy, I. P., Zemledeliye i agrarnyye otnosheniya v Irane. (Agriculture and Agrarian Relations in Iran), 13th and 14th centuries. (Moscow-Leningrad, 1960).
Smirnov, N. A., Ocherki istorii izucheniya islama v SSSR (Outline of the history of Islamic Studies in USSR) (Moscow, 1954).
Shmidt, A. E., Ocherki istorii islama kak religii. (The history of Islam as a religion) 'Mir Islama' (Islamic World) vols. I-III (St Petersburg, 1912).
Yakubovskiy, A. Yu., Istoriya Uzbekskoy SSR. (History of the Uzbek SSR) vol. I Bk One (Tashkent, 1955) Pt III, Chs 5–11.

'Abd al-Jalīl, I. M., *Brève histoire de la littérature arabe* (Paris, 1947).
Arnold, Th. and Guillaume A., *The Legacy of Islam* (Oxford, 1931).
Becker, C. H., *Islamstudien*, Bd I–II (Leipzig, 1924).
Brockelmann, C. *Geschichte der arabischen Litteratur*, Bd I–II (Weimar-Berlin, 1898–1902); Supplement-bände I–III (Leiden, 1937–42).
Browne, E. G., *A literary history of Persia*, vols. I–IV (Cambridge 1909–24); new edn (Cambridge 1951–6).
Caetani, L., *Annali dell'Islam*, vol. I–X (Milano, 1905–16).
Dozy, R., *Essai sur l'histoire de l'islamisme* (Leyde, 1879).
Encyclopaedia of religion and ethics, ed J. Hastings, vol. I–XII (Edinburgh, 1908–26).
Encyclopédie de l'Islam, ed M. Th. Houtsma, etc, vols. I–IV et Suppléments (Leyde-Paris, 1913–38). Parallel edn in English and German.
Gardet, L., *La cité musulmane: vie sociale et politique* (Paris, 1954).
Gibb, H. A. R., *Arabic literature: an introduction* (London, 1926).
——, *Mohammedanism* (London, 1949).
Goldziher, I., *Muhammedanische Studien*, Bd I–II (Halle, 1889–90).
——, *Vorlesungen über den Islam*, Bd I–II (Heidelberg, 1925) 2 Ausg.
Hitti, Ph. K., *History of the Arabs* (London, 1946) 3rd edn.
Hughes, T. B., *A Dictionary of Islam* (London, 1885).
Huart, Cl., *La littérature arabe* (Paris, 1923).
Juynboll, A. W. T., *Handbuch des islamischen Gesetzes* (Leiden, 1910).
Kremer, A. von, *Geschichte der herrschenden Ideen des Islam* (Leipzig, 1868).
——, *Kulturgeschichte des Orients unter den Chalifen*, Bd I–II (Wien, 1875–7).
Lambton, A. K. S., *Islamic Society in Persia* (London, 1954).
Lammens, H., *L'Islam, croyances et institutions* (Beyrouth, 1926).
Le Strange, G., *The lands of the Eastern Caliphate* (Cambridge, 1905).
Levy, R., *The social structure of Islam* (Cambridge, 1957) 2nd edn.
Macdonald, D. B., *Development of Muslim theology, jurisprudence and constitutional theory* (London, 1913).
Nicholson, R. A., *A literary history of the Arabs* (Cambridge, 1930).

Nöldeke, Th., *Der Islam 'Orientalische Skizzen'* (Berlin, 1892).
Pearson, J. D., *Index Islamicus 1906–56;* Supplement 1956–60 (Cambridge, 1962).
Polak, J. E., *Persien, das Land und seine Bewohner*, Bd I–II (Leipzig, 1865).
Rypka, J., *Iranische Literaturgeschichte* (Leipzig, 1959).
Sale, G., *The Koran* (London, 1821)
Sauvaget, J., *Introduction à l'histoire de l'Orient musulman: Elements de bibliographie* (éd refondue et complétée par Cl. Cahen) (Paris, 1961).
Schacht, J., *Der Islam* (Religionsgeschichtliche Lesebuch) (Tübingen, 1931).
Schwarz, P., *Iran im Mittelalter nach den arabischen Geographen*, Bd I–IX (Leipzig-Stuttgart, 1896–36).
Shorter Encyclopaedia of Islam, ed H. A. R. Gibb and J. H. Kramers (Leyden, 1953).
Wellhausen, I., *Skizzen und Vorarbeiten*, I–VI (Leipzig, 1887–99).
Wensinck, A. J., *Ka'ba*. EI vol. II
——, The Muslim creed (Cambridge, 1932).
Wüstenfeld, F., *Die Geschichtschreiber der Araber und ihre Werke* (Göttingen, 1882).
Zambaur, E. de, *Manuel de généalogie de l'Islam* (Hanover, 1927).
Zaydan, J., *Ta'rīkh tamaddun al-islam*, vols. I–V (Cairo, 1902–6) (in Arabic).

Introduction and Chapters I and II
Iran's obedience to Islam. Sunnīs, Shī'ites and Kharijites Dogma and Ritual

Sources

Anonymous Arab of the 11th century. Facsimile of (part of) Arabic text. Russian translation. Introduction to the Work and Commentaries. P. A. Gryaznevich, ed V. I. Belyayev (Moscow, 1960).
Balādhurī, Liber expugnationis regionum auctore . . . al-Beladsori . . ., ed M. J. de Goeje (LB, 1866) (Arabic text).
Dīnawarī, Abu Hanifa ad-Dinawari . . . . Préface, variantes et index, publiés par I. Kratchkovsky (Leyde, 1912).
Ibn Sa'd, Ṭabaqāt. Ibn Sa'd. Kitāb at-Tabaqāt al-Kabīr, ed E. Sachau cum aliis, vol. I–IX (LB, 1904–28) (Arabic text).
Ibn Qutayba, Ibn Qutaiba's 'Uyūn al-akhbar, trs C. Brockelmann, Bd I–IV (Berlin-Strassburg, 1900–8) (Arabic text).
Ibn Hishām, Das Leben Muhammed's nach Muhamnmed Ibn Ishaq bearbeitet von 'Abdelmelik Ibn Hischam (Sira sayyidna Muhammad) trs F. Wüstenfeld. Bd I–II (Göttingen, 1858–60) (Arabic text).
——, Sira, trs G. Weil (Stuttgart, 1864) (German translation).

Further aids to study

Bartol'd, V. V., Abu Mikhnaf, ZVORAO, vol. XVII (1906).
——, Dve neopublikovannyye stat'i o rannem islame. (Two unpublished

articles on early Islam) Foreword by L. I. Klimovich. 'Istorik-Marksist' (1939) No. 5–6

——, K istorii arabskikh zavoyevaniy v Sredney Azii (History of Arab Conquests in Central Asia) ZVORAO, vol. XVII (1906).

——, Museylima. Izvestiya Ros. acad. nauk. 'Musaylima'. (Transactions Russian Academy of Science) vol. XIX (Leningrad, 1925).

Belyayev, V. I., Anonimnaya istoricheskaya rukopis' kollektsü V. A. Ivanova v Aziatskom Muzeye. Zap. Kollegii Vostokovedov (Anonymous historical MS in V. A. Ivanov's collection at the Asiatic Museum.) Records of College of Orientalists, vol. V (1930).

Belyayev. Ye. A., Obrazovaniye arabskogo gosudarstva i vozniknoveniye islama v VII veke V serii: Doklady sovetskoy delegatsii na XXIII Mezhdunarodnom Kongresse Vostokovedov v Kembridzhe (The formation of the Arab state and rise of Islam in the 7th century). In series Reports of the Soviet delegation to XXIII International Congress of Orientalists in Cambridge (Moscow, 1954).

Belyayev Ye A. and A. Yu., Yakubovskiy, Araviya k nachalu VII v. V km. Vcemirnaya istoriya. I III (Arabia to the beginning of the 7th century) In *World History*, vol. III, USSR Acad. Sc. (Moscow, 1957) Chap. VII.

Inostrantsev, K. A., Sasanidskiye etyudy. (Sasanian Studies) (St Petersburg, 1909).

Kadyrova, T., Iz istorii Krest'yanskikh dvizheniy v Maverannakhre i Khorasane (History of peasant movements in Māwarannahr and Khurāsān) (Tashkent, 1965).

Krymskiy, A. Ye., Istochniki dlya istorii Mokhammeda (Sources for the history of Muḥammad) (Moscow, 1902).

Nadiradze, L. I., K voprosu o rabstve v Aravii v VII v. V sb: Voprosy istorii i literatury stran zarubezhnogo Vostoka. (The question of slavery in Arabia in the 7th century) In Questions of history and literature in countries of the East beyond the border (MGU, 1960).

Pigulevskaya, N. V., Araby u granits Vizantii i Irana v IV–VI vv. (Arabs in Byzantium and Iran in 4th–6th centuries) (Moscow-Leningrad, 1965).

——, Zarozhdeniye feodal'nykh otnosheniy na Blizhnem Vostoke. (Genesis of feudal relations in Near East) Records IVAN, vol. XVI (1958).

——, Obshchestvennyye otnosheniya v Nedzhrane v nachale VI v. (Social relations in Nejrān at the beginning of the 6th century.) 'Sovetskoye Vostokovedeniye' (Soviet Orientalism) vol. VI (Moscow-Leningrad, 1949).

Tolstov, S. P., Genezis feodalizma v kochevykh skotovodcheskikh obshchestvakh (Genesis of feudalism in nomadic cattle-raising societies) Transactions GAIMK No 103. (Leningrad, 1934).

——, Ocherki pervonachal'nogo islama (Outlines of early Islam) (Moscow, 1932).

——, Po sledam drevnekhorezmiyskoy tsivilizatsii (On the tracks of the ancient Khwarazmian civilization) (Moscow-Leningrad, 1948).

Yakubovskiy, A. Yu., Irak na grani VIII i IX vv. V kn: Trudy Pervoy sessii arabistov (Iraq at the turn of the 8th and 9th centuries) In Works of the First Session of Arabists (Leningrad, 1937).

——, *see also* Belyayev, Ye. A., and A. Yu. Yakubovskiy

Andrae, Tor, *Mohammed, the man and his faith* (London, 1936, German translation 1932).
Arnold, T. W., *The Caliphate* (Oxford, 1924).
Bartol'd, W., *Abu Muslim*, EI, vol. II.
Bell, R., *The origin of Islam in its Christian environment* (London, 1926).
Beveridge, W., *Ebionism*, ERE, vol. V.
Blachère, R., *Le problème de Mahomet: Essai de biographie critique du fondateur de l'Islam* (Paris, 1952).
Brandt, W., *Mandaeans*, ERE, vol. VIII.
Brockelmann, K., *Das Verhältnis von Ibn el-Athirs 'Kamil fi-t-tarich' zu Tabaris 'Tarikh ar-rusul'* (Strassburg, 1890).
Brünnow, R. E., *Die Charidschiten* (Strassburg, 1884).
Buhl, Fr., *Das Leben Mohammeds* (Heidelberg, 1955) 2 Ausg.
——, *Hanif*, EI vol. II.
Burckhardt, I., *Travels in Arabia* (London, 1829).
Casanova, P., *Mohammed et la fin du monde* (Paris, 1911).
Diez, E., *Manara*, EI, vol. III.
——, *Masdjid*, EI, vol. III.
——, *Mihrab*, EI, vol. III.
——, *Minbar*, EI, vol. III.
Fischer, A., *Kahin*, EI, vol. II.
Geiger, A., *Was hat Muhammad aus den Judentum aufgenommen?* (Bonn, 1833); new edn (Leipzig, 1902).
Godard, A., *Les anciennes mosquées de l'Iran*, 'Athar-e Iran', vol. II (Haarlem, 1937).
Goldziher, I., *Isma'*, EI, vol. II.
Grimme, H., *Mohammed*, Teil I: Das Leben (Münster, 1892).
Huart, Cl., *Histoire des Arabes*, vols. I–II (Paris, 1912).
Lammens, H., *Etudes sur le règne du calife Mo'awiya I* (Paris, 1908).
——, *Etudes sur le siècle des Omayyades* (Beyrouth, 1930).
——, *La Mecque à la veille de l'hégire* (Paris, 1924).
Le Strange, G., *Baghdad during the Abbasid Caliphate* (London, 1924) 2nd edn.
Macdonald, D. B., *Allah*, EI, vol. I.
Margoliouth, D. S., *Early development of Mohammedanism* (London, 1904).
——, *Mohammed and the rise of Islam* (London-New York, 1905).
——, *Muhammad*, ERE, vol. IX.
Montgomery Watt, W., *Muhammad at Mecca* (Oxford, 1953).
——, *Muhammad at Medina* (Oxford, 1956).
Muir, W., *Life of Mahomet* (Edinburgh, 1923) 2nd edn.
——, *The Caliphate, its rise, decline and fall* (London, 1924) 2nd edn.
Nöldeke, Th., *Das Leben Muhammeds* (Hanover, 1863).
——, *Ein Sklavenkrieg im Orient*, 'Orientalische Skizzen' (Berlin, 1892).
Snouck Hurgronje, C., *Mekka*, vols. I–II (Leiden, 1888).
Sprenger, A., *Das Leben und die Lehre des Mohammad*, Bd I–III (Berlin, 1861–5).
Spuler, B., *Die Chalifenzeit: Entstehung und Zerfall des islamischen Weltreiches* (Leiden, 1952).
——, *Iran in frühislamischer Zeit: Politik, Kultur, Verwaltung und öffentliches Leben (633–1055)* (Wiesbaden, 1952).

Weil, G., *Geschichte der Chalifen*, Bd I–III (Mannheim, 1846–61).
Wellhausen, J., *Das Arabische Reich und sein Sturz* (Berlin, 1902).
——, *Die religiös-politischen Oppositions-parteien im alten Islam* (Berlin, 1901).
——, *Reste arabischen Heidentums* (Berlin, 1897).
Wensinck, A. J., Salat. EI vol. IV.
Zaydan, J. Umayyads and 'Abbasids, translation by D. S. Margoliouth (Leyden, 1907) GMS IV.
Zwemers, S. M. The Moslem Christ (London, 1912).

See also General literature above

Chapter III
The Koran

Sources

Bayḍāwī, Commentarius in Coranum . . ., Bd I–II, ed H. Fleischer (Lipsiae, 1846–8).
Zamakhsharī, The Kashshaf 'an haqaiq at-tanzīl . . ., vols. I–II, ed W. Nassau Lees. (Calcutta, 1854–61) BI.
Maḥallī, Jalālu 'd-Dīn and Suyūṭī, Jalālu 'd-Dīn, Tafsīru' l-Jalālayn (Bombay, 1869) (Arabic text).
Rāzī, Fakhru 'd-Dīn, At-Tafsīru 'l-Kabīr, vols. I –VIII (Cairo, 1308 (1890)) (Arabic text).
Suyūṭī, See Maḥallī and Suyūṭī.
Suyūṭī, Jalālu 'd-Dīn, Soyuti's Itqan fi-'ulum al-Qur'an or the exegetic sciences of the Qoran, ed Mawlawies Basheer od-deen and Noor al-Haqq, with an analysis by Dr Sprenger, vols. I–II (Calcutta, 1852–4) BI (Arabic text).
Ṭabarī, Muḥammad b. Jarīr, Tafsīr, vols. I–III (Cairo, 1901).

For editions of the Koran and Concordances see General literature (Sources) above

Further aids to study

Krachkovskiy, I. Yu., Appendices to Russian translation Koran (*see Section General literature, Sources* above).
Krymskiy, A. Ye., Lektsii po Koranu (Lectures on the Koran) (Moscow, 1902).
Brockelmann, C., Baidawi, EI, vol. I.
Buhl, F., Kur'an, EI, vol. II.
Grimme, H., *Mohammed*, vol. II, Einleitung in den Koran (Münster, 1895).
Hirschfeld, H., *New researches in the composition and the exegesis of the Qoran* (London, 1902).
Jeffrey, A., *Materials for the history of the text of the Qoran* (London, 1937).

Nöldeke, Th., *Der Qoran*, 'Orientalische Skizzen' (Berlin, 1892).
——, Geschichte des Qorans, ed F. Schwally, Bd I–II, Leipzig, 1909–1919 (new revised edn).
Sale, G., *The Koran* (London, 1821).
Stanton, H. W., *The teaching of the Qoran* (London, 1920).
Weil, G., *Historisch-kritische Einleitung in den Koran* (Bielefeld, 1844, 2 Ausg. 1878).

See also General Literature Introduction and Chapters I–II (Further aids to study).

Chapters IV–VII Muslim Law. Sunnī Law. Public Law. Criminal and Civil Law.

Sources

Abū Yūsuf Ya'qūb, Kitābu 'l-Kharāj (Būlāq, 1302 (1885), new edn. Cairo, 1911) (Arabic text).
——, Abou Yusof Yaqoub, *Le livre de l'impôt foncier*, Notes and translation by E. Fagnan (Paris, 1921).
Bayhaqī, Tārīkh-ī Bayhaqī, ed Drs Ghanī and Fayyāz (Tehran, 1324 (1945)) (Persian text).
Bukhārī, Ṣaḥīḥ, *Le recueil des traditions mahométanes*, vols. I–III, ed L. Krehl (Leyde, 1862–8 new edn Leyde, 1907–8) (Arabic text).
Ibnu 'l-Athīr, Usdu 'l-Ghāba fī ma'rīfati 'ṣ-Ṣahaba (Cairo, 1280 (1863)) (Arabic text).
Ibn Ḥanbal, Musnad, vols. I–VI (Cairo, 1312 (1895)) (Arabic text).
Qābūs-nāma, Qābūs-nāma . . ., ed Reuben Levy. (London, 1951). GMS NS XVIII (Persian text).
Māwardī, Al-Aḥkāmu 's-Sulṭāniyya, Al-Māwardī, *Constitutiones politicae*, ed M. Enger. (Bonnae, 1853) (Arabic text).
Mālik b. Anas, Al-Muwaṭṭa' With comment. az-Zurkani vols. I–IV (Cairo, 1280 (1863–4) (Arabic text).
Marghīnānī, Burhānu 'd-Dīn, Hidāya, ed N. Grodekov, vols. I–IV. (Tashkent, 1893) (Russian translation) (Russian translation from French made from Persian from Arabic original).
Muslim, Aṣ-Ṣaḥīḥ, vols. I–II (Būlāq, 1290 (1873)) (Arabic text).
Shaybānī, Al-Jāmi'u 'ṣ-Ṣaghīr (Lucknow, 1311 (1893)) (Arabic text).
Shāfi'ī, Kitābu 'l-Umm (Būlāq, 1321 (1903)) (Arabic text).

Further aids to study

Ali-Zade, A. A., K voprosu ob institute ikta. Sb. statey po istorii Azerbaydzhana (On the institution iqṭā'.) Collection Articles on the history of Azerbaydzhan Issue I (Baku, 1949).

Bartol'd, V. V., Teokraticheskaya ideya i svetskaya vlast' v musul'manskom gosudarstve (The theocratic idea and the secular authority in the Muslim state) Report, St Petersburg University for 1902.

——, Ulugbek i yego vremya (Ulugh Bek and his time) (Petrograd, 1918).

——, Khalif i Sultan (Caliph and Sultan) 'Mir Islama' vol. I.

Berg, L. V. van den, *Basic principles of Muslim law*, Russian translation by V. Girgas (St Petersburg, 1882).

Charles, R., *Muslim law*, Russian translation with foreword by Ye. A. Belyayev (Moscow 1959).

Girgas, V. F., Prava Khristian na Vostoke po musul'manskim zakonam (The rights of Christians in the East under Muslim legislation) (St Petersburg, 1865).

Krymskiy, A. Ye., Istochniki dlya istorii Mokhammeda (Sources for the history of Muḥammad) Pt II (Moscow 1912).

Ostroumov, N. P., Shariat po shkole (mazkhab) Abu Khalify (The Sharī'a according to the school (madhhab) of Abu Ḥanīfa) (St Petersburg, 1913).

Petrushevskiy, I. P., Vinogradarstvo i vinodeliye v Irane v XIII–XIV vv (Viticulture and Wine-making in Iran in the 13th and 14th centuries) 'Vizantiyskiy vremennik', vol. XI (1956).

——, Primeneniye rabskogo truda v Irane i sopredel'nykh stranakh v pozdnem srednevekov'ye. v serii: Doklady delegatsii SSSR na XXV Mezhdunarodnom Kongresse vostokovedov v Moskve (Application of slave labour in Iran and neighbouring countries in the late Middle Ages) In the series, Reports of the USSR delegation to the XXV International Congress of Orientalists in Moscow (Moscow, 1960).

Yakubovskiy, A. Yu., Ob ispol'nykh arendakh v VIII v (Métayage leases in Iraq, 8th century) 'Sovetskoye Vostokovedeniye, vol. IV. (Moscow-Leningrad, 1947).

Abdul-Rahim, *The principles of Muhammadan jurisprudence* (London, 1911).

Ameer Ali, *Personal law of the Muhammadans* (Lucknow, 1880).

Baillie, N. B. E., *A Digest of Muhammadan law*, vol. I (London, 1869).

Becker, C. H., *Steuerpacht und Lehnwesen in den moslemischen Staaten*, 'Der Islam', 1914, Bd V, Heft I (1914).

Berchem, M. van, *La propriété territoriale et l'impôt foncier sous les premiers califes* (Genève, 1886).

Cahen, Cl., *L'évolution de l'iqta' du IX au XIII siècles*, *Annales* (*économies, sociétés, civilisation*) vol. 8. No 1 (Paris, 1953).

Clavel, E., *Droit musulman: le waqf ou habous . . .* (*rites hanafite et malekite*) vol. I–II (Paris, 1895–6).

Dennet, D. C., *Conversion and the poll-tax in early Islam*, Harvard historical monographs (1950).

Fyzee, Asaf, *Outlines of Muhammadan law* (Oxford, 1949; 2nd edn, 1955).

Goldziher, I., *Die Zachiriten* (Leipzig, 1884).

——, *Fiqh*, EI vol. II.

——, Muhammedanische Studien, Bd II (Halle, 1890) (rendered in Russian by V. R. Rozen in ZVORAO vol. VIII, 1894).

Gottheil, R., *The Cadi — the history of this institution* (London, 1908).

Guillaume, W., *The traditions of Islam* (Oxford, 1924).
Juynboll, Th. W., Hadith, EI vol. II.
Krehl, L., Über den 'Sahih' des Buchari, ZDMG, Bd IV, (1850).
Kremer, A. von, *Geschichte der herrschenden Ideen des Islams*, Bd III, Die Staatsidee des Islams (Leipzig, 1868).
Law in the Middle East, ed. M. Khadduri and H. Liebesny, vol. I, Origin and development of Islamic law (Washington, 1955).
Lokkegaard, F., *Islamic taxation in the classic period* (Copenhagen, 1950).
Poliak, A. M., 'Classification of lands in the Islamic law', *American Journal of Semitic Languages* (1940).
Rosenthal, E. I. J., *Political thought in medieval Islam* (Cambridge, 1962).
Snouck Hurgronje, C., 'Le droit musulman', in *Revue de l'histoire des religions*, vol. XXXVII, (1897).
Shoukry Bidair, *L'institution des biens dits habous ou waqf* (Paris, 1924).
Tischendorf, P., *Das Lehnwesen in den moslemischen Staatem* (Leipzig, 1872).

See also General literature, and literature on Chaps. I and II, above

Chapters VIII and IX
Theological disputes. A scholastic theology

Sources

Ghazālī, Abū Ḥāmid, Al-Munqidh mina 'ḍ-Ḍalāl (Cairo, 1303 (1886)) (Arabic text).
——, Iḥyā'u 'Ulūmi 'd-Dīn, vols. I–IV (Cairo, 1289 (1872)) (Arabic text).
——, Kimiyā-yi Sa 'ādat (Bombay, 1320). (Persian text).
——, Al-Munqidh mina'ḍ-Ḍalāl, French translation by Bardier de Meynard, JA 7, vol. IX
——, Tahāfutu 'l-Falāsifa, ed M. Bouyges (Beyrouth, 1927) (Arabic text).
——, *Widerspruch der Philosophen*, übersetz. von T. J. de Boer (German translation Tahāfutu 'l-Falāsifa').
Ibn Rushd (Averroes), Tahāfutu 't-Tahāfut (Cairo, 1303 (1886)) (Arabic text).
Subkī — Ṭabaqātu 'sh-Shāfi'iyya (Cairo, 1324 (1906)) (Arabic text).
Firdawsī, Shāh-nāma J. Mohl. Chah nama . . ., edn complète, vol. I (Paris, 1830) (Persian text).

Further aids to study

Bartol'd, V. V., Mir Ali-Shir i politicheskaya zhizn'. (Mīr 'Ali Shīr and political life.) In collection Mīr 'Alī Shīr (Leningrad 1928).
Goldziher, I., Saint-worship in Islam (Moscow, 1938). (Russian translation of five articles of I. Goldziher, with foreword by L. I. Klimovich).

Asín Palacios, M., Algazel — dogmática, moral, ascética (Zaragoza, 1901).
——, 'Sens du mot "tehafot" dans les oeuvres d'al-Ghazali et d'Averroes', *Rév. Afric.* Nos 261–2 (1906).
Bauer, H., *Die Dogmatik al-Ghazali's* (Halle, 1912).
Boer, T. J. de, *Die Widersprüche der Philosophen und ihr Ausgleich durch Ibn Roshd* (Strassburg, 1894).
——, *Geschichte der Philosophie im Islam* (Stuttgart, 1901). (English translation by T. J. de Boer, *The history of philosophy in Islam*, London, 1903).
Carra de Vaux B, *Ghazali* (Paris, 1902).
——, Ibn Rushd, EI vol. II.
Goldziher, I., Abdal, EI vol. I.
——, *Die islamische und judische Philosophie: Die Kultur der Gegenwart*, Bd I Hft 5 (1913).
——, *Vorlesungen über den Islam*, ed Fr Babinger (Heidelberg, 1925 (2nd edn)); French translation: I. Goldziher, *Le dogme et la loi de l'Islam* (Paris, 1920).
Horten, M., *Die philosophischen Systeme der spekulativen Theologen im Islam* (Bonn, 1912).
Kremer, A. von, *Kulturgeschichtliche Streifzüge auf dem Gebiete des Islams* (Leipzig, 1873).
Macdonald, D. B., 'Al-Mu'tazila' EI vol. III.
——, 'Ghazali', EI vol. II.
——, 'Kadar', EI vol. II.
——, 'Life of al-Ghazali', JAOS, vol. XX (1899).
——, *The religious attitude and life in Islam* (Chicago, 1909).
Margoliouth, D. S., 'Karramiya', EI vol. II.
Mehren, M. A., Exposé de la réforme de l'islamisme commencée par el-Ash'ari. Actes du III Congrès international des orientalistes à St Petersbourg, vol. II (St Petersburg, 1876).
Mez, A., *Die Renaissance des Islam* (Heidelberg, 1922).
Munk, S., *Mélanges de la philosophie juive et arabe* (Paris, 1859).
Rosenthal, Franz, *The Muslim concept of freedom* (London, 1960).
Salisbury, Muhammadan Doctrine of Predestination and Freewill. JAOS vol. VIII (1866).
Schreiner, Zur Geschichte des Asharitentums. Actes du VIII Congrès International des orientalistes à Stockholm. Sect. I (Leyde, 1891).
Spitta, W., Zur Geschichte Abu-l-Hasan's al-Ash'ari. Leipzig, 1879.
Strothmann, R., Tashbih. EI vol. IV.

Chapters X and XI
Moderate Shī'ites, Ismā'īlīs, Carmathians and Extreme Shī'ites

Sources

Bayhaqī, Abu 'l-Faḍl, Tārīkh-i Bayhaqī. ed Drs Ghani and Fayyaz (Tehran, 1324 (1945)) (Persian text)

——, *History of Mas'ūd (1030–1041)*, Foreword, Russian translation and Notes by A. K. Arends (Tashkent, 1962).
Bīrūnī, *Alberuni's India*, ed E. Sachau (London, 1877) (Arabic text).
——, *Alberuni's India*, translation by E. Sachau (London, 1888; 2nd edn 1910).
Bundārī, *Recueil de textes relatifs à l'histoire des Seldjoucides*, ed M. T. Houtsma, vol. II (Leyde, 1889) (Arabic text).
Juwaynī, *The Tārīkh-i Jahāngusha* . . ., ed Mirza Muhammad ibn 'Abd al-Wahhāb-i Qazwīnī, Pt III containing the history of Mangu-qaan, Hulagu and the Ismailis (Leyden-London, 1937) GMS XVI/3 (Persian text).
——, *The history of the world-conqueror*, by Ata Malik-i Juwaynī, translation by J. A. Boyle, vol. II (Manchester, 1958).
Guyard St, *Fragments relatifs à la doctrine des Ismaelis* (Paris, 1874).
Ibn Bābawayh al-Qummī aṣ-Ṣadūq, Kitābu man lā yaḥḍuruhu 'l-faqīh (Tehran, 1326 (1908)) (Arabic text).
Ikhwānu 'ṣ-Ṣafā, *Rasā'il*, vols. I–IV (Cairo, 1347 (1928)) (Arabic text).
Kotov, F. A., O khodu v Persidskoye tsarstvo (Journey into the Persian Kingdom) (Moscow, 1959).
Kulaynī, Muḥammad b. Ḥasan, Al-Kāfī fī 'ilmi 'd-Dīn, vols. I–II (Tehran, 1307 (1889)) (Arabic text).
Nāṣir-i-Khusraw, Sefer-nameh, ed Ch. Schefer (Paris, 1881) (Persian text, French translation and appendices).
——, Safar nāma, Russian translation by Ye. E. Bertel's (Moscow-Leningrad, 1933).
Nawbakhtī, Firaq ash-Shī'a, ed H. Ritter (Constantinople, 1931) (Bibliotheca Islamica).
Polo, Marco, *The Travels*, Russian translation by I. P. Minayev, ed V. V. Bartol'd (St Petersburg, 1902).
Rāwandī, The Rahat as-sudur . . ., ed Muhammad Iqbal, (London-Leyden, 1921) GMS NS II (Persian text and commentaries).
Rashīdu 'd-Dīn, Faḍlullāh, Jami'at-tawārīkh, part of the Ismailis' history . . ., ed Danesh Pajuh and M. Modarresy (Tehran, 1960) (Persian text).
Ṭūsī, Muḥammad b. Ḥasan, Fihrist (Calcutta, 1853) BI (Arabic text).
——, Tahdhību 'l-Aḥkām (Tehran, 1316 (1899)) (Arabic text).
Ḥillī, Najmu 'd-Dīn Ja'far, Sharāyi 'u'l-Islām (Tehran, 1300 (1882)) (Arabic text).
Ḥillī, Ḥasan b. Muṭahhar ('Allāmayi Ḥillī) Minhāju 'l-Karāma fī ma'rifati 'l-imāma. (Tehran, 1297 (1880)) (Arabic text).
——, Minhāj al-Karāma . . ., translation by the Revd W. M. Miller. In series Oriental Translation Fund (1928) (English translation chapter on the doctrine of the imamate).
Ḥurūfī Texts, Textes Houroufis, edited and translated by Clément Huart (Leyde-London, 1909) GMS, IX.
Shushtarī, Nūru'llāh, Majālisu 'l-Mu'minīn (Tehran, 1283 (1866)) (Persian text).

Further aids to study

Bartol'd, V. V., Rytsarstvo i gorodskaya zhizn' v Persii pri Sasanidakh i pri islame (Chivalry and urban life in Persia under the Sāsānids and under Islam) ZVORAO, vol. XXI (1913).

Bertel's, A. Ye., Nasir-i Khosrov i ismailizm (Nāṣir-i Khusraw and Ismā'īlism.) (Moscow, 1959).

Gordlevskiy, V. A., Kara Koyunlu. Izvestiya Obshchestva obsledovaniya i izucheniya Azerbaydzhana (Qāra Qoyūnlū, Transactions of the Society of Research in Azerbaydzhan) No. 4 (Baku, 1927).

Zhukovskiy, V. A., Sekta lyudey istiny — akhl-i Khakk v Persii (The Sect of the People of Truth — Ahl-i Haqq in Persia) ZVORAO, vol. I issue 2 (1887).

Zakhoder, B. N., Mukhammad Nakhshabi. K istorii Karmatskogo dvizheniya v Sredney Azii. Uch. zap. MGU (Muḥammad Nakhshabī. History of the Carmathian movement in Central Asia) Records MGU, issue 41 (1940).

Marr, Yu. N., Radeniye sekty 'lyudey istiny' (Ecstatic invocation of the People of Truth sect) In Yu. N. Marr, Articles and Reports, vol. II (Moscow-Leningrad 1939).

Minorskiy, V. F., Materialy dlya izucheniya persidskoy secty 'lyudi istiny' ili ali-ilakhi (Materials for the study of the Persian sect 'People of Truth' or Alī-ilāhī) (Moscow, 1911).

Smirnov, K. N., Persy, Ocherk religiy Persii (The Persians. Outline of the religions of Persia) (Tiflis, 1916).

Stroyeva, L. V., Vosstaniye ismailitov v Irane na grani XI–XII vv. V sb: Issledovaniya po istorii stran Vostoka (Revolt of the Ismā'īlīs in Iran at the turn of the 11th/12th centuries) In collection Research on the history of the countries of the East. LGU (1964).

——, Dvizheniye ismailitov v Isfakhane v 1100–1107. (Movement of Ismā'īlīs in Iṣfahān in 1100–1107) Vestnik, LGU (1962) No 14.

——, 'Den' Voskreseniya iz mertvykh' i yego sotsial'naya sushchnost'. Kratkiye soobshcheniya IVAN (The Day of the Resurrection of the Dead and its social import) Short reports IVAN, issue XXXVIII (Moscow, 1960).

——, Ismaility Irana i Sirii XI–XII vv. v zarubezhnoy i sovetskoy literature v sb: Istoriografiya i istochnikovedeniye istorii stran Azii. Materialy mezhvuzovskoy nauchnoy Konferenstii (The Ismā'īlīs of Iran and Syria in the 11th and 12th centuries in foreign and Soviet literature) In the collection Historiography and Sources for history of the countries of Asia. Material for inter-University-Conference. LGU, (1964).

——, K voprosu o sotsial'noy prirode ismailitskogo dvizheniya v Irane v XI–XIII vv. (The question of the social nature of the Ismā'īlī movement in Iran in the 11th to 13th centuries) Vestnik LGU (1963) No 20.

Baillie, A., *A Digest of Muhammadan law*, vol. II (Imamiya) (London, 1870).

Donaldson, D. M., *The Shi'ite religion* (London, 1933).

Feylesuf Riza (Riza Tewfiq) Dr, 'Etude sur la religion des houroufis', in *Textes houroufis*, ed Cl. Huart (London-Leyden, 1909) GMS XI.

Goeje, M. J. de, *Mémoire sur les Carmathes de Bahrain* (Leyde, 1886).

——, *La fin de l'empire des Carmathes de Bahrain*, JA, 9 series vol. V (1895).

Goldziher, I., *Beiträge zur Litteraturgeschichte der Shi'a und sunnitischen Polemik*, Akademie d. Wissenschaft, Philol.-Hist. Kl, I (Wien, 1874).

——, Das Prinzip der Takiya im Islam, ZDMG Bd LX (1906).
——, *Streitschrift des Ghazali gegen die Batiniya Sekte* (Leyden, 1916).
Hamdani, H., History of the Ismā'īlī Da'wat, JRAS (1932), No. 1.
Hodgson, M. G. S., *The order of assassins* (The Hague, 1955).
Huart, Cl., Ismā'īliya, EI vol. II.
Jacob, G., *Die Bektashiye*, Abhandlung d. Königl. Bayer. Akademie der Wissenschaft, I Kl, XXIV, Teil III. (Münich, 1909).
Ivanow, W., *A creed of the Fatimids* (Bombay, 1936).
——, *A guide to Ismaili literature* (London, 1933).
——, *Brief survey of the evolution of Ismailism* (Bombay, 1952).
——, 'Early Shī'ite movements', JBBRAS, vol. 17 (1941).
——, 'Ismailis and Qarmatians', JBBRAS, vol. 16 (1940).
——, *Studies in early Ismailism* (Cairo, 1948).
——, *The rise of the Fatimids* (London, 1942).
Lewis, B., *The origins of Ismailism* (Cambridge, 1940).
Macdonald, B. D., Ithna 'ashariya, EI vol. II.
——, Shi'a EI vol. IV.
Massignon, L., Esquisse d'une bibliographie qarmate, in *Ajab-nama*, a volume of oriental studies presented to E. G. Browne (Cambridge, 1922).
——, Karmates, EI vol. II.
Minorsky, V., *La domination des Dailamites* (Paris, 1932).
Nöldeke, Th., *Das Heiligtum Husain's zu Kerbala* (Berlin, 1909).
Querry, A., Droit musulman. Recueil des lois concernant les Musulmans-Chyites vol. I–II (Paris, 1871–2).
Riza Tewfiq, *see* Feylesuf Riza
Sadighi, G., *Les mouvements religieux iraniens* (Paris, 1939).
Sell, Canon, *Ithna 'Ashariya or the Twelve Shi'ah Imams* (Madras, 1923).
Tornauw, N., Le droit musulman exposé d'après les sources (Paris, 1860) (French translation from German).

Chapter XII
Mysticism in Islam

Sources

Abū Sa'īd al-Mayhanī, Shaykh, Life and sayings (Hālat o sukhanān-i shaykh Abī Sa'īd) ed V. A. Zhukovskiy (St Petersburg, 1899) (Persian text).
'Aṭṭār, Farīdu 'd-Dīn, Tadhkiratu 'l-awliyā, ed R. A. Nicholson, vol. I–II (London-Leyden, 1905–7) (Persian text).
Aflākī, Afḍalu 'd-Dīn, Manāqibu 'l-'Ārifīn, in Cl. Huart, *Les saints des derviches-tourneurs*, vol. I (Paris, 1918) (French translation).
Jāmī, Nūru 'd-Dīn, The Nafahat al-uns min hadharat al-quds, ed 'Abd al-Hamid and Kabir ad-din Ahmad (Calcutta, 1859) (Persian text).
Jullābī Hujwīrī, The Kashf al-Mahjub . . ., translation by R. A. Nicholson (London, 1911; GMS XVII.
Ibnu 'l- 'Arabī, Fuṣūṣu 'l-Ḥikam (Cairo, 1309 (1891); new edn Cairo, 1321 (1903). Both edns with commentary by 'Abdu 'r-Razzāq Kāshānī. (Arabic text).

——, Futūḥātu 'l-Makkiyya (Būlāq, 1274 (1857)) (Arabic text).
——, The Tarjuman al-ashwaq, a collection of mystical odes, ed R. A. Nicholson. In series Oriental Translation Fund, New Series, vol. XX (London, 1911) (Arabic text, English translation and commentary).
Ibnu 'l-Munawwar, Asrāru 't-Tawḥīd fī maqāmāti 'sh-Shaykh Abī Sa'īd (Secrets of the Divine Unity in the mystical progress of Shaykh Abū Sa'īd), ed V. A. Zhukovskiy (St Petersburg, 1899) (Persian text).
Kāshānī, 'Abdu 'r-Razzāq, Abdu-r-Razzaq's Dictionary of the technical terms of the Sufies, ed Sprenger (Calcutta, 1845). (Arabic text).
Kāshifī, Fakhru 'd-Dīn 'Alī b. Ḥusayni Wā'iẓ, Rashaḥāti 'Ayni 'l-Ḥayāt (Lucknow, 1308 (1890); also Tashkent, 1329 (1911)) (Persian text).
Kirmānī, Shāh Ni'matullāh Walī, Matériaux pour la biographie de Shah Ni'matullah Wali Kirmani: Textes persans publiés avec une introduction par Jean Aubin. (Tehran-Paris, 1956).
Lāhōrī, Rahīmullah, Khazīnatu 'l-Aṣfiyya (Cawnpore, 1312 (1894)) (Persian text).
Luṭf 'Alī Beg Ādharī Iṣfahānī, Ātash-Kada (Calcutta, 1249 (1833); also Bombay, 1277 (1860)) (Persian text).
Massignon, L., *Recueil de textes inédits concernant l'histoire de la mystique en pays d'Islam* (Paris, 1929).
Qushayrī, Abu 'l-Qāsim, Ar-Risālatu 'l-Qushayriyya (Būlāq, 1287 (1870)) (Arabic text).
Riḍā-qulī Khān Hidāyat, Majma'u 'l-Fuṣaḥā (Tehran, 1295 (1878)) (Persian text).
——, Riyāḍu 'l-'Ārifīn (Tehran, 1305 (1887)) (Persian text).
Rūmī, Jalālu 'd-Dīn, Mathnawī. The Mathnavi-i Ma'navi, ed from the oldest manuscripts . . ., by R. A. Nicholson, vol. 1–8 (London-Leyden, 1926–40). (Persian text, English translation and commentary).
Kharaqānī Abu 'l-Ḥasan, Shaykh. Ye. E. Bertel's. Nūru 'l-'Ulūm, biography of Shaykh Abu 'l-Ḥasan Kharaqānī. In collection Iran, vol. III (Leningrad, 1929). (Persian text, Russian translation and Introduction).

Further aids to study

Bertel's Ye. E., Osnovnyye momenty v razvitii sufiyskoy poezii. V sb: Vostochnyye Zapiski (Principal features in the development of Ṣūfī poetry.) In Oriental Notes. vol. I (Leningrad, 1927).
——, Sufiyskaya kosmogoniya u Farid ad-dina 'Attara (Sūfī Cosmogony in Farīd 'd-Dīn 'Aṭṭār) Yafeticheskiy Sbornik, III (1924).
——, Sufizm i sufiyskaya literatura (Sūfism and Sūfī literature.) Ye. E. Bertel's Selected Works. vol. III (Moscow, 1965).
Zhukovskiy, V. A., Chelovek i poznaniye u persidskikh mistikov. (Man and cognition in the Persian mystics) (St Petersburg, 1895).
Ivanov, P. P., Khozyaystvo dzhuybarskikh sheykhov (The economy of the Juibar Shaykhs) (Moscow-Leningrad, 1954).
Krymskiy, A. Ye., Ocherk razvitiya sufizma do kontsa III veka khidzhry. Trudy Vostochnoy komissii imp. Moscovskogo arkheologich. obshchestva (Outline of the development of Ṣūfism until the end of the 3rd century AH)

Works of Oriental Commission, Imp. Moscow Archeolog. Society, vol. II (Moscow, 1895).
Semenov, A. A., Bukharskiy Sheykh Bakha ud-din [Nakshband]. Vostochnyy sbornik v chest' A. N. Veselovskogo (The Bukhārā Shaykh Bahā'u 'd-Dīn [Naqshband]) Oriental Collection in honour of A. N. Veselovskiy (Moscow, 1914).

Abū Bakr Sirāj ad-dīn. The origins of Sufism 'Islamic Quarterly', vol. III No. 1. (London, 1956).
Affifi, A., *The mystical philosophy of Ibn al-'Arabī.* (Cambridge, 1939).
Arberry, A. J., *An introduction to the history of Sufism.* (Oxford, 1942).
——, *Le soufisme: Introduction.* Traduction française de J. Gouillard (Paris, 1952).
Asín Palacios, M., *Algazel* (Zaragoza, 1901).
Asín Palacois, M., La mystique d'al-Ghazzali. 'Mélanges de la faculté orientale de l'Université St Joseph', vol. VII (Beyrouth, 1914–21).
Browne, E. G., The Sufi Mysticism. In *A Literary history of Persia,* vol. I Chap. XIII.
Carra de Vaux, Djalal ad-din Rumi. EI vol. I.
——, *Ghazali.* (Paris, 1902).
Ethé H., Der Çufismus und seine drei Hauptvertreter in der persischen Poesie. Morgenlandische Studien. (Leipzig, 1870).
Gobineau, J. A., *Trois ans en Asie,* 1855–1858. (Paris, 1859).
Goldziher, I., Abdal. EI vol. I.
——, L'ascétisme aux premiers temps de l'Islam. Revue de l'histoire des religions. vol. 37 (1898).
——, Asketismus und Sufismus. In I. Goldziher. Vorlesungen über den Islam. Bd IV (Heidelberg, 1925).
——, Materialen zur Entwickelungsgeschichte des Çfismus. Wiener Zeitschrift für die Kunde des Morgenlandes. Bd XIII (1899).
Guyard St. 'Abd ar-Razzaq et son traité de la prédestination et du libre arbitre. JA 7 sér, vol. I.
Hartmann, R., Zur Frage nach der Herkunft und den Anfangen des Sufitums. 'Der Islam', Bd VI (1916).
Horten, Max, Indische Strömungen in der islamischen Mystik. Bd I–II (Heidelberg, 1927–8).
Macdonald, D. B., 'Abd ar-Razzaq Kashani. EI vol. I.
——, Al-Ghazali. EI vol. II.
——, Derwish. EI vol. I.
——, Emotional religion in Islam as affected by music and singing. JRAS, (1901–2).
——, The life of al-Ghazali with special reference to his religious experiences and opinions. JAOS vol. XX (1899).
Margoliouth, D. S., Kadiriya. EI vol. I.
Massignon, L., *Essai sur les origines du lexique technique de la mystique musulmane* (Paris, 1922, 2 ème edn Paris, 1954).
——, *La passion d'al-Halladj, martyre mystique de l'Islam.* (Paris, 1922).
——, Tarika. EI vol. IV.

——, Tasawwuf. EI vol. IV.
Merx, A., *Idee und Grundlinien einer allgemeinen Geschichte der Mystik.* (Heidelberg, 1893).
Nicholson, R. A., *The idea of personality in Sufism.* (Cambridge, 1923).
——, The lives of 'Umar ibn al-Farid and Ibn al-'Arabi. JRAS (1906).
——, *The mystics of Islam* (London, 1914).
——, *Studies in Islamic Mysticism.* (Cambridge, 1921).
Palmer, E. H., *Oriental mysticism.* 2nd edn with introduction by A. J. Arberry. (London, 1938).
Rose, H. A., *The Darvishes.* (Oxford, 1927).
Smith, Margaret, *Rabi'a the mystic* (Cambridge, 1928).
——, *Studies in early mysticism in the Near and Middle East* (London, 1931).
Tholuk, F. A., Sufismus sive theosophia Persarum pantheistica. (Berolini, 1821).
See also section 'General literature' and bibliographies to Chaps. VIII and IX

Chapter XIII
The triumph of Shī'ism in Iran

Sources

Angiolello, Discourse of . . . G. M. Angiolello, HS vol. 49, pt 2 (London, 1873) (English translation).
Anonymous Venetian merchant. The travels of a Merchant in Persia. HS vol. 49, pt 2 (London, 1873) (English translation).
Anonymous historian of Shah Ismā'īl I. The early years of Shah Ismail . . ., ed Denison Ross. JRAS (1896) (Persian text).
Waṣṣāf, Kitāb-i Mustaṭāb-i Waṣṣāf. (Bombay, 1269 (1852–3) Persian text (reprint Tehran, 1338 HS (1959)).
Ducas, Ducas. Historia. Corpus scriptorum historiae Byzantinae, ed J. Bekker (Bonnae, 1834) (Greek text and Italian translation).
Zāhidī, Ḥusayn b. Shaykh Abdāl. Ṣilsilat an-nasab-i Ṣafawiya . . . (Berlin, 1343 (1924–5)) (Serie 'Iranschahr') (Persian text).
Zeno, Caterino, Travels in Persia . . ., HS vol. 49, pt 2 (London, 1873).
Qazwīnī, Mīr Yaḥyā, Lubbu 't-Tawārīkh. Ed Sayyid Jalālu 'd-Dīn Ṭehrānī (Tehran, 1315 HS (1936)) (Persian text).
Qazwīnī, Ḥamdu'llāh Mustawfī, The Tārīkh-i Guzīda. Ed E. G. Browne (Leyden-London, 1910) GMS XIV/1–2 Facsimile of Persian MS and abridged English translation.
Mar'āshī, Ẓahīru 'd-Dīn, Sehir eddin's Geschichte von Tabaristan . . ., hrsg B. Dorn (St Petersburg, 1850).
Rashīdu 'd-Dīn Faḍlu'llāh, Jāmi'u 't-Tawārīkh. vol. III. Critical edn Persian text A. A. Alizade, and Russian translation A. K. Arends, (Baku, 1957).
——, Mukātabat-i Rashīdī. Ed Prof Khān Bahādur Muḥammad Shafī (Lahore, 1947). (Persian text).
Rota, G., La vita del Sophi, re di Persia . . . (In Appendix to R. du Mans. Etat de la Perse en 1660, éd Ch. Schefer) (Paris, 1890).

Sayfī, Sayf b. Muḥammad of Herāt. Tārīkh-nāma-yi Harāt. Ed Prof Muhammad Zubayr aṣ-Ṣiddīqī. (Calcutta, 1944) (Persian text).
Tawakkul, Ibn Bazzāz. Ṣafwatu 'ṣ-Ṣafā. (Bombay, 1328 (1910)) (Persian text).
Tadhkiratu 'l-Mulūk, The Tadhkirat al-muluk . . ., ed V. Minorsky. (Leyden-London, 1943) GMS NS, XVII (Persian text and English).
Faḍu'llāh b. Rūzbihān Khunjī, V. Minorsky. Persia in AD 1478–1490; an abridged translation of Fadlallah b. Ruzbihan Khundji's 'Tarikh-i 'Alamārā-yi Amīnī' (London, 1957).
Ḥasan Rūmlū, A Chronicle of the Early Safawis . . ., ed C. N. Seddon. Gaekwar's Oriental Series, No LVII (Persian text), LXIX (Abridged English translation) (Baroda, 1931–4) (Aḥsanu 't-Tawārīkh. vol. XII).
——, Aḥsānu 't-Tawārīkh. MS LGPB, Dorn's Catalogue No. 287 (vols. XI & XII, Persian text).

Further aids to study

Bartol'd, V. V., Narodnoye dvizheniye v Samarkande 1365 g. (Popular movement in Samarqand, 1365) ZVORAO vol. XVII (1906).
——, Novyy istochnik po istorii Timuridov (New source on the history of the Tīmūrids) Transactions IVAN vol. V (Leningrad, 1935) (Posthumous).
Gordlevskiy, V. A., Iz religioznykh iskaniy v Maloy Azii — Kyzylbashi (Of religious quests in Asia Minor — the Qizil Bāshes) 'Russkaya Mysl' (1916) No 11.
Ibragimov Dzhafar, Ardebil'skoye Vladeniye Sefevidov. (The Ardabīl dominion of the Ṣafawids) (Baku, 1960).
——, Feodal'nyye gosudarstva na territorii Azerbaydzhana XV v. (Feudal states on the territory of Adharbayjan in the 15th century) (Baku, 1962).
Ivanov, P. P., Khozyaystvo dzhuybarskikh sheykhov. (The economy of the Juibar Shaykhs) (Moscow-Leningrad, 1954).
Miklukho-Maklay, N. D., Shiizm i yego sotsial'noye litso v Irane na rubezhe XV–XVI vv. V sb: Pamyati akad. I. Yu. Krachkovskogo. (Shi'ism and its social facet in Iran at the turn of the 15/16th centuries) In Memorial vol. Academician I. Yu. Krachkovskiy. LGU (1958).
Molchanov, A. A., K kharakteristike nalogovoy sistemy v Gerate epokhi Alishera Navoi. V sb: Rodonachal'nik uzbekskoy literatury. (A description of the tax-system in Herāt in the time of 'Alī Shīr Nawā'ī) In collect. Father of Uzbek Literature. (Tashkent, 1940).
Novichev, A. D., Krest'yanskoye vosstaniye v Turtsii v nachale XV veka (Peasant rising in Turkey at the beginning of the 15th century) 'Problemy Vostokovedeniya' (1960) No 3.
Petrov, P. I., Dannyye istochnikov o sastave voinskikh kontingentov Ismaila I. (Data in the sources on the composition of the military contingents of Ismā'īl I) 'Narody Azii i Afriki' (1964) No 3.
Petrushevskiy, I. P., Vnutrennyaya politika Akhmeda Ak Koyunlu. Sbornik statey po istorii Azerbaydazhana (Home policy of Aḥmad Āk-Koyūnlū.) Collected articles on history of Ādharbāyjān. Issue 1 (Baku, 1949).
——, Gorodskaya Znat' v gosudarstve Khulaguidov. (Urban nobility in the

state of the Hūlāgūids) 'Sovetskoye Vostokovedeniye', vol. v (Moscow-Leningrad, 1948).
——, Gosudarstva Azerbaydzhana v XV v. Sbornik statey po istorii Azerbaydzhana (States of Ādharbayjān in the 15th century.) Collected articles on the history of Ādharbāyjān, Issue 1 (Baku, 1949).
——, Iz istorii Shirvana v kontse XV v. (History of Shīrwān at the end of the 15th century) 'Istoricheskiy Zhurnal' (1944) No 1.
——, Ocherki po istorii feodal'nykh otnosheniy v Azerbaydzhane i Armenii XVI — nach. XIX vv (Survey of the history of feudal relations in Ādharbāyjān and Armenia, 16th to early 19th centuries.) LGU (1949).
Stepanov, A. S., Trud Duki Kak istochnik po istorii vosstaniya Bërklyudzhe Must'afy. (Ducas' work as source on the history of the revolt of Börklüce Muṣṭafā) 'Vizantiyskiy Vremennik' vol. XI (1956).
Stroyeva, L. V., Serbedary Samarkanda. (The Sarbadārs of Samarqand.) Records LGU No 98 (1949).
Tveritinova, A. S., K voprosu ob izuchenii pervogo antifeodal'nogo vosstaniya v Turtsii. (An inquiry into the first anti-feudal rising in Turkey.) 'Vizantiyskiy Vremennik', vol. XI (1956).
Uspenskiy, F. I., Ocherki po istorii Trabezuntskoy imperii (Essays on the history of the Trebizond empire) (Leningrad, 1929).
Shakhmaliyev, E. M., K voprosu o diplomaticheskikh snosheniyakh pervykh Sefevidov c zapadnymi stranami (Diplomatic relations of the early Safawids with Western countries) Records Ādharbayjān State Univ. Hist. Series Issue 1 (1950).
Efendiyev, O.A., Iz istorii sotsial'noy i politicheskoy bor'by v Azerbaydzhane na rubezhe XV i XVI vv. (The history of the social and political struggle in Ādharbayjān at the turn of the 15th/16th centuries) Kratkiye Soobshcheniya IVAN, Issue XXXVIII (1960).
——, K nekotorym voprosam vnutrenney i vneshney politiki shakha Ismaila I. (Some questions of the home and foreign policy of Shah Ismā'īl I.) Hist. Inst. Ādharbayjān SSR Ac. Sc., vol. VII (Baku, 1957).
——, Obrazovaniye azerbaydzhanskogo gosudarstva Sefevidov v nachale XVI v. (Formation of the Ādharbāyjān state of the Ṣafawids at the beginning of the 16th century) (Baku, 1961).
Aubin, Jean, Etudes Safavides, I. Journal of the economic and social history of the Orient, vol. II pt I (Leiden, 1959).
Babinger, F., Marino Sanuto's Tagebücher als Quelle zur Geschichte der Safawijja. In *'Ajab-nama.* A volume of oriental studies presented to E. G. Browne (Cambridge, 1922).
——, Schejch Bedr ed-din . . . Ein Beitrag zur Geschichte des Sektenwesens im Altosmanischen Reich. 'Der Islam' Bd XI (1921).
Bayānī Kh, Les relations de l'Iran avec l'Europe occidentale à l'époque safavide (Paris, 1937).
Browne, E. G., Note on an apparently unique manuscript — History of the Safawy Dynasty, JRAS (1921) July.
Büchner, V. F., Serbedars. EI vol. IV.
Falsafī, Naṣrullāh, Tārīkh-i rawābiṭ-i Irān bā Urūpā dar dawra-yi Ṣafawiyya. (Tehran, 1334 HS (1955)) (In Persian).
Hinz, W., Irans Aufstieg zum Nationalstaat im XV Jahrhundert. (Berlin, 1936).

Iqbāl (Eghbal), ʻAbbās, Tārīkh-i mufaṣṣal-i Īrān az istīlā-yi Mughūl tā inqirāḍ-i Qājāriyya (Tehran, 1320 HS (1941)) (In Persian).
Kasravī, Aḥmad, Shaykh Ṣafī wa tabārash (Tehran, 1323 HS (1944)) (In Persian).
Minorsky, V., A Mongol decree of 720–1320 to the family of Shaykh Zahid. BSOS vol. XVI, pt 3 (1954).
——, Musha'sha' EI, Supplements, livre 4 (1937).
——, Shaykh Bali-efendi on the Safavids. BSOS vol. XX (1957).
——, The Aq Qoyunlu and land reforms. BSOS vol. XVII, pt 3 (1955).
——, The poetry of Shah Isma'il. BSOS vol. X, pt 4 (1942).
——, The supporters of the lords of Ardabil. In Tadhkirat al-muluk (Appendices) . . ., ed V. Minorsky. (London, 1943). GMS NS XVI.
Petrushevskiy, I. P., Nakhzat-i sarbadaran dar Khorasan. (Nahḍat-i Sarbadārān dar Khurāsān.) 'Farhang-i Īrān zamīn' vol. 5–6 (1341 HS (1962)). (Persian translation from Russian by Karim Kishavarz).
Roemer, H. R., *Die Safawiden* (Freiburg, 1953).
Spuler, B., *Die Mongolen* in Iran. 2 Aufl (Berlin, 1955).
Togan, Zaki Validi, Sur l'origine des Safavides. 'Mélanges Massignon'. vol. III. (Damascus, 1957).

Select Index